'My colleague Jan van Vliet has written a very interesting and intriguing study on the Puritan William Ames and his federal and volitional theology. He enhances the value of his book by delineating the influence Ames exerted on both Dutch and American Reformed experiential theology. Heretofore, nearly all Dutch researchers have assumed that Ames left little mark on the landscape of the *Nadere Reformatie* after his death in 1633. Van Vliet, however, is convincing in demonstrating that leading men of the *Nadere Reformatie*, such as Wilhelmus à Brakel and Petrus van Mastricht, were indebted to Ames on crucial points of their theological views. And these were not the only figures within the *Nadere Reformatie* to owe Ames a debt! In America, moreover, Jonathan Edwards was similarly influenced. This book will not, of course, be the last word on the topic, but not a single future researcher will be able to take the liberty of ignoring the results of the investigation that van Vliet submits in this book.'

W.J. op 't Hof, Affiliate Professor of the History of Reformed Pietism at VU University, Amsterdam, the Netherlands

Commendations for *The Rise of Reformed System*

'This is a masterful treatment of the thought of the great Puritan theologian William Ames. It sets out winsomely how, through the tools of covenant thinking and Ramist logic, Ames accomplished his goal of making Calvinism a properly experiential religion, and theology a system of practical instruction in "living unto God." It demonstrates how Ames served as the crucial link between his forebears in the Reformed tradition—especially John Calvin and William Perkins—and his successors in Puritanism and the Dutch Second Reformation. Clear, comprehensive, and marked by thorough scholarly command, the volume will be valued by novice and specialist alike.'
James D. Bratt, Professor of History, Calvin College, Michigan, USA

'In this scholarly monograph Jan van Vliet ably supplements Keith Sprunger's classic work on William Ames, giving us a fuller understanding of this influential Puritan theologian. Van Vliet carefully argues that Ames provides an example of how the graciously given covenant can be held together with an unapologetic call for the believer's vibrant response of obedience. But this study covers far more than just Ames; the reader is taken through the necessary background behind his theology (e.g., Calvin, Perkins) and given nuanced treatment of his influence (e.g., van Mastricht, Edwards). This work offers a helpful contribution to Puritan studies.'
Kelly M. Kapic, Professor of Theological Studies, Covenant College, Georgia, USA

'Jan van Vliet has given us so much with his comprehensive and wise work on William Ames. It is much more than a highly competent treatment of a meaningful episode in the history of the Reformed church—it helps us think clearly today about what is most important for us in our living for Jesus Christ. Ames believed that the important part of the sermon is its application for life—how many understand that today? Application to life based on solid work in understanding God's Word, isn't that exactly what we want and need today? Is faith understanding the truth? Or is desiring to do what God commands also important? There Ames went the crucial step further: understand, desire and then *do*! Isn't the gospel a true comfort, but Ames knew it as *joy*! Is Jesus your own Savior—why not add, the Savior of your church, all of you *together*! Most basic of all, what is it that God does in your salvation, what must you do—in what sense is the New Covenant conditional? The answers Ames gives are very deep, very helpful, just what we all need to know and believe. This is a remarkable and most necessary work. Saturate your mind and heart in it—and then *do* something with it.'
D. Clair Davis, Professor of Church History and Chaplain, Redeemer Seminary, Texas, USA

'A fine study of William Ames, the "learned doctor" of 17th-century English and American Puritanism and continental Reformed theology. He always taught – and practiced – that "theology is the doctrine of living to God." Van Vliet has given us the most thorough study of Ames to date and skillfully placed him into the context of his times.'
Keith L. Sprunger, *Oswald H. Wedel Professor of History Emeritus, Bethel College, Kansas, USA*

'*The Rise of the Reformed System* is a major contribution to Post-Reformation historical theology. Dr. van Vliet's thesis is that Ames left an influential legacy of experiential Calvinism in his covenantal marriage of sovereign grace and human obedience. The book traces the lines of influence linking Ames to a panorama of major Reformed theologians, including Calvin, Perkins, Cocceius, van Mastricht, Brakel, and Edwards. It also explores and offers a carefully nuanced perspective on Ames's "voluntarism" and ethics. Students of history, Puritan theology, and Reformed systematics will benefit from van Vliet's scholarship. We are in his debt for this book which helps to bridge the gap between Dutch and English-speaking scholarship on Reformed, experiential orthodoxy.'
Joel R. Beeke, *President, Puritan Reformed Theological Seminary, Michigan, USA*

'This is an astute and ambitious study of William Ames, among the most influential of English Puritan theologians. Its great strength is that it locates Ames within the broad sweep of the Reformed tradition from Calvin to Edwards, showing how his writings powerfully shaped its covenant theology, ethics, and experiential piety. The book will prove especially useful to English-speaking readers, for it opens up the Dutch context in fascinating ways.'
John Coffey, *Professor of Early Modern History, Leicester University, UK*

'Jan van Vliet's thorough intellectual history of William Ames documents the significance of this important Puritan theologian for the rise and development of the Reformed system. Arguing that Ames' contribution to Reformed thinking has been undervalued, van Vliet splendidly shows how the Amesian double emphasis on covenant theology and piety stands in continuity with the likes of Calvin and Perkins, and how it influenced subsequent Reformed leaders such as Cocceius and Edwards. Van Vliet's study convincingly conveys the thought and influence of Ames who called the church to an experiential Christianity which held doctrine and godliness together. Such an emphasis is still of vital importance for the Reformed faith today.'
John A. Vissers, *Professor of Historical Theology, Knox College, University of Toronto, Canada*

STUDIES IN CHRISTIAN HISTORY AND THOUGHT

The Rise of Reformed System

The Intellectual Heritage of William Ames

STUDIES IN CHRISTIAN HISTORY AND THOUGHT

The Rise of Reformed System

The Intellectual Heritage of William Ames

Jan van Vliet

Foreword by Donald K. McKim

Copyright © Paternoster 2013

First published 2013 by Paternoster

Paternoster is an imprint of Authentic Media
52 Presley Way, Crownhill, Milton Keynes, Bucks, MK8 0ES

www.authenticmedia.co.uk
Authentic Media is a division of Koorong UK, a company limited by guarantee

09 08 07 06 05 04 03   8 7 6 5 4 3 2 1

The right of Jan van Vliet to be identified as the author of this Work
has been asserted by him in accordance with the Copyright, Designs
and Patents Act 1988.

All rights reserved. No part of this publication may be reproduced, stored in a retrieval system, or transmitted, in any form or by any means, electronic, mechanical, photocopying, recording or otherwise, without the prior permission of the publisher or a license permitting restricted copying. In the UK such licenses are issued by the Copyright Licensing Agency, 90 Tottenham Court Road, London W1P 9HE.

British Library Cataloguing in Publication Data A catalogue record for this
book is available from the British Library

ISBN 978–1–84227–394-4

Printed and bound in Great Britain for Paternoster
by Lightning Source, Milton Keynes

In memory of Donald A. Leggett
(2 Tim. 3:14)

STUDIES IN CHRISTIAN HISTORY AND THOUGHT

Series Preface

This series complements the specialist series of Studies in Evangelical History and Thought and Studies in Baptist History and Thought for which Paternoster is becoming increasingly well known by offering works that cover the wider field of Christian history and thought. It encompasses accounts of Christian witness at various periods, studies of individual Christians and movements, and works which concern the relations of church and society through history, and the history of Christian thought.

The series includes monographs, revised dissertations and theses, and collections of papers by individuals and groups. As well as 'free standing' volumes, works on particular running themes are being commissioned; authors will be engaged for these from around the world and from a variety of Christian traditions.

A high academic standard combined with lively writing will commend the volumes in this series both to scholars and to a wider readership

Series Editors

Alan P.F. Sell	Visiting Professor at Acadia University Divinity College, Nova Scotia
D.W. Bebbington	University of Stirling, Stirling, Scotland
Clyde Binfield	Professor Associate in History, University of Sheffield, UK
Gerald Bray	Anglican Professor of Divinity, Beeson Divinity School, Samford University, Birmingham, Alabama, USA
Grayson Carter	Associate Professor of Church History, Fuller Theological Seminary SW, Phoenix, Arizona, USA
Dennis Ngien	Professor of Theology, Tyndale University College and Seminary, Founder of the Centre for Mentorship and Theological Reflection, Toronto, Canada

Contents

Foreword		xv
Preface		xvii
Abbreviations		xx
Chapter 1	Introduction	1
	Early Modern Thought and Method	1
	The Reformation Tradition	
Chapter 2	Situating William Ames: Culture, Corpus, Historiography	5
	At Home in England (1576-1610)	5
	An Expatriate in the Dutch Republic (1610-1633)	9
	Early Modern Dutch Culture	9
	Toward an Uneasy Reformed Hegemony	12
	Ames' Place in the Republic	16
	A Brief Summary of William Ames' Works	22
	William Ames in Historiography	23
Chapter 3	The Federal Theology of William Ames	27
	William Ames and Existing Covenant Thought	27
	Covenant Motifs in John Calvin, William Perkins, and William Ames	30
	The Pre-Temporal Covenant of Redemption	30
	A Covenant of Works	32
	The Covenant of Grace: Unity and Diversity	36
	"Covenant," "Testament," and Conditionality	42
	Covenant and Assurance	50
	Covenant and Church	53
	Concluding Remarks: Covenant as Architectonic	57
Chapter 4	The Voluntarism of William Ames	59
	Key Considerations and a Review of Calvin's Thought	59
	William Perkins and Voluntarism	61
	William Ames and Voluntarism	63
	An Established Trail	63
	The Intellectual, Theological and Ecclesiological Atmosphere	69
	Formalizing Ames' Voluntarism: The Influence of Ramism	71

	Voluntarism and the Guiding Theological Principles of Early Puritan Thought	75
	William Perkins	75
	William Ames	77
	Ames in the Context of Thomas, Calvin, and Perkins	78
	Concluding Observations	83
Chapter 5	The Legacy of William Ames in Johannes Cocceius in the Context of "Decretal Theology"	85
	"Decretal Theology" and Covenant Thought: Calvin to Ames	85
	The Covenant Thought of Johannes Cocceius	92
	The Amesian Inspiration for Cocceius' Covenant Thought	98
	Concluding Observations	103
Chapter 6	From Thomas' Casuistry to the Moral Theology of Westminster	105
	Introduction	105
	Reasons for Puritan Ethics	106
	A Dearth of Protestant Casuistry	106
	The Emergence of an Arid Orthodoxy	108
	Sabbath Desecration and Other Life-Style Practices	111
	Leaving Perkins and Medieval Ethics Behind	113
	The Theory of Conscience in Early Puritan Casuistry	113
	Wrapping Perkins' Medieval Casuistry in Biblical Dress	119
	Concluding Observations	125
Chapter 7	From Heidelberg to Westminster: William Ames in Confessional History and his Exposition of the *Heidelberg Catechism*	129
	Overview of the *Heidelberg Catechism*: Origins, Structure and Ethos	129
	William Ames' Commentary on the *Heidelberg Catechism*: Methodological Considerations	133
	Topical Examination of the *Heidelberg Catechism*, Ursinus' Commentary and Ames' Catechisme	136
	On Comfort: Lord's Day 1	136
	On Christ as Judge: Lord's Day 19	143
	On the Holy Spirit: Lord's Day 20	147

	On the Resurrection: Lord's Day 22	149
	On Doing Good Works: Lord's Day 24/32	153
	Miscellaneous Emphases	156
	Final Observations	158
Chapter 8	The *Nadere Reformatie* and William Ames	162
	Disputation at Franeker and the Synod of Dordt	162
	Johannes Maccovius	163
	The Heart of the Dispute: Faith or Morals?	167
	The Synod of Dordt (1618-1619)	171
	Experiential Christianity: The Beginnings of Dutch Puritanism	172
	Willem Teellinck	172
	Willem Teellinck and William Ames	177
	Unpacking Pietism, English Puritanism and the *Nadere Reformatie*	180
	Summary	183
Chapter 9	Amesian Contours in the Thought of Wilhelmus à Brakel and Petrus van Mastricht	185
	William Ames and Wilhelmus à Brakel	185
	Wilhelmus à Brakel	185
	Brakel's Amesian Emphases	186
	a) Prolegomena and Theology	186
	b) Theological Anthropology	190
	c) Christology	194
	d) Ecclesiology	196
	e) Soteriology	198
	f) Eschatology	209
	g) Administration of the Covenant of Grace – Brakel's Appendix	209
	Petrus van Mastricht, Expositor of William Ames	211
	Introduction	211
	General Observations: Method and Overview of Praktikale Godgeleerdheit	213
	Contents of Praktikale Godgeleerdheit	216
	a) Prolegomena	216
	b) Faith and the Will	220
	c) Conscience and Moral Theology	222
	d) Covenant Theology	224
	Concluding Observations: Ames, Brakel and Mastricht	228

Chapter 10	Covenant and Conscience: Amesian Echoes in Jonathan Edwards	233
	The Experiential Christianity of the Reformed Tradition – Covenant and Piety – in New England to Jonathan Edwards	233
	Biographical Parallels: Jonathan Edwards and William Ames	236
	Direct Amesian Influences in Edwards' Understanding of the Covenant	237
	The Pactum Salutis	237
	The Covenant of Works	238
	Covenant Conditionality	239
	The Role of Will, Once Again	240
	Edwards and Ames on the Heart of Informed Piety: Gracious Affections and Conscience	243
	Love to God	244
	Living to God	246
	Conscience and Authentic Experience	248
	Jonathan Edwards and Petrus van Mastricht	252
	Foreword	252
	Influence of Edwards' History of the Work of Redemption	253
	Introduction to Edwards' History of the Work of Redemption	254
	The Covenant as Architectonic of History of the Work of Redemption	255
	Summary	261
	Ames and Edwards: Closing Comments	262
Chapter 11	Summary and Concluding Remarks	266
Bibliography		269
	Primary Sources – William Ames	269
	Primary Sources – Others	270
	Secondary Sources	280
Indexes		317
	Author	317
	Scripture	321
	Subject	323

Foreword

The "learned doctor" William Ames (1576-1633) was one of the strongest English Puritan theologians who spent years teaching and writing in the Netherlands. His fame was widespread in Europe and beyond, especially in the New England culture where, in their early years, both Harvard and Yale used his books for the learning and edification of their students.

Ames was revered by Reformed theologians for an approach to theology which focused on the inseparable relationship of theology and ethics, or doctrine and piety. Ames' "practical divinity" owed much to his commitment to the philosophy of Pierre de la Ramée (Petrus Ramus, 1515-1572) transmitted through Ames' teacher William Perkins (1558-1602) at Christ's College, Cambridge. Ames consistently applied Ramist philosophy to Reformed, Puritan theology and produced both a "systematic theology," the *Medulla Theologiae* (1627) or *The Marrow of Theology* as well as an ethical manual, his *De Conscientia, et Eius Iure, vel Casibus* (1630) or *Cases of Conscience*. These two volumes were mainstays for clergy in both the Old World and the New. They were sources of theological and ethical understanding for pastors who needed clear direction in the midst of the thickets of theological controversies and ethical guidance in applying sound theological insights to the life of faith to lead parishioners in ways of faithful obedience to the Christian gospel. It is no wonder that, in 1637, when Ames' widow and children settled at Salem and later Cambridge, Massachusetts, the General Court granted forty pounds "to Mrs. Ames, the widow of Doctor Ames, of famos [*sic*] memory, who is deceased." Though Ames died before being able to emigrate to New England, his books and reputation preceded him and were deeply appreciated.

A great value of Jan van Vliet's study before us is that we now have a full-orbed discussion of Ames' intellectual history that delves into the works just mentioned, but also into a number of Ames' other works. Van Vliet shows the significant position of William Ames in the rise of Reformed theology, after the death of John Calvin (1509-1564), and how Ames contributed in mighty ways to the development of Reformed thought in a number of areas.

The systematization of Reformed theology in the post-Reformation period can be a thorny and complex issue. But van Vliet's persuasive presentation of the directions Ames set and the theological convictions he fostered give us a wider picture of Ames' influence. Van Vliet demonstrates ways major Reformed theologians such as Johannes Cocceius (1603-1669), Wilhelmus à Brakel (1635-1711), Petrus van Mastricht (1630-1706), and Jonathan Edwards (1703-1758) approached central elements of Ames' thought and incorporated these into their own detailed theological work. In some instances the appropriations of Ames are clear in the later writers. Sometimes they are camouflaged and it takes van Vliet's expert guidance to demonstrate their presence. Ames' impact exceeded that of his own books in themselves. His works were so seminal and persuasive that their insights were repackaged and developed further by theologians fittingly revered in their own right. But now we can see the Amesian influence with greater clarity. We find that it spread further than recognized before. For this, we owe a debt to van Vliet for providing this excellent and important exposition of Ames' thought and how it reached out in prevailing ways in the thought of other Reformed theologians.

Among the theological topics Ames advanced and van Vliet explores are Federal Theology, the issue of Voluntarism, "Decretal Theology" and Covenant Thought, Moral Theology, the Heidelberg Catechism, Experiential Christianity in relation to the *Nadere Reformatie* and the beginnings of Dutch Puritanism, Pietism, Piety, and Conscience. The thorough pursuit of these issues by van Vliet means we now have a more unified picture of who Ames was – in himself and in the ways he impacted other theologians.

To place Ames more clearly in the venerable Reformed theological tradition is to draw attention to the tradition itself. From its earliest days with Zwingli and Calvin, through its developments throughout Europe and into the British Isles, we encounter a tradition that is focused on strong theological reflection. The life of the Christian is grounded in theological understanding. The life of the Christian expresses its theological convictions about the God of the Scriptures who has come in Jesus Christ and lives in and through the church by the power of the Holy Spirit. The lives of Christian people witness to the Christian Gospel and are lives devoted to following the ancient maxim of St. Augustine that our theology is "faith seeking understanding." The Reformed tradition follows this trajectory.

Through Jan van Vliet's splendid work, we now have a deeper understanding of the theology of one of the Reformed tradition's most important theologians, William Ames. We are grateful to van Vliet for his labors. We also receive, with deep gratitude, a fresh look at "the learned Doctor William Ames" who began his *Marrow of Theology* with this key definition: "Theology is the doctrine or teaching [*doctrina*] of living to God" (1.1).

Donald K. McKim

Professor of Theology and Academic Dean, Emeritus
Author and editor of a number of books on Reformed theology, including *Ramism in William Perkins' Theology*

Preface

Puritan William Ames was a key and formative player as the narrative of the Reformed tradition was being written. Once the Augustinian doctrine of grace was reprioritized by first- and second-generation reformers, the next chapter recorded the struggle by theologians and pastors to blend an emerging theology of the covenant with a practical focus on Christian living. While the covenant is driven only by divine grace, the believer's response of obedience is absolutely vital to it and to true Christianity. William Ames was an early theologian who fused these two often contradictory elements of biblical teaching into a system giving structure and direction to a covenantally responsible religious life.

After setting the historical context and cultural backstory regarding the life, work and historiographical assessment of William Ames, I identify his central contributions to the Reformed system of thought and life. This involves a comparative analysis of Ames' covenant thought with that of John Calvin and William Perkins and is followed by considered reflection on Ames' much-debated and misunderstood commitment to voluntarism. His legacy in the work of covenant theologian Johannes Cocceius is observed, amidst the complications introduced by the emergence of "decretal theology." Establishing the biblical orientation of Ames' moral theology and his prescribed interface between covenant obedience and ethics completes the exposition of Ames' seminal contributions to the Reformed pillars of covenant and practical theology. Throughout I remain cognizant of the degree to which covenant theology was or was not part and parcel of developing Reformed thought at the time, beginning with Ulrich Zwingli (1484-1531), Heinrich Bullinger (1504-75), Zacharias Ursinus (1534-83), Caspar Olevianus (1536-87) and Scotsman Robert Rollock (c. 1555-99). Similarly, early Reformed ethics received a strong boost from Amandus Polanus (1561-1610).

Measurement of William Ames' systemic influence commences with a study of his practical emphasis as this appears in his commentary on the *Heidelberg Catechism* of 1563, lodged as he is between this early confessional document and the latter more developed systematization of the *Westminster Standards* of 1647 and 1648. His concern for authentic faith in personal and public life was shared by pious representatives of the seventeenth-century Dutch Republic as he provides theological structure to the efforts for further Reformation found there in the movement called *Nadere Reformatie*. Ames' model of covenant theology and piety is shown to be formative in the work of two contemporaries and chief representatives of the Reformed thought of this period of high orthodoxy, church theologian Wilhelmus à Brakel and scholar-theologian Petrus van Mastricht.

Ames' trail is picked up in the New World and enters the formative years of the American Reformed tradition, the early eighteenth century. The Amesian influence on the immensely creative mind of Jonathan Edwards, both directly and as mediated thorough Mastricht, is disclosed, recognizing that Edwards inherited an already very well-established Puritan tradition of covenant thought and moral theology. The historiographical literature abounds with studies of the presence and development of Puritanism in the colonies, notably in New England. From the founding of the first community, the first church, and the first college, the influence of the work and still recent memory of William Ames were singular and overwhelming.

My study closes with a historiographical reassessment of William Ames in the intellectual-theological history of the Reformed tradition.

John Coffey observed that this Reformed synthesis, as it were, should not be understood as monolithic or entirely uniform. I appreciate the reminder. As subsequent Reformed tensions through history have illustrated, merging thought and practice has not always been successful on a practical level, nor even agreed upon. The historical narrative is replete with ecclesiastical traditions laying claim to membership in the Reformed camp but representing some degree of variation in theological subscription and practical religion. And just a cursory glance across the Reformed landscape today shows the multiplicity of "brands" within the Reformed tradition, a veritable pluriformity of thought and practice. Indeed, this inherent fluidity could represent a Reformed distinctive in itself.

There will always be internal tensions within the Reformed tradition. This inclination to instability indicates how difficult – but vital – the struggle to unify doctrine with life is. For its part, English Puritanism, too, was riven by various disputes, notably after 1640. The following account should not be read to imply that English Puritanism/Dutch Reformed Pietism was a cohesive, stable system, rather than something more dynamic and even unpredictable at times.

My indebtedness for the completion of this project extends far and wide. My progress through the material was accompanied by an acute sense of gratitude for great thinkers, past and present. I have been truly privileged to stand on the shoulders of giants, and I trust my obligation is fairly reflected in the notes. The work originated with a doctoral dissertation over ten years ago, but has evolved, has changed emphases in some areas, and has gone significantly wider and deeper in others. Part of this endeavor was facilitated by a period of sabbatical leave from my prior area of service, Prairie Bible College, Three Hills, Alberta, Canada, for which I am grateful. I spent the 2010-11 academic year as visiting scholar at Denver Seminary in Littleton, Colorado. The gracious library staff there proved immensely helpful in the provision of personal study space and the gathering of materials.

My wife Joan of inexhaustible energy, who I had thought long-since overdosed on Puritan William Ames, found the strength to go one more long round with Ames and me; even my children remained supportive and encouraging throughout, although now from a distance.

Memories of my earliest seminary teacher, mentor, then good friend Don Leggett, and his unbending commitment to the truth of scripture, particularly the hard parts, continued to inspire as I encountered and unpacked many of the more difficult pieces of this narrative. I was also encouraged by the ever-kindly words of recently-passed John D. Eusden, who was "never too busy to talk about William Ames." Regrettably, the rich harvest of insightful correspondence from Willem J. van Asselt regarding further nuancing of Reformed Orthodoxy was reaped too late to make it into the manuscript before the deadline, but I am deeply appreciative of the time he took in engaging this work.

Finally, Editor Michael Parsons showed tremendous patience when this project entered his realm of responsibility, and I am grateful for Mike's help and advice. I take full responsibility for all deficiencies of this work.

Jan van Vliet, July 2013

Abbreviations

AKGNed	*Archief voor Kerkelijke Geschiedenis, inzonderheid van Nederland.*
AP	*American Presbyterians/The Journal Of Presbyterian History.*
AUSS	*Andrews University Seminary Studies.*
BIHR	*Bulletin of the Institute of Historical Research.*
BLGNP	D. Nauta et al. (eds.), *Biografisch Lexicon voor de Geschiedenis van het Nederlandse Protestantisme*, 5 vols. Kampen: J.H. Kok, 1978-2001.
BWG	B. Glasius, *Biografisch Woordenboek van Nederlandsche Godgeleerden.* 's Hertogenbosch: Gebr Muller, 1853.
CDP	Robert Audi (ed.), *Cambridge Dictionary of Philosophy*. New York: Cambridge University, 1995.
CH	*Church History.*
CSM	*Publications of the Colonial Society of Massachusetts.*
CTJ	*Calvin Theological Journal.*
DNR	*Documentatieblad Nadere Reformatie.*
EAL	*Early American Literature.*
GR	*Gordon Review.*
HJ	*The Historical Journal.*
HTR	*Harvard Theological Review.*
HWPh	Joachim Ritter et al. (eds.), *Historisches Wörterbuch der Philosophie*. 13 vols. Basel: Schwabe, 1971-2007.
Institutes	John Calvin, *Institutes of the Christian Religion*, John T. MacNeill, ed., Ford Lewis Battles, trans. 2 vols. Library of Christian Classics, no. 20-21. Philadelphia: Westminster, 1960.
JEH	*Journal of Ecclesiastical History.*
JETS	*Journal of the Evangelical Theological Society.*
KeTh	*Kerk en Theologie.*
MQR	*Mennonite Quarterly Review.*
NAK	*Nederlands Archief voor Kerkgeschiedenis.*
NDT	Sinclair B. Ferguson and David Wright (eds.), *New Dictionary of Theology*. Downers Grove, IL: IVP, 1988.
NEQ	*New England Quarterly.*
NedTT	*Nederlands Theologische Tijdschrift.*
NIDCC	James D. Douglas (ed.), *The New International Dictionary of the Christian Church*. Rev. ed. Grand Rapids: Zondervan, 1978.

ODNB	H.C.G. Matthew and Brian Harrison (eds.), *Oxford Dictionary of National Biography*. Oxford: Oxford University, 2004.
RefRev	*Reformed Review*.
RGG	H.D. Betz et al. (eds.), *Religion in Geschichte und Gegenwart. Handwörterbuch für Theologie und Religionswissenschaft*. 8 vols. and 1 index vol. 4th ed. Tübingen: Mohr Siebeck Verlag, 1998-2007.
SCH	G.J. Cumming (ed.), *Studies in Church History*. London: Nelson, 1965.
SCJ	*Sixteenth Century Journal*.
SJT	*Scottish Journal of Theology*.
SPAS	*Studies in Puritan American Spirituality*.
ThRef	*Theologia Reformata*.
ThT	*Theologisch Tijdschrift*.
USQR	*Union Seminary Quarterly Review*.
WTJ	*Westminster Theological Journal*.

Chapter 1

Introduction

Early Modern Thought and Method

The first couple of centuries of the early modern period were rich in philosophical and theological development as the intellectual heritage preserved in the medieval schools gained renewed traction with the recovery of particular biblical principles during the Reformation and post-Reformation period. During the era book-ended by the deaths of John Calvin and Jonathan Edwards these biblical-theological principles underwent a process of refinement and organization to bring us to the identifying features of the Reformed theological apparatus of the twenty-first century. Even as we are mindful of the medieval sources of Calvin's contributions to the intellectual world of Reformation thought, so too would this rich Reformed heritage be truncated if we were to neglect this post-sixteenth century evolution.

Moving forward from the late sixteenth century, post-Reformation thought was taken up by the later continental reformers, the English Puritans, the continental post-Reformation theologians of the seventeenth-century Dutch Republic, and from there by thinkers in North America, particularly Jonathan Edwards. Along the way, it evolved in the midst of philosophical discovery, theological challenge and cultural change and so informed and defined the Reformed tradition over the course of over four centuries to its current location on the theological landscape of the twenty-first.

R.A. Muller has described the development of post-Reformation thought during this stage of the early modern period – from approximately 1565 to 1725 – as proceeding in three distinct phases: "early" (c. 1565-1618/40) "high" (c. 1620/40-1685) and "late" (post-1685 and well into the eighteenth century) orthodoxy. During the former period, the thought of second generation Reformers was codified and received confessional status, amidst significant historical circumstances such as the Synod of Dort (1618) and the Thirty Years War. The second phase is characterized as a "broader theological synthesis" combining confessional summation with a rising controversy and a sharpening polemic around a number of issues, chief of which were questions of faithfulness to the traditional Reformed writers and to biblical piety. During late orthodoxy, traditional Reformed theology took on a certain degree of theological and biblical ambivalence as philosophical foundations seemed less secure and polemic was replaced with varying degrees of commitment to biblical standards and confessional subscription.[1]

This work traces the origins, transmission, and further evolution of select distinctives of the Reformed system of thought and life through this entire era of orthodoxy. The Reformation thought of first- and second-generation magisterial Reformers, notably Ulrich Zwingli and John Calvin, was mediated to the early orthodox writers such as Puritan William Ames and Johannes Maccovius (1588-1644), underwent systematic and scholastic development and was carried through into the late orthodoxy of the eighteenth century by faithful and creative successors.

The Reformed Tradition

The Reformed tradition represents a cohesive and internally consistent system of theological thought and life constructed through doctrinal accretions over a long period of expansion, refinement and evolving systematization. The subsequent richness of this system of life and thought can be summarized by at least the following sets of distinctives or principles.[2]

First, Reformed theology is highly doctrinal, a theology of the Word. It is a system of belief anchored in an abiding trust in the inspired, authoritative, and self-authenticating nature of scripture whose author is absolutely sovereign. *Sola scriptura* explains the emphasis on preaching and sacraments, the high view of creeds and confessions and the principle of the conjunction of Word and Spirit. Working out these theological issues through history, often in polemic, has given rise to a rigorous intellectual tradition as the challenges of

---

[1] R.A. Muller, "John Calvin and later Calvinism: the identity of the Reformed tradition" in *The Cambridge Companion to Reformation Theology*, D.Bagchi and D.C. Steinmetz, eds. (New York: Cambridge University, 2004; 3rd printing, 2009), 134-35; idem, *Post-Reformation Reformed Dogmatics: The Rise and Development of Reformed Orthodoxy, ca. 1520 to ca. 1725*. Vol. 1 2nd ed., (Grand Rapids: Baker, 2003), 30-32; hereafter *PRRD 1*. The periodization in *PRRD 1* has much tighter and more defined boundaries, even than those found in the first edition. Cf. the divisions of orthodoxy into early, high, and late in O. Weber, *Foundations of Dogmatics*, D.L. Guder, trans. (Grand Rapids: Eerdmans, 1981-82) I, 120-27.

[2] See such standard works as B.G. Armstrong, *Probing the Reformed Tradition: Historical Studies in Honor of Edward A. Dowey, Jr.* (Louisville, KY: Westminster/John Knox, 1989), I.J. Hesselink, *On Being Reformed: Distinctive Characteristics and Common Misunderstandings* (Ann Arbor: Servant, 1983), J.H. Leith, *Introduction to the Reformed Tradition* (Atlanta: John Knox, 1981), D.K. McKim, ed., *Major Themes in the Reformed Tradition* (Grand Rapids: Eerdmans, 1992), E.M. Osterhaven, *The Spirit of the Reformed Tradition* (Grand Rapids: Eerdmans, 1970). An accessible summary of the theological distinctives of Reformed theology are found in R.W.A. Letham, "Reformed Theology," *NDT*, 569-72. On the "theological boundaries" of the Reformed tradition, see J.H. Gerstner, "Theological Boundaries: The Reformed Perspective" in *The Evangelicals: What They Believe, Who They Are, Where They Are Changing*, rev. ed., D.F. Wells and J.D. Woodbridge, eds. (Grand Rapids: Baker, 1977), 21-37.

changing cultural climates and historical circumstances prompted further reflection and response. Yes, of theology and the church it must be said, *reformata et semper reformanda*, but only according to the Word of God, not the whim of men and women, nor the exigencies of the cultural, intellectual or theological climate. Significantly, the interpretative construct through which this theology of the Word is given meaning is its unique covenant theology.

Secondly, the Reformed tradition emphasizes a life of piety and holy circumspection in conformity to the will of God with the Ten Commandments as moral compass for Christian life and practice. The Reformed tradition takes seriously the apostle's direction to be holy, as God is holy. It prescribes an ethical and biblically-responsible Christian life, underscoring a life lived in covenant obedience. Intellectual subscription to precise theological formulations is not enough; true subscription includes lived submission since theology is both of the head and the heart, involving both orthodoxy and orthopraxy. Authentic covenant-status of God's redeemed, image-bearing creature is expressed through right living.

Thirdly, the Reformed system mandates cultural engagement. Covenant obedience, means the believer's worldview should be a decidedly biblical one; a covenant life is one committed to the vocation of seeking to bring a sinful world into conformity to scriptural principles and under the lordship of Christ. To the Reformed, therefore, both the delegation of creation-care in Genesis and the New Testament Great Commission are broadly considered as the cultural mandate to be vigorously pursued. There is not one inch of the created order over which Jesus Christ does not claim "This is mine!" This transforming vision is a communal and covenant responsibility. Life is lived *coram Deo*.

Finally, our four-fold typology holds that the Reformed tradition is a "church" tradition. It places a high priority on ecclesiastical organization and order. It highly esteems church membership – indeed, mandates it – because membership represents an organic community of the people of God, his covenant people. This covenant community has its own unique system of church government, worship and liturgy, spiritual oversight and discipline, as well as evangelism and mission.

These four sets of principles appear in the thought of Calvin in either mature of inchoate form. While he has been accused of intellectualizing the faith, he seamlessly interwove intellect and piety in his theological tapestry. While Reformed "worldview" architecture was developed by "neo-Calvinists," Calvin also spoke of believers' broader cultural responsibility. System-building of Reformed thought across time and space proved faithful to Calvin as the biblical center of the tradition was preserved through the ages. At the center of this tradition are found covenantally-centered belief and practice, a holistic faith tradition in which scriptural imperatives guide both faith and morals. The thought of Puritan William Ames is central in the formation, subsequent furtherance, and formal articulation of this system.

In order for the content of a tradition to remain faithful to its origins, it cannot be overtaken by form. Reformed system, as it developed through the periods of early, high, and late orthodoxy, employed different thought forms and philosophical constructs of the day. It is true that at times these structures controlled the substance of thought, possibly even hampering further development. Theology came to be handmaiden to philosophical systems, impairing its practical dimension and disabling useful orthopraxy. While all early modern thinkers navigated with remarkable ease and fluidity the world of ideas of the seventeenth century, not all were as successful as William Ames in distinguishing form from content. Ames had his philosophical favorites, to be sure, which he was not shy in disclosing and to which his theological system at times seemed bound. But his ability to preserve and further the theological and practical heart of the Reformed system is admirable. Working through Ames' thought will be a constant reminder of this but also of Calvin's dictum that we must transmit the tradition faithfully in the form we think will prove best.

Chapter 2

Situating William Ames: Culture, Corpus, Historiography

At Home in England (1576-1610)

Almost half-way into the reign of Elizabeth I (r. 1558-1603) and as the closing years of the first phase of Puritanism loomed, East Anglia had already established itself as the center of a robust and scrupulous Puritanism. Consequently, although the geographical distance from London to Ipswich, Suffolk County, is not great, the religious thought and practice of the two centers were separated by an unbridgeable chasm. Always prepared to apply biblical teaching to their sixteenth century context, the Puritans understood verse 113 of Psalm 119 as offering only one of two options: the impure "vayne inventions" of the Elizabethan settlement, or the unsullied purity of "God's law." When forced to choose between these two irreconcilable ways of understanding the God-human dimension, the interpretation of scripture, and the form of worship, East Anglian Puritanism knew where it would cast its vote. By the time Ames was born, therefore, in 1576, the Puritan stream there was flowing strong. It would be most surprising if someone born into this already established theological and ecclesiastical tradition would not be, at best, reflexively suspicious and, at worst, unapologetically hostile towards anything to do with the religious settlement imposed by the politically astute Tudor monarch. In this respect, Ames would not prove wanting, as his subsequent life and thought demonstrated.[3]

---

[3] Biographical accounts of William Ames of various length, detail and quality exist throughout the literature on the Puritans and their thinking and impact. The primary references however, are: K.L. Sprunger, *The Learned Doctor William Ames: Dutch Backgrounds of English and American Puritanism* (Chicago: University of Illinois, 1972); J.D. Eusden, "Introduction" in William Ames, *The Marrow of Theology*, trans. Eusden from the 3rd Latin ed., 1629 (United Church, 1968; reprint ed., Grand Rapids: Baker, 1997), 1-66; references to Eusden's work will hereafter appear as Eusden, "Introduction" in *Marrow*; K. Reuter, *Wilhelm Amesius: der führende Theologe des erwachenden reformierten Pietismus* (Neukirchen, Kreis Moers: Buchhandlung des Erziehungsvereins, 1940), trans. D. Horton as *William Ames: The Leading Theologian in the Awakening of Reformed Pietism* in Horton *William Ames by Matthew Nethenus, Hugo Visscher and Karl Reuter* (Cambridge: Harvard Divinity School, 1965), 155-278, (hereafter Horton, *Ames by Reuter*); H. Visscher, *Guilielmus Amesius: Zijn Leven en Werken* (Haarlem: J.M. Stap, 1894), trans. T.G. Hommes and D. Horton as *William Ames: His Life and Works* in Horton, *William Ames*, 23-154, (hereafter Horton, *Ames by Visscher*); M. Nethenus, *Praefatio Introductoria* (Amsterdam: John Jansson, 1668 [*sic*]), trans. D. Horton as *Introductory Preface in Which the Story of the Life of Master Ames*

It was fortunate for Ames that he had a benefactor, and a non-conforming Puritan at that. For his parents both died while he and his sister, Elizabeth, were quite young, and he came under the care of a maternal uncle from Boxford, a center known for its Puritan leaders. Mr. Snelling took his responsibility in the rearing of young Ames seriously, furthering Ames' religious and intellectual development in keeping with the familiar Puritan principles of solid learning, high piety, and unmitigated non-conformity. These emphases found fertile ground in young Ames.[4] He matriculated at the University of Cambridge in 1593 or 1594[5] and received the Bachelor of Arts degree in 1597-98, but it was 1601 that proved to be the crowning year for Ames' intellectual, ecclesiastical and spiritual development. He earned the Master of Arts, was elected a fellow at Christ's College, was ordained into the ministry, and experienced a profound, spiritual conversion. Already by his mid-twenties, therefore, Ames found himself well-positioned to establish his reputation and to perpetuate non-conforming Puritanism in both the academy and the church. He remained at Cambridge until 1610.[6]

The Puritans at Christ's College gladly welcomed Ames as one of their own. The school proved a hospitable intellectual and spiritual training ground for the young Puritan. Ames, in turn, embraced his college, the undisputed center of the undiluted Puritanism of the time, a wonderfully congenial and comfortably familiar school for a bright young student from Suffolk. It was here that highly-principled Puritans of the East-Anglian variety gathered to learn, discuss and further perpetuate their high ideals. Many famous Puritans came from Christ's, most notably William Perkins. Perkins and Ames overlapped only a year at Cambridge because Perkins moved to nearby St. Andrew the Great Church where he conducted a teaching ministry until his death in 1602.[7] But much of Perkins' thought on philosophy, pedagogy, theology, and piety he passed on to his protégé. This included not only the tireless promotion of Ramism and Calvinism, but also strident opposition to the papacy. In Cambridge, then – college and church – Ames' biblical and Puritan convictions on doctrine and life deep-

---

is *Briefly Narrated and the Excellence and Usefulness of his Writings Shown* in Horton, *William Ames*, 3-22, (hereafter Horton, *Ames by Nethenus*); and K.L. Sprunger, "Ames, William (1576-1633)," *ODNB*, vol. 1, 941-46.

[4] Sprunger, *Ames*, 8-10; Horton, *Ames by Visscher*, 28.

[5] On the University of Cambridge, see J.B. Mullinger, *The University of Cambridge*, 3 vols. (Cambridge: Cambridge University, 1873-1911). For the history of Christ's College, see J. Peile, *Christ's College* (London, 1900), and *Biographical Register of Christ's College, 1505-1905 and of the Earlier Foundation, God's House, 1448-1505*, 2 vols. (Cambridge: Cambridge University, 1910-1913). For Cambridge and the Reformation, see H.C. Porter, *Reformation and Reaction in Tudor Cambridge* (London: Cambridge University, 1958) and his related *Puritanism in Tudor England* (New York: MacMillan Co., 1970).

[6] Sprunger, *Ames*, 11-12.

[7] Sprunger, *Ames*, 11.

ened and flourished. This meant a life committed to the teachings of Calvinism and the practice of piety and a vocation dedicated to the promotion of true religion, both of which Ames pursued with unmitigated passion.

From the very beginning, the Puritan movement emphasized a life of piety sparked by an initial spiritual experience. For Ames this occurred under the preaching of Perkins.[8] By Ames' own account, despite his pious living he had never "passed through the climactic Puritan experience of conversion,"[9] and it was not until hearing the "rousing, awakening and quickening" preaching of Perkins that Ames learned that authentic Christian conversion, not moral living alone, constituted true religion. "A man may be *bonus ethicus*, and yet not *bonus Theologus*, i.e. a well cariaged man outwardly, expressing both the sense and practise of religion in his outward demeanor: And yet not be a sincere hearted Christian."[10] As a fellow at Christ's, Ames was known for administering the "salutary vinegar of reproof" to those in the college predisposed to gambling and "pagan ways."[11] For Ames' part, unsanctified ministers in Elizabethan England were an all too common occurrence, and ministerial students would learn from Ames the piety required of a man called to the ministry.[12]

At Cambridge Ames quickly adopted the philosophical and pedagogical system of French Huguenot Peter Ramus.[13] The prevailing philosophical ethos at Christ's College was one highly suspicious of Aristotle and since the middle of the sixteenth century influential thinkers at Christ's had promoted the relatively new and exciting practical system of Ramus. According to W.J. Ong, Ames was the most devoted non-continental Ramist.[14] In this regard as in many other

---

[8] Sprunger, *Ames*, 11; Horton, *Ames by Reuter*, 160.
[9] Sprunger, *Ames*, 12.
[10] William Ames, *A Fresh Suit Against Human Ceremonies in Gods Worship* (Rotterdam [?]: N.p., 1633), 131. Except for cases where I work with modern translations of Puritan work, I retain the spelling, grammar, and, in most cases, syntax, of the original. Hear Ames' own account of his teacher's emphasis in ministry: ". . . worthy Master Perkins . . . instructed [students] soundly in the Truth, stirred them up effectually to seeke after godlinesse, made them fit for the kingdome of God; and by his owne example shewed them, what things they should chiefely intend, that they might promote true Religion, in the power of it, unto Gods glory, and others salvation" (*Conscience with the Power and Cases Thereof. Devided into V. Bookes* [N.p., 1639], "To the Reader"). My convention in referring to this work is to cite book, chapter and section. At times, for greater precision, citation of a Question (Q) will be given.
[11] Horton, *Ames by Nethenus*, 4.
[12] William Ames, "An Exhortation to the Students of Theology delivered at Franeker Anno MDCXXIII," D. Horton, trans., (Boston, MA: Harvard Divinity School, 1958); English translation of "Paraenesis, ad Studiosos Theologiae, habita Franekerae, Aug. 22, anno 1623," delivered within eighteen months of his arrival to remind the theological students in the Franeker community of their faithful attendance to holy and moral living.
[13] Sprunger, *Ames*, 107; Eusden, "Introduction" in *Marrow*, 37. Ramus died in the St. Bartholomew's Day massacre in Paris on August 23/24, 1572.
[14] W.J. Ong, *Ramus, Method, and the Decay of Dialogue* (Cambridge: Harvard University, 1958), 304.

areas his commitment and influence surpassed even that of his Cambridge teachers.

Within this group of nonconforming Puritans at Christ's, Ames rapidly became the self-appointed watchman for moral living at the college. The college's vigorous criticism of the established religion – in particular the prelatical system and church ceremonies – earned the Cambridge Puritans a reputation as trouble-making agitators in the scholarly and ecclesiastical environment. But King James' tolerance had limits. Concerned for the internal stability that religious conformity and solidarity would surely lend his newly-acquired kingdom, and having thought the church had reformed enough, he called the Hampton Court conference in 1604. The results did not bode well for the Puritans throughout the kingdom. Legislated conformity was now strictly enforced resulting in repression at intellectual centers, particularly the venerable institutions of Oxford and Cambridge. Anyone opposed to conformity jeopardized reception of the academic degree or risked losing an already earned one.[15]

Even in the face of such official and severe recrimination, however, the Puritan solidarity was not deterred. It wasn't until the threats materialized that the college's non-conformity began to disintegrate. Chief Puritan spokesmen were punitively stripped of their academic responsibilities and dismissed. The end came in 1609 when the leadership of the college became vacant. When James I guaranteed the election of Valentine Cary as Master – a man whose anti-Puritan reputation preceded him – repression of the Puritan party intensified.[16] Although Carey turned out beneficial for the college it went not so well for the Puritans, who had lost their intellectual home with the official imposition and now strict enforcement of conformity. The "venerable Puritan tradition" was pacified[17] but not Ames whose opposition to and vocal renunciation of the established church and its practices continued unabated despite royal interference and official hostility to Puritan nonconformity. Finally his apparent impunity failed him. His unyielding commitment to the Puritan cause got him suspended from ecclesiastical duties and from all degrees. He was not actually expelled from the college but to remain at his alma mater promised a grim future at best so he chose voluntary and permanent leave. Indeed, the pressure of the universities and the church left all non-conforming Puritans with very limited options. Ames, in particular, became *persona non grata* in all official circles. He was hounded by the state even as city lecturer at Colchester, and, following only a

---

[15] Sprunger, *Ames*, 16-26.
[16] S.R. Pointer, "The Emmanuel College, Cambridge, Election of 1622: The Constraints of a Puritan Institution," in *Puritanism and Its Discontents*, L.L. Knoppers, ed. (Cranbury, NJ: Associated University, 2003), 118. In this 1622 Emmanuel College election, a campaign of secrecy was pursued because of what had happened in 1609 at Christ's College in the election of Carey. Pointer's account is fascinating.
[17] Pointer, "Emmanuel College Election," 118.

very brief time there, he left England for the Netherlands in 1610. He remained in exile there for the remainder of his life.[18]

An Expatriate in the Dutch Republic (1610-1633)

Early Modern Dutch Culture[19]
The seventeenth century was a period in which the Dutch Republic's fortunes and accomplishments plateaued in all respects. Located on the North Sea and with a well organized system of inland waterways, the Republic enjoyed unparalleled strategic advantages that facilitated trade, transportation, and communication resulting in the rapid accumulation of wealth. The protectionist tendencies and laissez-faire approach of government was augmented by economic passivity on the part of her European neighbors. It was not long before further riches poured into the Dutch coffers from the income of its colonial empire begun through the formation of the venerable Dutch East India Company.[20]

The Netherlands was an aristocratic country, both socially and politically. The power of the old landed nobility in the Republic remained slight, their outlook uncharacteristically resourceful and their ruling philosophy "simple and

---

[18] Sprunger, *Ames*, 20-23.
[19] This section draws on various sources describing the golden age of the Netherlands. Key among these are: M. Prak, *The Dutch Republic in the Seventeenth Century: The Golden Age*, trans. D. Webb (Cambridge: Cambridge University, 2005; reprint ed., 2008); J.I. Israel's majestic *The Dutch Republic: Its Rise, Greatness and Fall, 1477-1806* (Oxford: Clarendon, 1995); J.L. Price, *Holland and the Dutch Republic in the Seventeenth Century: The Politics of Particularism* (Oxford: Clarendon, 1992); S. Schama, *The Embarassment of Riches: An Interpretation of Dutch Culture in the Golden Age*, (London: William Collins & Sons, 1987); K.H.P. Haley, *The Dutch in the Seventeenth Century* (Norwich, England: Jarrold and Sons Ltd., 1972); J.H. Huizinga, *Dutch Civilization in the Seventeenth Century*, A.J. Pomerans, trans. (London: Collins Sons & Co. Ltd., 1968); P. Geyl, *The Netherlands in the Seventeenth Century: Part One, 1609-1648*, 2nd ed. (New York: Barnes & Noble, 1961); W.F. Dankbaar, *Hoogtepunten Uit Het Nederlandsche Calvinisme in de Zestiende Eeuw* (Haarlem: H.D. Tjeenk Willink & Zoon, 1946); J.L. Motley, *The Rise of the Dutch Republic*, 3 vols. (New York: Harper & Brothers, 1899); and D. Campbell, *The Puritan in Holland, England, and America: An Introduction to American History*, 2 vols. (New York: Harper & Brothers, 1892). The "Netherlands" in this section ("Low Countries" or "United Provinces") has reference to seventeen provinces, a geo-political unit, roughly comprising the present-day Netherlands ("Northern Provinces") and Belgium and Luxemburg ("Southern Provinces"). The nomenclature "Dutch Republic" pertains to the Republic of the United Netherlands, the seven northern provinces after 1588, approximately the same as the present-day Netherlands. Except where noted, all foreign language translations in this book are my own.
[20] Israel, *Dutch Republic*, 241-75, 307-27, 344-48, 400-10, 467, 473-74, 496-97, 540-42; Huizinga, *Dutch Civilization*, 10, 15-25; Geyl, *Netherlands*, 189-208; Campbell, *Puritan in Holland*, 2.316-2.317. This prosperity led to the development of modern banking institutions well before this concept arose anywhere else in Europe. The first commercial bank in Europe opened in Amsterdam in 1609 (Schama, *Embarassment of Riches*, 345).

patriarchal." Business and politics fused together, as the power of the waning medieval church combined with this weak nobility to leave a gap in the political and social structure – a gap rapidly filled by the rising merchant class.[21]

The urban nature of seventeenth-century Dutch culture made for an interesting cultural matrix of the body politic. On the one hand, the common people – made up of a large class of artisans, small businessmen, sailors, shipbuilders, fishermen and farmers – enjoyed a high standard of living. The wealthy townsmen, on the other hand – the merchants and financiers – became the government of the day and transformed into a true burgher aristocracy. But significantly, this aristocracy was surprisingly free of the corruption and inertia that characterized other European governments. Government was benevolent and the comparative simplicity of the wealthy classes bespoke a society that had not lost its virtuous moorings of an earlier day. The high sense of dignity and status among the ordinary people was displayed in their patronage of the arts and in their indulgence in cultural events that matched the propensities of the aristocracy. This cultural achievement was the result of economic prosperity that was shared by everyone, including those on poor relief. It is said that even the cobbler owned a painting.[22]

Life in the Golden Age was extremely sociable and this ethos was touched by simplicity and thrift. Intellectually, the influence of Erasmus over all of Dutch life was significantly greater than that of Calvin, whose influence in the Netherlands, for the most part, dated from around 1550, although it didn't really pick up steam until 1560 and beyond.[23] Huizinga asserts that "the Scottish Presbyterians were far churchier than their Dutch counterparts. . . . Humanism in a specifically northern form, and differing characteristically from the Humanism of the Italians, French and Germans, has always been the soil on which Dutch culture flourished."[24] And despite the Calvinistic doctrines that made prayer the "chief intellectual diet" of the people, Dutch society was one which

---

[21] For an excellent survey of the evolution of the merchant elite in Amsterdam and Antwerp, see Israel, *Dutch Republic*, 309-12, 344-48, 553-54; Huizinga, *Dutch Civilization*, 18-20. Schama paints a delightful portrait of the Golden Age Dutch mentalité in *Embarassment of Riches*.

[22] Israel goes on to say that the social welfare system became an effective means of enforcing social control (Israel, *Dutch Republic*, 358, 547-91). See also Huizinga, *Dutch Civilization*, 40.

[23] Israel, *Dutch Republic*, 101-5, 328-60. Huizinga, *Dutch Civilization*, 41-61. Israel identifies the primary political and ecclesiastical factors that pushed forward the spread of Calvinism after this period.

[24] Huizinga, *Dutch Civilization*, 53. Huizinga does not elaborate further on this northern form of humanism, except to say that he means humanism in the sense of the intellectual phenomenon of the late Middle Ages and that matured in the first half of the sixteenth century. We can only surmise that he means a particular humanism that resulted from (or motivated) a "fusion of piety with love of learning and culture" that had rooted in the Netherlands "long before Calvin proclaimed his hard doctrine in the year of Erasmus' death" (*Dutch Civilization*, 53). See also Israel, *Dutch Republic*, 44-54, 566-67, 575-81.

continued to embrace the cultural fruits of economic prosperity and political benevolence.

The broader political and intellectual culture to which Ames had emigrated differed significantly from that found at home. The Republic was driven by a number of republican ideals amidst post-Reformation confessional formulation and solidification in the ecclesiastical realm. These ideals were interrelated and were evidenced primarily in these three broad areas: the republican ideals of freedom and toleration, the interplay of theological development and enlightenment discovery, and the ecclesiastical hegemony of the public (Reformed) Church.

From its beginnings, the Republic held sacred the notions of freedom and privilege. These much-celebrated ideals had been part of the Dutch psyche, going back to fifteenth-century Burgundian Netherlands when the loosely federated seventeen provinces had always had the "privilege" of autonomous self rule.[25] Any attempt to impose a central-style government over the provinces was perceived as a flagrant violation of these agreed-upon self-governing "privileges" constituting a serious threat to the very independence of the Republic.

This more restrictive sense of political privilege and freedom came to evolve into a broader, more abstract, principle – the modern idea of toleration centered around the notion of freedom of conscience.[26] Indeed, this concept lay at the center of life in everyday encounter, from the simplest to the most complex, from determining the rules of engagement in human discourse to defining the features of rival ideological blocs, whether philosophical (Aristotle and Ramus), theological (medieval or Reformed), political (Orangist or republican), or ecclesiastical (Reformed or non-Reformed). In reality, however, there was no widespread agreement about how this ideal of toleration could or even should be enforced, notably in the area of religion. Toleration, as admirable as it was in the abstract proved a slippery principle upon which to reach accord and was even more elusive in practice. Despite the fact that the official policy after the Revolt was one of toleration – freedom to worship according to the dictates of one's conscience – all expressions of worship but the mainstream Reformed – the Calvinist – were subject to varying degrees and practices of intolerance, particularly when the Reformed Church became the public church. A non-agreeable mix of beliefs had found residence in the Republic by the late sixteenth century in the midst of the process of Reformed confessionalization. At points throughout the seventeenth century Reformed intolerance of Roman Catholics, Lutherans, Anabaptists, Mennonites, Remonstrants and Jews was relatively commonplace. And many of the agitators themselves were only loosely committed to Reformation doctrine – crypto-Protestants.[27]

---

[25] Prak, *Dutch Republic*, 15.
[26] Israel, *Dutch Republic*, 2-5.
[27] Israel, *Dutch Republic*, 372-77. R.P-C. Hsia and H. van Nierop have together assembled and edited an innovative and provocative group of essays probing this well-known

Toward an Uneasy Reformed Hegemony
Despite broader repression, persecution and execution by the Spanish authorities, the Reformation – if in "diverse hues" – made significant headway in the Netherlands in the first half of the sixteenth century. This can be attributable to the spread of Luther's work and the ongoing effects of reform promoted by movements such as the Brethren of the Common life.[28] Reformed thought took on a distinctly Calvinistic flavor, however, under the influence of Dutch refugees outside of the Republic's borders. "The main impulse behind the rise of the Reformed Church to dominance within the Netherlands Reformation flowed [from] the Dutch-speaking refugee churches in London and in Germany."[29] Because of the isolation from the centers of church hierarchy and government, the influential prelatical system of the established church prior to the Reformation was never firmly established in the north. By the turn of the century, most of the patriciate had received their education in the Protestant church, so unimpeded was the advance of Calvinism, and much of society at large was rooted in the Protestant faith.[30] Calvinist Protestantism became the officially recognized religion, particularly in the north while the southern Netherlands, being more firmly rooted in the medieval church, resisted.[31] In the north, Dutch appropriation of Calvinistic doctrines resulted in rapid formation of the Dutch Reformed Church with the development of the *Belgic Confession* by Guido de Brès in 1561, the translation of the *Heidelberg Catechism* from German into

---

Dutch tradition of religious tolerance. The volume successfully challenges the commonly-held thesis of Dutch permissiveness during the Golden Age and concludes that this established reputation is rooted in myth. See their *Calvinism and Religious Toleration in the Dutch Golden Age* (Cambridge: Cambridge University, 2002).

[28] Israel, *Dutch Republic*, 74-101; Huizinga, *Dutch Civilization*, 19, 47-48. An interesting eighteenth-century source for the historiography of the Reformation and the Netherlands of this period is found in G. Brandt, *The History of the Reformation and Other Ecclesiastical Transactions in and about the Low-Countries, from the Beginning of the Eighth Century, down to the Famous Synod of Dort*, 4 vols. (London: T. Wood, 1720-23; reprint ed., New York: AMS, 1979). See also *Documenta Reformata: Teksten uit de Geschiedenis van Kerk en Theologie in de Nederlanden sedert de Hervorming*, J.N. Bakhuizen van den Brink et al., eds., 2 vols. (Kampen: J.H. Kok, 1960-62). D. Nauta's work in this place and time of religious history is invaluable. See his *Het Calvinisme in Nederland* (Franeker: Wever, 1949) and *De Nederlandsche Gereformeerden en het Independentisme in de zeventiende eeuwe* (Amsterdam: H.J. Paris, 1935). See also Israel, *Dutch Republic*, 101-4, 146, 163-64, 221-22, 226-28, 361-72, 391-94, 422-24, 434-36, 598-603.

[29] Israel, *Dutch Republic*, 101.

[30] Huizinga, *Dutch Civilization*, 19, 47-48.

[31] There was also a Jewish community in Amsterdam (which produced Spinoza), in addition to Lutherans and Anabaptists (Huizinga, *Dutch Civilization*, 54-55). But although some Puritans considered Anabaptists as a "revolutionary conspiracy," Ames considered them no more than a "troublesome and annoying distraction for the Elect" (K.L. Sprunger, "William Ames, A Seventeenth-Century Puritan, Looks at the Anabaptists," *MQR* 39 [1965]: 73).

Dutch by Pieter Datheen, (Lat., Petrus Dathenus) in 1563 and the adoption of a constitution (church order) in 1571 modeled after that in Geneva. The *Genevan Psalter* was also translated into Dutch by Datheen and became the official hymnal of the Dutch Reformed Church in the Netherlands.[32] All the elements for an organized Calvinistic Church were in place within a quarter of a century of the introduction of Calvinism, and that under the persecuting reign of Charles V. When Ames entered the Republic the Netherlands had worked through almost half a century of ecclesiastical and theological reconstruction in the midst of political turmoil and continual war with Spain.[33]

But in the early decades of the seventeenth century, Protestantism was by no means overly dominant. This was a time of significant victory for the Roman Catholic Reformation in the northern Netherlands, notably between 1609 and the 1630s, a period coincident with Ames' life in the Republic. The Catholic faithful met with significant persecution in Friesland around 1620[34] when Ames was himself doing battle with the great Roman Catholic Jesuit scholastic Robert Bellarmine. In fact, confessionalization was characteristic of all religious groupings and had successfully taken hold amongst all traditions. Consequently, the province was divided into four blocs – Reformed, Mennonite, Catholic and the "libertines." All confessional groups were growing, but growth in the Reformed camp was most robust, most steady, and most permanent. The close interweaving of religion and politics made for complex relations. "Church allegiance and confessional rivalry were inextricably entwined in early modern times, with political life and statecraft."[35] Resurgent Catholicism notably in the north, with its attendant loyalty to Spain, was even considered anti-republican. The entire legitimacy of the Republic was viewed with considerable doubt by the Catholics. Thus, party factions and competing ideologies characterized life in the Dutch Republic as the seventeenth century opened.

The public church had existed uneasily within the religious pluralism that existed from around 1580, "when this new religion [Calvinism] was more or

---

[32] Israel, *Dutch Republic*, 102, 164.

[33] The Eighty Years War between the Netherlands and Spain commenced in 1568 with the rebellion of the Dutch against Spanish imperialism and tyranny. The revolt was led by Calvinist William the Silent, Prince of Orange, who was assassinated in 1584. Although Spain granted the Netherlands *de jure* independence at the Peace of Westphalia in 1648, (the occasion of which marked the practical end of the Holy Roman Empire), Dutch independence had been generally acknowledged by Spain as early as 1609 at the beginning of the Twelve Year Truce (Israel, *Dutch Republic*, 241-44); R.G. Clouse, "Thirty Years' War (1618-48)" *NIDCC*, 970; B.G. Armstrong, "Westphalia, Peace of (1648)" *NIDCC*, 1040; and J.W. van Loon, *Kerkgeschiedenis in Synchronistisch Verband met de Wereldgeschiedenis*, 2nd printing (Amsterdam: Hoveker & Zoon, 1878, 300-26).

[34] Israel, *Dutch Republic*, 383. Zeeland saw significant persecution as well at this time.

[35] Israel, *Dutch Republic*, 390.

less imposed on the people."[36] The ecclesiastical reorganization in the Netherlands that was required following the dismantling of the Roman Catholic system was a massive enterprise, somewhat chaotic, disorganized and resisted at points, in a country still engaged in battle with Spain. The more stable States of Friesland assured themselves of the right to intervene to assure purity of doctrine.[37] It was a time of ecclesiastical, political and theological uncertainty. W. Bergsma argues that the perception of Friesland as a country of "militant Calvinism" along these lines endured because the chief magistrate of Friesland, Willem Lodewijk (1560-1620) was a staunch Calvinist himself.[38]

Around the turn of the century, approximately 25 per cent of the Frisian population was Anabaptist and the Reformed had "the psychology of a minority." The following surprising claim has been made:

> In 1600 the majority of the people of Friesland were Lutheran, Mennonites, Catholics and neutrals, who preferred to make no choice, the rest being *heromnes* "who could not tolerate the burning of heretics." Add to this the fact that numerous people were undecided in religious matters, that indifference could lead to atheism, that some districts . . . had been no more than superficially converted to Christianity, that the doors of the Reformed churches were not open to all and sundry and that the majority of those who attended their services were not professed members but only 'adherents' who had as yet no desire to join the Church and it will be obvious that the situation at the beginning of the seventeenth century was much less clear-cut than has generally been assumed.[39]

The presence of crypto-Protestantism was problematic for Reformed pastors. From his study of the correspondence of the ministers of the time in which is shown their deep concern over the lack of piety in the general population, Bergsma concludes that "the new doctrines were not greeted with universal enthusiasm." The religious faith of the day constituted an "amalgam of Christian ideas, magic, *Aberglauben*, indifference and endemic ignorance." Yet Bergsma's study of the diaries of farmer Dirck Janszoon (1578-1636) indicate an individual who demonstrated a God-fearing piety, faithful devotion to scrip-

---

[36] W. Bergsma, "'Slow to hear God's Holy Word'?: Religion in everyday life in early modern Friesland" in *Experiences and explanations: Historical and sociological essays on religion in everyday life*, L. Laeyendecker, L.G. Jansma, and C.H.A. Verhaar, eds. (Leeuwarden: Fryske Akademy, 1990), 59-78; Israel, *Dutch Republic*, 361-98, 637-74.

[37] Bergsma gives the following reason for the establishment of the University of Franeker: In 1580 "when the priests went into compulsory retirement, the need for clergymen to take their place was obvious. Shortly afterwards, in 1585, it was therefore decided to establish a university in Franeker "for Christ and his Church." The professors would be required to sign the catechism and the Confessio Belgica in person" ("Slow to hear," 61).

[38] Bergsma, "Slow to hear," 62.

[39] Bergsma, "Slow to hear," 62. The execution of heretics was advocated by Beza in his *Een Christalijnen Bril* (1602), translated into Dutch and circulated in Friesland at this time.

ture and family, and who took his membership in the Reformed Church seriously. Bergsma concludes that between these two ends of the spectrum – careless mockery of the Reformed faith at one end and heartfelt love for this same faith at the other – existed the large majority of the population with adherence to a variety of denominations "on offer" but with no true commitment to any.[40] With "due caution" Bergsma suggests that "Dirck Janszoon represented, to a certain extent, the Reformed ideal in the early seventeenth century, but that the Preacher's story nevertheless reflects the true situation: most Frisians were . . . slow to hear God's Holy Word.[41] This view seems to be confirmed by well-known Dutch Reformed pietist Willem Teellinck who lamented that the large majority of the population had changed from Roman Catholicism to the Reformed faith in name only, maintaining their former lifestyle.[42]

While religious pluralism posed its challenges within the Republic's dominant Protestant ethos, the most divisive issue of the day erupted within the official church. It is a curiosity of history that of the many controversies, the most divisive of all was that within the Dutch Reformed Church itself in 1603.[43] The area of conflict into which Ames was drawn upon his appearance in the Netherlands was the theological battle just beginning to rage over the teaching of Jacobus Arminius (1560-1609), a professor of theology at influential and prestigious Leiden University.[44] Leiden had been established in 1575 to "bolster the political and religious separatism of Holland and Zeeland" as a center of study for the liberal arts and sciences, undergirded with theology, while the universities at Franeker, Utrecht and Groningen had been planted, first and foremost, as protectors and bastions of Calvinistic orthodoxy.[45] Because the universities

---

[40] Bergsma, "Slow to hear," 65-69.
[41] Bergsma, "Slow to hear," 71.
[42] Willem Teellinck, *Eubulus ofte Tractaet Vervattende Verscheyden Aenmerckingen over de tegenwoordige staet onzer Christelicker Gemeynte*, D.D. Theodorus and Johannes Teellinck, V.D.M., eds. (Utrecht: Hermannus Specht, Hermannus Ribbius, and Johannes van Waesberge, 1657), 21; H. Bouwman, *Willem Teellinck en de practijk der godzaligheid*, (Kampen: J.H. Kok, 1928; reprint ed., Kampen: De Groot Goudriaan, 1985), 10.
[43] Israel, *Dutch Republic*, 391-93.
[44] Interestingly, Arminius also embraced the logic of Ramism, a system to which he gave "enthusiastic espousal" while a student at Leiden (C. Bangs, *Arminius: A Study in the Dutch Reformation* [Nashville: Abingdon, 1971], 55). See also Israel, *Dutch Republic*, for excellent coverage of Leiden University, from its origins to its decline (198, 393-94, 430, 456-57, 565-94, 662-63, 901, 1049-51).
[45] Israel, *Dutch Republic*, 569-70; Huizinga, *Dutch Civilization*, 57-59. This strong position of Huizinga is challenged, however, by Dankbaar, who claims that if Huizinga is at all accurate, "it is only true insofar as there prevailed a more rigid conception of "orthodoxy" there [at Franeker, Utrecht, Harderwijk and Groningen] and that this position was much less official and less deliberately presented [in Leiden]; in actual fact, however, orthodoxy was equally present there" (Dankbaar, *Nederlandsche Calvinisme*, 141). Israel attributes the initial disappointing attraction of Leiden to its "less than solid reputation

were "unencumbered by the weight of the medieval past" considerable latitude was allowed in intellectual life.⁴⁶ This latitude was exercised by a group of counter-Calvinists – followers of Arminius – in the formal challenge they posed to a handful of central Calvinistic doctrines, thereby positioning themselves in direct opposition to the Calvinistic ecclesiastical (and political) establishment whose intellectual leader was Gomarus. Even the generally lax spirit of the day was unprepared for such overt challenge to orthodoxy – if loosely upheld – and this brash neo-Arminian offensive in state and church circles forced an assembly of divines to meet at the city of Dordrecht from 1618-1619. As mentioned, the Synod decided in favor of the Contra-Remonstrants (Calvinists) and purged church, state and university of all known Arminians.⁴⁷ Ames' appointment at Franeker placed him in the cradle of early modern Reformed orthodoxy.

Ames' Place in the Republic
The large English community in the Netherlands of the late-sixteenth and seventeenth centuries was made up of merchants, craftsmen, soldiers with the English and Scottish regiments and religious refugees.⁴⁸ This accounted for the presence of English churches and preachers in almost every large town of the western Netherlands. The golden age spirit was of a republican and tolerant nature and sacred sanctuary was held out for all, particularly for religious dissenters and non-conformists from England. Perhaps even more important for the Puritan cause was the success of continental publishers in broadening the Puritan audience.⁴⁹ Dutch participation (the English would say "complicity") in the dissemination of Puritan literature constituted a brisk business, a commercial venture introduced around the beginning of the seventeenth century and partly financed by English merchants. By the time Ames appeared on the scene, then, the Puritan agenda was not an unfamiliar one to Dutch ecclesiastical and theological life.⁵⁰ It was an interesting, if not altogether unexpected develop-

---

amongst strict Calvinists" who opted for Geneva or Heidelberg and, after 1585, preferred Franeker (*Dutch Republic*, 570-72).
⁴⁶ Israel, *Dutch Republic*, 565-87; Huizinga, *Dutch Civilization*, 58.
⁴⁷ An excellent and brief summary of the theological issues at stake and the church/state interests and how these were resolved is found in W. Walker et al., *A History of the Christian Church*, 4th ed. (New York: Charles Scribner's Sons, 1985), 538-42.
⁴⁸ A.C. Carter, "The Ministry to the English Churches in the Netherlands in the Seventeenth Century," *BIHR* 33 (Nov. 1960): 166. See also K.L. Sprunger, "Other Pilgrims in Leiden: Hugh Goodyear and the English Reformed Church," *CH* 41 (1972): 46-60.
⁴⁹ Hsia observes that religious toleration generally was most visible through the writing of the period – "the formation of a textual and intellectual community that crossed religious boundaries" (*Calvinism and Religious Toleration*, 6).
⁵⁰ The activity of Dutch printing houses in the translation and publication of the Puritan exiles' writing is well known. See, for example, K.L. Sprunger, *Trumpets from the Tower: English Puritan Printing in the Netherlands, 1600-1640*, Brill's Studies in Intellectual History, A.J. Vanderjagt, ed., no. 46 (Leiden: E.J. Brill, 1994) and W.J. op 't Hof, *Engelse Piëtistische Geschriften in het Nederlands, 1598-1622* (Rotterdam: Lindenberg,

ment, that the success in the advance of the Puritan, non-conformist movement in this tolerant environment "made English religion in the Netherlands distinctly more Puritan than at home."[51] The significance of this was not lost on the English establishment. Indeed, in a statement on church and political circumstances amongst the English in the Netherlands in 1632, it was reported with considerable alarm to the Privy Council in London that there existed

> ... about 25 or 30 English churches in the Low Countries, which are largely seminaries of disorderly preachers. And although some may think that the empire is finally rid of them because they are overseas, they actually do more damage there than they could do here by dishonoring our nation, writing provocative books and conducting ongoing correspondence with the recalcitrants in England.[52]

Of no individual would this assessment prove to be more apt than of the expatriate influential preacher/teacher, William Ames. Subsequent events would indeed confirm that it was only by death that the empire would be finally and permanently rid of Ames.

After a very brief stay in Rotterdam and a short chaplaincy in Leiden,[53] Ames, in 1611, took a position as chaplain to Sir Horace Vere, commander of the English forces at The Hague.[54] Vere was a "knight of Puritan persuasion"

1987). For a broader picture, see *Short-Title Catalog of Books Printed in England, Scotland, Ireland, Wales and British America and of English Books Printed in Other Countries, 1641-1700*, D.G. Wing, ed., 3 vols. (New York: Columbia University, 1945-51).

[51] Sprunger, *Ames*, 28-29; Horton, *Ames by Nethenus*, 4.

[52] J.N. Bakhuizen van den Brink, "Engelse Kerkelijke Politiek in de Nederlanden in de Eerste Helft der 17de Eeuw," *NAK* 39 (1952): 132-46; quote from p. 132. For an early record of the impact of some of the English exiles on the proceedings at the Westminster Assembly see T. Goodwin et al., *An Apologeticall Narration of Some Ministers Formerly Exiles in the Netherlands: Now Members of the Assembly of Divines, Humbly Submitted to the Honourable House of Parliament* (London, 1643).

[53] It was here, in this very brief visit, that Ames entered into discussions on the nature of the church and became a committed Congregationalist for the remainder of his life (Sprunger, *Ames*, 29-30 and 39-44 and Horton, *Ames by Visscher*, 42). Publications written in favor of congregational church government (and anti-prelatical by definition) would later be held against him during his chaplaincy at The Hague (Sprunger, *Ames*, 32-36). For an account of the congregationalism in the Netherlands during this period, see R.P. Stearns, *Congregationalism in the Dutch Netherlands: The Rise and Fall of the English Congregational Classis, 1621-1635* (Chicago: The American Society of Church History, 1940). Ames' ecclesiology has recently received scholarly attention by B.R. Davis in his "Reformation while tarrying for many: The radical Puritan ecclesiology of William Ames" (Ph.D. diss., Southern Baptist Theological Seminary, 2010).

[54] Sprunger, *Ames*, 30. See Sprunger's detailed accounting of the activities of the English speaking churches in the Netherlands at the time in his *Dutch Puritanism: A History of English and Scottish Churches of the Netherlands in the Sixteenth and Seventeenth Centuries*, Studies in the History of Christian Thought, H.A. Oberman, ed., no. 31 (Leiden: E.J. Brill, 1982). See 142ff. for activity of the church at The Hague and Ames' and

and, to the delight of the Puritans, he and his wife were devout believers. In an environment where the attention of the English presence directed itself to commerce and war, high piety and sound worship ranked low.[55] Maintaining such a religious disposition in this climate earned Vere the respect of the Puritan party, especially in the context of growing tension between the egalitarian Dutch and the intolerant English. The Dutch policy of harboring English expatriates and enabling them to promote their cause from legitimate platforms in church and school became a major source of international conflict between these two countries. Navigating the irritable sensitivities required political acumen. Although endorsement was not sought, placement of English ministers into Dutch ecclesiastical environments typically took into consideration, at least to some degree, the sentiments of the English authorities.[56] But Ames managed to serve as military chaplain and regular preacher to the English inhabitants in the town to 1618. It was during his tenure at The Hague that he married the daughter of John Burgess, his predecessor there, but she died shortly after marriage. Ames remarried and his wife bore three children.[57]

To appease the English establishment and wisely deciding in his own best interests, Ames largely left the Anglicans alone in favor of the Separatists and Arminians. These two groups quickly replaced the Church of England as the immediate targets of his efforts to promote, in the case of the former, "true religion and the power of it" and to convince, in the case of the latter, of the soundness of congregational ecclesiastical organization. Overwhelmingly, however, it was the anti-Remonstrant cause that Ames found himself championing. Arminian tendencies in the Netherlands were present everywhere, particularly at influential Leiden University – the haven of strict Calvinism – and battle lines were being drawn as Ames entered the public theological and ecclesiastical arena of the Netherlands in the Arminian controversy.[58]

Because Ames' Calvinist reputation was by now well-established through his much published polemic with leading Arminian controversialists, and in recognition of his unmatched proficiency in fighting the Arminian battle, the Dutch ecclesiastical establishment beckoned him for service to Dordrecht in

---

other Puritans' involvement and ministry. In this connection, see also F.O. Dentz, *History of the English Church at the Hague, 1586-1929* (Delft: W.D. Meinema, 1929).

[55] Horton, *Ames by Visscher*, 30, 42; Sprunger, *Ames*, 34.

[56] Carter, "Ministry to the English Churches," 168.

[57] Sprunger, *Ames*, 34, 250-53; Horton, *Ames by Nethenus*, 20. Ames' second wife, Joan, would outlive him, join the migration to Salem, Massachusetts, in 1637 and die in Cambridge in 1644. Both Ames' sons, William and John, attended Harvard and had already returned to England (Wrentham, Suffolk) by 1645, after William had graduated Harvard. William was a minister. See the fascinating story of the return to England of many New England "pilgrims," including William Ames' sons, in Susan Hardman Moore, *Pilgrims: New World Settlers and the Call of Home* (London: Yale University, 2007; reprint ed., 2010). The detailed appendices alone are invaluable.

[58] Horton, *Ames by Visscher*, 43-44.

1618, to help deal with those pesky Remonstrants. The Englishman Ames was tapped for the key (non-voting) position of theological advisor to the president of the synod, Johannes Bogerman. As synod-related theological issues came to consume all of his energies, it was perhaps propitious that the pressure from across the channel could no longer be resisted, and the English establishment in the Netherlands was successfully prevailed upon to dismiss Ames from his chaplaincy in The Hague for his continuing non-conformity.[59] He could devote himself to his new calling without reserve.

Even after Dort and the triumph of the Calvinists, the English church and state were relentless in their pursuit of William Ames. This chase had now gone on, with various degrees of enthusiasm, for the better part of a decade. Following the closure of the Synod many Remonstrants and their sympathizers were purged from centers of influence in state affairs and intellectual circles. When Leiden University (1575) elected Ames to fill a newly-formed chair in theological ethics, it seemed a foregone conclusion that he would receive an appointment to a professorial position at the world-famous academy.[60] But the formal protest of the English state and church, as sustained and severe as it was, trumped the resolve of the university and city council of Leiden and Ames was denied the chair. After three years of tutoring in the city to support his family, he was invited in 1622 to a theological vacancy at a much less prestigious university in Friesland: the Calvinist and orthodox University of Franeker (1585). With the prospects of signing such an illustrious and influential scholar to their faculty, Franeker blithely ignored the long reach of the English establishment and Ames embarked on a fruitful eleven-year tenure there.[61]

Successfully sustaining his defense of thirty-eight theses and four corollaries on moral theology and Christian ethics under Sibrandus Lubbertus (c. 1555-1625) earned Ames the Doctor of Theology degree. With this in hand he advanced to the professorial chair. It was from this occasion until his departure from the northern Netherlands that Ames made his greatest contributions to theology, casuistry and the Puritan cause, notably with his completion of *Medulla Theologiae* (*Marrow of Theology*)[62] and *De Conscientia, et Eius Iure, vel*

---

[59] Sprunger, *Ames*, 49-51; Eusden, "Introduction" in *Marrow*, 6. On Bogerman, see H.E. van der Tuuk, *Johannes Bogerman* (Groningen: J. B. Walters, 1868) and G.P. Itterzon, *Johannes Bogerman* (Amsterdam: Ton Bolland, 1980). On the transmission of information from the proceedings of the Synod, see J. Hales, *Letters from the Synod of Dort to Sir Dudley Carlton, the English embasssador at the Hague* (Glasgow: Robert and Andrew Foulis, 1765).
[60] "Documents Bearing upon the Recommendation of Ames to the Professorship at Leyden," Horton, *Ames by Visscher*, 151-53.
[61] Sprunger, *Ames*, 65-70; Horton, *Ames by Nethenus*, 53-55, 151-53; Eusden, "Introduction" in *Marrow*, 6.
[62] First published as *Medulla Theologiae, ex sacris literis, earumque interpretibus extracta, & methodice disposita*. Amstelodami: Joannem Janssonium, 1623 (fragments), 1627. [*The Marrow of Sacred Divinity, Drawne out of the holy Scriptures, and the In-*

Casibus (*Conscience with the Power and Cases Thereof*),[63] both works of which had seen partial pre-releases, of sorts, under the auspices of earlier projects.

Next on Ames' to-do list was the setting of a reforming agenda for which he would become famous, an agenda with which he would seek to elevate the Christian establishment to his high standards of faith and life. He remembered the slipping morality in his home country; he observed an arid orthodoxy in some quarters of the academy; he discovered a lack of piety – heart religion – in the Dutch church; and what he considered impiety and loose morality among colleagues and undisciplined students disappointed him. To a non-conforming Puritan these behaviors were anathema to vital Christianity, betraying something less than "religion and the power of it." Ames' reforming agenda constituted the reconstruction of vital practical divinity and the disciplined life.[64]

With such a plan for the renewal of orthodoxy in faith and morals, coupled with his unwavering Puritan commitment to see it through, it was not long before he found himself engaged in controversy with Johannes Maccovius whose emphasis appeared to be more in theoretical systematic theology and militant theological disputation and less in practical divinity. Indeed, while Ames saw Maccovius promoting Aristotelian metaphysics a little too enthusiastically, for his part Maccovius, took exception to Ames' piety and his Ramist pedagogical philosophy. It was during this time that Ames shifted from theological polemics to emphasizing the theological life, particularly for students called to the ministry. Although good and pious character was expected of all the students at the university, in students of theology was this most especially necessary. "One can be a good tailor, shepherd, or plowman, without being a good man," Ames declared. "But a man who is not good, and even something more, never comes out a good minister."[65] After all, Franeker had been committed *Christo et Ecclesia*.

Despite the school's location on the periphery of European intellectual life, it had a reputable faculty, notably in the areas of biblical studies, theology and philosophy. Ames' presence there upped the ante even further. As a result, students from all over the world were attracted to this remote corner of the United Provinces. With the help of similar-minded colleagues, Ames was at least partially successful in reform towards piety. In addition, before he was through, and against considerable opposition, Franeker officially adopted Ramist philos-

---

terpreters thereof, and brought into Method. London: Printed by Edward Griffin for John Rothwell, 1642.]

[63] First published as *De Conscientia, et Eius Iure, vel Casibus, libre quinque*. Amstelodami: Joannem Janssonium, 1622 (as doctoral thesis), 1630. Appearing at the end of *Conscientia* was an exhortation to the Franeker students entitled "Paraenesis, ad Studiosos Theologiae, habita Franekerae, Aug. 22, anno 1623"; the English language translation is the work of D. Horton, hereafter, "Exhortation."

[64] Sprunger, *Ames*, 78-85; Eusden, "Introduction" in *Marrow*, 8-10; Horton, *Ames by Visscher*, 120-40.

[65] Ames, "Exhortation."

ophy, logic and rhetoric, and became the center for Ramism in Europe.[66] The Puritan allegiance to creed was served well by Ramism, as was the passion for efficient scriptural interpretation; as an added bonus Ramist rhetoric guaranteed that this creedal subscription and biblical exposition would spur to action.[67]

By 1633 Ames personal and professional options were bright. Bermuda threw out the welcome mat: he had received an invitation from the Puritan governor there, where he was "most entirely beloved and reverenced."[68] New England was calling: since 1632 Ames had been under pressure to join a group of Puritan contemporaries and colleagues in the new plantation there.[69] And opportunities in Rotterdam beckoned. Consequently, Ames resigned from the university,[70] disheartened by the unyielding polemical spirit of his colleague Maccovius, weakened by the weather of the northern Netherlands and encouraged to leave by a wife who had never felt at home in Franeker. He chose in favor of Rotterdam, induced by a promised appointment as an associate minister, with Hugh Peter, in a large English Congregational church. This was a difficult invitation to resist, because it came with a teaching post at the soon-to-be-formed Puritan college, a tempting prospect for a Puritan who had already proven he could move effortlessly between church and academy.[71] And so, fol-

---

[66] Sprunger, *Ames*, 79-80, 88, 111; Horton, *Ames by Visscher*, 59-60. One of Franeker's more famous students was René Descartes (1596-1650).

[67] Miller, *Seventeenth Century*, 328-29.

[68] G.L. Kittredge, "A Note on Dr. William Ames," *CSM* 13 (1910): 61, cited in Sprunger, *Ames*, 251.

[69] *CSM* 13: 62. Noteworthy among these contemporaries was Thomas Hooker (1586-1647) who also had received a call to the English church in Rotterdam but who had gone on to New England. Curiously, Ames' earliest biographer, Matthew Nethenus, makes no mention of any tentative plans Ames may have had to advance from Rotterdam to New England. Nethenus' only reference to America in connection with Ames is regarding Ames' widow and children going on to America, "where, after she had lived for some time in respect and even, because she was Mrs. Ames, in honor, she bade farewell to this world and followed her husband" (Horton, *Ames by Nethenus*, 19-20). Eusden's very brief but excellent account of Ames' life mentions this last detail (Eusden, "Introduction" in *Marrow*, 9-11).

[70] An excellent account of the controversy swirling around Ames from the time of his arrival in Franeker to his departure has been written by C. van der Woude, "Amesius' Afscheid van Franeker," *NAK* 52 (1971-1972): 153-77. Of particular value is the record of the reaction of Franeker to Ames' departure and the attempts by the Academy to keep him there ("Afscheid," 165-77). See also K.L. Sprunger, "William Ames and the Franeker link to English and American Puritanism," in *Universiteit te Franeker: 1585-1811*, G.Th. Jensma, F.R.H. Smit, F. Westra, eds. (Leeuwarden: Fryske Academy, 1985), 264-74.

[71] Sprunger observes that by 1633 the concentration of English exiles in Rotterdam made this city the center of Puritan activity in the Netherlands (Sprunger, *Ames*, 92; Horton, *Ames by Visscher*, 60-62). On Hugh Peter, see R.P. Stearns, *The Strenuous Puritan: Hugh Peter, 1598-1660* (Urbana, IL: University of Illinois, 1954).

lowing the tenth anniversary of his sojourn in Friesland, Ames and his family took their leave.

But unfortunately the plan for ministry in Rotterdam was cut short. On November 11, 1633, two months after arriving in Rotterdam, Ames died of shock and exposure suffered when his house was flooded during a storm.[72] It is a curious footnote to the life of so influential an individual that all but his native land would unashamedly lay claim to him on behalf of country. Well-known Puritan and prolific New England historian Cotton Mather (1663-1728) could wistfully assert in 1702 that William Ames, that "angelical doctor," "was *intentionally* a New-England man, though not *eventually*"[73] while a more contemporary continental historian, J.N. Bakhuizen van den Brink, could declare, with confidence, that were it not for his premature death, Ames, who ". . . had been already for some time the spiritual father of the Independents in the Netherlands, would have become the great theologian there."[74] On the other hand, the official position of England's political and religious establishment was represented by Archbishop of Canterbury George Abbot, who intoned in a letter in March, 1611, that "if he [Amias] were here amoungst us . . . some exemplary Punishment would be his Reward."[75]

A Brief Summary of William Ames' Works

Here we provide only a very short summary of Ames' work. The theological, moral and teaching documents that he produced – his *Marrow*, his *Conscience* and his *Catechisme* – are each the subject of thorough study later in this work. His other works will be introduced and drawn upon where needed.

Ames' writing can be classified into two broad categories, each of which represents related foci of concern and interest. One group of literature relates to a period when personal circumstances, ecclesiastical developments, political currents and theological movements motivated Ames to pick up his pen. The second part of his corpus represents his life interest. In addition, his authorship also is evident in miscellaneous and often briefer writings more difficult to classify such as university addresses and various correspondences.[76]

The first category of writing can be classified as polemical and comprises, firstly, the anti-prelatic writing of the early part of his career at Cambridge and

---

[72] Sprunger, *Ames*, 94; Horton, *Ames by Visscher*, 62-63; Horton, *Ames by Nethenus*, 19.
[73] Cotton Mather, *The Great Works of Christ in America or Magnalia Christi Americana*, 3rd ed., vol. 1 (Hartford: Silas Andrus and Son, 1853; reprint ed., Edinburgh: Banner of Truth Trust, 1979), 236.
[74] Bakhuizen van den Brink, "Engelse Kerkelijke Politiek," 137.
[75] *Memorials of Affairs of State in the Reigns of Q. Elizabeth and K. James I, collected from the Original Papers of the Right honorable Sir Ralph Winwood*, vol. III, 346, cited in Horton, *Ames by Visscher*, 35, 40.
[76] Sprunger provides an excellent chronological listing of all of Ames' works in Sprunger, *Ames*, 263-66. See also Horton, *Ames by Nethenus*, 21 and Horton, *Ames by Reuter*, 278-79.

The Hague. This literature marked him as a radical non-conformist, aided in his removal from Cambridge, pre-empted a career at Leiden, and just generally cast a long shadow over the early part of his years as a minister, scholar and theologian. Then, in the Netherlands Ames turned his intellectual and literary energies to polemic with the antinomians and Remonstrants that were gaining strength there at the opening of the seventeenth century. His posting at Dort attests to his widely-recognized proficiency in defending orthodox Calvinism from the antinomian and Arminian assault of the time. Although much of this literature dates to his time in The Hague and at Dordrecht, this style of polemic writing Ames maintained throughout his entire life when he felt not only the papacy (in the person of Bellarmine, for example), but also fellow Protestants (such as the Church of England or Arminians) required correction.

The second category of the Ames corpus can be considered more didactic, although not exclusively so, and comprises his works on philosophy, theology, practical or moral theology, catechetical instruction and biblical commentaries. It is here that Ames made the greatest contribution to the development and codification of post-Reformation theological system. Ames' interest in these areas dates back to his early years in Cambridge. For example, although his philosophical interest commenced with his adoption of the Ramist system at Cambridge, Sprunger observes that his philosophical writings appear only sporadically throughout his career and as a whole were not even published in his lifetime but posthumously, in 1643, as a collection of six short treatises, *Philosophemata*.[77] It is his didactic work – theology, casuistry and catechism – which will be examined in great detail below in establishing Ames' intellectual history and value for the Reformed tradition.

William Ames in Historiography

Until relatively recently, the historiographical study of William Ames has been consigned to the German and Dutch scholarship.[78] From the earliest work done on the person and thought of Ames, he has generally been placed in the "pietist" camp. K. Reuter notes that, curiously, A. Ritschl overlooked Ames entirely in his 3-volume history of pietism.[79] H. Heppe made brief mention of Ames in discussing the influences of Puritanism on the Dutch church.[80] A. Schweizer

---

[77] Sprunger, *Ames*, 106.
[78] Biographies of Ames have been around since the seventeenth century, however. The first appeared in 1658 and was penned by Nethenus, colleague of Gisbertus Voet at Utrecht. This was published in the form of a "Praefatio Introductoria" to Ames' *Opera*. Much of Nethenus' is paraphrased in John Quick's account in the "Icones Sacrae Anglicanae" although there are significant additions to Quick's seventeenth-century biographical record which resides in Dr. Williams' Library. See Sprunger *Ames*, ix-x.
[79] A.B. Ritschl, *Geschichte des Pietismus in der reformirten Kirche* 3 vols. (Bonn: Markus, 1880-1886).
[80] H. Heppe, *Geschichte des Pietismus und der Mystik in der Reformirten Kirche, namentlich der Niederlande* (Leiden: E.J. Brill, 1879).

and C.E. Luthardt both classify Ames as a moralist and draw attention to his work in this connection only.[81] Alternatively, Reuter claims "the real character of his theology is left hidden" as in the work of H.E. Weber and P. Althaus.[82] And while Dutch historian H. Visscher credits Ames as a man of "great significance" for England, the Netherlands, and America, indeed, "a man of great achievement,"[83] W. Goeters placed Ames as the theological head of the church reform movement in the Netherlands.[84] It is Reuter's assessment that Ames developed a "new theological principle" arising out of the "basic meaning which Ames gave to the spiritual life." According to Reuter, Ames taught that theology was an art which was to be practiced according to its rules. For Ames theology is *eupraxia*, argues Reuter, and this "empirical principle" Ames carried over from philosophy into theology.[85] Ames' value for the history of theology, therefore, is that he was an anti-Arminian "pietistic voluntarist" who set out to theologically undergird Reformed pietism, who reacted against the scholasticism of developing Reformed system, and who laid the groundwork towards empiricism in theology which Schleiermacher carried consistently to its conclusion.[86] In so doing, claims Reuter, Ames sought to reunify the Calvinian understanding of theology as theoretical and practical, as knowledge and life. "Because of his empirical-psychological orientation," however, Ames did not quite pull it off.[87] "In this position Ames stands between Calvin and Schleiermacher. He is the theological representative of Reformed pietism."[88] Following Reuter's work, American scholar F. Ernest Stoeffler echoed this sentiment and regarded Ames as the "early theologian of the Pietistic movement in the Low Countries."[89]

---

[81] A. Schweizer, "Die Entwickelung des Moralsystems in der Reformirten Kirche," *Theologische Studien und Kritiken* (Zurich: 1850), 52-53, and C.E. Luthardt, *Geschichte der Christlichen Ethik* (Leipzig: 1893), both cited in Horton, *Ames by Reuter*, 157-58.

[82] H.C. Weber, *Der Einfluss der protestantischen Schulphilosophie auf die orthodox-lutherische Dogmatik* (Leipzig: A. Deichert'sche Verlagsbuchhandlung Nachf, 1908), and P. Althaus, *Die Prinzipien der deutschen- reformierten Dogmatik im Zeitalter der aristotelischen Scholastik* (Leipzig: Deichert, 1914; reprint ed., Darmstadt: Wissenschaftliche Buchgesellschaft, 1967), both cited in Horton, *Ames by Reuter*, 157-58.

[83] Horton, *Ames by Visscher*, 145-50.

[84] W. Goeters, *Die Vorbereitung des Pietismus in der reformierten Kirche der Niederlande bis zur labadistischen Krisis 1670* (Leipzig: J.C. Hinrichs'sche Buchhandlung, 1911; reprint ed., Amsterdam: Ton Bolland, 1974), cited in Horton, *Ames by Reuter*, 158.

[85] Horton, *Ames by Reuter*, 171-206.

[86] Horton, *Ames by Reuter*, 273-77.

[87] Horton, *Ames by Reuter*, 276.

[88] Horton, *Ames by Reuter*, 277.

[89] F.E. Stoeffler, *The Rise of Evangelical Pietism*, Studies in the History of Religions, no. 9 (Leiden: E.J. Brill, 1965), 117.

Following on the heels of this primarily German assessment, C. Graafland asserts that there is no such thing as the "school of Amesius."[90] This dean of the Dutch scholarship on the reform movement in the post-Reformation Netherlands credits Ames with providing and formulating the theological foundations for the pious character of the Christian life. One is to recall, states Graafland, that Ames originated from England and was therefore imbibed, not with Protestant scholasticism (which was the norm in continental development of Reformed system) but with the practical aspect of Reformed theology, particularly as this originated with Peter Ramus. Graafland asserts that "no one assumed [Ames'] doctrinal system in its entirety."[91]

Most recently, even as W. van 't Spijker applauds Ames' value for the intellectual and theological life of the post-Reformation Netherlands, he nonetheless concludes that Ames' theology, despite its far-reaching influence, "stood rather secluded from that of his reformed contemporaries" and that the "main flow of Reformed theology appeared to have passed him by."[92] Yet later seventeenth-century figures such as Jodocus van Lodenstein and Melchior Leydekker evidence strong affiliation with Ames' pietism; the former, himself a chief representative of this further reformation in the Dutch Republic, intentionally transmitted Amesian thought through his own teaching, while the latter declared that the three "roots of the *Nadere Reformatie* are the Synod of Dort, William Ames and the Puritans.[93]

Amesian historiography is finally provided a more balanced view by K.L. Sprunger with his *The Learned Doctor William Ames*. In this 1972 publication

---

[90] C. Graafland, "De Zekerheid van het Geloof: Een onderzoek naar de geloofsbeschouwing van enige vertegenwoordigers van reformatie en nadere reformatie" (Th.D. diss., State University of Utrecht, 1961), 139, n. 1. This was published as *De Zekerheid van het Geloof: Een onderzoek naar de geloofsbeschouwing van enige vertegenwoordigers van reformatie en nadere reformatie* (Wageningen: H. Veenman en Zonen, 1961).
[91] He concludes this statement with "except for P. van Mastricht who should be considered more of a copyist than a student of Ames" (Graafland, "Zekerheid," 139, n. 1). On the Amesian influence on Mastricht, Graafland is echoing a sentiment expressed much earlier by Reuter in Horton, *Ames by Reuter*, 177, 199. W. Geesink makes the same assessment (*Gereformeerde Ethiek*, 2 vols. [Kampen: J.H. Kok, 1931], 2.493-2.495). Geesink is cited by volume and page number. Later in our study we shall examine the Amesian-Mastrichtian connection.
[92] W. van 't Spijker, "Guilelmus Amesius (1576-1633)," in *De Nadere Reformatie en het Gereformeerd Piëtisme*, T. Brienen et al., eds. ('s-Gravenhage: Boekencentrum, 1989), 54, 60. Van 't Spijker attributes this, at least in part, to Ames' use of a peculiar, practically untranslatable Latin, which factor did not add to his popularity. According to van 't Spijker, however, the Puritan emphasis of piety and practical life did not immediately appeal to everyone.
[93] C. Graafland, "Jodocus van Lodenstein (1620-1676)," in *De Nadere Reformatie: Beschrijving van haar voornaamste vertegenwoordigers*, T. Brienen et al., eds. ('s-Gravenhage: Boekencentrum, 1986), 86-87. Graafland goes on to characterize Jodocus van Lodenstein as thoroughly Amesian ("Lodenstein," 87-163). Definitional aspects of the *Nadere Reformatie* are considered in a later chapter.

with which he can claim to be Ames' unofficial biographer, Sprunger rightly asserts that to see Ames chiefly for his contributions to Reformed piety, to "pious Christianity," is only "half a truth." Scholars must interpret Ames as equally responsible for re-introducing Christian action as an identifying tenet of the Christian life; for Ames this meant being a pamphleteer, a polemicist, an agitator, a church planter, an academy promoter – in other words, a militant nonconformist for the cause of Christ.[94]

The aim of the current project is to complete this historiographical re-orientation of William Ames, by identifying, tracing and measuring the impact of Amesian thought through the development of Reformed system. As such, it challenges the current Amesian historiography as imbalanced and only half-true. Sprunger's accurate observation invites a fully-orbed study of the theology and ethics of William Ames, and, further, is a motivating factor in setting about to sketch the intellectual history of this central figure through the formative years of the Reformed system.

---

[94] Sprunger, *Ames*, 261.

Chapter 3

The Federal Theology of William Ames

The exercise of both faith and obedience constitutes the redemptive center of the divine-human encounter. Inherent in the biblical injunction to believe and obey, however, appear several ostensibly irreconcilable contradictions which are really best addressed through the hermeneutical model offered by covenant theology. It is through covenant relationship that God not only acts in gracious condescension to effect the redemption of his people, but also imbues the redeemed with both the desire and the enablement to fulfill the covenant "conditions." What are these conditions? Is the covenant mutual, or one-sided? How does the concept of an unconditional covenant and the requirement for good works combine smoothly together in the theological system of a federal theologian?

Puritan William Ames shows these questions to be answered in a unique, creative way, embraced by a theological system that is covenantally-structured. We explore his thought by identifying chief "markers" of covenant theology – markers that would be included in the thought of any well-informed, committed federal theologian – and determine to what degree these were present in the thought of his predecessors. Because Ames appeared on the theological landscape at a time and place when the presence of a theology of covenant was fairly commonplace in the thinking of post-Reformation divines, we turn to the work of Ames' chief theological influences, John Calvin and William Perkins.

William Ames and Existing Covenant Thought

Although some scholars maintain a distinction between "covenant" and "federal" theology following the logic that the former has reference to a broader theological category of which the latter is a particular expression or manifestation, this work follows the convention of using the terms "federal" and "covenant" interchangeably because of etymological similarities and the commonality between the broader conceptual categories. This fairly standard approach can be further justified on the basis of linguistic origins and the historical, cross-disciplinary use of these two designations, reaching all the way back to social and institutional formation in early modern Europe.[1]

---

[1] C.S. McCoy and J.W. Baker, *Fountainhead of Federalism: Heinrich Bullinger and the Covenantal Tradition with a Translation of De testamento seu foedere Dei unico et aeterno (1534) by Heinrich Bullinger* (Louisville, KY: Westminster/John Knox, 1991), 12-13; P.A. Lillback, *The Binding of God: Calvin's Role in the Development of Covenant Theology*, Texts & Studies in Reformation and Post-Reformation Thought, R.A.

By the late sixteenth century, the idea of covenant to describe the divine-human relationship was not new; covenant thought was standard fare in the theology of Reformed divines well before the time of William Ames.[2] Even more categorically, D.A. Weir states that after 1590, federal theology was so commonplace "all over Europe" that it becomes impossible to "draw historical connections between the various concepts of covenant."[3] While the first comprehensive treatise on the subject was written by Heinrich Bullinger, the idea itself predates even him and can be traced back to Irenaeus, Chrysostom and Augustine.[4] The medieval church utilized some idea of covenant in various church doctrines[5] – notably in the nominalism of Gabriel Biel and in connection with justification and sacramentalism[6] – but it was really during the Reformation, in the covenant thinking of Zwingli and Bullinger, that the origins

---

Muller, ed. (Grand Rapids: Baker, 2001), 26-28, 29-57. W.J. van Asselt describes the distinction in *Federal Theology of Johannes Cocceius (1603-1669)*, Studies in the History of Christian Thought, no. 100, R.A. Blacketer, trans. (Leiden: Brill, 2001), 325.

[2] See particularly the following: Lillback, *The Binding of God*, 29-109; van Asselt, *Federal Theology of Johannes Cocceius*, 325-332; McCoy and Baker, *Fountainhead of Federalism*. A valuable contribution of the latter volume is the translation of Bullinger's treatise on covenant, "the first work that organizes the understanding of God, creation, humanity, human history, and society around the covenant" (McCoy and Baker, *Fountainhead*, 9); J. von Rohr, *The Covenant of Grace in Puritan Thought*, American Academy of Religion, Studies in Religion, C. Hardwick and J.O. Duke, eds., no. 45 (Atlanta: Scholars, 1986). This volume is an excellent examination of theological topics understood within the covenant theology of Puritanism; D.A. Weir, *The Origins of the Federal Theology in Sixteenth-Century Reformation Thought* (Oxford: Clarendon, 1990). For a recent critical assessment of Weir's work see B.J. Lee, *Johannes Cocceius and the Exegetical Roots of Federal Theology*, Reformed Historical Theology, vol. 7 (Gottingen: Vandenhoeck & Ruprecht, 2009); hereafter, *Cocceius and Federal Theology*.

[3] Weir, *Origins of the Federal Theology*, vii-viii. Weir argues that the pre-lapsarian "covenant of works" is the hallmark of federal theology and he traces the origins and development of this covenantal concept.

[4] H.A. Oberman, *The Harvest of Medieval Theology: Gabriel Biel and Late Medieval Nominalism* (Grand Rapids: Eerdmans, 1967), 174; R.S. Clark, summarizes like this: "The theology of the early 17th century Reformed theologians William Ames (†1633), Johannes Wollebius (†1629) and Amandus Polanus (†1610) was written in the same direction as that of Olevian and Ursinus. The high point of Reformed federal theology was doubtless the work of Johannes Cocceius (†1669), Francis Turretin (†1687), J.H. Heidegger (†1698) and Herman Witsius (†1708)" at http://rscottclark.org/2001/09/a-brief-history-of-covenant-theology/ [accessed June 19, 2013]. Superceded by"Christ and Covenant: Federal Theology in Orthodoxy," in *Companion to Reformed Orthodoxy* Herman Selderhuis, ed. (Leiden: Brill, 2013).

[5] Oberman, *Harvest*, 81-82, 146-50, 166-78, 243-48.

[6] J.S. Preus, *From Shadow to Promise: Old Testament Interpretation from Augustine to the Young Luther* (Cambridge, MA: Harvard University, 1969), 123-25, 130-31, 261-62.

of a Reformed covenant theology can be found.[7] Building on this foundation, Calvin made extensive use of the covenant idea in his *Institutes*, commentaries, and elsewhere. How committed Calvin was to federal theology is a highly controverted question, often based on the seemingly impossible task of reconciling the apparent incompatibility between predestination and covenant theology. Indeed, a number of interpretive schools have arisen around this very question, all well represented, as one would expect, by highly-esteemed Calvin scholars.[8] Although it is not our purpose to sort through all these different viewpoints – this has been done by many – it is important that we take a fresh look at the commitment to covenant in Calvin's thought to help us determine whether and how Ames built on this in the construction of his own theological system. Thus it is against John Calvin's work, firstly, that the theology of William Ames will be compared.

In exploring Ames' unique contributions to the already existing stream of covenant thought we must, secondly, be cognizant of any development of the idea of covenant as this may have occurred between Calvin and Ames. For this reason, William Perkins becomes our other touchstone. As Ames' theological and spiritual inspiration was found in this father of English Puritanism, it is undoubtedly the case that much of Ames' thinking in the area of covenant, as in many other areas, came from his teacher. We therefore ask: How much covenant theology did Perkins imbibe? Again, the assessment is mixed. Mid-twentieth century Puritan scholar P. Miller has stated that the "three great names in the early development" of covenant thinking were William Perkins, William Ames and John Preston.[9] While Preston was the popularizer of the doctrine, it was Ames who was federal theology's "chief architect."[10] Miller notes that while Perkins wrote no treatise on covenant theology, his *Workes* contain various references to covenant thought.[11] In agreement, I. Breward judges Perkins' significant contribution in this area certainly noteworthy but

---

[7] L.D. Bierma, *German Calvinism in the Confessional Age: The Covenant Theology of Caspar Olevianus* (Grand Rapids: Baker, 1996; reprint ed., *The Covenant Theology Of Caspar Olevianus*, Grand Rapids: Reformation Heritage, 2005), 31-62.
[8] A good summary of these schools is provided in Lillback, *The Binding of God*, 13-28. See also R.A. Muller, *The Unaccommodated Calvin: Studies in the Foundation of a Theological Tradition* (New York: Oxford University, 2000), 3-4.
[9] P. Miller, *The New England Mind: The Seventeenth Century* (Cambridge: Harvard University: 1939), 374, 502.
[10] P. Miller, *The New England Mind: From Colony to Province* (Cambridge: Harvard University, 1953), 54. See also his *Seventeenth Century*, 502-5.
[11] Miller, *Seventeenth Century*, 502; Miller also states that while Ames' work on covenant must be "extracted" from relevant sections of his published work, it was Preston's work which was controlled by the covenant idea. In fact, Preston devoted one work entirely to the subject of covenant (*Seventeenth Century*, 502-3).

not central to his teaching.¹² And although K. Barth provides a brief and very helpful sketch of the development of covenant theology and the key players, he ignores Perkins altogether while his more protracted discussion focuses on the thought of Johannes Cocceius, whom he sees as representing federal theology "in a form which is not only the most perfect, but also the ripest and strongest and most impressive."[13]

It appears many historiographers have made judgments based on Perkins' infrequency of reference to the notion of covenant. But playing this numbers game can be deceiving; unstated assumptions and presuppositions are important in the formulation of any system of thought. V.L. Priebe, for example, observes that Perkins' entire theological system had the idea of covenant as central (particularly his teaching on soteriology and the godly life), regardless of the (few) times this was made explicit. He concludes that while Perkins mentions the covenant idea only seventeen times in the three volumes comprising his *Workes*, the concept of covenant provides the underlying structure for his thought.[14] It is probably fair to conclude that even if the work of William Perkins was not explicitly or architectonically covenantal, current scholarship entertains no lingering doubts about the commitment of William Perkins to the theology of covenant and his work thus constitutes a necessary second touchstone against which to compare that of William Ames.[15]

Covenant Motifs in John Calvin, William Perkins and William Ames

The Pre-Temporal Covenant of Redemption

It is generally thought that one of the hallmarks of covenant theology is the existence of a prior agreement between the Father and the Son, a compact whereby these two persons of the trinity agreed that Christ would atone for those the Father would give him. It is thus a pre-temporal, intra-trinitarian mutual assent whereby the Son agrees to ratify the Father's covenantal promise of salvation for the elect through his own temporal and mediating work as the incarnate Son. This is designated as the covenant of redemption (or, alternatively, the eternal "counsel of peace" or the *pactum salutis*). Although nowhere does Calvin explicitly identify an intra-trinitarian covenant of redemption, his work does intimate the view that there was an eternal Father-Son agreement

---

[12] I. Breward, "The Life and Theology of William Perkins 1558-1602" (Ph.D. diss., University of Manchester, 1963), 60. For a relatively early study on Perkins, see J.R. Tufft, "William Perkins, 1558-1602," (Ph.D. diss., University of Edinburgh, 1952).
[13] K. Barth, *Church Dogmatics*, vol. 4 (New York, Charles Scribner's Sons, 1956), 60.
[14] V.L. Priebe, "The Covenant Theology of William Perkins" (Ph.D. diss., Drew University, 1967), 32, 255.
[15] For example, Y.J.T. Song, "System and Piety in the Federal Theology of William Perkins and John Preston" (Ph.D. diss., Westminster Theological Seminary, 1998).

within the Godhead.[16] "We call predestination God's eternal decree," asserts Calvin, "by which *he compacted with himself* what he willed to become of each man."[17] In commenting on Jeremiah 22:29-30, Calvin states that "God is ever so consistent with himself, that his covenant, which he has made with Christ and with all his members, never fails. . . ."[18] While no emphasis on the *pactum salutis* is discovered in the work of William Perkins,[19] William Ames very clearly and explicitly teaches an intra-trinitarian covenant of redemption. The application of redemption, says Ames, is effecting the mediating work of Christ in "certain men." This application – the responsibility of the Spirit – depends on three things: the Father's decree and "donation" of Christ, Christ's intention to make satisfaction for those identified by the Father, and the Father's own acceptance of this satisfaction.[20] Ames continues:

> This agreement between God and Christ was a kind of advance application of our redemption and deliverance of us to our surety and our surety to us. Upon that latter redemption, to be completed in us, it has the effect of a kind of an efficacious example; the former is a representation of the latter and the latter is brought into being by the former.[21]

The pre-temporal covenant of redemption, the agreement between the Father and the Son, then, is interpreted by Ames as being a surety or guarantee of redemption actualized in time in God's elect.[22]

---

[16] A helpful study into the origins of the *pactum salutis* is found in B. Loonstra, *Verkiezing-Verzoening-Verbond. Beschrijving en beoordeling van de leer van het pactum salutis in de gereformeerde theologie* (The Hague: Boekencentrum, 1990), 105-47.

[17] Calvin, *Institutes* 3.21.5, my emphasis. Citations from Calvin's *Institutes* are by book, chapter and section.

[18] Cited in Lillback, *The Binding of God*, 213.

[19] William Perkins, *The Workes of that Famous and Worthy Minister of Christ in the Universitie of Cambridge, Mr. William Perkins*, 3 vols. (London: John Legatt, 1612-1613). Citations from Perkins' *Workes* are by volume and page number and, at times, the particular book in which the citation is found. Priebe emphatically asserts this claim as well ("Covenant Theology of Perkins," 46).

[20] Ames, *Marrow*, 1.24.1-1.24.3.

[21] Ames, *Marrow*, 1.24.3.

[22] This might be a good place to comment briefly on L. Berkhof's representation of this facet of Reformed theology. He states that theologians, "since the days of Coccejus, distinguish two covenants, namely, the covenant of redemption (*pactum salutis*) between the Father and the Son, and, as based on this, the covenant of grace between the triune God and the elect, or the elect sinner" (*Systematic Theology*, 4th ed. [Grand Rapids: Eerdmans, 1972], 265). In his teaching on the covenant of redemption, Ames refers to many scriptural texts Berkhof cites as the biblical/historic warrant for this theological locus. This constitutes one place (in several) where Johannes Cocceius' indebtedness to William Ames has not been detected. Ames' presentation of this covenant – as introductory to the covenant of grace, indeed, almost subsumed by it – Berkhof attributes to Cocceius. Furthermore, Ames also uses the designation for Christ as "surety" and

A Covenant of Works

Scholars of covenant theology are in general concurrence that in the work of John Calvin can be found the unmistakable attributes of a covenant of works, even if the specific nomenclature is absent. Building on the earlier thought of individuals such as Ulrich Zwingli and Johannes Oecolampadius (1482-1531), Calvin makes use of this theological category which receives creedal formulation by his late contemporaries Caspar Olevian (1536-87) and Zacharias Ursinus, who saw this covenant as representing the law and requiring strict obedience. Thus, while compared to the later federal theologians Calvin's conception of this covenant is somewhat undeveloped, it is there nonetheless. P.A. Lillback shows how this conclusion cannot be escaped when examining Calvin's teaching on Adam's pre-fall state as exposited in his commentary on Genesis 1-3. Furthermore, relying on Calvin's copious exegetical and theological work germane to this matter, evidence for such an inchoate theological category in Calvin's thought becomes persuasive. It is beyond the scope of our work to summarize all the evidence, but included are the following: 1) Calvin's reliance on Augustine's thought where one finds the concept of a pre-fall covenant; 2) the logic behind Calvin's placement of his covenant discussions in the *Institutes*; 3) his use of theological concepts that can be considered covenantal; 4) the conditional nature of the pre-lapsarian agreement in Adam's state of innocency, an agreement which rubric followed closely the covenantal stipulations of promise, obedience and reward; 5) Calvin's treatment of the *imago Dei*; 6) the sacramental nature of the tree of life, which he sees, with Augustine, as a figure of Christ and which, further, proves consistent with his own view of the (synonymous) relationship between sacrament and covenant; and 7) the affirmation of merit only in the context of grace in the covenant of the law.[23]

Therefore, while it is true that nowhere does Calvin use the designation "covenant of works" and although none of these arguments in and of themselves would be sufficient to prove the existence of a pre-lapsarian covenant in the thought of Calvin, taken together the evidence seems insurmountable. Calvin built on the work of earlier architects of Reformed theology and through the incorporation of pre-lapsarian covenantal attributes in his thought and work he unmistakably furthered the structural move towards a later, fully developed covenant of works. A precisely-articulated, most comprehensive federal theology in the Reformed tradition would not be long in coming. Muller confirms this evolutionary nature of covenant concepts and nomenclature.[24] He summarizes the areas of significance that must be considered in any study of this pre-

---

"head" (*Marrow* 1.24.3, 1.24.6), the twin characteristics that Berkhof attributes to Christ in this *pactum salutis* (*Systematic Theology*, 266-67).

[23] Lillback, *The Binding of God*, 287-304.

[24] R.A. Muller, "The Covenant of Works and the Stability of Divine Law in Seventeenth-Century Reformed Orthodoxy: A Study in the Theology of Herman Witsius and Wilhelmus à Brakel," *CTJ* 29 (1994): 75-100.

lapsarian covenant and examines the scholarly debate surrounding this "derivative" doctrine including its place in the developing Reformed tradition, the interrelationship between the two covenants (works and grace) and law and grace, and the caricature of Reformed federalism presented by those who argue that the older legalistic Reformed language of covenant of works indicates a "radical priority of law over grace." Muller concludes:

> The elements of the Reformed doctrine of the covenant of works . . . indicate the result of a process of doctrinal development in the Reformed tradition. As such, the language of the doctrine is certainly different from the language of the Reformers and even from that of earlier successors to the original Reformers like Ursinus and Olevian or, indeed, in a slightly later time, William Perkins. Yet, the fundamental points of the doctrine . . . remain virtually identical. The free gift of grace in the one covenant respects the stability of law in the other, while the presence of law under different uses in both covenants echoes both the immutability of the divine nature and the constancy of the divine promises.[25]

Given the evolving nature of federal theology as a theological category, organizing principle, and hermeneutical tool, it is not surprising that William Perkins appears somewhat more assertive in identifying a covenant of works. In various places, mention is made of his understanding of a pre-fall covenant between the Creator and the creature and he explicitly designates this as the covenant of works.[26] What is surprising, however, is what surfaces upon careful examination. In fact, Perkins' understanding of the covenant of works is somewhat different from that held by later federal theologians. Whereas Perkins, following through with Calvin's intimations, explicitly designates the moral law, the decalogue, as the covenant of works,[27] the more developed notion holds that the covenant of works was the primitive law printed on the heart of Adam at creation. This was decidedly not Perkins' understanding. As J.G. Møller points out, Perkins did not know of a pre-fall covenant as federal theologians understand it.[28] He never actually connects the covenant of works to Adam's pre-fall state,[29] but uses the covenant of works, the moral law, the Ten Commandments, as preparatory to grace. The function of the covenant of works, for Perkins, is to convict of sin and drive men and women to Christ and thus to the covenant of grace.[30] For Perkins, the covenant of works is always present and functioning with the covenant of grace through history to bring men and women to Christ.[31]

---

[25] Muller, "Covenant of Works," 100.
[26] Perkins, *Workes*, 1.32.
[27] "The covenant of workes, is Gods covenant, made with condition of perfect obedience, and is expressed in the morall law" (*Workes*, 1.32).
[28] J.G. Møller, "The Beginnings of Puritan Covenant Theology," *JEH* 14 (1963): 60-61.
[29] As Priebe also observes in "Covenant Theology of Perkins," 42.
[30] Perkins, *Workes*, 1.70, 1.299; Priebe, "Covenant Theology of Perkins," 43-46.
[31] Priebe argues for two uses of the covenant by Perkins: for the experience of salvation and for the godly life of obedience ("Covenant Theology of Perkins," 48).

Only once does Perkins show the law to be in nature by creation (and thus linked to pre-fall Adam). This leads Priebe to conclude that "while this one reference to the law being in nature by creation could presumably imply a covenant of works, when it is evaluated in the total context of Perkins' thought, it does not appear to be of central importance."[32] On this basis, he is prepared to state categorically that one of the "commonly accepted distinguishing marks of covenant theology . . . the covenant of works made with Adam at creation . . . [is] not evident in Perkins' thought."[33] While Perkins may be more explicit than Calvin in identifying a covenant of works, his understanding of the concept does not appear to improve or clarify over that of his Reformed predecessor.[34] It is worth repeating that Perkins saw the two covenants as working simultaneously through history in the life of the believer: the covenant of works – the moral law – being used by God in a preparatory way to bring sinners into the pale of the covenant of grace.

A review of Ames' *Marrow* on this aspect of covenant theology yields some agreement with the views of both Calvin and Perkins regarding the pre-fall condition and relationship between God and humanity. But Ames also moves federal theology forward significantly. He explains that "government is the power whereby God directs and leads all his creatures to their proper end."[35] This government includes the means and the empowerment for attaining that end. This governance of God over his creatures is two-fold: "common government" and "special government." To the former belongs the law of nature (in which all creatures participate by virtue of the divine image in them), an inclination to obedience, an instinct to higher activities where these can be ascertained by reason and a certain power to obey. In addition to this common government, God governs his rational creatures, secondly, "in a moral way" by special government which is his revealed will, the same "in substance" . . . "as the moral law of the decalogue."[36] This special government operates by a system of commandments and proscriptions, rewards and punishments. This conjunction in God's moral governance gives rise to a covenant between God and humanity, "a kind of transaction of God with the creature whereby God com-

---

[32] Priebe, "Covenant Theology of Perkins," 43.
[33] Priebe, "Covenant Theology of Perkins," 46. For the contrary position, Song observes that there is more than just "circumstantial evidence" that Perkins' teaches a pre-lapsarian covenant of works (Song, "System and Piety in Perkins and Preston," 108). He has in mind, for example, the following statement found in Perkins' casuistry: "The law was once given to Adam & imprinted in his heart in his first creation, and in him, as being the roote of all mankind, it was given to all men . . . ." (*A Discourse of Conscience*, in *Workes*, 1.523).
[34] This seems to confirm Priebe's comment that "[Perkins'] entire interpretation of the Legall covenant is strikingly similar to that of Calvin," ("Covenant Theology of Perkins," 42).
[35] Ames, *Marrow*, 1.9.19.
[36] Ames, *Marrow*, 1.10.16.

mands, promises, threatens, fulfills; and the creature binds itself in obedience to God so demanding."[37] Ames also holds to an "intermixture" of the covenant of works with the covenant of grace through salvation history, if not in precisely the same manner as Perkins.[38] Finally, with generous scriptural appeal, Ames unambiguously identifies the federal headship or representative nature of Adam's existence, disobedience and fall.[39]

While Calvin attached sacramental significance to only the tree of life in the pre-fall garden as a figure or type of Christ (understanding the banishment of Adam and Eve from the garden as an excommunicative act on the part of God), Ames holds to the sacramental significance of the covenant of works as centering on two "symbols or sacraments:" the tree of life was the reward for obedience; this was the sacrament of life. The punishment for disobedience, on the other hand, was the tree of the knowledge of good and evil; this was the sacrament of death.[40] This covenantal period of integrity came to a conclusion when Adam, through the fall, "showed . . . contempt for the whole covenant."[41]

Ames' indebtedness to, and advance upon, the existing Calvin/Perkins track here are unmistakable. First, Calvin's teaching of the close relation between natural law and moral law are picked up by Ames but given further refinement in the context of a clearly-defined and so designated covenant of works, the concept for which Calvin provides only adumbrations.[42] Second, while it might appear that Ames sees a distinction between the natural law and the moral law, he carefully articulates that both reside in the conscience of pre-fall Adam as common government (law of nature) and special government (moral law *added to*[43] the law of nature). The covenant of works is characterized by the moral law which subsumes the law of nature. Third, Ames further articulates the relationship between the law of nature and the decalogue with more specificity then does Calvin who also considers the conscience and the decalogue to assert the same things.[44] Indeed, it is in the introduction to his moral theology that Ames investigates "What proportion the Morall Law beares to the Law of Nature." Note the care Ames takes in articulating his very judicious response:

> All the Precepts of the Morall Law, are out of the Law of Nature, except the determination of the Sabbath-day in the fourth Commandment, which is from the positive law. . . .

---

[37] Ames, *Marrow*, 1.10.9.
[38] Ames, *Marrow*, 1.39.4.
[39] Ames, *Marrow*, 1.10.1-1.10.16, 1.10.25-1.10.32, 1.11.30.
[40] Ames, *Marrow*, 1.10.33.
[41] Ames, *Marrow*, 1.11.8.
[42] Ames uses the designation "covenant of works" in 1.39.4 and 1.39.9.
[43] "This special government does not exclude the basic government [law of nature] of the reasonable creature, which is common to all creatures, but it is rather added to it" (*Marrow*, 1.10.3).
[44] Calvin, *Institutes*, 2.8.1.

> *Object.* But it may bee objected, that if the Morall were the same with the Law of Nature, it had no need to bee promulgated either by voyce or writing for it would have beene writ in the hearts of all men by Nature.
>
> *A.* That to Nature upright *(i.e.) as it was in the State of innocency*, there was no need of such a Promulgation. But ever since, the corruption of our Nature, such is the blindnesse of our understanding and perversnesse of our will and disorder of our affections, that there are onely some Reliques of that Law remaining in our hearts like to some dimme aged picture, and therefore by the voyce and power of God it ought to bee renewed as with a fresh pencill. Therefore is there no where found any true right practicall reason, pure and complete in all parts, but in the written Law of God. *Psalme 119.66.*[45]

Here Ames very clearly describes the character and the dynamics of the covenant of works. The decalogue, save the Sabbath law, is "*out of*" the law of nature. For Ames, because of the Edenic breach, the principle, existence and character of the moral law is necessitated by the earlier principle, existence and character of the unblemished law of nature resident in the *imago dei*. This primitive law written on the tablets of the heart of the prefall creature as a covenant of works was, in fact, except for the addition of the sabbath law, repeated later and given as the Sinaitic moral code written on the tablets of stone for the postfall administration of the covenant of grace. Ames furthers Calvin's thought and teaches it in fuller form and with greater force.

Two final emphases: both the Calvin/Perkins and Amesian tracks see a place for the moral law in the covenant of grace. In addition, for both tracks obedience is the condition whereby Adam could have obtained the reward, whereas disobedience invoked the divine punishment, although Ames holds to a somewhat more symmetric view of the sacramental signs of the covenant of works.

The Covenant of Grace: Unity and Diversity

There is no shortage of evidence in Calvin's work to maintain the position that Calvin insists on the unity, identity and continuity of the covenant of grace as it advances through salvation history, from its earliest traces in the promise to Adam. It is a common theme in his writing.[46] The formal establishment of the covenant with Abraham is that point to which Calvin repeatedly returns. The differences in the inter-temporal administration of the covenant he explains in terms of the progressive nature of revelation, until, finally, the covenant is consummated in Jesus Christ and its full meaning is disclosed:

> The covenant made with all the patriarchs is so much like ours in substance and reality that the two are actually one and the same. Yet they differ in the mode of

---

[45] William Ames, *Conscience*, 5.1.27-5.1.28.
[46] See Lillback, *The Binding of God*, 142-61; E.M. Osterhaven, "Calvin on the Covenant," *Readings in Calvin's Theology*, D.K. McKim, ed. (Grand Rapids: Baker, 1983), 98-106; and A.A. Hoekema, "The Covenant of Grace in Calvin's Teaching," *CTJ* 2 (1967): 136.

dispensation. . . . What else does [Moses] do but call them back to the covenant begun with Abraham? . . . The Lord held to this orderly plan in administering the covenant of his mercy: as the day of full revelation approached with the passing of time, the more he increased each day the brightness of its manifestation. Accordingly, at the beginning when the first promise of salvation was given to Adam (Gen. 3:15) it glowed like a feeble spark. Then, as it was added to, the light grew in fullness, breaking forth increasingly and shedding its radiance more widely. At last – when all the clouds were dispersed – Christ, the Sun of Righteousness, fully illumined the whole earth.[47]

William Perkins agrees that the covenant of grace is one in substance, its progression represented by the Old and New Testaments in movement from promise to fulfillment:

The old testament or covenant is that, which in types and shadowes prefigured Christ to come, and to be exhibited.
The new testament declareth Christ already come in the flesh, and is apparently shewed in the Gospell.[48]

Additionally, Perkins saw the covenant to be the means by which God worked out his decree of election[49] locating the *ordo salutis* – effectual calling, justification, sanctification, and glorification – within the broader context of the covenant of grace.[50] Full systematic integration, however, across time and space of the *ordo salutis* with the covenant of grace would have to wait for the more advanced thought of William Ames and the detailed structuring provided somewhat later by Johannes Cocceius. Never does Perkins connect the *ordo salutis* to the covenant of grace in a direct way.

With Calvin, William Ames holds that the covenant of grace first appeared in redemptive history in God's initial pronouncement of the promise to Adam.[51] Furthermore, he teaches the identity and unity of the covenant and its continuity through time with logic similar to that of Calvin (and the brief attention paid it by Perkins) but in considerably more detail:

Although the free, saving covenant of God has been one and the same from the beginning, the manner of the application of Christ of the administration of the new covenant has not always been so. It has varied according to the times during which the church has been in process of being gathered. In this variety there has always been a progression from the imperfect to the more perfect. At first the

---

[47] Calvin, *Institutes*, 2.10.2, 1.8.3, 2.10.20.
[48] Perkins, *Workes*, 1.70.
[49] The covenant is the "outward means of executing the decree of election" (Perkins, *Workes*, 1.31).
[50] Priebe, "Covenant Theology of Perkins," 129-66.
[51] Ames, *Marrow*, 1.38.13.

mystery of the gospel was manifested in a general and obscure way and later more specifically and clearly.[52]

At the heart of this question of the inter-temporal administration of the covenant of grace lies the more specific issue of the relationship between the covenants (testaments). In other words: Did the meaning of the covenant change as the biblical story advances? Having established their unity, what are the differences, if any, between the old and new covenants?

Calvin illustrates five ways by which this bi-covenantal distinction can be argued from the progressive nature of the covenant of grace.[53] The old covenant conveyed new covenant blessings typologically. It did this in two ways: firstly, the old covenant used material (temporal) blessings as representative of spiritual (eternal) blessings wherein members of the new covenant were able to participate directly. With respect to the Jews' inheritance of the land of Canaan, Calvin states that "in the earthly possession they enjoyed, they looked, as in a mirror, upon the future inheritance they believed to have been prepared for them in heaven."[54] Secondly, the ceremonial system of law and sacrifice was a system of types and shadows that pointed to an as yet unfulfilled reality – the reality of Christ. "The second difference between the Old and New Testaments consists in figures: that, in the absence of the reality, it showed but an image and shadow in place of the substance; the New Testament reveals the very substance of truth as present."[55] These types were symbols of the confirmation of Christ, by whom the New Testament was ratified and through whom the Old Testament actually became the New.

Related to this distinction is the third: on the basis of Jeremiah 31 and 2 Corinthians 3, the new covenant is characterized by the presence and work of the Holy Spirit. The old covenant is of the "letter" while the new is of the "spirit," written on the heart. Significant here is the enabling work of the Spirit – by which forgiven men and women are empowered to keep that law of the old covenant, that rule of righteousness. This same letter becomes spirit when conjoined with the Holy Spirit. In this understanding, Moses can be seen "narrowly" as a lawgiver whose message produced only death, or more "broadly" as a preacher of the gospel, a type of Christ. And the Old Testament saints were equally partakers of the new covenant benefits, although not to the same degree. This was so because of the greater power of the Holy Spirit, the greater dispensing of mercy, and the greater clarity of revelation in the new covenant. Thus it is a movement, an evolution, from lesser to greater.

---

[52] Ames, *Marrow* 1.38.1-1.38.3.
[53] Lillback, *The Binding of God*, 150-58; Osterhaven, "Calvin on the Covenant," 99-100; and W. van den Bergh, *Calvijn over het Genadeverbond* ('s-Gravenhage: W.A. Beschoor, 1879), 79-85.
[54] Calvin, *Institutes*, 2.11.1.
[55] Calvin, *Institutes*, 2.11.4.

Calvin points to the bondage of the old covenant and the liberty of the new as the fourth distinction between them. "Scripture calls the Old Testament one of 'bondage' because it produces fear in men's minds; but the New Testament, one of 'freedom' because it lifts them to trust and assurance."[56] The fifth and final point of distinction between the two covenants lies in their application: the old covenant applied only to the nation of Israel, while the new covenant is made accessible to all of humanity through Christ. In these five ways does the latter covenant have superiority over the former.[57]

While William Perkins devotes much of his chapter on the covenant of grace to identifying this covenant with the gospel,[58] Ames shows greater creativity in outlining the relation between the old and new dispensations of the covenant of grace. But first we must review what he had to say about the relationship between the two covenants themselves. With this as background, then, it becomes easier to understand how covenant theology is architectonic of Ames' system as he employs it to characterize the entire history of redemption. Ames holds to a covenant of grace that is one-sided and absolutely unconditional. He enumerates the differences between the covenant of works (which, in this connection, he also calls the "old covenant" or "transaction") and the covenant of grace (the "new covenant"). The old differed, first, in kind: the old was a covenant of friendship, but the new is a covenant of reconciliation between enemies; secondly, in action: in the old covenant, two parties covenanted but, in the new only God covenants; thirdly, in object: the old was extended to all humanity while the new was extended to the elect only, "to certain men," to those "who God intended;" fourthly, in moving cause: in the old this was God's sovereignty as expressed in his wise justice and counsel but in the new it is only mercy; fifthly, in its basis: the old was founded on human ability but the new on Jesus Christ; sixthly, in the reward promised: only life in the old but righteousness and "all the means of life" in the new; seventhly, in the conditions: perfect obedience in the old and no conditions in the new, although faith, by grace, appropriates the promise. As if anticipating the issue of covenant conditionality, Ames pauses for a moment here, to address it in a somewhat more exact manner and to strongly promote the monopleuric nature of the covenant of grace. God requires faith as a condition of covenant, he says. But do not consider this a "prior condition." Rather, this faith is a "following or intermediate condition."

---

[56] Calvin, *Institutes*, 2.11.9.
[57] Van den Bergh, *Genadeverbond*, 84-85. Following his exposition of these five distinctions that Calvin makes, van den Bergh devotes considerable space to a comparative study between the *Institutes* and the commentaries of Calvin with respect to this theme. He does this to controvert Schweizer and others who argue that Calvin's teaching in this area is found only in the *Institutes*. Van den Bergh finds that this teaching in Calvin's *Institutes* is largely substantiated by all of his commentaries that touch on this subject with particular attention paid to Jer 31 (*Genadeverbond*, 87-107). This confirms the position Muller vigorously makes throughout *Unaccommodated Calvin*.
[58] Perkins, *Workes*, 1.70-1.71.

What's more, it is "given by grace as a means to grace, which is the proper nature of faith." Thus, God freely and gratuitously supplies the condition of faith which in turn becomes the believer's access to grace itself. The final two distinctions Ames identifies between the covenant of works and of grace are, seventhly, in the effect: the teaching of righteousness, a dead letter in the old versus the bestowal of righteousness, a "quickening spirit" in the new; and, finally, in duration: the old is antiquated, the new is eternal.[59] Thus the conditional covenant of works, the transaction, the old covenant that was broken, has been replaced with a new, unconditional covenant, and is the means by which the Holy Spirit applies the redemption, purchased by Christ, to the elect.[60]

At this point, Ames introduces a creative and insightful contribution to the architecture of the federal theology of the Reformed system, and in so doing, sets the stage for Johannes Coccius. This is found in his description of the movement, within the covenant of grace, from initial inauguration to ultimate consummation. Ames argues for the unity of the two covenants (testaments) using the determinative plumb line of the *ordo salutis*. Using predestination as a starting point, Ames tracks the covenant object through the stages of spiritual renewal: calling, justification, adoption, sanctification and glorification. By way of this taxonomy, the covenant becomes the vehicle through which the elect, redeemed sinner both "moves" through the *ordo salutis* (a "vertical movement") and advances through time (a "horizontal movement"), while shrugging off the covenant of works. This "intermixture," then, of the covenant of works and the covenant of grace gradually is lessened as the covenant child moves along the path of sanctification until, finally, all Adamic traces disappear, or, more precisely, until the believer's spiritual condition asymptotically converges to the state of full sanctification, which state one reaches in fully consummated form only and finally at death.

In explaining the progressive nature of the administration of the covenant of grace Ames first outlines the distinction between the Old and New Testament administration which, with Calvin and Perkins, is two-fold: in the old economy, the covenant anticipates Christ and in the new, the covenant testifies to His presence. In the first dispensation two additional and distinct periods are identified: one before Moses and one from Moses to Christ. Continuing in typical Ramist fashion Ames notes two further divisions in the pre-Mosaic period: from Adam to Abraham and from Abraham to Moses. The redemption by Christ and the application of Christ was promised in the Adamic covenant, from Adam to Abraham in a very "general" way – i.e., to all humankind. The dispensation from Abraham to Moses saw the covenant promises narrowed to the family and posterity of Abraham. The covenant through the Mosaic economy was unique in that the same Christocentricity of the covenant of grace was prefigured by "ordinary" means (the ceremonial law) and "extraordinary"

---

[59] Ames, *Marrow*, 1.24.13-1.24.22.
[60] Ames, *Marrow*, 1.24.1-1.24.10.

means (deliverance from Egypt). From the time of Christ to the end of the world this same covenant of grace, "new not in essence but in form," is administratively unique in both quality and quantity. In quality, the doctrines of grace and salvation are expressed "not in types and shadows" but in the reality. And in quantity, the covenant administration has wider application inter-spatially ("is diffused through the whole world") and inter-temporally (until Christ returns). In addition, the application of the Spirit is more effectual (letter and spirit) and the new administration produces a more spiritual life.[61]

With Calvin, Ames agrees that the new covenant is an improvement upon the old in terms of: application (broader), "clarity" (from type to antitype), effect (from ritual and ceremony to obedience), and spirituality (from letter to spirit). Uniquely, however, Ames sees an "intermixture" of the previous covenant of works with the old (pre-Christ) administration of the covenant of grace as the liberating effects of this covenant gradually take hold:

> Freedom comes, first, in doing away with government by law, or the intermixture of the covenant of works, which held the ancient people in a certain bondage. . . . Second, the yoke of ceremonial law is taken away in that it was a mortgage bond held against sinners, forbade the use of some things in their nature indifferent, commanded many burdensome observances of other things of the same nature, and veiled the truth itself with many carnal ceremonies. Col. 2:17, "Which are a shadow of things to come, but the body is of Christ."[62]

To Ames, then, the new covenant is significant in that it completely abolished any residual traces of the covenant of works found in the old covenant. His focus is not so much on the gracious liberty provided by the new covenant. Rather, it is on the dynamics underlying this acquisition of grace. Existentially, old covenant bondage is lifted in successively greater stages as redemptive history advances progressively nearer the approach of Christ.

Ames' understanding of the bi-covenantal distinctions are very Calvinian (and Perkinsian where Perkins commented at all) in their point of departure. But he has nuanced some key covenantal themes much more assertively and, in so doing, advances considerably the teaching of both Calvin and Perkins while laying the groundwork for Cocceius. His understanding and delineation of the conditions of the covenant of works indicate the prominence of this covenant in Ames' thinking, something not seen in either Calvin or Perkins. The continued presence of the covenant of works in the old covenant and its successively phased disappearance sets the stage for the more formal system of covenant abrogation developed by Cocceius. This apparent covenant "admixture" no doubt comes from Perkins' undeveloped and atypical thought on the covenant of works. Ames' concatenation of covenant renewal instances to mark periodicity, and his use of this system as the organizing tool dominating the inter-

---

[61] Ames, *Marrow*, 1.38.4-1.39.14.
[62] Ames, *Marrow*, 1.39.9.

temporal administration of the covenant of grace, are both unique and clearly architectonic.

"Covenant," "Testament," and Conditionality
As one works through the early and subsequent evolving nomenclature and language used in articulating covenant thought, it is helpful to maintain the fine distinctions in meaning between the covenantal designations "covenant" (or "pact") and "testament." B.J. Lee's recent appraisal of the evolution of covenant terminology uncovers the problematic nature of coming to terms with the terminological use in the Hebrew and Greek scriptures, the Vulgate and through the exegetical and theological concerns of the sixteenth and seventeenth centuries.[63] While "terminological consensus was never achieved" he concludes persuasively that synonymous use of the designations *foedus* (covenant, "pact") and *testamentum* (testament) is misleading at best and erroneous at worst and that the fine distinctions in meaning should be maintained.[64] Von Rohr explains the distinction we are using in the present work:

> A testament is grounded only on the will of the testator and involves the bequeathing of promised legacies, with no requirement for action on the part of the recipient. A covenant, however, is different . . . for it is a mutual agreement and commitment, in which the consent of each of the participants is essential.[65]

With this mind, let us turn first to the thought of Calvin. Calvin appears to use the word "covenant" as a synonym for "testament." First, in a general way he observes that "the Old Testament or covenant that the Lord has made with the Israelites had not been limited to earthly things, but contained a promise of spiritual and eternal life."[66] But in his commentary on Galatians, his interchangeable employment of the terms appears to be with more conscious deliberation:

> [The] difference between us and the ancient fathers lies in accidents, not in substance. In all the leading characters of the testament (*testamentum*) or covenant we agree: the ceremonies and form of government, in which we differ, are mere additions. . . .
> *These are two covenants*. I thought it better to adopt this translation, in order not to lose sight of the beauty of the comparison; for Paul compares the two *diathekai* to two mothers, and to employ *testamentum*, which is a neuter noun, for denoting a mother, would be harsh. The word *pactio* appears to be, on that account, more

---

[63] Lee, *Cocceius and Federal Theology*, 23-72.
[64] Lee, *Cocceius and Federal Theology*, 27.
[65] Von Rohr, *Covenant of Grace in Puritan Thought*, 35.
[66] Calvin, *Institutes*, 2.10.23.

appropriate; and indeed the desire of obtaining perspicuity, as well as elegance, has led me to make this choice.[67]

Calvin's main thrust here is really not a concern for the "elegance" of gender agreement but to distinguish covenant from testament. Calvin needs to preserve the distinction in meaning between these two words because he adheres to *both* the monopleuric nature generally associated with "testament" *and* the dipleuric meaning commonly understood of covenant or mutual pact. We will presently show just exactly how Calvin works out this apparent theological contradiction in practical terms.

William Perkins also uses "covenant" and "testament" interchangeably in his work:

> This covenant is also named a Testament: for it hath partly the nature and properties of a testament or will. For it is confirmed by the death of the testatour. . . . Secondly, in this covenant we do not so much offer, or promise any great matter to God, as in a manner only receive even as the last will and testament of a man, is not for the testators, but for the heires commoditie.[68]

In his commentary on Galatians 3, Perkins expands:

> it is a Covenant or compact, because God for his part promiseth remission of sinnes and life everlasting, and *requireth faith on our part*. In respect of this *mutuall obligation*, it hath in it the forme of a covenant. It is also a Will, or Testament in two respects. First, because the promise is confirmed by the death of the mediatour, *Hebr.* 9. 15. Secondly, the things promised, as remission of sins, and life everlasting, are given after the manner of legacies, that is, freely, without our desert or procurement. In this we see the great goodnes of God, who vouchsafeth to name them in his Testament, that have made covenant with the devill, and are children of wrath by nature, as we all are.[69]

Because Perkins sees God as freely choosing to bind himself to humanity, the latter receives freely. For Perkins, this unconditional divine love, this free mercy towards humanity, makes humanity none other than the "grateful recipient of the benefits of God's sovereign pleasure."[70] A study of Perkins' *Golden Chaine or a Description of Theology*[71] reveals that the covenant is the means by which God, solely in his good pleasure, executes the decree of election.[72] We have already mentioned this. Another way Perkins describes this covenant relationship is in terms of "donation:" the concept of the "Mysticall Union" must

---

[67] Calvin on Gal 4:1 and 4:24 in *Commentary on Galatians*, Calvin Translation Society (Grand Rapids: Baker, 1979).
[68] Perkins, *Workes*, 1.70.
[69] Perkins, *Workes*, 2.243, my emphasis.
[70] Priebe, "Covenant Theology of Perkins," 61.
[71] Perkins, *Workes*, 1.9-1.116.
[72] As Priebe puts it in "Covenant Theology of Perkins," 63.

be seen, he argues, in terms of a "Donation or giving of Christ unto man."[73] While it is tempting to maintain that Perkins is prepared to use the designations covenant and testament synonymously to emphasize the one-sidedness of the covenant relation, there are places where we read the opposite. In *Golden Chaine*, Chapter XIX entitled "*Concerning the Outward meanes of executing the decree of Election, and of the Decalogue*," Perkins says this:

> After the Foundation of Election, which hath hitherto beene delivered, it followeth, that wee should intreat of the outward meanes of the same.
> The meanes are God's covenant, and the seale thereof.
> God's covenant, is his contract with man, concerning the obtaining of life eternall, upon a certen condition.
> This covenant consists of two parts: Gods promise to man, Mans promise to God.
> Gods promise to man, is that, whereby he bindeth himself to man to bee his God, if he performe the condition.
> Man's promise to God, is that, whereby hee voweth his allegeance unto his Lord, and to performe the condition betweene them.
> Againe, there are two kindes of this covenant. The covenant of workes and the covenant of grace....[74]

Outside of any further elaboration regarding the divine and gracious source of humanity's enablement to obedience, it appears that while Perkins may wish to use testament and covenant synonymously, he appears to favor the dipleuric covenant.

Coming a generation later, William Ames also identifies "covenant" with "testament," describing the covenant of grace as a testament, God's freely given word of assurance:

> The application by which God fulfills with greatest firmness what was contained in a covenant formerly made and broken is called in the Scriptures the *new covenant*, Heb. 8:8, 10; ... It is called a covenant because it is a firm promise. In the scriptures every firm determination, even though pertaining to lifeless things, is called a covenant. Jer. 33:20, 25, "*My covenant with the day and my covenant with the night.*" ... Yet because it is a free gift and confirmed by the death of the giver, it is more properly called a testament, not a covenant, Heb. 9:16. This sense is not in a firm determination, which is not so properly called a testament as a covenant.[75]

Yet note that Ames unambiguously prefers "testament" over "covenant" on the same basis as the less-precise reasoning of Perkins: belief in the one-sided, unconditional nature of the covenant. The remainder of this chapter will demonstrate Ames' consistency in this respect.

---

[73] Perkins, *Workes*, 1.298.
[74] Perkins, *Workes*, 1.31-1.32.
[75] Ames, *Marrow*, 1.24.10-1.24.12.

Even as we detect some internal struggle in the thought of each of the three theologians under consideration here,[76] they demonstrate unanimous preference for the designation "testament" over "covenant." While Calvin attaches to the term both a monopleuric and dipleuric meaning, Perkins seems to prefer, although quite ambiguously, the one-sided nature of the covenant relation. Similarly in the case of Ames; his preference for the word testament appears to be because of the monopleuric, free, one-sided nature of the relation so designated. The difference between the three is primarily a question of degree: Ames is consistently unambiguous in his contention that the covenant of grace is entirely one-sided. This seemingly trivial difference between Calvin, Perkins, and Ames will assume greater significance.

Because of the centrality of the issue of covenant conditionality for the development and understanding of covenant theology, it is worth pursuing this matter a little further. Since the publication of the landmark "Trinterud thesis," many scholars have pursued Trinterud's hypothesis that the Rhineland Reformers (chiefly Zwingli and Bullinger) taught a conditional covenant while Calvin held to an unconditional covenant of grace.[77] The former was dominated by a "law-covenant" understanding that was anchored in the political theory of natural law and social contract.[78] Thus, although grace motivated God to enter into covenant relationship with humanity, major emphasis was placed on humanity's obedience for covenant fulfillment. This understanding was, if not antithetical, then surely in contradistinction to the position that placed stress on the sovereign electing act of God in grace, a position clearly taught by Calvin. Trinterud summarizes:

> For Calvin, and so in the Geneva Bible, the covenant of God is God's promise to man, which obligates God to fulfill.... In the covenant theory of the Rhineland ... the covenant is a conditional promise on God's part, which has the effect of drawing out of man a responding promise of obedience, thus creating a mutual pact or treaty. The burden of fulfillment rests upon man, for he must first obey in order to bring God's reciprocal obligation into force.[79]

As attempts have been made to clarify Puritan covenant thought, the position has developed that this Rhineland conception was mediated to English Puritanism through the writings of William Tyndale. So widespread and dominant was

---

[76] No doubt for reasons explained by Lee in *Cocceius and Federal Theology*, 23ff. See particularly his study on Calvin's terminological use on pp. 41-44.

[77] L.J. Trinterud, "The Origins of Puritanism," *CH* 20 (1951): 37-57. Among other leaders in the Reformation movement in Rhineland cities such as Zurich, Basel, and Strassbourg, Trinterud identifies Zwingli, Jud, Bullinger, Oecolampadius, Capito, Bucer, and Martyr ("Origins," 37).

[78] Trinterud, "Origins," 41-42. Trinterud argues that the Rhineland reformers imported most of the ideas found in medieval social contract theories into the religious realm of just developing covenant theology.

[79] Trinterud, "Origins," 45.

this view, it is claimed, that Rhineland covenantal thinking became the normative theological system of the Westminster Assembly.[80] Lillback has examined Calvin's views on covenant conditionality in attempts to establish a consensus between Calvin and the Rhineland Reformers and so close the chasm which has developed in a major area of Reformed and Puritan scholarship.[81] We have already noted Calvin's unique monopleuric/dipleuric position and it is Calvin's views that we now develop further.

From his comments on Genesis 17, it is apparent that Calvin understands God as requiring mutual fidelity from his own children. According to Lillback, Calvin, in fact, is "quite comfortable with the use of the terms of a conditional covenant."[82] God has bound himself in mutual pact with humanity, offering covenantal blessings and demanding covenantal obedience. Calvin believes that God places himself under condition:

> Since therefore the Lord has entered into covenant with us on the condition of undertaking our cause, let us not doubt that he will actually fulfil it, and will shew that the insults which are offered to us are offered to himself. In a word, he is joined to us in such a manner that he wishes all that belong to him and to us to be in common.[83]

From the divine vantage-point, the covenant is an act of free sovereign grace. For commenting on the phrase "mercies of David" in Isaiah 55:3, Calvin says:

> By this phrase he declares that it was a covenant of free grace; for it was founded on nothing else than the absolute goodness of God. Whenever, therefore, the word "covenant" occurs in Scripture, we ought at the same time to call to remembrance the word "grace." By calling them "the faithful mercies of David," he declares that he will be faithful in it, and at the same time states indirectly that he is faithful and steadfast, and cannot be accused of falsehood, as if he had broken his covenant . . . .[84]

When viewed from the perspective of the creature, the covenant is made conditional in the required response the sovereignly-executed covenant provokes. In commenting on ignoring or abandoning the covenant, Calvin remarks that "by their own defects and guilt . . . Ishmael, Esau, and the like were cut off from adoption" for violating the conditions of the covenant.[85] How can the covenant be both conditional and unconditional?

---

[80] Trinterud, "Origins," 38-40.
[81] Lillback, *The Binding of God*, 169-72. See also his "The Continuing Conundrum: Calvin and the Conditionality of the Covenant," *CTJ* 29 (1994): 42-74.
[82] Lillback, "Conundrum," 59.
[83] Calvin, commenting on Isa 37:23, cited in Lillback, "Conundrum," 64.
[84] Calvin, commenting on Isa 55:3, cited in Lillback, "Conundrum," 66.
[85] Calvin, *Institutes*, 3.21.6.

A close reading of Calvin in both his *Institutes* and his commentaries yields the Calvinian teaching of both an unconditional and a conditional covenant. From the point of view of the divine, the covenant is unconditional; from the vantage point of humanity, the covenant is conditional. Thus Calvin solves the apparent contradiction by holding that the requirement of covenant obedience is a must – a response to a gracious God who freely chose unconditionally to covenant with humanity.[86] This is God's self-binding act of unconditional love. As Hoekema astutely observes: "In the covenant of grace both God's sovereignty and man's responsibility meet."[87] And this doctrine of a freely-given, one-sided-yet-mutual, conditional-yet-unconditional covenant, Calvin ably integrated with his doctrine of predestination.[88] The challenge that this particular take on Calvin presents to adherents to the Trinterud thesis is obvious.

If there is any substance to Trinterud's claim that the early Puritans were responsible for importing the conditional covenant theory from the Rhineland Reformers to the *Westminster Standards*, then a quick glance at Perkins' words on covenant conditionality would surely qualify him as a prime and early candidate for such an instrument of mediation. It is therefore helpful to repeat Perkins' definition of covenant as found in his *Golden Chaine*:

> This covenant consists of two parts: Gods promise to man, Mans promise to God.
> Gods promise to man, is that, whereby he bindeth himself to man to bee his God, if he performe the condition.
> Man's promise to God, is that, whereby hee voweth his allegeance unto his Lord, and to performe the condition betweene them.[89]

Here Perkins clearly states his understanding of covenant as a conditional transaction, an agreement between God and the creature, a "contract" as he states earlier in the same paragraph. There are further passages where Perkins underscores the conditional nature of covenant. But the particular conditionality of which Perkins speaks here appertains only to his conception of the covenant of works, because, after a lengthy exposition of the decalogue (which, recall, for Perkins, is the covenant of works), he comes to his description of the covenant of grace.[90] If his "contractual" definition of covenant is applied to his understanding of the covenant of grace it becomes clear very quickly that Perkins understands humanity's responsibility in covenant to be obedience to the "condition" of the covenant of grace – faith and repentance: "The covenant of grace is that whereby God freely promising Christ, and his benefits, exacts againe of

---

[86] Lillback, "Conditionality of the Covenant," 64-68.
[87] Hoekema, "Covenant of Grace," 144.
[88] This is ably demonstrated by Lillback, "Conditionality of the Covenant," 71-73.
[89] Perkins, "*A Golden Chaine: or, The Description of Theologie*," in *Workes*, 1.32.
[90] Perkins, *Workes*, 1.32-1.70; Priebe observes this as well ("Covenant Theology of Perkins," 72-77).

man, that hee would by faith receive Christ, and repent of his sinnes."[91] But this repentance and faith, is itself a gift of grace, as Perkins ably shows in various places in *Workes*.[92] Thus, while faith and repentance are "conditions" of the covenant they are also free gifts of grace given simultaneously within the covenant relation.

Perkins teaches that after entering into (God-initiated) covenant, humanity responds in obedience, both passively and actively.[93] *Passively*, the will is moved by God to desire to obey. The will is *active* because of this prior action of God and is faulty by reason of the continuing sinful nature. This is how people are "co-workers with the grace of God" in fulfilling the conditions of the covenant and it is for this reason that Perkins can say "we doe not utterly deny the co-operation of mans will with God's grace."[94] This helps clarify Perkins' sense of the mutuality of the covenant of grace.

Discussions on covenant conditionality require us to examine both the monopleuric or dipleuric aspects. Should God's dealings with humanity be understood as only gracious, as entirely one-sided? The answer to this question is, unreservedly, yes. This emphasis undergirds the monopleuric understanding of covenant conditionality. But then the related question must be asked: Is there a place for obedience in God's dealings with humanity? Again, the answer is a resounding yes. This is the priority of the dipleuric camp. How can such apparently contradictory answers both be right?

These two perspectives on covenant conditionality each have an overwhelming strength and weakness. The strength of the monopleuric "school" is its proper biblical emphasis on God's grace, the entirely unconditional, gracious act of God in calling sinners back into relationship with himself. The weakness of this school is that undue reliance on only grace often risks a descent into dead orthodoxy, as good works – acts of obedience – are ignored on the grounds that all is of grace and one's works count for nothing. Evidence of such arid scholasticism is something that Ames faced in the Netherlands. His reaction against it was part of his systemic reconstructive effort there. On the other hand, the dipleuric school, with its emphasis on obedience and good works could lead to legalism, to a justification by works, as it were, as untenable to the Reformed as it is unbiblical. Yet history provides ample illustrations within branches of the Reformed tradition where such descent into legalism has occurred. The concept of obedience, the doing of works, is extremely important to particular traditions coming out of the so-called Radical Reformation in deliberate antipathy towards the Lutheran (over)emphasis on faith alone. In contra-

---

[91] Perkins, *Workes*, 1.70.
[92] Perkins, *Workes*, 1.124 and 1.165 (in his exposition of the *Apostles' Creed*), and 1.362 (*Treatise Tending Unto a Declaration, Whether a Man be in the Estate of Damnation, or in the Estate of Grace*). Priebe also presents this understanding of Perkins' position on covenant conditionality ("Covenant Theology of Perkins," 75-86).
[93] Perkins, *A Treatise of God's Free Grace and Man's Free Will*, in *Workes*, 1.736.
[94] Perkins, *Workes*, 1.736.

distinction to this, the strength of the dipleuric camp rests in its position that the Christian response to the free offer of the gospel, extended only by grace through faith, is *necessarily* obedience and good works. Consequently, the obedient life of the redeemed is non-discretionary, and, as such, serves as an excellent barometer of one's residency in Christ.

Not surprisingly, William Ames maintained both the unconditional nature of the covenant of grace and the call for obedience. In fact, his affirmation of the one-sided nature of the covenant of grace is so unambiguously strong that he is judged to be an exception to the otherwise stereotypical (Trinterudian) alignment of English Puritanism with the Rhineland Reformers. Recall his heavy emphasis on the testamental nature of the definition of covenant. Although Ames' position on the question of covenant conditionality appears close to that of Perkins, it must be recalled that Perkins cast his definition of covenant in terminology and with certain ambiguities unfamiliar to Ames. For Ames, the singular, explicit, and clear emphasis was that God works in grace, humanity responds in obedience. Ames' enumeration of the differences between the covenant of works and the covenant of grace stressed that God applies Christ's redemption by the covenant of grace – a "firm promise" and a "free gift." Echoing Perkins, Ames explains that in this new covenant, only God promises because humanity is disabled by sin to enter into a spiritual covenant with God.[95] And as if anticipating the question of covenantal mutuality, Ames concedes, almost grudgingly: "But *if two parties are necessary in the strict sense of a covenant*, then God is a party assuming and constituting and man is a party assumed."[96] Only out of sheer mercy does God establish this one-sided covenant with humanity.

What then of covenantal response? While the covenant of works required perfect obedience of humanity in its own strength, Ames' compelling and precisely-nuanced position on covenant conditionality in reference to the covenant of grace bears repeating: "the present covenant requires no properly called or prior condition, *but only a following or intermediate condition (and that to be given by grace as a means to grace), which is the proper nature of faith.*"[97] It is almost as if Ames is saying: "If you insist on attaching a condition to the covenant, then I will grant you an *intermediate* one and that only *following* freely-given grace." Then following Perkins, he asserts that the offer of Christ is received both passively and actively – the former through infusion of the "principle of grace in the will of man" and the latter by an "elicited act of faith."[98] So although Ames does teach an unconditional covenant, he co-mingles the conditional with the absolute (unconditional) in his understanding of salvation and, additionally, affixes a high priority to covenantal responsibility. He avers that

---

[95] Ames, *Marrow*, 1.24.10-1.24.14.
[96] Ames, *Marrow*, 1.24.14, my emphasis.
[97] Ames, *Marrow*, 1.24.19, my emphasis.
[98] Ames, *Marrow*, 1.26.21-1.26.27.

this response, the response of obedience, will be the working-out of faith by divinely-granted grace as well.

Although the position of Ames might appear similar to Perkins and Calvin before him, Ames' true intent can be appreciated only when seen in the context of his very unique definition of theology as the doctrine of living to God. The genuine implications of this unique Amesian priority, come clearly to the fore in his identification of the will as central in this entire drama of regeneration and obedience:

> The will is the proper and prime subject of this grace; the conversion of the will is the effectual principle in the conversion of the whole man. Phil. 2:13, it is God that works in you both to will and to do of his own good pleasure.
> The enlightening of the mind is not sufficient to produce this effect because it does not take away the corruption of the will. Nor does it communicate any new supernatural principle by which it may convert itself.[99]

This is the true context in which all of Ames' thought on covenant – in this case, covenant conditionality – must be understood. Eusden accurately captures the spirit of Ames' covenantal understanding when he affirms that, for Ames, "the covenant of grace was that which a man sought to *experience* as he lived to God."[100] Humanity *must* exercise the will in faithfulness to the covenant, and this not only in covenant *obedience* but also in covenant *entry*. Otherwise, the covenant is violated. Ames is clarifying what Calvin emphasized – that theologizing serves piety; i.e., knowledge of God should always lead to godliness in life. The way in which this message was communicated however, demonstrates just how far Ames had moved, beyond Calvin, in embracing this principle in an architectonically-covenantal framework. In addition, Ames focused on the volition as the instrumental means by which such piety, such (covenantal) life is pursued.

Covenant and Assurance

As intimated above, for Calvin, the assurance of salvation offered by the covenant of grace is one of its chief characteristics and endearing features. "Let us always remember that this promise, like all others, would not bear fruit for us if the free covenant of his mercy had not gone before, upon which the whole assurance of our salvation depended."[101] There is assurance of certainty in doubt, happiness in despair, peace in suffering and hope in adversity.[102] The very heart and attraction of the covenant, other than its redemptive quality, is the objective assurance it proffers. In fact, Calvin elaborates at length on the assuring nature

---

[99] Ames, *Marrow*, 1.26.23-1.26.24.
[100] Eusden, "Introduction" in *Marrow*, 53, my emphasis.
[101] Calvin, *Institutes*, 3.18.7.
[102] Lillback, *The Binding of God*, 268-72.

of covenant and predestination; the doctrine of election provides assurance and enables perseverance.[103]

Locating predestination at the head of his *Golden Chaine* identified Perkins' overwhelmingly supralapsarian commitment. Yet for Perkins, too, the doctrine of predestination carries a faith-assuring quality. In explaining predestination in his commentary on the *Apostles' Creed*, he follows his explanation of "Universall grace" with the "uses" to which this hard teaching can be applied. "Endlesse consolation" heads up the list.[104] Because of the covenant, perseverance carries the divine guarantee of life; despite sin's dreadful power unleashed upon the elect, at times with such force, that "they be hardly saved,"[105] covenant means assurance.

Its immediate and practical use in the life of the elect is to motivate one to work at making one's calling and election sure by abstaining from worldly attraction in search for security. Moreover, the elect are to live as those appointed to newness of life, because they are "vessels of *honour*." This status conveys assurance notably in suffering, which is a sure sign of the elect's conformity to Christ.[106] It is obvious that, while Perkins considered covenant first and foremost as the outward means of executing the decree of election, the decree was, simultaneously, the grounds for assurance of covenant status.[107] Breward remarks that Perkins' teaching on assurance constituted his "third major contribution to the theology of grace and predestination," the other two being his defense of predestination on rational grounds and his conjoining of predestination and covenant theology.[108]

In Puritan thinking generally, the work of the Spirit was based on the covenant of grace which is itself grounded in God's sovereign election.[109] As inti-

---

[103] Calvin, *Institutes*, 3.24.3-3.24.7.
[104] Perkins, *Workes*, 1.291.
[105] Perkins, *Workes*, 1.291.
[106] Perkins, *Workes*, 1.291-1.293, original emphasis.
[107] Song discusses Perkins' views on covenant and assurance and argues that the doctrine of assurance is preeminent in the theology (and piety) of Perkins. He enumerates a number of Perkins' publications in which assurance is the dominant theme. Within the context of the *ordo salutis*, Song argues that assurance is, with faith, in the category of the "first grace" of justification, rather than sanctification where it has generally been placed. According to Song, Perkins holds that the "covenant serves as the 'chain' that bridges the decree and piety in redemption." Because of this interconnectedness of covenant and assurance, the covenant becomes, for Perkins, the chief instrument of assurance ("System and Piety in Perkins and Preston," 128-29, 132, 143-44).
[108] I. Breward, ed., *The Work of William Perkins*, The Courtenay Library of Reformation Classics, vol. 3 (Abingdon, England: Sutton Courtenay, 1970), 88-89, 94-95. In citations included in Breward's (much-shortened) reproduction of Perkins' *Workes*, I follow Breward's English modernization of Perkins.
[109] J.R. Beeke, *Assurance of Faith: Calvin, English Puritanism and the Dutch Second Reformation*, American University Studies, Series 7, Theology and Religion, vol. 89 (New York: Peter Lang, 1994), 144. Beeke rightly observes that "election and covenant

mated above, William Ames' concern, in line with this thinking, was that assurance was something to be sought, to be coveted, and to be encouraged in the life of the believer. Only in this way could doubt be overcome. Yet the reality of the presence of uncertainty – lack of assurance – was of great concern for Ames. True justifying faith was required for the following reason:

> The feeling of persuasion is not always present. It may and often does happen, either through weakness of judgment or various temptations and troubles of mind, that a person who truly believes and is by faith justified before God may for a time think that he neither believes nor is reconciled to God. . . . Believers obviously do not have the same assurance of grace and favor of God, nor do the same ones have it at all times.[110]

It is a relief, therefore, that a fruit of justifying faith is assurance.[111]

Evidences of God's divine favor in one's life are to be sought in the dynamic of the *ordo salutis* itself. In his teaching on the theological virtues of faith, hope, and love, Ames asserts that associated with the movement of the Christian life towards sanctification, the covenant subject exercises fruits of the Spirit. Ames identifies these fruits with virtues. As such, Ames could say both that these virtues profit humanity and that "holiness with all the virtues is called not only a fruit of the Holy Spirit *but also our fruit*."[112] A life lived in covenant must thus produce fruit and these evidences serve as assurance of salvation. The forensic act of justification is not sufficient to produce the living faith and evidences out of which issue the sought-after assurance. The place to start, according to Ames, is in the preparation of the mind, for this will lead to the act of faith whereby alone the believer has hope of experiencing the covenant faithfulness of God.[113] He reasons:

> Hope is strengthened and increased by all evidences which assure us that the good hoped for belongs to us. Rom. 5:4, *Experience produces hope.* . . . The inward signs of divine grace have first place among such evidences. 1 John 3:14, 19, *We know that we are translated from death to life, because we love the brethren.* . . . [H]ope is strengthened, increased, and stirred up by faith, repentance, good works, and a good conscience. True and lively hope exists through these, so to speak, antecedents Heb. 10:22, 23; 1 Peter 3:15, 16.[114]

We can summarize this section as follows: Calvin placed assurance within the more objective aspect of the covenant of grace. Perkins did this as well but took

---

ride in tandem, reinforcing each other . . . . God's absolute promises in election and covenant are solid pillars for increasing weak faith" (*Assurance*, 145).
[110] Ames, *Marrow*, 1.27.19.
[111] Ames, *Marrow*, 1.28.24.
[112] Ames, *Marrow*, 2.2.22, my emphasis.
[113] Ames, *Marrow*, 2.6.1-2.6.20.
[114] Ames, *Marrow*, 2.6.19-2.6.21.

the next step by teaching that one found one's assurance by denying the world and by living as children of light. Ames embraced both Calvin and Perkins but also moved in the direction of a more subjective approach, seeking evidences of assurance in living the life of covenantal obedience. This led to different emphases in the manner of Christian living. For example, for Calvin, the third use of the law was most significant here. This was important for Ames also, but with much greater refinement. How one lived the covenantal life was to be examined in the court of one's conscience as one progressed through the *ordo salutis*. This, for Ames, was what living to God was all about. Undoubtedly this gave rise to Ames' concern with casuistry – cases of conscience – following his teacher, Perkins. Finally, however, "God's constancy, truth and faithfulness appear in his decree."[115] Thus, while all three theologians anchored assurance in the decretive will of a covenantally-faithful God who promised, it was Ames who more than Calvin and Perkins understood assurance to be evidenced in a life of holy piety and covenant obedience.

Covenant and Church
Almost thirty-four per cent of Calvin's *magnum opus* is devoted to his teaching on the church. This teaching is inseparably connected and deeply couched in Calvin's covenantal understanding. In an editorial note it is remarked that throughout Book 4 "the church is treated as the divine institution to assemble and minister to the elect in the earthly condition in which they are . . . shut in the prison of the flesh."[116] The church is an aid to redeemed humanity's ongoing weakness, a place where the elect assemble and receive ministry in the covenant promises.

As early as the prophetic writings, says Calvin, God has promised the existence of a church. This is that collection of individuals that covenant people, a "holy Jerusalem" where God's people, as blemished as they are, "zealously aspire to holiness and perfect purity."[117] It is that place to which admittance is gained through forgiveness of sins and in which all those, so justified by faith, experience the covenant bonds.[118] In fact, Calvin's emphasis on the ongoing presence of the church despite "very serious sin" within it constitutes a profound ecclesiological principle, a principle found already in the work of the earliest church fathers. It underscores the high view of the church within the Christian tradition. That is why, for Calvin, separation and schism were so sinful; by these acts, the covenant community itself – the very body of Christ – is rent. He declared that "some fault may creep into the administration of either

---

[115] Ames, *Marrow*, 1.7.3. In addition, however, as Beeke argues, the Puritans made use of both the practical syllogism (objectively based on the believer's evidences of obedience and sanctification in daily life) and the mystical syllogism (subjectively based on the internal evidences of the Spirit in progression in grace) in (*Assurance*, 158ff.).
[116] Calvin, *Institutes*, 4.1.1, n. 2.
[117] Calvin, *Institutes*, 4.1.17.
[118] Calvin, *Institutes*, 4.1.20.

doctrine or sacraments, but this ought not to estrange us from communion with the church."[119] Voluntary desertion from the "outward communion of the church (where the Word of God is preached and the sacraments are administered) is without excuse."[120]

> For the Lord esteems the communion of his church so highly that he counts as a traitor and apostate from Christianity anyone who arrogantly leaves any Christian society, provided it cherishes the true ministry of Word and sacraments. He so esteems the authority of the church that when it is violated he believes his own diminished.[121]

Calvin held that rupturing the church through unlawful separation from it constitutes a heinous sin because it brings despite to the covenant. It is via this selfsame covenant which God has established with his people that sinners can be continually restored to God's favor. The covenant of God speaks to the inviolability of the divine promises; come what will, the church will remain until the return of Christ, at the consummation of the age.[122] As Calvin has entitled this massive topic in his *Institutes*, the church is "the external means or aids by which God invites us into the society of Christ and holds us therein."[123] For Calvin, church and covenant are closely, intimately, and organically related.

Perkins couches his discussion of the church within the language and concepts of predestination. He defines that church as "a peculiar company of men predestinated to life everlasting, and made one in Christ."[124] With this introduction, he enters a long discussion on predestination – twenty pages on this, the "efficient cause of the church" – before enlarging on "the *Mysticall Union*, which is the very forme of the Church, whereby all that beleeve are made one with Christ, Gal. 3:28."[125] Here Perkins makes clear intimations of the covenant relationship of the church. In mystical union, there is a mutual giving – Jesus to humanity by the free act of God's grace. Meanwhile, humanity is given to Jesus by the "altogether celestial and spiritual" indeed, "supernatural," gift of faith.[126] He calls this a relationship of "mutual consent," the "Evangelicall Covenant."[127] Perkins very much identifies the mystical union between Christ and his elect to be that moment where the "transaction" of "mutual consent" takes place.

---

[119] Calvin, *Institutes*, 4.1.12.
[120] Calvin, *Institutes*, 4.1.19.
[121] Calvin, *Institutes*, 4.1.10.
[122] Calvin, *Institutes*, 4.1.17.
[123] Calvin, *Institutes*, title of Book 4.
[124] Perkins, *Workes*, 1.277.
[125] Perkins, *Workes*, 1.298.
[126] Perkins, *Workes*, 1.298.
[127] Perkins, *Workes*, 1.299.

So closely does William Ames identify the church with the covenant of grace that it is at times difficult to discern where discussion of the one leaves off and of the other begins:

> The manner of administration of the covenant is twofold: One points to the Christ who will appear and the other to the Christ who has appeared. The Old and New Testaments are reducible to these two primary heads. The Old promises Christ to come and the New testifies that he has come. While Christ was still to appear, all things were more outward and carnal, afterwards more inward and spiritual. John 1:17, *The law was delivered by Moses; grace and truth came by Christ.* The church then had a double aspect: first as an heir and second as a child. Gal. 4:1 ff., *So long as the heir is an infant he differs not at all from a servant, though he be lord of all.* As an heir the church was free; as a child, in a certain way, not free, Gal. 4:1. As an heir it was spiritual; as a child carnal and earthly, Heb. 9:10; Rom. 9:7. As an heir it had the spirit of adoption, but as a child the spirit of fear and bondage.[128]

Perhaps unwittingly Ames maintains perfect identity between the covenant of grace and the church. Covenant terminology segues into church terminology. In the old covenant, the church was an infant looking forward with anticipation to the full covenantal blessing that would accrue to it as it advanced toward maturity. But it was yet in a servile condition, bound by the law. In the new covenant, the church is accorded liberty in Christ and becomes an heir to all the covenant blessings in its spiritual life.

A particular emphasis in Ames' discussion of the church concerns its empirical nature.[129] The church is the collective response of faith to God's gracious work in Christ. It comprises that body of believers who covenant with a God who has covenanted with them. There exists also a special bond among believers because the church covenant binds people to God and to each other. The church represents that place where the moral law is best exemplified. Further, Ames suggests that this bond be renewed frequently in public profession because "profession of the true faith is the most essential mark of the church."[130] Although Ames affirms the pre-eminence of preaching and the sacraments, for him the true mark of the church finds itself, more subjectively, in the community of faith covenanting with God and each other, a notion of "church covenanting" highly consistent with his focus on the subjective dimension of the church. Ames saw the church as a group of covenanted individuals, deeply involved with developing a congregation-centered church life (which included Puritan agitation). In the context of the broader church, such focus expresses itself in ecclesiastical independence. This accounts for Ames' well-known position of

---

[128] Ames, *Marrow*, 1.38.4-1.38.9.
[129] Horton, *Ames by Reuter*, 215-19.
[130] Ames, *Marrow*, 1.32.29-1.32.30.

ecclesiastical independence and also explains his ongoing debate regarding ecclesiological matters with Separatist Puritans such as John Robinson.[131]

In summary, Calvin sees the church as essential to the covenant community, a principle echoed by Perkins but overshadowed by his emphasis of the church as a product of God's predestinating work. Ames, meanwhile, practically identifies the church with the covenant community. If for Calvin the church and covenant are closely related, for Ames they are synonymous. It is that corporate body that God has instituted as separate from the world, a body of covenant people who are nurtured in the faith and who experience fellowship within the covenant bonds that exist amongst the members. Nuancing further, while Calvin draws more attention to the church as an object instituted by God as "external means or aids" by which covenant benefits are appropriated, Ames considers the church the "subject of redemption."[132] It is not so much the "object of the application" of salvation, but more the "subject of appropriation" of salvation.[133]

Some of these distinctions lie more in emphasis than anything else, but they are noteworthy. For instance, consider the view of the sacraments. Generally speaking, the sacraments are largely seen as signs and seals of the covenant of grace and of membership in the covenant community, the church. They are "exercises which make us more certain of the trustworthiness of God's Word"

---

[131] Because this section on covenant and church is largely theoretical, an explicit treatment of Ames' so-called "Congregationalism" is not covered here. As Sprunger shows in his work, both Independents and Congregationalists claim him as one of their key founders. Some claim him as the master of the "New England Way." Recall that when Ames left Franeker for Rotterdam it was not for an academic appointment but to co-pastor, with Hugh Peter, the English Reformed Congregation there (Sprunger, *Ames*, 29, 37, 38-44, 92, 97, 100, 185-88, 193-200, 201, 202-5, 219, 220-25, 256, 257-58). An interesting question in the context of the current work would be to ask whether Congregationalism/Independency is compatible with the Reformed tradition.

[132] Ames, *Marrow*, 1.31.1-1.31.2.

[133] Horton, *Ames by Reuter*, 215. This fine distinction comes from Reuter's reading of Ames' more philosophical works. Eusden astutely paraphrases Reuter's circumlocutious elaboration as follows: "In the *Marrow*, Ames depends on a distinction between *materia*, material or basic matter, and *forma*, constitutive force first offered in his *Principles of Logic*. The *materia* of a thing can be examined, in which process the thing under consideration is treated in a passive sense as an object. Or, the constitutive force may be examined, in which case the thing is viewed as a subject with attention focused on its living form or ability to give itself shape and power. Ames prefers to discuss the church as a subject or to concentrate on its *forma*. The *materia* of the church is the people, called together by God's will and providence the operation of which he has already discussed in the *Marrow*" (Eusden, "Introduction" in *Marrow*, 56). See also R.C. Walton, "The Visible Church: A Mixed Body or a Gathered Church of Visible Saints. John Calvin and William Ames," in *Calvin: Erbe und Auftrug*, W. van 't Spijker, ed. (Den Haag: Koninklijke Bibliotheek, 1991), 168-78. Recall as well, the recent work by Davis on Ames' ecclesiology in his "Puritan ecclesiology of William Ames."

says Calvin.[134] Moreover, despite differences in the old and new covenant sacraments, the promise remains the same – redemption and covenant membership.[135] Calvin makes appeal to the covenant as justification for both paedobaptism and the Lord's Supper.[136] Perkins emphasizes the assuring nature of the sacraments.[137] The sacrament is a "proppe and stay for faith to leane upon."[138] It is the sacraments and the proclamation of the Word that are "the *outward* means of executing the decree."[139] Ames underscores a more reciprocal meaning to the sacraments in their assuring quality, for this sealing of the covenant occurs not only on God's part but "secondarily on ours . . . in our thankfulness and obedience towards him."[140]

Concluding Remarks: Covenant as Architectonic

As part of an evolving tradition in Reformed theology that numbered many notable representatives, much of the thought of William Ames with respect to covenantal or federal categories was not unique and exhibited much concurrence with earlier thinkers. His contributions to the Reformed system of federal theology were clearly conditioned by that of his immediate Reformed predecessors. In that connection, then, this is certainly not the first work to challenge Miller's declaration that covenant theology was an "imposition . . . upon the system of Calvin"[141] Covenantal theological principles had long been introduced prior to the early modern period of Ames' world.

Yet the employment of covenant theology as the conceptual framework of developing system was really not evident until the work of William Ames. Here Miller was accurate in his (largely unsupported) claim of covenant architect for Ames. The latter's careful delineation of the covenant of redemption, works, and grace, and the construction of this federal covenantal principle around the axis of the *ordo salutis* in his theological predication, is uniquely architectonic. Ames truly was "a transitional figure – one of the very first in the Reformed tradition to seize upon the centrality of the covenant of grace."[142] In a way which has been underappreciated in Amesian scholarship, he was very much an original thinker and creatively progressive. The following summary identifies those areas in which Ames' contributions to federal theology are most unique:

---

[134] Calvin, *Institutes*, 4.14.6, 4.14.17, 4.19.2.
[135] Calvin, *Institutes*, 4.16.24; van den Bergh, *Genadeverbond*, 123-24.
[136] Calvin, *Institutes*, 4.16.7, 4.16.30, 4.17.6, 4.17.33, 4.17.44; Lillback, *The Binding of God*, 242-63.
[137] Perkins, *Workes*, 1.72.
[138] Perkins, *Workes*, 1.31.
[139] Perkins, *Workes*, 1.76, 2.255.
[140] Ames, *Marrow*, 1.36.31.
[141] Miller, *Seventeenth Century*, 367.
[142] Eusden, "Introduction" in *Marrow*, 55.

1) An explicitly identified and well-articulated *pactum salutis*, only adumbrated by Calvin and curiously ignored by Perkins;

2) A well-articulated, precisely-defined, and sacramentally-symmetric covenant of works, a concept inferred in "rudimentary" form in Calvin and found in rather undeveloped maturity in Perkins;

3) A unique structure of progression of the covenant of grace, dominated by a pattern of covenant renewal concatenation with intimations of a decreased "intermixture" of the covenant of works. Inseparably connected with this chronological mapping of covenant progression is Ames' unique means of demonstrating a logical, existential progression by means of the *ordo salutis*;

4) A preference for "testament" because of its primarily monopleuric meaning over "covenant" and its dipleuric connotations. This leads to great stress on the one-sided nature of the covenant of grace. This concept of unmitigated unconditionality is clearer than the ambiguous mutuality at times indicated by Perkins and the peculiar, somewhat logically asymmetrical, but creative Calvinian view on the covenant as both conditional and unconditional;

5) A more subjective location of assurance in the activism of the believer. This activism (hand-in-hand with Ames' moral and practical teaching, as we shall see) constitute an "informed piety." It represents a life of covenantal obedience lived along the lines of the decalogue, and monitored by the conscience as to conformity to the whole law; and

6) A subjective, empirical view of church, considered almost synonymous with covenant, in which the focus is more on the organic union of covenant children, compared to a more objective view in which through election, the church is called into mystical union with its head.

With his conflation of the concepts of faith and obedience as characterizing the renewed heart of those who truly own Christ, William Ames balanced both the gracious and the demanding character of the covenant of grace. While grace was always prior, obedience was not to be sacrificed on the altar of God's presumed beneficence. While grace is of utmost importance, obedience is no less so. For Ames obedience was the corollary to grace. The moral and practical nature of theology as living to God was a non-negotiable, and the theological architecture within which his practical impulses received formulation was covenant theology.

Chapter 4

The Voluntarism of William Ames

Key Considerations and a Review of Calvin's Thought

Much has been made of William Ames' commitment to "voluntarism," a medieval and early modern category of thought that raises both definitional and theological concerns in contemporary debate. First, the formal definition and meaning of voluntarism post-dates the period of early orthodoxy and is, in fact, of relatively recent origin. F. Tönnies coined the term in an 1883 publication[1] and S.K. Knebel asserts that the term had no theological referent prior to 1892.[2] It is only as the concept enters the theological realm that its area of meaning and the associated definitions assume a more theological bent. Second, the conversation on voluntarism is often misguided from the outset by setting the will and the intellect in diametric opposition to each other, outside any considerations of divine grace. Ignoring both of these definitional and theological nuances risks considerable misrepresentation and misunderstanding.

R.T. Kendall's discussion on Calvin's doctrine of faith is often provided as representative of just such a contemporary misreading: "faith [is] an act of the will *in contrast to* a passive persuasion in the mind."[3] This division between volition and intellect discounts two things: the dynamic interplay between these two faculties and the psychological unity of creatures made in the image of God. As a result of emphasizing the one over the other, either the Remonstrant ghost has reappeared or the biblical faith has been eviscerated by an arid orthodoxy. This "colloquial," either-or approach to understanding the psychological makeup of humanity is patently wrong, yet many have pursued it and declared Calvin guilty of intellectualizing the Christian faith with his emphasis on faith as knowledge.[4]

R.A. Muller has provided the medieval philosophical context in which this entire discussion is to be located, particularly with reference to Calvin's understanding of faith.[5] The referents of voluntarism – knowledge (*cognitio*) and the will (*voluntas*) – understood more technically and in their relation to faith,

---

[1] According to E. Herms, *RGG* 7 (2005): 1204.
[2] S.K. Knebel, *HWPh* 11 (2001): 1143.
[3] R.T. Kendall, *Calvin and English Calvinism to 1649* (Oxford: Oxford University, 1979), 3, my emphasis.
[4] Muller, *Unaccommodated Calvin*, 162.
[5] Muller, *Unaccommodated Calvin*, 159-73. See also the superb study of Dewey J. Hoitenga, Jr. in *John Calvin and the Will: A Critique and Corrective* (Grand Rapids: Baker, 1997).

speak to their relative primacy as the constitutive elements of the two faculties of the soul – the intellect and the volition. Primacy of the intellect, a more contemplative or speculative act, underscores the view of God as "being and truth" while, from a more practical angle, primacy is assigned to the volition and God is seen, ultimately, as the "highest object of human love." This medieval context makes it clear that neither view has in mind the idea of human thinking, willing, or acting outside of grace and where Calvin does address the volition he does so not in a philosophical sense but from a soteriological perspective wherein he addresses the age-old theological problem of human inability.[6]

Further study of Calvin's concept of faith must recognize the far-ranging meaning of *cognitio* in his thought. This is something either neglected or misunderstood in Calvin historiography.[7] Calvin understands faith both as a "certain and firm knowledge" and as trust (*fiducia*), and in his discussion of the soul he appears to place equal emphasis upon both the intellect and the will as the truly foundational human faculties. Troubling to some, therefore, is Calvin's apparent backpedalling in statements such as this:

> The understanding is, as it were, the leader and governor of the soul; ... the will is always mindful of the bidding of the understanding, and in its own desire awaits the judgment of the understanding. ... No power can be found in the soul that does not duly have reference to one or the other of these members.[8]

Later in the *Institutes* this primacy of the mind appears to be confirmed as Calvin defines faith:

> Now we shall possess a right definition of faith if we call it a firm and certain knowledge of God's benevolence toward us, founded upon the truth of the freely given promise in Christ, both revealed to our minds and sealed upon our hearts through the Holy Spirit.[9]

Can we assume from this, as many have, that the faith of Calvin is non-volitional and that Calvin has essentially a more intellectualistic understanding of true religion?[10]

---

[6] Muller, *Unaccommodated Calvin*, 166.
[7] Muller, *Unaccommodated Calvin*, 159-61.
[8] Calvin, *Institutes*, 1.15.7.
[9] Calvin, *Institutes*, 3.2.7.
[10] Kendall argues that the overwhelming tendency to intellectualism and passivity in Calvin is to be distinguished from the active and voluntarist dispositions of those who place faith in the will. For Beza, Calvin's successor, it is ultimately the will that must surrender to the gospel promise which leads him to conclude that faith is an act of the will. On this basis, Kendall classifies Calvin as an intellectualist and Beza a voluntarist, and carries this dichotomy through his entire study of English Calvinism to the Westminster Assembly. This bifurcation becomes the driving apparatus in Kendall's thesis – that there was a radical discontinuity between this perceived passivism of Calvin and the activism of the Puritans, including the Westminster Divines. See *Calvin and English*

Perhaps Calvin's famous definition of faith has been more quoted than understood. Closer reading of the latter passage and many others uncovers an equal balance of head and heart. "Faith," he said, "can in no wise be separated from a devout disposition." True assent to the gospel promise is "more of the heart than of the brain, and more of the disposition than of the understanding." The heart, said Calvin, not the mind, is "the chief part of faith;"[11] but this includes the mind for it "indicates affections, desires, volitions: there is a difference between thinking of a thing and striving for it . . . ."[12]

Admittedly, some individual Calvinian statements could be taken as privileging the intellect over the will in matters of faith. Yet in light of his entire body of work, the charge that Calvin intellectualized the faith cannot be maintained. In his assessment, Muller reminds us of the Augustinian provenance of much of Calvin's thought and, against the medieval philosophical backdrop, emphasizes Calvin's soteriological (rather than philosophical) concern. From this Muller concludes that primacy belongs to the volition, not the intellect, in Calvin's doctrine of faith:

> Calvin's theology falls, in its basic attitude toward the problems of human knowing and willing in their relation to the temporal working out of salvation, into a voluntarist rather than an intellectualist pattern . . . The will, not the intellect, stands at the center of the soteriological problem . . . . Faith, for Calvin, is a matter of intellect and will in conjunction – with the highest part, not merely the instrumental part, of faith belonging to the will.[13]

William Perkins and Voluntarism

Before we examine William Perkins' views on voluntarism, we take a brief glance at Beza because Perkins, although unquestionably a Calvinist, stood in the more direct shadow of Beza and is seen by many scholars as consequently owing more of his emphases to Beza than to Calvin. There is no question that Calvin's Genevan successor furthered his thought. But even more explicitly than Calvin did Beza center the faith act in the will because he understood the

---

Calvinism, 3, 19-29, 34, and his essay "The Puritan Modification of Calvin's Theology," in *John Calvin: His Influence in the Western World*, W.S. Reid, ed. (Grand Rapids: Zondervan, 1982), 197-214. Kendall's thesis, which identifies Beza as the source of "later Calvinism," has been soundly criticized for its presuppositions, method and implications. See, for example, Muller, *Unaccommodated Calvin*, 159-73; Beeke, *Assurance*, 20ff.; G.W. Harper, "Calvin and English Calvinism to 1649: A Review Article," *CTJ* 20 (1985): 255-62; and P. Helm, *Calvin and the Calvinists* (Edinburgh: Banner of Truth, 1982). This debate comes up again.

[11] Calvin, *Institutes*, 3.2.8, 3.2.33.

[12] Calvin, Sermon on Deut 6:4-9, cited in Muller, *Unaccommodated Calvin*, 169.

[13] Muller, *Unaccommodated Calvin*, 171. In agreement, Hoitenga, Jr. closes his study by stating that (fortunately, if inconsistently) while Calvin opens his discussion of the created will with an intellectualist account of it, he closes it with a voluntarist view (*Calvin and the Will*, 125).

emphasis to lie more explicitly upon volitional assent in the expression of faith. On this basis he has been seen, notably by the "Kendall school of discontinuity," as the originator of the voluntarist tradition, a tradition characterized by two opposing streams of developing Reformed orthodoxy that pitted Calvin against his theological descendants. But even if it could be successfully argued that voluntaristic tendencies were evident in Beza, outright voluntarism was avoided by his belief that what was required in the faith act was a *surrender* of the will and this surrender was facilitated only by dependence on God's enabling grace.[14]

Introducing case divinity as the vehicle through which many of life's moral ambiguities could be examined and resolved, Perkins' first casuistic exercise was to determine "whether I be a child of God or no." When we explore Perkins and voluntarism we find ourselves in the middle of his teaching on assurance of faith. When Perkins intimated that assurance of faith could come from what one *did* – evidences gleaned from the Christian life in which the elect lived as children of light – these voluntaristic traces entered the theological tradition and voluntarism became the hallmark of English Puritanism. This Bezan emphasis "gained ascendancy in the Perkins tradition" and all the divines coming after the father of Puritanism moved gradually down this voluntaristic track.[15]

In his judgment of continental theological developments after Calvin, Reuter avers that the heavy reliance upon the thought of Franciscus Gomarus (1563-1641) and Antonius Walaeus (1573-1639) resulted in the orthodoxy of scholasticism in post-Calvinian Reformed thought. For Gomarus, claims Reuter, "the home of faith is assigned to the mind possessed exclusively of intellectual qualities." When prominence is given to faith as no more than "conviction of the truth about God," trust – *fiducia* – is consigned to the sideline. This results in a "heavy line of demarcation between the mental functions of knowledge and will, far beyond the theology of Calvin" for whom "*assensus* (assent) is related rather to *fiducia* (trust) than to *notitia* (knowledge)." The whole of orthodoxy, more or less "decayed into an intellectualization of the faith."[16] With such theological evolution came a conception of faith as divided into psychological functions. This, according to Reuter, was a perspective not shared by the English Puritans, beginning with Perkins:

> In Perkins one still senses the power of the intellectual idea of faith which Beza held. . . . The acceptance of Christ in faith does not come by any act of the will but through a supernatural power of understanding. . . . [However], though he attributes the origin of faith to knowledge, he also recognizes a turning to faith which consists in the preparation of the heart by God for His gift of grace. And the highest step of faith exhibits real infallible trust coupled with complete convic-

---

[14] Beeke, *Assurance*, 47-89.
[15] Kendall, *Calvin and English Calvinism*, 3.
[16] Horton, *Ames by Reuter*, 183.

tion of the heart – the certain conviction of the complete forgiveness of sins and eternal life. There is a remembrance of Calvin here not only in the reference to knowledge but also in the desire to see the believing man as a unity. This keeps Perkins from the rigid sundering of the provinces of *mens* (intellect) and *voluntas* (will) in the mind. For him faith is not divided into psychological functions which have to be kept separate . . . .[17]

Regardless of Reuter's judgment on the (negative) developments leading up to Protestant scholasticism, our examination of Calvin's teaching on faith confirms the accuracy of Reuter's alignment of Perkins with Calvin over against the misguided assessment of the "discontinuity school." No doubt, the voluntaristic traces in Perkins, somewhat more explicit than in Calvin, result from the commitment to obedience evidenced in Christian activism undergirded by an understanding of covenant commitment as obligation and duties and intimated in his understanding of theology as "the science of living blessedly forever," a much more activistic perspective on theology than Calvin and one touched by Ramist convictions. To Perkins, only those works were "meritorious" as markers of obedience that issued out of faith and in reliance on God's enablement:

Whatsoever good thing thou goest about, whether it be in word or deede, doe it not in a conceite of thyself, or in the pride of thy heart, but in humilitie, ascribing the power whereby thou doest thy worke, and the praise thereof to God; otherwise, thou shalt finde by experience, God will curse thy best doings.[18]

His predestinarian system and the careful balance he struck between predestination's origin (the will of God) and predestination's "use" (the assurance of the elect and motivation to live as those conforming to the image of Christ) demonstrates an emphatic dismissal of the value of works outside of grace, but, at the same time, an awareness that the life of the elect entailed responsibility and obedience. This active and obedient walk of faith Muller has labeled "Christian voluntarism," an activity that can be held in tandem with election because it is "intelligible only in Christ. Christ himself has become the center of the predestinarian schema. Causal theocentricity [election] is paralleled by soteriological Christocentricity [obedience]"[19] We can conclude, then, that Perkins' voluntaristic tendencies arose out of his more activistic view of theology's center of gravity ("living blessedly").

---

[17] Horton, *Ames by Reuter*, 184.
[18] Perkins, *A Graine of Mustard Seede*, in *Workes*, 1.644.
[19] R.A. Muller, "Perkins' *A Golden Chaine*: Predestinarian System or Schematized *Ordo Salutis*?" *SCJ* 9 (1978): 77.

William Ames and Voluntarism

An Established Trail

William Ames prioritized the volition in a way and to a degree remarkably more emphatic than that of both Calvin and Perkins in his teaching on faith and the subsequent conduct of the Christian. Building further upon Perkins' view of theology, Ames' announces that theology is "the doctrine of living to God" and from this emphatic assertion one immediately comes to expect a more activistic view of faith and the Christian life. So pronounced is Ames' teaching on (obedient) Christian action, that "voluntarist" seems an apt term. Such a view of the primacy of the will seems completely consistent with an understanding of theology as a lived reality. With a nod to this unique Amesian definition, and recognizing the theological climate of Ames' adopted home, Sprunger rightly remarks that Ames' emphasis on the will was in response to "the chill of orthodoxy that leaves men too comfortable. . . . Theologically and propositionally Ames preached the omnipotence of God, but on the practical level man was responsible."[20] He judges that Ames' emphasis on the will rather than intellectual assent "pulled Ames from the mainstream of Reformed theology," because it was a position which few held.[21] According to Reuter, Ames' thought is to be considered analogous to that of medieval "practical voluntarism," and on that basis he locates Ames in the company of Anselm, Bernard, St. Francis, Henry of Ghent, and other medieval voluntarists.[22] Did Ames really depart from the mainstream of Reformed theology with such emphasis on the volition?[23]

Gisbertus Voet (or "Voetius," 1589-1676), Dutch theologian and leader of a post-Reformation renewal movement in the Dutch Republic addresses the question of faculty priority in the formal act of justifying faith and summarized the three prevailing positions that had currency in the theological formulation of the seventeenth century. The most common Reformed position was that justifying faith requires both intellectual assent enabled by "general faith" and "application of the will" that flowed from "special faith." The second perspective was the less common but still popular opinion held by leading lights and well known divines such as – and Voet lists them – Zanchius, Beza, Perkins, Gomarus and Maccovius who maintained the primacy of the intellect as the subject from which flows the faith act. The position of the third group, a clear minority, is that the faith act must be attributed to the will. "I have known one, Ames, who has defended this publicly," Voet announced.[24] It is notable that

---

[20] Sprunger, *Ames*, 147.
[21] Sprunger, *Ames*, 146.
[22] Horton, *Ames by Reuter*, 185, 202.
[23] Other prominent scholars maintaining this position are Kendall in *Calvin and English Calvinism*, 151-64 and Geesink in *Gereformeerde Ethiek*, 2.473-2.477. The latter attributes Ames' voluntarism to his adherence to Ramist logic.
[24] Gisbertus Voetius, *Disput.* V, 289, cited in Horton, *Ames by Reuter*, 184, 202. The literature on Voet is vast. This man was a giant in the movement to return the theology

from the standpoint of a close contemporary and passionate like-minded reformer, Ames' theological emphasis was judged to be a minority one.

This central theological principle is encountered immediately in the opening statements of *Marrow* where Ames defines theology as "the doctrine (or science) of living to God." Observe the logic behind this conviction: "The first and proper subject of theology is the will," he states, because one "is brought to enjoy God and to act according to his will . . . ."[25] Men and women are spiritual beings, whose lived reality as believers constitutes their "spiritual work" which is, in turn, evidenced by what they believe and how they act. Further, enjoying and obeying God is a condition one is "brought to" from the influence of the Holy Spirit on the heart, nothing less. The volitional activity of "living to God" is responsive to prior divine activity. Because Scripture's anthropology is heart-centered, this is Ames 'apparatus as well. To make his point, he employs the teaching of a most practical scripture to remind us of the procession of faith and obedience from the heart. Proverbs 23:26, enjoins one to surrender in faith and trust ("Give me your heart") while Proverbs 4:23 reminds us that the source of all obedience and observance is the heart ("From the heart come the acts of

---

of the *Nadere Reformatie* period to an informed piety or experiential Christianity of the sort we have discussed in the previous chapter. His work and influence have been much studied. He is heavily indebted to Ames for much of his thought but the scholarly literature has pointed out areas where Voet disagreed with Ames. On Voet, see A.C. Duker, *Gisbertus Voetius* (Leiden: E.J. Brill, 1897-1914) and C. Steenblok, *Gisbertus Voetius, zijn leven en werken* (Gouda: Gereformeerde Pers, 1975). On Voet and the *Nadere Reformatie*, see the following: *Theologische aspecten van de Nadere Reformatie*, T. Brienen et al., eds. (Zoetermeer: Boekencentrum, 1993); Brienen, *Voornaamste vertegenwoordigers*; Brienen, *Gereformeerd Piëtism*; J. van Oort, *De Kerkvaders en Reformatie en Nadere Reformatie* (Zoetermeer: Boekencentrum, 1997); F.A. van Lieberg, *De Nadere Reformatie in Utrecht ten Tijde van Voetius* (Rotterdam: Lindenberg, 1989); and S. van der Linde, "Gisbertus Voetius' Gedachten over de Prediking," *ThRef* 19 (1976): 256-67. For two recent studies examining Voet's epistemology and piety see J.R. Beeke, "Gisbertus Voetius: Toward a Reformed Marriage of Knowledge and Piety" in *Protestant Scholasticism: Essays in Reassessment*, 227-43, and W. van 't Spijker, *Vroomheid en Wetenschap bij Voetius* (Apeldoorn: Theologische Universiteit, 1998). For a good English language introduction to the work of Voet and prominent near-contemporaries, see J.W. Beardslee, III, ed. and trans, *Reformed Dogmatics: J. Wollebius, G. Voetius, and F. Turretin. A Library of Protestant Thought* (New York: Oxford University, 1965; reprint ed., Grand Rapids: Baker, 1977). Gisbertus Voet's thought is also found in a sampling of his work: *Geestelijke Verlatingen* (Utrecht: Lambert Roeck, 1646; reprint ed., n.p.: Het Traktaat-genootschap "Filippus," 1898) [*Spiritual Desertion*. Classics of Reformed Spirituality, trans. J. Vriend and H. Boonstra, ed. M. Eugene Osterhaven. Grand Rapids: Baker, 2003.]; *Disputationes theologicae*, 5 vols. (Ultrajecti: apud Joannem à Waesberge, Anonium Smytegelt, 1648-69); *Te asketica sive Exercitia Pietatis* (Gorinchen: Vink, 1654); *Proeve van de Kracht der Godzaligheydt* (Utrecht: Simon de Vries, 1656); and *Catechisatie over den Heidelbergschen Catechismus*, A. Kuyper, ed., 2 vols. (Rotterdam: Gebroeders Huge, 1891).

[25] Ames, *Marrow*, 1.1.9.

life").²⁶ Interestingly, there are unmistakable parallels here to Paul's opening verses in Romans 12 where the believer is urged first to renew the mind in order to determine ("approve") God's will. This is faith, and is necessarily followed by the offering up of one's being ("the whole man" as Ames puts it) as a living sacrifice. This, says Paul, is one's "spiritual act of worship," a sentiment echoed by Ames with his assertion that "this life is [one's] spiritual work."²⁷ Ames' Pauline reading informs his understanding of this spiritual work as conformity of the human to the divine will. Siding with Paul, then, and against Thomas, Ames concludes that because of its practical and lively nature, theology cannot be a speculative discipline; it must be practical.

Further, Ames' simple presupposition – that in the heart are located both the will and the intellect – aligns with the philosophical and theological thinking of the day. Speaking soteriologically, to surrender the heart to God is to submissively relinquish one's own desires and supplant these with the desire for faith and obedience. Faith and obedience are both acts of the will – the "possessing the true good" and the "doing the true good." The act of faith "depends partly upon an inborn principle or attitude toward grace and partly upon the action of God moving before and stirring up. Both faith and repentance "have the same subject; both have their seat in the heart or will of man."²⁸ In his discussion on effectual calling the "inward" offer of Christ, explains Ames, represents a spiritual enlightenment resulting in a "receiving of Christ." With an eye on Philippians 3:12 ("I apprehend, because I have been apprehended"), Ames differentiates between the "passive" and "active" nature of this "receiving" and elaborates:

> The *passive receiving* of Christ is the process by which a spiritual principle of grace is generated in the will of man. . . . This grace is the basis of that relation in which man is united with Christ. . . . The will is the proper and prime subject of this grace; *the conversion of the will is the effectual principle in the conversion of the whole man.* . . . The enlightening of the mind is not sufficient to produce this effect because it does not take away the corruption of the will. Nor does it communicate any new supernatural principle by which it may convert itself. Yet *the will in this first receiving plays the role neither of a free agent nor a natural bearer, but only of an obedient subject.* . . .
> *Active receiving* is an elicited act of faith in which he who is called now wholly leans upon Christ as his savior and through Christ upon God. . . . ²⁹

Volitional activity is executed only in response to prior overtures of grace. Ames is careful to identify the will as the *passive recipient* and the locus of the *first receiving* of supernatural grace. This passive receiving is conjoined with

---

²⁶ Ames, *Marrow*, 1.1.9.
²⁷ And this is the guiding principle of the *magnum opus* of late-seventeenth/early-eighteenth century Dutch divine Wilhelmus à Brakel, studied in a later chapter.
²⁸ Ames, *Marrow*, 1.26.27-1.26.30.
²⁹ Ames, *Marrow*, 1.26.21-1.26.25, my emphasis.

an "active receiving" of the grace proffered. But even this active receiving is an "*elicited* act of faith," a movement Godward but only subsequent to divine invitation and persuasion. This divinely-begun, volitionally-centered, work of faith presupposes the cognitive process of the intellect, for while it is true that the mind is in bondage to the corruption of the unredeemed will and cannot "produce" the "effect" of union with Christ, elsewhere Ames insists unequivocally that "the understanding's assent . . . is necessary to faith . . . ."[30] Surely this makes it difficult to maintain the charge of a voluntaristic-based faith disconnected from the intellect and from divinely-required obedience (or, as Ames puts it, "observance"). He quotes Philippians 2:13: "It is God that works in you both to will and to do his own good pleasure." If the clear Calvinian notion of the primacy of the volition in the conjunction of both intellect and will in the act of faith dimmed somewhat in Perkins' work, it is recovered here with vigorous insistence.

Once Ames has established the primary role of the will in the act of faith – both passively in receiving and actively in resting on Christ – his concern turns to the question of the choice of one's course of action. In other words, it is now time to "inquire into the actions, and conversation of his life" and this topic gets extended treatment in *Conscience*. Sandwiched between his exposition on both the cardinal virtues and the moral law, Ames asks:

> Quest 1. Whether in a good or evil act there be necessarily required an inclination of the will?
> 1. Ans. First, *the will is the principle and the first cause of all humane operation* in regard of the exercise of the act. For we therefore doe this or that rather then another thing, because we will; As God himselfe is said to do all things of his owne Will. Eph. 1:11. So also doth man who is made after the Image of God. *The first cause therefore of the goodnesse or sinfulnesse* of any Act of man, is in the Will.
> 2. Secondly, liberty also of election is formally in the will: that therefore any one doth yield obedience to God, or refuseth to do so, proceeds from the will.
> 3. Lastly, our obedience stands in our conformity to the Will of God: and the disobedience, in our unconformity thereunto. Now our *conformity with the Will of God is first and principally in our will*. Apoc. 2:6[31]

The operation of the faculty of the will is as primary in Christian action as it is in justifying faith. But here, too, Ames' position is so nuanced as to locate ultimate responsibility in the divine initiative. While the will is the "principle and the first cause" of any action in one's Christian life, it is not a self-determining desire towards such action but it is rather a *responsive* reaction to gracious overtures which elicit a desire to obey. This desire is the natural outworking of the prior act of faith and its consequent resting of the heart on God.

---

[30] Ames, *Marrow*, 2.5.48.
[31] Ames, *Conscience*, 3.19.1.

Ames, with Calvin, employs the philosophical and more technical understanding of the constitutive makeup and dynamic of faculty psychology. Frequent reference to the *summum bonum* found throughout Ames' work brings to mind the centrality of this concept in medieval thought. Ames' key sentiment, that "we love God as the chief good"[32] has a centuries-old lineage back to the medieval doctors and their vision of God as the highest good, the highest object of human love. For Ames the will is clearly the nobler faculty, objectively greater, more perfect, deserving of greater respect.[33] Borrowing further, Ames assets that "we desire God for ourselves, because we hope for perfect and eternal blessedness from him." This explains why "the highest end of this love should be God himself."[34] This focus is apparent particularly in his commentary on the Heidelberg Catechism in the context of "comfort" and "happiness" or "blessedness." Ames favors a more practical approach to the view of God, where God is seen as the "highest object of human love" as contrasted to the more contemplative (intellectualist) view of God as "being and truth." This medieval understanding receives a biblical overlay in which the realities of sin and disability are taken seriously and divine grace is always seen as prior. This is in line with Calvin's more soteriological view of human spirituality, or psychology. Neither faith nor obedience can be abstracted from grace, or exercised independently, or wrought synergistically. Ability to do the good is given by the inner strength and work of that same Holy Spirit that produced the prior act of faith in the Christian. So while Ames could say that "the first and proper subject of theology is the will,"[35] equally significant was his conviction that this was only and singularly due to the divine initiative, and it was out of obedience that "living well is more excellent than living happily."[36]

Ames' strong view of the primacy of the will stems from his unambiguous commitment to the principles of covenantal thought and the associated obligations that befall the child of God within the federal framework. Ames opens his third book in *Conscience*, "Of Man's Duty in General," with chapter one, "Of Obedience in General."[37] He inquires after the signs of "true obedience" and then follows this with the question of motivation. Why, he asks would the believer obey? Citing Hebrews 8:10, the key New Testament passage quoting at length the new covenant teaching found in Jeremiah 31, Ames succinctly answers that we are to "remember how we are bound by a most firme covenant to serve God" because "the end [purpose] of Gods greatest mercy is obedience."[38] Recall Ames' view of the covenant: it is a "kind of transaction of God with the

---

[32] Ames, *Marrow*, 2.7.1.
[33] From P. Kreeft's description of the medieval understanding of "noble." See his *A Summa of the Summa* (San Francisco: Ignatius, 1990), 40, n. 16.
[34] Ames, *Marrow*, 2.7.9-2.7.10.
[35] Ames, *Marrow*, 1.1.9.
[36] Ames, *Marrow*, 1.1.8.
[37] Ames, *Conscience*, 3.1.
[38] Ames, *Conscience*, 3.1.14[sic]-3.1.16.

creature" whereby God commands, threatens, promises and fulfills and the creature binds itself in obedience. Ames considered even God's commands and threats as examples of God's mercy.

Even while Ames emphasized the *practical* angle, God appealed also to the rational faculty of humans when he entered into covenant with them. Following Calvin, Ames holds that it is the informed intellect upon which the Holy Spirit has moved that motivates the will. With Calvin, Ames identifies the heart as the domicile of the will: "the conversion of the will is the effectual principle in the conversion of the whole man" because the enlightening of the mind is insufficient to purge the will of corruption.[39]

Ames was much more explicit and vigorous in his voluntarism than either Calvin or Perkins. This would explain Voet's assertion that Ames stood near alone in attributing such primacy to the will. But broadly speaking, Ames' voluntarism is solidly found in the intellectual stream of both Calvin and Perkins. Recognizing this modifies Kendall's thesis that voluntarism in English Calvinism began with Perkins, and gradually came to be appropriated by later Puritans, with the exception of Ames who gave it his "weighty sanction." With some overstatement, Kendall concludes that "Ames' voluntarism appears to be the key to all he believes."[40]

The Intellectual, Theological and Ecclesiastical Atmosphere
Our discussion must also consider the philosophical, theological and ecclesiastical atmosphere of the seventeenth century Dutch Republic. It is surely the case that Ames was forced to steer a clear path between the Arminianism and the Aristotelianism of the day, in both his active service and his formal writing. To his deep dismay, both were found in the Dutch academy and church, and it is against both that he inveighed unrelentingly. Firstly, there surfaced a more scholastic view of the faith in some quarters in the Netherlands, uncomfortably close to home. He found himself engaged in battle against the ghost of Aristotle in the form of fellow faculty who, in Ames' judgment, clearly over-rationalized the faith, in continuity with the intellectualism that came through in some of the Gomarism of the Counter-Remonstrants. Secondly, the mood was certainly charged with the Remonstrant controversy, and Kendall speculates that Ames may have received some Arminian overexposure. "It seems likely that Ames read Arminius' *Examination of Perkins' Pamphlet on the Order and Mode of Predestination* (1612)" and in the 1613 debate with Remonstrant Nicholaas Grevinchovius, Ames did not protest the former's claim that faith is an act of will.[41] Whether that piece of evidence – an argument from silence, really – can be used to support the presence of such a forceful theological principle in Ames' thought is highly unlikely, but the more general sentiment of Kendall's

---

[39] Ames, *Conscience*, 1.26.23-1.26.24.
[40] Kendall, *Calvin and English Calvinism*, 151, 154.
[41] Kendall, *Calvin and English Calvinism*, 152.

observation has some merit. Commenting on Ames' voluntarism and echoing Reuter, Eusden remarks in somewhat more measured tone, that in his polemical interaction with the Remonstrants, some of their protestations may have resonated with him, particularly as he was engaged in controversy with Aristotelians:

> Ames, almost alone in the orthodox party, found that the Remonstrant insistence on man's response in the drama of salvation was a needed corrective for Reformed theology. . . . It is not being suggested here that Ames was an Arminian-within-the-gates or a quasi-Remonstrant, but it is true that among orthodox theologians he was the most sensitive to the criticisms advanced by the opposition party."[42]

And it is precisely in this discussion with the Remonstrants more than anywhere else, observes Eusden, that Ames shows himself to be a child of Augustine in that love for God is determined most of all by what a person wills.[43] Eusden is correct in grounding Ames' thoughts in the work of Augustine and recognizing the importance of the primacy of the will in Augustine's thought.

With respect to his engagement with these two major matters of controversy – Arminianism and Aristotelianism – swirling in his adopted home, it is worth noting that Ames behaved no differently here than he had when at Cambridge. He was completely in character and held true to his theological convictions in the face of contemporary challenges. It would be difficult to maintain that Ames was not constantly forced to ponder his soteriology and his theological anthropology – notably the interplay of the intellect and the will – when discussing the determination of a person's standing before God. This reflection obviously yielded a theological position similar to that of Calvin but with a demonstrated sensitivity to the realities of his own day. This careful reconsideration of the faculties at play in the faith act itself resulted in a return to Calvin, in fact, further back than that – all the way to Augustine.[44] Ames' view of theology and the primacy of the will must be understood to represent the soteriological emphasis of Calvin but also a return to a more holistic understanding of faith (against both the Aristotelians and Arminians). The voluntarism of Ames, therefore, had a long and rich legacy; it was his emphatic declaration of activism that set him outside the bounds of Reformed thinking, outside the mainstream, as it were, in a creative attempt to set before the believer the responsi-

---

[42] Eusden, "Introduction" in *Marrow*, 7.
[43] Ames, *Marrow*, 1.26.23, observed earlier in Horton, *Ames by Reuter*, 184-87 and cited in Eusden, "Introduction in *Marrow*," 14-15.
[44] *Ames by Reuter*, 184-87. Citing multiple places in Augustine, Reuter says this: "Here and there faith is understood by Augustine in a voluntaristic way; faith is the will through which we believe, the will which God operates; faith is the vessel by which God's love is taken in and shared with other people as the fulfillment of the Law" (*Ames by Reuter*, 185, 202). Muller shares this assessment in *Unaccommodated Calvin*, 166-67.

bilities entailed by a pious life devoted to God, the doctrine according to godliness. What remained was a formal structuring of this voluntaristically-oriented theological system and precisely such a framework Ames discovered in the work of an earlier sixteenth-century philosopher and educational reformer.

Formalizing Ames' Voluntarism: The Influence of Ramism

With the Aristotelian renaissance of the late Middle Ages and into the early modern period, the privileged position held by revelation fell before the challenge posed by reason. Lost was faith in a metaphysic and epistemology anchored in divine revelation.[45] This faith in reason had its much earlier beginnings with Aristotle and was wholly adopted by the Schoolmen. They retained Aristotelian (dialectic) form and content in their claims that the *summum bonum* can be achieved through reason and tested against empirical and scientific observation, even as they sought to synthesize it with the Christian revelation. This was especially true of Thomas Aquinas, who "embraced Aristotle's thought whole-heartedly as a philosophy, but revised it as he found necessary"[46] and endeavored to demonstrate, against many Aristotelian rationalists, that reason and faith are not contradictory. As scholasticism declined by the middle of the fourteenth century, it was reduced to partisan squabbling over dialectical subtleties on theological issues more and more remote from the church.[47] It was this rationalistic system that the Reformers and the Humanists before them mistrusted, but the Puritans held Aristotle and the scholastics in particular disdain. In his chapter on "virtue" William Ames approvingly quotes Peter Ramus who opined the following:

> I had rather that philosophy were taught to children out of the gospel by a learned theologian of proved character than out of Aristotle by a philosopher. A child will learn many impieties from Aristotle which, it is to be feared, he will unlearn too late. He will learn, for example, that the beginning of blessedness arises out of man; that the end of blessedness lies in man; that all virtues are within man's power and obtainable by man's nature, art, and industry; that God is never present in such works, either as helper or author, however great and divine they are; that divine providence is removed from the theater of human life; that not a word can be spoken about divine justice; that man's blessedness is based on this frail life.[48]

---

[45] A. Vos, "Scholasticism," *NDT*, 621-23. The write-up on Scholasticism proper is excellent and concise covering its history, chief thinkers and strengths and weaknesses. Protestant scholasticism receives scant notice.
[46] A. Vos, "Aristotelianism," *NDT*, 43-45.
[47] Vos, "Scholasticism," 622-23.
[48] Ames, *Marrow*, 2.2.18, quoting Peter Ramus in, *Petri Rami Veromandui pro philosophica Parisiensis academiae disciplina oratio, ad Carolum Lotharinguum Cardinalem* (Parisiis, 1551), or *An Oration by the French Belgian Peter Ramus on Behalf of the Philosophical Training at the University of Paris, Delivered to Charles Cardinal Lorraine*, 40.

Much of Ames' passion is surely accounted for by his reaction against a scholasticism he perceived in both the theoretical theology of the academy and the crypto-Protestantism of the larger body politic, particularly in the public church. Yet Aristotle, especially as mediated by Thomas, was invoked by William Ames where it furthered his program of theology and ethics. Indeed, scholasticism, as method, still prevailed, and was perpetuated in the post-Reformation development of Protestantism, if in somewhat more Christian form.[49]

Ramus opposed what he considered to be the artificial, highly subjective and speculative system of Aristotle which majored in theoretical abstractions and was present to varying degrees in the official theological curricula of the day.[50] He developed a new, more objective system of thought that focused on liberating the schools "entangled in a decadent scholasticism" and offered a new program of practically-oriented learning that overcame Aristotle's division between theory and science.[51] In developing his system for study of the arts, Ramus developed a new framework for logic, grammar, rhetoric and religion along lines more akin to natural reasoning yet along the deductive method of Aristotle, whereby the movement in logic is from general to specific, a passing from universals to particulars.[52] For "By this methode we proceade from the antecedent more absolutely knowen to prove the consequent, which is not so manifestly knowen: & this is the only methode which Aristotle did observe."[53] This method was primarily a system of organization discernible by dichotomy with practical ends in view. In addition, Ramus was not only a philosopher, logician, and pedagogue. He was also a French Protestant, concerned with making the faith accessible to the common man and woman. This concern led to an interest in making theology precise, methodical and teachable, one cleansed from the scholastic influence. Indeed, Ramus raises dialectic, as a tool for elucidation of scripture, to divine proportion in the opening poem of his *Dialectica*:

---

[49] Muller, *PRRD 1*, 27-84.
[50] Horton, *Ames by Reuter*, 232-34; Eusden, "Introduction" in *Marrow*, 39; Sprunger, *Ames*, 106-7.
[51] Horton, *Ames by Visscher*, 71; Horton, *Ames by Reuter*, 232; Miller, *Seventeenth Century*, 125, 140, 150.
[52] Sprunger, *Ames*, 107-9. We have already mentioned that in many respects, the scholastic emphasis on logic and reason is utilized in Ramist logic (Sprunger, *Ames*, 110; Eusden, "Introduction" in *Marrow*, 15).
[53] Peter Ramus, *The Logike of the Moste Excellent Philosopher P. Ramus Martyr*, R. MacIlmaine, trans., C.M. Dunn, ed. Renaissance Editions, no. 3 (Northridge, CA: San Fernando Valley State College, 1969), 54-55.

In Laudem Scientiae Dialectieae sacrae

The sacred Sciences doe prayse deserve,
And merit laud because that they conserve.
The use of manners also doe declare,
What things in man most acceptable are.
But mongst them all ther's none so high in reach
As Dialectica, which reasoning doth teach.

This at the first from God almighty came,
From heaven descended this bright shining flame.
God reason taught, and man he did inspire
With faculties, which Logicke doth require.
The matter precepts, forme Methodicall,
The end is reasons use, to teach th'unlearned all.

Th'effects are diverse which I cannot tell,
Except I had a tongue which did excell.
The artes before confusedly did lie,
Till Logicks use compos'd them curiously.
But what doe I discoursing of this thing,
When prayses to the worth the learned cannot sing?[54]

Such a practical system, with its emphasis on method to make theology more usable and understandable, found a devoted disciple in William Ames. This new, use-oriented approach had high appeal to his practical nature, and Ramism became the structure within which Ames developed his system of thought and ethics. Ames' work is a model of the application of Ramism in developing system beginning with his very definition of theology. There were many Ramists at Christ's College, and this philosophical position was continued well into the seventeenth century through John Milton. It is noteworthy that William Ames became the foremost seventeenth-century Puritan Ramist.[55]

---

[54] Peter Ramus, *Peter Ramus of Vermandois, the King's Professor, his Dialectica in two bookes*, trans. R.F. Gent (London: W. J[ones], 1632; Ann Arbor, MI: University Microfilms, n.d.), front page.

[55] Eusden notes that at Christ's College, Cambridge, a long line of Ramist teachers, beginning with Laurence Chaderton (1536?-1640), included: Gabriel Harvey (1545?-1630), Perkins (1558-1602), George Downham (d. 1634), Ames, William Chappell (1582-1649) and John Milton (1608-1674). Ong points out the inroads the Huguenot's system made in the intellectual circles of the Palatinate and the Netherlands and compares this favorably to Ames' devotion to Ramism: "English Ramists are outdistanced by the Germans and the Dutch. The one Englishman under Ramist influence who stands out as a possible competitor is William Ames . . . who lived for a long time in the Netherlands" (S.J Ong, *Decay of Dialogue*, 304, cited in Eusden, "Introduction" in *Marrow*, 37, 38); Sprunger, *Ames*, 15. For an early study on the theology of Ramus, see P. Lobstein, *Petrus Ramus als Theologe* (Strassburg: G.F. Schmidts Universitäts-Buchhandlung, 1878).

Sensitive to possible criticism on his method, Ames defends his Ramism in his introduction to the *Marrow* with the following apologetic:

> There will be some who condemn the precision of method and logical form as curious and troublesome. But we wish them sounder reason, for they separate the art of learning, judging, and memorizing from those things which most deserved to be learned, known, and memorized.[56]

Aristotelian metaphysics and ethics were common fare in the Dutch academies and especially at Franeker. Despite synodical admonition at Dort with especial regard to Ames' colleague Johannes Maccovius at Franeker, the Dutch Aristotelians' attack on the Ramism introduced by Ames continued unabated.[57] Yet in the face of this considerable opposition, Franeker officially adopted Ramist philosophy and logic and became the center for Ramism in the Netherlands.[58]

It was not only the Aristotelian philosophy and method against which Ramus reacted. Close to Ramus' heart was a concern for ethics. Biblical ethics knew nothing of the ethics of Aristotle, said Ramus. Before his short life was so violently brought to an end, he had written a treatise on ethics which was one revision away from publication.[59] Yet enough of Ramus' thoughts on ethics survive in extant publications to provide a reasonably complete reproduction of his system. At the basis of his ethical system lies an entirely different conception of God which accounts for the vehemence with which Ramus attacks Aristotle. But as F.P. Graves points out, Ramus was not above exclusive appeal to reason for he "treats ethics from the standpoint of the four cardinal virtues and almost in the terms of Plato and Cicero. As a rule, however, Ramus does not desire any such complete emancipation" from the authority of scripture.[60]

For Ames, faith and works are one and indistinguishable in the life of the believer. In *Technometry* he demonstrates his disgust with those who treat theology and ethics separately.[61] If it is true that "the commonly accepted division of

---

[56] Ames, *Marrow*, "A Brief Forewarning of the Author concerning His Purpose."
[57] Sprunger, *Ames*, 111.
[58] Sprunger, *Ames*, 88, 111; Horton, *Ames by Visscher*, 59-60.
[59] F.P. Graves, *Peter Ramus and the Educational Reformation of the Sixteenth Century* (New York: Macmillan, 1912, text-fiche), 173; citing Ramus' *Oratio de Professione liberalium artium* (Paris, 1563), 104.
[60] Graves, *Ramus*, 176-77. Graves observes that Ramus' destruction of Aristotle is based, in part, on his failure to understand the great Greek philosopher; "as an ardent Christian he evidently holds it incumbent upon him to combat the paganism of that philosopher." Yet Graves also remarks about Ramus: "at times he shows that the ancient philosopher had anticipated the true Christian doctrine and accepts his positions, even at the expense of certain usages of the Church" (*Ramus*, 174, 176).
[61] William Ames, *Technometry*, L.W. Gibbs, trans. and ed. Haney Foundation Series of the University of Pennsylvania, vol. 24 (Philadelphia: University of Pennsylvania, 1979), theses 63, 88-94, 118; all citations from Ames' *Technometry* will have reference to this volume and appear by thesis number. (First published as *Technometria, Omnium & singularum Artium fines adæquatè circumscribens* [London: Milo Flesher, 1633] and

art into theoretical and practical is defective in many ways and therefore must be rejected"[62] how much the more must be anathematized those who would teach a discipline or "art of ethics" separate and distinct from the doctrines of theology. Repudiation of this essentially Aristotelian distinction between practical and theoretical philosophy appears at length in this work and Ames' attack against the ethicists or moral philosophers, those practitioners of natural ethics, is unrelenting. God's revealed will in scripture teaches thorough integration of theology and ethics; attempts to drive a wedge between the two are nothing less than metaphysical speculation and sophistry. Ames concludes:

> Hence, being thoughtless or ungrateful and yet not impious by law, do they listen who – educated in the bosom of the Church, have thoroughly learned both about the obscurity of these principles . . . and about the new revelation in the Scriptures – yet flee from these Scriptures to search after the principles of what they call "practical philosophy" and of law and seduce others with themselves.[63]

To summarize, the significance of the new Ramist system over the ancient one of Aristotle was great, not just for its pedagogical usefulness but also for its practical purposes. In the Ramist system, the Christian pilgrim is forced to make a decision, a response, based on God's law and the observable data of his or her faith and morals. We will see presently that the tool used – the hypothetical syllogism – was essential to the promotion of the vital Christianity so important to Ames.

Voluntarism and the Guiding Theological Principles of Early Puritan Thought

William Perkins

"Theology" said William Perkins in *Golden Chaine*, "is the science of living blessedly forever." What did Perkins mean by this "blessed" life? With clear echoes of Calvin, he continues: "Blessed life ariseth from the knowledge of God and therefore it ariseth likewise from the knowledge of ourselves, because we know God by looking into ourselves."[64] This theme is further developed with five chapters on theology proper (God's existence/nature, life, glory, trinity, works and decree) followed by teaching on predestination and creation. Living blessedly is clearly for Perkins, as it was for Calvin, sourced more in an intellectual apprehension of who and what God is. It will be helpful to see how and to what degree first Perkins and then Ames appropriated the method of Peter Ramus in their definitional and methodological principles.

---

itself part of a six-piece work published posthumously (1643) as one volume, *Philosophemata*).
[62] Ames, *Technometry*, thesis 62.
[63] Ames, *Technometry*, thesis 63.
[64] Perkins, *Workes*, 1.11. See also Breward, *Perkins*, 177.

I. Breward remarks that Perkins' *Golden Chaine* (first published in 1590) "marked the beginning of a series of English systematic theologies like Ames' *Medulla* and Usher's *A Body of Divinitie*." We have already seen that the Swiss and Rhineland reformers provided the theological premises of the English theologians. It is worth repeating that the chart of salvation introducing Perkins' *Golden Chaine* draws heavily from Beza's *Summa Totius Theologicae* in its presentation of theology and in its doctrinal arrangement. Breward notes that Beza, in turn, was much indebted to Lombard's *Sentences*. Perkins' theological writing, therefore, can best be characterized as a synthesis of medieval theological concerns addressed in the thinking of the Reformers but clothed in the philosophical *haute couture* of the day, the style of logician Peter Ramus.[65] Perkins' methodological commitment has been well-documented by D.K. McKim, who judges that the Perkins' *Creed* is "as close as Perkins came to producing a complete systematic theology," representing more mature thought and coming some five years after his *Chaine*."[66] But in terms of method, both works McKim shows to be entirely Ramist. A glance at the tables and schematics in both *Golden Chaine* and *Creed* bears out McKim's claim. In *Golden Chaine* Perkins posits that scripture is comprised of two categories of sacred sciences, theology and "others" which he labels "handmaids" or "retainers."[67] *Golden Chaine* is devoted to the exposition of the former. Theology ("the science of living blessedly forever") is seen both in God (his character and nature) and in God's works. The latter are evident through God's decree and the execution of his decree. The execution of God's decree comes about through his operation and his operative permission.[68] God's foreknowledge operates in predestination and reprobation. And there is further dichotomizing: predestination is broken down into "infants baptized" and "men of years of discretion."[69] Meanwhile, *Creed* is also introduced with a Ramist chart.[70] It has two parts: the *Apostles' Creed* is to be seen in its actions and its object. The former divides into believing a thing and believing God, while the object of the *Creed* is also twofold; God and the church.[71] Both works continue their further exposition through dichotomous arrangement.

It is not our purpose to review all of Perkins' dependence on the method of Peter Ramus; this has been masterfully done by McKim. What is significant is that William Perkins set the stage for those Puritans who would come after him and refine his method and theology even further. McKim underscores the im-

---

[65] Breward asserts that Beza "detested" Ramus (*Perkins*, 171).
[66] D.K. McKim, "Ramism in William Perkins" (Ph.D. diss., University of Pittsburgh, 1980), 218. Recall Muller's assertion that Perkins' *Golden Chaine* represented less a system than an exposition of the route to personal salvation.
[67] Perkins, *Workes*, 1.10.
[68] Perkins, *Workes*, Table between pages 1.95 and 1.96.
[69] Perkins, *Workes*, Table between pages 1.95 and 1.96.
[70] Perkins, *Workes*, Table between pages 1.120 and 1.121.
[71] Perkins, *Workes*, Table between pages 1.120 and 1.121.

portance of Ramism also for the preaching of sermons and the writing of commentaries of the day, and traces Ramus' influence from Paul Baynes, Perkins' immediate successor at Great St. Andrews Church in Cambridge, through all of Perkins' students there, with Ames representing the "prime example."[72]

William Ames

William Ames' *Marrow*, originally a series of lectures during his three-year interval at Leiden before his appointment at Franeker, appeared first in fragmentary form in Latin in 1623 and then in its final form in 1627 as *Medulla Theologiae*. It was reprinted many times and translated into many languages and presented theology as the domain of everyone, not just the scholar, with an emphasis on the affective utility of theology in addition to its intellectual basis. "The book was a declaration of the Puritan position that theology was an art with its own rules and practice."[73]

The first curiosity to strike the reader familiar with the prolix and discursive style of Puritan writing is the relative directness and terseness of this book. Ames' own diversion from this Puritan propensity requires further explaining:

> Some people, including those not unlearned, dislike this whole manner of writing, that is, of placing the main body of theology in a short compendium. They ask for great volumes in which they may establish themselves or wander about as they will. But I intend this for all those who have neither the ample leisure nor the great skill to hunt the partridge in mountain and forest. Their situation calls for showing them the nest itself, or the seat of what they are pursuing, without ado. . . . The dryness of style and the harshness of words will be criticized by the same persons [as those accusing me of obscurity]. And I confess that I share that heresy which bids me, when teaching, not to say in two words what may be said in one and which allows me to choose the key which best opens the lock. The key may well be of wood, if the golden key does not work.[74]

The *Marrow* is a good place to observe Ramist logic integrated with theology – an early Puritan system whose defining characteristic, Sprunger rightly observes, is the combined concern for pure doctrine and practical divinity.[75] Ramist tables are generously sprinkled throughout the pages of *Marrow*. The Ramist arrangement organizes Ames' entire system of theology and casuistry. Living to God, divinity, is done by faith (Book 1) and observance (Book 2). Faith in God must account for his efficiency (carried out in his decree) and sufficiency. God's efficiency is observed in his creation and providence. God's providence is by common ("ordinary") government (natural law) and special

---

[72] McKim, "Ramism in Perkins," 273-79.
[73] Eusden, "Introduction" in *Marrow*, 1-2.
[74] Ames, *Marrow*, "Brief Forewarning."
[75] Sprunger, "Ames, Ramus," 133. Sprunger shows that this integration of faith and obedience is the distinguishing characteristic of, also, the *Westminster Standards* (Sprunger, "Ames, Ramus," 149).

government (the covenant of works). Special government divides into humanity's fall and humanity's restoration. And this restoration is redemption, accomplished by Christ and applied by the covenant of grace. The remainder of Book 1 of *Marrow* takes the reader through a dichotomous arrangement of the path of the administration of the covenant of grace to the end of the world. In Book 2 we actually have the first part of Ames' casuistry or moral theology.[76] It is devoted to the "remaining part" of theology, "observance toward God," which he defines as "that whereby the Will of God is performed with subjection to his glory."[77] Ames has woven together *Marrow* and *Conscience* in such a way, that the two cannot be separated without seriously compromising his Ramist construction and without completely destroying his fully-integrated system of covenant theology with informed, practical piety. Remember, the title page for *Marrow* pointed out that it was "drawne out of the holy Scriptures, and the Interpreters thereof, and brought into Method." The "Method" he brought his system into – Ramism – was the glue holding together one of the earliest systems of Reformed theology.

It is worth noting, one more time, the conscious connection Ames draws between his theology and casuistry. In *Marrow* Ames defines divinity in Book 1, chapter 1, paragraph 1 as "the doctrine of *living* to God." Theology, for Ames, is all about right living. No doubt Ames was one of the earliest theologians to unwittingly democratize the science of theology, a change of massive proportion to the church of the day which had appropriated theology as the exclusive domain of its own educated elite. In this he much advanced the stream of thinking begun by William Perkins, that religion must be practical, and established this as a key tenet of the Reformed tradition.

Ames in the Context of Thomas, Calvin, and Perkins
As we conclude our examination of Ames' philosophical commitment into which were rooted both his theology and his informed piety, it might be useful to locate him in the philosophical/theological tradition he inherited to illustrate just how far Ames progressed along his own path. What was the position of the medieval Doctor on the nature of theology. Thomas opens his discussion by asserting the necessity of theology ("sacred science") for "man's salvation," *as well as that of* the philosophical sciences. This is necessary, he maintains, because the philosophical sciences are based on reason; for the salvation of humanity, however, revelation is needed as well:

---

[76] This is a good place to remind the reader that the designation "practical divinity," as used in its sixteenth- and seventeenth-century sense, refers to an experiential Christianity, whose trademark was an informed pietism or scripture-based ethic. This differs greatly from our conception today, where it refers to the art of preaching and other aspects of contemporary ministry.
[77] Ames, *Marrow*, 2.1.1.

> [The] whole salvation of man, which lies in God, depends on the knowledge of this truth [God]. . . . There is no reason, then, why the same things, which the philosophical sciences teach as they can be known by the light of natural reason, should not also be taught by another science as they are known through divine revelation.[78]

And this sacred science is "nobler" than the other sciences "in every way," transcending them because, as a speculative science, it deals with things more certain and above reason. For it is "concerned with divine things more fundamentally than with the actions of men" although it has an interest in these actions insofar as they bring men to the perfect knowledge of God. From this practical perspective, sacred doctrine is wisdom, says Thomas, and wisdom's end is eternal happiness.[79]

Although Thomas defines theology as more of a theoretical than practical science, it is clear that he recognizes its practical nature. This practical dimension is rooted in knowledge of God as this knowledge brings one into contemplation of things divine. For this is why Thomas designates theology as speculative: ethics is concerned with the actions of men and therefore is a practical science. But sacred doctrine concerns God, making it speculative. Not surprisingly, therefore, God is the subject of theology as well, while the object is "a power of habit."[80] Thomas follows this teaching on theology with the question of God's existence, nature and attributes.[81] We note that the separation Thomas makes between ethics and theology is reminiscent of Aristotle's bifurcation and is one to which Peter Ramus and William Ames after him took such great exception.

We have seen that the methodical and logical categories of Peter Ramus were shared by both William Perkins and his pupil William Ames. But our comparison has uncovered as well that Perkins used Ramism as his organizing categories only – his *Workes* demonstrate the typical Puritan propensity for words although he never scaled the heights to prolixity that some of the later Puritans would attain. At times McKim has had to dig deep, indeed, to find the Ramist organizing principles at work in Perkins. Ames, on the other hand, followed Ramus much more closely. His exposition is crisp and concise, very uncharacteristic of Puritan writing generally.

Peter Ramus held that "theology is the doctrine of living well."[82] Recall that Perkins, coming after Ramus maintained that theology is "the science of living

---

[78] Thomas Aquinas, *Nature and Grace*, Library of Christian Classics, vol. 11, A.M. Fairweather, trans and ed. (Philadelphia: Westminster, 1954), 1.1.1. I cite this work by book, chapter and section.
[79] Aquinas, *Nature and Grace*, 1.1.4-1.1.6.
[80] Aquinas, *Nature and Grace*, 1.1.7.
[81] Aquinas, *Nature and Grace*, 1.2-1.4
[82] Ramus, *Commentariorum de Religione*, cited in Sprunger, *Ames*, 132.

blessedly forever."[83] But for Ames, coming a generation later, it had to be even more precise: theology is the "doctrine of living to God."[84] What are we to make of this progression?[85] While one could argue that these definitions say essentially the same thing a comparative development of this theme will uncover just how vast the difference is. Perkins found the source and fountain of living blessedly forever in the knowledge of God. True knowledge of God was secured by way of epistemological dialectic which involved knowledge of self. We saw, as well, that Perkins then elaborates on just who and what God is and his work. Perkins could have been transcribing straight from John Calvin's *Institutes* when he penned this first chapter of *Chaine*. For Calvin, the knowledge of God the Creator was obtained through cognitive dialectic: "Without knowledge of self there is no knowledge of God" and "Without knowledge of God, there is no knowledge of self."[86] And although Calvin does not explicitly offer a definition of theology in the precise format of Ramus, Perkins and Ames, he does provide us with one, nevertheless. To what purpose does the knowledge of God tend? He answers that "our knowledge should serve first to teach us fear and reverence; secondly, with it as our guide and teacher, we should learn to seek every good from him, and, having received it, to credit it to his account." Or, as he put it elsewhere, only there is God known where there is religion or piety. "Here indeed is pure and real religion: faith so joined with an earnest fear of God that this fear also embraces willing reverence, and carries with it such legitimate worship as is prescribed in the law.[87] For Perkins, "theology is the science of living blessedly forever" and "the body of scripture is a doctrine sufficient to live well."[88] Clearly Perkins derives his understanding of theology and its nature from Calvin – knowledge of God and knowledge of self

---

[83] Perkins, *Workes*, 1.11.
[84] Ames, *Marrow*, 1.1.1.
[85] In quoting Peter Ramus, William Ames and Henry More in sequence, in their respective definitions of theology, S.T. Logan, Jr., cogently demonstrates that the philosophical commitment to Ramism was a contributing factor to the vast theological change at Christ's College, Cambridge, in the late sixteenth and early seventeenth centuries. See his "Theological Decline in Christian Institutions and the Value of Van Til's Epistemology," *WTJ* 57 (1995): 145-63. Logan's observations regarding the reasons for the intellectual shift in direction at the University of Cambridge are acute. For Cambridge Platonists, especially John Smith (1616-1652) and Benjamin Whichcote (1609-1683), theology was "more a Divine life than a Divine science" (A. Gabbey, "Cambridge Platonists," *CDP*, 99-101). This echoes strongly the emphasis on the practical, originated by Peter Ramus a century earlier and perpetuated by William Perkins at Christ's College, Cambridge. The influential neo-platonist in this College was More (1614-1687) who taught that "ethicks are defined to be the art of living well and happily" (Logan, "Decline," 157). The transition from Ramus through Ames to More is unmistakable, as Logan asserts.
[86] Calvin, *Institutes*, 1.1.1-1.1.3.
[87] Calvin, *Institutes*, 1.2.1, 1.2.2.
[88] Perkins, *Workes*, 1.11.

with a view to living blessedly forever.[89] Breward was correct when he said that "[Perkins'] definition of theology was a combination of Peter Ramus and John Calvin, and the arrangement of the whole work, prefaced as it was by a formidable looking diagram, owed a good deal to Ramist categories of arrangement and Aristotelian logic."[90]

It appears Ames diverges considerably from this Calvinian/Perkinsian emphasis in his stress on *doing*. Knowledge, intellectual apprehension, qualified as this might be with statements of "living blessedly" was not sufficient for Ames. He was seeking something much more activistic; theology is the doctrine of living to God. It is called doctrine because it is divinely revealed. But more than that, humanity, made in the image of God, must emulate him and "since the highest kind of life for a human being is that which approaches most closely the living and life-giving God, the nature of theological life is living to God." This is accomplished by living in accord with God's will and to his glory. And then, as if consciously wishing to refine Perkins' definition, Ames asserts that "although it is within the compass of life to live both happily and well, living well is more excellent than living happily."[91] Here Ames re-emphasizes Ramus' definition of theology – living well. Lest Perkins' definition of theology might lead one to believe that living blessedly could be self-serving, Ames makes the following clarification: "What chiefly and finally ought to be striven for is not happiness which has to do with our own pleasure, but goodness which looks to God's glory. For this reason, theology is better defined as that good life whereby we live to God than as that happy life whereby we live to ourselves."[92]

Ames provides a corrective to Perkins' more open-ended definition, and a solution to what Peter Ramus considered to be a chief problem in theology: the relation between living blessedly and living rightly.[93] Ramus concluded that the latter was to be preferred over the former, that "the righteous life was to be set over the blessed life; a life rightly lived is a life of response to God, the source of all righteousness."[94] Eusden is to the point as well when he asserts that "for Ames the end of theology was never to produce blessedness, which he felt re-

---

[89] The editors of Calvin's *Institutes* very astutely observe that "the word "knowledge" in the title, chosen rather than "being" or "existence" of God, emphasizes the centrality of revelation in both the structure and the content of Calvin's theology. Similarly, the term "Creator," subsuming the doctrines of Trinity, Creation, and Providence, stresses God's revealing work or acts rather than God in himself" (*Institutes*, 1.1.1, n. 1). The latter strictly ontological *(a priori)* and cosmological approaches are more prominent in medieval Scholastic doctrines of God, but make regular appearances in early modern "Calvinist" thinking as well. See, for example, Anselm's *Proslogium* or Thomas' *Summa*.
[90] Breward, *Perkins*, 85-86.
[91] Ames, *Marrow*, 1.1.5-1.1.6.
[92] Ames, *Marrow*, 1.1.8.
[93] Horton, *Ames by Reuter*, 175-76.
[94] Ramus, *Commentariorum*, 6, cited in Horton, *Ames by Reuter*, 175.

lated chiefly to man's ultimate aspiration and desire. In a search for his own blessedness, man could miss God, the very object of his living rightly."[95] In this area as in many others, Ames consciously strove to add precision to the thought of his teacher.

It is within these definitional and methodological considerations that we must now readdress the issue of volitional primacy in Amesian thinking. Ames' radical focus on the place of the will caused him to locate it as "the first and proper subject of theology"[96] with an emphasis that Calvin and Perkins never made and Thomas diametrically opposed, holding that God is the subject of theology. This differing emphasis plays out in the distinctive definitions of theology, particularly between Perkins and Ames. Not entirely disagreeing with Perkins who maintained that the intellect is to the soul "as the wagginer to the waggin," to Ames, living blessedly would never have been a science to the degree it was for Perkins. It was a doctrine. It was a covenantal responsibility. It was something centered in the will; it engaged the volitional faculty of men and women more than the intellectual. Having established this theological principle, how does Ames further develop his dogmatics – a treatise which, as we judged earlier, can be considered the first full-fledged systematic theology of post-reformation Elizabethan England of which Perkins' work was the harbinger? So non-negotiable was this particular view of theology that Ames' entire theological enterprise, Ramist of course, was undergirded by the responsibility of the creature in living to God: faith and observance. These comprise the division or parts of theology – not emphasizing knowledge of God and of self but rather *observance* (the doctrine of living to God), and *faith* (rooted in the sound theological principles of the Reformation). Ames' entire theology unfolds along this dichotomy. That this two-fold arrangement was similar to the non-Ramist structures of theological systematization as it was developing during this period was, no doubt, a happy convenience for Ames.

Closely connected with this, of course, is the question of the determination of the proper subject of faith. It is not surprising that the will receives the vote in this category as well. For faith "is true and proper trust."[97] One must join oneself to God in faith. "That special assent, whereby we declare that God is our God in Christ, is not the first act of faith but an act flowing from faith. . . . Since faith is the first act of our life whereby we live to God in Christ, it must consist of union with God, which a mere assent to the truth concerning God cannot effect."[98] And finally, faith necessarily involves surrender "to God in Christ as a sufficient and faithful Savior. But he cannot make that surrender through any assent of the understanding – only through a consent of the will."[99]

---

[95] Eusden, "Introduction" in *Marrow*, 47.
[96] Ames, *Marrow*, 1.9.
[97] Ames, *Marrow*, 1.3.13.
[98] Ames, *Marrow*, 1.3.17-1.3.18.
[99] Ames, *Marrow*, 1.3.19.

In refining both Calvin and Perkins (and others who place faith in the understanding *and* the will), Ames closes this chapter with a lengthy and cogent justification for his placement of faith exclusively in the will on the grounds that faith is a single virtue and therefore indivisible.[100] Only after he has established the will as the subject of faith is Ames prepared to enter into discussion on God, the object of faith. Only after he has underscored his disavowal of intellectual faith and placed faith solidly in the will (with greater force than both Calvin and Perkins, as we have seen) is he prepared to consider discussing God, creation and providence. Following his teaching on the knowledge of God comes, as we saw earlier, work on God's decrees and his covenant relationship with humanity.[101]

Although their respective theological systems liberally employed Ramist methodological and logical categories, Perkins was less a disciple of the French philosopher than was Ames whose commitment to Ramism dominated his entire system. In addition and perhaps more importantly, their theological priorities were markedly different. William Perkins was heavily indebted to John Calvin and to shadows of Thomas before him; William Ames cleared a new theological path because of his commitment to the view that theology could only be understood first and foremost as a practical doctrine – the doctrine of living to God. Here Peter Ramus can be said to have had a stronger influence on Ames than did Calvin, for Ramus tossed out both Aristotelian philosophy and method in favor of his own. As Perkins and Ames appear on the horizon, the former recasts Calvin and Beza in Ramist categories while the latter's commitment to Ramist logic, method and philosophy has resulted in significant modifications to some Calvinian priorities. We have seen that the chief of these had to do with the subject and object of theology – for Ames the faculty of the will, and God, respectively. Calvin showed more Thomistic tendencies, but began diverging into a direction carried on by Perkins and finessed by Ames. Perkins owed much more to Calvin than did Ames, who blazed his own theological trail through the Thomist, Calvinian, Ramist and Perkinsian paths before him.

Concluding Observations

We can be quite certain of the Calvinian origins of William Ames' volitional emphasis. There appears neither a Calvin-Perkins/Ames dichotomy (Reuter) nor a Calvin/Perkins-Ames dichotomy (Kendall and others representing the discontinuity school in various forms). It is clear that for all three of Ames' theological forebears under consideration here, regardless of the respective priorities each assigns to the volitional faculty, this must be understood against the background of medieval "faculty psychology." Ames held to Augustinian mon-

---

[100] Ames, *Marrow*, 1.3.22.
[101] Ames, *Marrow*, 1.4-1.10.

ergism as strongly as did not only Calvin and Perkins but other earlier and contemporaneous representatives of evolving Reformed theological system.

The medieval tradition, Calvinism, covenant thought and Ramism came in handy for a practical theologian swimming in an ecclesiastical and theological pool whose currents drifted towards an emphasis on right knowing to the neglect of right living on the one hand and to Arminianism on the other. Ames' distinctive emphasis on the will should be seen as a summary of his theological commitment as it is expressed in his definition of theology, and this commitment played out in his battle, as we shall see later, against what he considered the overly-philosophical commitment of his colleagues at Franeker, and in his attempts to permanently and broadly insinuate a vital piety into the church of the seventeenth century Dutch Republic. Neither faith nor practice by itself is adequate. For faith divorced from practice leads to "cold orthodoxy" on the one hand, while singular emphasis on good works "runs straight to Arminianism."[102] The story of Ames' life is that of determining the proper biblical balance between the two. The key to this balance was covenantal obedience.

---

[102] Sprunger, *Ames*, 146.

Chapter 5

The Legacy of William Ames in Johannes Cocceius in the Context of "Decretal Theology"

"Decretal Theology" and Covenant Thought: Calvin to Ames

It has been postulated that the doctrinal co-existence of predestination and covenant throughout the period of Reformed orthodoxy has led to a decretal theology that has crippled any cohesive development of Reformed doctrine. Ultimately, it is argued, all theology is dominated by the teaching of predestination. C. Graafland has come to this position after analyzing the tensions that developed between decretal and covenant thinking through the mid-eighteenth century and exploring attempts to resolve emerging doctrinal polarities.[1] He main-

---

[1] C. Graafland, *Van Calvijn tot Comrie: Oorsprong en ontwikkeling van de leer van het verbond in het Gereformeerde Protestantisme*, 3 vols. (Zoetermeer: Boekencentrum, 1992-96), 1.7-1.11, 3.393-3.403. I cite from Graafland's work by volume, and page number. For a full review of Graafland's momentous project, see my "Decretal Theology and the Development of Covenant Thought: An Assessment of Cornelis Graafland's Thesis with a Particular View to Federal Architects William Ames and Johannes Cocceius," *WTJ* (63) 2001, 393-420. Graafland asserts that this work confirms his earlier findings in *Van Calvijn tot Barth: Oorsprong en ontwikkeling van de leer der verkiezing in het Gereformeerde Protestantisme* ('s-Gravenhage: Boekencentrum, 1987), 593-94. On the relationship between the development of the doctrine of the covenant and scholasticism, see also S. Strehle, *Calvinism, Federalism, and Scholasticism: A Study of the Reformed Doctrine of Covenant*, Basler und Berner Studien zur historischen und systematischen Theologie, band 58 (New York: Peter Lang, 1988). The single dogma thesis represents only one aspect of the larger "continuity/discontinuity" debate that identifies doctrinal discontinuity between Calvin and his successors as the central feature of the development of Reformed orthodoxy. Earlier we mentioned strong support for this position in Kendall, *Calvin and English Calvinism*; others are B. Hall, "Calvin against the Calvinists" in *John Calvin*, G.E. Duffield, ed. (Grand Rapids: Eerdmans, 1966). For incisive and cogent critiques of this thesis and relevant collateral literature, see Muller, *PRRD 1*; idem, "The Myth of 'Decretal Theology'," *CTJ* 30 (1995): 159-67; idem, "Calvin and the "Calvinists": Assessing Continuities and Discontinuities Between the Reformation and Orthodoxy," parts 1 and 2, *CTJ* 30 (1995): 345-75; 31 (1996): 125-60; idem, *Christ and the Decree: Christology and Predestination in Reformed Theology from Calvin to Perkins* (Durham, NC: Labyrinth, 1986); P. Helm, *Calvin and the Calvinists* (Edinburgh: Banner of Truth Trust, 1982); idem, "Calvin, English Calvinism and the Logic of Doctrinal Development" *SJT* 34 (1981): 179-85; C.R. Trueman, "Calvin and Calvinism," in *The Cambridge Companion to John Calvin*, D.K. McKim, ed. (Cambridge: University of Cambridge, 2004). For an accessible introduction and summary of this area of debate see R.A. Muller, "Scholasticism and Orthodoxy in the Reformed Tradition: An Attempt at Definition," (Calvin Theological Seminary: Inaugural Address,

tains that Calvin reformulated the existing covenant thinking of Zwingli and Bullinger into a theological system so dominated by an emphasis on predestination, that covenantal themes were always subservient to, "locked up" in, the eternal divine decree of election and reprobation.[2] Calvin's thought, so Graafland, was indebted to more than just Luther; in fact, it was controlled by neo-Platonism (through Calvin's teacher John Major, the Greek Fathers and Augustine) and by Aristotle.[3] To reinforce the philosophical tendencies of Calvin, Graafland draws attention to the fact that, in H.M. Kuitert's opinion, Calvin's exegesis owes much to the neo-Platonic thought of Origen.[4]

Calvin's commentary on Romans, in particular chapters 9-11, clearly demonstrates the complementary relationship he understood to exist between election and the covenant. Already Hoekema had earlier outlined this Calvinian "solution" to this perceived antithesis.[5] For Calvin, within the covenant of grace bestowed upon humanity, the truly elect constitute a subset of the covenant community. Covenant membership due to presumption or hypocrisy carries an expiry date. In other words, birth into a Christian home and a non-genuine faith are both invalid and non-sustaining reasons for covenant membership, and individuals in the covenant by virtue of these two means of entry are cut off. Only those truly converted constitute the authentic elect. These are the real recipients of the blessings of Christ's redemptive work, while those in covenant but not recipient of these blessings, fall out, finally, as covenant children who have turned their back on the covenant promise.[6] Calvin offers this explanation for Israel's fall from covenant in the old administration before Christ. Not all who are members of the covenant community by election are the truly chosen subjects of a "more limited degree of election." This "secret election," reasons Calvin, pertains only to a portion of the larger, corporate covenant community whose membership is obtained by "corporate covenant." This larger covenant is not efficacious in spiritual effect. Rather, it is a "middle way" between election and rejection of humanity.[7]

Sept. 7, 1995). For an early assessment of the "Muller thesis" see M.I. Klauber, "Continuity and Discontinuity in Post-Reformation Reformed Theology: An Evaluation of the Muller Thesis," *JETS* 33 (Dec. 1990): 467-75. A recent and spirited critical assessment of Muller is found in C. Partee, *The Theology of John Calvin* (Louisville, KY: Westminster John Knox, 2008), 13-27.

[2] Graafland, *Calvijn tot Comrie*, 1.81, 3.395.
[3] Graafland, *Calvijn tot Comrie*, 1.171-1.185.
[4] Graafland, *Calvijn tot Comrie*, 1.184-1.185. See esp. 1.184, n. 31.
[5] Hoekema, "Covenant of Grace," 148-55. See also Lillback, *The Binding of God*, 210-30.
[6] Lillback, *The Binding of God*, 221-22; Hoekema, "Covenant of Grace," 148-49; Osterhaven, "Calvin on the Covenant," 93-95.
[7] Calvin, *Institutes*, 3.21.6-3.21.7; Lillback, *The Binding of God*, 214-17; Hoekema, "Covenant of Grace," 149, 150.

Covenant-breaking in the new covenant – spurning the covenant promises – proceeds by way of hypocrisy or apostatizing. The harsh act of covenant removal is judgment with a pedagogical purpose for the authentic covenant family; it serves as an admonition to the elect to persevere and to continue faithful in spiritual warfare. This theological predication issues from the letter-spirit distinction so key to Calvin's hermeneutic. This distinction is not absolutized and does not mean synonymity with an old covenant-new covenant bifurcation, but rather should be seen in a true biblical-theological sense as progression from lesser to greater which means movement from old to new, from shadow to reality, from promise to fulfillment. As Lillback explains:

> the law agrees with the New Covenant in its continual progress in all the ages of redemption. So Calvin asserts that the relationship of the Old and New Covenants is a matter of comparing the lesser to the greater. There is not an absolute dichotomy between them. . . . Calvin's interpretation of a comparison from lesser to greater explains the Old Covenant saints' experience of salvation, how David can delight in the law and Paul can be terrified by it, and how there can be covenant-breaking even in the New Covenant.[8]

Thus, election and covenant are neither identical nor antithetical. Calvin conjoins human responsibility with God's divine sovereignty. Authentic salvation is reserved only for those who "participate" in the covenant and "ratify it by faith." Such a seal of covenant membership – participation and ratification – brings human responsibility to the fore while simultaneously affirming that this faith is truly owned only by those whom God has selected as targets of divine choice. Divine sovereignty is the efficient cause of those who believe.[9] With abrogation of human responsibility within the corporate covenant community, the covenant, which is "potential letter" becomes the letter that kills. Conversely, for those who appropriate covenant promises through the exercise of faith and obedience, the covenant becomes the spirit that quickens, for it is ratified from the divine perspective by special or secret election.[10] This is the crux of the matter for Calvin, this very crucial distinction between general and special (or "secret") election, and explains the complementary nature Calvin saw between covenant and decretal thought.

In assessing the Puritan origins of covenant theology, Graafland takes Perkins as representative and interprets his thought as dominated by the polarity between decree and covenant.[11] Graafland seems to concur with P. Miller who argues that Calvin's inheritors introduced a reciprocal covenant to reconcile covenant with predestination.[12] Yet historian G.M. Marsden, while commend-

---

[8] Lillback, *The Binding of God*, 223-24.
[9] Hoekema, "Covenant of Grace," 151.
[10] Lillback, *The Binding of God*, 225-26.
[11] Graafland, *Calvijn tot Comrie*, 2.111-2.264, 3.398.
[12] Miller, *Seventeenth Century*, 365-97.

ing Miller for reminding us of the predominance of the Puritan mind in the intellectual life of early America, has argued that the lack of objectivity in Miller's endeavor has actually impeded our access to authentic Puritan thought.[13] This bias has caused Miller to misrepresent the covenant of grace as "a juridical relationship slyly substituted for the divine decree."[14] Marsden continues that, in fact, the Puritan conception of covenant was very much like that of their theological ancestor, and indeed significantly builds on it.[15] But this is often overlooked in Calvinian and Puritan scholarship because "Miller has created a myth that has been so elegantly presented and widely repeated that it will be difficult to destroy."[16]

It is true, predestination as a theological *locus* has pride of place in Perkins' supralapsarian scheme.[17] As Breward asserts, Perkins "spent most of his effort in the exposition of predestination and its implications for Christian life, giving it a prominence that Calvin had avoided."[18] A glance at his *Golden Chaine* exhibits the degree to which all of his teaching is secondary to God's eternal decree in predestination and reprobation, for the covenant is the "outward means of executing the decree of election."[19] But while the dynamic interplay between the doctrines of predestination and covenant do not receive a lot of explicit attention in Perkins' thought, Muller's study of Perkins leads him to conclude that this is, in fact, "a central issue of *A Golden Chaine*."[20]

Muller argues that the key to reconciliation of these two doctrines is to see the covenant as God's provision for humanity's inability to meet the condition of faith. This answers both the dipleuric nature of early federal covenant thought where the covenant represents a mutual pact between God and humanity, and the monopleuric character of early Calvinism where the testamental nature of covenant is more prominent. Muller asserts that Perkins' definition of covenant places him in the dipleuric camp and implies "a certain voluntarism."[21] Because of one's inability to keep the covenant of works, God has instituted the covenant of grace, the condition for which is faith. This covenant is

---

[13] It is Marsden's judgment that Miller is modifying Puritanism by injecting into Puritan intellectual life his own view which is decidedly not anchored in scripture, in doctrine, in the person and work of Christ, and in Calvinism. See G.M. Marsden, "Perry Miller's Rehabilitation of the Puritans: A Critique," *CH* 39 (1970): 91-105.
[14] Marsden, "Miller's Rehabilitation," 99.
[15] Observed also by Møller, who mentions Ames in this connection in "Beginnings of Puritan Covenant Theology," 49, n.4.
[16] Marsden, "Miller's Rehabilitation," 105.
[17] ". . . our first parents were indeed created perfect, but mutable: for so it pleased God to prepare a way to the execution of his decree" (Perkins, *Workes*, 1.18).
[18] Breward, *Perkins*, 92.
[19] Perkins, *Workes*, 1.31.
[20] Muller, "Perkins' *A Golden Chaine*," 78.
[21] "Perkins' primary definition of covenant derives directly from the federalist theology and is reminiscent of Ursinus' and Bullinger's formulations" (Muller, "Perkins' *A Golden Chaine*," 78).

also called a testament, "confirmed by the death of the testator," not by any effort of the beneficiary. "In this covenant," said Perkins, "we do not so much offer, or promise any great matter to God, as in a manner only receive . . . ." And this covenant is the gospel, in its fullest manifestation.[22] Perkins understood covenant to be the bridge between God's promise and humanity's inability. Within the covenant, a divinely-renewed will enables choosing both repentance and obedience, an impossibility ouside the covenant.[23] This decree/covenant interplay clearly explains what Perkins meant when he asserted that the covenant is the "outward means of executing the decree; he saw covenant as a divinely-ordained means to a divinely-ordained end.

William Ames addresses predestination following his discussion of the application of Christ's saving work through the covenant and before his description of the nature of the Christian pilgrimage (the *ordo salutis*). Ames saw predestination serving a transitional function, conjoining objective and subjective soteriology. The saving action of God is procured through the accomplished work of Christ and is appropriated in the life of the believer through predestination.[24] Ames' system is not at all based upon the leading *locus* of predestination. One single statement appears in his chapter on predestination, and this is really only a very cryptic and rather general affirmation of the eternal existence of the divine decree.[25] Clearly Ames' supralapsarian commitment was less rigid than that of Perkins. This position is reinforced by a glance at Ames' organizing structure in Book 1 of *Marrow* and the careful way in which his terminology is cast. The lengthy chapter on God's decree, which runs fifty-four sections and at times draws heavily from scholastic philosophy, says nothing about predestination.[26] One of the key statements he makes in this section, as profound as it is brief, is simply this: "The will of God is therefore the first cause of things"[27] adding further that "He wills the end before the means to the end because he works according to the most perfect reason."[28] Even in this context – the execution of the most perfect will of God – Ames is silent on the soteriological implications of decretal theology and diverges here from Perkins' clear emphasis.

Immediately following, Ames addresses God's providence, the second means used by God to execute his decree and counsel. Then comes theological

---

[22] Perkins, *Workes*, 1.70.
[23] Muller, "Perkins' *A Golden Chaine*," 79.
[24] According to Eusden, "William Perkins, in the *Golden Chain: Or the Description of Theology*, following Beza, had discussed predestination under the general heading of the work of God. Ames did not follow his teacher, but considered predestination as a transitional theme between the work of Christ and the description of the Christian life" ("Introduction" in *Marrow*, 27).
[25] "Predestination has existed from eternity. Eph. 1:4" (Ames, *Marrow*, 1.25.2).
[26] Ames, *Marrow*, 1.7.
[27] Ames, *Marrow*, 1.7.38.
[28] Ames, *Marrow*, 1.7.51.

anthropology. It is significant that, prior to his teaching on humanity's fall, sin and death, he inserts "Special Government of Intelligent Creatures" in which he describes the covenant of works.[29] Following his anthropology and Christology comes soteriology, introduced by Chapter 24, "The Application of Christ," in which key theological principles of the new covenant – the covenant of grace – are laid out. Finally comes Ames' teaching on predestination which segues seamlessly into the *ordo salutis*: calling, justification, adoption, sanctification, and glorification.[30] Although K. Reuter is technically correct when he asserts that with Ames "predestination has not yet become the first step in the order of salvation, as it shows itself in Witsius,[31] it does appear that Ames saw it as the launch-pad to the *ordo salutis* even if it had a primarily assuring function. It is H. Visscher's judgment that although Ames was a supralapsarian, he did not see a significant difference in the various lapsarian distinctions made by, notably, the Remonstrants.[32] In disparaging those who made much of this distinction, Ames had this to say:

> We can explain this simple yet infinite matter only in an imperfect manner and with various interpretations. These interpretations vary only in the matter of timing of the decrees, but all agree that the source of predestination is in God alone, in his own good pleasure. Outside of Him neither in man nor anywhere else can any cause be found. On the timing of the decrees, no one takes serious objection to the Remonstrants. *The essence of the matter remains the same, even when the timing is reversed.*"[33]

Although Ames could philosophize with the best of them, his philosophy was never of a speculative type. He saw little practical usefulness in constructing a system upon something so opaque as the ordering of God's decrees.

Because Ames refused to consider predestination as the *locus* of theology, the hypothetical question of incongruity between covenant and decretal thinking received scant attention. For Ames, covenantal responsibility within a predestinarian system is paramount. This is all part and parcel of assurance of faith and perseverance. Although the elect can sin and fall, their predestinated state will ensure that they do not fall away, finally. In his commentary on 1 Peter, Ames underscores the reassuring character of predestination: "The beginning and fountaine of all our happinesse and consolation consists in this, that we are

---

[29] Ames, *Marrow*, 1.10.
[30] Ames, *Marrow*, 1.25-1.30.
[31] Horton, *Ames by Reuter*, 253; Reuter concludes this statement with "But *the decisive step of freeing it from the doctrine of God has been taken* . . . .", my emphasis.
[32] Horton, *Ames by Visscher*, 92.
[33] William Ames, *Animadversiones in Synodalia Scripta Remonstrantium* (1629) and appearing in later editions as *Anti-Synodalia Scripta* (1646, 1661), 1.1, my emphasis, cited in Horton, *Ames by Visscher*, 92. See also Sprunger, *Ames*, 77, 264. These writings represent that part of Ames' corpus directed against the Remonstrant position at Dort 1618-19.

the elect of God."[34] In this connection, it might be helpful to remember that Ames' concern was that undue faith in election could be turned into license to sin; to ensure one's elect state, therefore, one's focus turned inward – predestination carries with it requirements for covenantal living. With Calvin, Ames locates the teaching of predestination from the doctrine of God in theology proper to the teaching on assurance in soteriology.[35] Moreover, this election and perseverance themselves are a part of God's covenanting, for Ames taught, with Calvin and less emphatically than Perkins, that the covenant was the vehicle that made the divine decree efficacious.[36]

Providing yet more insight into the relationship between decretal theology and covenant thinking is the further issue of the apparent inconsistency between the gospel offer and particularism. Calvin asserts that the "doctrine of salvation . . . is falsely debased when presented as effectually profitable to all" but its *reception* will be limited, because true faith resides only in those so called, since faith takes second place to election.[37] In large measure, this is the opinion of Perkins and Ames as well. Perkins dwells on this at length in his writing on predestination which comprises over ten percent of his commentary on the Apostles' Creed.[38] Predestination, says Perkins, is the "efficient cause of the Church."[39] Concurring, William Ames explicitly states that the free offer can only be appropriated by those called into covenant, the elect.[40] Keep in mind that Ames has not yet introduced his concept of double predestination at this point. This comes much later. Ames' careful language in reference to those recipients of the general gospel call, yet, ultimately, outside the covenant, is noteworthy. While the atonement was surely *sufficient* to satisfy all humanity, the "intention of application" was limited only to those so chosen: "Because these counsels of God are hidden to us, it is the part of charity to judge well of

---

[34] William Ames, *An Analyticall Exposition of both the Epistles of the Apostle Peter, Illustrated by Doctrines Out of Every Text. And Applyed by their Uses, for a further progresse in Holinesse*, Foreword by A.B. (London: Edward Griffin for John Rothwell, 1641), 3. First released as *Explicatio Analytica Utriusque Epistolae Divi Petri Apostoli* (N.p., 1635).

[35] Calvin, *Institutes*, 3.21. The editor's note is worth repeating: "While predestination is much stressed by Calvin, the formal treatment of the topic falls under the head not of the doctrine of God but of the doctrine of salvation, and is reserved to this point after the main outlines of the latter doctrine have been made clear. Calvin argues from Scripture, with much aid from Augustine" (*Institutes*, 3.21, note 1).

[36] Observe that altogether absent from Ames' thought is the Calvinian concept of a group of "special elect" within the broader fellowship of the "general elect" (the corporate covenant community), to explain the "falling away" and the "cutting off" from the covenant of grace, in both of its administrations.

[37] Calvin, *Institutes*, 3.22.10.

[38] Perkins, *An Exposition of the Symbole or Creed of the Apostles*, in *Workes*, 1.117-1.322.

[39] Perkins, *Workes*, 1.298.

[40] Ames, *Marrow*, 1.24.9, 1.26.13.

everyone, *although we may not say of all collectively, that Christ equally pleads the cause of each before God.*"[41] In fact, one of the defining improvements of the covenant of grace is that although the first covenant pertained to all humanity, the new "belongs in a special way only to certain men" despite the fact that it is "often offered indiscriminately to all."[42] The predestined, called into covenant membership, are the true and "limited" final recipients of universal gospel proclamation. For Ames, the broader structure of covenant thought explains the apparent incongruity between evangel and election just as certainly as it pre-empts discussion on hypothetical covenant-predestination polarities.

The Covenant Thought of Johannes Cocceius[43]

Our review of the famous covenant theology of Johannes Cocceius begins with Graafland's assessment of Cocceius' theological location in post-Reformation thought.[44] As Graafland views Cocceius' theological contribution within the

---

[41] Ames, *Marrow*, 1.24.9, my emphasis.

[42] Ames, *Marrow*, 1.24.15.

[43] See his *Summa Doctrina de foedere & Testamento Dei* (Franeker, 1648). Cocceius' major other works are: *Summa Theologiae* (1662); *Opera Omnia Theologica, Exegetica, Didactica, Polemica, Philologica*, 3rd ed. 10 vols. (Amstelodami: P. & J. Blaer, 1701); and *Opera Anecdota Theologica et Philologica*, 2 vols. Supplement to 3rd ed. (Amstelodami: P. & J. Blaer, 1706). I use both the original Latin and the Dutch translation, *De Leere Van het Verbond en Testament Gods*. Trans. from the Latin. 2nd printing (Amsterdam: Johannes van Someren, 1689).

[44] Cocceius' thought has received significant attention in the German scholarship, particularly in the nineteenth and early twentieth centuries; for a historiographical summary see van Asselt, *Federal Theology of Johannes Cocceius*, 2-16. According to van Asselt, Swiss theologian Karl Barth was preoccupied with Cocceius (*Federal Theology of Johannes Cocceius*, 9, n. 20). Although the study performed by C.S. McCoy constitutes a much earlier and also much referenced twentieth-century scholarly work on the thought of Cocceius, McCoy's Barthian commitment has obliged his perspective on Cocceius. McCoy's two major works on Cocceius are "Johannes Cocceius: Federal Theologian," *SJT* 16 (1963): 352-70, and "The Covenant Theology of Johannes Cocceius" (Ph.D. diss., Yale University, 1956). McCoy's dismissal of William Ames as insignificant in the development of federalism disappointingly continues the Amesian historiographical tradition. While McCoy is right in emphasizing the practical stress in Johannes Cocceius, scholars must account for other tendencies in Cocceius such as his philosophical disposition (and relationship with the Cartesians) and his anti-precisionist position. With respect to the former, the record is mixed. For example, in his opening statement on theology, Cocceius says that "theology is knowledge and speech; . . . speech about God, from God, in the presence of God, to his own glory" (in *Summa theologiae ex scripturis repetita*, 1.1, cited in McCoy, "Cocceius: Federal Theologian," 357). It is not before he has grounded all theology in that knowledge provided by the *source* of theology – revelation – that Cocceius is prepared to unpack the covenantal underpinnings of his concern that theology be practical. Could this concern be motivated by, and a deliberate attempt to stem, the contemporary focus on reason and philosophy of the Cartesian schools of the day? Was Cocceius usurping Descartes' dominance of the intellectual landscape? T.

broader stream of the Protestant tradition, he concludes that, when it comes to covenant theology broadly understood, Cocceius' thought is in line with the tradition as it developed through the period of Reformed orthodoxy and as it was viewed by his contemporaries, even if there was some disagreement between them. What is markedly different in Cocceius' covenant theology, however, is his original method of combining covenant thought with decretal thinking through his unique understanding of the relationship between the covenant of works and grace.[45] This derives from his emphasis on election (*verkiezing*) as sourced in Christ and the *pactum salutis* rather than in the double decree of predestination (*predestinatie*). The focus becomes Christological, not decretal. Re-centering the theological emphasis in this fashion enabled Cocceius to place significant distance between election and God's decree of double predestination, while concomitantly drawing the covenant of grace and election closely together. This accounts for his emphasis upon believers' act and life of faith, including the *ordo salutis* that both brought them to faith and determines their progression through faith. This is in contrast to laying the stress upon God's decretal nature as manifest in, especially, double predestination. According to Graafland, however, regardless of where one places the focus, including Cocceius' attempt to find correspondence or virtual coincidence between the *pactum salutis* and election, one is ultimately forced to return to the decree of predestination as the true divine origin of one's elect status. Graafland concludes that Johannes Cocceius, although uniquely creative, continues the tradition of Reformed orthodoxy wherein the development of covenant theology has run a

---

Verbeek, argues that in opposition to the theology of the (staunchly anti-Cartesian and philosophically-oriented) "Voetian Orthodox," "Coccejanism proved to be Cartesianism's natural ally" (*Descartes and the Dutch: Early Reactions to Cartesian Philosophy, 1637-1650* [Carbondale and Edwardsville: Southern Illinois University, 1992], 87). With respect to his perspective on precisionism, Cocceius' unique covenant theology illustrates his opposition to the precisionist views of Gisbertus Voet. Because both Cocceius and Voet must be designated covenant theologians, their respective conceptions of covenant must have diverged to account for such different ideas of what theology meant by "practical." *Nadere Reformatie* divine and Voetian Wilhelmus à Brakel, coming a generation after Cocceius, makes the concepts "covenant of grace" and "faith and conduct" practically synonymous (Wilhelmus à Brakel, *The Christian's Reasonable Service*, B. Elshout, trans., J.R. Beeke, ed. 4 vols. [Morgan, PA.: Soli Deo Gloria Publications, 1992-1995], 1.34); citations from this work are by volume and page number.

[45] Graafland, *Calvijn tot Comrie*, 323. Cocceius' unique covenant doctrine stems from his entire view of revelation, avers Graafland: "In his doctrine of revelation, Cocceius has placed much greater emphasis on the progress of revelation, to which he, among other things, gave shape, by placing stress upon the deficiency of the Old Testament as time of promise as compared to the New Testament as time of fulfillment. From this, Cocceius drew both dogmatic and ethical consequences" (Graafland, *Calvijn tot Comrie*, 323).

sad course in its inability to seamlessly fold together covenant thought and predestination teaching.[46]

In the most recent study on the thought of Johannes Cocceius conducted by W.J. van Asselt, considerable attention is paid to the former's epistemology, theology proper, and soteriology, in an attempt to come to a fuller appreciation of Cocceius' unique covenant theology.[47] In an extended analysis of his writing on the doctrines of the decrees and covenant, the reader is shown in some detail how Cocceius weaves together both decretal and covenant thought. Van Asselt concludes that the attention paid to the doctrine of the decrees by this federal theologian and the profile this doctrine assumes in all of Cocceius' thought, is proof positive that he saw no tension in the coexistence of predestination and covenant.[48] What we said above of Calvin, and demonstrated in the work of Ames as well, can be said with equal confidence about the position of Cocceius: "It is apparent that covenantal thinking and predestination are not mutually exclusive; they are complementary."[49] Cocceius accomplishes this convergence of covenant and decree in a comprehensive representation of God's plan of salvation, an understanding of scripture that folds together the temporal and eternal aspects of salvation history. Cocceius sees this conjoining of time (the horizontal dimension) and eternity (the vertical dimension) as most faithfully represented by establishing the proper and balanced relationship between the covenant of works and the covenant of grace.[50]

Coccceian historiographers have not acutely sensed this Cocceian balance, maintains van Asselt, and, as a consequence, have attenuated the scriptural teaching of theology proper. Emphasis has fallen on one of two views: scholars have tended to gravitate either towards an "evolutionary" model, in which this inter-covenantal relationship is seen to be solely chronological, or a "synthetic" model, in which it is seen to be singularly logical.[51] The former emphasizes the historical movement through time of redemptive history, the progress of covenant, or the *ordo temporum*. It overemphasizes the horizontal dimension and does not give the "eternity moment" its just due. Redemption is shown to pro-

---

[46] Graafland, *Calvijn tot Comrie*, 3.279.

[47] Van Asselt, *Federal Theology of Johannes Cocceius*; idem, *Johannes Coccejus: Portret van een zeventiende-eeuws theoloog op oude en nieuwe wegen* (Heerenveen: J. J. Groen en Zoon, 1997); hereafter, *Coccejus*. This volume is a revised version of his doctoral dissertation: "Amicitia Dei: Een Onderzoek naar de structuur van de theologie van Johannes Coccejus (1603-1669)" (Ph.D. diss., State University of Utrecht, 1988); hereafter, "Amicitia Dei." The dissertation develops technical detail that appears in the monograph only in summary form. I make use of all three works. See also Lee, *Cocceius and Federal Theology*, for an emphasis on the exegetical development of Cocceius' federal thought from his study of Heb 7-10.

[48] Van Asselt, *Federal Theology of Johannes Cocceius*, 197-287.

[49] Van Asselt, *Federal Theology of Johannes Cocceius*, 204.

[50] Van Asselt, *Federal Theology of Johannes Cocceius*, 197-287, 295-321.

[51] Van Asselt, *Federal Theology of Johannes Cocceius*, 273-76.

gress by gradually leaving behind the covenant of works and appropriating, by historical gradations, the covenant of grace (only fully realized at glory). The shortcoming of this theological interpretation is that Coccapeius' doctrines of the trinity, of decrees, and of predestination are not adequately represented. In other words, in this strictly chronological representation of salvation, predestination and the *ordo salutis* as such are transposed into strictly salvation-historical categories, resulting in overstatement of the horizontal dimension and understatement of the vertical dimension. This yields a particular view of Coccapeius not true to his genuine thought and contributions: he is considered an "original philosopher of history" whose thought is a harbinger of the principles of enlightenment thought, rationalism and idealism, and introduces into theology an evolutionary concept of history. Scholars holding this view (Barth, for example) wish to classify Coccapeius as a forerunner of the Enlightenment, but van Asselt concludes that Coccapeius cannot be so claimed as a Protestant philosopher of history.[52]

On the other hand, the synthetic model has the opposite deficiency: all the emphasis is on the vertical moment, on the doctrines of predestination and the way of salvation. Stress is placed upon the act of redemption along the lines of the *ordo salutis*, the "ordered salvation character" within the covenantal framework. This view concentrates on the intercourse within the covenant and by combining time and eternity in Jesus Christ it de-emphasizes the salvation-historical process. This emphasis results from utilizing, as interpretative grid, the concept of the eternal plan of salvation imposed by a decretal trinity. Scholars holding to this view argue for this position from the high christological content that they perceive Coccapeius to have given to the notions of predestination, the council of peace and the covenant of grace. The limited value of this model lies in its attenuated stress on the redemptive acts of God through real history. This interpretation presupposes unity of the predestination decree (*decretum praedestinationis*) and the salvation decree (*testamentum*), and draws a very close connection between Christology and predestination.[53] The decree of predestination precedes the salvation decree in this model: i.e., the Father chooses his own and gives them to the Son.[54] This christological interpretation of the

---

[52] Van Asselt, *Federal Theology of Johannes Coccapeius*, 3, 5, 304-5.

[53] As Graafland maintained as well.

[54] Van Asselt's detailed examination of Coccapeius' teaching in these areas and the distinctions and nuances of each (e.g. with respect to his decretal teaching: *decretum praedestinationis*, *testamentum*, and *pactum salutis*; and with respect to his covenant doctrine: *foedus*, *lex*, and *oeconomia* and *abrogatio*) are very luminous (van Asselt, *Federal Theology of Johannes Coccapeius*, 197-226). It is asked: Which factor dominates: a bilateral, bi-covenant doctrine or a singular, unilateral decree? Most important is the decree which embraces and is exercised over all of reality, comprising all aspects of God's rule; he is the *potentia Dei*, and the decree is with respect to the creature as such (*Federal Theology of Johannes Coccapeius*, 197-211). Only *then* comes the doctrine of (double) predestination, a subset of the divine decree which embraces the decision to elect or to

covenant of works and its abrogations, as a function of God's gracious act, compromise the two-sided nature of Coccceius' theology and unduly transposes the redemptive historical moment of Coccceius' theology into *ordo salutis* and predestination categories. By this interpretation, Coccceian scholars (such as McCoy) see him as a forerunner of German pietism, of which K. Barth is a worthy successor.[55] What both representations of Coccceius' federal theology do have in common is failure to consider the pneumatological factor as the key element bringing together both emphases on salvation history and salvation order. In both models the work of the Holy Spirit is entirely neglected.[56]

Discovering Coccceius' pneumatological emphasis in a combined evolutionary-synthetic model explains his characterization of the covenantal interaction between God and humanity as a relation of *friendship*, captured in the phrase *amicitia dei*, the friendship of God.[57] It is the Holy Spirit, through the course of redemptive history, who has given integration to both the chronological and the logical aspects of the plan of salvation:

> The Holy Spirit wrote the ways of God's covenant in time, and in doing so, sanctified time. The Holy Spirit followed a path, from the general work in creation and maintenance, through salvation history to the revelation of Christ in the history of the Kingdom. . . . Coccceius maintained the Holy Spirit to be the most important continuity factor [which] explained the doubleness and plurality of his theology. He believed that there was no single fulcrum from which the rest derived. God's deeds did not terminate one act, and therefore the relation of God to history could not be formulated in any single way. . . . The relation between history and existence was expressed in his theology through the idea of friendship with God.[58]

---

abandon. The reprobate are objects of the decree but not of the testament; this is reserved for the elect and underscores the immutability of God's eternal will for their salvation. The elect are chosen *in* and *through* Christ, not *because of* Christ; Coccceius is careful to ground election in the eternal good pleasure of God. And finally comes the testament which presumes the eternal pact between the Father and Son as legal ground. The pact is directed to the *terms* of the pact's negotiation (between Father, Son and Spirit) while the testament is directed to the *result* of the pact's negotiation, played out in time (*Federal Theology of Johannes Coccceius*, 212-26, 222). The relationship that Coccceius strikes between decree and covenant van Asselt represents as follows: "The testament describes the salvation-economy aspect of God's eternal will, and, as the result of the inter[sic]-trinitarian transaction, it remains directed towards history. The eternal pact between the Father and the Son is a description of the inter[sic]-trinitarian aspect of God's eternal will, which forms the legal foundation for the economy of salvation described in the testament, which is subsequently realized in the course of the covenant of grace" (*Federal Theology of Johannes Coccceius*, 225).

[55] Van Asselt, *Federal Theology of Johannes Coccceius*, 305-6.
[56] Van Asselt, *Federal Theology of Johannes Coccceius*, 284-87, 301-2, 306-10.
[57] Van Asselt, *Federal Theology of Johannes Coccceius*, 310-21.
[58] Van Asselt, "Amicitia Dei," 246-47. Yet, despite this emphasis on the pneumatological dimension as being truly representative of the varied (and, for some, contradictory) components of Coccceius' theology, van Asselt is unprepared to designate him as a "theologian of the Holy Spirit" (van Asselt, *Coccejus*, 111).

Within the framework of this pneumatologically-driven integrated model is found Cocceius' teaching of abrogations, the "hermeneutical key" through which his entire theological enterprise is accessed. He uses a unique doctrine of abrogations to mark the believer's path, the covenant child's progress, from initial existence to consummated glory.[59] In movement from the covenant of works to the covenant of grace both by way of salvation history (horizontal) and salvation order (vertical), the covenant of works is slowly abrogated by distinct historical and existential moments. Cocceius identifies five successive periods in this advance, each of which represents further abrogation of the covenant of works until, in the eschaton, the covenant of works has fully disappeared (is fully abrogated) while the covenant of grace has been fully appropriated. These five stages are: 1) with the fall when the covenant of works is rendered ineffectual; 2) with the establishment of the covenant of grace in which friendship and communion are offered humanity, not by works but by faith in a promised Savior; 3) with the incarnation of Jesus Christ; 4) with the death of the body and the final victory over sin; and 5) with completed sanctification, in the eschaton.[60] Returning to the question of whether these abrogations are historical occurrences along a chronological time-line or existential occurrences representing progression in the subjective experience of faith in the believer, it must be recalled that the pneumatological approach to Cocceius' theology conflated the historical/chronological with the existential/logical to result in a conjoining of time and eternity. This answer explains the very essence of the doctrine of abrogations – it is a combination, a blending, of the two models:

> With each new abrogation, the sphere of influence of the covenant of works on history and on the experience of the believer is diminished, while the influence of salvation and of the covenant of grace increases. . . . This interpretation combines the salvation-historical and the salvation order – or the historical and the existential – elements. . . . Each period in salvation history coincides with a corresponding state or condition in the believer.[61]

The uniqueness of this doctrine of abrogations is evidenced by the fact that there were no theologians who actually furthered this particular thinking[62] although there was no shortage of parties to both sides of what became a significant theological debate. On the one hand, those in the Voetian camp (the *ordo salutis* group) jealously guarded the decretal character of God and charged

---

[59] Van Asselt, *Federal Theology of Johannes Cocceius*, 271-87; idem, "The Doctrine of the Abrogations in the Federal Theology of Johannes Cocceius (1603-1669)," *CTJ* 29 (1994): 101-16; hereafter, "Doctrine of Abrogations."

[60] Cocceius, *Verbond*, 43, 54, 167, 328, 370; The Dutch version of Cocceius' work translates *abrogation* variously as *vernietiging*, *veroudering* and *afschaffing*. Cocceius scripturally anchors his doctrine of abrogations in Heb 8:13; van Asselt, *Federal Theology of Johannes Cocceius*, 271-73.

[61] Van Asselt, *Federal Theology of Johannes Cocceius*, 280-81.

[62] Van Asselt, *Federal Theology of Johannes Cocceius*, 287.

Cocceius with introducing a "monstrous dogma" into theology by injecting a historicizing moment into the covenant which confused the *substance* of the covenant of grace with its *administration*. On the other hand were found those (the *ordo tempora* group) who wanted to dismiss any notion of eternal decree and pact, holding fast to only the redemptive-historical relationship between the two covenants.[63] But rather than seeing this as a case of either/or, Cocceius' doctrine of covenant abrogations represents a more careful integration of both the historical and eternal dimensions of God's plan of salvation and of the Christian life.[64] This more fully captures both the static and dynamic elements in sanctification, the former having reference to the decretal activity of God whereas the latter represents the processive nature of the Christian life. The process of spiritual renewal is exactly that – a process – and in this context the doctrine of abrogations, pneumatologically speaking, makes perfect sense, since it "is federal theolgy's [*sic*] version of the traditional doctrine of sanctification. . . . [It] is at its deepest level a history of sanctification as the work of the Holy Spirit, in which an analogy or coordination can be discerned between the process of salvation history and the process within the *ordo salutis*."[65]

Van Asselt's elucidation of Cocceius' thought and its internal consistency carries more cogency than that of Graafland which emphasized its internal tension. This can be explained by Cocceius' pneumatological orientation in explaining the seemingly irreconcilable time/eternity and the associated historical/existential contradictions. Satisfactory resolution can only be found in the presence and activity of the Holy Spirit in the initial act of redemption, but also in redemption's sanctifying progression, from the covenant of works to the covenant of grace, both historically and in the spiritual life of the believer.

How does William Ames' see this covenantal interplay? Recall Graafland's observation that the notion of abrogations is not entirely unique with Cocceius, but that, in fact, ideas along similar lines can be found in the much earlier thought of Calvin, Beza and Zanchius.[66] He does not mention Ames.

The Amesian Inspiration for Cocceius' Covenant Thought

Johannes Cocceius' covenant theology received its inspiration in Bremen from federalists Matthias Martini (1572-1630) and Ludwig Crocius (1586-1655) before he went to Franeker to study under the famous philologist Orientalist Sixtinus Amama (1593-1629). Cocceius was, first and foremost, a philologist

---

[63] Van Asselt, *Federal Theology of Johannes Cocceius*, 282-84; van Asselt, "Doctrine of Abrogations," 112. It was Antonius Hulsius (1615-1685) who denounced the doctrine of abrogations as a *monstrosum dogma* (*Federal Theology of Johannes Cocceius*, 283). Graafland touches on this controversy as well in *Calvijn tot Comrie*, 3.279-3.284.
[64] Van Asselt, *Federal Theology of Johannes Cocceius*, 286.
[65] Van Asselt, *Federal Theology of Johannes Cocceius*, 286-87.
[66] Graafland, *Calvijn tot Comrie*, 3.318-3.319.

and exegete.⁶⁷ But it is also true that he studied under William Ames at Franeker, "one of the most astute theologians of the Second Reformation." It is therefore not surprising that in many areas of theology, uniquely Amesian emphases found welcome reception in the thought of Cocceius: the very definition of theology, its practical nature, the place of human responsibility, and the centrality of the volition in the act of faith, to name a few.⁶⁸ Noteworthy too is the emphasis both ascribe to God *qua* God. Cocceius' Christology held that the elect were not elect *in* Jesus Christ but *through* Jesus Christ due solely to the eternal good pleasure of God. Along similar lines, and much earlier, Ames had very carefully nuanced the concept of faith to give God his due; the *object* of faith is not Christ, but God. To underscore, faith in God is obtained by faith in Christ. Christ becomes the *mediate* object of faith; God himself is the *ultimate* object.⁶⁹

But the most noteworthy dependence of Cocceius on Ames appears to be in his covenant theology. In particular, the nature of the relationship both theologians draw between the covenant of works and the covenant of grace needs to be explored. For the concern is identical: how to relate the existential growth of the believer with the chronological unfolding of redemptive history. Solidly in back of this dynamic inter-covenantal relationship looms the nature of that between the decree and covenant. Ames, followed by student Cocceius, sets forth his theology along highly covenantal lines. But before he introduces the covenant as descriptive of the relationship between God and humanity comes a chapter on "The Decree and Council of God." Before any dialogue on covenant is entertained, it must be established that all things happen on account of God's eternal good pleasure⁷⁰ as demonstrated in both his creation and providence.⁷¹ The government of the "intelligent creature," in God's creation, is by way of covenant which has two sacraments.⁷² But this covenant of works is violated, humanity sins, and sin has consequences, a key one of which (condemnation) is overturned by the restoration of fallen humanity to fellowship with God through the person and work of Christ, and all solely for God's good pleasure and out of his benevolence.⁷³

The distinguishing feature of Ames' architectonic covenant theology is found as he works out the "application" of Christ. The means through which would be exercised the already-established covenant of redemption between "God and Christ" which entailed Christ's surety-ship (of a reciprocal nature in

---

⁶⁷ Van Asselt, *Federal Theology of Johannes Cocceius*, 25-26; Graafland, *Calvijn tot Comrie*, 3.324; McCoy, "Cocceius' Theology," 72-84, esp., 78, 81, 83.
⁶⁸ Van Asselt, *Federal Theology of Johannes Cocceius*, 27-28, 102, 153, 256.
⁶⁹ Ames, *Marrow*, 1.3.1, 1.3.7-1.3.9.
⁷⁰ Ames, *Marrow*, 1.7.
⁷¹ Ames, *Marrow*, 1.8, 1.10.
⁷² Ames, *Marrow*, 1.10.
⁷³ Ames, *Marrow*, 1.9-1.23.

which God would deliver the faithful to Christ and Christ to the faithful) is the covenant of grace.[74] Following this, Ames ties together decree and covenant:

> Thus our deliverance from sin and death was not only determined by the decree of God but also granted and communicated to Christ and to us in him before it was known by us. . . . Therefore, the application is the end result of the obtaining. Since the end is intended by God the Father and Christ the obtaining, as the means to that end, has a firm connection with it. The application by which God fulfills with great firmness what was contained in a covenant formerly made and broken is called in the Scriptures the *New covenant*.[75]

Redemption is *accomplished* by the decretal decision of God, and *applied* in covenantal relationship. This application – redemptive history – is ordered along covenantal lines from start to finish. Beginning with the intra-trinitarian *pactum salutis*, and moving from the covenant of works through to the covenant of grace – the "New covenant" – Ames, the astute theologian, maintained that there could exist no contradiction between decree and covenant.

Ames' exposition of the *ordo salutis* significantly opens with "application in general," as he labels predestination, before moving through the "parts:" calling, justification, adoption, sanctification and glorification. This is the "application of redemption considered in itself." The *subject* of the application of redemption (the church) is acted upon by the *way* or *means*: ministers, scripture, sacraments and ecclesiastical discipline. Finally, then, comes covenant administration.[76]

Recall that Ames focuses on the chronological aspect of the covenant of grace by dividing the covenantal dispensations into distinct periods through to Christ's return when "the application which has only been begun in this life will be perfected."[77] This administration of the covenant of grace we saw to be further divided into three dispensations: before Christ, from Christ to the end, and at the end.[78] With this classification, Ames finds opportunity to remain true to his Ramist convictions, for within the first dispensation there is to be distin-

---

[74] Ames, *Marrow*, 1.24.

[75] Ames, *Marrow*, 1.24.4, 1.24.7.

[76] Ames, *Marrow*, 1.25-1.30, 1.31 opening statement, 1.33-1.37, 1.38, 1.39, 1.41. Chapter 1.40 addresses Ames' teaching on the sacraments of baptism ("the sacrament of initiation or regeneration" which "seals the whole covenant of grace to all believers") and the Lord's supper ("the sacrament of nourishment and growth for the faithful in Christ") [Ames, *Marrow*, 1.40.5, 1.40.6, 1.40.16].

[77] Ames, *Marrow*, 1.41.1.

[78] With this particular three-fold division of dispensations, Ames, no doubt reluctantly, must compromise his commitment to the method of Petrus Ramus, for he must now chart his model from an uncharacteristic trichotomy, rather than the standard Ramist dichotomy. While such diversion is quite uncommon, it does appear from time to time in Ames' work. In fact, this commitment to dual arrangement is so strong in places, that it appears to unduly strait-jacket some Amesian explanations that could easily have been fleshed out more. Could content have come to serve form in places?

guished distinctive covenant administration from Adam to Moses and from Moses to Christ. Ames further dichotomizes the Adam-to-Moses dispensation into two periods: from Adam to Abraham and from Abraham to Moses.[79]

What is noteworthy here is Ames' integration of his just-explained elements of the order of salvation with what is clearly a chronological scheme. We hinted at this feature of Ames' covenant system earlier. Ames has embedded the eternity aspect of the life of the faithful into the temporal/historical progression of that faithful group at that particular stage of redemptive history. The logical, existential elements of the *ordo salutis* are integrated with the chronological periods of the *ordo temporum*. The horizontal movement and vertical progression are continually in a state of intersection; the recipients of God's electing power receive covenantal benefits with ever-increasing clarity and assurance as predestination and covenant meet in unity in a perfect blending of decretal theology and covenant doctrine. Note the following example of this conflation, as redemptive history unfolds from the time of Abraham to Moses:

> First, election was set forth in the persons of Isaac and Jacob who were beloved before Ishmael and Esau . . . . Second, redemption along with its application was majestically shown in the person and blessing of Melchizedek – also in the promise and covenant of blessing to come to all nations from the seed of Abraham . . . . Third a calling came in the leading of Abraham from Ur of Chaldees to a certain new and heavenly country . . . . Fourth, justification was illustrated by the express testimony of God that faith was reckoned to Abraham for righteousness, as the father and pattern of all who should believe . . . . Fifth, adoption was declared by giving God's name to Abraham and all the sons of the promises, and by assigning the inheritance to the sons of the promises, the family of the free woman through grace . . . . Sixth, sanctification was prefigured by circumcism [*sic*], which stood for the taking away and abolishing of the corruption of sin and the old man so that a new creature might come in their places . . . . Seventh, glorification was pointed to in the blessing promised in the land of Canaan, which was a type of the heavenly country.[80]

Of note in this illustration is that predestination, or, more specifically, election, is folded into the *ordo salutis*; through seamless intercourse the eternal and the historical, the logical and the chronological are combined. Although this is not always so obviously the case in Ames' depiction of this dynamic within the other periods of covenant administration, in this instance it serves to clearly underscore the close relation he saw between the decree and the covenant. In addition, we saw in a previous chapter the large amount of space Ames was prepared to devote to an enumeration of the differences between i) the covenant of works and the covenant of grace, and ii) the Old Testament and New Testament administration of the covenant of grace.[81] Particularly noteworthy is the

---

[79] Ames, *Marrow*, 1.38.
[80] Ames, *Marrow*, 1.38.22-1.38.28.
[81] Ames, *Marrow*, 1.24, 1.39.

fact that each period in salvation history is coordinated with a corresponding series of conditions or states of believers. Each of these periods in the history of salvation has coordinated with it all of the elements of the order of salvation. The wheel of salvation history moves relentlessly forward while the cogs (the aspects of the *ordo salutis*), although generically identical through time, take on different expressions of these aspects. And these cogs anchor the rim to the hub of faith. Not all believers are at the same place in the *ordo salutis* at any given moment in historical time. The points of coordination of the historical dimension (horizontal) with any one of the components of the existential or ontological (vertical) are dissimilar among believers. Not only this, but perhaps more significantly, Ames seeks to eliminate any time dimension from the *ordo salutis*. Different and distinct moments in redemptive history serve continually as evidence of one's predestination, calling, justification, adoption, sanctification and glorification. Obviously the believer is forensically justified, once and for all. Redemptive history is not only the field in which the entire *ordo salutis* is played out but also the terrain upon which history progresses by specific historical instances that remind believers of their status in Christ.

From this it is clear that Johannes Cocceius formalized a view of covenantal execution of which intimations existed in the earlier thought of William Ames, the comfortable coexistence of decree and covenant, the dominance of neither in the wedding of eternity thinking and historical thinking. Cocceius provided a more solid and generic theological (pneumatological) substance to this marriage (the work of the Spirit, according to van Asselt) which advanced by covenant abrogation and covenant appropriation. This staging of the appropriation of the promises of the covenant of grace received initial inspiration from Ames. Although Ames preferred to revise only slightly (and Ramistically) the simpler sketch of the administration of the covenant of grace as Calvin had laid it out, Cocceius raised this model of covenant administration to an art form no doubt to lend cohesion to his rather unique doctrine of abrogations.

Finally, Ames holds to an inchoate form of abrogation of the covenant of works. Although it was truly the trademark of Cocceius' creative system, Ames provided an explanation of the dynamic relationship between the covenant of works and of grace in a way that was, at the same time, somewhat opaque, more measured and less fanciful.[82] In contrast to Cocceius, Ames teaches that the demands of the covenant of works are gradually diminished, but not in distinct step form. This also was intimated in a previous chapter. With the introduction of the New Testament at the coming of Christ, Ames is satisfied to say, if somewhat cryptically, the following:

> the testament is new in relation to what existed from the time of Moses and in relation to the promise made to the fathers. But it is new not in essence but in form.

---

[82] Recall Antonius Hulsius' assessment.

> In the former circumstances the form of administration gave some evidence of the covenant of works, from which this testament is essentially different.[83]

Further, "freedom comes, first, in doing away with government by law, or the intermixture of the covenant of works, which held the ancient people in a certain bondage."[84] The spirit of adoption in the New Testament delivered believers from the bondage of the covenant of works. Freedom came also with the lifting of the yoke of ceremonial law.[85] All this is because the Holy Spirit has been more effectually applied and his gifts are more perfect in the New Testament (liberty in the Spirit) than in the Old Testament (bondage of the letter).[86] At the eschaton, finally, "the application [the covenant of grace] which has only been begun in this life will be perfected."[87] The chronological becomes the ontological. Time translates into eternity. All aspects of the *ordo salutis* are fully actualized and fulfilled; final and total abrogation of the covenant of works, with the concomitant full appropriation of the covenant of grace, comes only at the resurrection, when hope becomes certainty, and faith, sight.[88] Following this clear lead established by William Ames before him, Johannes Cocceius also considers this reality to be the fifth and final stage of the abrogation of the covenant of works.[89]

Concluding Observations

The work of covenant theologians William Ames and Johannes Cocceius demonstrate the misdirection of the single dogma thesis. The idea of such theological conflict was entirely foreign to these originators and architects of the federal theology. Moreover, located where he was between Calvin/Perkins and Cocceius, Ames advanced considerably further than the former the idea of covenant as life, but stopped short of the more detailed covenantal speculations and constructions of the latter, notably the highly-refined doctrine of abrogations. The broad conceptions for Cocceius' covenant system, characterized by the conflation of the historical and existential and by the doctrine of abrogations, had its origins in the earlier theological work of William Ames. In fact, Cocceius emphasizes the notion of *amicitia dei* – "friendship with God" – as the un-

---

[83] Ames, *Marrow*, 1.39.4.
[84] Ames, *Marrow*, 1.39.9.
[85] Ames, *Marrow*, 1.39.9.
[86] Ames, *Marrow*, 1.39.9-1.39.12.
[87] Ames, *Marrow*, 1.41.1.
[88] Ames, *Marrow*, 1.41.1-1.41.6; the called will be in "eternal glory;" the effects of justification and redemption "will then be completed;" the adopted "will enter into the possession of their inheritance;" in the sanctified the "image of God will be perfected;" and, finally, "the glory and blessedness hoped for will shine forth in all fullness, not only in the soul but also in the very body. . . . This final perfection of administration requires the coming and personal presence of Christ himself" (Ames, *Marrow*, 1.41.2-1.41.9).
[89] Cocceius, *Verbond*, 370-89.

derlying principle of his covenant doctrine.[90] To regain fellowship with God, those who became his enemies through the fall can regain his friendship via his covenantal relationship with them. Interestingly this concept is not unique with Cocceius but is found earlier in the thought of Ames in a passage we addressed in an earlier chapter. Ames discusses the improvement of the covenant of grace over that of works where "the old was a covenant of friendship, so to speak, between the creator and the creature, but this is a covenant of reconciliation between enemies."[91] This idea of reconciliation represents a major idea in the covenant thought of Ames, although, as in all of his covenant doctrine, Cocceius fleshed it out in much greater detail, providing a covenantal understanding where the Holy Spirit is at the center of this reconciliation between enemies. For Cocceius this central principle constitutes the very basis for his unique and pneumatologically-understood covenant theology. It is indeed true what Cocceius said of his relationship with Ames: it was not superficial (*non perfunctorie*).[92]

Finally, it is important to remember that Ames' unique fusion of predestination and covenant thinking is necessary for the internal coherence of his system of covenant theology and informed piety, or, faith and obedience. With the internal consistency of Ames' system of theology demonstrably intact, we now turn to a fuller examination of the second aspect of his theological system, observance, with a view to uncovering the biblical/theological underpinnings upon which he builds his system of Christian life and piety.

---

[90] Van Asselt, *Federal Theology of Johannes Cocceius*, 256-57.
[91] Ames, *Marrow*, 1.24.13.
[92] Reported in van Asselt, *Coccejus*, 18.

Chapter 6

From Thomas' Casuistry to the Moral Theology of Westminster

Introduction

In considering the Christian walk of faith, William Ames identifies the covenant relationship as foundational in establishing the responsibility of the obedient believer. Ethical behavior is covenant-grounded. Further, while covenant is the vehicle through which God governs rational creatures,[1] the divine law is the imperative standard for such governance.[2] Conformity to the moral law's requirements results in either the (undeserved) reward of felicity or the (deserved) punishment of unhappiness, an adjudication that takes place in the court of one's conscience:

> From this special way of governing rational creatures there arises a covenant between God and them. . . . Hence arises the force and reason of conscience which is an intelligent creature's self-judgment in his subjection to God's judgment.[3]

Because of the covenant, then, one is constrained to maintain the stipulations of the moral law, with conscience as both guide and arbiter.

Unfortunately, however, maintaining covenant obligations in a life of obedience is not often so clear-cut: it can be fraught with uncertainty – even confusion – arising from instances of apparent moral ambiguity. Such instances give rise to "cases of conscience" which must be resolved if covenant obedience is to be taken seriously and the conscience is to be clear. What, then, are the *broader* principles of moral theology extending beyond the *direct* imperatives of the ten commandments? What is the procedure to follow in both determining and applying the relevant laws of conduct in custom and case-based analysis? These questions lie at the very center of casuistry, which addresses serious moral issues on an individual, case-by-case basis.

Interestingly, this is not just an out-dated and irrelevant concern. While the formal practice of casuistry and its nomenclature have long since fallen out of

---

[1] Ames, *Marrow*, 1.10.
[2] On God's means of governing by law, Ames says this: "A law is made by commanding or forbidding. A law is established by promising or threatening" (*Marrow*, 1.10.6-1.10.7). This imperative mood of expressing divine law causes L.W. Gibbs to observe the implied "ethical voluntarism" of Ames' understanding of natural law and conformity to it ("The Puritan Natural Law Theory of William Ames," *HTR* 64 (1971): 37-57, 40-41).
[3] Ames, *Marrow*, 1.10.13.

favor, casuistry is still very much a common contemporary activity in the resolution of a specific moral case or problem. This can be seen from the very definition itself: "Casuistry, most broadly understood, is a process of reasoning that focuses upon specific cases or moral problems, as opposed to the general study of ethical theories or concepts."[4] In the rational process of the casuistic exercise, reasoning moves from the more to the less certain in resolving the conflict. It is the very nature of the case that evangelical Christians, in their pursuit of life *coram Deo*, navigate with difficulty that often uncertain terrain between Christian liberty and prescribed rules owing to disagreement on the former because of ignorance of the latter.

In the Christian tradition, of course, the "more certain" to which all moral behavior makes appeal is scriptural teaching. This tradition took some time to develop. The initial Puritan blend of medieval/early modern casuistry evolved into a purer system of practical theology which received full confessional consolidation in the Westminster Standards. William Ames' moral theology proved pivotal in this development.

Reasons for Puritan Ethics

A Dearth of Protestant Casuistry

Although the literature on Christian case divinity is generally thought to have had its beginnings in the medieval period, K. Kirk provides an extended discussion of the lineage of casuistry all the way back to the New Testament. In fact, if we are to ascribe to "casuistry" the widest meaning possible, then "Christ was the greatest of casuists." Problems of morality were evident in the gospels and in the many behavioral issues that Paul confronted, while the church fathers and councils also dealt with such questions in the early years of theological development and ecclesiastical organization. Therefore, by the time of the medieval thinkers a body of literature had been in development for some time. The medieval doctors, markedly Thomas Aquinas, furthered this trajectory by setting their pens to the writing of a formal system of moral theology and casuistry.[5] At the time of the Reformation and with the jettisoning of all things Roman Catholic, this rich and long-established tradition was cast away. But once formal Reformation theological principles had been established and Reformed

---

[4] D.H. Smith, "Introduction" to *Conscience and Its Problems: An Introduction to Casuistry*, by K.E. Kirk, Library of Theological Ethics, R.W. Lovin, D.F. Ottati, W. Schweiker, eds. New ed. (Louisville, KY: Westminster, John Knox, 1999), xiii; hereafter, *Conscience and Its Problems*. This volume was first published in 1927, underwent a number of revisions, and continues to be a preeminent source book in the field of theological ethics.

[5] Kirk, *Conscience and Its Problems*, 150, 150-202.

thinkers turned to theological systematization and codification, the need for teaching on sticky ethical issues again became apparent.[6]

It is true that the earliest Puritan casuistic concern over issues regarding grace and assurance had been addressed by William Perkins before more practical casuistry appeared. In fact, Perkins considered the question of assurance of salvation the greatest case of conscience there ever was, penning an entire, if brief, volume on just this topic.[7] But more than a treatise addressing issues of spiritual formation was required. Practical moral guidance was considered an essential task of ministers of the gospel and the demand for written guidance – a moral compass, as it were – was keenly felt by early post-Reformation divines.[8] Perkins responded to the call. With his *Cases of Conscience* an official body of Protestant moral theology had its beginnings.[9]

No doubt the concern at the newly-formed Academy at Franeker was how the recently-acquired Professor Ames would teach his uniquely-defined theology – living to God – without a corresponding pedagogical plan for the practice of piety. Thus the venerated Englishman wrote his own treatise, to "excite to this kind of study."[10] And although Ames, somewhat more judiciously than his

---

[6] For a summary of the method and practice of medieval casuistry, notably that of the Jesuits, and a broader application of the casuistry of early English Puritanism, see my "Gambling on Faith: A Holistic Examination of Blaise Pascal's Wager," *WTJ* 62 (2000): 33-63.

[7] Perkins, *Workes*, 1.421-1.438.

[8] K. Thomas, "Cases of Conscience in Seventeenth-Century England," *Public Duty and Private Conscience in Seventeenth-Century England*, J. Morrill, P. Slack, and D. Woolf, eds. (Oxford: Oxford University, 1993), 32, 36, 37. Excellent introductions to Puritan casuistry appear in Sprunger, *Ames*, 153-66; T.F. Merrill, ed. and intro., *William Perkins. 1558-1602. English Puritanist. His Pioneer Works on Casuistry: "A Discourse of Conscience" and "The Whole Treatise of Cases of Conscience."* (Nieuwkoop: B. De Graaf, 1966), x-xx; and H.R. McAdoo, *The Structure of Caroline Moral Theology* (London: Longman's, Green and Co., 1949).

[9] Kirk notes the medieval dependence of the initial casuistry of the Reformed Churches, (*Conscience and Its Problems*, 202).

[10] Ames, *Conscience*, "To the Illustrious and Mightie Lords, the Staes of Zeland," Dedicatory Epistle. In his study of the development of casuistry in England, Elliot Rose surely understates with the following: "Ames has some light to cast on the spirit of the school . . . [but] since he spent most of his active career in Holland he cannot be expected to apply himself directly to English problems" (Rose, *Cases of Conscience* [Cambridge: Cambridge University, 1975], 185). But Ames' casuistry clearly addresses issues both in the Dutch Republic and at home in England. On the state of morality in seventeenth-century England, see Campbell, *Puritan in Holland*, 2.350-2.375, 2.453-2.457. He portrays Elizabethan England as a society morally adrift, where the religious elite enjoyed lives of self-aggrandizement. He notes that the English were "not so laborious as the French and Hollanders, preferring to live an indolent life, like the Spaniards" (*Puritan in Holland*, 2.350-2.375, 2.453-2.457). In more measured tone, Lawrence Stone observes the difference between the freer morality of English society and the circumspection found on the continent and notes that as early as 1499, Erasmus, on a visit to England, reported the propensity of the English to kiss strangers on the lips, not

teacher Perkins, made liberal use of thinkers and theologians of the church of Rome, it remained his preference that "the children of Israel should not need to goe downe to the Philistims (that is, our Students to Popish Authors) to sharpen every man his share, his Mattocke, or his Axe, or his weeding Hooke . . . ."[11] After lecturing on cases of conscience for eight years, Ames crowned his teaching in 1630 with the publication of *Conscience*, a preeminent and salutary work on moral theology that filled an "unwarranted gap in the contemporary study of theology."[12]

The Emergence of an Arid Orthodoxy
The theological ethos of the Republic, the crypto-Protestantism found in the official Dutch Reformed Church, and the academy's emerging emphasis on theoretical theology was matched by the benign neglect of practical divinity. A diminishing piety became evident in some quarters of the public church – an absence of "heart religion." This changing religious climate was reinforced by the lack of confessionary zeal evidenced in the Church. Since the very late sixteenth century it had been in a state of opposition to "heavy-handed official insistence on Catholic allegiance" and it was not prepared to substitute, what many saw as a newer dogmatism, for the old.[13]

The revival of Dutch Catholicism during this period, notably in the north Netherlands, brought with it unabated confessional rivalry.[14] Within the Reformed Church, itself, increasingly greater friction developed between the orthodox Calvinists and the "libertines." This mounting tension evolved into two competing blocs, a rivalry that broke through ecclesiastical borders and spilled out into the public sphere, affecting the entire body politic. The orthodox were significantly intolerant towards all but their own and advocated growth in church power over society in general. On the other hand, the libertines exhibited much more tolerance not only towards those outside the official Dutch Reformed Church, but also with respect to theological matters within the

---

only in greeting but for every other occasion (*The Family, Sex and Marriage in England* [New York: Harper & Row, 1979], 325). See also his *Road to Divorce: England, 1530-1987* (Oxford: Oxford University, 1990), *Uncertain Unions: Marriage in England, 1660-1753* (Oxford: Oxford University, 1992), and *Broken Lives: Separation and Divorce in England, 1660-1857* (Oxford: Oxford University, 1993).

[11] Ames, *Conscience*, "To the Reader." On the basis of statements like this, claims Kirk, "the Reformed casuists all give[the papists] more or less grudging mention [and] quote them continually . . . ." (*Conscience and Its Problems*, 202).

[12] Horton, *Ames by Reuter*, 166. Kirk blames the independent-mindedness of the Reformers and Puritans when he judges that the century of Reformation casuistry – particularly its consistency and systematization – is not to be compared to that of "its counter-Reformation sister. . . . Perkins and Ames produced what can at best be called mere sketches of the subject" as compared to "indefatigable pioneers" such as Suarez (*Conscience and Its Problems*, 204, 205, 207).

[13] Israel, *Dutch Republic*, 362-64.

[14] Israel, *Dutch Republic*, 377-98.

Church.[15] In the midst of this confusing mosaic, many Reformed churches of the day housed preachers whose pulpiteering made a mockery of that office, trotting out evidence of their learning in theoretical theology and ancient languages while betraying ignorance of scripture and "the Doctrine according to Godlinesse."[16] Ames' contemporary, Willem Teellinck, was one of the few Dutch theologians interested in more than just doctrinal precision and was not prepared to sacrifice the systematic study of ethics on the altar of dogmatic formulation. He found himself looking to the Puritans in England, attracted as he was by their practical theology and having experienced Puritan pietism firsthand during a stay in England.[17] Further through the seventeenth century, Ames late-contemporary Gisbertus Voet and "the leading spokesman of Calvinist orthodoxy in the Republic" would incorporate Puritan morality into Dutch Calvinism from his chair at the University of Utrecht.[18]

The "Reformed Thomas à Kempis," as Voet described Teellinck, had an immediate impact on the culture of the early Golden Age. Although the state of morality in England was judged to be inferior to that of the Republic, the prosperity of the time and the philosophy of government encouraged experimentation in moral laxity.[19] And despite the emergence of "a new ethic of Christian mercy" resulting from the long struggle between the Netherlands and Spain, it was apparent this was not matched with an accelerated Christian ethic. As in England if for slightly different reasons, attention turned from pious living to an often less-than-pious focus on the life that could be obtained from recently-found economic prosperity. Such an interest in a newly-accessible life was finding expression and promotion in the arts and literature, especially amongst the poets.[20] Bucking this trend, however, was Pensionary Jacob Cats, an influ-

---

[15] Israel, *Dutch Republic*, 390-95.
[16] Ames, *Conscience*, Dedicatory Epistle. In preparation for pulpit ministry in seventeenth-century Netherlands, mastery of the biblical languages was non-negotiable. See W.J. van Asselt, "'Hebraïca Veritas': Zeventiende-Eeuwse Motieven Voor de Bestudering van het Hebreeuws door Predikanten," *KeTh* 46 (1995): 309-24. On occasions of pulpit misuse of such study see Horton, *Ames by Visscher*, 141-44.
[17] For purposes of this section, I mention Teellinck's involvement only in passing and conduct a deeper examination of his thought in a further chapter.
[18] Israel, *Dutch Republic*, 662; Horton, *Ames by Visscher*, 120; Geyl, *Netherlands*, 216. Quote from Israel, *Dutch Republic*, 444.
[19] The government did not explicitly encourage loose living. Rather it espoused the "laissez-faire" attitude we addressed earlier. In fact, the government promoted peace and order. Geyl notes "even Descartes, the Frenchman, who, devout Catholic but revolutionary philosopher, passed the best part of his life in Holland, praised next after liberty, which men enjoyed more in that country than elsewhere, the order and security reigning there" (*Netherlands*, 214); Israel, *Dutch Republic*, 585, 587.
[20] C.J. Cadoux, *Philip of Spain and the Netherlands: An Essay on Moral Judgments in History* (London and Redhill: Lutterworth, 1947), 65, 225. See also T. Watt, *Cheap Print and Popular Piety, 1550-1640*, Cambridge Studies in Early Modern British History, A. Fletcher et al., eds. (Cambridge: Cambridge University, 1991).

ential politician and social commentator whose views on morality and piety owed much to Teellinck's English wife. By extolling Calvinist values and promoting the agenda of the Further Reformation, Cats poured principles of piety into the cultural ethos of the north Netherlands.[21] That Teellinck applied a moral theology to the churches in Zeeland with some success is attested by none other than Ames himself. He lauds the faithfulness of this recently-departed "worthy Servant of the Lord," now reaping his reward for his zealous and tireless dedication to the cause of godliness.[22] But Ames and Teellinck were clearly in the minority. It was therefore high praise, indeed, that despite the aspersions thrust upon Ames by colleagues and opponents in intellectual circles, his work was generally considered complete, exact and "most accurate and orderly" by, among many others, colleague Amama and theological faculty at Leiden University.[23]

Clearly Ames was disappointed with this low level of demonstrated piety in the Dutch Republic of the day. To forestall the obvious dangers of what he considered to be a lifeless orthodoxy, he promoted sound and searching preaching because, after all, "the principall worke of the Sermon, if it be not Catecheticall, is in the use and application."[24] And to the application of a life of piety his casuistry was certainly directed. Following the 1630 publication of *Conscience*, translations and new editions continued for forty years, often by rival publishers.[25] Even his detractors esteemed it highly and it was immediately placed on the curriculum of theological faculties. Why the demand? Because, observed Reuter, glancing back four centuries from his own mid-twentieth century perspective, Ames' moral theology "served as an excellent pathfinder in the burning questions of the Christian life and succeeded not in looking at all possible cases of conscience but in pointing out the ground of faith common to them all."[26] Frequent translation was matched with widespread distribution of *Con-*

---

[21] Jacob Cats, *Houwelijk Dat is Het Gantschebeleyt des Echten Staets* (Amsterdam, 1655) and *Alle de Werken* (Amsterdam, 1658 and Amsterdam/Utrecht, 1700), cited in Schama, *Embarassment of Riches*, 398-99, 436-38; Israel, *Dutch Republic*, 531; Geyl, *Netherlands*, 65, 230. Geyl observes that "as late as the nineteenth century all respectable Protestant households possessed, alongside the Bible, a copy of [Cats'] *Collected Works*" (*Netherlands*, 231). A public position dating back to the fifteenth century, a "pensionary" was a powerful political figure in the Dutch Republic. This town secretary and legal adviser also held membership in town delegations in the provincial States (assemblies). The pensionaries of the provinces of Holland and Zeeland were notably influential and, by the end of the 16th century, virtually dominated certain city governments (Encyclopedia Brittanica, "Pensionary," Britannica.com. http://www.britannica.com/EBchecked/topic/450291/pensionary [accessed June 18, 2013]).

[22] Ames, *Conscience*, Dedicatory Epistle.

[23] Horton, *Ames by Visscher*, 60, 67 n. 43, 121.

[24] Ames, *Conscience*, 4.26.28.

[25] In 1635, publishing houses in both Amsterdam and Franeker issued the book (Horton, *Ames by Reuter*, 166-67).

[26] Horton, *Ames by Reuter*, 166-67.

science beyond the sacred halls of the academy and the church and into believers' homes,[27] making his teaching on ethics a useful and necessary complement to his more theoretical work. This was, no doubt, Ames' further purpose in writing so extensively on preachers, and homiletics, and the need to prick the conscience and motivate to right living.[28] This obvious and documented preoccupation with the practical nature of theology, and its proper introduction into the church by well-trained preachers, made Ames' contribution in moral theology all the more beneficial for Christian living, in a time and culture when people professed the letter, but not the spirit, of scripture. Ames challenged this with his "empirical principle"[29] of theology, that faith and spiritual life are inseparable, that theology is the doctrine of living to God.

Sabbath Desecration and Other Life-Style Practices
The early Puritans had very strong convictions on Lord's Day observance – it should be spent in worship and the practice of piety. At home and before Ames came to the Netherlands he had been involved in similar controversy over the Sabbath because of the strong anti-Sabbatarian sentiment of both church and civil authorities.[30] The issue accompanied Ames to the Dutch Republic, where the controversy took on a life of its own because of the theological crisis precipitated by Teellinck as he sought to stem anti-sabbatarianism in Zeeland and crypto-Protestantism in general. All got caught up in the storm – church and academy alike – as Teellinck's efforts at church reform soon garnered national attention.[31] The theological horsepower on this issue, as with so many others, came from Ames: rejecting all ceremonial (and thus obsolete) associations with the Sabbath, he argued that the institution of the Sabbath commandment was a moral one on grounds of its permanency. Not only did it appear in the moral code but in fact it dated back before that, to the beginning of creation, long before the institutionalization of the ceremonial system that prefigured Christ.[32] Sunday was a specially sanctified day in which public worship and further spiritual exercises such as preparation for worship services, edifying discussion afterwards, and the day-long practice of piety were added to one's daily spiritu-

---

[27] Horton, *Ames by Reuter*, 167.

[28] Ames, *Conscience*, 4.26, "On making sermons." Here Ames provides extremely useful and detailed instructions for proper biblical preaching, all the way from initial text selection through exegesis and application to appropriate homiletical styles. See also Horton, *Ames by Visscher*, 141-44.

[29] Reuter designates it as such and elaborates in Horton, *Ames by Reuter*, 171-81.

[30] Recall that in addition to the considerable coverage of the Sabbath question in both *Marrow* and *Conscience*, Ames wrote a tract on the issue.

[31] Horton, *Ames by Reuter*, 167.

[32] Ames, *Marrow*, 2.15; idem, *Conscience*, 4.33; idem, *Sabbati*, 1, 2, 23-27, cited in Horton, *Ames by Visscher*, 134-36.

al life.[33] This was Ames' desire for the Netherlands where he noticed widespread desecration of the Lord's Day, a common complaint by the English there and confirmed by a contemporary of the time.[34] Ames expended tremendous energy on this matter as he sought to combat this lax attitude, terminate the practice of Sabbath violation, and restore much stricter Sabbath observance society-wide. In this effort he was joined by various Dutch pietists who gave this issue considerable attention.[35]

Amongst the many problematic lifestyle issues of the day, some stood out as particularly egregious examples of the culture's moral laxity.[36] These were the questionable practices of gambling and dancing.[37] As with all controversial issues, both defendants and opponents of these activities could be found in both the academy and the church, continuing a controversy that had plagued the church from its beginning.[38] However, this life-style question rapidly moved beyond the purely theoretical and practical, and into the realm of the spiritual, when a prominent member of the academy connected it to the sacrament of the Lord's Supper. Should one who demonstrated gambling or dancing propensities gain admission to the table of the Lord?[39] Posing it this way, of course, only encouraged pulpit activity on the morality of these issues and exhortations to self-examination were common lest the table be dishonored and the Lord blasphemed. Such attention to communicant eligibility represented a "trademark of Reformed Pietism"[40] and this particular question soon became a battlefield in the area of moral theology. On gambling, Ames' position was that it should be proscribed because of the typically unsavory character and behavior of the participants, and the sinful consequences of continually frustrated expectations effected by the profane use of something with sacred roots.[41] The serious addic-

---

[33] Ames, *Conscience*, 4.33, Question 4; Horton, *Ames by Visscher*, 133-40, 138. Visscher mentions the 1617 royal order of King James encouraging people to participate in all manner of entertainment on the Sabbath.

[34] W. Brereton, *Travels in Holland, the United Provinces, England, Scotland and Ireland, MDCXXXIV-MDCXXXV*, E. Hawkins, ed. Remains, Historical and Literary Connected with the Palatine Counties of Lancaster and Chester, 1844, vol. 1 (Reprint ed., New York: The Chetham Society, n.d.), 6; Israel, *Dutch Republic*, 475.

[35] W.J. op 't Hof, *Voorbereiding en bestreiding* (Kampen: De Groot Goudrian, 1991), 115, 124-55. He assesses the implications of this long, drawn-out controversy for the *Nadere Reformatie* and provides brief geographic connections of many pious representatives of Puritan-style Sabbatarianism. Included in his list, of course, is Ames (*Voorbereiding*, 143).

[36] Schama, *Embarassment of Riches*, 375-480.

[37] Horton, *Ames by Visscher*, 126-32.

[38] Visscher observes that the majority opinion of the Church fathers and councils stood unambiguously opposed to gambling (Horton, *Ames by Visscher*), 126.

[39] Simon Episcopius, *Antwoord op LXIV Theologische vragen* (Amsterdam: 1648), 193ff, cited in Horton, *Ames by Visscher*, 126, 131.

[40] Op 't Hof, *Voorbereiding*, 17, 22-29, 41.

[41] Ames, *Marrow*, 2.11.23-2.11.34; idem, *Conscience*, 4.23, 5.45.

tive quality of "gaming" stems from the "nothing to lose" philosophy engendered by such expectations.[42] Although some theologians, such as fellow Puritan Thomas Gataker, attempted to find middle ground in the debate by distinguishing between the game itself and its consequences and by providing detailed instruction on playing dice games, the reality of gambling in the Netherlands demonstrated such fine distinctions to be wishful thinking for an unattainable moral ground, mere *pia vota*.[43] Considering the holy nature of the lot, Ames warns against its inappropriate use in betting and gaming, while dancing was proscribed because of its immodesty and the associated danger of compromising chastity.[44]

To Ames and like-minded pietists, the perceived need for moral direction in England and the Dutch Republic was apparent. It was not only a rising dogmatism that threatened a practical life of high piety. Godliness, as the Puritans understood it, was also jeopardized by the growing immorality associated with the advantages and liberties of the Golden Age. New philosophies, progress in the political and social realms, and newly-discovered economic opportunity and wealth worked against a biblically-oriented ethic. Such moral drift William Ames sought to reverse by developing the initial efforts of Perkins and thus doing for the Protestant cause what a long tradition of medieval casuists had already done for the Roman Catholic.

Leaving Perkins and Medieval Ethics Behind

The Theory of Conscience in Early Puritan Casuistry
William Perkins published two major works on moral theology in which he provides both his philosophy of conscience and its practical application to real life cases.[45] His first work, *Discourse*, supplies the theoretical structure upon which he then places the logical construct employed for the practical resolution of specific cases. First and foremost, construction of a sound moral theology is to be based upon the organic relationship between God and humanity. Once

---

[42] Ames, *Marrow*, 2.11.32.

[43] For a good example of Ames' involvement and writing on the topic of gambling and providence, and the crisis which this precipitated, also known as the "Ames-Gataker debate" see M. Todd, "Providence, Chance, and the New Science in Early Stuart Cambridge," *HJ* 29 (1986): 697-711. Recall the sermon on gambling that Ames preached at the university church, St. Mary's, on St. Thomas Day, December 21, 1609, the tipping point to his ouster. See Todd, "Providence," and Sprunger, *Ames*, 22, 176. Gataker's involvement in the controversy in England is nicely summarized in Horton, *Ames by Visscher*, 126-32, although the quarrel did not begin prior to 1610 as Visscher claims. *Pia vota* is Visscher's phrase in *Ames by Visscher*, 126-30.

[44] Ames, *Marrow*, 2.11, 2.19.45; idem, *Conscience*, 5.45, 5.39.23-5.39.25.

[45] For two relatively recent studies on the casuistry of William Perkins, see M.R. Shaw, "The Marrow of Practical Divinity: A Study in the Theology of William Perkins" (Th.D. diss., Westminster Theological Seminary, 1981) and C.C. Markham, "William Perkins' Understanding of the Role of Conscience," (Ph.D. diss., Vanderbilt University, 1967).

established, this relationship calls forth conscience's duties, varieties, and application.[46]

Perkins maintains that the proper subjects of conscience are reasonable creatures – men and angels. According to Perkins' taxonomy, the soul has two faculties – the understanding and the will.[47] The former is "the more principal part serving to rule and order the whole man: and therefore it is placed in the soul to be as the wagginer to the waggin." Conscience resides in the intellect because actions of the conscience are directed by reason which itself determines the volition. Further, the intellectual faculty can be dichotomized into theoretical and practical classes – the former distinguishes between truth and falsehood while the latter determines the "goodness" or "badness" of actual situations, and this determination is within the purview of conscience. Thus it is the practical side of the intellect that houses conscience because its job is to pass moral judgment on one's behavior. It does so in its capacity as a natural power, a faculty, a created quality, issuing forth in knowledge and judgment, for scripture ascribes to conscience such actions as accusing, excusing, comforting, terrifying – actions which obviously must be driven by such a (divinely-) created quality for the autonomous mind would be incapable of such action. Conscience is thus an operative faculty of the mind. Perkins argues here for conscience as faculty because the mind's observations (the "principles and conclusions of the minde") must be applied in order to render a verdict of innocence or guilt. Again, the whole function of conscience is to adjudicate one's particular actions.

Finally, conscience is a divine gift from God that he placed between himself and humanity, combining two parties in the knowledge of a secret. Deriving the meaning from its Latin origins, Perkins reasons that this combination (*con*, "with," and the verb *scire*, "to know") has in view a special knowledge – "some one secret thing" – between God and creature. "God knows perfectly all things of man though they never be so hid and concealed: and man by a gift given him of God; knowes togither with God, the same things of himselfe: and this gift is called Conscience." Conscience both provides testimony and renders judgment. It is the arbitrator, working on behalf of the Creator, to pronounce either for or against one as it passes sentence on all of one's thoughts, words and deeds.[48]

William Ames' casuistry, although penned to address the same concern as that of Perkins, is a much more integral part of Ames' works. It flows directly from his definition of theology and his practical concern for godly living. Recall the explicitly tight connection Ames makes between covenant and conscience and that he sees *Conscience* as part of a unified system of doctrine and

---

[46] Perkins, *Workes*, 1.517-1.554. See Shaw, "Perkins," 82-110, for a study of Perkins' theoretical approach to the concept of conscience.
[47] McKim demonstrates the Ramist approach of Perkins' casuistry in "Ramism in Perkins," 226-39. Not surprisingly, Ames follows Perkins' lead.
[48] Perkins, *Workes*, 1.517-1.518.

life as he promises in *Marrow*: "if there are some who desire to have practical matters better explained, especially those of the latter part [Book 2] of this *Marrow*, we shall attempt, God willing, to satisfy them in a special treatise, which I mean to write, dealing with questions usually called 'cases of conscience.'"[49] This "special treatise" saw the light of day as *Conscience*, a collection of five logically-arranged books in which the theory and practice of conscience is very clearly presented. Respectively, Ames lays out the general philosophy of conscience, addresses its soteriological concerns, attends to the exigencies of the Christian life as lived out in obedience to the will of God, and reminds the reader of the responsibilities entailed by living to God and each other.

Ames defines conscience much more carefully than does Perkins and intentionally corrects what he sees as unjustified – and possibly risky – speculation. "The conscience of man (for I doe not intend to treat of the conscience of angels) is a mans judgement of himself, according to the judgement of God of him."[50] With Perkins he explains that conscience results from exercising the intellect, not the will, because it utilizes judgment which belongs to the faculty of reason. This intellectual exercise is more than just bare assent to facts or "apprehension of the truth;" rather, this judgment presupposes an already "firm and settled" truth. Consequently, it is not a "*contemplative judgement*, whereby truth is simply discerned from falsehood: but a *practicall judgement*," whereby this truth is personally applied to the situation at hand, with a view to ruling the volition.[51] And as to whether conscience is a power (faculty), habit or act, Ames argues that Perkins misclassifies conscience as faculty:

> He gives this reason of his opinion, namely, because the act of Accusing, Comforting, Terrifying, etc. cannot bee ascribed to the Conscience, if itselfe were an act. But this reason is weake: because in the Scriptures such kinds of effects are attributed to the thoughts themselves, which undoubtedly are acts. *Rom. 2.15. Their thoughts Accusing one another, or Excusing*. The reason is, because things done, are the effects not onely of the Mover, but also of the motion itselfe. Besides, Master *Perkins* maketh Conscience, Understanding, Opinion, Knowledge, Faith, and Prudence, to be of one kind or sort; but none would define these so, as that they should be taken for distinct faculties of the soule.[52]

Neither can conscience be designated a habit, argues Ames, distinguishing himself from the (Franciscan) Schoolmen such as Scotus, Bonaventure and Durand, since the only function of a habit is to quickly motivate to action, while conscience, more comprehensively defined, has other functions such as accusing, comforting, and so forth. It remains, therefore, to designate conscience, "with

---

[49] Ames, *Marrow*, "Brief Forewarning."
[50] Ames, *Conscience*, 1.1, Preamble; idem, *Marrow*, 1.10.13.
[51] Ames, *Conscience*, 1.1.2-1.1.3.
[52] Ames, *Conscience*, 1.1.4.

the best Schoolemen," (of which group Thomas reigns supreme) as *act*, for it is "an act of practicall judgement, proceeding from the Understanding by the power or meanes of a habit." Following Perkins, Ames argues that these acts of judgment can be properly effected only through the logical discourse afforded by the operation of the practical syllogism.[53]

This intellectual construct is indispensable in the adjudication of behavior, an adjudication which process, from start to finish, takes place in the court of one's conscience. This three-statement formulation is the field of operation of both the mind and the memory, movement through which results in the rendering of a verdict on questions of moral behavior. The syllogism comprises the proposition, the assumption and the conclusion and by deduction renders a judgment. To illustrate, Ames (again, following Perkins) presents the syllogistic workings of the conscience of an unbeliever in the following fashion:

> He that lives in sinne, shall dye:
> I live in sinne;
> Therefore, I shall dye.[54]

Ames fleshes out a more precise picture than Perkins on the spiritual dynamics within the discursive sequence of the syllogism. The major premise, the *proposition*, begins the process. This is the *law*, the objective and authoritative body of writing (biblical teaching) against which the rightness or wrongness of actions is measured. It asserts the truth of the law with respect to particular behavior. In Ames' example, this assertion is simply the scriptural truth that sinners die, a claim made by the intellect as it apprehends the biblical law. This is followed by the *assumption*, the minor premise, the *index* or a *book*, i.e., an assertion about the state of things: "I live in sinne." This is where memory is operative as it considers the state of affairs of one's lived experience. Finally comes the *conclusion*, designated the *judge*: "Therefore, I shall dye." A verdict is rendered, when one's behavior (step 2) is measured against the biblical assertion regarding that behavior (step 1). Ames concludes:

> In that Syllogisme alone is contained the whole nature of Conscience. The Proposition treateth of the Law; the Assumption of the fact or state, and the Conclusion of the relation arising from the fact or state, in regard of that Law; The Conclusion either pronounceth one guilty, or giveth spirituall peace and security.[55]

---

[53] Ames, *Conscience*, 1.1.4-1.1.8; Perkins, *Workes*, 1.535.
[54] Ames, *Conscience*, 1.1.8.
[55] Ames, *Conscience*, 1.1.11.

Whereas Perkins has by now left the Schoolmen, at least in his theory of conscience, Ames is not yet through with them. He observes that it is the "synteresis" which provides the proposition.[56] What is meant by this concept?

Synteresis has reference to the conscience as being the internal repository of the laws of right and wrong. Ames refers to *synteresis* as the "storehouse of principles." It is this storehouse of principles out of which the law of God – the biblical law – is drawn. It is a "habit of the understanding" (the realm of the intellect) because it houses those principles governing moral actions that God has implanted in the mind of humanity and which continue to reside there post-fall. It is part of humanity's image-bearing capacity. Broadly understood, *synteresis* encompasses not only general conclusions determined by principles of justice deduced from natural law, but also those practical truths to which believers can give assent because, by faith, they are made privy to divine revelation in the matter under consideration. Thus it is, that *synteresis* is divided into "natural" and "enlightened" conscience.[57] The former embraces the principles of nature as law; the latter recognizes the legally binding character of scriptural principles. Both elements are contained in the revealed will of God which both displays this law and demands the creature's duty. To re-emphasize, the revealed will of God, or the law of God, incorporates both the moral principles within created humanity and the additional laws that God "hath injoyned." Thus Ames can uphold that the conscience can be bound only by the revealed will of God, the law of God understood as all those things commanded in the Gospel. Further, it is the law of God that requires submission to the laws of the creature; the latter do not carry self-referential authority. To be bound in conscience by the laws of men (or children by parents or a promise by an oath) is idolatry, since only God knows the inward workings of the conscience.[58] This Amesian view of the conscience follows very closely Thomas' understanding of *synteresis* as habit. Thomas calls *synteresis* the "law of our understanding inasmuch as it is the habit of keeping the precepts of natural law, which are the first principles of human activity."[59] Of course these precepts of natural law are common for all people: "with respect to general principles of both theory and practice, what is true or right is the same for all and is equally recognizable."[60] Moreover, Thomas asserts that although natural law precepts are fully covered in the Old and New Law, not everything found there is of natural law since

---

[56] Recall the direct connection Ames draws between the law of nature in primitive humanity and the moral law. By adding the notion of conscience into this mix, he has painted a full portrait of the responsibilities of the creature to maintain covenant faithfulness through obedience to all the principles that extend from the moral law. This is where case divinity comes in. (Calvin had an inchoate sense of this in *Institutes*, 2.8.1.)
[57] Ames, *Conscience*, 1.2.1-1.2.7.
[58] Ames, *Conscience*, 1.2.9-1.2.15.
[59] Aquinas, *Law and Political Theory*, 77.
[60] Aquinas, *Law and Political Theory*, 89.

"many things there imparted are above our nature."[61] In agreement, Ames discusses the "natural" and "enlightened" conscience as representing, respectively, the principles of natural law and additional principles found in scriptural law.

Clearly both Perkins and Ames make generous use of scholastic categories in their teaching of the theory of conscience. But whereas Perkins appropriates some of these concepts as a working base from which to develop his casuistry, Ames pauses to penetrate into the theory underlying the abstractions of conscience's dynamics. These abstractions and their incorporation in syllogistic representation are rooted, for the most part, in Thomas Aquinas' theory of natural law. As the discourse on casuistry unfolds further throughout *Conscience*, it will be observed that Aristotelian characteristics used extensively in Thomas' *Summa* regularly come to the fore. Early Puritanism poured much indeed of Aristotle, and Thomas after him, into Peter Ramus' model. For William Ames, Thomas was indeed the "best Schoolman."[62]

Because of its implications for Christian obedience, Ames' deliberate definition of conscience as *act*, and not as *faculty* (Perkins) or *habit* (Scotus and other Schoolmen) is particularly noteworthy. Only with conscience as *act* can Ames' consistently argue that Christian experimentalism (or experientialism) is voluntary and is more than an inherent aptitude to assess and adjust behavior. Thoughts of conscience are themselves *act*, argues Ames. With conscience as act, the judgment of the intellect, stirs the habit (capability or predisposition),

---

[61] Aquinas, *Law and Political Theory*, 91. Thomas follows Gratian who says that "natural right is what is contained in the Old and New Laws [Law and Gospel] . . . by which everyone is commanded to do to others what he would have done to himself, and forbidden to do to others what he would not have done to himself [*Decretum* I, I. Preface. Leipzig I, I]," (*Law and Political Theory*, 91). Thomas asks whether natural law can be abolished from the human heart. His answer: no, but "lust or some other passion" can impair the reason from applying general principles of law while "other and secondary precepts" of natural law can be "effaced" by "wrong persuasions" or "perverse customs and corrupt habits" (*Law and Political Theory*, 95-97).

[62] Ames' dependence on the Thomistic tradition, notably as mediated through Spanish Jesuit Francisco Suarez (1548-1617) is significant and cannot be overstated. Compare Ames' construct of the theory of law (*Conscience*, 5.1-5.1.11) to that of Aquinas (*Law and Political Theory*, 19-37, 165-71) and to Suarez's *De Legibus ac de Deo legislatore* (*A Treatise on Laws and God the Lawgiver*) in *Opera Omnia*, Vols. V-VI. A good analysis and demonstration of the implications of Ames' natural law teaching for the formulation of modern democracies, notably in the areas of citizens' inalienable rights, social contract theory and the right of resistance is provided by Gibbs,"The Puritan Natural Law Theory of William Ames," 37; G.L. Mosse also develops the political dimension of Puritan casuistry, touching on, among other things, the doctrine of resistance, in "Puritan Political Thought and the 'Cases of Conscience'," *CH* 23 (1954): 109-18; on p. 110 Mosse asserts that "flexibility and practicality, as opposed to "Utopianism" were to be the hallmarks of this Puritan approach towards building the godly society." McAdoo traces the ancestry of the Caroline definition of "conscience" back to the scholastics; he, too, demonstrates the scholastic dependence of Ames' understanding of conscience (*Caroline Moral Theology*, 64-97).

and motivates change. Habit predisposes and enables change, is a tendency or disposition to change (presumably from unbelief to belief, from disobedience to obedience, etc.). Faculty is an inherent power or capability that could effect change. But *act is change*. Hand-in-hand with the practical syllogism, conscience as act *must* produce an effect in keeping with the judgment or verdict arising from a comparison of behavior to its standard. Ames is in pursuit of *act*, not just a propensity to act, because only pure act is a mark of obedience to the grace given in the covenant relationship. Nothing less than act will do for William Ames, and this understanding of conscience is key in the construction of the theoretical foundations for his case divinity. In all its simplicity, this is the philosophical/logical instrument that best suits Ames' program of living in Christian obedience when confronted with the truth of the God's law, the truth of one's behavior, and the truth of the subsequent verdict.

Wrapping Perkins' Medieval Casuistry in Biblical Dress
Perkins' practical ethics proceeds under three chief headings, each of which is subdivided into any number of Ramist dichotomies.[63] Book 1 is "man simply considered in himselfe without relation to another" and is essentially a treatise on human nature, spiritually conceived. It covers such topics as confession, sin, salvation (a large part devoted to preparationism), assurance and five "distresses of mind" and the comfort afforded these.[64] He also summarizes briefly some of his earlier teaching on the nature of conscience. Perkins' comes across gentle, highly sympathetic, practical and extremely pastoral, especially in his excursus on comforting the distressed. All remedies begin with repentance and faith. In just one of many statements that could easily have application to contemporary spiritual formation he counsels the afflicted to live "not . . . by feeling but by faith."[65] Hovering in the background is the constant reminder of Perkins' concern for a believer's assurance of faith and salvation.[66] Striking as well

---

[63] William Perkins, *The Whole Treatise of the Cases of Conscience, Distinguished into Three Bookes* (London: John Legat, Printer to the University of Cambridge, 1606; reprint ed., The English Experience: Its Record in Early Printed Books Published in Facsimile, no. 482. Amsterdam: Theatrum Orbis Terrarum Ltd., and New York: Da Capo, Inc., 1972). I cite from this work by book, chapter and section.

[64] See Shaw, "Perkins," 111-53, for a discussion on Perkins' concept of conversion.

[65] Perkins, *Conscience*, 1.8.5.

[66] Perkins' teaching on assurance of faith appears in an entirely separate and small casuistic work entitled *A Case of Conscience, the Greatest thatever was: how a man may know whether he be the child of God, or no* in *Workes*, 1.421-1.428. The resolution to this case of conscience is anchored in Ps 15 and 1 John and proceeds in discourse form between the Church and the Apostle (for 1 John) and Jehovah and David (for Ps 15). See Shaw, "Perkins," 154-213, for a study of Perkins' doctrine of assurance in connection with worship. Ames did not afford the issue of assurance of faith the priority Perkins did.

are random appearances of medieval thought such as his apparent approval of the scholastic distinction between mortal and venial sins.[67]

Next Perkins examines "Man as he stands in relation to God." The focus is fourfold: theology proper, scriptures, worship, and the Sabbath. Again, Thomas looms large. His exhaustive coverage of the arguments for the existence of God carries this qualifier:

> I doe not meane to dispute the question, whether there be a God or no; and thereby minister occasion of doubting and deliberation in that which is the onely maine Ground and pillar of Christian religion: But rather my purpose is, in shewing that there is a God, to remooue, or at least to help an inward corruption of the soule that is great and dangerous, whereby the heart and conscience by nature denieth God and his providence. The wound in the bodie that plucks out the heart, is the most dangerous wound that can be: and that opinion that takes away the Godhead, doth in effect rend and plucke out the very heart of the soule.[68]

In addition to their reassuring value, Perkins considers these proofs as preparatory to faith.[69]

---

[67] Perkins, *Conscience*, 1.2.3-1.2.11, especially 1.2.10-1.2.11.
[68] Perkins, *Conscience*, 2.2, Introductory question.
[69] Perkins, *Conscience* 2.2. Very closely following Thomas, Perkins explains that the existence of God can be seen from nature, grace and glory (cf. Aquinas, *Nature and Grace*, 1.2.3). From the realm of nature and creation, he advances five arguments which are judged useful for all to consider, from skeptical atheist to "setled" believer" (*Conscience*, 2.2.1). God's existence is seen, first, in the creation of the world (Rom 1:20), through the beauty and the coherence of the created order. Thomas' cosmological thinking is explicitly anchored in biblical revelation. Perkins explains, for example, how all creatures (in heaven and earth), from the simplest to the most advanced, fulfill the particular and unique purpose for which they were created. Secondly, God's preservation and governance of the created order attest to his being (Acts 14:17). Food and clothing, rain and sunshine, the hatching of an egg and the developmental process of a butterfly all bear witness to God. The rational creature's innate knowledge of good and evil (natural law), of which conscience is the indisputable evidence, is a third proof of God's existence, while a fourth is the inherent knowledge, in every creature, that there is a God. Each of these proofs for God's existence is fleshed out at length. Perkins, finally, offers the "fifth and last argument from nature . . . that which is used by all Philosophers" – the cosmological argument straight from *Summa* (*Conscience*, 2.2). Perkins' "proofs" from nature can be characterized as grounded in scriptural revelation and viewed from a cosmological and teleological perspective; he cannot let go of Thomas completely. On the other hand, however, Anselm's argument from pure abstract thought, is absent altogether from Perkins. A second set of proofs – those from the light of grace – briefly follows. Perkins asserts that the superiority of God's self-disclosure by grace is far superior to the evidence of God's existence obtained from natural theology. For while the latter is useful for faith in a preparatory way, through grace one comes to know God savingly, and this in three ways: propositional statements, prophecy (both fulfilled and unfulfilled), and miracles, all found in scripture (*Conscience*, 2.2) Finally, on the basis of 1 Cor 13:12, "the third ground of proofes, is fetched from the light of glorie" (*Conscience*, 2.3). Because of our creatureliness we see only adumbrations of God now, knowing him

The remainder of this section addresses christology, the scriptures, religion and worship. Perkins' coverage of the Sabbath is the longest chapter in this book, which length is approached only by the chapters on baptism, the scriptures and the godhead (primarily the cosmological arguments). The nature of the work is highly practical and pastoral, with corrections to current (typically papist) views made clear. Thus, although the writing is robustly anti-papist, it is generally not vehement, except where Perkins considers practices of the Roman Church to be especially detestable and heretical. At times Perkins employs an Aristotelian style of discourse, and rapidly disposes of any opposition to his casuistic teaching with biblical texts. It could be said that this second book follows a very general pattern of commands found in Table 1 of the moral law.

"Man as he stands in relation to Man" constitutes Book 3 of Perkins' casuistry. Both the organizing principles and the content of this book are truly surprising. Perkins begins with an excursus on virtue, which he defines as "a gift of the Spirit of God, and a part of regeneration, whereby a man is made apt to live well."[70] His case divinity focuses on the virtues of prudence, clemency, temperance, liberality and justice, under which are addressed moral dilemmas arising in the course of human relations against the backdrop of the social issues of the day. Such issues as forgiveness, self-defense, use of money, proper dress, recreation and reputation are discussed and resolved.

William Ames gathers all his casuistry in one five-volume work. He enlarges his theory of conscience – with Perkins-style elaboration[71] and concludes with a brief summary including four corollaries that were publicly debated "to encourage and stirre up to the study of Practicall Divinity."[72] It is not surprising that Ames' pedagogical technique is almost entirely Ramist.

Next Ames inquires into "those things that belong to the state of man."[73] The first order of business is to define a case of conscience as "a practical question, concerning which, the Conscience may make a doubt."[74] This volume is devoted, primarily to soteriological issues such as sin, entry into the state of grace, preparationism, the ongoing flesh/spirit battle and conduct in the Christian life.[75] It could easily pass for a compendium of Reformed theology, structured loosely around the *ordo salutis* and compares most uniformly with that of Perkins. Ames closes with an appendix, of sorts, comprised of further teaching on

---

only as he has revealed himself to us. But in glory, the creature shall see the Creator perfectly when faith becomes sight (*Conscience*, 2.3).

[70] Perkins, *Conscience*, 3.1.

[71] Ames, *Conscience*, 1.3-1.15.

[72] Ames, *Conscience*, 1.49-1.55, the 38 theses and four corollaries defended by Ames for his doctoral degree at Franeker under Sibrandus Lubbertus on May 27, 1622 (Sprunger, *Ames*, 74).

[73] Ames, *Conscience*, 3.1.

[74] Ames, *Conscience*, 2.1.1.

[75] Ames, *Conscience*, 2.2-2.19.

the problem of temptation from thirteenth century medieval theologian William Paris.[76]

On the other hand, "Of Man's Duty in Generall" – is an inquiry into "the actions, and conversation of [man's] life."[77] This is meant to address the whole question of obedience to God, a distinctively Amesian priority. Ames asserts that the signs of true obedience are submissively placing God's will ahead of the creature's, even when the divine will appears prejudicial. How is this to be accomplished? By exercising those characteristics that conduce to an obedient life, viz., the cardinal virtues of prudence, courage, temperance and justice (or, in expanded form, wisdom, humility, sincerity, zeal, peace, prudence, fortitude, patience, temperance, etc.) and by avoiding those tendencies that thwart an obedient walk (such as drunkenness, sins of the heart, sins of the mouth, etc.).[78] Thus, whereas Perkins saw these virtues as organizing principles for instruction in man's social intercourse, Ames emphasized more their nature as characteristic of the *obedience* that underscored theology as the doctrine of living unto God. Following Perkins, the concept of virtue in general is accorded a high priority, and the honored place assigned the cardinal virtues, as hallmarks of the life of obedience, is noteworthy.[79] On the other hand, and equally obvious, is the absence of any arguments for God's existence. Only one statement in Ames' work suggests a possible usefulness for natural theology. In the context of his exposition of the theological virtues in *Marrow*, Ames addresses the question of love for God (which logically follows faith and hope). He elaborates: "An unclear and remote inclination toward God preceeds faith, a certain shadow of which is found to some degree in all creatures."[80] But this kind of love, says Ames, is an ungrounded optimism, and does not constitute true love of God. In distinction from Perkins, Ames wariness of natural theology is clearly borne out here.[81]

These three books comprise just over a third of *Conscience*, and constitute the preliminary matters, as it were: definitional and conceptual elaborations on conscience, instruction on entry into and maintenance of the Christian life, and

---

[76] Ames, *Conscience* 2.49-2.54. William [of] Paris was actually William of Auvergne (1180/90-1249), a highly-regarded medieval theologian and bishop of Paris 1228-1249. His *Opera Omnia* appears on the first page of the Auction Catalogue of Ames' library. Ames is quoting from the Opera's "De tentationibus & resistentiis," 282-97 (Sprunger, *Ames*, 179). See also the excellent summary of William of Paris' life and work in N. Lewis, "William of Auvergne," *The Stanford Encyclopedia of Philosophy*, E.N. Zalta, ed. (Stanford University, Winter 2010 edition) http://plato.stanford.edu/archives/win2010/entries/william-auvergne/ [accessed June 18, 2013].

[77] Ames, *Conscience*, 3.1.

[78] Ames, *Conscience*, 3.2-3.22.

[79] As in other places, Ames adds here to the already considerable literature he has written on virtue in *Marrow*, 2.2.

[80] Ames, *Marrow*, 2.7.4.

[81] Also observed by Eusden, "Introduction" in *Marrow*, 49.

exhortation to obedience through the exercise of the cardinal virtues. Ames can now concentrate on his real concern, one which takes seriously the complexities that arise in the Christian life and that give rise to cases of conscience because not specifically addressed in scripture. How are these cases of conscience to be adjudicated? The simple answer is: By a proper understanding and application of the *full sweep* of the moral law.

This is Ames' organizing framework – the biblical decalogue. It is precisely because the law does not explicitly cover all possible eventualities in the believer's walk of obedience that explicit scripture-based instruction on case divinity is needed. That Ames frames his entire casuistry with the moral law demonstrates just how wide a net the law does cast. Thus, the final two books of Ames' casuistry attend to one's duty toward God and toward neighbor. With respect to the former, the entire spectrum of the obedient Christian's view and worship of the one true God is surveyed.[82] In fact, judging from his location of the case divinity associated with the first table of the law within the broader framework of worship, one could say that, for Ames, God can only be properly understood and related to through true worship. All of life, *coram Deo*, is worship. A worshipful context for truly knowing God is not an unexpected Amesian emphasis, since he feels so strongly that the community of God must join the church. In fact, church membership is a non-negotiable: nothing short of incumbent upon the believer; it is a covenantal responsibility. One adheres to the true church "in respect of the Covenant and promise of God."[83] In Ames' tone one detects undercurrents of anti-papism; although Ames could be an aggressive controversialist, his casuistry does not appear to be the place for strident polemic. Even in his teaching on heresy Ames' manner is measured.[84]

His commentary on the first two commandments (proscribing both substitute gods and idols) is introduced with a chapter on "Religion" and centers on cases of conscience arising out of the theological virtues of faith, hope and love, and opposing vices such as heresy, apostasy, presumption, and consulting with the devil. The sin of opposition to God is addressed, and edifying instruction on acts of worship such as prayer, confession and song is provided. Under commandment three, proscribing blasphemy, Ames teaches on the biblical use of the oath, the lot, and the sacraments, again, all in the context of worship. The book closes with a brief chapter on commandment four, the Lord's Day, "supposing those things which are spoken of this point in the *Marrow*."[85] The topics range from the more general (the true and false church) to the more specific (the gesture of prayer and singing), and receive varying amounts of attention. Ames prepares the reader for his final book on interpersonal relations by first settling any uncertainty the believer may have about his relationship to God. He

---

[82] Ames, *Conscience*, 4.1-4.33.
[83] Ames, *Conscience*, 4.24.4.
[84] Ames, *Conscience*, 4.4.
[85] Ames, *Conscience*, 4.33, chapter introductory note.

covers much the same ground as Perkins' but structures his casuistry somewhat more explicitly within the framework of the ten commandments.

In his elaboration of the second tablet of the decalogue (Book 5), the possibilities for discussion are vast. Ames has deep concern regarding "the duty of man towards his neighbour" and no topic is off limits, from acts of suicide on the high seas (commandment six) to the need for spousal intimacy in marriage ("mutuall communication of bodies," commandment seven).[86] Ames affords the reader some wonderful insights into seventeenth century society in both the Dutch Republic and England and the associated concerns regarding all aspects of human behavior that gave rise to cases of conscience. The book stretches for a total of fifty-seven chapters and is twice as long as his elaboration on the first table of the law. Commandment five covers such topics as justice, revenge, restitution, favoritism, love for neighbor, intercessory prayer, schism, humility, pride, and the mutual obligation between opposite classes of people, all for which the commandment on honoring of parents is the springboard. Here the hallmarks are respect for others and their reputation, and obedience of one class of citizen over against another. Then follows commandment six, or, as Ames labels it, "Precept 6," and the associated teaching on meekness, patience, long-suffering, slowness to wrath, goodwill, equanimity, manslaughter, duels, and war. The seventh commandment, proscribing adultery, addresses the "solemnities of matrimony," the already mentioned "mutual duties of man and wife" and divorce and polygamy. Basic issues of fairness in economic enterprise are addressed by chapters on "contracts," profits, lending of money ("usury"), poverty, wealth, saving and spending, and theft, all with respect to commandment eight and the proscription against theft. Under commandment nine one finds teaching not only on a "lye" but also on "public judgments, the judge, accusers, witnesses, advocates and defenders." Apparently gossip is part of the human condition. It was as much a seventeenth-century problem as a contemporary one, for "revealing a secret" gave rise to a case of conscience. Ames' casuistry closes with an exposition of the tenth commandment, centering on "contentment" which guards against covetousness.[87]

Ames carefully scrutinizes the constitutive elements of human character and how these interact in the social setting in morally ambiguous ways that, in his judgment, are inconsistent with scriptural direction and thus create cases of conscience. For example, we mentioned his teaching on the ethics and conduct of men and women as social beings and how this applies directly to the "mutual

---

[86] Ames, *Conscience*, 5.31.14, 5.37.4.
[87] Ames, *Conscience*, 5.5-5.57. Ames' classification of the temporary or permanent nature of some laws appears somewhat ambiguous if not arbitrary. This is because of his lack of precision in the classification of the judicial laws: Are these judicial laws part of the moral law, or do they relate to the ceremonial law or do they have relevance to the civil law of the theocracy? In keeping with the spirit of the day, Ames appears to underappreciate the forgiveness and grace that are the hallmark of the New Testament age. His position on capital punishment for adultery is a case in point.

obligations" between different classes of persons.[88] This overwhelming interest in social intercourse might suggest that there is simply more possibility for ambiguity in the interpretation of the law with respect to humans as social beings than there is with respect to their relationship with God. Or it might suggest that the casuistry required by the exigencies of seventeenth-century morality was more extensive in the human relations sphere than in the area of relations with the Divine.

The practical divinity of Ames bears much resemblance to that of Perkins, but he differs where it matters – in the conceptually organizing framework. Perkins' organizing tool is the system of cardinal virtues – the medieval authority of Thomas reigns here as in many other places.[89] Ames identifies the cardinal virtues as a feature of humanity's obedience to God but his case divinity is structured by the scriptural moral law.[90]

Concluding Observations

The ethical system represented by Ames' casuistry represents the earliest blueprint for a life of high piety and morals to which the Reformed believer is expected to subscribe through the course of a life of covenant obedience. This is the *sine qua non* of the Reformed system. Ames' case divinity met the need for a post-Reformation Protestant casuistry by addressing particular theological, ecclesiastical and social exigencies of his cultural context. He made use of prevailing philosophical and logical concepts to construct the casuistical model he then applied to the workings of conscience. This process acted as an aid in adjudicating the moral ambiguities that would arise in the believer's pursuit of a

---

[88] Ames, *Conscience*, 5.19-5.26. He addresses the "mutual obligations" between: the aged and gifted and their "inferiors," rulers and subjects, man and wife, parents and children, masters and servants, ministers and flock, and magistrates and subjects.

[89] "Virtue" said Perkins, "is a gift of the Spirit of God, and a part of regeneration, whereby a man is made apt to live well." How was this different from the schoolmen? "And this I put in the first place, to confute the received error of the wisest Heathen Philosophers, which call Vertue an habite of the minde, obtained and confirmed by custom, use, and practice" (*Conscience*, 3.1). Yet Ames was willing to borrow yet again from these "Heathen Philosophers" when he defines virtue as "a condition or habit by which the will is inclined to do well." But he placed it in the will because, as we have already observed, the will "is the true subject of theology" (*Marrow*, 2.2.4-2.2.7). An important distinction between Ames and the Schoolmen on this point is that, for Ames, virtue was a result of faith; for the scholastics, it made one acceptable to God (*Marrow*, 2.2.8-2.2.9).

[90] In fact, one searches in vain for coverage of these scholastic categories in standard, Reformed systematic theologies; nor do they surface in theological dictionaries. In a popular dictionary of philosophy under the entry "theological virtues," the reader is directed to J.F. Wippel's entry "Aquinas" (*CDP*, 31-34, 842). To define the four cardinal virtues as principles of the morally honorable life, an emphasis picked up by first Perkins and then, to a somewhat lesser degree, by Ames, is to reach back to Cicero and to Plato before him, according to J.L.A. Garcia, "Cardinal virtues," *CDP*, 103.

life of Christian obedience. Covenant theology guaranteed the inner coherence and inseparable fusion of both the creator's condescending grace and the creature's obedient response. For Ames, this obedient response was enjoined by the believer's renewed will. *Theologia est doctrina Deo vivendi*. This is heart religion.

While giving William Perkins, the first Puritan casuist his due, and employing his emphasis in matters of case divinity as a springboard to the further development of post-Reformation ethics, it was with Ames that decalogue-grounded Puritan casuistry in particular took on the character of Reformed piety more generally through the period of early orthodoxy. The offer of the gospel, freely extended by the divine covenant-maker in a one-sided act of unconditional grace would be met by obedient Christian living measured against the moral law as *synteresis*. Through his restructuring of the medieval form of the casuistry of William Perkins, and through defining conscience as act, Ames has provided a theoretical/practical model which, with the will at center, is the model to be followed in the life of the obedient covenant child, saved by grace through faith.

A final observation on Ames' method is in order. Like Perkins, his use of the Schoolmen was frequent but, unlike Perkins, it was more judicious.[91] For

---

[91] This chapter touches on the use of scholastic philosophy by the early Puritans. Over a quarter of a century ago, Breward observed that "Hooker's thomism has long been common knowledge, but there has been little investigation into the thomism of the puritans and second generation protestant theologians" (*Perkins*, 53). Although more is known now of the Puritan's intellectual indebtedness, for our purposes we have established that this debt is huge indeed, especially to Thomas, and notably in the work of William Ames. It appears that William Ames was much more apt to seek the advice and input of medieval Roman Catholic scholars than was William Perkins. We have mentioned only a few names, scratched the surface as it were. Roman Catholic Cardinal Robert Bellarmine (1542-1621) and already-mentioned medieval theologian William of Paris also make appearances in Ames' work, respectively in polemic and in approval. For Ames controversy with Bellarmine, see his *Scriptum Elenchticum contra Papistas vid. Bellarminus Enervatus in 4 Tomos Divisus* (1625-29). Noteworthy, too, is Ames' ambivalence toward Spanish Jesuit philosopher Francisco Suárez (1548-1617), a colleague of Bellarmine at a Jesuit college in Rome, "the most outstanding writer of the Jesuit order. . . . He was a worthy disciple of St. Thomas: he was the last of the Schoolmen" (*Histoire de la science politique dans ses rapports avec la morale* [2 vols., 4th ed., Paris, 1913], vol. 2, 55-56), cited in "Introduction." This excellent sampling of the thought of Suárez appears in *Selections from Three Works. De Legibus, AC Deo Legislatore, 1612 Defensio Fidei Catholicae et Apostolicare Adversus Anglicanae Sectae Errores, 1613 de Triplici Virtute Theologica, Fide, Spe, et Charitate, 1621*, Vol. Two, The Translation, prepared by G.L. Williams et al. with certain revisions by H. Davis, S.J., Introduction by J.B. Scott (Oxford: Clarendon, and London: Humphrey Milford, 1944; reprint ed., Buffalo: William S. Hein & Co., Inc., 1995). Suárez's dualism Ames abhorred, but his Thomistic theory of law is almost straight from this Jesuit. According to Eusden, the sabbatarianism of the Reformed tradition owes much to the findings of the late scholastics, particularly Suárez (Eusden, "Introduction" in *Marrow*, 19, n. 40).

Ames, medieval philosophy was an indispensable tool, but always only in the capacity of handmaiden.[92] At the same time as he borrowed from the ancient philosophers, he reviled their non-biblical presuppositions and formulations. The Aristotelian bifurcation of ethics and theology Ames assailed *ad infinitum*; he meets this dualism head on with Titus 2:12 that a lived theology is righteous and honorable *living*.[93] Indeed, the theme dominating *Technometry* was that "knowledge is judged by its performance, not by its theory."[94] Yet while the philosophical categories and theories of the medieval theologians and casuists were vigorously denounced, some of their teaching found reception in Ames who acknowledged that "the Papists have laboured much this way, to instruct their Confessors: and in a great deale of earth and dirt of Superstitions, they have some veines of Silver: out of which, I suppose, I have drawne some things that are not to be despised."[95] It is in his theoretical work on the dynamics of conscience that we see real evidence of this disclaimer. Here Ames mined quite liberally from the veins of silver that the Papists had previously quarried.

Ames' work in moral theology gives evidence of a judicious blending of an existing intellectual stream with the biblical directive to holy living. This model represents the sort of holistic teaching that Increase Mather detected when he lauded this "angelical Doctor": "It is rare for a *scholastic wit* to be joined with an *heart warm in religion*, but in him it was so"[96] This Amesian joining of "scholastic wit" with piety constitutes a very early example of the ease with which Reformed thinkers have historically been disposed to wed biblical piety with the intellectual streams of the time. Such philosophies and ideologies have been most effectively utilized by the Reformed to advance the cause of Christ along the lines of the Reformation *solas*. The transmission of this tradition has always been, in the words of John Leith, that of a "living, growing reality, not of an impersonal thing."[97] The fusion of faith and obedience that represents Ames' moral theology and that was to evolve into the informed piety of the Reformed tradition is a key example of this. This torch of piety was passed on

---

Ames' library was very well supplied by the medieval philosophers and theologians. See J.H. Tuttle, "Library of Dr. William Ames," *CSM* 19 (1911): 63-66.

[92] It is worth noting that despite Perkins' stated opposition to the Church of Rome, he was comparatively gentle. It is curious that Thomas Pickering's highly anti-papist introduction to Perkins' *Conscience* contrasts markedly with Perkins' own *Preface*, a model of tender pastoral exposition of Christ's burden recorded in Isa 50:4 and the need of the church of the day for just such a healer of souls. The Catholic Church isn't even mentioned.

[93] German Protestant theologian Bartholomäus Keckermann (c. 1571-1609), a contemporary exponent of this dualism and favorite of Ames' Franeker colleague Maccovius, is quoted scornfully at length in *Marrow*. See Eusden, "Introduction" in *Marrow*, 8, 48.

[94] Sprunger, *Ames*, 168.

[95] Ames, *Conscience*, "To the Reader." However, the sentence immediately following reads: "But they are without the life of this Doctrine: and death is in their pot."

[96] Mather, *Magnalia*, 236.

[97] Leith, *Reformed Tradition*, 17-18.

from William Ames to Puritan Richard Baxter, while it reached its most mature creedal expression in the exposition of the decalogue found in the *Westminster Larger* and *Shorter* catechisms.[98] Meanwhile, this biblical system of Puritan ethical teaching would intersect with an already-developing Reformed moral theology and lay the groundwork for the best experimental Calvinism that would follow, particularly in the Netherlands, where, since the Revolt of 1584, the Reformed Church had state sanction as the official Church of the Dutch Republic, and where Reformation doctrine had already received creedal expression in the widely-accepted *Heidelberg Catechism*. It was no doubt, with some anticipation, that Ames embarked on his commentary upon that already famous document.

---

[98] Richard Baxter's work represents Puritan casuistry in its most developed (some might say "over-developed") form. See particularly his *A Christian Directory: or, A Summ of Practical Theologie, and Cases of Conscience* (London: By Robert White for Nevil Simmons, 1673). See also the following: *The Life of Faith, as it is the Evidence of Things Unseen* (London: Printed by R.W. and A.M. for Francis Tyton and Jane Underhill, 1660) and *The Practical Works of Richard Baxter*, Introduction and life by W. Orme, 23 vols. (London: James Duncan, 1830; reprint ed. in 4 vols., London: George Virtue, 1857 and Ligonier, PA: Soli Deo Gloria, 1990-91). See also J.M. Phillips, "Between Conscience and the Law: The Ethics of Richard Baxter (1615-1691)," (Ph.D. diss., Princeton University, 1959).

Chapter 7

From Heidelberg to Westminster: William Ames in Confessional History and his Exposition of the *Heidelberg Catechism*

Overview of the Heidelberg Catechism: Origins, Structure and Ethos

The distinguishing features of the *Heidelberg Catechism*, focusing on issues from authorship to ethos have been recently examined by W. Verboom.[1] He summarizes various theories of the origins of the *Heidelberg Catechism* – its original version and its later revisions – with a view to determining the primary author of, and inspiration for, this confessional standard.[2] He concludes that

---

[1] W. Verboom, *De Theologie van de Heidelbergse Catechismus. Twaalf Themas: De Context en de Latere Uitwerking* (Zoetermeer: Boekencentrum, 1996), 15-25. The literature on the *Heidelberg Catechism* and its origins and intent is immense. I will not repeat that here. Suffice to say that the *Catechism* was composed by two individuals. One of these was Zacharias Ursinus, professor at the university in the city of Heidelberg in the Palatinate, during the Lutheran Reformation. The Calvinist, Frederick (III) the Elector (1515-76), had just succeeded Otto Henry to this post in 1559 and sought a manual of instruction that would teach a system of the Reformed faith in place of the then prevailing *Augsburg Confession* (1530, authored by Luther and Melanchthon). Along with Ursinus, Caspar Olevianus, a minister in Heidelberg and predecessor of Ursinus at the university, was the second individual commissioned to this task. The *Catechism* was adopted as one of the three Forms of Unity of the Dutch Reformed Church at the Synod of Dort (the others being the *Belgic Confession* (1561) and the *Canons of Dort* (1618-19). See also: L.D. Bierma et al., *An Introduction to the Heidelberg Catechism: Sources, History, and Theology*, Texts and Studies in Reformation and Post-Reformation Thought, R.A. Muller, ed. (Grand Rapids: Baker, 2005). A particular strength of this excellent volume includes translations of the Smaller and Larger Catechisms of Zacharias Ursinus; H. Hoeksema, *The Triple Knowledge: An Exposition of the Heidelberg Catechism* 3 vols. (Grand Rapids: Reformed Free, 1970), 10-15; C. Buchanan, "Catechisms" *NIDCC*, 199-201; Caspar Olevianus, *A Firm Foundation: An Aid to Interpreting the Heidelberg Catechism*, L.D. Bierma, trans and ed. Texts and Studies in Reformation and Post-Reformation Thought, R.A. Muller, ed. (Grand Rapids: Baker, 1995), xiii-xlii; hereafter "Olevianus by Bierma," *Firm Foundation*; and B. Thompson et al., *Essays on the Heidelberg Catechism* (Philadelphia: United Church, 1963).

[2] Verboom, *Heidelbergse Catechismus*, 16-17. This is, in itself, interesting. Verboom shows how subsequent editions of the *Heidelberg Catechism* were altered in response to issues of the day. Before the passing of the first century since its inception, differing theories regarding the precise origins of the *Heidelberg Catechism* arose. Much of this debate concerns the nature of the respective contributions of each of the two authors. Verbeek provides a useful and brief summary on pages 15-17. For defense of the signif-

although the primary inspiration was Ursinus' teacher Melanchthon, the *Catechism* demonstrates the influence of multiple existing catechisms, chief of which are the *Catechism* of Calvin and the *Larger Catechism* of Polish theologian Johannes à Lasco. The earliest version included only 128 (unnumbered) questions and answers. The 129th on the Roman Catholic mass was included as the Reformed Church responded to the anti-Protestant anathemas of the Council of Trent (meeting in three stages, 1545-47, 1551-52, and 1562-63), and is found in the second and third printings of the *Heidelberg Catechism* in 1563. Synodical meetings convening shortly after the 1563 publication all gave approval and strongly encouraged the use of the *Heidelberg Catechism* as the teaching manual of the churches.[3] It would be fair to say that by the time William Ames arrived on the Dutch scene in 1610, the ecclesiastical air would have been heavy with Heidelberg.

In comparison with the catechisms of the sixteenth century, Verboom points out that the *Heidelberg Catechism* is of a different and unique orientation, which then sets the tone for the remainder of the instruction found therein. Some early catechisms have a distinct "ecclesiological" tone, a tone established with their opening question which emphasizes the catechist as a candidate by baptism, for church membership. Others emphasize the created nature of the student, turning then to the question of the purpose or end of this created being of God. This is Calvin's approach.[4]

The *Heidelberg Catechism*, however, is different and unique in its entire theme – introduced by its distinctive initial orientation – in that its entire tenor is at once revelatory and experiential. In fact, Verboom characterizes the *Heidelberg Catechism* as *anthropological-experiential*, a highly spiritual document. And although the designation "covenant" does not appear in the entire document, he asserts that the entire teaching of the *Heidelberg Catechism* is anchored in covenant thought. He points out that the *Major Catechism* (1562) of Ursinus is introduced with the theme of covenant; the *Minor* (1562), on the other hand, begins with the question of the comfort of the Christian. And because of the well-known covenantal emphasis of Olevianus and his contribution in the drafting of the *Heidelberg Catechism*, this entire experiential and pastoral teaching of the *Heidelberg Catechism* must be seen as covenantal in character.[5]

---

icant contribution of Caspar Olevianus, see Bierma's argument in "Olevianus by Bierma," *Firm Foundation*, xv-xxviii.

[3] Verboom, *Heidelbergse Catechismus*, 17-22. Verboom briefly chronicles, first the ascending, and then descending use of the *Heidelberg Catechism* in the churches in the Netherlands (currently, Nederlandse Hervormde Kerk) as prescribed by respective Church Orders (Books of Church Order or Constitutions).

[4] Verboom, *Heidelbergse Catechismus*, 19.

[5] This is pointed out by Verboom on page 19, and also in "Olevianus by Bierma," *Firm Foundation*, xv-xxxi. Both scholars, Bierma in considerable detail, demonstrate the striking stylistic and linguistic parallels between Olevianus' *Firm Foundation* and the *Heidelberg Catechism*. The co-authorship of Ursinus and Olevianus had already been

Thus, "covenant and experience, the objective with the subjective, move wonderfully together in the HC. This is the unique, the peculiar, also the surprising and the captivating [nature] of the HC."[6]

The theme of comfort that pervades the *Heidelberg Catechism* from its very opening had its origins, claims Verboom, with the emphasis of the irenic Melanchthon, Ursinus' instructor. The law convicts, the gospel comforts. Luther and Olevianus, as well, place emphasis upon "comfort." It is pointed out that this theme of comfort must be understood internally and externally. In the case of the former, it is only through Jesus Christ that spiritual strength is found, strength to provide comfort for the Christian in his or her ongoing striving with Satan. In the case of the latter, to own Christ in this world is to suffer persecution. Any fear or threat of physical danger obtains mollification with the assurance of a covenant God's unswerving guardianship over even the hairs on one's head. Comfort is received in the midst of not only spiritual, but also physical, exigencies.[7]

This motive of comfort is explicated in the *Heidelberg Catechism* in a format of instruction commonly referred to as the "triple knowledge": misery, deliverance and thankfulness. Although it is generally acknowledged that this particular format has its origins in the ordering of Paul's letter to the Romans, in drawing our attention to the *Locus* of Melanchthon (as well as some earlier Lutheran catechisms) Verboom sees this Reformer as an early source of inspiration for the unique emphases as these are captured in the instructional framework of the *Heidelberg Catechism*. Verboom further notes that each part of this three-fold knowledge is closely tied with the three chief aspects of the Christian life: faith, law and prayer.[8] It is immediately apparent that in the *Heidelberg*

---

proposed by the earliest scholars and historians of the *Heidelberg Catechism* (Verboom, *Heidelbergse Catechismus*, 15-16 and "Olevianus by Bierma," *Firm Foundation*, xv-xvii). See also L.D. Bierma, "The Covenant Theology of Caspar Olevian" (Ph.D. diss., Duke University, 1980). For catechetical and covenantal emphases of Olevianus, including the work Bierma draws on, see the following: *An Exposition of the Symbole of the Apostles, or rather of the Articles of Faith. In which the chief points of the everlasting and free covenant between God and the faithful is briefly and plainly handled*, trans. J. Field (London: H. Middleton, 1581); *De substantia foederis gratuiti inter Deum et electos, itemque de mediis, quibus ea ipsa substantia nobis communicavit* (Genevae: apud Eustathius Vignon, 1585); and *Geschriften van Caspar Olevianus. Verklaring van: "De apostolische Geloofsbelijdenis," "Het wezen van het Genadeverbond," "De getuigenissen van het Genadeverbond"* (Den Haag: Het Reformatorische Boek, 1963).
[6] Verboom, *Heidelbergse Catechismus*, 19, drawing comparisons with R. Bohren's *In der Tiefe der Zisterne* (Munich, 1990).
[7] Verboom, *Heidelbergse Catechismus*, 20.
[8] Verboom, *Heidelbergse Catechismus*, 21-22. Verboom helpfully demonstrates how the Law of God is employed twice in the instructional framework of the *Heidelberg Catechism*. It is through the knowledge of this Law that one comes to know one's misery (Q&A 3 and 4). It is through the knowledge of the Law that one comes to know how to live a life in thankfulness to God for his redemptive work in Christ (Q&A 92 through

Catechism, this format of instruction of the threefold-knowledge around the theme of comfort has become architectonic.

Verboom's luminous introduction points to the existential nature of the *Heidelberg Catechism*. The experiential faith taught by the *Catechism* and introduced by Q&A 2 is a knowledge of the head and the heart. This gives it a practical function, distances it from an arid intellectualism, and harks back to the Hebrew concept of knowledge as found in the Torah – knowledge pertaining to life experience. Faith encompasses the whole of one's being – one's intellect, volition and affections. It is emotional and full of personal feeling and experience, representing the heights and depths of the life of faith. Verboom argues that this emotional theme is borrowed from Psalms. The emotions exhibited in the *Catechism* have, as end, love and service for God and neighbor.[9] In this connection, H. Hoeksema emphasizes the *Catechism's* highly spiritual tone and character.[10] Against the charge that the *Heidelberg Catechism* is anthropocentric in its subjectivity and in its emphasis upon the creature's perspective, Hoeksema argues that it speaks of the appropriation of a theocentric truth by the believer:

> The Heidelberg Catechism considers the truth which, of course, is always theocentric, from the viewpoint of its being appropriated and experienced by the believing Christian in this world, and, more particularly, from the point of view that it is his comfort, his sole comfort in life and death.[11]

A reminder of the theological character of the *Heidelberg Catechism* concludes the introduction. It binds and unifies the thought of the earlier Reformers: Melanchthon's emphasis on the Law looms large in this teaching document; Bullinger's stress on Covenant is evident throughout the highly personal interaction between the creature and the Creator; and, Calvin's awe for the Creator and his relationship with his creation permeates every theme. It is interesting, Verboom notes, that Ursinus was a student of all three. In this sense the *Heidelberg Catechism* is "authentically Reformed" and not the statement of faith of a "generalized evangelical confession" as K. Barth has claimed.[12] Finally, the *Catechism* is an irenic document and its tender spirit belies the bitter and tempestuous the-

---

115). Verboom very helpfully points out that in the former, Jesus' own words are used to point one to one's misery. This demonstrates, so Verboom, that the Law, at its very depth, is grounded in the love of God. In the latter, the broad exposition of the decalogue emphasizes the positive nature of the Law as a rule for both faith and practice in that all the questions but two are posed in the form of prescriptions (teaching, amplification, permissive actions, requirements) and not proscriptions (*Heidelbergse Catechismus*, 22, 278-79).

[9] Verboom, *Heidelbergse Catechismus*, 22-24.
[10] Hoeksema, *Triple Knowledge*, 1.14.
[11] Hoeksema, *Triple Knowledge*, 1.22.
[12] Verboom, *Heidelbergse Catechismus*, 24.

ological, political and ecclesiastical climate of the Dutch Republic in which it was born.

This early Reformed teaching apparatus, observes Verboom, stood at the close of an age in theological development, because shortly after its appearance, an arid scholasticism would make its appearance, a mood starkly contrast with the warm, personal and experiential character of the *Catechism*.[13] Hoeksema summarizes well this continental Reformed confessional document that William Ames took in hand:

> The Heidelberg Catechism is a veritable treasure of that triple knowledge of which it speaks in the second question and answer, and which is indispensable for the possession of the true comfort in life and death. It is the most widely known and generally used of all the Reformed symbols. It is rich in content, beautifully simple in form, highly spiritual in tone and content. . . . [It] is one of the most beautiful and masterful compositions of all times. And our Reformed fathers gave evidence of their sound practical judgment when they ordained that one of the sermons on each Sabbath should be based on one of the Lord's Days of this precious little book.[14]

William Ames' Commentary on the Heidelberg Catechism: Methodological Considerations

In 1635 William Ames' catechetical teaching entitled *Christianæ Catecheseos Sciagraphia* came off the press. This posthumously published work was released in English in 1659 and entitled *The Substance of Christian Religion: Or, a plaine and easie Draught of the Christian Catechisme in LII Lectures, on Chosen Texts of Scripture, for each Lords-day of the Year, Learnedly and Perspicuously Illustrated with Doctrines, Reasons and Uses*.[15] This lengthy title underscores both close similarities and differences in method, in emphasis and in content with the model from Heidelberg upon which his exposition is based.

According to the author introducing the work, Ames ". . . takes up an especially appropriate text from the word of God, breaks it apart and explains it succinctly, draws out lessons containing the catechetical doctrine, and finally

---

[13] Verboom, *Heidelbergse Catechismus*, 15-25.

[14] Hoeksema, *Triple Knowledge*, 1.15.

[15] Guilielmus Amesius, *Christianæ Catecheseos Sciagraphia* (Franekeræ: Bernardum A. Berentsma, 1635). The 1635 posthumous publication was most likely the work of Hugh Peter, Ames' friend in Rotterdam. The first English language version came from London as *The Substance of Christian Religion: Or, a plaine and easie Draught of the Christian Catechisme, in LII Lectures, on Chosen Texts of Scripture, for each Lords-day of the Year, Learnedly and Perspicuously Illustrated with Doctrines, Reasons and Uses* (London: T. Mabb for Thomas Davies, 1659; Ann Arbor, MI: University Microfilms); hereafter, *Catechisme* (Mabb ed.) A much more readable version is found in *A Sketch of the Christian's Catechism: William Ames (1576-1633)*, T.M. Rester, trans., J.R. Beeke, ed. (Grand Rapids, Reformation Heritage, 2008). I am largely making use of this text; occasionally I cite the 1659 Mabb ed.

applies them to their use."[16] With Ursinus, Ames judged the teaching of the "Substance of Christian Religion" to be presented most effectively in Sunday preaching over the course of the year. Ames topical choice is also borrowed from his Reformed predecessors – there is one-to-one topical correspondence between each of Ames' fifty-two Lord's Days and those of the *Heidelberg Catechism*.

It is in method that the differences are most notable. First is the absence of the unifying topical structure which gives the *Heidelberg Catechism* its characteristic designation as a manual of instruction for teaching the "three-fold" or "triple" knowledge. Ames certainly teaches of misery, deliverance, and thankfulness, but he ignores the way in which this thematic connection is brought forward in the *Heidelberg Catechism* through its employment of this triple-headed motif. Second, the pedagogical sub-structure along which these two instruction manuals are organized can also be distinguished. Following true scholastic form, Ursinus' *Heidelberg Catechism* moves systematically forward in *quaestio* format.[17] By contrast, Ames' *Catechisme* is in lecture form, "designed," after all, "for the use of his students . . . dictated . . . at their request."[18] Ames self-consciously distances himself from the *quaestio* method employed in Ursinus' own commentary as well. This *Commentary* commences with the opening question and answer and provides very detailed exposition occasionally leading to further questions which often take on a polemical nature. Ursinus' entire work attests to his mastery of the Reformed doctrines of the day.

Ames is more exegetical in his approach, introducing each Lord's Day topic with a brief exposition of a leading scriptural passage taken from the *Heidelberg Catechism's* own proof-texting apparatus.[19] This leads to a theological explanation in the form of "Doctrines" or "Lessons," each of which is applied very practically. These uses vary. They could be informational, instructional, or directional. Some uses lend themselves more readily to the preacher for "exhortation," even "admonition" and "reproof." Others invite polemic use to refute and thus reform the enemies of the orthodox Reformed faith, chiefly the "Arminians" and "Papists." Warnings of "condemnation" follow stern rebuke.

---

[16] Ames, "To the kind and fair reader," *Catechisme*, 3; in citing this work, I use the designation *Catechisme* to eliminate confusion with the more conventional reference to the *Heidelberg Catechism*.

[17] From this point forward I refer to Ursinus rather than Ursinus and Olevianus because I will be referring to Ursinus' own commentary. I am using a number of versions for this comparison, but the chief one is *The Commentary of Dr. Zacharias Ursinus on the Heidelberg Catechism*, G.W. Williard, trans. (Columbus: Scott and Bascom, 1852; reprint ed., Phillipsburg, NJ: Presbyterian and Reformed, 1985); hereafter Ursinus, *Commentary*.

[18] Ames, "To the kind and fair reader," *Catechisme*, 3.

[19] Proof-texts were a later addition to the *Heidelberg Catechism*. Verboom notes that the first edition had marginally-noted scripture chapters only (*Heidelbergse Catechismus*, 17).

While the biblical teaching can serve to the "humiliation" of believers and non-believers, the encouraging theme of "comfort" and "consolation" makes frequent appearances. The reader is reminded of the pastoral dimension of Ames, first introduced in his ethical teaching and most characteristic of the soul doctors that graced ecclesiastical life in the early modern Dutch Republic. Occasionally, and true to the emphasis of this work as being a guide for ministers of the Gospel, Ames provides "special admonition to ministers of the Word." Randomly scattered throughout this prescribed format Ames raises sets of "objections" and "questions" on the more controversial topics such as the Reformed teaching of paedo-baptism (Lord's Day 27) and the use of the Law (Lord's Day 2). Finally, being much more laconic than Ursinus (except when it came to his teaching on the Sabbath), Ames combines some Lord's Days based on topical similarity.

Consider briefly his teaching on the topic of the Lord's Supper. The controversial nature of this article of faith caused it to be a highly controverted element in the theological and ecclesiological climate of the day and therefore presents itself as a good subject for examination of Reformed expositors at their most prolix. In the *Heidelberg Catechism*, this topic runs for three Lord's Days (28-30) and eight questions and answers (Q&A 75 through 82), comprising about ten per cent of Ursinus' entire catechetical commentary as compared to less than five per cent of Ames' *Catechisme*. Through Ursinus' long description of the doctrine of communion, he addresses questions regarding this sacrament's essence and design, its distinction from baptism, its verbatim meaning, its Roman Catholic counterpart the mass, its lawful and unlawful use, its institution and its recipients. The nature of the nine introductory questions as he has raised them, give him occasion to fully address the error of the celebration of the mass, of transubstantiation and of consubstantiation, as well as of the teaching of the Sacramentarians. He draws on arguments from, for example, the analogy of faith as expressed in Christ's human nature, parallel passages of scripture and church tradition, to advance the Reformed understanding of Jesus' words as he instituted this sacrament. He brings in the Church Fathers, quoting from Tertullian, Clement of Alexandria, Cyprian, Basil, Hilary, Gregory Nazianzus, Ambrose, Chrysostom, Theodoret and, most liberally, from Augustine. Ursinus' anti-papal corrective runs almost thirty pages, forty-five per cent of the total allotment for this particular topic covered in the three Lord's Days mentioned above. As much of his exposition on the Lord's Supper is devoted to refuting the errors of the papists as it is to "positive" instruction. In the last few pages he demonstrates the supercessionist nature of the Lord's Supper over the Jewish Passover.[20]

The penetrating and exhaustive nature of Ursinus' commentary is in marked contrast to the more "prudent" method of William Ames which presents itself as a more directly accessible teaching instrument for preachers asked to provide

---

[20] Ursinus, *Commentary*, 377-440.

practical guidance. We see the classic Puritan homiletical method at work: text, doctrine, and use. Ames' *Catechisme* is one of the earliest teaching documents in which this "Plain Style" pattern is clearly employed and illustrated, a style introduced by William Perkins.[21] The textual exposition often includes brief contextual highlights, the doctrinal lecture is expositional and apologetic in nature, and the applicatory emphasis is meant to ensure that preachers of God's Word exhort their congregations to be not only *hearers* but also *doers*. "The receiving of the word consists of two parts: attention of mind and intention of will."[22] Under Ames' guiding hand, the *Heidelberg Catechism* is transformed, enlarged as it were, from being primarily an exhaustive manual of instruction in the reformed faith to now serving as more of a manual for pulpit use. Preachers need to be concise and practical in their orientation, clearly enunciating the use to which each doctrine must be put.

Topical Examination of the Heidelberg Catechism, Ursinus' Commentary and Ames' Catechisme

On Comfort: Lord's Day 1

Ames' commentary on the opening theme of the *Heidelberg Catechism* is his longest chapter, comprising almost four percent of his entire *Catechisme* and contrasts with the brevity of Ursinus who devotes less than one percent of his *Commentary* to this topic. This fact alone invites close comparison.

---

[21] For the earliest and best illustration of this "plain style" model, see William Perkins, *The Art of Prophesying with The Calling of the Ministry*, with a Foreword by S.B. Ferguson (Edinburgh: Banner of Truth Trust, 1996). This combines the following two volumes: *The Art of Prophesying* (first published as *Prophetica, sive de sacra et unica ratione concionandi* [Cambridge, 1592] and translated into English as *The Arte of Prophecying, or, A Treatise concerning the sacred and onely true manner and methode of Preaching* [Cambridge, 1606]), and *The Calling of the Ministry*, 1605. Ferguson summarizes: "The form of the plain style was as follows: the preaching portion, be it text or passage, was explained in its context; the doctrine, or central teaching of the passage was expounded clearly and concisely; and then careful application to the hearers followed in further explanation of the 'uses'" (*The Art of Prophesying*, ix). In *The Art of Prophecying*, Perkins adheres very closely to the Ramist method of exposition and logic. In the introduction to his translation and commentary on William Ames' *Technometria*, Gibbs notes that Perkins' "one fully Ramistic work" was written when Perkins was a fellow at Christ's College, Cambridge, a position he held for 11 years. Gibbs observes that Perkins "is probably the first Englishman to have written on preaching within the framework of Ramist philosophy" (*Technometry*, 27). See also J.A. Pipa, Jr., "William Perkins and the Development of Puritan Preaching," (Ph.D. diss., Westminster Theological Seminary, 1985).

[22] Ames, *Marrow*, 2.8.7. L.M. Gordis provides a highly readable and luminous study on the Puritan use of scripture and style of preaching in *Opening Scripture: Bible Reading and Interpretive Authority in Puritan New England* (Chicago: University of Chicago, 2003).

By way of quick review, Q&A 1 teaches, in pastoral tone, that one's only comfort in life and death resides in Christ and his redeeming, preserving grace. The answer is highly personal, warmly engaging the catechumen with the comfort found in partaking of the spiritual felicity granted by the saviorhood of Christ. The emphasis is overwhelmingly spiritual, that comfort obtained from ownership of Christ. Although the comfort in view is meant to refer to this-worldly concerns as well, the stress is clearly on spiritual deliverance and the assurance of future hope that Jesus Christ yields.

Ursinus begins by noting that comfort "results from a certain process of reasoning, in which we oppose something good to something evil, that by a proper consideration of this good, we may mitigate our grief, and patiently endure the evil."[23] Only the "highest good" is sufficient to oppose the evil spoken of, the greatest of which is "sin and death." This highest good is represented by different entities in the variety of philosophical systems Ursinus enumerates as having currency during the sixteenth century. This good, however, is found in none of these systems. Rather, it is only in the "doctrine of the church" that such a good is found; it is only this doctrine that "imparts a comfort that quiets and satisfies the conscience;" this teaching alone reveals human misery and deliverance through Christ:

> This, therefore, is that christian comfort, spoken of in this question of the catechism, which is an only and solid comfort, both in life and death – a comfort consisting in the assurance of the free remission of sin, and of reconciliation with God, by and on account of Christ, and a certain expectation of eternal life, impressed upon the heart by the holy Spirit through the gospel, so that we have no doubt but that we are the property of Christ, and are beloved of God for his sake, and saved forever, according to the declaration of the Apostle Paul: "Who shall separate us from the love of Christ? Shall tribulation, or distress," &c. (Rom. 8. 35.)[24]

The nature of this comfort is for reconciliation with God through Christ's blood, for deliverance from the miseries of sin and death, for preservation of this reconciliation, deliverance, and all other benefits Christ purchased for us, for the turning of our evil into good, and, finally, for "our full persuasion and assurance of all these great benefits, and of eternal life." In fact, the only place where the comfort of which Ursinus speaks might be interpreted to apply directly, in a more practical way, to this present life, is in his paragraph on the necessity of this comfort which is twofold: "on account of our salvation" and "on account of praising and glorifying God." For, after all, "the substance of our comfort, therefore, is briefly this: – That we are Christ's, and through him

---

[23] Ursinus, *Commentary*, 17-18.
[24] Ursinus, *Commentary*, 18.

reconciled to the Father, that we may be beloved of him and saved, the Holy Ghost and eternal life being given unto us."[25]

Only this comfort is "solid" because it is unfailing and unshaken. The Christian is empowered to withstand the various assails of Satan by pointing to Christ's satisfaction, reconciliation, redemption, preservation, perseverance on the "long and difficult" spiritual pilgrimage, and assurance of the Holy Spirit's reassuring presence in times of doubting faith and weakness. He summarizes: "In this most severe and dangerous conflict, which all the children of God experience, christian consolation remains immoveable, and at length concludes: therefore Christ, with all his benefits, pertains even to me."[26]

In answer to Q&A 2 (also Lord's Day 1) Ursinus teaches that a knowledge of one's misery is necessary to awaken a desire for deliverance (as sickness awakens a desire for medicine), to motivate to thankfulness, and to enable profitable hearing of the law and gospel. Knowledge of the deliverance through Jesus Christ saves from despair, awakens desire, provides comfort, prevents human substitutes in place of Christ's redemption, enables faith, (for "faith cannot be without knowledge") and engenders gratitude.[27]

Finally, a knowledge of gratitude is necessary to one's comfort because firstly, God will "grant deliverance only to the thankful." Secondly, gratitude acceptable to God must be properly exercised according to the rule of his word. Thirdly, in gratitude we acknowledge the non-meritorious nature of our service to God and neighbor, while, finally, expressions of gratitude work to increase our faith and comfort.[28]

A study of the remainder of the catechism will reveal an unfolding of this almost exclusively soteriological dimension. The spiritual overtones of the primary theme upon which the entire catechism is constructed call to mind Verboom's judgment that the *Heidelberg Catechism* is soteriological, theological and existential, and that, as demonstrated in the pervasive theme of the appropriation of knowledge that yields comfort, it is a document that challenges both the head and the heart.

Practical theologian William Ames commences with Psalm 4 as opening text: "The aim of this Psalm is to teach us, by the example of David, how we ought to conduct ourselves when we are whirled into great dangers." Theology is the teaching of living to God. Ames, the logician, is quick to employ Peter Ramus' system at the first opportunity. Through a system of dichotomies Ames asserts that, in this psalm, David accomplishes two things: he prays for deliverance from imminent danger and he shows the encouragement offered his soul through this prayer. David demonstrates that his highest good (*summum bonum*, nomenclature also used by Ursinus) is found in divine favor. This felicity

---

[25] Ursinus, *Commentary*, 19-20.
[26] Ursinus, *Commentary*, 20.
[27] Ursinus, *Commentary*, 21-22.
[28] Ursinus, *Commentary*, 22.

brings a joy far surpassing that of any earthly goods as recipients of such favor are delivered from fear and given to bask in security and safety. And "'good' is understood as all that appears delightful, useful, pleasing, or any other thing that seems desirable." Because David's consolation in affliction and life was this *summum bonum*, so must it be for us.[29] Ames continues:

> Moreover, "highest good" is specifically understood as that in which our blessedness consists. In this blessedness is contained the confluence of all desirable goods. Moreover, the highest good is called a "consolation," just as it is in the Catechism, since it is like a uniting (consolidation) of the soul and a confirmation against griefs, sorrows, or opposing terrors. A proper consolation is a mitigation of griefs, sorrows, and fears.[30]

Ames methodically elaborates on this chief good. He explains its teleological nature, the careless risk and cost of ignoring it in favor of this life's "trifles," its governance over, and proper grounding of, all our actions, and its inherent dignity and excellence. Finally, this doctrine should reprove and refute the irrational and unchristian disregard of those who ignore such chief good at their own peril.[31]

From verse 6 of the psalm Ames draws his second doctrinal lesson, that man's felicity is not found in the here and now, in material wealth, sensual delight, or reputation. Since such worldly goods are but ephemeral, often bring sin and misery with them, and are held in common with the beast, incapable of the "capacity for blessedness," the soul and spirit are not perfected by this type of good. In fact, disregard for such worldy wealth is a virtue, a mark of spiritual maturity. This teaching is to be used for reproof towards those involved in pursuit of blessedness through such external possessions.[32]

Ames finally comes to the heart of the psalm's teaching: "Our true and highest good consists in the union and communion we have with God."[33] This is "deduced" from verse 6b: "Lift up upon us the light of Your face, O Jehovah." "God Himself," asserts Ames, "is the true and highest good," both practically and objectively because God is the instrument of that blessing, both in its communication and as its appropriation. In this scripture, God self-identifes as the God of the covenant; thus, this communion is true to the covenant axiom: "I will be your God; I will be your ample reward."[34] He explains:

> [O]ur communion with God is our formal blessedness and is commonly called the *vision of God* and the *beatific vision*. Now to "see God," in the phrasing of Scripture,

---

[29] William Ames, *Catechisme*, 5-6.
[30] Ames, *Catechisme*, 6. Again, notice the remarkable similarity in language between Ames and Ursinus at this point; cf. Ursinus, *Commentary*, 17-18.
[31] Ames, *Catechisme*, 6-7.
[32] Ames, *Catechisme*, 7.
[33] Ames, *Catechisme*, 8.
[34] Ames, *Catechisme*, 8.

does not signify either the sight of the eyes of the mere speculation of the intellect, but every sort of enjoyment of God, inasmuch as it causes our blessedness. Moreover, we arrive at this enjoyment or communion through Jesus Christ our Lord, and it is precisely this consolation that the Catechism appropriately says is caused by Christ. Everything we receive that pertains to our blessedness refers back to Christ.[35]

Fully half-way through this, his longest Lord's Day, Ames finally explains (if ever so briefly) that this chief good, this consolation, is attained through Jesus Christ. But then, Ames, the philosopher, is again quick to leave Christ and move directly to the reasons for having God as chief good, supplemented by texts from the Old Testament (Psalms and Isaiah). These reasons focus on the peace that communion with God yields; that God is the first and efficient cause of all things, as well as the end, and therefore in him alone can be found the goal and perfection of life; God alone is independent and therefore trust in him is certain; he represents the only infinite good since only he can be imparted to all; and only God is free of any hint of imperfection. There is no further elaboration on Jesus Christ as chief good. And the value of this teaching lies in its motivating power to seek God as chief good, and its encouraging tone in reinforcing the blessedness of those in Christ despite life's setbacks"[36]

The doctrinal teaching of Lesson 4 expands on the all-surpassing "sweetness" of communion with God, the highest good, contrasting it with the fleeting, false and counterfeit joys of the world, joys often overcome by affliction and "suffocating vexations of conscience." True spiritual joy and its consoling power overcomes the whole person – body, soul, and spirit – and is eternal; armed with Acts 5:41 and James 1:2 Ames asserts that, as counter-intuitive as it may seem, worldly affliction often gives cause for rejoicing. The reader is thus warned against the deceptive power of the material delights of the world and the duplicity of the ungodly who promote such delight in their opposition to piety. The faithful are encouraged to "eagerly contend" for this joy, overcoming impediments through ongoing repentance and amendment of life. The spiritual discipline of uninterrupted fellowship with God is strongly encouraged as the thankful believer meditates on the gift of God's promises and blessings given in Christ Jesus.[37]

Ames' commentary on this Lord's Day closes on the strong note of assurance found in the final passage of the psalm: "This joy and holy consolation convey a certain security to the consciences of the faithful." This assurance contrasts with worldly security because it is grounded in God's protecting presence and immutability, features obtained through the means of grace including God's Word – both read and preached – and prayer. Again, in contradistinction from the security of the world, based as it is on "vain imagination" and human

---

[35] Ames, *Catechisme*, 8.
[36] Ames, *Catechisme*, 8-9.
[37] Ames, *Catechisme*, 9-11.

traditions, only this authentic assurance will deliver from all anxieties and discouragement.[38]

The key similarities and differences between Ursinus and Ames on the *Heidelberg Catechism's* introductory chapter can be enumerated as follows:

1) Both emphasize intellectual apprehension of the Christian faith in attaining comfort. The existential dimension is somewhat attenuated.
2) In this rational process, the philosophical concept of *summum bonum* – the "chief good" or "highest good" is introduced by Ursinus to demonstrate the remedy for sin and to explain the failure of all competing philosophies as solutions, including the doctrine of the Church of Rome. Sin is overcome only through the *summum bonum* – reconciliation with God through Christ. William Ames more loosely follows Ursinus' reasoning at this point. He is certainly more loathe to let go of the designation "chief good" and his focus is primarily philosophical and practical. The concept regularly reappears throughout his *Catechisme*. Fully half way through his exposition of Psalm 4 Ames underscores the consoling function of Jesus Christ as the means to that chief good. Although no full scale Christology and soteriology is expected, Ames' teaching on Christ seems rather abbreviated. In fact, while Ursinus points directly to the saviorhood of Jesus, nowhere in Lord's Day 1 does Ames mention the saving, reconciling work of Jesus Christ. This has to wait until much later, Lord's Day 11.
3) Permeating Ames' doctrinal exposition is the surpassing nature of that "joy" and "happiness" located in the summum bonum."[39] There is a not-so-

---

[38] Ames, *Catechisme*, 11.

[39] This use of the English word "happy" in Lord's Day 1 requires investigation. The Latin version of Ursinus' *Commentary*, by Ursinus' friend and disciple David Pareus, uses the word "beate" in Q&A 2. (Davidis Parei Silesii, *Explicationum Catecheticarun D. Zachariae Ursini Silesii* [Neostadii Palatinorim: Excudebat Matthaeus Harnisch, 1593], 34). Ursinus' subsequent exposition, as we mention, nowhere uses the word "happy" to connote the felicity that comfort brings to those so comforted. Should the English translation of "beate" not have been more properly translated as "blessed"?
In a much earlier English translation, the word "beate" is translated "happy." (*The Summe of Christian Religion: Delivered by Zacharias Ursinus in his Lectures upon the Catechisme*, translated by D.H. Parry [Oxford: Joseph Barnes, 1601], 58]. According to the title page, this work was "translated into English first by D. Henrie Parry, and lately conferred with the last and best Latine Edition of D. David Pareus." Both Dutch language translations I am employing throughout this study translate "beate" as "geluk." This term more clearly encompasses the idea of "blessedness" that "beate" communicates. The biblical understanding of "beate" is best seen in Jesus' teaching on the Sermon on the Mount, the "beatitudes." Blessedness and spiritual felicity, I am sure, is Ursinus' meaning of the word here. Both of these Dutch editions are prepared by Festus Hommius and include other associated works (sermons, addresses, etc.) as well. The first is *Het Schat-Boeck Der Verklaringhen over de Catechismus der Christelicke Religie*, "translated from the Latin exposition of the Learned Zacharias Ursinus including others who wrote about this catechism, and translated and assembled by Festus Hommi-

subtle shift from an emphasis on "comfort" and "consolation," to one of "joy" and "happiness" obtained through Jesus Christ our Lord. While certainly having reference to spiritual issues, this-worldly concerns are predominant, if only to warn of their imperfect, ephemeral and sinful nature. Ursinus, on the other hand, never uses the word "happy" or "joy;" "comfort" is everywhere synonymous with "spiritual comfort" and is always to be taken soteriologically.[40] The soteriological and eschatological character of the *Heidelberg Catechism* receives less emphasis from Ames right from the opening theme.

4) Ames provides an argument from covenant very early in his work. Although only briefly and in passing, Ames teaches that it is by the formula of the covenant ("I will be your God . . . I will be your ample reward") that God asserts himself as both the efficient cause and objective reality of one's happiness. The covenant is the vehicle whereby God communicates himself to humanity. Indeed, the name "Jehovah" underscores this relational, covenantal character of God. Blessedness and comfort derive from the *hesed* with which Jehovah engages his chosen family. This is in sharp contrast to early covenant theologian Ursinus who waits until his teaching on Christ as mediator (Lord's Day 6) before he introduces his covenant teaching.[41] Psalm 4 serves as Ames' scriptural foundation for grounding comfort and consolation in covenant theology from the very outset.

5) Yet Psalm 4 warrants further mention. Although everything that Ames says could legitimately, with some imagination, be drawn from this passage, it is curious that even one of the many New Testament texts on the comfort of Christ is not employed. The *Heidelberg Catechism* illustrates a few of these in its prooftexting apparatus, texts which clearly point to the over-

---

us" (Amsteldam: Joannes van Ravesteyn, 1650). The title page of the other and much later edition is much the same as the earlier one but specifies the Latin work of David Pareus as the original source from which Hommius translated. This edition appeared in two volumes and is by Johannes Spiljardus, who clarified the translation and cleansed the existing version of "non-Germanic words" (*onduitsche woorden*), all, it is asserted, in comparison with the Latin translation. It received the approbation of the theological faculties of the University of Leyden and the University of Utrecht, the former on 9 December, 1656, and the latter on 7 February, 1657. Abrahamus Heydanus, Johannes Cocceius and Johannes Hoornbeek signed from Leyden while Gisbertus Voetius, Andreas Essenius and Matthias Nethenus signed for Utrecht. This edition has a very long introduction by Joan van den Honert of Leiden. It was published in Gorinchem, by Nicolaas Goetzee in 1736.

[40] Ursinus, *Commentary*, 18.
[41] Ursinus, *Commentary*, 96; Christ is mediator who reconciles opposing parties, says Ursinus, for this is the task of mediators and in their work, which consists of mediating an agreement, they bring reconciliation. So it is with Christ: "This reconciliation is called in the Scriptures a Covenant, which has particular reference to the Mediator . . . . Hence the doctrine of the Covenant which God made with man, is closely connected with the doctrine of the Mediator" (*Commentary*, 96).

whelming soteriological "comfort" of the Gospel. Although it could be argued that David, as a type for Christ, would somehow be aware of the fulfillment of Old Testament promise in the coming of the anti-type himself, (2 Samuel 7, for instance) it is highly unlikely that he would have known of a personal Savior. The question of the Holy Spirit does not even come up. This work of comfort, argues Ursinus, is a trinitarian task from the start. Perhaps this usage of Old Testament scripture as his point of departure has obligated Ames' exposition in a direction of muted Christology. This is a marked difference from the biblically more holistic sweep of the *Heidelberg Catechism*. Ames exhibited the typical Puritan adherence to the Old Testament, sometimes at the expense of the more illuminated teaching of the New as fulfillment of promise and prophecy. This would explain attenuated teaching on many themes, but, chiefly, on the fulfillment of the gospel promises in Jesus Christ. Comfort involves the entire Godhead, as Ursinus emphasized (Q&A 1).[42]

These differences in emphases between the *Heidelberg Catechism*/Ursinus' commentary and that of William Ames are not without consequence for the remainder of these respective teaching documents. The expositions of the *Heidelberg Catechism* and Ursinus have an unmistakable inner coherence, a three-dimensional structure through which the opening theme carries forward smoothly, almost seamlessly, as it weaves its way through the remaining 51 Lord's Days. Each of the following 128 questions enlarges upon the first. Each points back to this "comfort," understood primarily soteriologically. Although William Ames has borrowed each of his 52 "lecture" topics from the *Heidelberg Catechism*, and even though much of his exposition borrows from Ursinus, it will become clear that the comfort of which Ames' *Catechisme* speaks does not carry the inner coherence of the *Heidelberg Catechism*, and its elucidation of the notion of "comfort" from a more concrete, this-worldly perspective, sets the stage for a more practical approach to the subsequent exposition. At this point one might also pause to consider whether Ames' more didactic and practical transformation of the *Heidelberg Catechism* may have been carried forward into the *Westminster Standards*, notably the *Larger* and *Shorter Catechism*.

On Christ as Judge: Lord's Day 19
In both the *Heidelberg Catechism* and Ursinus' *Commentary*, this topic appears as an exposition of the phrase in the *Apostles' Creed* regarding Christ's role as judge. It is couched within the broader context of the knowledge of "Deliverance." For true, saving faith, argues Ursinus, one must have belief in the *Apostles' Creed*. First comes the Godhead. In this particular instance, Christology is in view and Christ's session and return comprise Q&A 50, 51 and 52 of Lord's

---

[42] Ursinus, *Commentary*, 18-22.

Day 19 (and Articles 6b and 7 of the *Apostles' Creed*). Ames essentially ignores addressing Christ's session in his commentary on Lord's Day 19, focusing only on the final judgment and Christ's role as judge (Q&A 52).

The comfort provided by this knowledge is that this Christ-the-judged becomes Christ-the-judge, meting out both God's mercy and justice. Ursinus' teaching on this phrase is extensive, covering all topics related to the future judgment; he discusses its timing and reality (because of "the decree of God" as "chief cause," but also to bring glory to himself), its essence, the judge's coming and action, the judgment's sentence, execution and objects, its deferment and its desire. Comfort is derived from the gracious nature of the judge "who is our brother, redeemer and defender."[43]

Noteworthy is the Objection posed regarding the scriptural teaching that all people will be judged according to their works. If this is true, it is asked rhetorically, will not all come under the judgment of the Law as opposed to the mercy of the Gospel? Echoing James, Ursinus answers that the works in view here are those arising from faith; the judgment will thus be, properly speaking, according to the effects of faith, i.e., "according to the gospel."

> [Christ the judge] will prove from the fruits of their faith, that it was a true faith which they possessed, and that they are the persons to whom eternal life is due according to the promise. He will, therefore, exhibit to the wicked the works of the righteous, and bring them forward as evidences for the purpose of convincing the ungodly that they have applied unto themselves the merits of Christ. God will also render to the faithful according to their works, that we may take comfort therefrom in this life, having the assurance that we shall be placed at his right hand.[44]

There is comfort to be found in Christ's role as judge from the grace demonstrated to the elect, a grace played out in the ultimate separation of the righteous and the wicked. With anticipation, therefore, the godly join Paul as they yearn to be delivered from the body of death when Christ delivers his church. Significantly, of the scriptural references in the *Heidelberg Catechism*, the two passages referenced from Matthew 25 focus on soteriology/eschatology: the righteous are sent to their eternal felicity (v. 34) and the unrighteous consigned to their eternal woe (v. 41). No mention is made of the significance, for the judgment, of Jesus' parables in the same chapter.[45]

Although he does mention that salvation was prepared from the beginning of the world, Ames points to the judgment as serving God's glory rather than the decree which Ursinus emphasized. In fact, Ames avoids using decretal language altogether and explains that part and parcel of the glory of God is the joy of the faithful and just condition of the unfaithful. Moreover, Ames' and Ursinus' Christological angles on the judgment also differ. While Ursinus sees

---

[43] Ursinus, *Commentary*, 260, 269.
[44] Ursinus, *Commentary*, 264.
[45] Ursinus, *Commentary*, 269-70.

Christ's role as judge in closer association with his mediatorship or his priestly function, Ames understands it more as Christ's kingly role: judgment "belongs to his Kingly office and power, whereby he was made Lord and King and had all judgement committed to him."[46] Christ's priestly function in the judgment is not so much a chief doctrine as it is a source of consolation for the faithful.[47]

Ames' choice of Matthew 25 agrees with that of the *Heidelberg Catechism*. It is clearly a central place in scripture where Jesus teaches the absolute necessity of good works. In his exposition of this text, and prior to the doctrinal lessons arising from it, Ames systematically reasons, again through a long chain of dichotomies, from the occasion of Christ's return to the necessity of good works. Christ's sentence will be twofold: salvation and condemnation. The cause of the former is the benevolence of God to which good works is an "adjunct," an *adjoined* sign. Further, "by synecdoche of the specific for the general, [these works] are designated by works of mercy and are amplified by the relation that these works have to Christ personally while they are being exercised towards His members."[48]

Ames does not choose those passages in Matthew that speak only of the soteriological dimension of Christ's judgment while Ursinus' more existential emphasis obligates this selectivity. Ames wants to take a holistic view of this opening chapter to set the proper pace for what comes after. Following both the *Heidelberg Catechism* (Q & A 52) and Ursinus' *Commentary*, he draws attention to the gospel's teaching regarding the judgment's certainty, the imcomparability of the glory of the presider, and the finality of the ultimate separation, all lessons for encouraging information (2 Peter 3: 3, 4), for admonition and for consolation.[49] Salvation is due to God's mercy since all good resides in the *summum bonum*, while destruction is due to rebellious "neglect and contempt" for God's gratuitous blessing. God's glory is thus enlarged; unbelievers have no one but themselves to blame. Respectively, therefore, the pious and the impious magnify God's glory; the former in communion with him; the latter in separation.[50]

Now Ames is ready to press home some of his own emphases. A significant part of Ames' entire exposition of this Lord's Day comes up in the reasons offered for the next and final doctrinal lesson drawn from this passage in Matthew. We saw that Ursinus' only mention of good works was in response to an objection posed by those who argued that if all are judged according to works, the Law must apply convictingly because all are lawbreakers. We saw as well that this key chapter in Matthew was used quite selectively in the scriptural apparatus accompanying the *Heidelberg Catechism*. Indeed, in Ursinus' *Com-*

---

[46] Ames, *Catechisme*, 97-99.
[47] Ames, *Catechisme*, 99.
[48] Ames, *Catechisme*, 97-98.
[49] Ames, *Catechisme*, 98-100.
[50] Ames, *Catechisme*, 101.

mentary, the soteriological tone of these verses is completely dominant and represents the force of Ursinus' teaching. But Ames, our practical theologian, always concerned that orthopraxy match orthodoxy, takes a closer look at Jesus' teaching in this passage. He avers that the blessings of the chief good are, themselves, evidenced by good works: "The signs and certain verdicts (*judicia*) of this blessing are good works, and the signs and certain verdicts of this cursing are evil works."[51] Rationalizing, Ames continues:

> The good works of the pious come from the same grace of God by which the blessing [of his communion] is conveyed to them. In contrast, evil works conjoined to defiance proceed from the same malice that God has cursed and [against which He] adjudges a perpetual curse.
> God out of grace has promised a blessing on good works and out of justice has adduced a curse on evil works.
> In good works there is a certain disposition and preparation of the way for the blessing that will follow [in the future]. On the other hand, in evil works not only is there a certain disposition and preparation of the way [for the curse that will follow], but the curse is in proportion to the merit.[52]

We are admonished, by this lesson, towards a "meticulous reckoning" of the actions in our lives. *Qualis est vita, finis ita*. "Such as the life is, such is the end."[53]

Ames' argument for good works is carefully constructed. Taken out of context, many statements could lead to charges of voluntarism or "Amesian Arminianism." But the message of the epistle of James looms large and reinforces the sage's teaching that God is to be feared, and his commandments to be kept, for "this is the whole duty of man." He closes with a dire warning: "For God shall bring every work into judgment, with every secret thing, whether it be good, or whether it be evil." Indeed, such as the life is, such is the end.[54]

If Ames' explanation of this Lord's Day demonstrates an attenuated soteriology to those accustomed to thinking more theologically, it does so because the inspired sage and apostle did so first. Easier to detect in some instances than others, the soteriological message so pronounced in the *Heidelberg Catechism* hovers more in the background. Ames' wrote his manual of instruction with

---

[51] Ames, *Catechisme*, 102.
[52] Ames, *Catechisme*, 102.
[53] Ames, *Catechisme*, Mabb ed., 137; (literally: "As the quality of the life is, so is its end" [*Catechisme*], 102.)
[54] Caspar Olevianus' sentiment is much the same when he says that this Article in the *Creed* serves to admonish us of four things: to live temperate lives, to diligently pray (for escape from the punishments of the Last Judgment), to expectantly await his return, and to separate oneself from the "idolatry of the Roman Anti-Christ" ("Olevianus by Bierma," *Firm Foundation*, 87-88).

Ursinus close by but with greater attention to practical use for the person in the pew.[55]

On the Holy Spirit: Lord's Day 20
Continuing his exposition of the *Apostles' Creed*, Ursinus now comes to that place in the Godhead that speaks of the Holy Spirit. He expands on the singularly soteriological and trinitarian aspect given briefly in the *Heidelberg Catechism* to explain, in considerably more detail, the Spirit's person, office and gifts.

Ursinus dwells on the essence, the personhood and the procession of the Holy Spirit. The Spirit is consubstantial with the Father and Son, yet both distinct and equal. He enlightens, regenerates, unites in Christ, rules his children by directing their actions to the service of God and neighbor as articulated in the decalogue. The Spirit has a comforting and strengthening presence for the endangered and the weak in faith. He provides gifts at his discretion, both common (to all people) and charismatic (to the early church only). The Spirit is received by faith, and, although he is given invisibly to the church through word and sacrament, he has been known to have been given visibly (e.g., at Jesus' baptism), "at particular times, and for certain causes." The presence of the Holy Spirit is secured through diligent religious exercises (preaching, sacraments, gospel meditation, prayer, faithful exercise of gifts, penitence and avoidance of sins that "offend" the conscience). While the truly regenerate never lose the Spirit's gifts, "hypocrites and reprobate sinners" do since they were never truly numbered with the elect. The Holy Spirit is necessary for our salvation, understood broadly to include regeneration, thinking and doing good, knowing and obeying God and inheriting the kingdom of heaven. Finally, one may authentically know of the Holy Spirit's indwelling through faith and repentance.[56] The exposition of Ursinus is littered with biblical texts attesting to the doctrinal points he makes.

The much briefer exposition of William Ames covers much the same territory and borrows heavily from the *Heidelberg Catechism* and from Ursinus' *Commentary*. The nature and being of the Holy Spirit within the trinity is explored freely given to the faithful. But Ames' deliberately more practical angle is demonstrated by the scriptural text employed. Ames' emphasis is purity of body: In 1 Corinthians 6:19 Paul asks: Are you ignorant, brethren, that your body is the temple of the Holy Spirit, who is in you, whom you have from God, or that you do not have a right to yourself?" Although this text appears in the

---

[55] Notice the place of "good works" in Ames' *Marrow*. Recall that theology is the doctrine of living to God. Such life is conducted through faith and observance. Observance is comprised of virtue and good works. The latter, good works, are "known in" religion (worship) and "justice and charity toward our neighbor" (*Marrow*, 72-73, 77, 79, 219). In *Marrow*, this section introduces Ames' exposition of the second table of the law, commandments five through ten (*Marrow*, 300-7, 308-31).
[56] Ursinus, *Commentary*, 270-85.

Heidelberg Catechism and in Ursinus' explanation as well, it is only one among many texts brought to bear from both testaments, and is a minor force in the highly soteriological context in which this teaching of the Holy Spirit is cast. Ames' pneumatology focuses on purity of the body:

> These words contain the most efficacious argument against whoring and similar sins. It is sought from the opposite end, because, of course, the purpose of Christian bodies is plainly opposed to this sin. This purpose is declared by the possessor and inhabiter of the subject: the Holy Spirit. The subject is explained through the metaphor of a temple, because certainly our bodies are like houses consecrated for Him. Indeed, in order to render this argument more evident and effective, the apostle adds: The Holy Spirit is the one who has made it subject, as it is also adjoined that He possesses our bodies so that He may have them for his own dwelling place. Further on he illustrates in both respects the relation we have to the Holy Spirit: by His efficient cause, because we have Him from God, and from the consequent effect and its adjunct – that is, by faith and by certain knowledge of the relation that exists between the Holy Spirit and our bodies, which is illustrated by the words "Are you ignorant, brethren . . . ?"[57]

Key to Ames' conception of purity of life is the centrality of the physical body which is both the possession and habitation of the Holy Spirit. Ames pneumatology is essentially cast in terms of moral theology. Yet the theological lessons Ames draws from this text – certainly the first two – curiously bear an uncanny resemblance to Ursinus' exposition, one grounded in more traditional and directly soteriological biblical teaching on the Holy Spirit.[58] Ames anchors both these lessons in the doctrine that one's body, in its capacity as the Spirit's temple, is consecrated to God and thus sacred. The application of this text is to give proper Trinitarian direction to faith and to refrain from grieving or quenching the Holy Spirit.[59] That Ames derives these doctrines from his opening text is rather amazing; he clearly prefers Ursinus' commentary with its theological emphasis based on scriptures with explicit soteriological overtones.

It is with Ames' third doctrinal lesson that the reason for his scriptural choice becomes more obvious – again, of course, the importance of maintaining purity of body since the Holy Spirit resides in the complete person, soul and body. Ames is now ready to pay attention to the overwhelmingly practical, this-worldly dimension of Paul's teaching anchored firmly in the opening biblical text from 1 Corinthians 6. Believers must purge sin from their bodies which must be employed to God's glory. Elaborating, Ames explains the contradictory nature of having both sin and the Holy Spirit reside in the temple of God. Application of this teaching is, as would be expected, overwhelmingly adjuring: the believer is pointed specifically to Christ's behavior at the commerce enthusiastically transpiring in the temple. The implication is clear; cast your

---

[57] Ames, *Catechisme*, 103.
[58] Ursinus, *Commentary*, 271; Ames, *Catechisme*, 103-4.
[59] Ames, *Catechisme*, 104-5.

demons – lust, carnality, etc. – out of your body, the Holy Spirit's temple.[60] Recall Ursinus' comment that one of the Holy Spirit's offices was to rule the actions of men and women to ensure conformity to both tables of the decalogue.[61] Of the sixteen pages Ursinus devotes to explicating the doctrine of the Holy Spirit, this one line will have to suffice as to the practical, immediate use of this doctrine for the believer.

Note that Ursinus' brevity is at the same time much more comprehensive than Ames. Ursinus points to the whole Law; Ames only mentions fornication and physical impurity. This particular Pauline statement is obviously all about physical impurity and this clearly explains Ames' focus, but he is not at all prepared to leave the practical implications of pneumatology quite so skimpy with respect to proper care of the physical body, the Holy Spirit's temple. For Ames, it is the idea of the Holy Spirit's ownership over and residency within the physical body, which lies at the core of the doctrine of the Holy Spirit as he teaches it in *Catechisme*. The point is brought home in the fifth and last lesson on this Lord's Day, a final warning to self examination, and further encouragement to experiential knowledge of the Holy Spirit's indwelling and purity of life.[62]

Thus ends the pneumatological teaching of Ames' *Catechisme*. Using a curious scripture the whole meaning of which conjures up the idea of moral behavior, and liberally borrowing soteriological emphasis from Ursinus' teaching, Ames again manages, even in his doctrine of the Holy Spirit, to "direct" and "instruct" preachers-in-training to focus the attention of their listeners upon purity of life in morals. The pneumatology of Ames, as it appears here in his *Catechisme*, is a quintessential example of putting a scripture with a clearly overriding practical emphasis to theological, soteriological use. Whereas most theologians would generally have taken a theological teaching and pointed to its practical implications (as Ursinus does, for example), Ames reverses the order, and converts a primarily theological teaching to an exhortation in practical divinity. While not neglecting the soteriological dimension, the Amesian emphasis in pneumatology is the overcoming of sin's reign in the body, the Holy Spirit's temple.

On the Resurrection: Lord's Day 22
The teaching of the *Heidelberg Catechism* on this, the penultimate article of the *Apostles' Creed*, is entirely soteriological and eschatological. It gives no immediate practical instruction, whatsoever, regarding the value of this doctrine to the faithful living in the moment. It is entirely other-worldly. The believer's comfort rests in the fact that the physical body shall be reunited with the soul and glorified as Christ's.

---

[60] Ames, *Catechisme*, 105-6.
[61] Ursinus, *Commentary*, 278.
[62] Ames, *Catechisme*, 106.

William Ames begins on a much more practical note. In his exposition of this creedal point which he anchors in Philippians 3:20-21, Ames begins immediately with the temporal comfort and practical motivation to the sanctified life. It is about our conduct in the present. In the here and now, true followers emulate the apostles' heavenly focus over the earthly priorities of "false teachers." These heavenly aspirations arise from present faith and hope of future resurrected glory, a state of being that is assured by an omnipotent God.[63]

In contrast, Zacharias Ursinus opens his elaboration of this doctrine with a discussion on the immortality of the soul (established by various scriptures and presupposed by the doctrine of the resurrection of the body), the soul's location upon physical death (the wicked in hell, not purgatory as the papists insist, and the faithful in Abraham's bosom), and the meaning of the term "resurrection" in this article of the *Creed*.[64] Although scripture sometimes uses the term to speak of one's conversion, Ursinus explains that here is meant "the restitution of the substance of our bodies after death out of the very same matter of which they now consist, and the re-animating, or quickening of the same bodies with an incorruptible and immortal life by the same immortal soul, by which they now subsist."[65] He appeals to Augustine's emphasis on the distinction between the pre- and post-resurrection body. When the Apostle refers to a spiritual body, he has in mind a body ruled by the Holy Spirit, argues Ursinus.[66]

On the nature of the resurrected body, Ames is much more precise. "The bodies that rise again are the same [as the previous bodies] in their natural essence, but not in the mode of their disposition."[67] For it is only logical that those bodies involved in good or evil are the same as those receiving reward or punishment. After all, it is "so easy" for God to do this. A substantively different physical resurrected body, as taught by heretics, must be refuted.[68]

William Ames agrees with Ursinus that the certainty of the resurrection is assured by scriptural promises, but he requires two declarations to construct his

---

[63] Ames, *Catechisme*, 111.
[64] Ursinus, *Commentary*, 309-12.
[65] Ursinus, *Commentary*, 312.
[66] Ursinus, *Commentary*, 316.
[67] Ames, *Catechisme*, 112.
[68] Ames, *Catechisme* 112. In his work, Ames' contemporary and friend, Gisbertus Voet, joins Ames in echoing Ursinus. Still following Ames, he explains that the heavenly body described in 1 Cor 15 should be understood as different from the physical "not with respect to the essence or being of the body, but with respect to the quality and the disposition thereof, its mortality and ruinousness" (Voetius, *Catechisatie. Dat is Een grondige ende eenvoudige onderwijsinge over de Leere des Christelicken catechismi: Bestaende in Vragen en Antwoorden* compiled by Cornelius Poudroyen [N.p., 1653], 557). In addition to sharing Ames' concern for practical theology, Voet's capacity as physician to the soul is demonstrated in his responses to peripheral issues regarding the resurrection. For example, he explains that the body of the handicapped will be perfected in glory since the imperfection of physical handicaps is due to evil (*quaet*) and in glory there is no evil (Voetius, *Catechisatie*, 559).

dichotomy so he tacks on God's power (already mentioned) as a second "ground" for the resurrection.[69] In fact, Ames' entire exposition, from his first doctrinal statement to his last, focuses exclusively on the power of God in Christ and both the immediate and teleological purpose of the resurrection – the display of God's glory, but in a highly practical vein.[70] The resurrection's demonstration of God's glory through the mediatorial power of Christ is also the central theme in both Ursinus' *Commentary* and the *Heidelberg Catechism* itself, but the practical angle is absent from these documents.[71]

To elaborate on the certainty of the resurrection, Ames asserts that man was initially created to be an eternal being; this involves reunion of soul and body. Further, the commensurability of eternal rewards with temporal deeds is required by the "equity of the divine dispensation: that deeds done in the sinful body have a proportionate reward in the resurrected body, whether for good or evil.[72] Not only logical, but ever consistent, Ames held fast the axiom that a lived faith is demonstrated by a holy life; anything else would invoke the wrath of God. Ursinus, supported by scriptural passages and the teaching of Ambrose, makes precisely the same point when he says: "The justice of God demands that the bodies of the saints which have fought, should also be crowned; and that the wicked be punished in the same bodies in which they have blasphemed, and opposed God."[73]

The likeness of the resurrected body to that of Christ's glorified body should move to thankfulness and to eschewing of the world and should compel to faithfulness in spiritual exercises and to a lifestyle that commends our souls to Christ. There are temporal implications of the future physical resurrection: we must, "in some way lead a heavenly [life]" even as we anticipate future glory and all its blessedness, since where our *summum bonum* is, there will our heart and whole person be. This means heavenly discourse, self-denial and Christ-likeness. Our degree of conformity to such behavior should drive us to self-examination – whether we be a child of God or no (Perkins' "greatest case of conscience there ever was") – and further pursuit of holiness.[74]

For Ursinus, the purpose of the doctrine of the resurrection is to glorify God. A "subordinate" end is "the salvation and glory of the elect; and on the other hand, the punishment and rejection of the reprobate."[75] As exhaustive as Ursinus attempts to be, the reader can draw no practical use for the faithful who still inhabit the pre-resurrection body.

In his instructional manual employed to prepare preachers for the pulpit ministry Ames has ensured that listeners in the pew will be instructed in holiness of

---

[69] Ursinus, *Commentary*, 313-15; Ames, *Catechisme*, 112-13.
[70] Ames, *Catechisme*, 111-15.
[71] This theme of power is shared with Voet as well (Voetius, *Catechisatie*, 557).
[72] Ames, *Catechisme*, 112.
[73] Ursinus, *Commentary*, 315.
[74] Ames, *Catechisme*, 113-15.
[75] Ursinus, *Commentary*, 317-18.

life. He asserts that the future hope of the resurrection has an application by way of exhortation and admonition to godly living in the now. In so doing he has addressed both the "already" and "not yet" aspects of the believer's ultimate kingdom citizenship long before this theological principle became standard fare in Reformed thinking.

The most significant teaching arising out of the doctrine of the resurrection is, for both theologians, teleological. But whereas for Ursinus the purpose of the resurrection is God's glory, Ames' focus is more on the real, material implications: the active pursuit of a life consistent with God as chief good[76] and the overcoming of sin's reign in the body, the Holy Spirit's temple. For both Ursinus and Ames this doctrine demonstrates the power of God in Christ; but while for Ursinus this doctrine has a consoling use, Ames does not explicitly mention "comfort" or "consolation;" this central theme is, in fact, conspicuous by its absence. The primary purpose of this doctrine is an injunction to present holiness. Theology both generally but in its specifics as well, is living unto God.

We conclude this section by briefly connecting the doctrine of humanity's physical resurrection with Lord's Day 17. Here the *Heidelberg Catechism* speaks of the resurrection of Jesus Christ, Article 5 of the *Apostles' Creed*. Christ's resurrection serves as comfort to the faithful since it shows Christ's victory over death. In this manner, believers are both guaranteed their share in Christ's righteousness and assured of their own resurrection, which the power of Christ obtains for them and of which Christ's resurrection is a pledge. Ursinus' *Commentary* carries much the same emphasis, adding an affirmation of the resurrection's historicity from scripture while it serves a multi-faceted purpose that confirms Christ's merit, the Holy Spirit's inauguration, and the Church's preservation and final glorification.[77] The teaching is entirely soteriological, or, as Verboom would describe it, existential.

For Ames, any comfort derived from humanity's physical resurrection flows directly from Christ's. Ames sees this Lord's Day as a continuation of the previous one, where he explained the *death* of Christ. Both Lord's Days use, as text, John 10:17-18. Ames follows Ursinus in underscoring the consolation afforded by the resurrection of Christ. By his own power, Christ rose from the dead, vicariously victorious over "death, the devil, sin, hell, and all our enemies," most certainly an assuring deposit, as it were, of the believer's physical and spiritual resurrection.

Yet while the value of the doctrine of the resurrection of Christ is overwhelmingly existential and soteriological, Ames is right to find the practical

---

[76] Ames, *Catechisme*, 132-33.
[77] Ursinus, *Commentary*, 233-40. The purposes of Christ's resurrection are: for the sake of his own and his father's glory, fulfillment of prophecy, consistency with his dignity and power, assurance of his continued mediatorial work, and security of believers' salvation as seen in their justification, regeneration, resurrection and glorification.

angle. But his application is brief and somewhat novel: the believer is admonished, rather opaquely, to "spiritually imitate rising again from the dead."[78] Ames overlooks clear biblical passages that underscore the practical value of Jesus' resurrection. Ephesians 1:19-20 is one such passage, for example, and teaches that Christ's resurrection enables human victory over sin. Romans 6:4 is another: If Jesus is living, then the faithful are enabled to a life of genuine, if incomplete, holiness. The small successes believers have over sin in the present are only because of the resurrection's power which brings newness of life in the midst of death. Yet Ames opts for something less obvious, ignoring the clearly practical applications of these passages in favor of an admonition couched in the obscurity of "spiritual imitation."

On Doing Good Works: Lord's Day 24/32
Our final thematic examination of the *Catechisme* of William Ames addresses the place of good works in the Christian life. Within the *Heidelberg Catechism*, both the location of this theme and the theme itself are highly significant. This Lord's Day introduces the third and final section of the "triple knowledge," the subject of "Gratitude." Within this section are found expositions of the decalogue and the Lord's Prayer. The authors of the *Heidelberg Catechism* held to good works (as expressed in the moral code) and to prayer, as the chief instruments whereby the believer can render thankfulness to God for deliverance from the misery of sin and death through the mediatorial work of Jesus Christ. This gratitude is comprised of conformity to this law (Lord's Days 34-44) and religious exercises, specifically prayer (Lord's Days 45-52). We should note that the *Heidelberg Catechism* does not place this three-dimensional instruction on comfort, misery and deliverance in a vacuum. Rather, this deliverance is anchored in free sovereign grace. Lord's Day 24 makes that clear. In this soteriological scheme, therefore, what value, do good works have? This is the logical question with which this section opens.

The answer to the question (Q&A 86) is brief: good works are motivated out of thankfulness, are an expression of praise, serve to the believer's assurance (since good works are the fruit of faith), and serve as a witness to neighbor; believers perform good works "for the sake of *God, ourselves and our neighbor*."[79] In the context of the assuring nature of good works Ursinus brings forward the passage in James 2:17, and concludes that "it is by our good works, therefore, that we know that we possess true faith, because the effect is not without its proper cause, which is always known by its effect."[80] Be reminded again that in Q&A 87, the *Heidelberg Catechism* declares that good works have

---

[78] Ames, *Catechisme*, 88-91.
[79] Ursinus, *Commentary*, 483; Olevianus makes exactly these three points but only very briefly and without elaboration in Q&A 170 of "Olevianus by Bierma," *Firm Foundation*, 116-17.
[80] Ursinus, *Commentary*, 483.

no salvific value.[81] That is because they are a fruit of faith. Conversely, "all those who perform evil works, and continue in their wicked and ungrateful lives, cannot be saved, inasmuch as they are destitute of true faith, and conversion."[82]

Somewhat oddly Ames moves smoothly from Lord's Day 31 (the keys of the kingdom: gospel preaching and discipline) to Lord's Day 33 (the Law of God), appearing to altogether ignore Lord's Day 32. A trip to the publisher's Table of Contents reveals cryptic instructions to the reader: "XXXII, As in the 24, lecture"[83] concerning the value of good works. Practically speaking, the Preacher making weekly use of Ames' *Catechisme* to instruct the parishioners in the ways of practical divinity would speak for two Sundays in the year on Lord's Day 24. Ames has accomplished both his goals: economy of words and exhortation to godliness. So back we go to his exposition of the 24th Lord's Day for his comments on the nature and value of good works.

As expected, Ames' opening text is from the book of James. Chapter 2, verse 22, reads: "Do you see that faith was a helper of his works, and out of the works faith was led to its goal?" Yet there is something rather out of place about the use of this text in teaching the doctrine of the merit of good works in the context of justification, the context set by the *Heidelberg Catechism* (and, of course, Ursinus' *Commentary*). But Ames is anxious to teach the positive value of good works and cannot until Lord's Day 32, where it would be contextually better placed. The *Heidelberg Catechism* more properly waits for Lord's Day 32 to teach the positive value of good works (in the context of the definition of good works (Q&A 91), logically following the explanation of true conversion (Q&A 88-90) and introducing the exposition of the decalogue as the only rule of life. The authors, more concerned about proper context and the inner cohesion of the *Heidelberg Catechism*, understandably explain the overwhelmingly negative value of good works in Lord's Day 24. Much of his commentary is directed in polemic with the Church of Rome.[84]

It is in the context of his answer to one of the thirteen objections posed by the Roman Catholic Church to Q&A 64 ("does not this doctrine make men careless and profane?") that Ursinus ascribes a positive value to good works, but only cautiously. His detractors quote James 2:24: "Ye see then how that by works a man is justified, and not by faith only." This, say his opponents, is a counterargument to Ursinus' teaching that works have no justifying function. Ursinus' reply is that in the passage brought forward by the Roman Catholics, there is a "double ambiguity": "If the term justify, as used by the apostle James, is understood properly, of justification before God, then the term faith signifies a dead faith; and if we understand the faith here spoken of as true, or justifying

---

[81] Ursinus, *Commentary*, 464-66.
[82] Ursinus, *Commentary*, 467.
[83] Ames, *Catechisme*, Mabb ed., Table of Contents.
[84] Ursinus, *Commentary*, 333-40.

faith, then the ambiguity in it is the word justify."[85] All positive value that can be attributed to good works Ursinus leaves to his teaching on Lord's Day 32 where it appears more properly in context.

We move back to William Ames on Lord's Day 24 and see that he almost immediately brings to the fore the issue of the meritorious nature of good works. But not before he denies works any soteriologically justifying power, as argued by the Papists. In fact, even "many of our own" hold the mistaken notion that good works justify us before men and women. He concludes: "justifying faith is such that it is effective through good works."[86]

From this theological truth and from a (Ramistic) exposition of the subsequent verses in the James passage under consideration, he summarizes James' message:

> (1) True and justifying faith is productive of good works, and (2) works are the goal and perfection of faith. For faith is said to cooperate with good works, because together with the command of God it conveys its own force and efficiency for producing all good works. Moreover, because works are said to be the perfection of faith, they should not be understood to constitute a formal or inward perfection of faith . . . but to contain the external perfection of faith, to the degree that they flow from faith, just as the effect somehow has a perfection in itself from its own cause, to the degree that it partakes of the force and the virtue that are the internal perfection of the cause.[87]

This cause/effect connection receives very brief mention in Ursinus' explanation of Lord's Day 24.[88]

Thus, the lesson to be taken from this explication is twofold: good works are the effects and not the cause of justification and good works are non-discretionary. In fact, they accompany faith by "necessary coherence."[89] Covenant theology is brought in to argue the point: "The faithful are not under the covenant of works, and thus they cannot be justified by their works." since all good works are a gracious gift, non-meritorious since owed to God, and imperfect and filthy in any event. They only serve to condemn. Here Ames follows Ursinus' thought quite closely. This lesson should deepen both our sense of dependence on the grace of God and the utter incapability of self in doing good.[90]

To argue the necessary accompaniment of good works, Ames again, closely tracks with Ursinus' explanation (found, remember, in his exposition of Lord's Day 32) that good works are due God for his glory, serve to assure oneself, and

---

[85] Ursinus, *Commentary*, 338.
[86] Ames, *Catechisme*, 121.
[87] Ames, *Catechisme*, 121.
[88] Ursinus, *Commentary*, 333.
[89] Ames, *Catechisme*, Mabb ed., 162-64.
[90] Ames, *Catechisme*, 122-23.

help for witness to others.[91] Ames enlarges that good works are done out of "Gospel thankfulness." In fact, our election and calling are precisely for this end: the performance of good works. Internal sanctity is expressed in external holiness. Good works flow naturally from our election, redemption, vocation, with the purpose of living righteous, pious and God-focused lives. In addition to gratitude, covenant obedience obliges believers to pursue good works "with virtue and all strength." This covenant theme is uniquely Amesian; it does not make an appearance in Ursinus' exposition.

In closing this Lord's Day, Ames also has encouragement for those faithful whose good works are not apparent and whose faith stumbles. The seed may be there, says Ames, but the fruit may not be "discerned." This is not the norm, however; in such a case faith's degree and consoling power are weakened.

The biblical teaching on good works should make believers zealous in pursuit of the fruit of faith and warn all those who deny that works and faith are intrinsically connected.[92] In two brief doctrines William Ames has addressed the vast territory covered in two Lord's Days in the *Heidelberg Catechism* and Ursinus' *Commentary*. All he has to say, formally, on good works appears in the five pages of his commentary on Lord's Day 24. Yet Ames' concern for praxis, the dominant and unifying theme in all his teaching, comes to the fore within the framework of his covenant thought. Here, in his *Catechisme*, this connection is made clear and explicit.[93]

Miscellaneous Emphases
It is worthwhile to briefly underscore some uniquely Amesian emphases. While some of these simply represent Ames' view of what was important in the practice of theology, other emphases, although now part of standard reformed theological thinking, were only just beginning to develop at this time and must therefore be seen as newly-emerging components of Reformed theology.

In the category of the former we can mention his curious departure from the more precise and systematic model of the *Heidelberg Catechism*. Thus, for example, Ames discusses only the article in the *Apostles' Creed* on Christ's death, neglecting to examine the topic of his burial and descent into hell (Lord's Day 16).[94] In Lord's Day 31, where the topic in the *Heidelberg Catechism* concerns the keys of the kingdom, what they are and how they function, Ames chooses to address the topic by introducing God as a God of order who

---

[91] Ames, *Catechisme*, 122; cf. Ursinus, *Commentary*, 483.
[92] Ames, *Catechisme*, 123-24.
[93] This is one of only two places in the entire *Catechisme* where Ames presents "objections." In Lord's Day 24, Ames considers two objections posed by the Roman Catholic thinking on merit: 1. Good works can be perfect to the degree that they originate in the Holy Spirit, and 2. "recompense is given according to works" (*Catechisme*, 122). The other occurs in Lord's Day 15, where the objection asserts, by means of a syllogism, that Christ suffered against his will (*Catechisme*, 81).
[94] Ames, *Catechisme*, 83-87.

has appointed ministers to oversee the church through their ministerial powers. The means used for the exercise of this power are identified only briefly at the very end of the exposition of the Lord's Day. Discipline is barely mentioned and left entirely unexplained.[95] Not surprisingly, the doctrine of the Sabbath is expounded at great length, and he grounds it, with Ursinus, in the example set by God at creation.[96]

Our comparison of Ames' and Ursinus' respective expositions of the Ten Commandments introduces Ursinus as an early practitioner of casuistry. Extended development of the teaching of the commandments, while in some cases only hinted at in the *Heidelberg Catechism*, receive full coverage in his *Commentary*. So, for example, the fifth commandment – to honor one's father and mother – can be extended to cover all relationships between superiors and inferiors. Ames does this as well. And both commentators make frequent use of the term and the concept of "synecdoche" explaining it frequently to ensure the reader knows the means whereby generalizations are made from specifics.[97] Finally, Ames' doctrine of the church is introduced with the Pauline teaching on the relationship between husbands and wives (Ephesians 5:25-27). Paul exhorts husbands to love their wives even as Christ loved the church and gave himself for it.[98] What is at first glance a very practical, unsoteriological passage Ames uses to introduce a rather existential theme – the doctrine of the church. Although the coverage is much briefer than that of Ursinus, many of the same elements regarding the church's essence and character are covered.[99] And "because the "Common Place of the eternal predestination of God, or of election and reprobation naturally grows out of the doctrine of the church: and is for this reason correctly connected with it,"[100] Ursinus chooses to handle that central doctrine at this point in his *Commentary*. His exposition on the doctrine of predestination is half again as long as his teaching on the doctrine of the church.[101] In the *Catechisme* of William Ames, on the other hand, one looks in vain for formal and prolonged teaching on the doctrine of predestination.

One area where Ames showed himself to be at the forefront of the development of theological thought occurs in Lord's Day 15. The issue here has to do with the suffering of Christ. Here Ames brings in the idea of the pre-temporal covenant between God the Father and God the Son. Christ's expiation, Ames explains, "was the covenant initiated (*pactum initum*) between the Father and Christ: if he should offer this obedience for us, then, since we have been liberated from disobedience and death, we should live in Him (Isa. 53:10). This suf-

---

[95] Ames, *Catechisme*, 144-46.
[96] Ames, *Catechisme*, 169-75; cf. Ursinus, *Commentary*, 557-74.
[97] Ursinus, *Commentary*, 577-83; Ames, *Catechisme*, 176-79; cf. idem, *Conscience*, 5.19-5.20, 5.23; cf. idem, *Marrow*, 2.17.66.
[98] Ames, *Catechisme*, 107-10.
[99] Ursinus, *Commentary*, 285-93.
[100] Ursinus, *Commentary*, 293.
[101] Ursinus, *Commentary*, 293-305.

fering was the consummation of every obedience."[102] The concept of a pre-temporal agreement within the Godhead was not yet part and parcel of received covenant theology, and its appearance here is somewhat surprising. Ursinus, one of the earliest covenant theologians certainly makes no mention of such a covenant when he asks: "What was the Impelling Cause of the Passion of Christ?" He answers: God's love for the human race, God's compassion for those "fallen in sin and death," and his desire and purpose to avenge Satan who spoiled God's image in humanity.[103] This pre-fall covenantal agreement between the Father and the Son, asserts Ames, is of comfort to the faithful because it represents the remedy for sin – its guilt and terror, while admonishing us to abhor sin.[104]

Final Observations

It should be observed that the "ecclesiastical tone" mentioned by Verboom as characteristic of earlier catechisms, if absent from the *Heidelberg Catechism* proper, is quite prominent in Ursinus' *Commentary*. The prolegomena of Ursinus is dominated by his "Doctrine of the Church."[105] He begins: "These Prolegomena are partly general, such as treat of the entire doctrine of the Church: and partly special, such as have respect merely to the Catechism." The doctrine of the church "reveals the only way of escape through Christ."[106] In the midst of his ecclesiology, he introduces and expands on decretal theology, a central and growing locus in the theological development during this period of early orthodoxy. Moreover, while the pathos and the personal nature of the *Heidelberg Catechism* certainly are its domineering spirit, Ursinus' *Commentary* shows that he can engage in polemic with detractors of the Reformed faith when the need arises.

Ames' method, like that of Ursinus, is replete with Ramism and, to a lesser extent, syllogistic reasoning. It does not carry the soteriological focus of Ursinus even if the overall theme of *Catechisme* is in agreement with Ursinus. Although it is obvious that Ames is prone to wander from this theme, the areas from which he borrows from Ursinus for his own exposition are clear and unmistakable. Furthermore, Ames ably demonstrates that no theological truth, be it ever so theoretical or existential, can be without some exhortation to *eupraxia*.[107] This eupraxia was not conducted in a vacuum, but rather proceeded ac-

---

[102] Ames, *Catechisme*, 82.
[103] Ursinus, *Commentary*, 216.
[104] Ames, *Catechisme*, 82.
[105] Ursinus, *Commentary*, 1.
[106] Ursinus, *Commentary*, 18.
[107] In the opening thesis of his *Technometria*, Ames asserts: "Art is the idea of *eupraxia*, or good action, methodically delineated by universal rules," Ames, *Technometry*, 93. Theology was, for Ames, one of the arts and thus subject to these rules even though it had as source divine revelation and not nature (Sprunger, *Ames*, 115).

cording to scriptural rules set out in God's revelation. The *Heidelberg Catechism* is grabbing, pithy, personal, pastoral and overflows with pathos. While Ursinus' *Commentary* is more expository, it also communicates a warm and pastoral sentiment to the heart of the reader. Although there are instances where William Ames does touch the heart in a pastoral way, such pathos does not flow from his mind and pen in a consistent way in his commentary. His concern here is simply for greater immediate application to one's present lived experience. This accounts also for hortative tendencies found in his commentary. The preacher sitting in Ames' counsel for guidance in directing the faithful in their soul struggle could not aspire to being the kind of physician of souls bred by the *Heidelberg Catechism* on the strength of his *Catechisme* alone. For this they would have to go to his *Conscience*.

The *Heidelberg Catechism* has often been charged with inserting a strong anthropocentric flavor into the teaching of the church. This point is made in the context of comparisons with the *Westminster Standards*, the catechisms of which, it is argued, are more theocentric from the very outset where the theme is established in Q&A 1 in both the *Larger* and the *Shorter Catechism*. To enter into this debate, at this point, will take us too far afield, but our study of William Ames has demonstrated, if anything, that one can move in both directions on this score. For example, on the one hand, the possibilities for putting an anthropocentric gloss on the *Heidelberg Catechism* are very real. The "Amesian gloss," as he has given it to us in his *Catechisme*, shows the possibility of that, with its emphasis on practical divinity and eupraxia. On the other hand, this same document clearly shows instances where it is highly theocentric as well. Ames' long and exhaustive discussion on "God himself" as the "true chief good, as well effectively as objectively" underscores the God-centeredness of this work in the context of the source of comfort for the believer. Perhaps we should remember that, prior to all theologies, Calvin's *Institutes* set the standard by underscoring the need for an understanding of both the Creator and the creature, and the chasm between the two. In the *Heidelberg Catechism*, Q&A 1 teaches that the creature's only comfort is in the re-creative work of the Creator. In both the *Larger* and *Shorter* catechisms of the *Westminster Standards*, Q&A 1 teaches that while the Creator is to be glorified, the creature is to do the enjoying of him forever.

For Ames it is essential that the *Heidelberg Catechism* be adapted to pulpit use – to plain-style preaching form. For when it comes to priorities in preaching a sermon, "which part is most to be insisted on, the explication of the Text, the handling of the Doctrines, or the Use and Explication of them?" The answer: while "some speciall occasion may make the large explication of the text, or handling of the Doctrine to be necessary, . . . regularly, and ordinarily the principall worke of the Sermon, if it be not Catecheticall, is in the use and application."[108] Ames' commentary has modified the *Catechisme* to perfectly fit his recipe for effective preaching.

At this point, it might also be instructive to be reminded that the *Westminster Larger* and *Shorter* catechisms closely duplicate this Amesian method of exposition and instruction. In the *Larger Catechism*, Q&A 1-90 teach of God; Q&A 91-196 teach that "Having seen what the scriptures principally teach us to believe concerning God, it follows to consider what they require as the duty of man." And the *Shorter Catechism* is so organized as well: Q&A 1-38 teach doctrine; the second half begins with the question posed in Q 39: "What is the duty which God requires of man?" The remainder of the *Shorter Catechism*, through the final question and answer (107), enlarges on this.[109]

In establishing its theme, it is interesting to note that in the opening question of the *Westminster Larger* and *Shorter* catechisms, the Divines have skipped back over the *Heidelberg Catechism* to revert back to the first question in Calvin's catechism which seeks to establish the chief end of man, to know God. But it is not enough to know God. That the Divines appropriated William Ames' emphasis is clear here in their amended (from Calvin's) declaration of humanity's goal or chief end. For Ames it was not enough to "know" God, however experientially this might be interpreted. Men and women, throughout their daily existence, must work to actively glorify God in thought, word and deed. Yes, through faith by grace alone was salvation secured. And only through divinely-empowered covenantal obedience would the child of God enter into the felicity reserved for the saints and begin, even in this life, to fully enjoy him forever. This chapter has demonstrated that William Ames did all he could to ensure that this living and very practical faith was not lost on the continental catechumen nurtured on the *Heidelberg Catechism*. Ames deliberately revised this popular teaching document to ensure that this emphasis would be impressed upon the student in faith, from both pulpit and podium, through his very practical overlay of the already warm, personalistic and experiential *Heidelberg Catechism*.

In his brief but useful introductory section on some of the historical issues surrounding the origins and development of the *Heidelberg Catechism*, Verboom mentions approvingly the four-fold purpose that K. Barth understood that doctrinal standard to serve:

> 1. The Heidelberg Catechism is a textbook for instruction in the faith for church, home and school.
> 2. The Heidelberg Catechism is a guide and rule for preachers, students and others.

---

[108] Ames, *Conscience*, 4.26.Q11-4.26.Q12.
[109] *The Confession of Faith (1647), The Larger Catechism (1648), The Shorter Catechism (1648), The Directory of Public Worship* (Toronto: Presbyterian Publications, n.d.).

3. The Heidelberg Catechism has a liturgical aspect. According to the Church Order of 1563, each Sunday [Lord's Day] ensures that a portion of it is read during the church service.

4. The Heidelberg Catechism is a guiding principle for the catechism sermon that is held in the Sunday afternoon lesson.[110]

To these, William Ames would indubitably add purpose number 5: The *Heidelberg Catechism* is a textbook for living to godliness.

---

[110] K. Barth, *Einführung in dem Heidelberger Katechismus* (Zurich, 1960), cited in Verboom, *Heidelbergse Catechismus*, 18-19.

Chapter 8

The *Nadere Reformatie* and William Ames

Disputation at Franeker and the Synod of Dordt

The European intellectual climate through the early modern period under consideration was overwhelmingly Aristotelian. Until 1650, the Philosopher's metaphysics prevailed in intellectual circles; a scholastic Aristotelianism was the *philosophia recepta*, "the officially and ecclesiastically sanctioned philosophy prevailing in universities and academies . . . ." An Aristotelian synthesis ruled in the European world of thought.[1]

This is the world Ames entered when he landed on the continent in 1610, bringing with him little more than the building blocks – sound doctrine and high piety – for the further construction of an incipient intellectual and practical system of godliness and purity of life. It was in the seventeenth-century Dutch Republic that his thought was further systematized in interaction with the philosophical, theological, cultural and ecclesiastical affairs of the day. A movement of further reformation was taking hold – the *Nadere Reformatie* – and Ames was quickly drawn in.[2] Officially this was a movement committed to an ongo-

---

[1] See J.I. Israel's superb summary of the intellectual preconditions that gave rise to the "radical enlightenment" commencing in about 1650 with Cartesian thought in *Radical Enlightenment: Philosophy and the Making of Modernity, 1650-1750* (Oxford: Oxford University, 2002), 3-22; quotation from p. 16. Israel observes it would be almost a half-century before a new "philosophical radicalism" (Cartesianism) set in which, after 1650, drove all new streams of thought to a defense of the truth of revealed religion (*Radical Enlightenment*, 15).

[2] W.J. op 't Hof provides a brief but carefully-nuanced synopsis and explanation of the movement and its exponents. He asserts that a century's worth of research into Dutch Pietism and the *Nadere Reformatie* has yielded little insight into precise definitional considerations. He clarifies: "Dutch Reformed Pietism (De Nadere Reformatie) . . . was the movement of Dutch Pietists in the national Church." He postulates that Dutch Pietism can be dated quite precisely to 1588 (when Dutch translations of pietist J. Taffin's works rolled off the press) and that the *Nadere Reformatie* (the Second Reformation), as movement commenced in 1608 with the first publication of W. Teellinck. See his "Stellingen," or "theses" – a list of twenty-four propositions for the defense of his dissertation of which this volume is the published version (*Engelse Piëtistische Geschriften*, 641-45). See Beeke's excellent discussion in *Assurance*, 383-413. See also L.F. Groenendijk, "De Oorsprong van de uitdrukking 'Nadere Reformatie'," *DNR* 9 (1985): 128-34. On various aspects of the *Nadere Reformatie*, see a representative sampling of C. Graafland's work as follows: "Macarius, F.A. Lampe en de Nadere Reformatie (n.a.v.: J.H. van de Bank, Macarius en zijn invloed in de Nederlanden)," *ThRef* 21 (1978): 56-60; "De toekomstverwachting der Puriteinen en haar invloed op de Nadere Reformatie,"

ing reformation of faith and morals, spearheaded by the doctrinal and ecclesiological reforms of the sixteenth century Reformation. Specifically:

> The Dutch Second (or "Further") Reformation is that movement within the Dutch Reformed Church during the seventeenth and eighteenth centuries, which, as a reaction to the declension of absence of a living faith, made both the personal experience of faith and godliness matters of central importance. From that perspective the movement formulated substantial and procedural reformation initiatives, submitting them to the proper ecclesiastical, political, and social agencies, and pursued those initiatives through a further reformation of the church, society, and state in both word and deed.[3]

Johannes Maccovius
At the Academy in Franeker and after an initial period of cordiality, Ames' system of thought and life collided with that of a colleague whose living faith fell short of the mark in the judgment of the more pious, and who appeared eager for militant theological disputation and mockery of Ames' piety and Ra-

---

DNR 3 (1979): 65-95; "Nadere Reformatie. G. Voetius, W. à Brakel, J. Verschuir," in *Bij Brood en beker. Leer en gebruik van het heilig avondmaal in het Nieuwe Testament en in de geschiedenis van de westerse kerk*, W. van 't Spijker et al., eds. (Kampen: De Groot Goudrian, 1980), 248-78; "De invloed van het Puritanisme op het ontstaan van het Gereformeerde Piëtisme in Nederland," *DNR* 7 (1983): 1-24; "De Nadere Reformatie en haar culturele context," in *Met het Woord in de Tijd*, L. Westland, ed. ('s-Gravenhage: Boekencentrum, 1985), 117-38; "Kernen en contouren van de Nadere Reformatie," in *Voornaamste vertegenwoordigers*, 349-67; "Gereformeerde Scholastiek V: De Invloed van de Scholastiek op de Gereformeerde Orthodoxie," *ThRef* 30 (1987): 4-25; "Gereformeerde Scholastiek VI: De Invloed van de Scholastiek op de Nadere Reformatie (1)," *ThRef* 30 (1987): 109-31; "Gereformeerde Scholastiek VI: De Invloed van de Scholastiek op de Nadere Reformatie (2)," *ThRef* 30 (1987): 313-40; "Het eigene van het Gereformeerd Piëtisme in de 18e eeuw in onderscheid van de 17e eeuw," *DNR* 11 (1987): 37-53; "De Nadere Reformatie en het Labadisme," in *Gereformeerd Piëtisme*, 275-346; and "Schriftleer en schriftverstaan in de Nadere Reformatie," *Theologische aspecten*, 29-97. See particularly 40-61. S. van der Linde was one of the first scholars in this relatively new category of study. See, for example, his "De betekenis van de Nadere Reformatie voor Kerk en Theologie," *KeTh* 5 (1954): 215-25, "Het Werk van de Heilige Geest in de gemeente: Een appreciatie van de Nadere Reformatie," *NedTT* 10 (1956): 1-13, "De Prediking van de Nadere Reformatie," *ThRef* 19 (1976): 6-21, "Calvijn, Calvinisme en Nadere Reformatie," *DNR* 6 (1982): 73-88, "'De Nadere Reformatie', Een Nieuwe Start," *ThRef* 29 (1986): 188-97, "De Heilige Geest in Reformatie en Nadere Reformatie," in *Leven door de Heilige Geest*, A. Noordegraaf, ed. (Amersfoort: N.p., n.d.), 49-81. An examination of the representatives of the *Nadere Reformatie* is also found in W. van Gorsel, *De Ijver voor Zijn Huis: De Nadere Reformatie en haar belangrijkste vertegenwoordigers* (Groede: Pieters, 1981). Recall the much earlier Graafland dissertation.

[3] C. Graafland, W.J. op 't Hof, F.A. van Lieburg, "Nadere Reformatie: opnieuw een poging tot begripsbepaling." *DNR* 19 (1995): 108. I use the English translation found in Willem Teellink, *The Path of True Godliness*, A. Godbehere, trans., J.R. Beeke, ed. (Grand Rapids: Baker, 2003), 7-8.

mism.[4] Polish-born theologian Johannes Maccovius had studied philosophy under the Aristotelian Bartholomäus Keckermann at Danzig. After spending time debating at other universities in Eastern Europe, he went to the Dutch Republic in 1613 to facilitate the legal studies of the aristocratic family in whose employ he was as governor.[5] Arriving in the Friesen town of Franeker, Maccovius was asked to join the two-man faculty there, one of which, Lubbertus, was a theologian well known throughout Europe.[6] Under the promotion of Lubbertus, Maccovius received the doctoral degree in theology in 1614, the first individual to earn the theological doctorate from this school since its inception in 1585. He became professor in 1615 after failed attempts by the school to secure more experienced faculty (among which was Bogerman, later president of the Synod of Dort, who served at Franeker after the synod). Maccovius remained at Franeker until his death in 1644, wielding tremendous influence in the education of theological students from all of Europe and greatly advancing the method and teaching of what we now know as Protestant scholasticism. This was the primary vehicle for the development of Protestant orthodoxy through the post-Reformation period and is has to do more with the method, logic and a distinctly Protestant approach to academic disciplines than with an overwhelmingly philosophical (e.g., Aristotelian) or distinctively theological (e.g., predestinarian) commitment. The final form of theological premises and doctrines, not worked out by the first- and second-generation reformers, was carefully refined and established by these "orthodox" or "scholastic" Protestants.[7] The contribu-

---

[4] Horton, *Ames by Visscher*, 60, 120-40. For superb (and sympathetic) coverage of this period in Maccovius' life see the biography by A. Kuyper Jr., *Johannes Maccovius* (Leiden: D. Donner, 1899). This is the published version of his dissertation, "Johannes Maccovius" (Th.D. diss., Free University of Amsterdam, 1899). On p. 315 Kuyper indicates that a point of most serious contention between the two Franeker colleagues was regarding the Ramist system of philosophy and logic as Ames incorporated these into his theology.

[5] This brief biography of Maccovius from Kuyper, "Maccovius," 4-27 and recapped in M.D. Bell, "Propter Potestatem, Scientiam, AC Beneplacitum Dei: The Doctrine of the Object of Predestination in the Theology of Johannes Maccovius" (Th.D. diss., Westminster Theological Seminary, 1986), 10-13.

[6] For an excellent study on the life and thought of this central figure in the early period of the Dutch Further Reformation see C. van der Woude, *Sibrandus Lubbertus, leven en werken, in het bizonder naar zijn correspondentie* (Kampen: J.H. Kok, 1963).

[7] Muller, *PRRD I*, 33-37. For two recent studies of Protestant scholasticism, see *Reformation and Scholasticism*, W.J. van Asselt and E. Dekker, eds. Texts & Studies in Reformation and Post-Reformation Thought, R.A. Muller, ed. (Grand Rapids: Baker, 2001) and *Protestant Scholasticism: Essays in Reassessment*, C.R. Trueman and R.S. Clark, eds. (Carlisle, Cumbria: Paternoster, 1999). The latter volume includes essays covering the presence of Protestant scholasticism in the work of European thinkers from Luther and Calvin to the Enlightenment. On the development of Reformed orthodoxy amidst prevailing philosophical traditions, see S. van der Linde, *Het gereformeerde protestantisme* (Nijkerek: G. F. Callenbach, 1957), *Vromen en Verlichten: Twee eeuwen Protestantse Geloofsbeleving 1650-1850* (Utrecht: Aartbisschoppelijk Museum Utrecht:

tion of English theologians such as Ames has ensured that Protestant scholasticism, essentially a continental phenomenon in its origins, assumed a truly international character.[8]

Cordial relations between Lubbertus and Maccovius were short-lived. Struggles between the two colleagues centered on Maccovius' popularity with the student body, his rigid supralapsarianism and a dubious lifestyle. Lubbertus, the infralapsarian, carefully guarded a pious life style and was an older professor without the charisma of the much younger Maccovius. But serious charges against Maccovius by Lubbertus resulted from the former's promotion of a thesis developed by Thomas Parker for the M.Phil. degree at Leiden. Parker's father, Robert, had accompanied Ames from England to the Netherlands. In the period 1611-1619, while Ames was serving as chaplain to Vere in The Hague Parker studied at Leiden. In the absence of suitable Leiden faculty to examine Parker, Ames was instrumental in securing Maccovius' involvement for his fellow-countryman. Lubbertus took great exception to Parker's scholastic, "highly technical and philosophical" study on the process of conversion and brought charges at the Classis of Franeker in 1618 against Maccovius for his involvement. Although they were not, strictly speaking, theological theses but, rather, "philosophical theses with theological import and consequences," the case was sent to the provincial synod for adjudication. But it was decided to try the case at the Synod of Dort which meetings opened in November of that year.[9] At what became known as the "heresy trial" of Maccovius which commenced in April 1619 after Dort had decided against the Arminians, Maccovius responded to these charges and further accusations leveled at his teaching. His teaching and Parker's theses were characterized as being "speculative, metaphysical, obscure and false." Ames spoke strongly in defense of both Maccovius and Parker and an international panel was established to adjudicate the case.

1974), "Mystiek en bevinding in het Gereformeerde Protestantisme," in *Mystiek en bevinding*, G. Quispel et al., eds. (Kampen: Kok, 1976), 45-61, "Het 'Griekse' Denken in Kerk, Theologie en Geloofspraktijk," *ThRef* 28 (1985): 247-68, and "Gereformeerde Scholastiek IV: Calvijn," *ThRef* 29 (1986): 244-66. On this same subject, see W. van 't Spijker, "Gereformeerde Scholastiek II: Scholastiek, Erasmus, Luther, Melanchthon," *ThRef* 29 (1986): 7-27 and "Gereformeerde Scholastiek III: Zwingli en Bucer," *ThRef* 29 (1986): 136-60.

[8] Muller, *PRRD I*, 66-67. Muller argues that lack of study of the influence of English theologians in Europe during the late-sixteenth through seventeenth centuries has led to an understanding of Protestant scholasticism in strictly continental terms, as a primarily continental phenomenon. Although it is true that the movement was essentially continental in origin, the English Puritans contributed immensely to theological formulation within a scholastic framework.

[9] Van der Woude, *Lubbertus*, 338-430; Sprunger, Ames, 30, 60, 61. The chapter entitled "On Shaky Ground with Maccovius" in *Lubbertus* chronicles the contentious relationship between the two scholars. So preoccupied was Lubbertus with these Parker-related theses and Maccovius' that he missed the opening of the Synod of Dordt on 13 November, 1618 (*Lubbertus*, 357); Sprunger, *Ames*, 30, 60, 61.

The upshot of the trial, which was finally decided after a number of conferences between the parties in question, was the rendering of, first, a "preliminary" judgment and, then, a final judgment. The latter was less severe than the former and in it Maccovius received full acquittal but was warned to refrain from using the scholastic language of Robert Bellarmine and Francisco de Suárez. Synod's major concern was for Maccovius' perspicuity in teaching. Particularly, he was proscribed from teaching against infralapsarianism which had a strong promoter in Lubbertus. Maccovius' accusers were warned against any further harassment of Maccovius without clear evidence of the latter's heterodoxy.[10]

Ames played a key role in the defense of Maccovius and in the final resolution of the dispute. This puts in sharp relief the bitter acrimony that developed between Ames and Maccovius following both Ames' appointment as Franeker's third faculty member upon his promotion to doctor of theology in 1622 and Lubbertus' death in 1625. Seven years after defending his colleague at Dort, in 1626, Ames (as university rector) and a group of colleagues found reason to bring charges against Maccovius centering primarily on the latter's lifestyle with a view to securing his dismissal. Although we can't be sure what was prior in Ames' mind – the impious living of his Franeker colleague or the latter's philosophical commitment to Aristotle and the schoolmen – we can speculate that it was most likely the former since against the latter he was ably defended by Ames and exculpated by Synod. What is clear and no doubt played a role as well was the short-lived pietistic "revival" at the school. In any event, the school did not act on the petition against Maccovius and for his remaining time at Franeker to his departure to Rotterdam in 1633, Ames remained embroiled in controversy with his colleague, holding fast his position that true godliness involved not only precise and sound theological discourse but also "outward as well as inward obedience."[11]

---

[10] Kuyper, "Maccovius," 27-100; Bell, "Maccovius," 14-27; Sprunger, *Ames*, 59-62. Excellent earlier coverage of the controversy in the English language is provided by Nethenus in Horton, *Ames by Nethenus*, 7-13. A verbatim English translation of Ames' defense of Parker's theses and the final "Judgment of the Deputies" Nethenus also provides in these pages. For more detail on the issues at stake in this synodical investigation into the charges against Maccovius, see also J. Heringa, "De twistzaak van den hoogeleeraar Johannes Maccovius, door de Dordrechtsche Synode, ten jare 1619 beslecht," *AKGNed* 3 (1831): 503-664 and M.I. Klauber, "The Use of Philosophy in the Theology of Johannes Maccovius (1588-1644)," *CTJ* 30 (1995): 376-91. A recent sympathetic interpretation of Maccovius is offered by W.J. van Asselt, "The Theologian's Tool Kit: Johannes Maccovius (1588-1644) and the Development of Reformed Theological Distinctions," *WTJ* 68 (2006): 23-40.

[11] Kuyper, "Maccovius," 315-96; Sprunger, *Ames*, 88-90. Both Kuyper and Sprunger find evidence indicating the general dislike for the character of Maccovius (Sprunger, *Ames*, 75; Kuyper, "Maccovius," 43); W.B.S. Boeles is unable to find even one favorable report on Maccovius. See his *Frieslands Hoogeschool en het Rijks Athenaeum te Franeker*. 2 vols. (Leeuwarden, 1878-70), 2.93, cited in Sprunger, *Ames*, 75. Van Asselt

The Heart of the Dispute: Faith or Morals?
The theological controversy with Maccovius involved both personal and theological affairs.[12] Kuyper's study of the primary areas of discord between the two supralapsarianists reveals the central issue to have been whether such a thing as preparatory grace prior to regeneration exists, followed by a subsidiary query as to whether the unregenerate hear the declaration of the gospel savingly. In keeping with his ascription of volitional power to the creature, Ames taught preparatory grace (reflecting the Puritan preparationist teaching he learned from Perkins) and gospel benefit for the unregenerate who could exercise their volition to hear the word savingly. Whereas Maccovius asserted an immediate regeneration by the Holy Spirit, Ames held to the power of the Word to regenerate the sinner.[13] Maccovius emphasized unyieldingly the primacy of the intellect in the regenerate mind: the will is renewed through the mediacy of the intellect. The intellect is the *terminus a quo*, the will the *terminus ad quem*. Ames held equally stubbornly to the primacy of the volition. Kuyper concludes that "here too it must be conceded that Ames, in this polemic, deviated from the pure Reformed position confessed and defended by Maccovius."[14]

Ames also opposed the philosophical theologians of the scholastic tradition who held to a distinct bifurcation between theology and ethics. Keckermann had developed theology (spiritual good) and ethics (moral good) as separate studies. This Aristotelian characteristic was particularly repugnant to Ames. In the seventeenth section of the chapter on virtue, one of his longest single sections in *Marrow*, Ames inveighs against this Aristotelian tendency:

> 16. . . . There can be no other teaching of the virtues than theology which brings the whole revealed will of God to the directing of our reason, will, and life.
> 17. They who think differently have no reasons which move an understanding and sound man. They hold that the end of theology is the good of grace and the end of ethics is moral or civil good (as if no moral or civil good were in any way spiritual or the good of grace). This is to say that the proper good, blessedness, or end of man is not a single good, and that a man's virtue does not lead him to his end and chief good. They say that theology is concerned with the inward affections of men

---

laments, then disputes, this record and discovers some evidence to the contrary. He describes Maccovius as "a Polish aristocrat" with a "rather flamboyant temperament," ("Maccovius," 23-24). Last phrase quoted from Ames, *Marrow*, 2.2.16-2.2.17.

[12] Ames, *Marrow*, 1.1.1-1.3.22, 2.2.1-2.2.16, 2.3.1-2.3.32.

[13] Kuyper, "Maccovius," 315-96. Bell, "Maccovius," 26. The two other main areas of debate between the two theologians concerned: 1) whether all that is revealed to individuals in God's name is to be understood as His real will. This Ames affirmed but Maccovius denied; and 2) whether Christ is to be worshipped as mediator which Ames held to but Maccovius denied (a practical implication of which involved the question of directing prayer to Christ). See Kuyper, "Maccovius," 57 and 315-96. The first citation is a succinct statement of the four areas of difference between the two colleagues.

[14] Kuyper, "Maccovius," 365.

and ethics with outward manners – as if ethics, which they consider the prudence which governs the will and appetite, had nothing to do with inward affections, and theology did not teach outward as well as inward obedience. . . . [15]

Ames' clear and unequivocal teaching on right living set him on a collision course with Maccovius from the very beginning.

Bell carefully nuances the root cause of the difference between the two theologians as a divergence of opinion on style of living:

> [Most] of the actually verifiable differences in lifestyle between Maccovius and Lubbertus/Ames came about because of a different perspective on the Reformed practice of piety. Ames, of course, was a very strict puritan in his theology and practice and mirrored that lifestyle to all his students. He typified the kind of piety that was prevalent in England and New England among the puritans. Some of this carried over into the Netherlands because of the great number of puritan exiles in the Low Countries and a similar, but less strict view of Christian living became the norm among the Reformed here. In the rest of Europe, the Reformed were not as strict in their practice and made more leeway for differences in the outworking of one's faith. Maccovius, of course, had grown up in this less restrictive atmosphere and it seems likely that his practice of piety would remain closer to the German or Swiss Reformed viewpoints, even when he moved to the Netherlands. This is not to excuse those aspects of his life where he may actually have been improper in his actions, but it is meant to show that some of [sic] reasons for these conflicts over lifestyle may have arisen over some differences in the practice of Christian living that were always allowed to co-exist within Reformed theological circles.[16]

We believe the difference between the two individuals may have been a little bit more complex than this. To be sure, "Maccovius' life never quite equaled his theology, and for a theologian this was unfortunate, especially when the school was trying to upgrade standards" as explicitly stated in the university statutes.[17] Absolving Maccovius of any unacceptable theological or philosophical deviation does not excuse his aberrant lifestyle. Both van Asselt and Bell rightly justify Maccovius' use of highly refined scholastic classes of distinctions in his *Distinctiones* on the grounds that this necessarily reduced ambiguity in theological discourse. If lack of clarity is an undesirable theological attribute at the best of times for the most theologically mature scholar, then surely the *novitii* of the academy at Franeker who were, for the most part, encountering this terminology for the first time required precision in teaching.[18] From that perspective Maccovius' efforts were laudable. But it must be remembered that this is precisely where Maccovius was admonished at the Synod of Dort. If it is true that for Maccovius, as for Calvin before him, the practical side of theology

---

[15] Ames, *Marrow*, 2.2.16-2.2.17, opposing the Aristotelianism of Keckermann.

[16] Bell, "Maccovius," 25; Bell's entire argument is found in "Maccovius," 14-76.

[17] Sprunger, *Ames*, 87.

[18] Bell, "Maccovius," 49; van Asselt, "Maccovius," 28.

(or what Calvin called "true piety") represented true knowledge of God,[19] then Maccovius fell shy of the mark in teaching and in practice. For Puritan William Ames, Maccovius' scholastic philosophical commitment with its tendencies to abstraction, his demonstrated lack of piety, and his polemical spirit properly invited disputation. It might be an overstatement to contend, as Kuyper does, that Maccovius was responsible for the introduction of an Aristotelian scholasticism to Dutch theology.[20] On the other hand, was he only a "pioneer" as Bell suggests?[21] Regardless, keep in mind that the Franeker professors were teaching candidates for ministry – future leaders and teachers of orthodoxy in thought and in life. With that goal in view, it must be remarked that Ames proved more faithful to the task. The two theologians parted, the issues unresolved.[22]

The message of Christian piety was communicated to students most effectively, not in rarefied theological debate, but in teaching them how to preach. Ames' concern for the sanctity of the preaching office and the purity of the minister of the gospel is nowhere made as explicit as in both his formal and moral theology.[23] The reader is taken on a guided tour of instruction in practical theology. Ames is very precise: The text must come from scripture itself, not the catechism, although "some select places of Scripture may be propounded for a foundation of the Catechisticall instruction" to demonstrate the catechism's agreement with scripture. The whole counsel of God must be taught, not just "certaine Parcels and Sections" (as the Church of Rome was accustomed to doing). Plagiarism is "altogether unworthy" of a minister of the gospel, although the use of commentaries and "godly sermons" are recommended in sermon preparation. Writings and sayings non-divine in origin are to be shunned on the pulpit, while the "sentences of Fathers" are to be used very sparingly, only when needed "to convince the pertinaciousnesse of some, to refute the slanders of the enemies, and to help the weaknesse of others . . . the

---

[19] Bell, "Maccovius," 61.
[20] Kuyper, "Maccovius," 130.
[21] Bell, "Maccovius," 76; Bell names many earlier theologians (all from Leiden), "transitional figures, if not true scholastics," including Danaeus, Junius, both Trelcatius senior and junior, and Gomarus, among others ("Maccovius," 76-77). For a study of the Leiden faculty, see A. Eekhof, *De Theologische Faculteit te Leiden in de 17de Eeuw* (Utrecht: G.J.A. Ruys, 1921).
[22] It is an interesting footnote to this study that shortly before his death in 1644, Maccovius promoted student Johannes Coccelus to the theological doctorate. Cocceius gave Maccovius' a highly commendatory funeral oration (van Asselt, "Maccovius," 24) and was appointed to replace him. Bell argues that with covenant theologian Johannes Cloppenburg as colleague, Cocceius, whom Bell labels the "father of covenant theology," transformed Franeker from a school of scholastic thinking to one which thought in covenantal categories. "This symbolized in a real way the waning of the era of the Reformed dogmaticians and the rise of the era of the proponents of 'Biblical theology' within the Reformed schools" ("Maccovius," 27-28).
[23] Ames, *Conscience*, 4.26; idem, *Marrow*, 1.35, esp. 1.35.15-1.35.70.

word of God, and the edification of Beleevers requiring no such thing."[24] "Words of Art, Latine words, Greeke, Hebrew, etc." are to be avoided since they "hinder the understanding" and "they favour of ostentation in the Minister."[25] The risk here is that listeners will become accustomed to learned eloquence and come to despise the simplicity of the gospel. And although allegories are allowed, unbiblical allegorical interpretation is forbidden. The choosing of a text should be sensitive to time, place, and audience; usually the text itself should be explained in terms of doctrine, use and application, while in-depth doctrinal teaching is left to catechetical instruction.[26] The sermon is to be kept simple, absent of teaching of heresies, biblical obscurities and controversies. When drawn into controversies, these must be prudently shown to differ from the "principles of the doctrine of Christ." Finally, in keeping with the example set in the "Primitive Church," not only ordained ministers, but also others "of the brethren" may speak an edifying word and this practice "ought not to be contemned."[27]

Visscher provides evidence that this Amesian *desideratum* was the exception rather than the rule. As late as 1684, a half-century after the death of Ames, a sermon was preached in The Hague on "The Illustrious Prophecy of Malachi 3:1."

> First appears a series of Hebrew, Greek, and Latin quotations, then a quotation from the Talmud and the Jewish exegetes, and the practical purpose of the sermon except for a few exhortations to conversion, is almost completely forgotten. Even Hellenbroek, who is not the most impractical of men, very often has Latin, Greek, and Jewish exegetes speak from his pulpit.[28]

Visscher goes on to applaud Ames' attempt to cleanse the pulpit of this corruption by emphasizing only the biblical text, doctrine and uses.

Ames' direction for ministers of the gospel emphasizes the faith walk, the personal sanctity, the "integrity of life" and the intimate knowledge of scriptures that must characterize those called to this sacred office. Even though men may occasionally mount the pulpit without divine calling, "yet for one to invade the proper duty of a Minister without a speciall calling is altogether un-

---

[24] Ames, *Conscience*, 4.26.14.
[25] Ames, *Conscience*, 4.26.15. However, a high priority was placed on the necessity of *learning* and *knowing* the original biblical languages. In 1623 the young and already-famous linguist Sixtinus Amama appealed to the Synod of Friesland to turn down applicants to ministry who were unable to consult scipture's original languages. This appeal appeared in pamphlet form in Franeker in 1624. See van Asselt, "Bestudering van het Hebreeuws door Predicanten," 309-24.
[26] Ames, *Conscience*, 4.26.28-4.26.29; idem, *Marrow*, 1.35.19.
[27] Ames, *Conscience*, 4.26.16.
[28] Horton, *Ames by Visscher*, 142. Visscher is referring to a copy of a sermon in his possession: "The Illustrious Prophecy of Malachi 3:1, delivered by Fredericus Ragstat à Weille, Minister of the Gospel in the Church of Christ in Spijk, The Hague, 1684."

lawful" for such high vocation represents "an undertaking of a singular, and weighty function, the author and dispenser of which is God himselfe."[29]

No doubt it was Ames' desire to fill the pulpits in the Netherlands with men who showed evidence of vital piety and high learning, men who were spiritually alive and could take their listeners with them into communion with God. One of Ames' earliest biographers, Matthew Nethenus wrote in 1658 that "he prayed and preached with lively emotion, word, and gesture, so that eyes became wet with tears."[30] Such compassion Ames no doubt instilled in all his students, much to the chagrin of, and in diametric opposition to, the impiety Ames found in corners of the Dutch theological professoriate of which he unquestionably considered Maccovius the Franeker standard-bearer.

The Synod of Dordt (1618-1619)
As significant as Ames's involvement at Dordt was for Maccovius and the Franeker Classis of the Reformed church, Ames' presence in Dordrecht was of greater moment when viewed from the perspective of both the history of the development of Reformed thought internationally and ecclesiastical developments in the Netherlands.[31] Ames was tasked with formulating the opposition

---

[29] Ames, *Conscience*, 4.25.1-4.25.4.
[30] Horton, *Ames by Nethenus*, 20.
[31] As can be expected, the literature on the issues at the Synod of Dort is vast. A helpful, luminous, and immediately accessible history, including hundreds of photographs and brief biographies of individuals present at the Synod including their significance, is found in *De Synode van Dordrecht in 1618 en 1619*, W. van 't Spijker et al., eds. (Houten: Den Hertog, 1987, 1994). An introduction to the issues is provided in the following, from contemporary observers to later scholars: some earlier commentators were: Festus Hommius, *Oordeel des Synod: Nationalis Der Gereformeerde Kercken van de Vereenichde Nederlanden* (Dordrecht, 1619); Petrus Molinaeus, *Anatome Arminianismi, seu enucleatio controversiarum quae in Belgio agitantur: super doctrina de providentia, de praedestinatione, de morte Christi, de natura & gratia*, editio secunda (Lugduni Batavorum: ex officina Jacobi Marci, 1620) translated (by Pierre Du Moulin) as *The Anatomy of Arminianisme: or the Opening of the Controversies lately handled in the Low-Countries, concerning the Doctrine of Predestination, of the Death of Christ, of the Nature of Grace* (London: T. S., 1620); William Twisse, *The Doctrine of the Synod of Dort and Arles, reduced to the practise* (Amsterdam: 1631); *The Articles of the Synod of Dort, and its Rejection of Errors: with the History of Events which made way for that Synod*, trans. and ed., Thomas Scott (Utica: William Williams, 1831); B. Glasius, *Geschiedenis der Nationale Synode in 1618 en 1619 gehouden to Dordrecht*, 2 vols. (Leiden: E.J. Brill, 1860-61). In the more recent literature, see the following: H. Kaajan, *De Groote Synode van Dordrecht in 1618-1619* (Amsterdam: N.V. de Standaard, 1918); *Crisis in the Reformed Churches: Essays in Commemoration of the Great Synod of Dort, 1618-1619*, P.Y. de Jong, ed., (Grand Rapids: Reformed Fellowship, Inc., 1968); H.D. Foster, "Liberal Calvinism: the Remonstrants at the Synod of Dort in 1618," *HTR* 16 (1973): 1-37; R.W. Godfrey, "Tensions within International Calvinism: The Debate on the Atonement at the Synod of Dordt, 1618-1619," (Ph.D. diss., Stanford University, 1974). A study on theological disputes in the Netherlands at the time of William Ames' residency there has been done by D. Nobbs in *Theocracy and Toleration: A Study in the*

and advancing the Calvinist position at the Synod of Dort, with expectations that the theological, intellectual, and ecclesiastical landscape would be purged of the heresies of that Dutch theologian from Leiden, Jacobus Arminius, and his ilk.[32] From his perspective, no doubt, a happy incidental was that the political landscape was cleansed as well.

History has shown the decisive formal victory that was won by the Calvinists at Dort, even if informally things were less clear as they ultimately played out on the ecclesiastical and political landscape. Perhaps it was here that Ames was more sensitized to the need for biblically-responsible living in the crypto-Protestant climate of the public church. No doubt many of Arminius' and Ames' concerns were similar; the practical method of Ramus proved attractive to Arminius as well. It was Arminius' assertion that supralapsarianism offered no present assurance of final salvation; it led either to despair or "unwarranted security."[33] It is entirely possible that in opposing the Arminians, Ames took note of their concern, even if his answer was radically different from theirs.

Experiential Christianity: The Beginnings of Dutch Puritanism

Willem Teellinck

We saw that the growing prosperity of the Netherlands through the late sixteenth and seventeenth centuries encouraged a life style that was more comfortable than it was Christian amidst the crypto-Protestantism of the public church. Despite this, however, theological debate raged, albeit, as we saw above, at the theoretical level only. M.H. Prozesky identifies a second theological controversy coming somewhat later towards the middle of the seventeenth century. Disagreement arose over Johannes Coccejus' covenant theology.[34] Recall the rather creative system of covenant theology that Cocceius had developed, a much more speculative systematization of the thought of Ames. The "Coccejan" school underscored the bifurcation that existed between theoretical correctness and what they considered to be spiritual impoverishment in the Netherlands. The stage had been set by Ames before him who had, as we saw, moved theol-

---

Disputes in Dutch Calvinism from 1600-1650 (Cambridge: Cambridge University, 1938) while G.F. Nuttall wrote on the period shortly after Ames' death in "English Dissenters in the Netherlands, 1640-1689," *NAK* 59 (1978): 37-54.

[32] Arminius' reaction to Beza and his supralapsarianism were no doubt responsible for his appropriation of the logic of Ramus. Ramus, in turn, was suspicious of Beza himself and of Beza's use of scholasticism especially in regards to the Lord's Supper. Ramus cautions Heinrich Bullinger against "l'esprit subtil et le caractere dominateur de Theodore de Beze;" see Bangs, *Arminius*, 61. Arminius' work is available as *The Works of James Arminius*, trans. from the Latin by J. Nichols and W.R. Bagnall, 3 vols. (London: Printed for Longman, Hurst, Rees, Orme, Brown and Green, 1825-28; reprint ed., Grand Rapids: Baker, 1956).

[33] Bangs, *Arminius*, 56-63, 347-48.

[34] M.H. Prozesky, "The Emergence of Dutch Pietism," *JEH* 28 (January, 1977): 29-37.

ogy "away from the arid intellectualism of most of his professional colleagues and towards a practical and redemptive emphasis,"[35] an emphasis, we have shown, on covenantally-obedient living.

The short life of Willem Teellinck (1579-1629), like that of his contemporary and close friend Ames, was devoted to the promotion of godly living in a society characterized by confession of strict theological principles with somewhat less rigorous application to lived experience.[36] We have shown that this contradiction was promoted, if not actively then certainly passively, by some professional theologians in the Dutch academies. Born in Zeeland, Teellinck studied abroad at St. Andrews and Poitiers and spent nine months with the Puritan community in England in 1604.[37] His exposure to the Puritans and his lodging with a highly pious family in Bambury left permanent impressions upon him. Upon his return to the Netherlands he studied briefly (with Voet) under Trelcatius, Gomarus and Arminius at Leiden and went into pastoral ministry in 1606. He married a Puritan woman, had four children and died at the age of fifty.[38]

The pietism of Teellinck was of a different character than that of Jacob Spener, properly considered the "father of Pietism." The German Pietism was

---

[35] Prozesky, "Dutch Pietism," 35.
[36] For a sketch of Teellinck's life and contribution to the pietism of the *Nadere Reformatie* see K. Exalto, "Willem Teellinck (1579-1629)," in *Voornaamste vertegenwoordigers*, 17-47. See also the considerable research conducted by op 't Hof into the vast writing of Teellinck in "Willem Teellinck in het licht zijner geschriften," *DNR* 1 (1977): 3-14, 33-41, 69-76, 105-114; 2 (1978): 1-12, 33-62, 65-88, 97-105; 3 (1979): 33-40, 97-100; 4 (1980): 1-9, 33-38, 97-103; 5 (1981): 1-5, 34, 70-82, 107-108; 6 (1982): 1-4, 37-45; 7 (1983): 25-30, 37-42, 117-25; 8 (1984): 9-17, 37-40, 73-80, 109-113; 9 (1985): 37-42, 73-77, 109-118; 10 (1986): 31-36, 64-66, 73-76. Teellinck had a godly brother, Eeuwoud, who was a highly-educated (in law) and much-published public servant. Although not formally educated for the ministry, Eeuwout served as an elder in the consistory of the church at Middelburg, Zeeland. When Willem came here at the end of 1613, they worked together in consistory to return the area to "Zeeuwse piëtisme." He joined his brother in the struggle for greater discipline in church and culture and is considered to have had a great influence in the movement to pietism there. The two brothers died within six months of each other (*Eeuwout Teellinck in handschriften*, W.J. op 't Hof et al., eds. (Kampen: De Groot Goudriaan, 1989), 9.
[37] Beeke has Teellinck receiving a theological doctorate from Leiden in *Assurance*, 118; Both Bouwman and Engelberts, relying on the biography of Teellinck by his son Maximilian, have Teellinck promoted to doctorate (in law) in 1603 at Poitiers. See respectively, Bouwman, *Teellinck*, 14 and W.J.M. Engelberts, *Willem Teellinck* (Amsterdam: Ton Bolland, 1973), 9. Although it is always possible that Teellinck had a doctorate each in law and theology, his very brief stay at Leiden makes this rather implausible. See Engelberts, *Teellinck*, 20-21.
[38] Op 't Hof, *Engelse Piëtistische Geschriften*, 494-99. See also Engleberts, *Teellinck*, 3-21 and Bouwman, *Teellinck*, 7-15. The record is unclear whether he was married in England or the Netherlands. Engelberts thinks the former is most likely (*Teellinck*, 19-20, n. 2-n. 3).

characterized by a decidedly anti-dogmatic stance and sought reformation in the church differently than was pursued by the English Puritans and the Dutch "experientialists."[39] For Spener, whose understanding of the organic church of Jesus Christ was primarily in terms of the "church invisible," the need for ecclesiastical reform could be met by the establishment of conventicles and the practice of the priesthood of all believers in ministering to each other. This ground-level infusion of new spiritual life in the church would manifest itself, finally, in church reformation. But the primary concern of the Dutch experientialists was purification of church and life, both personal and social. This meant a strong balance between sound teaching and visible piety.[40] And in this they were faithful to Calvin "who not only was zealous for sound doctrine, but also for a sanctified life."[41]

Teellinck was a powerful preacher in the mold of William Perkins. His compassionate preaching was of an intensely biblical and practical nature, even if short on great oratorical flourish. His effect upon his listeners was so profound that highly-regarded theologian Voet relates, after hearing him only three or four times that "since that time my heart's desire has been that I and the teachers of this land could duplicate such form and power of preaching."[42] His preaching against a dead orthodoxy brought him under suspicion by the Reformed orthodox; meanwhile Arminians censored him for his very devotion to that Reformed orthodoxy.[43] It was his emphasis upon holy living that, paradoxically, earned him the opprobrium of voluntarist and pietist alike. As well, his writings demonstrate a remarkable similarity to Perkins in the "stepped" approach to salvation.[44] Teellinck produced a massive corpus in his lifetime,[45] the

---

[39] I use this designation advisedly and avoid the word "pietist" because of the uncomplimentary connotations with German Pietism that the label conjures. I shall further develop this concept presently. On Dutch experientialism, see W. van 't Spijker, "Experientia in reformatorisch licht," *ThRef* 19 (1976): 236-55.
[40] Bouwman, *Teellinck*, 11-12; op 't Hof, *Engelse Piëtistische Geschriften*, 639-46; Beeke, *Assurance*, 383-95.
[41] Bouwman, *Teellinck*, 13.
[42] Voet, cited in Bouwman, *Teellinck*, 16.
[43] Exalto documents this in "Willem Teellinck (1579-1629)," in *Voornaamste vertegenwordigers*, 23, 24ff. See also Beeke's summary in *Assurance*, 120, and op 't Hof in *Engelse Piëtistische Geschriften*, 499-508.
[44] Willem Teellinck, *Sleutel der Devotie Ons opende de Deure des Hemels*, 1624, vol. 3 in *Alle de wercken van Mr. Willem Teellinck*, 3 vols. (Utrecht: Johannes van Someren, 1659-1664), cited in Stoeffler, *Evangelical Pietism*, 132-33 and Beeke, *Assurance*, 120-29. See also the following by Teellinck: *The Ballance of the Sanctuarie, shewing how we must Behave our selves when wee see and behold the People of God in Miserie and Oppression under the Tyranny of their Enemies*, C. Harmar trans., T. Gataker, ed. (London: I.D. for William Sheffard, 1621); *The Christian Conflict and Conquest* (London: John Pawlar for I. Bellamie, 1622); *Huys-boeck, of te een Voudighe Verklaringhe en toe-eygheninghe, van de Voornaemste Vraeghstucke des Nederlandschen Christelijcken catechismi* (Middelburgh: voor Gillis Horthemels, 1650).

bulk of which was directed to *praxis pietas* and the fruits of conversion, in conformity to the primary emphasis of the *Heidelberg Catechism*.[46] Teellinck was followed by a small but vocal and influential minority, one of whom was Johannes Polyander, professor at Leiden. In his correspondence with Teellinck, he grieves the rampant hypocrisy of crypto-Protestantism, deeply regretting that "many Christians do not worship God in spirit and in truth." He strongly encourages Teellinck to continue his writing ministry whereby people will become not only better informed but also holier.[47]

Teellinck stresses in *Eubulus* that the Christian church of this period had brought upon itself the "heaviness" under which it was laboring by abandoning its first love. Unity in the church must come about in three ways: through the conviction of the truth, through the persuasion of love and the external compulsion (constraint) of the public authorities.[48] If, for example, the Remonstrants were not overcome by the overpowering, convincing power of the gospel, a demonstration of love, in all its power, must be applied with a view to steering the wayward individual towards the true faith. Continual resistance to the truth must be corrected by the public authorities, the "fosterlord" (*voedsterheer*) of the church. It was the responsibility of the state to drive individuals to the true faith and to use all its might to protect all that Christ has commanded and to keep out all human invention not commanded by Christ. Teellinck allowed tremendous power to the state – recall he was seeking reform of the public church.[49]

Additionally, Teellinck was compelled to motivate to right living. The Arminian controversy and the corresponding concern with purity of church and doctrine occupied the attention of the Reformed orthodox to the neglect of an authentic, vital, and vibrant Christian devotion.[50] In fact, in his Preface to a 1631 publication by Teellinck, Voet expressed this concern and observed that people had neglected to busy themselves with the writings of William Perkins and Jean Taffin, in his opinion two great theologians devoted to holiness of life.[51] He claimed that a living godliness was being forgotten because these

---

[45] Teellinck produced 127 manuscripts only some of which saw print (Goeters, *Vorbereitung des Pietismus*, 13). Four of his works were translated into English in his lifetime, the titles of which provide a good window on the concerns of Teellinck's heart (Stoeffler, *Evangelical Pietism*, 127, n. 1). Teellinck had a difficult, unpolished writing style which seriously limited his already great influence (Beeke, *Assurance*, 135-36, n. 80).

[46] Beeke, *Assurance*, 120-24.

[47] W.J. op 't Hof, "Johannes Polyander en Willem Teellinck: Een vergeten brief en nog meer," *DNR* 7 (1983): 126-43.

[48] Teellinck, *Eubulus*, 84. He fleshes out these three ways on pages 85-106, 106-221 and 221-342 respectively.

[49] Teellinck, *Eubulus*, 223, 227, 242, 255.

[50] Bouwman, *Teellinck*, 19-20.

[51] Jean Taffin (1529-1602) was a Pietist born in present-day Belgium and whose translated works had a tremendous influence in the movement of Reformed pietism. See the

practical/experiential-writers (*practijk-scribenten*) and their unwavering commitment to spurring one to reformation of life were being neglected.[52] The most irreproachable orthodoxy, Teellinck agreed, was worthless if one's confession did not reside in the heart. Only a vital piety would lead to the power of godliness.[53] On the basis of this emphasis, Teellinck was charged with being an "emotionalist," too subjective in theological emphasis and thus in league with the Arminian position. To this charge Teellinck responded that he too was concerned with sound doctrine but that many Reformed in doctrine were very un-Reformed in life. It was not his intention, he asserted, to criticize those promoting sound doctrine; rather, he was determining whether the "unsanctified confessors of doctrine" (*onheilige belijders der leer*) could be stirred to more holy thoughts."[54] It is equally his burden, he averred, to strive for sound doctrine, since "I truly know that Godliness is a true fruit of the knowledge of the Truth, Tit. 1:1, from which follows that is there to be any growth, this doctrine must be maintained."[55] So concerned was he for reformation of life in the Netherlands, that he advised the government the rescue of the country could come about only through grassroots reformation of morals and life.[56]

---

following two titles to obtain a good sense of his emphases: *De merck-teeckenen der kinderen Godts, ende de vertroostinghen in hare verdruckingen*, trans. J. Viverius (Amsterdam, 1620). [*Of the Marks of the Children of God, and of their Comforts in Afflictions*, trans. A. Prowse for Thomas Man (London: Thomas Orwin, 1590). A more accessible version is the recent *The Marks of God's Children*, P.Y. De Jong, trans., J.A. De Jong, ed. (Grand Rapids: Baker, 2003], and *De boetveerdicheyt des levens, vervaet in vier boeken*, trans. J. Crucius (Amsterdam, 1620). [*The Amendment of Life, Comprised in Fower Books* (London: G. Bishop, 1595).] According to W.J. op 't Hof, it was in Taffin's writings that a first identifiable program for further reformation was developed. See more detail in his "Taffin, Jean" in *BLGNP* 4:412-14. S. van der Linde judges Taffin to be the first passionate promoter (*pleiter*) of a further reformation in "Jean Taffin: eerst pleiter voor 'Nadere Reformatie' in Nederland," *ThRef* (1982): 6-29. See also his *Jean Taffin: Hofprediker en raadsheer van Willem van Oranje* (Amsterdam: Ton Bolland, 1982). Connections between the Reformation and the thought of the *Nadere Reformatie* as seen by contemporaries of the latter period are found in, for example, W.J. op 't Hof, "De visie op de Reformatie in de Nadere Reformatie tijdens het eerste kwart van de zeventiende eeuw," *DNR* 6 (1982): 89-108 and "Gisbertus Voetius' Evaluatie van de Reformatie," *ThRef* 32 (1989): 211-42.

[52] Voet, in his Preface to Teellinck's *De Worstelinge eenes bekeerden Sondaers* (1631), cited in Bouwman, *Teellinck*, 18-19.

[53] .Bouwman summarizing Teellinck in *Teellinck*, 19-21.

[54] This was the primary focus of his devotional writings according to Engelberts, (*Teellinck*, 157-78).

[55] Teellinck, "Geestelycke Couranten," (1626), 62-65, cited in Bouwman, *Teellinck*, 19, 61.

[56] Teellinck, "Zions Basuyne," (1621), cited in Bouwman, *Teellinck*, 20.

Teellinck's burning passion was "new life in Christ."[57] This was evidenced and perfected through godly living, the "true goal of life" which he summarized as glorifying God and promoting the salvation of self and neighbor.[58] Thus, during the raging theological and ecclesiastical battles between scholastic Calvinism and Arminianism, Teellinck tried "upon these troubled waters . . . to sail the fragile barge of Pietism, contending in all of his writings that to the soundness of doctrine must be added the power of godliness expressed in truly Christian conduct"[59] at both the personal and public level. We have seen that he found himself looking to the Puritans in England, attracted as he was by their practical theology and having experienced Puritan pietism firsthand during a stay in England. No doubt he considered it the greatest convergence of providences that had brought William Ames so near at hand at a time like this.

Willem Teellinck and William Ames
In distinguishing Teellinck's thought from that of Ames, Bouwman observes Heppe's assertion that Teellinck's written works comprise nothing other than the clear and devotional development of the teachings of the church.[60] In agreement, Bouwman notes that for Teellinck, theology was the doctrine of knowing God and serving him, as distinguished from Ames for whom theology meant the doctrine of living to God.[61] Our study of Ames indicates that obedience is understood in the Christian ideal of living to God in covenantal relationship.

It is instructive at this point to again review the intellect/will distinction, right understanding of which is so much a part of any effort to come to terms with Ames' teaching and that of his contemporaries. It will be remembered that Ames departed significantly from his teacher Perkins in the relative position of these two faculties. Perkins' famous simile that the intellect is to the soul as the driver is to the wagon is picked up by Teellinck as he sought to articulate his understanding of these two faculties in defending himself from the accusations of voluntarism, while at the same time distancing himself from the Arminians with whom his scholastic enemies sought to align him.[62] In line with the (mis)understanding of his day, Bouwman points out that this is the same distinction made by Calvin, although that incorrect reading of Calvin we ad-

---

[57] M.E. Osterhaven, "The Experiential Theology of Early Dutch Calvinism," *RefRev* 27 (1974): 181.
[58] Teellinck, *True Godliness*, 128-36.
[59] Stoeffler, *Evangelical Pietism*, 128.
[60] Heppe, *Geschichte des Pietismus*, 129, cited in Bouwman, *Teellinck*, 25.
[61] Bouwman, *Teellinck*, 25. Teellinck's definition of theology is found in "Adam rechtschapen, wanschapen, herschapen," 224.
[62] As pointed out by W. van 't Spijker in "Teellinck's Opvatting van de menselijke wil," *ThRef* 7 (1964): 126 and Bouwman, *Teellinck*, 25. Teellinck's self-alignment with Perkins is found in his "Adam rechtschapen, wanschapen, herschapen," 242.

dressed in an earlier chapter.[63] With a similar bias, Engelbert places Teellinck among the voluntarists, a position challenged by W. van 't Spijker who locates Ames in this category not through comparisons with Calvin, but rather from his comparative study of Ames and Teellinck.[64]

Even though Ames, in this respect, did not share the nomenclature or phrasing of both Calvin and Perkins, he shared their view that the volition is spurred into action by an informed intellect. The will, then, both savingly appropriates and makes life application of true faith. In concord with Ames' high view of the volition, Teellinck asserted, if somewhat ambiguously, that "the will is the highest power of the soul with respect to its own action . . . whereby one desires good, resists evil, and holds the doubtful (*twijfelachtige*) in suspense."[65] It was the *twijfelachtige* that Ames sought to minimize with his casuistry. Clearly Ames' moral theology in the midst of this ethos was welcomed by Teellinck, a true kindred spirit.[66] And Ames had high esteem for Teellinck. When his *Conscience* was published the year following Teellinck's death at the age of fifty, Ames devotion of almost a third of the dedication (earlier cited) to Teellinck carried highly eulogistic overtones:

> That worthy servant of the Lord, Master William Teeling, who was by [promoting the *Doctrine according to Godlinesse* held] in great admiration, and famous throughout all the Low-Countrey churches, (to say nothing of others, that both have, and doe take the same course) tooke such painfull paines this way, both publikely and privately, by word and writing, that it may be truely said, *The zeale of Gods house hath eaten him up*: whereby also, (Envy the follower of such a virtue, being now overcome) he hath obtained that Crowne, which God hath prepared for those that have instructed many unto righteousnesse.[67]

It is time to identify more clearly the system Ames brought to the *Nadere Reformatie*. English Puritan concern for practical theology or experiential Christianity spurred the development of a moral theology that vigorously enjoined reformation of life and thought. Upon examination, that Ames cast this within a covenantal framework simply confirms the central role given the covenant concept going all the way to Calvin. From Perkins on, Puritanism en-

---

[63] Bouwman, *Teellinck*, 25.
[64] Van 't Spijker, "Teellinck's Opvatting," 125-42. On accusations of voluntarism against Teellinck, see J. de Boer, *De Verzegeling met de Heilige Geest, volgens de opvatting van de Nadere Reformatie* (Rotterdam: Bronder, 1968), 97-98, and Engelberts, *Teellinck*, 111-12. In this respect, Beeke comes to Teellinck's defense as well in *Assurance*, 121-24. Regarding Ames as voluntarist, van 't Spijker affirms Goeters' misguided historiography found in Goeters, *Vorbereitung des Pietismus*, 70.
[65] Teellinck, "Adam rechtschapen, wanschapen, herschapen" 243, cited in van 't Spijker, "Teellinck's Opvatting," 18, and Bouwman, *Teellinck*, 27.
[66] Geesink notes that Reformed ethics appropriated Puritan principles through the mediation of Ames (Geesink, *Gereformeerde Ethiek*, 2.473-2.477).
[67] Ames, *Conscience*, "Dedicatory Epistle."

deavored to address matters regarding one's personal relationship with God within the covenant of grace.[68] Muller's comments are apposite:

> [English Puritan casuistry is the] English Reformed resolution of the problem of human responsibility in a system of salvation by grace alone. . . . Perkins emphasized the work of Christ and its application in covenant. . . . This balance of system and piety focused on the work of Christ and the covenant was carried forward by Perkins' foremost pupil, William Ames.[69]

In agreement, W. Orme observes that "William Perkins is, properly, the first original writer in our language on the theory and practice of religion, in a regular systematic form."[70] Yet we have seen that although Perkins incorporated both mutuality and one-sidedness in his covenantal understanding of theology, it was Ames who constructed a system of covenant theology based on the unambiguously monopleuric covenant of grace in which the believer had covenantal responsibility for obedience and observance in a life of Christian activism. This was the system Ames brought to the *Nadere Reformatie*; this is what made it such an attractive theological package to the continental theologians such as Willem Teellinck who were so concerned with high ethical norms within the Christian life but lacked system. If Beeke is right when he says that Perkins was the father of English Puritanism, and Teellinck the father of the Dutch Second Reformation,[71] then surely Ames was the connecting link, even if he was preceded across the North Sea by the translated writing of Perkins. Ames introduced to the continent an informed, system-based theology and an experiential Christianity, careful always to guard against an overly-pietistic subjectivism by measuring the Christian life against the objective standards of scripture. This is the essence of the informed pietism of the Reformed system. And his burden for applied and moral theology led, as we have seen, to his concern for proper ministerial preparation and training, focusing on the preacher's responsibility to prick the conscience and motivate to right living. Was this not Teellinck's agenda too?

There is further evidence of, perhaps, a more direct sort to demonstrate a likely kinship between Ames and Teellinck. Teellinck sent both his older sons Maximiliaan and Justus to study under Ames at Franeker; both sons named Ames in their publicly-defended disputations. Second, Franeker's theological faculty provided strong approbation to Teellinck's agenda for

---

[68] R.A. Muller, "Covenant and Conscience in English Reformed Theology: Three Variations on a 17th Century Theme," *WTJ* 42 (1980): 308-34.
[69] Muller, "Covenant and Conscience," 311, 309-10.
[70] W. Orme, *The Life and Times of Richard Baxter*, vol. 2 (London: James Duncan, 1830), 163.
[71] Beeke, *Assurance*, 105.

reform by setting their signatures to a number of his written works. Ames' signature is prominent.[72]

We conclude this section with a reminder that comes from Engelberts regarding the cross-Atlantic connection between the spiritual and ecclesiastical life of the Dutch Republic and England:

> [Teellinck's] deepest impressions were received from what he saw and heard in the district in which he resided in England. What was the spirit that reigned there? A type of pietism, . . . the Puritan Pietism. . . . The quiet simplicity, the deep sincerity, and the tireless perseverance with which the "practice of godliness" was pursued must not only have commanded the respect of all those who witnessed it but also unwittingly, in those hearts, sown a seed which bore not insignificant fruit. And this seed fell also in the heart of Teellinck when, after considerable travel, he set up his tent in the vicinity of Bambury.[73]

Thus it was that Teellinck, the Dutch theologian permanently influenced by English Puritanism, and Ames, the English expatriate, became the two pre-eminent Reformed contemporaries of the early seventeenth-century Further Reformation in the Netherlands. "At the side of Amesius," remarks Reuter, "stands Teellinck as witness to the intimate relationship between Puritan pietistic piety and the religious core of Augustine's system."[74] Their program involved a return to well-informed, biblical, pious living. They worked in tandem to reform life, church and academy in the theological context of scholasticism and Aristotle within a society and a public church that had drifted some distance from its orthodox Reformation moorings.

Unpacking Pietism, English Puritanism and the Nadere Reformatie

Because German Pietism as espoused by its founder Jacob Spener has many elements in common with Amesian teaching, briefly examining the differences will help us appreciate even more clearly the contributions of Ames to Reformed system.[75] Spener read the Puritans' criticisms of conventional Christianity and emphasis upon personal sanctity. He inveighed against scholastic theology, emphasized the "living faith" of the believer, and called people to account for their ungodly life, most notably tendencies toward drunkenness and litiga-

---

[72] W.J. op 't Hof, *Engelse Piëtistische Geschriften*, 497-99; idem, "Een onbekende zoon van Willem Teellinck," *DNR* 25 (2001): 84-89.

[73] Engelberts, *Teellinck*, 95-96.

[74] Horton, *Ames by Reuter*, 187. Reuter is citing Heppe, *Geschichte des Pietismus*, 131ff. Reuter observes that Augustine's predication that the true bond between God and humanity is love has its origins in Plato who opined that "the true philosopher is a lover of God." Conjoining love for God with faith "goes beyond ordinary Reformed and orthodox doctrine" asserts Reuter, citing Heppe. Reuter continues, "Ames was the first to work through this new standpoint theologically" (*Ames by Reuter*, 187).

[75] Jacob Spener, *Pia Desideria*, T.G. Tappert, trans. and ed. (Philadelphia: Fortress, 1964).

tion. He taught sound stewardship and Christian service, lamenting over lawbreakers and calling for church reform. This reform would come about through more "extensive use of the Word of God among us," especially the New Testament, and through the re-introduction of "the ancient and apostolic kind of church meetings." Other recommendations include "the establishment and diligent exercise of the spiritual priesthood," emphasis on Christian practice in addition to the faith, proper conduct in religious controversies, and a well-trained, well-read, well-practiced and pious clergy to introduce and supervise these changes.[76]

It cannot be disputed that Ames' concerns paralleled those of Spener. But Spener's ecclesiastical context was the Lutheran church and his teleological context was almost solely eschatological, looking forward to a better day.[77] Ames, meanwhile, was concerned with living to God as a goal in the here and now, convinced of the biblical teaching of *coram Deo*; such as the life is, such is the end.

A 1929 survey of the distinguishing features of Puritanism still holds considerable value for us today. R. Bronkema comes up with three predominant characteristics: "Biblicism, Ethicism and Mysticism" although the latter he qualifies by stating that "the most one can say is that Puritanism inclines in a mystical direction.[78] In comparing Pietism and Puritanism, Bronkema concludes that, in areas where Puritanism and Pietism were similar, the latter: was "more confessionally indifferent," "emphasized to a greater extent the supremacy of the will" and placed more emphasis on the subjective aspect of the practice of piety. Its religious enthusiasm bore a "more mystical character." Furthermore,

> Pietism arose largely as a reaction against formalism, Puritanism as a reaction against Romanism and immorality.... Pietism had as primary purpose the cleansing of the life of the individual; Puritanism, at least in the Puritan age, the cleansing of church life. Pietism withdraws from Church and world, Puritanism aims to reform them. Thus Pietism was strongly individualistic; Puritanism, at least at first, was not. Pietism was emotional, exalting feeling. Puritanism was more stolid, austere, and in a certain sense intellectual. For the basis of Pietism was experi-

---

[76] Spener, *Pia Desideria*, 9, 52-53, 58-75, 87-118.
[77] P.C. Erb, ed., *Pietists: Selected Writings*. The Classics of Western Spirituality, R.J. Payne, ed. (New York: Paulist, 1983), 6.
[78] R. Bronkema, "The Essence of Puritanism" (Th.D. diss., Free University of Amsterdam, 1929), 70. See also the following: J. Brown, *The English Puritans* (London: Cambridge University, 1912); L.J. Trinterud, "The Origins of Puritanism;" J.C. Brauer, "Reflections on the Nature of English Puritanism," *CH* 23 (1954): 98-109; B. Hall, "Puritanism: The Problem of Definition" in *SCH*, vol. 2, 283-96; and Trinterud, ed., *Elizabethan Puritanism* (New York: Oxford University, 1971). On the connections between Puritanism and Pietism, see S. van der Linde, "Puritanisme en Piëtisme," *ThRef* 31 (1988): 196-212. On Puritanism and Christian piety, see G.S. Wakefield, *Puritan Devotion: Its Place in the Development of Christian Piety* (London: Epworth, 1957).

ence, that of Puritanism the Bible. Pietism can be called subjective, Puritanism aimed at the objective results of religion. Pietism emphasized love, Puritanism emphasized faith and works. The predominant tone in Pietism was joy, while Puritanism became somber through its emphasis on righteousness, wrath, hell and damnation. The tendency of Pietism was to neglect Scripture; that of Puritanism was strongly scriptural. Pietism lacked all central control; Puritanism had its strength in Bible authority. The hearth of Pietism was Germany; that of Puritanism England.[79]

J.T. McNeill comes up with essentially the same features in his brief survey.[80] He emphasizes as well the internal differences within Pietism.[81] To this otherwise good summary should be added, however, the Puritan theology of covenant through which tapestry these other characteristics were interwoven. As it stands, William Ames is located solidly in the Puritan camp, but he borrowed heavily from his fellow Pietists and was unique in formulating theology as the doctrine of living to God in covenant. Undoubtedly Ames leanings toward godliness in life conflated nicely with the emphasis on personal and public piety he found in concerned spiritual leaders in the early seventeenth-century Dutch Republic, and helped construct the theological architecture of the *Nadere Reformatie*. In fact, it seems reasonable to postulate that his formal thought represented the center of the *Nadere Reformatie* of his day. In addition to the "formal" definition of the movement, Beeke provides a helpful summary of the characteristics of the movement from Graafland's work:

> Generally speaking, the complex Dutch Second Reformation focused on a variety of major themes. In summarizing the movement, Graafland addresses the following contours: election, regeneration, sanctification, the family and the congregation, the church, creation and natural theology, eschatology, and theocracy. Through promoting a pious lifestyle and a theocratic concept of all social relationships based on family worship, the parish, and the church as a whole, the Second Reformation aimed to establish and enforce moral and spiritual discipline in all spheres of life. Second Reformation sermons addressed all of these mostly active themes, but simultaneously stressed the fall of Adam, the natural man's inability to aspire to good, the absolute sovereignty of divine predestination and grace, dependence on God, the necessity of adequate conviction of sin, the experience of conversion, and the simplicity of true worship.[82]

Osterhaven refers to William Ames as a "representative of this experiential theology of early Dutch Calvinism"[83] remarking that Ames "differs noticeably

---

[79] Bronkema, "Puritanism," 77-78.
[80] J.T. McNeill, *Modern Christian Movements* (Philadelphia: Westminster, 1954; reprint ed., New York: Harper & Row, 1968), 71-74.
[81] McNeill, *Modern Christian Movements*, 49-71.
[82] Beeke, *Assurance*, 393-94, summarizing Graafland, "Kernen en contouren," in *Voornaamste vertegenwoordigers*, 349-67.
[83] Osterhaven, "Experiential Theology," 180-89.

from the more mystical pietists in that the description of love [in *Marrow*] mentions sweetness and joy but places the emphasis on doing God's will."[84] To be sure, areas in Ames' writings confirm his tendency to travel in a pietistic direction, but never along a road unmarked by the signposts of the covenant of grace. For Ames, the covenant's very essence and structure represent the truth of God's Word. This emphasis on covenantal obedience prevented him from moving into an unbiblical mysticism. Ames provided, as it were, a "covenantal framework" to healthy pietism in the Netherlands. If one were to place all of the above-cited characteristics within the covenantal framework designed by Ames, then one would have a well-constructed Reformed system for faith and life.

Thus sound doctrine combined with high piety distinguished this movement from all others. Osterhaven probes its "mood," "method" and "model men." With respect to the first, "these Calvinists . . . were zealous for spiritual perfection." They promoted this zeal by, secondly, criticizing the existing church through "existential personalism," "the claim that the whole man, feeling and will, as well as intellect, must be affected by religious experience and that this experience must be one in which the individual becomes aware of the centrality of his relationship to God."[85] And, thirdly, the two "model men" whom Osterhaven identifies as most actively promoting such a program of experientialism are William Ames and Theodorus Jacobus Frelinghuysen (1692-1747).[86]

Osterhaven summarizes the experiential theology of the *Nadere Reformatie* as "that broad stream of Reformed teaching which, accepting the creeds of the church, emphasized the new birth, the conversion, and the sanctification of the believer so that he might acquire an experiential or personal knowledge of Christ's saving grace."[87] This led to a sense of *gelukzaligheid*, best translated as "holy felicity," and to active pursuit of a life of obedience. Ames saw this obedience anchored in the covenantal relationship between God and his people.

Summary

Ames went to the Netherlands and sharpened his unified and covenant-based theological program of faith and obedience in the face of opposition on the continent, where, paradoxically, his agenda received both approbation and further fuel. Ames interacted full-bore with the emerging experiential Calvinism of the Netherlands, defining its tenets and defying its opponents.

---

[84] Osterhaven, "Experiential Theology," 186.
[85] Osterhaven, "Experiential Theology," 183. This focus on the "whole man" was a deliberate attempt to explicitly shift the prevailing emphasis from the intellect.
[86] The latter of whom was "a pastor of incalculable influence in the life of the Reformed Church in America," especially in bringing evangelical pietism into the Middle Colonies (Osterhaven, "Experiential Theology," 180, 186). Frelinghuysen comes up again later.
[87] Osterhaven, "Experiential Theology," 182.

Even as we reflect on the largely misguided historiographical assessment of William Ames, we must remember that he maintained a distinctly Calvinistic emphasis; Calvin's *Institutes* were, after all, intended for direction in godliness.[88] "Calvinism was intrinsically oriented toward piety"[89] and Ames remembered this as he supplied formal theological infrastructure to Dutch pietistic tendencies through his utilization of covenantal principles and categories in an architectonic way.

The experiential Christianity close to Ames' heart he considered lacking in Maccovius, in the public church, and in society, but not in Willem Teellinck, together with whom he set about reorienting the culture of the Dutch Republic towards a practical and vital Christianity, towards a godliness that focused on sound doctrine, taught visible piety and religious affections and emphasized the volitional aspect of a life of covenant obedience in the power of godliness.

This combination of system and practice with its peculiar Amesian emphases places this "solid, judicious and learned divine"[90] squarely at the head of the *Nadere Reformatie*.

---

[88] Calvin, "Subject Matter of the Present Work," *Institutes*, 6-8. See also, Erb, *Pietists*, 4.
[89] Stoeffler, *Evangelical Pietism*, 116.
[90] Benjamin Brook, *The Lives of the Puritans*, vol. 2 (London: James Black, 1813; reprint ed., Pittsburgh: Soli Deo Gloria, 1994), 407.

Chapter 9

Amesian Contours in the Thought of Wilhelmus à Brakel and Petrus van Mastricht

William Ames and Wilhelmus à Brakel

Wilhelmus à Brakel
The late seventeenth-century pastor/theologian Wilhelmus à Brakel represents a prime example of the experiential Christianity of the Dutch Second Reformation with its twin emphasis upon sound doctrine and pious, sanctified living. Brakel was born and schooled in Friesland in the northern Netherlands and pastored there his entire life. He belonged to the period of "high" orthodoxy, among theologians such as Petrus van Mastricht, Francis Turretin (1623-1687) and Gisbertus Voet.

As we attempt to identify the seminal influence reflected in Brakel's work in theoretical and practical divinity, it will be helpful to introduce this chapter with a very brief biographical sketch to help further contextualize Brakel's theological orientation.

Wilhelmus à Brakel was born in Leeuwarden, the Netherlands in 1635, two years after the death of William Ames.[1] He was schooled in the University of Franeker, known for its commitment to doctrinal precision and, after Ames' tenure there, to the pious life as well. We cannot underestimate the influence that the legacy of Ames had at that institution. It was soon after Brakel entered the academy in 1654, fully twenty one years after Ames' departure, that he learned the need for an educated ministry and the value of scholarship.[2] Being

---

[1] These biographical details are from W. Fieret, "Wilhelmus à Brakel – A Biographical Sketch," Wilhelmus à Brakel, *Reasonable Service*, xxxi-lxxxi. The original treatise appeared in two volumes and was published in numerous editions throughout the eighteenth century. I have also made use of Volume 1 of the original first edition of 1700: Wilhelmus à Brakel, *Redelyke Godts-Dienst, In welke de Goddelijke Waarheden des Genaden-Verbondts worden verklaart, tegen allerleye partyen beschermt, ende tot de praktijke aangedrongen*, 2 vols. ['s-Gravenhage: Cornelis van Dyck, 1700]. The new edition released in 1881 in "modernized" Dutch has been invaluable in this study (Wilhelmus à Brakel, *Redelijke Godsdienst*, 2 vols. [Leiden: D. Donner, 1881]). I cite from *Service* by volume and page number. See also F.J. Los, *Wilhelmus à Brakel* (Leiden: G. Los, 1892).

[2] Wilhelmus à Brakel, no doubt, learned much of this from his father, Theodorus, himself a Reformed minister who, according to Wilhelm Goeters, "came under the influence of Ames" (Goeters, *Vorbereitung des Pietismus*, 93). For the thought of the elder Brakel, and to examine his Amesian emphases, see, for example, his *Het geestelijke leven, ende de stand eens geloovigen menschen hier op aarde* (Amsterdam: Abraham Cornelis,

declared a candidate for ministry he was unable to find a pulpit in a time when ministers of the gospel were in oversupply, so he studied under Voet and Andreas Essenius at Utrecht. But subsequent to receiving his first call in 1662, he served four congregations in the northern Netherlands, preaching in distinctively experiential fashion and enduring the theological controversy and ecclesiastical conflict of the day. He thus labored for twenty-one years in William Ames' adopted home of Friesland, before spending the remainder of his career and life in Rotterdam, his fifth pastoral charge.

At the very beginning, therefore, of Pastor Brakel's journey, he embarked on a geographical and theological pilgrimage which consisted in a series of divinely appointed steps that brought him to intersect with the Learned Doctor at every turn.[3]

Brakel's Amesian Emphases
a) Prolegomena and Theology
"The substance or *contents* of the Word is the covenant of grace, or to state it differently, it contains the perfect rule for faith and practice."[4] With this statement, Brakel immediately introduces the body of his theological work with a notable Amesian distinctive – covenant theology – expressed in Amesian nomenclature.[5] That the covenant relationship is the grid through which all of humanity interacts – with each other and with God – is made apparent in the second half of Brakel's assertion. Both faith and practice can be properly understood only covenantally – this means living to God. And for Ames this living to God has the divine word as touchstone. He claims that the Bible is the "rule of faith and conduct" the "perfect rule of faith and morals,"[6] whose style and function "affects the will by stirring up pious motives, which is the chief end of theology."[7] From the outset, then, we detect more than faint traces of the spirit of Ames in Brakel's work. In fact, in his opening definition Brakel combines Ames' two key distinctives – covenant theology and informed piety, but does a better job of explicitly grounding his thought in scripture from the very outset.[8] A perceived attenuation or deficiency of Ames' view of scripture has

---

1648) and *De trappen Des Geestelijken Levens*, 8th ed. (Amsterdam: Abraham Cornelis, 1670).

[3] It is a curiosity of providence that both divines, after spending so much time in the northern Netherlands, should conclude their lives in Rotterdam.

[4] Brakel, *Service*, 1.34.

[5] Although by the time Brakel was writing covenant theology was fairly commonplace in Reformed thought, a journey through Brakel's four volumes will evidence the degree to which an explicit covenant framework is the organizing principle for all of his theology, with Amesian conceptual categories and nomenclature.

[6] Ames, *Marrow*, 1.34.2, 1.34.10, 1.34.16.

[7] Ames, *Marrow* 1.34.19.

[8] For a study of Brakel's view of scripture, see C. Graafland, "Schriftleer en schriftverstaan," *Theologische aspecten*, 29-97.

been observed by scholars. When seen in the context of the high view of scripture prevalent in the period of the Reformed orthodoxy of the day, Ames' view falls short.[9] Graafland studies the view of scripture of many representatives of the *Nadere Reformatie* and has this to say of Ames' relative place in that movement: "It can be said of Voetius, more so than of Amesius, that he strove to combine further reformation (*nadere reformatie*) of the church with existing Reformed orthodoxy."[10]

Both Ames and Brakel emphasize the importance of reading and hearing this Word of God. Ministers must faithfully attend to that "divine obligation" says Ames.[11] Because the Bible in the original autographs is the only "authentic" word of God since error creeps into translations, ministerial preparation must include training in the original languages.[12] But despite all the shortcomings of translations, the international, multiethnic and multilinguistic nature of the church of Jesus Christ makes universal accessibility and thus the project of Bible translation paramount.[13] Ames' counsel in this matter sounds very contemporary: "We must not rest forever in any accepted version, but faithfully see to it that a pure and faultless interpretation is given to the church."[14] This emphasis on the Bible's universal intelligibility receives enthusiastic endorsement from Brakel. While Ames clearly places more stress on the inspiration of scripture,[15] both men explicitly counter the Roman Catholic claims to authority at length and share other, by now typically Reformed, emphases as well such as scripture's necessity, perspicuity, sufficiency, authority, etc. In the context of the Cartesian controversy which had been swirling in the Dutch Republic, Brakel adds a long section on the interplay of reason and faith in the exposition of scripture, but ultimately, reason must give way to faith: "intellect and reason are absolutely necessary to understand Scripture and thereby to exercise faith" but, finally, "reason must surrender itself to the Word; the Word must never surrender itself to reason."[16] Descartes would shudder.

Recall that for Ames, the object of faith is God who is understood in his efficiency and sufficiency. God's sufficiency Ames further dichotomizes into his essence and subsistence. And God's essence lies in his attributes, communicable and incommunicable, while his subsistence lies in his trinitarian nature.[17] This taxonomy could have been the blueprint for the exposition of Brakel who, like Ames, feels it necessary to distinguish between the ontological and eco-

---

[9] Graafland, "Schriftleer en schriftverstaan," *Theologische aspecten*, 31-34.
[10] Graafland, "Schriftleer en schriftverstaan," *Theologische aspecten*, 35.
[11] Ames, *Conscience*, 4.11.
[12] Brakel, *Service*, 1.33-1.34; 1.67-1.72, 2.132; Ames, *Marrow*, 1.34.24-1.34.34; idem, *Conscience*, 4.26.
[13] Brakel, *Service*, 1.69.
[14] Ames, *Marrow*, 1.34.33.
[15] Ames, *Marrow*, 1.34.1-1.34.7.
[16] Brakel, *Service*, 1.59-1.60.
[17] Ames, *Marrow*, 1.4-1.5.

nomic trinity. "We must distinguish here between the divine essence and divine persons,"[18] said Brakel, before going on to sketch a somewhat fuller portrait of God's nature (essence) and trinitarian character (subsistence).[19] Finally, "the Father, the Son and the Spirit," says Brakel, "reveal themselves, interact with, and exercise believers in an individual and distinct manner."[20] Ames had called these the "boundaries of action" of the divine persons of the trinity, "that aspect in which one person's working or manner of working shines forth most clearly."[21] It is the work of the trinity to execute the covenant of grace, a covenant whose benefits and desirability are revealed and confirmed to believers by the very names of the persons of the trinity.[22]

The efficiency of God, says Ames, is his absolute power (*potentia absoluta*) and his ordaining or actual power (*potentia ordinata sive actualis*).[23] Brakel refers to these as, respectively, power in its "primary meaning" and in its "second meaning."[24] Both theologians agree that God does nothing that contradicts his character or that is "contrary to the essential nature of things,"[25] or that "involve a contradiction, either in God or in created things."[26]

While the introductory comments to Ames' and Brakel's respective chapters on the decrees of God are very similar (focusing primarily on the characteristics of God's decretive activity), it is clear that Brakel's concern is of a more polemical nature. Brakel's major burden is to withstand the objections of the proponents of "free will."[27] Ames, on the other hand, offers a three-way emphasis on the counsel of God. God's decree is a perfect expression of this counsel, and Ames focuses on the purpose or end of this counsel (God's glory), the mental conception of this end (by divine knowledge) and the intention and agreement of the will. The better part of the chapter discusses the nature and characteristics of God's will.[28] Brakel does not follow Ames' unique coverage in this regard.

Brakel proceeds immediately to the doctrine of predestination: election and reprobation and presents the well fleshed-out Reformed thinking on this doctrine.[29] The detail of this exposition of "double-predestination" match quite

---

[18] Brakel, *Service*, 1.146.
[19] Brakel, *Service*, 1.83-1.191.
[20] Brakel, *Service*, 1.177.
[21] Ames, *Marrow*, 1.6.27-1.6.31.
[22] Brakel, *Service*, 1.171-1.184.
[23] Ames, *Marrow*, 1.6.18.
[24] Brakel, *Service*, 1.130-1.131.
[25] Brakel, *Service*, 1.131-1.132.
[26] Ames, *Marrow*, 1.6.17. As scripture, Ames adds 2 Tim 2:13, "He cannot deny himself."
[27] Brakel, *Service*, 1.198-1.207. Although Ames may not formally denunciate Arminianism here, his strong anti-Arminian stance is well known.
[28] Ames, *Marrow*, 1.7.
[29] Brakel, *Service*, 1.211-1.250.

closely that of Ames.[30] What is noteworthy, however, is the respective placement of this topic in the work of the two theologians under consideration. Earlier we noted how Ames followed Calvin in locating the doctrine of predestination at the beginning of his soteriology, directly after the chapter of the application of Christ which is Ames' key expository chapter on the covenant of grace (presented, remember, by way of comparison to the covenant of works).[31] For Ames, Christ's work is applied in covenant and by a predestinating God. But in systematizing his theology, Brakel gives predestination a much higher priority in the development of doctrine by placing it up front as he does. For Brakel, because predestination is part and parcel of God's decretive will, he locates his exposition of it in his theology proper, his doctrine of God. William Ames' position is more faithful to Calvin, while Brakel follows the path of Perkins and Beza. Finally, while Calvin's inchoate teaching on the covenant of redemption received explicit affirmation in Ames, it is presented in full force by Brakel.[32]

The closing section in Brakel's theology proper addresses creation (and angels and devils). It appears that Brakel is following Ames' Ramist classification here as well, for in introducing the chapter on creation he begins with: "Having considered the intrinsic works of God, we proceed to consider His extrinsic works – in the realm of nature and in the realm of grace. His works in nature are *creation* as well as His *providence* in regard to His creation. We shall first discuss creation."[33] Recall that Ames has just completed his teaching on God's decree, itself an expression of God's "efficiency" or "working power." This could be designated his "intrinsic" work," to use Brakel's expression. Ames is now ready to show how this intrinsic "efficiency" is demonstrated: "The efficiency of God may be understood as either creation or providence."[34]

Ames sees a particular sequence in the divine generation of matter and life in the created order:

> His wisdom is seen, first, in that simple elements were created before things elementary, condensed, or compound; second, in that among the simple things the more perfect were made first, being closest to the nature of God; third, in that those things were created first which have only being, then those which have life as well as being, then those that have sense as well as being and life, and last of all those which have reason besides being, life, and sense; fourth, in that simple things were created in order from the more perfect to the less perfect, but com-

---

[30] As Eusden observes, Ames "was not completely orthodox" in the matter of predestination (Eusden, "Introduction" in *Marrow*, 7).
[31] Calvin, *Institutes*, 3.21-3.24; Ames, *Marrow*, 1.24.
[32] Calvin, *Institutes*, 3.21.5; Ames, *Marrow*, 1.19.2-1.19.5 and 1.24.1-1.24.3; Brakel, *Service*, 1.251-1.263. Brakel entitles his chapter "The Covenant of Redemption Between God the Father and God the Son Concerning the Elect; or, the Counsel of Peace."
[33] Brakel, *Service*, 1.265.
[34] Ames, *Marrow*, 1.8.1.

pound things in order from the less perfect to the more perfect (plants before men, for example).³⁵

Brakel, too, wishes to emphasize the specific pattern followed in creation:

> In the creation of lifeless objects God began with that which is most sophisticated: light, from which he proceeded to air, from air to water, and from water to the earth, which is the least sophisticated structure. In creating living creatures, however, God began with the lowest degree of complexity, the irrational animals, and ended with His most magnificent creature, man.³⁶

In his understanding of the creation of heaven as being the "third heaven" referred to in 2 Corinthians 12:2 and 1 Kings 8:27, Brakel also borrows from Ames, prooftexts included.³⁷ Much of the detail is also similar, as well as the coverage of the creation of angels (good and apostate), but it is generally standard Reformed fare on the doctrine of creation, much of it from Calvin.

b) Theological Anthropology

The theological anthropology of William Ames and Wilhelmus à Brakel follows closely that of John Calvin and subsequent Reformed development. Humanity is body and soul, the soul immortal.³⁸ But there are some noteworthy, peculiarly Amesian distinctives to be found in Brakel. Of particular note, is Brakel's view on conscience. "The conscience," explains Brakel, "is man's judgment concerning himself and his deeds, to the extent he is subject to God's judgment."³⁹ Writing three-quarters of a century earlier, Ames had said that "The conscience of man . . . is a man's judgement of himself, according to the judgement of God of him."⁴⁰ As we have already seen, in places Ames shows himself to be a "most eminent disciple"⁴¹ of William Perkins who had incorporated many of these elements in his understanding of conscience.⁴²

Wilhelmus à Brakel's treatise betrays considerable dependence on Ames as he discusses the essence and dynamics of conscience. Using layman's terminology (rather than the language of the schoolmen of which Ames was so fond), Brakel too presents a syllogistic understanding of conscience, "a constitutive element of the intellect" comprised of three elements: knowledge, witness, and acknowledgment. He explains:

---

[35] Ames, *Marrow*, 1.8.58.
[36] Brakel, *Service*, 1.272.
[37] Brakel, *Service*, 1.273; cf. Ames, *Marrow*, 1.8.34.
[38] Brakel, *Service*, 1.309-1.317; Ames, *Marrow*, 1.8.63-1.8.80.
[39] Brakel, *Service*, 1.317.
[40] Ames, *Conscience*, 1.1.Preamble.
[41] Merrill, *Perkins*, xviii.
[42] Perkins, "A Discourse of Conscience" in Merrill, *Perkins*, 5-7; Perkins, *Conscience*, 1.3.

> First, there is *knowledge* of the will of God, commanding or forbidding every man with promises and threats. . . . Secondly, there is the element of *witness*. After man's obligation is held before him, it determines whether or not he has acted according to light and knowledge. . . . Thirdly, there follows an *acknowledgement* that the righteous God is also cognizant of this and will reward or judge him accordingly.[43]

It is evident that Brakel's view on conscience appropriates wholesale the syllogistic system of Ames and the Schoolmen.[44] For Brakel, Ames' "proposition" – the major premise in the syllogism – is the *knowledge* of the will of God, the moral law, as it was for Ames. The minor premise – Ames' "assumption" (alternatively "index" or "witness" or "book") is Brakel's *witness*. Finally, Ames' "conclusion" which "either pronounces one guilty or giveth spiritual peace and security" Brakel designates as *acknowledgement* of God's cognizance of the action under review in the court of conscience, and the reward or penalty associated therewith. Brakel supports his exposition of the nature and workings of the conscience with the same biblical texts as does Ames.

In his comments on the nature of the human soul, Brakel describes the interrelatedness of the intellect and the will in a way that very clearly echoes Ames. Brakel declares that

> . . . it is the intellect, not the will, which judges in a given matter. It is the intellect which presents a matter to the will as being either desirable or contemptible, prescribing the course of action to be taken under the current circumstances. The will embraces this practical judgment blindly and acts accordingly.[45]

Ames had said that conscience is a "practical judgement," "proceeding from the understanding" "to the end that it may be a rule within him to direct his will."[46] Rather than explore further into the workings or conscience as Ames had, Brakel is satisfied to ask only one further question: Can the conscience be in error? He answers in the affirmative and at great length.[47]

Close similarity is seen also in Brakel's tripartite treatment of the image of God. This image requires a basis ("or that which is prerequisite, . . . man's soul"); it requires the form ("relating to the quality of its inherent powers . . . knowledge, righteousness, and holiness"); and it requires the consequence ("the exercise of dominion over the entire earth").[48] With slight deviation, a very similar taxonomy had been advanced by Ames:

---

[43] Brakel, *Service*, 1.317.
[44] Although we should be careful not to read too much into the use of the hypothetical or practical syllogism since this style of reasoning is, in a sense, nothing more than a logical deductive process of critical thinking.
[45] Brakel, *Service*, 1.320.
[46] Ames, *Conscience*, 1.1.3, 1.1.6.
[47] Brakel, *Service*, 1.318-1.320.
[48] Brakel, *Service*, 1.323-1.325.

> [1] In man the true basis for an image is found. . . . [2] This image then is the conformity of man to the highest perfection of God. [3] The image of God in man was both inward and outward. The inward is the perfection of body and soul. The perfection of body was seen in its embodiment of beauty and usefulness conforming to God's will. Gen. 2:25; Rom. 6:13. The perfection of the soul consisted in its immortal nature, seen not only in the faculties whereby it has freedom in its actions – in the understanding and the will – but also in its endowment with gifts whereby man is rendered able and fit to live well, that is, in wisdom, holiness and righteousness, Eph. 4:24; Col. 3:10. The external perfection of man consisted of his dominion over other creatures. . . .[49]

We have seen that Brakel probes extensively into the faculties of the soul. The extent to which he borrows from Ames is considerable and unmistakable.

Recall William Ames' treatment of the efficiency or "working power" of God, demonstrated in his decree to be worked out in creation and providence. The latter Ames defines as that "efficiency" whereby God's provision for existing creatures conforms with the counsel of his will." This providence is either "conservational or governmental." And while the former refers to God's activity in retaining in existence and essence all things "universal and particular," God's government "is the power whereby God directs and leads all his creatures to their proper end."[50] It is common and special.

Wilhelmus à Brakel follows Ames closely here as well. Providence is the "execution of God's decree" in preservation, cooperation and government. Preservation is "the immediate, energizing power of God whereby all creatures in general and every creature in particular is preserved in its being and existence." Cooperation is "the concurrence of the power of God with the motions of his creatures." And government is that activity whereby God "governs all things in general and each thing in particular for purposes predetermined by him."[51]

In his exposition of the "special" governmental providence of God – the latter half of yet another Ramist dichotomy – Ames' unique contribution to federal theology commences, a contribution that has received full and elaborate treatment through the history of the development of theological thought until the present day in which it is very much a part of accepted Reformed thinking. Recall Ames crisply asserting: "From this special way of governing rational creatures there arises a covenant between God and them. This covenant is, as it were, a kind of transaction of God with the creature whereby God commands, promises, threatens, fulfills; and the creature binds itself in obedience to God so demanding."[52] Brakel agrees: "The covenant of works was an agreement between God and the human race as represented in Adam, a pact in which God promised eternal salvation upon condition of obedience, and threatened eternal

---

[49] Ames, *Marrow*, 1.8.66-1.8.78.
[50] Ames, *Marrow*, 1.9.1, 1.9.14, 1.9.15, 1.9.19.
[51] Brakel, *Service*, 1.331-1.343.
[52] Ames, *Marrow*, 1.10.9.

death upon disobedience. Adam accepted both this promise and this condition."[53] That the standard for Adam was the ten commandments, "all agree."[54] This understanding of the interrelatedness of natural law and moral law receives much elaboration by Ames who, as we saw, advances the natural law thinking of Aquinas in a much more biblical direction.[55] Typically Brakel provides a much more detailed exposition, no doubt reflecting the doctrinal development of that thinking through the course of the seventeenth century. The concept of the federal headship of Adam to which Brakel alludes in his definition, Ames explains near the end of his chapter on the covenant of works, or, as he calls it, the "special government of intelligent creatures." For "because Adam was the first of mankind, from whom all men come, a law was given to him not only as a private person, as among the angels, but as a public person or the head of the family of man."[56] These fleshed out Amesian distinctives, only faint adumbrations of which appeared in Calvin, are appropriated wholesale by Brakel and given a practical bent.[57] But while Ames identifies two sacraments – the tree of life symbolic of the reward for obedience and the tree of the knowledge of good and evil symbolic of the punishment for disobedience – Brakel is explicit in denying sacramental significance to the latter. He recognizes only the tree of life as a sacrament.[58]

The covenant of works has been breached, but both Ames and Brakel consider the obligations still binding upon humanity. As Brakel puts it, "this covenant remains in full force, obligating the entire human race (that is, who have not been translated into the covenant of grace) to obedience and subjecting men to punishment, since the fulfillment of the promise continues to be contingent upon obedience."[59]

Many other close resemblances can be found in the theological anthropology of William Ames and Wilhelmus à Brakel. Clearly it must be expected that the more established doctrinal concepts as these evolved through seventeenth century Reformed theology would be similar in the thinking of both these great theologues. But this section has demonstrated that Brakel has appropriated some uniquely Amesian thinking in his own theology. We have discovered also that not only is Brakel very Amesian in some points of content, but his style is often very much that of the learned expatriate doctor who preceded him on his home turf in the northern Netherlands.[60]

---

[53] Brakel, *Service*, 1.355.
[54] Brakel, *Service*, 1.359.
[55] Ames, *Conscience*, 5.1.1-5.1.2.
[56] Ames, *Marrow*, 1.10.30.
[57] Brakel, *Service*, 1.367, 1.379-1.380.
[58] Ames, *Marrow*, 1.10.33; Brakel, *Service*, 1.259, 1.362-1.365.
[59] Brakel, *Service*, 1.375.
[60] In this connection the reader is directed to Brakel's exposition of "Sin's Dominion over the Ungodly" in the chapter currently under review (*Service*, 1.396-1.398) and invited to read it alongside Ames' "Of the State of Sin" (*Conscience*, 2.2).

c) Christology
As we compare the christology of William Ames and Wilhelmus à Brakel there is a striking difference in their respective introductory chapters. Whereas Brakel chooses to introduce his teaching on the person and work of Christ with an exposition of the covenant of grace, Ames reserves this seminal chapter as opening act for his soteriology.[61] To be sure, not too much should be read into this distinction. Yet some remarks are in order to explain the sequence in which these christological and soteriological doctrines are introduced.

Recall that for Ames, Christ is the *application* of the covenant of grace. After humanity's fall, restoration (or salvation) was effected through redemption and its application. Redemption was the "matter" of this restoration while its application was the "form." And this matter was Jesus Christ, the mediator, while the form – the application – was by means of the covenant of grace. Ames' Ramist system proceeds systematically along to his soteriology. The motivation for this topical sequence seems to be that we must understand Christ and his work before we can understand Christ applied.[62]

Brakel, on the other hand, chooses to anchor his entire christology in covenantal foundations since it was grace that interposed to redeem humanity from the breached covenant of works, a grace with Christ as surety.[63] The further teaching on the person and work of Jesus Christ are Calvinian for both theologians under review and represents standard Reformed thinking of the day. However, the notion of the states of Christ's person as he effected his work of redemption (i.e., his humiliation and his exaltation) and the elaboration of these states and degrees is a concept which was very new, if not unique with Ames.[64]

---

[61] Francis Turretin, from whom Wilhelmus à Brakel has also very clearly received considerable inspiration, placed the chapter on the covenant of grace before his christology as well. See Francis Turretin, *Institutes of Elenctic Theology*, G.M. Giger, trans., J.T. Dennison, Jr., ed., 3 vols. (Phillipsburg, NJ: P&R, 1992-1997), 2.169-2.269. I cite volume and page. L. Berkhof places it at the close of his theological anthropology, thus introducing his christology (Berkhof, *Systematic Theology*, 272-301). C. Hodge, whose christology is subsumed under the larger heading of soteriology, likewise locates his exposition of the covenant of grace before his teaching on the person of Christ in his *Systematic Theology*, 3 vols. (Grand Rapids: Eerdmans, n.d. [1962]), 2.354-2.377; I cite Hodge by volume and page).

[62] Ames, *Marrow*, 1.18.1-1.18.10, 1.24.1-1.24.22.

[63] Brakel, *Service*, 1.427. Brakel's views on the essence of the covenant of grace are Amesian. Of note is the unambiguous way in which Brakel votes for an unconditional covenant of grace. "God places no conditions upon man at all, nor does man promise anything as a condition upon which he would enter this covenant" (*Service*, 1.439).

[64] I make this statement very tentatively. This understanding of Christ's person/work did not appear in Calvin. Berkhof has this to say on the history of the development of this doctrine: "The doctrine of the states of Christ really dates from the seventeenth century, though traces of it are already found in the writings of the Reformers, and even in some of the early Church Fathers. It was first developed among the Lutherans when they sought to bring their doctrine of the *communicatio idiomatum* in harmony with the humiliation of Christ as it is pictured in the Gospels, but was soon adopted also by the

Brakel's view of Christ's execution of his offices in history (prophet, priest and king) comport with Ames' teaching that "there are two parts to redemption: the humiliation of Christ as our mediator, and his exaltation."[65] Christ's humiliation has "two elements" said Brakel: "His suffering for the purpose of making satisfaction, and the placing of Himself under the law in order to merit salvation for His elect."[66] Ames stresses the satisfaction of Christ's death – his humiliation consists of "his subjection to the justice of God in order to perform those things necessary for the redemption of man"[67] and both agree that Christ suffered in body and soul.[68] In the next area of examination – the degrees (or steps) within each of these two states – Ames and Brakel exhibit some disagreement on one or two of the finer points, establishing a tradition of disagreement that remains in some Reformed camps to this day. Was Christ's birth (the act of incarnation) a step in his humiliation? Ames says yes; Brakel, no, it was a "qualifying of his person." In the same way, the conceptualization of Christ's descent into hell is framed differently.[69]

Reformed. They differed, however, as to the real *subject* of the states. According to the Lutherans it is the human nature of Christ, but according to the Reformed, the person of the Mediator. There was considerable difference of opinion even among the Lutherans on the subject. . . ." Berkhof attributes the loss of this theological teaching in "many present day works" on the pantheizing tendencies of Schleiermacher's teaching and the jettisoning of the idea of objective right, the concomitant difficulty in maintaining the idea of a judicial position, and, consequently, the loss of the idea of a state of the Mediator (*Systematic Theology*, 332-33).

[65] Brakel, *Service*, 1.575; Ames, *Marrow*, 1.20.1.

[66] Brakel, *Service*, 1.576.

[67] Ames, *Marrow*, 1.20.2; Eusden claims that "Ames presents basically an Anselmic interpretation of the atonement, stressing Christ's "satisfaction" ("Introduction" in *Marrow*, 20, n. 44). This is certainly Ames' emphasis in 1.20.5-1.20.6: "The end of this humiliation is satisfaction and the achievement of merit. It is called satisfaction because it is for the honor of God as a kind of recompense for the injury done to him by our sins." But then further in that same and in subsequent sections Ames does teach the substitutionary nature of Christ's suffering and death (*Marrow*, 1.20.6-1.20.22). To be sure, his emphasis is clearly on "the achievements of merit and satisfaction by Christ" (*Marrow*, 1.20.13). In this sense he seems to follow in the tradition of the Latin Church. What is the orthodox view? "The two great objects" says Charles Hodge "to be accomplished by the work of Christ are, the removal of the curse under which mankind laboured on account of sin; and their restoration to the image and fellowship of God. Both these are essential to salvation. We have guilt to be removed, and souls dead in sin to be quickened with a new principle of divine life. Both these objects are provided for in the doctrine of redemption as presented in the scriptures and held in the Church. In the opposing theories devised by theologians, either one of these objects is ignored or one is unduly subordinated to the other. It was characteristic of the early Greek church to exalt the latter, while the Latin made the former the more prominent" (*Systematic Theology*, 2.563).

[68] Brakel, *Service*, 1.576-1.581; Ames, *Marrow*, 1.22.

[69] Ames, *Marrow*, 1.20-1.22; Brakel, *Service*, 1.575, 1.623. Brakel opines that "it is fitting that one understand "was buried" to refer to His lying in the grave, and "descend-

Finally, in discussing the state of Christ's exaltation, both Ames and Brakel find three steps – resurrection, ascension and session – during the latter of which Christ exercises his prophetic, priestly and kingly offices. But Brakel adds the return of Christ as a fourth and final step in his exaltation.[70]

The christology of Wilhelmus à Brakel, although significantly closer in development to what is today considered to be received Reformed orthodoxy, has borrowed considerably from William Ames at points.

d) Ecclesiology
The doctrine of the church was an important theological head for Wilhelmus à Brakel. The editor of his translated work observes that the location of Brakel's ecclesiology deviates from the traditional sequence of Reformed thinking and offers possible explanations centering on Brakel's commitment to covenant theology.[71] We saw that about a third of Calvin's *magnum opus* is devoted to ecclesiology. Recall that for Calvin the church is the covenantal abode where the struggling believer received strengthened faith. For Calvin, church and covenant are inseparable. Recall further that Ames saw perfect identity between the covenant of grace and the church.

In the various distinctions made in what constitutes a church, Ames' love of dichotomy takes him in the following direction. The church is militant and triumphant, visible and invisible. Further bifurcation of the visible church yields the "hidden" and the "manifest" church. The former is found "where the number is fewer and profession less open. This is likely to occur in time of heresies, persecutions, or godless morality." The manifest church, on the other hand, is found "where a greater number of saints exist and profession is freer and more public."[72] Finally, all churches professing the faith "which belongs to the catholic church" are constituent members of the true catholic ("uniquely universal") church. "Our church at Franeker may rightly be called catholic."[73]

Brakel exposits in precisely the same manner, distinguishing between the essential form (invisible) and accidental form (visible) of the church. Some confusion arises in his exposition when he uses these visible/invisible designations

---

ed into hell" to refer to the suffering of Christ's soul" (*Service*, 1.583). Ames, meanwhile, proposes that the "reign of death for three days . . . is usually and properly described as existence in hell. The burial of Christ for three days was a testimony and representation of this state" (*Marrow*, 1.22.29-1.22.30). Berkhof covers quite extensively the issues revolving around the statement "he descended into hell" concluding with the by now standard Reformed position that it is best to consider the phrase as referring to "(a) that Christ suffered the pangs of hell before His death, in Gethsemane and on the cross; and (b) that He entered the deepest humiliation of the state of death" (*Systematic Theology*, 340-43).

[70] Ames, *Marrow*, 1.23.9-1.23.34; Brakel, *Service*, 1.625-1.658.
[71] Brakel, *Service*, 2.xv.
[72] Ames, *Marrow*, 1.31.21-1.31.39.
[73] Ames, *Marrow*, 1.31.19, 1.31.20.

in two different senses. His first meaning carries the traditional visible church/invisible church connotation. The second meaning in which he uses these terms reflects the Amesian manifest/hidden conception of the visible church.[74] But Brakel's understanding is clearly Amesian, emphasizing the organic nature of the church, be it "the church of England, of the Netherlands, or of Rotterdam"[75] and asserting that the unity and catholicity of the church means it transcends geographical location – "be it Jerusalem, Rome, or any other locality." The primary focus of both Ames and Brakel is the membership and constitution of the church which follows, broadly speaking, the Calvinian understanding.[76] The covenantal underpinnings of the church are made explicit by Calvin, Ames and Brakel. "The church is founded upon the covenant" writes Brakel.[77]

The marks of the church are four-fold for Brakel: biblical purity of doctrine, "holiness of her members," "proper administration of the sacraments," and the exercise of discipline.[78] Ames holds aloft one primary mark and three secondary ones: The "most essential mark" of the church is profession of the true faith,[79] ensured by the way of application of redemption – sound preaching and sacraments – "to which some ecclesiastical discipline must be added."[80] For both theologians, the blessings of the church are identified with the benefits of the covenant of grace.[81] Thus men and women are duty-bound to join the church, although Ames exhibits a more passive understanding of church membership than does Brakel. Ames asserts that the church is constituted by "calling." The church is the "company of men who are called."[82]

To leave the true church is to "break the covenant."[83] Both Ames and Brakel devote large sections of their writing to reasons why men and women may not leave the church;[84] these reasons are qualified by instances when severing connections with a church is acceptable. Brakel's exposition is very much condi-

---

[74] At first glance this double-purpose use of the words "visible" and "invisible" appears to be a problem in translation. But Brakel indeed uses the terms "sichtbare" and "onsichtbare" in these two different senses. The translators, no doubt having to make a judgment call between faithfulness to the precise terms used by Brakel or clarity of meaning of the text chose the former (Brakel, *Redelyke Godts-Dienst*, 1.558). In this context it is rather ironic that the translators have sub-titled this section "Clarification of the Invisible/Visible Church Distinction."
[75] Brakel, *Service*, 2.5.
[76] Although, as we noted earlier, Ames focuses more than Calvin on the *subjective* character of the church.
[77] Brakel, *Service*, 2.11.
[78] Brakel, *Service*, 2.29-2.37.
[79] Ames, *Marrow*, 1.32.30.
[80] Ames, *Marrow*, 1.33.3-1.33.4.
[81] Ames, *Conscience*, 4.24; Brakel, *Service*, 2.59.
[82] Ames, *Marrow*, 1.31.6-1.31.7; idem, *Conscience*, 4.24.1; Brakel, *Service*, 2.55-2.86.
[83] Brakel, *Service*, 2.62. This too is Calvin's view in *Institutes*, 4.1.10.
[84] Ames does this in, primarily, *Conscience*, 4.24.

tioned by what he saw to be degeneracy in the churches of some of his less orthodox contemporaries.[85]

In their discussion of the offices of the church, Brakel appropriates Ames' language in his designation of "extraordinary offices" of "apostles, evangelists and prophets" while "ordinary offices" are ministers, elders and deacons. These are the categories Ames uses to explicate the way of application of the covenant of grace – extraordinary ministers through the Word, the establishment of the church and miracles; ordinary ministers through their office of preaching, administration of the sacraments and exercise of discipline.[86] Both Ames and Brakel lay great stress and exposit at length on the calling of men and their preparation to the gospel ministry, for, as Ames so gravely puts it, they are the "successors" of the extraordinary ministers. This prolixity is matched, in both theologians, only by the practical advice of what to do once in that office, especially in the capacity of preaching (preparation and delivery). We already mentioned that for both, learning in the original languages is paramount; for "the Holy Scriptures are recorded in this language."[87] Yet ministers must exhibit gravity, approachability, humility, self-denial, diligence; these are among the qualifications for the ministry. The practical and pastoral bent of both William Ames and Wilhelmus à Brakel shines here. It does appear that Brakel was working with two sets of tools as he recorded his thoughts in this field: the reality and exigencies of his own contemporary world, and Ames' *Marrow* and *Conscience*.[88]

e) Soteriology

In Romans 8:29-30 the Apostle Paul presents the *ordo salutis* that has been the basis for Reformed thinking on the logical or existential "stages in the Christian life" ever since. "For those God foreknew he also predestined to be conformed to the likeness of his Son, that he might be the firstborn among many brothers. And those he predestined, he also called; those he called, he also justified; those he justified, he also glorified." Elsewhere the Apostle adds adoption and sanctification.[89]

As soteriological thinking evolved after the Reformation, so did the understanding of this *ordo salutis*. L. Berkhof traces this changing understanding of

---

[85] Brakel, *Service*, 2.60-2.86.
[86] Brakel, *Service*, 2.117-2.129; 2.131-2.187; Ames, *Marrow*, 2.35-2.37.
[87] Brakel, *Service*, 2.132.
[88] Ames, *Marrow*, 1.33.12-1.33.17; 1.35.4-1.35.70; idem, *Conscience*, 4.25-4.26; Brakel, *Service*, 2.132-2.142. Of such paramount importance was the ministerial office to Ames, that he devotes over six pages in *Marrow* and seventeen pages in *Conscience* to the calling, preparation, and responsibilities (chiefly preaching) of the minister of the gospel. The exigency of the time no doubt was an important motivation in Ames' concern. In this respect he follows William Perkins. And Brakel follows Ames.
[89] We emphasize that the *ordo salutis* is to be understood in a *logical*, not temporal, sense.

both the number and sequence of these "steps" as fundamental conceptions of this "way of salvation" have changed over the course of the development of Reformed theology.[90] A brief glance at this will help place our comparative examination of William Ames and Wilhelmus à Brakel into context.

John Calvin was the first to attempt to systematize these various "parts" of the order of salvation in any way but his work was criticized by A. Kuyper for being too subjective, emphasizing the human activity rather than the divine.[91] Reformed soteriology generally wishes to emphasize the legal dimension of humanity's spiritual condition – its relation to the law, forensic justification and the imputation of Jesus Christ's righteousness. According to Berkhof:

> In view of this precedence of the legal over the moral, some theologians, such as Maccovius, Comrie, A. Kuyper Sr., and A. Kuyper Jr., begin the *ordo salutis* with justification rather than regeneration. In doing this they apply the name "justification" also to the ideal imputation of the righteousness of Christ to the elect in the eternal counsel of God. . . . The great majority of Reformed theologians, however, while presupposing the imputation of the righteousness of Christ in the *pactum salutis*, discuss only justification by faith in the order of salvation, and naturally take up its discussion in connection with or immediately after that of faith. They begin the *ordo salutis* with regeneration or with calling, and thus emphasize the fact that the application of the redemption of Christ is in its incipiency a work of God. This is followed by a discussion of conversion, in which the work of regeneration penetrates to the conscious life of the sinner, and he turns from self, the world, and Satan, to God. Conversion includes repentance and faith, but because of its great importance the latter is generally treated separately. The discussion of faith naturally leads to that of justification, inasmuch as this is mediated to us by faith. And because justification places man in a new relation to God, which carries with it the gift of the Spirit of adoption, and which obliges man to a new obedience and also enables him to do the will of God from the heart, the work of sanctification next comes into consideration. Finally the order of salvation is concluded with the doctrine of the perseverance of the saints and their final glorification.[92]

It seems then, that in Berkhof's view, the "Reformed consensus" of the *ordo salutis* is the following: calling/regeneration, conversion, justification, sanctification and glorification; more precisely, this becomes calling, repentance, faith, justification, sanctification and glorification. Whether calling or regeneration has priority is discussed at length by Hoeksema, precisionist *par excellence*.[93]

Berkhof makes a final comment on the seventeenth-century understanding of the term "regeneration" that is germane to our discussion. Although now this

---

[90] Berkhof, *Systematic Theology*, 415-22.
[91] Berkhof, *Systematic Theology*, 417.
[92] Berkhof, *Systematic Theology*, 418.
[93] His exhaustive treatment of this aspect of soteriology leads him to the following conclusion regarding the *ordo salutis*: 1) regeneration; 2) calling; 3) faith; 4) conversion; 5) justification; 6) sanctification; 7) preservation and perseverance; 8) glorification (H. Hoeksema, *Reformed Dogmatics* [Grand Rapids: Reformed Free, 1966], 446-51).

designation is primarily understood in terms of the divine impartation of the principle of the new life to humanity, broadly understood it also has reference to the new birth or to the "first manifestation of the new life." But Berkhof adds that the term regeneration "in the theology of the seventeenth century frequently occurs as synonymous with conversion or even sanctification."[94]

It is noteworthy that William Ames followed the Pauline example set in his letter to the Romans and did not seek to finesse the *ordo salutis* to the degree his theological heirs have. This is not because the *ordo salutis* – its essence and application – was unimportant for Ames. We have seen that it constituted the very organic structure by which Ames demonstrated the administration of the covenant of grace through its various dispensations. But Berkhof's comment on seventeenth-century thought is confirmed by Ames' (and Brakel's) understanding. In fact, as if foreseeing subsequent controversy over this in the Reformed camp, Brakel wisely counsels that "although we can make a distinction between calling, regeneration, conversion, and sanctification, considering them to be sequential – that is, the one issuing forth from the other – Scripture does not always use this distinction. Instead, Scripture comprehends all these in either one word or the other.[95] Ames, meanwhile, opined that "a common confusion of regeneration and sanctification" arises when sanctification is related "to calling or that first rebirth in which faith is communicated as a principle of new life."[96]

Ames identifies predestination, calling, justification, adoption, sanctification and glorification as the stages in the Christian life, or, the "way of salvation."[97] In *Conscience* and as if anticipating Berkhof, Ames further inserts faith and repentance.[98] We have commented before on his use of the doctrine of predestination in commencing his soteriology and say nothing further about that here. Absent predestination, Brakel follows Ames very closely in this regard. He commences with calling and adds regeneration and faith (conversion) before proceeding to justification in which are subsumed adoption, peace and joy. "Justification includes spiritual sonship,"[99] "justification . . . engenders peace with God,"[100] and "justification also engenders joy."[101] The remainder of his

---

[94] Berkhof, *Systematic Theology*, 419.

[95] Brakel, *Service*, 2.233.

[96] Ames, *Marrow*, 1.29.6.

[97] In *Conscience* he puts it this way: effectual vocation ("the first entrance into the state of saving grace"), faith ("the work of effectual vocation"), repentance, justification, adoption, sanctification and glorification from which issues obedience (*Conscience*, 2.2.5-2.2.19). Book 2 of *Conscience* is an elaborate explanation of the interrelatedness of the conscience with the various "states of saving grace." In the first chapters (1-4) Ames discusses the essence of a case of conscience, the state of sin, and preparationism.

[98] Ames, *Conscience*, 2.6-2.8.

[99] Brakel, *Service*, 2.415.

[100] Brakel, *Service*, 2.439.

[101] Brakel, *Service*, 2.455.

soteriology represents exhaustive coverage of glorification and the Christian life.

Following his chapter on predestination, Ames delineates the calling into an "external" act ("the offer is an objective presentation of Christ"[102]) and an "internal" act ("the receiving of him . . . a kind of spiritual enlightenment, whereby the promises are presented to the hearts of men, as it were, by an inner word").[103] Brakel follows closely in Ames' train.[104]

William Ames commences his theological project with the following discussion on faith:

---

[102] Ames, *Marrow*, 1.26.8.

[103] Ames, *Marrow*, 1.26.7, 1.26.14.

[104] Hoeksema declares that where one makes a distinction between the internal and the external call, the "very nature of the case" requires that regeneration precede calling. In his discussion of Petrus van Mastricht's view of the *ordo salutis* (in which regeneration follows upon calling), he observes that this is due to Mastricht's neglect in distinguishing between the external call (the objective preaching of the Word) and the internal call (the subjective, Holy Spirit-induced appropriation). He then continues: "The same order we find also in Brakel. . . . Also with Brakel this order of calling and regeneration follows from the fact that he does not make distinction between that which the Holy Spirit works immediately in the very depth of our being and that which he works through the means of the preaching of the Word in our consciousness. If we fail to make this distinction, it stands to reason that the calling is strictly first in the ordo salutis" (*Dogmatics*, 447-48). Hoeksema's view of Brakel is a puzzle. The chapter preceding "Regeneration" Brakel has entitled "The External and Internal Call." In distinguishing them, he asserts: "They both proceed from God, occur by means of this Word, pertain to the same matters, and are presented equally to all. Both calls are addressed to human beings who by nature are the same. They are, however, distinguishable. The one functions externally only by means of the Word, to which also the Holy Spirit does join Himself in His common operation, resulting in common illumination and historical faith. The other, however, penetrates the very heart of man, powerfully illuminating it with wondrous light, revealing spiritual mysteries to man in their essential form, and powerfully inclines the will to embrace those mysteries in Christ, and to the obedience of faith" (*Service*, 2.193-2.194). Brakel's exhaustive treatment of the distinction between external calling and internal calling is then followed by the chapter on "Regeneration," introduced thus: "Having considered the work of God in the conversion of man, we shall now proceed to the consideration of the person who is the recipient of this divine operation, and thus is regenerated" (*Service*, 2.233). I am assuming Hoeksema is aware of Brakel's chapter on the calling. With this distinction between internal and external call so explicitly made and exhaustively explained in this chapter, it is difficult for me to understand how Hoeksema can make such a judgment of Brakel. Hoeksema appears to be seeking an even greater nuancing in the distinction. For him, internal calling is not mediated by the Word of God; it is the Holy Spirit's immediate work. External calling, on the other hand, is mediated by the Word of God. But I am not sure how distinguishing between the Holy Spirit's work in "the very depth of our being" (without the Word – internal calling) and the Holy Spirit's work through "the preaching of the Word in our consciousness" (external calling) is useful, or whether it is even a correct distinction to make. Does the Holy Spirit ever work without the Word?

> Faith is the resting of the heart on God . . . . To believe signifies ordinarily an act of the understanding as it gives assent to evidence. But since as a consequence the will is wont to be moved and reach out to embrace the good thus proved, faith may rightly designate this act of the will as well. So it is to be understood in this book: Faith is a receiving. John 1:12, As many as received him, or who believe. In this way, faith comes by the good which then becomes ours through faith. It is an act of choice, an act of the whole man – which is by no means a mere act of the intellect. . . . True Christian faith which has a place in the understanding always leans upon divine testimony, as far as it is divine. But it cannot be received without a genuine turning of the will towards God . . . the object of faith. Christ as redeemer is the mediate but not the ultimate object of faith, for we believe through Christ to God. . . . Some place true faith partly in the understanding and partly in the will. This is not quite correct, for it is a single virtue . . . .[105]

This is how one lives to God and how the central tenet of such commitment plays out in the life of the believer.

Brakel, following closely, asserts that "the *subject* or *seat* of faith is man, more particularly the will. . . . The *object* of faith is first of all the Word of God . . . but proceeds by means of the Word to Christ . . . but proceeds through Christ to God." Because "true saving faith . . . consists in a heartfelt trust to be brought to salvation by Christ . . . we immediately establish that faith is not seated in the intellect, but in the will."[106] Brakel's coverage of the interrelationship and interrelatedness of the intellect and the volition closely mirror that of Ames.[107] He even has a response for "Those who Object to Faith Being the Exercise of One's Will."[108] And, with Ames, he sees Christ as a "stepping stone" to God, as it were, the bridge between the fallen creature and the divine Creator.

Brakel, again with Ames before him, asserts the will as central in the act of faith, favoring this conception over the primacy Calvin appears to accord the intellect in the language used.[109] Brakel includes very practical and pastoral teaching and guidance on what constitutes the marks of saving faith, since assurance is not of the essence of faith. Indeed, this chapter could have been penned in response to Perkins' quest for the answer to the greatest case of conscience that ever was. In fact, Brakel does broach this precise topic in his pasto-

---

[105] Ames, *Marrow*, 1.3.1-1.3.22.
[106] Brakel, *Service*, 2.266, 2.274, 2.278.
[107] Brakel, *Service*, 2.278-2.282.
[108] Brakel, *Service*, 2.282. J. van Genderen judges that Brakel has an "anti-intellectualistic" view of faith. He remarks on Brakel's emphasis in the following way: "in that time faith was understood by some to reside more in the intellect, others associated it equally with the intellect and will, and still others connected faith more with the will. Brakel committed to this third and last conception which we find particularly with Amesius," ("Wilhelmus à Brakel (1635-1711)," in *Voornaamste vertegenwoordigers*, 178).
[109] Calvin, *Institutes*, 3.2.7.

ral section in the discussion of adoption some chapters further: "The Need to Examine One's Self Whether He Is a Child of God."[110]

All of the Calvinian soteriological distinctives appear in both Ames and Brakel, more crisp and succinct in the former than the latter, as we would by now expect. For Brakel's work is an exposition second to none in its efforts at precision and pastoral application. Justification is forensic, involves the imputation of Christ's righteousness and is effected by faith alone.[111] Adoption is illustrated with human /divine analogies of sonship, involves freedom in Christ (liberty but not license), and involves assurance (which both theologians note is not of the essence of faith).[112] Teaching on the sacraments is similar, although Ames places the topic near the end of his theology (Book 1 of *Marrow*) while Brakel brings the sacraments in after a chapter on the sealing of the believer by the Holy Spirit and sacraments. Brakel closes his second volume with two lengthy practical chapters in which he discusses matters of the life of faith and warnings against practitioners of "a natural and spiritless religion."[113] In the major heads of doctrine and soteriological tenets, Ames and Brakel are in agreement, while some differences in emphases are detected in some of the details.[114]

The final topic considered in this major head of doctrine is sanctification (and glorification). This theme opens the third volume of Wilhelmus à Brakel's work and can rightly be said to represent his teaching on the Christian life. Both theologians agree that sanctification differs from justification, is imperfect in this life, involves the transformation of the intellect, will and affections, involves mortification and vivification and results in the exercise of virtues issuing from holiness as this is expressed in the law of the ten commandments.[115]

In his general considerations of the law of God, Brakel's use of Amesian natural and moral law thinking is extensive.[116] We saw in a previous chapter how the moral law is subsumed by the natural law except for the Sabbath commandment which Ames sees as part of the positive law.[117] The natural law is eternal (because divine) and so designated; the positive law is also eternal

---

[110] Brakel, *Service*, 2.433.
[111] Ames, *Marrow*, 1.27.6-1.27.26; Brakel, *Service*, 2.341-2.411.
[112] Ames, *Marrow*, 1.28; Brakel, *Service*, 2.415-2.438; Brakel's teaching on assurance does not appear until the last volume: 4.214-4.217.
[113] Ames, *Marrow*, 1.36, 1.39; idem, *Conscience*, 4.27-4.28; Brakel, *Service*, 2.601-2.699.
[114] For example, the sacraments are signs, seals and symbols of the covenant of grace. There is a peculiar meaning given to the sacrament of the Lord's Supper which is uniquely Amesian: he asserts that communion is a "sacrament of nourishment and growth" (*Marrow*, 1.40.19-1.40.20). Nowhere is to be found the concept of "remembrance." Both Ames and Brakel devote much space to anti-papal (and anti-Lutheran) polemic (Brakel, *Service*, 2.535-2.565; Ames, *Marrow*, 1.40.22-1.40.31).
[115] Brakel, *Service*, 3.3-3.35; Ames, *Marrow*, 1.29.
[116] Brakel, *Service*, 3.35-3.81, especially 3.55; Ames, *Conscience*, 5.1.
[117] Ames, *Conscience*, 5.1.27; idem, *Marrow*, 2.15.12.

(because divine) but not so designated. "That Positive Right was in the mind of God from eternity as well as the Natural. But in respect it is not so easily apprehended by Human Reason, therefore it is not usually termed the Law Eternal."[118] In his exposition, recall Ames' heavy reliance upon the scholastics, especially Thomas and Suárez. Ames rounds out his theory of law by establishing that not only the moral law, but also the law of nations, the civil law, and the judicial law are part and parcel of natural law.[119] In addition, "we acknowledge the law of nature in brutes" in the sense of the natural urges of the creatures in the animal kingdom such as "the safeguard and defense of life and liberty, the coition of male and female, etc."[120] Not surprisingly, Christ's teaching in Matthew 7:12 (the "Golden Rule") is also imprinted upon the soul of humanity by natural law.[121]

Our earlier study of the covenant of works outlined Ames' teaching on the relationship between the moral law and the law of nature. We saw how strongly and precisely he equated the two as compared to the somewhat weaker intimations of Calvin and Perkins. Brakel teaches, with Amesian assertion, that "the law of the ten commandments is . . . identical to the law of nature as far as contents are concerned" and therefore they are eternal.[122] Additionally, while Ames had said that in the Mosaic economy "the form of administration [of the covenant of grace] gave some evidence of the covenant of works,"[123] Brakel advances that while there is no covenantal "intermixture" (as Ames puts it)[124] the "contents or substance [of the decalogue] is identical to the demands [but not the purpose] of the covenant of works."[125] The ten commandments are the rule of life for New Testament believers.[126]

Ames treats all case-divinity relating to the decalogue in Book 4 and Book 5 of *Conscience*. As Brakel outlines his understanding of the moral law and its application in broad terms, the principles he sets forth owe a great deal to those in Ames' casuistry but also to the developing Reformed thinking on the commandments. They are more than just sins forbidden; they also enjoin virtues. Thus the teaching on the decalogue is followed by chapters that speak of hope, love, prayer, patience, uprightness, self-denial, contentment, etc.

In this connection it is important to make some clarifying remarks about volume three and four of Brakel's work. The subtitle to this second half of his teaching appears as "Dealing with the sanctified life of covenant members in

---

[118] Ames, *Conscience*, 5.1.7.
[119] Ames, *Conscience*, 5.1.17-5.1.36.
[120] Ames, *Conscience*, 5.1.13-5.1.15.
[121] Ames, *Conscience*, 5.1.20.
[122] Brakel, *Service*, 3.55.
[123] Ames, *Marrow*, 1.39.4.
[124] Brakel, *Service*, 3.50.
[125] Brakel, *Service*, 3.41.
[126] Brakel, *Service*, 3.59.

their growth, decline and struggle"[127] and bears strong resemblance to the emphasis William Ames originated with his very definition of theology and from which the dichotomous structuring of his work flows. Consider Ames' stated intention that his *Marrow* and his *Conscience* are actually one cohesive unit. His theological teaching (introduced by faith) is exposited in Book 1 of *Marrow* structured within a strictly covenantal framework. Book 2 explicates the second half of Ames' Ramist system of theology – observance – and it is here that he provides a blueprint for the Christian life as this is expressed in the exercise of the theological virtues in humanity's dealing with God (for which the first table of the law is guide) and with itself (Table 2 of the decalogue). Of particular note is the lengthy treatment afforded the topic of the Sabbath, the longest chapter in all of *Marrow*.[128] That *Marrow* and *Conscience* are unified is demonstrated not only by the subject matter and the way in which *Conscience* so naturally flows from and is an in depth commentary of Book 2 of *Marrow*, but also by Ames' express and stated intent: "if there are some who desire to have practical matters better explained, especially those of the latter part of this *Marrow*, we shall attempt, God willing, to satisfy them in a special treatise, which I mean to write, dealing with questions usually called 'cases of conscience'."[129]

It can be clearly demonstrated that Ames' unique view of theology and his presentation of "theory and practice" flowing from this definition are appropriated by Brakel as the organizing principles of his work. That Brakel borrows more than just the organizational structure from Ames has already been demonstrated in reference to his exposition of theology to this point (the close of Volume 2). Brakel's remaining two volumes borrow substantively as well from Ames' *Marrow* but now Brakel's indebtedness to Ames' *Conscience* becomes especially apparent. This is most evident in Brakel's explication of sanctification, which progresses through the ten commandments, to glorification (the last "step" in the *ordo salutis*) and which covers the Lord's Prayer and the exercise of the theological and the cardinal virtues. Interspersed throughout are highly pastoral chapters emphasizing experiential Christianity and identifying Wilhelmus à Brakel as a true physician of souls to a greater degree than the earlier

---

[127] Brakel, *Redelijke Godsdienst*, Book 2, subtitle page preceding title page. This subtitle does not appear in the translated volume. It is clear that Brakel is following the Amesian pattern: first doctrine, then more explicit application. The application, Brakel's experiential divinity, bears striking resemblance to casuistry.

[128] As a point of interest, the chapter on the Sabbath stretches for thirteen pages. This compares with seventeen pages on his doctrine of God (but in four chapters) and twenty pages (but seven chapters) on his Christology (Ames, *Marrow*, 2.15). In *Conscience*, Ames provides three more pages of instruction on this topic (in addition to his tract *Sabbati*). This is only one place of several in *Conscience* where Ames explicitly provides a cross reference to his previous work – in a subtitle he helpfully explains: "Supposing those things which are spoken of this point in the *Marrow*" (Ames, *Conscience*, 4.33).

[129] Ames, *Marrow*, "Brief Forewarning."

Puritan soul doctors William Ames and William Perkins. It is at this point in the evolution of Reformed system, with the conflation of the decalogue's teaching and casuistry, that Ames' moral/practical theology or piety becomes the informed piety of the Reformed tradition.

Wilhelmus à Brakel's exposition of the decalogue follows closely that of Ames' in both *Marrow* and *Conscience*. To be sure, it is difficult to ascribe all similarities to Ames' uniqueness, because the theological literature to which Brakel has access was vast at the end of the seventeenth century. But one does detect Amesian distinctives throughout, in addition to the entire tenor of Brakel's exposition which borrows heavily from Ames' casuistry.

In explaining the first table of the law and in his exposition of the second commandment, for example, Brakel first notes that the command is "presented within a covenant context."[130] Then, in his reasons for the prohibition of the worship of images, Brakel follows Ames' presuppositions almost identically. Ames had condemned the use of images in worship for these reasons:

> first, because they are not sanctified by God to such an end; second, because they can represent to us neither God himself nor his perfections; third, because they debase the soul and call our attention away from the spiritual contemplation of the will of God; fourth, because once admitted into the exercise of worship, by the perversity of man's mind, the worship itself is transferred, at least in part, to them.[131]

And this was all based upon an earlier proposition that "opposed to instituted worship is will-worship which is devised by men and is unlawful, Matt. 15:9, Col. 2:23."[132]

Three quarters of a century later, hear Brakel's reasons for the unlawfulness of image-worship:

> First, this is absolutely forbidden in this commandment and in many other passages. . . . Secondly, God cannot be depicted and it is therefore God's will that such ought not to occur. . . . Thirdly, it highly dishonors God. . . . Fourthly, it corrupts man.[133]

And he goes on to explain that image-worship is, "at the very least will-worship, which is forbidden in Matthew 15:9." This sin of will-worship "consists in serving God in a manner of our own devising, or in a manner which has been suggested to us by men. . . . The Lord Jesus rejects this in Matthew 15:9." With identical biblical texts, both have grounded the unlawfulness of image-worship in will-worship, and presented much the same reasons for the proscription. It is also noteworthy that, at one point, Brakel first states and then opposes

---

[130] Brakel, *Service*, 3.105.
[131] Ames, *Marrow*, 2.13.33.
[132] Ames, *Marrow*, 2.13.23.
[133] Brakel, *Service*, 3.109-3.110.

the position of Roman Catholic casuist Cajetan[134] (always one of Ames' favorites). However, Brakel is much more expansive in his exposition of the commandment than is our sometimes cryptic Ramist, William Ames.

As another example, both theologians find it necessary to teach at length on the proper and improper use of lots. Recall Ames' position in this regard: it brought him into trouble with many of his contemporaries, particularly Thomas Gataker (1574-1654).[135]

A final example: Brakel also gives extensive consideration to the doctrine of the Sabbath, much of it in the same vein as Ames. Like Ames, his comments on this subject run the longest of any of the other commandments by far.[136]

The theme running through Book 5 of *Conscience* is that of "mutual obligation," a phrase used over and over again as Ames shares his thoughts on the case-divinity of the second table of the law. Wars are allowed, duels are forbidden. And in his consideration of the sixth commandment, Ames defines "meekness" as the "virtue which moderates anger" while Brakel designates it the "foundational virtue." Exposition of the seventh commandment is extensive, from "immodest caressing" to "the mutual duties of man and wife" which comprise "fulfilling the obligations which love requires." But while both broach the topic of adultery, Ames is the expert, waxing at length on what constitutes adultery, justification for divorce (adultery and abandonment) and reconciliation. Ames was clearly addressing contemporary problems in the country he had left and to the degree these existed in his adopted homeland at the time this was written. We have seen that in his attenuated understanding of the progressive nature of New Testament teaching, Ames also maintains the capital nature of the crime of adultery. All of this detail is absent from Brakel's more advanced exposition.

---

[134] Brakel, *Service*, 3.110-3.114.

[135] Brakel, *Service*, 3.123-3.128; Ames, *Marrow*, 2.10.1, 2.11, esp. 2.11.9, 2.11.23; idem, *Conscience*, 4.23; Sprunger, *Ames*, 23-24, 175-76; Eusden, "Introduction" in *Marrow*, 18. Puritan divine Thomas Gataker held that lots were indifferent by their very nature. The will of God could only be determined by careful study of scripture. See Gataker's *Of the Nature and Use of Lots* (London, 1619) and the follow-up *A Just Defence of Certain Passages in a Former Treatise Concerning the Nature and Use of Lots* (London, 1623). His works are available in *The Works of Thomas Gataker* (London: Jacob Benjamin, 1659). William Ames, on the other hand, with Brakel in later agreement, maintained the sacred nature of the lot because it had "a certain relationship to a singular and extraordinary providence of God which controls a purely contingent event" (*Marrow*, 2.11.9). Recall Ames was anathematized at Cambridge for a strong sermon against what he saw as injudicious and flippant use of something holy – students at the University were playing dice and card games. This proved to be the tipping point of his already tenuous position there and led to his permanent departure for the Netherlands (Sprunger, *Ames*, 23-24).

[136] Brakel, *Service*, 3.139-3.183. The 44 pages Brakel uses to explain the Sabbath commandments compare to an average of 8-10 pages for each of the remaining nine commandments.

The teaching on commandments seven through ten shows many parallels. More than once both theologians underscore the thread of their thinking with a reminder that Christ's teaching in Matthew 7:12 provides the basis and justification – the divine *imprimatur*, as it were – for their thought. Brakel's coverage of the Lord's Prayer is extensive, covering each petition in minute detail, while in that most significant portion of Ames' work under consideration only a few explicit references to the Lord's Prayer are found: In *Marrow*, Ames first teaches that prayer arises from faith, hope and love, then asserting that "love toward our neighbors is necessary in prayer that is acceptable to God – hence, the fifth petition of the Lord's Prayer."[137] Moreover, Ames advises that it is only "an example or pattern according to which we are to direct our prayers . . . . It is not expedient to stick to this form . . . because by this means it is become among the papists like a charm."[138] Perhaps that is why there is no drawn out exposition of the Lord's Prayer.[139]

The pastoral chapters borrow extensively from Ames' casuistry and this is where Brakel exposits the cardinal virtues. These follow his exposition of the decalogue; he designates them as either "virtues" or "propensities" and they are part and parcel of the final stage in the Christian life – glorification. They are matched by strikingly similar chapters in Ames' *Conscience*.[140] Both Ames and Brakel spare no space in addressing the questions of temptation, backsliding, rebellion, spiritual decline and spiritual growth.[141] Many of Brakel's conceptual definitions are from Ames; many emphases are similar. And Brakel's presentation style bears much closer resemblance to Ames' *Conscience* than his *Marrow*. In the former, questions are posed, answers provided, objections raised

---

[137] Ames, *Marrow*, 2.9.4-2.9.8; idem, *Conscience*, 4.14.8.

[138] Ames, *Conscience*, 4.17.11-4.17.12.

[139] Although in his *Catechisme* he gives abundant teaching on the Lord's Prayer.

[140] These include, among others (with corresponding chapters by Ames in parentheses where these are entitled differently): love toward God, fear of God, obedience (the entire subject of Book 3 in *Conscience*), hope in God, spiritual strength or courage ("of fortitude" and "of boldness which is contained under fortitude"), the profession of Christ and his truth ("of the external profession of faith"), contentment, self-denial ("of temperance"), patience ("of patience" and "of patience towards God"), uprightness ("of a lie"), prayer, fasting, watchfulness, singing, vows ("of an oath"), love for one's neighbor ("of charity towards our neighbour"), humility ("of humility towards God"), diligence ("of constancy"), compassion ("of charity toward our neighbour"), and prudence.

[141] It is noteworthy that to the end of Book 2 of *Conscience*, in which the way of salvation is presented (the *ordo salutis* again), Ames appends "Certaine Collections out of the Booke of William Paris concerning temptations, and the resisting of them, which I thought good here to set down for the further illustration of the Doctrine of temptations, because they are not read in the Author except by a very few" (*Conscience*, 5.2.Appendix).

and confidently refuted.[142] This is Brakel's entire apparatus. And both theologians took their cue from the Schoolmen.

The exhaustive treatment of soteriology ends, for both, with teaching on the perseverance of the saints.[143]

f) Eschatology
Both William Ames and William Perkins hold to an eschatology that represents Reformed thought at that period in its development. The former introduces his final theological head – the final chapter in Book 1 of *Marrow* – in the following way: "So far we have considered the administration of the covenant before the end of the world. In that end, the application which has only been begun in this life will be perfected. . . . This final perfection of administration requires the coming and personal presence of Christ himself, Acts 10:42."[144] The resurrection is a miracle, the last judgment will be "exercised by Christ as king," "the sins of the faithful will not come into judgment. . . . It would not be right that they should again be brought to light" and "after the day of judgment Christ will remain king and mediator forever."[145]

For Brakel, the eschaton will unfold in pretty much this manner also.[146] This section, also for Brakel, is uncharacteristically short, although, in his inimitable way, he covers more ground than does Ames. And although Brakel acknowledges that opinions vary regarding judgment-day publication of the sins of believers, he votes in the affirmative, since so doing brings even greater glory to God. In any event, it is not a "fundamental doctrine of faith."[147]

g) Administration of the Covenant of Grace – Brakel's Appendix
It remains to comment briefly on Brakel's Appendix to Volume 4, entitled "The Administration of the Covenant of Grace in the Old and New Testaments." How important is the covenantal concept for Wilhelmus à Brakel?

The long title to Brakel's *magnum opus* reads "The Christian's Reasonable Service in which Divine Truths concerning the Covenant of Grace are Ex-

---

[142] In that sense, Ames' *Marrow* is a more pure and unfettered Ramistic delineation. While *Conscience* is also Ramist, scholastic method – proposition, argument and refutation – dominates in places, resulting in the coverage of a vast field of inquiry.

[143] Brakel, *Service*, 3.275-3.300; Ames, *Marrow*, 1.30.10-1.30.26.

[144] Ames, *Marrow*, 1.41.1, 1.41.9. See also, 1.15, 1.16; idem, *Conscience*, 2.17.

[145] Ames, *Marrow*, 1.41.10-1.41.34.

[146] We must comment here on Brakel's very strong statements, which he grounds in Rom 11 and other biblical passages, regarding the conversion of the Jewish nation (*Service*, 4.511-4.535). It is worth noting that his massive, formal, theological/pastoral work ends on this note. To the original version of *Redelijke Godsdienst*, Brakel added an exhaustive commentary on the Revelation of St. John. This was not translated, explains the editor, "due to its controversial nature." The editor promises, however, that this commentary will be translated as a separate volume "out of respect for à Brakel and for the sake of historicity" (*Service*, 4.535, n. 2).

[147] Brakel, *Service*, 4.344-4.346.

pounded, Defended against Opposing Parties, and their Practice Advocated as well as The Administration of this Covenant in the Old and New Testaments."[148] In the introductory paragraph of his soteriology, Brakel states: "Thus far we have discussed the Surety of the covenant and the partakers of this covenant, the church. We shall now proceed to consider the way the Lord brings these partakers of the covenant into the covenant, and how he leads them to the ultimate goal of eternal felicity."[149] The covenant of grace is the architectonic principle of all Brakel's thought.

Ames' unique covenantal design, constructed as an organizing principle for the administration of the covenant of grace and as a unifying vehicle for the Old and New covenants through the analytical grid of the *ordo salutis* is assumed by Brakel. The covenant of grace is administered through the identical Amesian biblical economies: from Adam to Abraham, from thence to Moses, from thence to Christ, and from thence to "the Revelation of John."[150] Using predestination as a starting point, Ames tracks redemptive history through the (existential) stages of the Christian life: calling, justification, adoption, sanctification and glorification. Brakel taxonomy bears close relation. The chapter sequence follows the Amesian construct and the content of the chapters focuses primarily on the uniqueness of the period under examination. Because the *ordo salutis* has, for Brakel, no central place as an organizing principle in his teaching of the administration of the covenant of grace, it does not appear anywhere. Brakel has different emphases. Especially important to him is that there be no confusion as to what the "covenant made at Horeb" represents – a confirmation, not a commencement of the covenant of grace. This appendix serves as a compendium, as it were, of redemptive history: all of the significant moments in redemptive history are identified and connected with the administration of the covenant of grace through that particular time. The ceremonial system, for example, is divided into three sections: location (tabernacle), persons (priests and Levites) and ceremonies (sacrifices), and shown to point to Christ.[151] The nature of Christ's suretyship for Old Testament believers is explored at length.

The greatest curiosity, however, is Wilhelmus à Brakel's concern for the future of the Jewish nation. The final chapter in this appendix – chapter 6 – runs for thirty-three pages; eight pages summarize the history of Jesus Christ's life and ministry, the gospel among the Gentiles and differences in worship between the Old and New Testament church. Twenty-five pages are devoted to arguing, from primarily New Testament texts but also from Old, for the future conversion of the Jews. For, after their return to the land, "Canaan will be ex-

---

[148] The title of the original also went on to include "*and the Meeting of the Church in the New Testament presented in an exposition of the Revelation of John.*" This part of the title is dropped in Elshout's translation.

[149] Brakel, *Service*, 2.191.

[150] Brakel, *Service*, 4.373-4.535.

[151] Brakel, *Service*, 4.421-4.433.

traordinarily fruitful, the inhabitants will be eminently godly, and they will constitute a segment of the glorious state of the church during the thousand years prophesied in Revelation 20."[152] Brakel's work closes with a brief pastoral application: "Various Reasons Given for Focusing upon the Conversion of the Jewish Nation." It is indeed a curious note upon which to end not only such a *magnum opus* but especially an exposition of the administration of the covenant of grace.

Brakel's understanding of the administration of the covenant of grace is clearly Amesian in structure. Even the condensed nature of his exposition has traces of Ames, although the centrality of the *ordo salutis* is absent altogether. The central motif for Ames through the administration of the covenant of grace is the church as an organic unity through space and time.[153] So it is also for Brakel in his entire exposition.

Petrus van Mastricht, Expositor of William Ames

Introduction
Petrus van Mastricht was born in 1630 in Cologne and received his theological education at Utrecht where he was sent in 1647 to study under Gisbertus Voet.[154] After a stop at Heidelberg, he received his doctorate in theology and philosophy from Duisburg in 1669. He was called to pastor a Reformed church in Xanten of district Wesel in North Rhine-Westphalia in 1652, and commenced service in early 1653 after spending some time in Glückstadt in the provincial area of Schleswig-Holstein.[155] Subsequent to this he was appointed

---

[152] Brakel, *Service*, 4.531.
[153] Ames, *Marrow*, 1.38.7-1.38.10.
[154] Many of these biographical details from W.J. van Asselt, "Mastricht, Petrus van," *BLGNP* 5: 360-62, many of which are disputed and amended by A.C. Neele. See the latter's *Petrus van Mastricht (1630-1706): Reformed Orthodoxy: Method and Piety*, Brill's Series in Church History, vol. 35, W. Janse, ed. (Leiden: Brill, 2009), 27-63. This volume is a marginally corrected reprint of the author's University of Utrecht doctoral dissertation and appeared earlier as *The Art of Living to God: A Study of Method and Piety in the* Theoretico-practica theologia *of Petrus van Mastricht* (1630-1706), Perspectives on Christianity, series 8, vol. 1, J.W. Hofmeyr, ed. (Pretoria: Department of Church History, 2005).
[155] Henricus Pontanus, "Lyk- en Lof-reede [eulogy]," in the introductory matter to Mastricht's *magnum opus, Beschouwende en Praktikale Godgeleerdheit, waarin door alle de Godgeleerde Hoofdstukken henen, het Bybelverklarende, Leerstellige, Wederleggende, en Praktikale deel, door eenen onafgebroken schakel, onderscheidenlyk samengevoegt, voorgestelt word: Hier By Komt een volledig Kort-begrip der Kerklyke Geschiedenisse, een vertoog der Zedelyke, en een schets der Plichtvermanende Godgeleertheit, enz*. Met eene Voorrede van den Heer Cornelius van der Kemp, including a eulogy by Henricus Pontanus, trans. unknown (Rotterdam: Hendrik van Pelt, de Wed. P. van Gilst, Jacobus Bosch, en Adrianus Douci, and Utrecht: Jan Jacob van Poolsum, 1749-1753), 14 (page numbering mine). My convention in citing from *Praktikale Godgeleerdheit* is by book, chapter and page number; Van Asselt, "Mastricht,"

professor of oriental languages and practical theology at Frankfort an der Oder in 1667, relocating to Duisburg in 1670. Six years later he crossed the border and entered the Dutch Republic, taking the professorial chair at the University of Utrecht in 1677, a position recently vacated by Voet's death.[156]

Mastricht entered the epicenter of the swirling Cocceian-Voetian controversy. Historiographers observe that although he "appreciated the scholarly merit of Cocceius, Mastricht showed himself to be a sharp critic of his ideas."[157] His disagreement with the Labadists[158] of the day and their subjectivism and separatist tendencies was grounded in the objective character of Reformed doctrine and its corresponding idea of the church. Further, his developing concern for balance between theology and observance, a balance entirely absent from the Labadists and pietists generally, gave rise to his *magnum opus*, *Theoretico-Practica Theologia*, (or *Praktikale Godgeleerdheit*), in short, a demonstrated conviction that true theology exhibited consonance between theory and practice. Highly reminiscent of Ames' Franeker address and guided by very similar principles, Mastricht's own inaugural oration focused on the designation "theologian" and the task of theology as knowledge.[159] According to his funeral orator Henricus Pontanus, Mastricht was the only Reformed professor who carried

---

360; A.E. van Tellingen, "Het leven en enige aspecten uit de theologie van Petrus van Mastricht (1630-1706)," (M.A. thesis, University of Utrecht, 2003), 13-14, cited in Neele, *Mastricht*, 32.

[156] Of Voet, Mastricht recalls affectionately: "He was the last living member of the Synod of Dort, my ever-present renowned teacher, whose memory I shall always hold in high esteem. . . . I became his successor in the professor's office in the year 1677" (*Praktikale Godgeleerdheit*, 8.3.409). On the faculty at Utrecht during the tenure of Voet, see J.A. Cramer, *De Theologische Faculteit te Utrecht ten tijde van Voetius* (Utrecht: Kemink en Zoon, 1932).

[157] Van Asselt, "Mastricht," 360.

[158] These were followers of the earlier-mentioned Jean de Labadie (1610-1674) who separated from the mainstream church and founded a Dutch quietistic and separatist sect in search of church purity. They were highly subjectivist and held that no one was in a state of grace who did not have absolute assurance. They withdrew not only from the church but from civil affairs as well and were considered mystics. Such separatist movements, however, continued to influence the larger movement of church reform and spiritual renewal that characterized the *Nadere Reformatie* (Beeke, *Assurance*, 176, 392-93, 407, 410; Goeters, *Vorbereitung des Pietismus*, 139-286; Stoeffler, *Evangelical Pietism*, 162-69; Graafland, "De Nadere Reformatie en het Labadisme."

[159] Van Asselt, "Mastricht," 360; cf. Ames' opening address. Drawing from the "ancients" – a veritable philosophical and theological treasure chest commencing with Socrates – Ames' "exhortation" to the theological students at Franeker moves along the following outline as I have determined it: i) the end of theology (the "noblest" of all disciplines), i.e., the purpose of the minister; ii) the "fitting" of our minds for study of the 'divine discipline;'" iii) the exercising of this discipline (1 Tim 4:13, 15); iv) the preaching (doctrine, method, practice) and living of theology (following Luther's dictum); v) and the pursuit of personal godliness, "Exhortation," n.p. (Amesius, "Paraenesis" in *Conscientia*, 1670), 452-65, my page numbering. Neele confirms Mastricht's passion for the inseparability of theology and preaching (*Mastricht*, 67).

the title "Professor of Practical Theology."[160] With his colleagues (Cocceian) F. Burmann and M. Leyendecker, the academy at Utrecht reached new heights. In 1682, Mastricht served as rector of the school. Dogged with failing health, he died in Utrecht in 1706. His biographer notes that Petrus van Mastricht never married and upon his death his status as a man of means was evidenced by the fact that he bequeathed over ƒ20,000 to the Academy for the support of students at Utrecht.[161]

If we include a smattering of much earlier preliminary disputations and separate writings in moral theology, Mastricht invested over thirty years of energy into his masterpiece, *Praktikale Godgeleerdheit*.[162] According to B. Glasius, the book focuses on precision and clarity and "breathes a sharp, anti-Cocceian spirit."[163] His work remained in use for well into the eighteenth century, representing the cream of late seventeenth-century Reformed system.

General Observations – Method and Overview of Praktikale Godgeleerdheit
The work of Mastricht is generally Ramist in arrangement, probably because he follows both Ames' convictions and train so closely. However, although in broad sweep his arrangement of subject matter follows that of Ames' *Marrow*, his detailed and highly expository management show that, more than anything, Ramist arrangement was a great convenience for him. Mastricht, with Ames, appropriated the Huguenot's idea that theology must be active. Thus, to aug-

---

[160] Van Asselt, "Mastricht," 361.
[161] The precise amount of the gift is unsure. Van Asselt mentions ƒ20,000 ("Mastricht," 362); a more likely number of 24,000 guilders is given by, among others, Isaac le Long, *Hondert-Jaarige Jubel-Gedachtenisse der Academie van Utrecht* (Utrecht: M. Visch, 1736), xii, cited in Neele, *Mastricht*, 58.
[162] According to Neele, *Mastricht*, 74. Van Asselt claims "more than twenty years" in "Mastricht," 362. Following many years of preliminary and "contributive publications" (Neele's phrase, *Mastricht*, 300), the first volume of an enhanced earlier edition was released in Amsterdam in 1682; the second volume in 1687. In 1698 an expanded edition was published in Utrecht as *Theoretico-Practica Theologia: Quâ, per singula capita Theologica, pars exegetica, dogmatica, elenchtica & practica, perpetuâ successione conjugantur*, ed. nova, priori multo emendatior, & tertiâ saltem parte auctior (Trajecti ad Rhenum: Prostant apud Gerardum Muntendam, 1698). This edition includes a presentation of Christian ethics and a brief sketch of the practice of godliness and was re-released in 1715 and 1724. The 1724 edition was translated into Dutch in the period 1749-1753 by an unknown translator in four volumes as *Praktikale Godgeleerdheit*, cited above. A translation of this work into the English language is currently underway and will prove to be of immeasurable benefit to English-speaking scholarship. I am using this 1924 Dutch version for my purposes in the present work. For the English-language reader, the meaning of chapter titles, etc., is often clearer from the original than from the Dutch translation. I therefore frequently cite the Latin as well. I also consult the original where questions in the translated edition arise. Both works are cited by book, chapter and page number. Sprunger's publication date (1655) for Mastricht's *magnum opus* is incorrect (Sprunger, *Ames*, 260).
[163] B. Glasius, *BWG* 2:470-72.

ment the highly practical tenor of his theology in *Praktikale Godgeleerdheit*, Mastricht devotes a considerable amount of space to the coverage of issues in moral theology as well. It is here that his reading of Ames is very close. In many cases, in fact, Mastricht is hardly more than an expositor of the English expatriate's casuistry, often repeating word for word what the Franeker Professor said three-quarters of a century earlier. In summary, while Mastricht's late seventeenth-century system represents an advance over Ames in the systematization of Reformed theology by expanding on areas in theoretical theology where Ames was more cryptic, he appropriated wholesale the general theological position of Ames, notably in the areas of covenant and moral theology. In so doing, he guaranteed the perpetuation of the heart of the theology and informed piety of the Reformed system in the development of Reformed thought through the eighteenth century.[164]

Praktikale Godgeleerdheit follows a *loci* approach and, as such, represents the by now familiar systematic arrangement of the subject matter one would expect to find in expositions of Reformed systems. He moves from prolegomena (Volume 1, Book 1 on the nature, source and divisions in theology), to theology proper (Books 2 and 3 on the being and works of God respectively). His theology proper ends in Volume 2 with an exposition of the covenant of works. It is the breach of this covenant which introduces Book 4, his theological anthropology. In Book 5, the covenant of grace is explained before Christ is introduced as the mediator of this covenant. This book covers the person and work of Christ while Book 6 discusses soteriology, the Holy Spirit's application of redemption along the lines of the *ordo salutis*. In Book 7 Mastricht has over 200 pages on ecclesiology.[165]

It is in Book 8 (commencing in Volume 3 and continuing through much of Volume 4) that Mastricht devotes a massive amount of space – over twenty percent of the entire work – to his exposition of the administration of the covenant of grace. This section is essentially an explication of the history of the world, divided into four periods. The last and briefest chapter of this long section represents Mastricht's teaching on eschatology – a short 30-page exposi-

---

[164] At this point it is important to remember that the theological literature and system to which Mastricht had access was vast indeed. Some of the key individuals of the high orthodox era (c. 1640-1725) wrote significant theological treatises as well, some much earlier than Mastricht. A few of these individuals are: Franz Burmann, (1632-79, Mastricht's colleague at Utrecht), Johannes Cocceius, to whose thought Mastricht took great exception), Abraham Heidanus (1597-1678), Johannes Hoornbeeck (1617-66, also an anti-Cocceian), Johannes Marckius (1656-1713), Benedict Pictet (1655-1724), Francis Turretin (1623-87), Gisbertus Voetius, and Hermann Witsius (1636-1708); Muller provides a helpful enumeration of the significant individuals of this period of high orthodoxy in *PRRD 1*, 31-32. To this can be added the influence of many English Puritans through their translated writings in the Netherlands (Muller, *PRRD I*, 66-67). Think only of op 't Hof's massive *Engelse Piëtistische Geschriften*.

[165] Mastricht, *Praktikale Godgeleerdheit*, 7.1.475-7.7.708.

tion of chapters seven through eleven of the book of Revelation.[166] Book 8 will be explored some more below.

It is immediately apparent that the exposition of his subject matter follows the well-known and pedagogically highly effective method of Ames as the latter made use of this in his *Catechisme*. In fact, the long title of Mastricht's work communicates precisely the subject matter of his massive work: it is the teaching of theoretical and practical divinity by way of the typical four-fold typology, now commonly employed in seventeenth-century textual commentary.[167] Following an introductory presentation of the biblical text under consideration, it is further addressed in this characteristic four-dimensional way: textual explanation or exposition (*verklarende*), doctrinal (*leerstukkig*) teaching, polemic or "argumentative" (*wederleggende*) assertion (in which objections are raised and rebutted), and practical (*betrachtende*) application. It is this classic pedagogical technique in the instruction of the theory and practice of theology that characterizes Petrus van Mastricht, the Reformed Professor of Practical Divinity. His ethical writing is subdivided into Moral Theology (*Zedelyke Godgeleerdheit*) and Practical Theology (*Plicht-Vermanende Godgeleerdheit*).[168]

Mastricht provides a helpfully accessible brief user's manual at the opening of his exhaustive, over-3000 page work. This he entitles "Thoughts on the Most Effective Preaching to Enjoin Theoretical-Practical Theology."[169] He introduces this address with complimentary words for the evangelical preaching of Puritan writers such as Perkins, Ames, Bowles, and Saldenus. Practical evangelical preaching, he says, has a four-fold benefit: the preacher is edified, the listener is advantaged, the subject matter is faithfully discerned and the practice of godliness is advanced. Citing Ames as authority on these matters, Mastricht judges that the value of the sermon will be diminished, the "thread of the sermon" lost, if the hearer is not provided with clarity in exposition and motivation to godliness. The book is a brief lesson in sermon preparation and homiletics, including examples of text-exposition and application.[170] The pre-eminence of this task for the student of theology was Mastricht's conviction.

---

[166] Mastricht, *Praktikale Godgeleerdheit*, 8.1.709-8.4.520.
[167] That such four-fold typology is classic for the age is noted by Muller in *PRRD 1*, 219 and R.A. Muller, *After Calvin: Studies in the Development of a Theological Tradition* (Oxford: Oxford University, 2003), 58.
[168] Mastricht, *Praktikale Godgeleerdheit*, Volume 4, 521-840. The arrangement of this work, all found in Volume 4, is somewhat different from his theological section. My convention in citing from this part of Mastricht's work is by title (*Zedelyke Godgeleerdheit* or *Plicht-Vermanende Godgeleerdheit*), book, chapter, and page number.
[169] *Nagedachten over de beste Predik-Wyze tot Gebruikmakinge van de Beschouwende-Praktikale Godgeleerdheit*, *Praktikale Godgeleerdheit*, pages 841-70. (*De Optima concionandi Methodo Paralipomena. In usum Theologia Theoretico-Practica, Practica Theologia*, pages 1225-36.)
[170] *Beste Predik-Wyze*, 841-70.

Content of Praktikale Godgeleerdheit
a) Prolegomena
Mastricht's prolegomena addresses the many aspects entailed in the study of theology: its nature, its source and rule of conduct (viz., scripture), and its description. The nature of theology is itself divided into three components: its teaching method or pedagogy, its task, and its description. His biblical point of departure for his exposition is 1 Timothy 6:2-3. In elaborating on each of these subcategories, Mastricht repeatedly asserts, first and foremost, what theology is:

> In this chapter, following some introductory remarks regarding the teaching-method for instruction in theology, we shall address the task, that is, Christian theoretical-practical theology, considered as *the doctrine (or teaching) of living to God through Christ*. As foundation for all we say, we shall expound the above-mentioned passage. . . .
> Theoretical-practical Christian theology is none other than the doctrine to live for God through Christ; or the doctrine after Godliness, Tit. 1.1.[171]

This is the only divinity that Timothy learned from Christ and the prophets and apostles, argues Mastricht. For this reason, and because only theoretical-practical divinity can be both learned and admonished as a teaching after godliness, it must be insisted that this is the only divinity to appropriate. In fact, the Apostle proscribed the learning of any other doctrine. This is the teaching of scripture.[172]

Ames' and Mastricht's respective definitions of theology, as similar as they are, are further buttressed by similar scriptural texts although Mastricht is somewhat more expansive, elaborating on the greater degree of precision of his definition, that theology is the doctrine of living to God *through Christ*. Mastricht emphasizes that not only is theology theoretical-practical, but it is always of a Christian sort as well, more explicit than Ames that the ultimate *summum bonum* – God – is necessarily mediated through Christ. Christ is the stairway to heaven.

---

[171] Mastricht, *Praktikale Godgeleerdheit*, 1.1.2; cf. "hoc capite, post præliminare de *methodo* Theologiæ tradendæ, contemplabimur *definitum*, quod præstat *Theologia Christiana Theoretico-Practica*, ejusque *definitionem*, quâ, *doctrina* est *vivendi Deo per Christum*. Omnibus, pro fundamento struemus, exegesin textus præmissi I. Tim. VI. 2. 3. . . . Theologia ista Christina, theoretico-practica, non est, nisi *doctrina vivendi Deo per Christum*; seu *doctrina, qua est secundum pietatem* 1. Tim. VI. 3. item *cognitio veritatis, qua est secundum pietatum* Tit. 1.1 (*Practica Theologia*, 1.1.1, 1.2.12). Neele remarks, mistakenly, that Ames' definition of theology follows "explicitly" that of Ramus, who defined theology as "the doctrine of living well" (Neele, *Mastricht*, 96). See my discussion on the paradigmatic shift represented by Ames' definition of theology over against that of Ramus in a previous chapter. In the same way, Mastricht's more refined articulation is a significant improvement over that of Ames.

[172] Mastricht, *Praktikale Godgeleerdheit*, 1.1.10; idem, *Practica Theologia*, 1.1.4.

Moving on to the doctrinal nature of theology, Mastricht again echoes Ames. Here is what Ames has to say in the section immediately following his assertion that theology is the doctrine of living to God:

> It is called doctrine, not to separate it from understanding, knowledge, wisdom, art, or prudence – for these go with every exact discipline, and most of all with theology – but to mark it as a discipline which derives not from nature and human inquiry like others, but from divine revelation and appointment. Isa. 51:4 . . . Matt. 21:25 . . . John 9:29 . . . Gal. 1:11-12 . . . John 6:45.[173]

Now hear Mastricht:

> Theology is therefore a doctrine, Is. 51:4 . . . Ps. 19:8. That is why it is generally called a doctrine, a teaching, likewise a form of teaching, Rom. 6:17, a teaching after Godliness 1Tim 6:3, cf. Joh. 7:16, 17. 1 Tim. 4:6. We call it a doctrine, not that we scorn and reject the designations of philosophical habit such as understanding, knowledge, wisdom, prudence, and art. For in Holy Scripture we see that these names are so used, first understanding Pro. 2:6, Col. 2:2, then knowledge or acquaintance . . . then wisdom . . . then prudence . . . and that instead of the name "art" as, similarly, use is made of phrases that function to differentiate between good and evil, Hebr. 5:14. Not that theology is so bound to any one of these peculiarities to the exclusion of the others; but rather because it incorporates the perfection and consummation of all other designations. For this reason we prefer to use the broader term doctrine, as that within which all other names can be included. However, there is yet another reason subsumed in this designation, and that is that sacred divinity exists preeminently through doctrine or revelation Is. 51:4, Matt. 16:17, Joh. 1:18, Gal. 1:11, 12.[174]

As we move on in our examination, there are many more similarities (identities, actually) that could be pointed out. A distinguishing feature of Mastricht's system, compared to that of Ames, is the location of his doctrine of Holy Scripture at the very beginning of his work as part of his prolegomena.[175] Based upon the opening scripture of 2 Timothy 3:16 and 17, this 74-page chapter is inserted between the first and third chapters of Book 1. Thus, his opening chapter on the Nature of Theology (cf. Ames, *Marrow*, 1.1) and his third chapter on the divisions or parts of theology (cf. Ames, *Marrow*, 1.2) are wisely augmented with a chapter on Holy Scripture. Although not too much should be read into this, this ordering of the theological *loci* is more in keeping with the systematic ordering of Reformed system we have today, and certainly represents some methodological progression from that of Ames. Recall that although Ames first refers to the Scriptures in his chapter on faith (*Marrow*, 1.3), it is not addressed as a locus of

---

[173] Ames, *Marrow*, 1.1.2.
[174] Mastricht, *Praktikale Godgeleerdheit*, 1.1.31-1.1.32.
[175] The opening statement of Mastricht's work is that theology should be understood "in two divisions: those things which are known beforehand, and those things of the system itself" (*Praktikale Godgeleerdheit*, 1.1.1).

theology until chapter 34, and then in his teaching on the extraordinary and ordinary offices of the church (the apostles and present ministers, respectively) within his ecclesiology.[176]

Although much more could be said about Mastricht's teaching on the nature of theology and the scriptures, we have demonstrated the Amesian inspiration of many of Mastricht's ideas and concepts. In some cases, Ames' very words are used by Mastricht in his exposition of the components of his prolegomena just studied.

The third and final chapter of Book 1, "Of the Divisions of Theology" constitutes a brief commentary on 2 Timothy 1:13. Mastricht explains his two-fold division of theology into faith and obedience:

> The art or feat of living to God of which Scripture is the measure and rule of conduct can be presented in particular divisions, and is profitable both for one's judgment and one's memory, as the Apostle teaches and advises in the above-mentioned words . . . where the Apostle admonishes Timothy to hold fast and maintain the fundamental divisions of holy divinity which are faith and love.[177]

Mastricht then conducts an exposition of the (Greek) text through thorough word study and concludes, in his expository section, that: "One must take note that faith has mostly to do with those things that must be believed, and love

---

[176] Graafland notes that Ames shows a more functional understanding of scripture by placing his doctrine of scripture within the context of the proclamation of the church. This is dissimilar to the prolegomenal perspective of Reformed orthodoxy. In observing that the teaching of the church is the teaching of scripture, Graafland asserts that Ames' thinking was entirely in line with Reformed orthodoxy (Graafland, "Schriftleer and schriftverstaan," *Theologische aspecten*, 31). A further emphasis unique to Ames is that "[in] form of expression, Scripture does not explain the will of God by universal and scientific rules, but rather by stories, examples, precepts, exhortations, admonitions, and promises. This style best fits the common usage of all sorts of men and also greatly affects the will by stirring up pious motives, which is the chief end of theology" (Ames, *Marrow*, 1.34.19). Graafland sees this passage as demonstrating that Ames has consciously imbued his doctrine of scripture with his Puritan piety. Scripture is the possession of the common man or woman, not of the educated elite. Scripture does not first and foremost gratify the intellect, but rather it moves the will to make a heartfelt choice for God. Graafland notes that this is clear evidence of Ames' voluntaristic view of faith. For Ames, the intellect serves the purpose of judging between genuine and counterfeit doctrine but to experience this doctrine in true faith is an act of the will. Ames' congregational leanings are also evident in his doctrine of the church ("Schriftleer en schriftverstaan," *Theologische aspecten*, 32). Graafland also points to this emphasis on praxis in Ames' casuistry where his instructions on hearing the word of God lay special stress on the doing, rather than listening (cf. Ames, *Conscience*, 4.11). Graafland notes that Mastricht's doctrine of scripture is a thorough elaboration of that of Ames (in the same way Brakel's doctrine of scripture elaborates that of Voet), ("Schriftleer en schriftverstaan," *Theologische aspecten*, 32, 61-68).

[177] Mastricht, *Praktikale Godgeleerdheit*, 1.3.117.

must be focused upon those things that must be done, or obedience."[178] Further, it is Timothy's (and the reader's) responsibility to: i) acquire the standard for your own life, carry it with you and guard it; ii) maintain it and watch that you conform your life to it and teach your students the same; iii) let it direct your apologetic against the opposition; and, iv) let your entire life, and that of yours, be suited and directed to these, which are the most important aspects both of the standard and the divisions of theology, that is faith and love.[179]

Earlier that same century Ames had taught:

> The two parts of theology are faith and observance. 2 Tim. 1:13 . . . . 1 Tim. 1:19. . . . The theology of Paul consisted of these parts: Acts 24:14-16 . . . . The same parts made up the theology of Abraham: Gen. 15:6 and 17:1 . . . . Christ demands the same of his disciples when he requires, beyond faith, that they *Observe everything which he commanded*, Matt. 28:20. Paul covers the same matters in his Letter to the Romans which manifestly contains the sum of theology. Finally he wanted to have these things taught in the churches. Titus 3:8 . . . .[180]

The explanation of this passage and its teaching are further conducted in the doctrinal section. Here Mastricht follows the passages cryptically introduced by Ames in the above quote, in much more detail and draws from the earlier wealth of writing found in the literature of the church fathers (such as Cyril of Jerusalem, Anastasius of Nicea) before making further reference to Ames by name and citation (*Marrow*, 1.2.2). Mastricht's point is that many revered names through the history of the church have emphasized that the consummate Christian is one who has both faith and good works. In fact, the witness of scripture, Psalm 37:13, 1 Timothy 1:19, John 13:17, Acts 24: 14, 15, 16, and Titus 3:8 all underscore theology as faith and observance. This was recognized, formally captured, and powerfully expressed (*krachtig uitgedrukt*), says Mastricht, by William Ames:

> Also, there is no shortage of reasons for this division. Because in the first place, as men consider the topic of divinity, they shall discover that this division agrees precisely with the parts of theology, which Amesius strongly emphasized as such.[181]

The section cites a long quotation from Ames (the entire section of *Marrow* 1.2.1) before Mastricht closes with: "and we distinguish them in such a way

---

[178] Mastricht, *Praktikale Godgeleerdheit*, 1.3.118.
[179] Mastricht, *Praktikale Godgeleerdheit*, 1.3.118.
[180] Ames, *Marrow*, 1.2.1. The evidence casts doubt on Neele's assertion that Ames' Ramist division of theology into faith and observance was driven by primarily methodological considerations as opposed to the more biblical motivation of Mastricht who, contrary to Calvinists and Puritans following in Ames' train, "based the division on the biblical text and its exposition" (Neele, *Mastricht*, 109, n. 20).
[181] Mastricht, *Praktikale Godgeleerdheit*, 1.3.119.

that faith has the prior position and obedience the second."[182] And that love is expressed in obedience is best seen in moral theology, "as Ames expresses in the already-noted citations."[183] William Ames would have been gratified with Mastricht's sound biblical defense of his Ramist framework.[184]

Following this doctrinal section comes a brief discussion of the arguments of the Socinians and the Arminians, before Mastricht unfolds the practical aspect of theology (the longest of the three). Here the *uses* of theology as faith and observance are laid out. Chiefly, he teaches that this division of theology (or rather, clarifies Mastricht, not the division itself but each *part* of this division) ensures that theologians as well as Christians in general will, firstly, do theology justice by seeing it as a unified whole, comprising these two necessary parts, and not emphasizing one part at the expense of the other. In fact, divinity students are exhorted not to abandon love when urging the faith (1 Corinthians 13: 1, 2) because that would show they care more about polemics of the faith than about faith itself. Confession of the mouth must be confirmed and not denied by works, lest by living inconsistently individuals show their faith to be dead (quoting James 11:18 here). Secondly, those things which the Holy Scripture tied so closely together should motivate one to believe and do good works, not for works' own sake but for the sake of true faith and obedience. Following further exposition of the duties devolving upon one who seeks to live in a fashion after godliness, Mastricht's Book 1, prolegomena, concludes.[185]

b) Faith and the Will
Book 2 of *Praktikale Godgeleerdheit* unpacks faith. The exposition is schematically laid out in a manner almost identical to the Ramist framework employed by Ames.[186] As the first element of this dichotomous arrangement, Mastricht explains faith by taking John 1: 11-12 as his opening scripture and explaining it at length. Employing the identical passage, Ames had asserted that faith involved the heart's repose on God. In opposition to, for example, Beza, Macco-

---

[182] Mastricht, *Praktikale Godgeleerdheit*, 1.3.120.

[183] Mastricht, *Praktikale Godgeleerdheit*, 1.3.119.

[184] Section 5 is the final section in Eusden's translation. Eusden observes in a note that "Posthumous editions add a concluding section [Section 6] to this chapter in which the distinction between faith and observance is held to be similar to the traditional distinction between metaphysics and ethics. Francisco Suárez (1548-1617), *Disputatio I* or *First Disputation*, v, n. 44 is quoted. . . ." ("Introduction" in *Marrow*, 80, n. 8). Eusden explains that these "later editors," in this Section 6, pointed out that the Amesian understanding of faith and observance sees the two as essentially connected and unified acts, while the Scholastics overemphasized the divisions of theology and philosophy. Although this is indeed the content of this section, I doubt Eusden's assertion that this is necessarily the work of later editors. One of the Latin editions of *Medulla* I am using is that of 1628 which most certainly does include Section 6; cf. *Medulla* (1628 and 1643), 1.2.6. Recall Ames died in 1633.

[185] Mastricht, *Praktikale Godgeleerdheit*, 1.2.120-1.2.123.

[186] Mastricht, *Praktikale Godgeleerdheit*, opening pages.

vius, and Keckermann, who argued that believing involved the intellect's assent to evidence, Ames insisted that ultimate movement toward God comes from the will. Thus, because it is necessary for the faith to be embraced, it is a volitional act of reception – an act of choice, an undertaking of the whole man. This is not merely the intellect at work. [187] True faith "cannot be received without a genuine turning of the will towards God . . . who is the object of faith . . . . [while] Christ as redeemer is the mediate but not the ultimate object of faith, for we believe through Christ in God."[188] This surrender to Christ cannot come through any "assent of understanding – only through a consent of the will."[189] This true faith is true and proper trust in God and, while "some place true faith partly in the understanding and partly in the will . . . this is not quite correct for it is a single virtue."[190]

Mastricht follows this reasoning very closely. He repeats Ames' contention that faith is an *act* in accepting (*aannemen*) God as the ultimate *end* or *object* and Christ as the only mediator. He repeatedly emphasizes that faith is a deed. It is a deed of the entire rational soul – "for with the soul man believes, and that is with the entire heart."[191] While the intellect receives knowledge of the gospel promises and gives its approval primarily to the proposition of Christ as Messiah, it is in the will that saving faith receives concurrence and whereby we sincerely desire to have God and the Mediator. For:

> a theoretical knowledge and consent is not sufficient; a practical act is required whereby men are convinced, and the will moved, to reach for the proffered God and Mediator (Rom. 7:18). . . . In the will saving faith receives concurrence by which we earnestly desire God and the mediator who offered themselves to us in the gospel and whom we accept and receive John 1:12.[192]

Mastricht's understanding of the interplay of the intellect and the volition in saving faith and his emphasis on the soul as the habitation of these faculties is similar to Ames' intellect-volition dialectic and his stress on the heart as the residence of humanity's faculties. Reuter seems mistaken, then, when he remarks that Mastricht was more "eclectic" in locating faith in the soul, thus underscoring a more unified intellect-volition connection.[193]

The act of "accepting" is explicated in terms of receiving, consenting, choosing, covenanting. And as mentioned, while Mastricht, with Ames, sees God as the object of faith, the *focus* of the faith is the mediator in his offices as proph-

---

[187] Ames, *Marrow*, 1.3.1-1.3.3.
[188] Ames, *Marrow*, 1.3.5-1.3.8.
[189] Ames, *Marrow*, 1.3.19.
[190] Ames, *Marrow*, 1.3.22.
[191] Mastricht, *Praktikale Godgeleerdheit*, 2.1.129.
[192] Mastricht, *Praktikale Godgeleerdheit*, 2.1.129.
[193] Horton, *Ames by Reuter*, 195.

et, priest and king.[194] Interestingly, Mastricht opens his next chapter on the existence and knowledge of God with an introductory sentence pointing to the goal of saving faith as the seeking, the longing and the acceptance of God as our "highest end" (*hoogste einde, summum finem*).[195] We are reminded of Ames' similar use of the concept *summum bonum* in *Catechisme*. The remainder of Mastricht's exposition on faith (recall, the first division of theology, the second being obedience) represents reasonably well-developed Reformed theology of the day. The penultimate chapter on ecclesiology is followed by a long chapter on the administration of the covenant of grace, mediated by Christ. We will return to this chapter presently; for now we will examine the second half of his work in which Mastricht, like Ames, focuses on obedience.

c) Conscience and Moral Theology
Mastricht's teaching on the concept of conscience is introduced as early as his chapter on the existence and knowledge of God. Following a long discussion on the reasons for the existence of God (following Perkins and *contra* Ames) Mastricht presents as witnesses to this existence the three-fold testimony of the world, of God himself, and of the conscience.[196] Citing Romans 1:19 (what may be made known about God is made plain to them) and Romans 2:15 (conscience excuses or accuses, comforts or frightens) we again see clear Amesian dependence.[197]

As explained elsewhere, Mastricht's exposition of the active part of theology – obedience – is found in his work on moral theology. An examination of his overview and a reading of his teaching in this area reveal such close correspondence to that of William Ames' casuistry, in both form and content, that our study could easily conclude with this assertion. Mastricht is truly a perpetuator of the informed piety of William Ames and, as such, has carried this well through the thought of Reformed system via his own work. But cogency demands a brief comparative study here.

Mastricht's moral divinity comes to us as *Moral Theology* (*Zedelyke Godgeleerdheit*) and *Practical Theology* (*Plicht-Vermanende Godgeleerdheit*). The first comes in three books: "Obedience in General," "Worship," and "Just and Unjust Treatment of Neighbor." Under the first, Mastricht leans heavily on the first section of Chapter 1 of Ames' *Marrow*, ("On Obedience") and Chapter 3 of Ames' *Conscience*, where Ames (and Mastricht) describes the cardinal virtues, their opposites and good and evil works. Book 2 of Mastricht's moral theology describes such things as the theological virtues, prayer, oaths, the lot, and the Sabbath; this compares closely with Ames' *Marrow*, Book 2, sections two through fifteen, and all of Book 4 of *Conscience*. The content coverage of

---

[194] Mastricht, *Praktikale Godgeleerdheit*, 2.1.129-2.1.132.
[195] Mastricht, *Praktikale Godgeleerdheit*, 2.2.162; idem, *Practica Theologia*, 2.2.65.
[196] Mastricht, *Praktikale Godgeleerdheit*, 2.2.143-2.2.170.
[197] Cf. Ames, *Conscience*, 1.4.

Mastricht's final book on Moral Theology, "Just and Unjust Treatment of Neighbor," is drawn from Book 5 of Ames' *Conscience* and chapters 16-22 of Book 2 of *Marrow*, viz., the proper, biblical of treatment of neighbor, structured around the second table of the decalogue.[198]

Mastricht divides his teaching of conscience (*conscientie*) into four components. Under the first he addresses the nature of conscience ("a man's judgment of himself according to his submission to God").[199] From this very Amesian definition of conscience, Mastricht continues to follow closely Ames' exposition in all four divisions (nature, types, care, and neglect of conscience).[200] It is at the very opening of his exposition that, following Ames, he explains the dynamics and components of syllogistic reasoning in arriving at a judgment and Mastricht employs one of Ames' precise syllogisms to demonstrate how conscience works in actual fact ("All that believe shall be saved; I believe; Therefore, I shall be saved and preserved").[201]

Mastricht's second volume on moral divinity is actually a more specific elaboration on cases of conscience and compares with the more detailed cases found in Books 2, 4 and 5 of Ames' *Conscience* (and relevant areas of *Marrow*, Book 2) and not addressed by Mastricht in *Moral Theology*. In this volume, Mastricht focuses on the *practice* of the moral theology just learned. He entitles this volume *Theologiæ Asceticæ* (Dutch: *Plicht-Vermanende Godgeleerdheit*) and explains the distinction of this volume from the preceding one:

> We have completed the short coverage of *Moral* Theology studied from the perspective of particular virtues and vices. Thus we proceed to the *practice* of these virtues. Although the virtues, when considered *in themselves and in their own nature* are very much different from each other, in their activity and practice they are really very closely tied and blended together. For the practice of these virtues through the many contingencies of the Christian life brings them together in many respects . . . . We call the doctrine of this uniting of virtues, in view of the various cases and circumstances of the Christian life, "duty-bound godliness" or the "practice of godliness (*Theologia ascetica*)" in conformity with the Apostle, Acts 24:16 . . . 1 Tim. 4:7 . . . . In agreement as well with various divines of an earlier age as, for example, Basilius, . . . as well as with those of more recent times, particularly of the Reformed divines, such as, for example, Bayle . . . Wilhelm Teellinck . . . Joh. Gerardi . . . and particularly, Gysbertus Voetius, in his . . . *Practice of Godliness*. . . .[202]

---

[198] Mastricht, *Zedelyke Godgeleerdheit*, 1.522-1.563; 2.564-2.628; 3.628-3.668.
[199] Mastricht, *Zedelyke Godgeleerdheit*, 1.3.525.
[200] Mastricht, *Zedelyke Godgeleerdheit*, 1.3.525-1.3.526.
[201] Mastricht, *Zedelyke Godgeleerdheit*, 1.3.525; cf. Ames, *Conscience*, 1.1-1.11.
[202] Mastricht, *Plicht-Vermanende Godgeleerdheit*, Foreword. A good recent study into Voet's practice of godliness of which Mastricht speaks can be found in C.A. de Niet, *Gijsbertus Voetius. De Praktijk der Godzaligheid*, 2 Vols. (Utrecht: De Banier, 1996).

This "Practice of Godliness" is considered in general, regarding God, regarding neighbor, and regarding self.[203] We will resist the temptation to point out each area of similarity. Enough has been shown by way of example to demonstrate the indebtedness of the moral divinity of Petrus van Mastricht to that of William Ames.[204] What is Mastricht's guiding theological and hermeneutical framework?

d) Covenant Theology

The entire eighth book of *Praktikale Godgeleerdheit* is devoted to the administration of the covenant of grace from the time of creation to eternity and amounts to what could be considered to be a highly-detailed exposition of the history of the world. Although in general terms if follows the major sub-categories of Ames' three chapters on the administration of the covenant of grace, the detail that Mastricht adds to the Amesian sketch is considerable. We will provide a brief overview of Mastricht's covenant system as he lays it out for us in Books 1-7, focus on Book 8, and close our study of Mastricht's thought with some conclusions.

Covenant theology permeates books one through seven of the work of Mastricht. His book on the "Works of God" (Book 3) concludes with a chapter on the covenant of works (*Verbondt der Nature, De fœdere naturæ*).[205] Book 4 which covers anthropology and is entitled "Of Man's Fall from God" (*van's menschen Afval van Godt, de hominis apostasiâ à Deo*) runs for four chapters, opens with a chapter on the breach of the covenant of works and closes with the

---

[203] Mastricht, *Plicht-Vermanende Godgeleerdheit*, 1.1.671-1.1.681; 1.2.682-1.1.724; 1.3.725-1.3.775; 1.4.776-1.4.840.

[204] Yet I cannot resist noting one more example, the last lesson in Mastricht's *magnum opus*. Under the title "The Duties of Godliness with respect to Death," chapter 15 of the fourth book of *Plicht-Vermanende Godgeleerdheit* provides Mastricht's wisdom on how to die "well," i.e., "blessedly" or "felicitously" (*wel-sterven* [*Plicht-Vermanende Godgeleerdheit*, 4.15.837]; cf. *benè beateque moriendi* [*Theologiæ-Asceticæ*, 4.15.1223]). Ames handles this topic in a four-fold manner: the nature of death, the desirability of death, comfort in the face of death, and how a believer is to enjoy this consolation (Ames, *Conscience*, 2.17.1-2.17.18). Mastricht chooses to address the topic in a three-fold manner: the nature of dying blessedly, the advantages of dying blessedly, and the means to die blessedly. His exposition runs parallel to that of Ames and part three is, in fact, a long quotation from Ames, whom he cites (*Conscience*, 2.17.10-2.17.18), representing an answer to Question 4 posed by Ames; cf. Amesius, *Conscientia et Eius Iure vel Casibus*, 2.17.10-2.17.18 and Mastricht, *Theologiæ Asceticæ*, 4.15.1223-4.15.1224. Interestingly, the Dutch translation misquotes various Amesian scriptural references that Mastricht has rendered faithfully in his own Latin original. The key misquote, in fact, is in the actual citation itself (the translator cites *Ames. Cas. Conscient. Lib. II Cap. xviii*; the proper citation is, as I have noted, the *seventeenth* chapter of Book 2 of *Conscience*; cf. *Plicht-Vermanende Godgeleerdheit*, 4.15.840).

[205] Mastricht, *Praktikale Godgeleerdheit*, 3.12.181; idem, *Practica Theologia*, 3.12.413; cf. Ames, *Marrow*, 1.10.

punishment of sin (original and actual).²⁰⁶ Mastricht's Christology is the subject of Book 5 and is introduced with a chapter on the covenant of grace (*Verbondt der Genade, De fœdere gratiæ*). What is most interesting is that Christ is introduced as the Mediator of the covenant of grace. It is this mediatorial title that figures prominently in the entire exposition of Mastricht's Christology, as he works through Christ's (or rather, the Mediator's) names, persons, offices, and states.²⁰⁷ Book 6, of the "Application of Redemption" follows and is a fleshed out exposition of Ames' teaching on the *ordo salutis*.²⁰⁸ The second last book in Mastricht's theology is concerning ecclesiology (*De Kerke en Kerkelyke Zaken, De Ecclesiâ & Ecclesiasticalibus*).²⁰⁹ In the overall organizing structure, as well as in the subheads, Mastricht has followed Ames very closely. From Mastricht's use of covenant as a theological principle and as structural concept in Books 1-7, and notably his employment of the covenantal framework in Book 8 examined below demonstrate unambiguously that Mastricht's entire theological system is architectonically covenantal.²¹⁰

To understand just how much the concept of covenant represents the skeleton around which the body of his entire system is constructed, consider this. Recall the fundamental dichotomous arrangement of Faith and Obedience. The former division constitutes the details of Mastricht's theological system; the latter focuses on his moral divinity along the lines explained above. The first section on faith introduces the covenant structure beginning with the book on anthropology. From here on, the entire work is structured around the concept of the covenant of grace. Again, we let Mastricht speak for himself as he introduces his thought on the plan of his work from Book 5 on and as he exposits Genesis 3:15:

---

[206] Mastricht, *Praktikale Godgeleerdheit*, 4.1.216-4.4.362; idem, *Practica Theologia*, 4.1.327-4.4.388; cf. Ames, *Marrow*, 1.11-1.17.

[207] Mastricht, *Praktikale Godgeleerdheit*, 5.1.363-5.18.166; idem, *Practica Theologia*, 5.1.389-5.18.636; cf. Ames, *Marrow*, 1.18-1.23.

[208] Mastricht, *Praktikale Godgeleerdheit*, 6.1.167-6.9.474; idem, *Practica Theologia*, 6.1.637-6.9.765; cf. Ames, *Marrow*, 1.14-1.30.

[209] Mastricht, *Praktikale Godgeleerdheit*, 7.1.475-7.7.708; idem, *Practica Theologia*, 7.1.766-7.7.862; cf. Ames, *Marrow*, 1.31-1.37.

[210] Despite Neele's disagreement (*Mastricht*, 110, n. 24). His wish is that "... our study invites a specific study on the doctrine of the covenant of Mastricht. . . . One study should consider Jonathan Edwards's indebtedness to Mastricht regarding covenant theology. . . . Another study should consider Mastricht's indebtedness to Coccejus, not only as an exegete but also as covenant theologian" (*Mastricht*, 286). Our current work goes some distance in accomplishing this. Further, Neele asserts, with considerable opaqueness, that "the citations and references to Ames's works are not dominant [*sic?*] present" (*Mastricht*, 79). On the contrary, our work demonstrates that Amesian citations and references, including long and direct (both attributed and unattributed) quotations are numerous, as were the resources at his disposal during this period of the formation of Reformed system. What is eminently most significant is that both the letter and the spirit of Ames so demonstrably surface in Mastricht.

> In the previous book we spoke of the fall of humanity and the extreme misery of the transgressors through the breach of the covenant of works. Now follows man's recovery whereby he is restored and lifted out of a state of sin and death into a state of grace and life. This subject-matter will be handled in two parts: redemption and the application of this redemption. Both components recognize the covenant of grace as the standard and rule of conduct, which has been established in place of the violated covenant of works. This redemption, God willing, we hope to explain in the fifth book, and its application in the sixth. . . .
> [Now] in this book [Seven] we move to her subject and to the means. The subject with which redemption and its application are both concerned and active is the Church . . . Eph. 5:25. . . .
> It remains that we say something worthwhile [in Book Eight] with regards to her various divisions, which can also be designated as the administration of the Covenant of Grace.[211]

This is how William Ames introduces his Christology, soteriology, ecclesiology, and his chapters on the administration of the covenant of grace in which his eschatology is very briefly considered.

> After the fall of man, we next consider his restoration. The restoration of man is the lifting from a state of sin and death to a state of grace and life. . . . There are two parts in this restoration, redemption and its application. . . . These parts are of one and the same compass. For the end of redemption is its application, and the first reason, rule, and measure of application is the same gracious will of God which brings about this redemption. . . .The mediator is Jesus Christ alone. . . .
> So much for redemption; we now consider its application [in chapters 24-30]. . . .
> So much for the application of redemption considered in itself. Now we take up the matter of the subject to which and the way in which it is applied [in chapters 31-37]. The subject is the church. Eph. 5:25-27. . . .
> Although the free, saving covenant of God has been one and the same from the beginning, the manner of the application of Christ or the administration of the new covenant has not always been so. It has varied according to the times during which the church has been in process of being gathered [in chapters 38-41].[212]

We have now come to Book 8 of Mastricht's work. This compares closely to the last few chapters of Ames' *Marrow*, with a couple of exceptions. These exceptions will be noted presently. In this book, the final one of his system, Mastricht presents an exhaustive exposition of the administration of the covenant of grace. Mastricht, following Ames, has identified four chief periods of the administration of the covenant of grace as follows: "Under the Patriarchs" (cf. Ames, "Before Moses"), "Under Moses" ("cf. Ames, "Moses to Christ,") "Under Christ" (cf. Ames, "Christ to the End of the World"), and "In and Under Eternity" (cf. Ames, "The End of the World"). The age which represents the period under Christ is characterized by God's covenant renewal activity.

---

[211] Mastricht, *Praktikale Godgeleerdheit*, 5.1.363-5.1.64, 7.1.475, 8.1.709.
[212] Ames, *Marrow*, 1.18, 1.24, 1.31, 1.38.

Of greatest interest in these respective schemas is the massive commentary that Mastricht provides for each of the periods. As we have seen above, Ames applies the *ordo salutis* to various historic events in the life of the church in each of the dispensations of the covenant of grace. As well, he describes the nature of the church through these respective periods. Mastricht does this as well, but he does much more. With Ames, he comments on the soteriological significance of each of the periods under consideration and makes observations on the preservation and activity of the church.[213] But here the comparison with Ames ends for Mastricht then proceeds to write an entire history of redemption, structured by each of these periods and contemporized by events in the history of the world until the present. In fact, at the beginning of his work Mastricht provides a very helpful "Sketch of Church History, According to the Eighth Book."[214] Again, to summarize the content of this book we let Mastricht introduce the subject matter of Book 8 himself as he explains it in his foreword to the entire manuscript:

> In the eighth book regarding the administration of the covenant of grace, I have added church history, in its entirety and perfection, if succinctly; here you shall find, with respect to the Old Testament, the champions of the particular ages of the church, civic and ecclesiastical, patriarchs, judges, kings, (of both kingdoms, the Jewish as well as the Israelite), and the most noteworthy things from each in particular. And with regard to the New Testament, you shall meet the Roman emperors and Popes, each in particular, regarding that in which they were most significant. Then you shall see the various states of theology, and the deviations into heresy and error. And also the states of the church, and her propagators, patriarchs, prophets, apostles, evangelists, each of whose history has been recorded. You shall read as well of the means of propagation, namely, the ecclesiastical writers, synods, schools, forms of government, persecutions, martyrdoms, and whatever else belongs to the church, by which things, I believe, all prerequisites for a complete record of church history are satisfied; however, I have done this succinctly because otherwise I would have been required to produce many thick books.[215]

---

[213] The *ordo salutis* is also very prominent in Mastricht. For example, the period of the flood is characterized by these soteriologically significant events: "Regarding the external call, Noah, the preacher of righteousness, called the world to repentance; similarly with the internal call, in inducing Japheth to Shem's tent; regarding justification . . . Noah believed God . . . ; regarding sanctification, Noah was a righteous man, blameless among the people of his time . . . ; regarding glorification, this is seen in the deliverance of Noah and his family from the misery of the flood: compare 2 Pet. 2:9 and the opposite judgment upon the idolatrous world . . . ." (Mastricht, *Praktikale Godgeleerdheit*, 8.1.744).

[214] Mastricht, *Praktikale Godgeleerdheit*, introductory comments in the un-numbered preliminary pages; idem, "Diatyposis Historiæ Ecclesiasticæ, juxta librum octavum," *Practica Theologia*, introductory matter.

[215] Mastricht, *Praktikale Godgeleerdheit*. Mastricht concludes that his earlier plans for a larger church history (which work had already been begun and was now at the history of the life of Isaac) had to be put aside due to his advanced age and thus to better serve the

This introduction summarizes the work for what it is: a massive, not so succinct exposition of the pattern of redemptive history first established by William Ames and soon after so typical of post-Reformation theological systems.

Mastricht subdivides his four-period description of the history of the church into the following sub-heads (with the four major heads in parentheses): (1. *Under the Patriarchs*) i) Adam to Noah; ii) Noah to Abraham; iii) Abraham to Moses; (2. *Under Moses*) iv) Moses to David; v) David to the Babylonian Exile; vi) Babylonian Exile to Christ; (3. *Under Christ*) vii) The first Age of the New Testament under the first Seal (Revelation 6: 1-2); viii) the second Age of the New Testament under the second Seal (Revelation 6: 3-4); ix) the third Age of the New Testament under the third Seal (Revelation 6: 5-6); x) the fourth Age of the New Testament under the fourth Seal (Revelation 6: 7-8); xi) the fifth Age of the New Testament under the fifth Seal (Revelation 6:9-11); the sixth Age of the New Testament under the sixth Seal (Revelation 6: 12); and, finally (4. *Under Eternity*) xii) the seventh age of the New Testament under the seventh Seal (Revelation 7:1-11:19). This entire scheme is an exposition of the history of the church from creation to eternity and it is in only a few closing sections under the final period (period xii) that Mastricht presents his eschatology.[216]

Concluding Observations: Ames, Brakel and Mastricht

This chapter of our study on the legacy of Ames has been sufficient to establish incontrovertibly the indebtedness of, firstly, Wilhelmus à Brakel's theoretical and practical divinity to Amesian thought. We have attempted to focus on streams of thought that are particularly distinctive of William Ames, not always an easy task. Wilhelmus à Brakel's own uniqueness lay not in any formative contribution to Reformed theology. Rather, it is found in his recognition of both the gracious nature of a sovereign God combined with the absolute necessity for obedience. This was communicated by way of the best pastoral application of the period. Brakel's contribution rests in the manner in which he was able to plumb the very depths of spiritual experience in the Christian walk.[217] In Brakel, grace and obedience come together in complete unity and in a highly pastoral context. This is the mark of experimental Calvinism. Brakel followed Ames in viewing theology as a combination of sound doctrine and sober life made practical by an appreciation for covenant theology and an application of

---

church. In the meantime, however, for readers desiring an exhaustive volume on church history, Mastricht highly recommended the work of Spanheim printed at Leiden.

[216] Mastricht, "Schets der Kerkelyke Geschiedenisse volgens het Achtste Boek," *Praktikale Godgeleerdheit*, preliminary pages, table of contents.

[217] The four volumes of *Service* used here total approximately 2400 pages of script, 2230 without the Appendix. Of these 2230 pages, I consider 830 pages of a purely practical, pastoral nature. This is 37 per cent. There are only two pages of practical instruction in the Appendix.

informed piety. Surely in spirit, Brakel's definition of theology, too, was "the doctrine of living to God" in his concern for piety and godliness of life. Indeed, in areas Father Brakel excels even the Learned Doctor in his penetrating but judicious soul-searching. He carries forward the gentle and tender spirit of William Perkin's casuistry but with the scholarly apparatus and full-bodied practical divinity given him by William Ames. That he was spiritual physician *extraordinaire* is especially evident beginning with the third volume of his *Service* and through to eschatology where his insights on sanctification are so closely modeled on the theory and practice of the Amesian system of ethics.[218]

There is no doubt that Brakel drew from many of the resources available at the end of the seventeenth century to inform his own thinking. On occasion we have drawn attention to the fact that unity in thought demonstrates not so much Brakel's intellectual indebtedness to Ames, but rather the coherence of Reformed thinking of the day and the adherence of each individual to the then-received tradition. To be sure, Amesian thought would also have been mediated to Wilhelmus à Brakel by others during this period of high orthodoxy.[219] In this connection, the observations appearing in the preface of the translated work used in this present study are apropos: "One cannot but be struck by its kinship with English Puritan literature. This is especially evident in the third and fourth volumes which are devoted almost entirely to the life of sanctification. As is true for the Puritans, à Brakel was a most able physician of souls."[220] But the true extent of William Ames' influence can be better gauged in the context of the following comment:

> The obvious similarity between à Brakel's writings, which represent the cream of Dutch Second Reformation literature, and Puritan literature is highly significant. It proves that the Puritans and the Dutch Second Reformation divines (sometimes referred to as the Dutch Puritans) were essentially cut from the same cloth. It will be difficult to find essential differences between à Brakel and such English Puritans as John Owen, Thomas Goodwin, and John Bunyan.[221]

Only when we remember that William Ames and his major works on theology and ethics predated most of the more influential Puritan divines and all those here listed can we fully appreciate the influence he wielded from his professorial chair in Franeker. For the emphases on experiential religion and piety had

---

[218] Referring to the second volume of Brakel's original two-volume work, Geesink observes, interestingly, that Brakel's system is very much "in the spirit of Voetius, although deprived of Voetius' power by his [Brakel's] 'subjective rules'" (Geesink, *Gereformeerde Ethiek*, 2.494). A formal comparative study of the thought of Ames and Voet is required.

[219] See Muller, *PRRD 1*, 27-32. Brakel's indebtedness also extends to Francis Turretin. In this regard, we have mentioned the influence of Voet many times. See W. van 't Spijker, "Gisbertus Voetius," in *Voornaamste vertegenwoordigers*, 49-84.

[220] Beeke, "Preface" in Brakel, *Service*, xxi.

[221] Beeke, "Preface" in Brakel, *Service*, xxi-xxii.

their provenance in the Amesian understanding of theology. Ames' case-divinity probed the spiritual life and, by the godliness found there, established not only a *determination* of William Perkins' greatest case of conscience there ever was but also the *depth* of that experience. In such spiritual probing, Wilhelmus à Brakel excelled.[222]

On the title page of the original edition of *Redelyke Godts-Dienst* appears a pertinent pictograph.[223] A cherubic-like character designated "De Waarheydt" (The Truth) is flanked on either side by two characters: "Beschermt" (Defended) appears on the left and "Beleeft" (Experienced) on the right. All characters are facing westward as if in motion. Beschermt is dressed in battle armor, carrying a sword in a posture of defense, a picture of Christian fortitude and courage. Beleeft is wearing robes, much like those in which De Waarheydt is clothed, flanked on each side by a small, innocent child, a picture of Christian faith, hope and love. Just in front of Beleeft's face is a small cross, suspended, as it were, in the air. De Waarheydt, meanwhile is holding aloft a tuft of grass or a sheaf of wheat to denote nourishment, following confidently in the train of Beschermt. This was Brakel's view of Truth: Protected and Experienced.

This poignant pictorial representation applies just as easily to the view of theology of Ames for whom "living to God" was centered on the Truth protected by Faith and experienced in Obedience. "Let all things be done unto edifying," advised the English translators of Ames.[224] Within the covenant community of the church of Jesus Christ in the Reformed tradition, the godly legacy of the covenantal and experiential faith of William Ames and Wilhelmus à Brakel continues to edify.[225]

---

[222] For example, H.W. Laman, *Geloofsbezwaren opgelost door Wilhelmus à Brakel* (Kampen: J.H. Kok, 1929).

[223] I am describing the pictograph appearing in the 1700 first edition, *Redelyke Godts-Dienst*. The pictograph reappears, with minor modification, in the twentieth edition, *Redelyke Godtsdienst*, used by the translators for these four volumes comprising the English edition.

[224] Ames, *Marrow*, quoting 1 Cor 14:26 on the title page.

[225] In connection with Brakel's (and Ames') emphasis on preaching, it might be interesting to examine the lives and emphases of *Nadere Reformatie* preaching divines to determine whether and how the distinctives of these two theologians may have been transmitted from the academy, to the pulpit, and from thence to the pew. Did the ecclesiastical and spiritual life of the *Nadere Reformatie* Reformed reflect the covenantal and pietistic emphases of Ames and Brakel? For a look at some examples of ministers and preaching in this period, see the following: K. Exalto, *Beleefd Geloof: Acht Schetsen van Gereformeerde Theologen uit de 17e Eeuw* (Amsterdam: Ton Bolland, 1974); T. Brienen, *De Prediking van de Nadere Reformatie* (Amsterdam: Ton Bolland, 1974); K. Exalto, *De Kracht Der Religie: Tien Schetsen van Gereformeerde 'Oude Schrijvers' uit de 17e en 18e Eeuw* (Urk: De Vuurtoren, 1976); and T. Brienen, "De 22 regels van Willem Teellinck over het maken van preken," *DNR* 6 (1982): 16-22. For an individual who conducted typical catechetical preaching in the time of the *Nadere Reformatie*, see Bernardus Smytegelt, *Des Christens Eenige Troost in Leven en Sterven, of Verklaringe over den Heidelbergschen Catechismus in LII Predicatien; Benevens V Belydenis-*

We have demonstrated, secondly, that there exists a clear, unambiguous connection between the thought of William Ames and that of a foremost theologian/scholar of the *Nadere Reformatie*, Petrus van Mastricht. The dependence of the latter upon the former, however, had already been acknowledged by Mastricht in his brief foreword to the reader. Following some introductory words regarding the nature of this work of *Praktikale Godgeleerdheit*, Mastricht discusses his moral divinity: "I have followed the subject arrangement of the highly-renown *Amesius*, in his *Marrow* and *Cases of Conscience*, which struck me as so suitable and convenient that I neither required, nor desired to have, any other."[226] Our examination has demonstrated just how suitable and convenient Ames turned out to be for Mastricht's purposes. In addition, it appears that the recasting of Ames' ideas in more contemporary language is one of Mastricht's strengths. Thus, in capturing the focus on faith and obedience, doctrine and life, Mastricht can say that faith has everything to do with believing, and love has everything to do with obedience. It is love for a covenantal God which motivates to obedience. Faith, for Mastricht, is an act of the will, assenting to Christ and the gospel offer. Conscience arrives at judgment through syllogism.

It was more than Ames' moral divinity which provided such rich fodder for the work of Mastricht. The organizing structure, expositional method, key conceptual definitions, and process of thought all bear remarkable resemblance to Ames' work. Even Mastricht's prolegomena is closely patterned after his inspirer, but with added and welcome improvements. Two examples of such development are the addition of a christological dimension to Ames' definition of theology, and the bringing forward of the doctrine of scripture into prolegomena where it more properly belongs. Thus Mastricht brings a slight refocus to developing Reformed system by grounding it more explicitly and immediately than did Ames in both the living and written word.

Predicatien (Middelburg: Ottho en Pieter van Thol, Den Haag, en A.L. en M.H. Callenfels, 1747). On Smytegelt, see Marinus Johannes Antonie de Vrijer, *Ds. Bernardus Smytegelt en zijn "gerookte riet"* (Amsterdam: H. J. Spruyt, 1947). Finally, on the "oude schrijvers" [literally *old writers*] see also W. van Gent, *Bibliotheek van oude schrijvers* (Rotterdam: Lindebergs, 1979). Because Jodocus van Lodenstein has been presented as thoroughly Amesian, a study of the former's sermons would be of particular interest. In that connection, see the following: *Het Vervolg van den Geestelyken Opwekker, Voor-gestelt in Negen Predicatien* (Amsterdam: Jacobus Van Hardenburg, 1707); *De Heerlykheyd Van en Waar Christelihke Leven. Uytblinkende in God-saligen Wandel, volgens het Geestelijke Licht des Evangeliums, te sien in Jezus heerlyk Voorbeeld, nedrige Geboorte en Armoede, om ons te Wederbaren, en Rijk in God te maken* (Amsterdam: Jacobus Van Hardenburg, 1711); *Beschouwinge van Zion* (Amsterdam: J. Van Hardenburg, 1718); and *J. van Lodensteyn's Negen Predicatien*, Everardus van der Hooght, ed. (Rotterdam: Gebr. Huge, n.d.). See also D. Slagboom, *Jodocus van Lodensteyn* (Utrecht, 1966) and, more recently, J.C. Trimp, *Jodocus van Lodensteyn, Predicant en dichter* (Kampen: Kok, 1987).

[226] Mastricht, *Praktikale Godgeleerdheit*, "Foreword of Petrus van Mastricht."

Significantly, the architectonic character of Mastricht's covenant theology is also patterned after that of the highly-acclaimed Puritan. His theological system is constructed around the covenant of grace as organizing principle. While the first half of his work grounds all "formal" theology in faith, the second half grounds all "practical" theology in obedience. The Ramist faith/observance structure of Ames is taken over intact but for some further nuancing as Mastricht does his part to advance the letter and spirit of the Reformed tradition – covenantally-grounded experiential Calvinism. Finally, as Mastricht traces the administration of the covenant of grace through the old and new dispensations he sketches an exhaustive schema for the history of Christ's work of redemption. This comprehensive "Sketch of Church History" concludes with an elaborate eschatology.

Ames' emphasis on a gracious covenant that demanded obedience as formally systematized in his theology and piety was transported into the formal theological systems of two Reformed divines whose impact on the construction of Reformed system and on the thought and life of their day and beyond was incalculable. [227]

---

[227] According to W.J. op 't Hof, "no puritan in the [Dutch] Republic commanded as wide an appeal and so great an influence as Ames" (*Het puritanisme. Geschiedenis, theologie en invloed* [Zoetermeer: Boekencentrum, 2001], 310). In addition to others and the already mentioned Teellinck family, op 't Hof also identifies the following individuals as highly Amesian in their theology, casuistry, or both: Adrianus Cocquius (1617-?), Johannes Hoornbeek (1617-66), Simon Oomius (1630-1707), Caspar van Wallendal (1624-79), Lodewijk Meijer (?-1681), and Guilielmus Saldenus (1627-94). See his "Kennis van hoofd en hart: Dogmatische themas in de Nadere Reformatie," *Geloofsleer en Geloofs(be)leven in de Nadere Reformatie*, 8-17, first paper of the 8th Winter Course of the SSNR, 2002-2003, and also *Het puritanisme*, 310-12. Yet, despite this appropriation of Ames' thought, his congregationalist ecclesiology found no home in the Netherlands (*Het puritanisme*, 310).

Chapter 10

Covenant and Conscience: Amesian Echoes in Jonathan Edwards

The Experiential Christianity of the Reformed Tradition – Covenant and Piety – in New England to Jonathan Edwards

Through his influence in theology, method and ethics, William Ames cast a much wider net after his death than during his life. P. Miller's assessment of the significance of Ames in New England is based on early college curricula. Ames' teaching was primary among the Non-Separatist Congregationalists which constituted the "content of Harvard's ministerial training" into the late 1600s[1] and at the Collegiate School in New Haven through the early 1700s when Jonathan Edwards was student.[2] The "reformulation of Protestant theology" commenced by Ames and Preston had become "the distinctive badge of

---

[1] Miller, *From Colony to Province*, 221. In the 1670s, Ames' theology was replaced at Harvard by John Wollebius' *The Abridgment of Christian Divinity* (*Seventeenth Century*, 96). Eusden writes that "only when Puritanism radically changed its character to a semiarid legalism in the late seventeenth century did his name cease to appear with regularity in New England theological annals. . . . In early American theological and intellectual history, William Ames was without peer" ("Introduction" in *Marrow*, 11). N. Fiering asserts "reading of Ames at Harvard was mandated until at least as late as 1726, and probably for long after that" (*Moral Philosophy at Seventeenth-Century Harvard: A Discipline in Transition* [Chapel Hill: University of North Carolina, 1981] 28, 28 n. 52). For the extent to which Ames' thought was present in the Harvard curriculum well over a century after his death in Rotterdam, see R.F. Seybolt, "Student Libraries at Harvard, 1763-1764," *CSM*, vol. 28, 449-61. See also A.O. Norton, "Harvard Text-Books and Reference Books of the Seventeenth Century," *CSM* vol. 28, 361-438. This document includes S.E. Morison's intriguing "Note on the Education of Thomas Parker, of Newbury," *CSM*, vol. 28, 261-67. In this essay William Ames ranks prominent. An item of great historical interest is the imprint, inserted between pages 262 and 263, of Thomas Parker's (controversial) M.A. degree received at Franeker on April 1, 1617. Finally, see also "Three Early Massachusetts Libraries" by C.F. Robinson and R. Robinson, *CSM*, vol. 28, 107-85. For a study of the presence of scholasticism at early Harvard College see W.T. Costello, *The Scholastic Curriculum in Early Seventeenth Century Cambridge* (Cambridge: Harvard University, 1958), S.E. Morison, *The Founding of Harvard College* (Cambridge: Harvard University, 1935), idem, *Harvard College in the Seventeenth Century* (Cambridge: Harvard University, 1936), and idem, *The Intellectual Life of New England* (Ithaca: Cornell University, 1956).

[2] G.M. Marsden, *Jonathan Edwards: A Life* (New Haven and London: Yale University, 2003), 76, 102; I.H. Murray, *Jonathan Edwards: A New Biography* (Edinburgh: Banner of Truth Trust, 1987; reprint ed., 1996), 31.

New England" and Ames' *Marrow* was the students' "standard textbook survey."[3] On matters of form and structure, Miller avers that theological method in New England was descended from a "line of logicians and scholars" of which Richardson and Ames were "chief."[4] In the third area, that of casuistry, this "guidebook for earthly existence" was a reference that every parson had on his shelf to steer him through "problems of moral regulation."[5] Small wonder Cotton Mather judged Ames to be "one of the most eminent and judicious persons that ever lived in this world."[6]

While it is important to recognize the presence and entrenchment of the hallmarks of the Reformed tradition in New England prior to Jonathan Edwards, it is equally significant to understand the Amesian provenance and mediation of these central tenets. Correspondence on the 29th of December, 1629, between William Ames and John Winthrop indicates Ames' plans to join his friend in New England.[7] Ames never made the trip but his family and his thinking did. Early New England leaders were imbibed with the thought of Ames. Similar to the situation in the Dutch Republic a century earlier, the beginning of the eighteenth century saw spiritual power of the colonial churches significantly diminished, and piety was rare. The form of religion was present but not its power.[8] A "perfunctory orthodoxy" had set in.[9] When a *Nadere Reformatie* divine, Dutch Reformed minister Theodorus Jacobus Frelinghuysen fervently preached evangelical repentance and faith, held to Dutch Reformed church discipline and introduced visitation, revival followed. Mistaken by some for a German Pietist, Frelinghuysen had been raised in a pietistic climate and come under the influence of Voet and van Lodenstein (1620-76).[10] When targeted with pietistic epithets he cited the Church Fathers, Calvin and Beza in defence. Not stopping there, Frelinghuysen made further appeal to teaching of men like Ames and Brakel, often quoting the *Heidelberg Catechism* in his defense. Gilbert Tennent recognized in Frelinghuysen a kindred spirit, was impressed by the spiritual vitality in the latter's congregations in New Jersey, and was himself exhorted by Frelinghuysen for a flagging zeal which Frelinghuysen saw as the cause for Tennent's poor ministry. Tennent began speaking with greater power – a "rousing" preaching – and the Great Awakening began.[11] It was

---

[3] Miller, *From Colony to Province*, 233.
[4] Miller, *From Colony to Province*, 428.
[5] Miller, *Seventeenth Century*, 48, 428, 40, 291.
[6] Cotton Mather, *Magnalia*, 236.
[7] Sprunger, "Ames and the Franeker Link," 270.
[8] A. Messler, *Annals of the American Pulpit*, W.B. Sprague, ed., vol. 9, "Reformed Dutch" (New York: Robert Carter & Brothers, 1869; reprint ed., New York: Arno & The New York Times, 1969), 8-15.
[9] L. Trinterud, *The Forming of an American Tradition: A Re-examination of Colonial Presbyterianism* (Philadelphia: Westminster, 1949), 54.
[10] J.H. van de Bank, "Frelinghuysen, Theodorus Jacobus," *BLGNP* 4:139-40.
[11] Trinterud, *American Tradition*, 54-58.

George Whitefield's considered opinion that Frelinghuysen was "the beginner of the Great Work."[12] As would be expected, at such a time of spiritual awakening the character of God's emissaries was scrutinized. In a sermon warning of the dangers of "unconverted" ministers, Gilbert Tennent quotes the thought of Wilhelmus à Brakel and Gisbertus Voet as authorities in emphasizing the personal conversion of ministers in promoting piety and gospel truths.[13] Thus from the time of the Massachusetts Bay colony, to that of Jonathan Edwards, the Reformed tradition had already taken deep root in the spiritual soil of the New World.[14]

Although the impact of William Ames upon Jonathan Edwards has been noted in the history of New England, formal study connecting the two divines awaits. We will attempt to demonstrate just how indelible the Amesian imprint was upon the thinking of third generation New England Puritan Jonathan Edwards.

---

[12] Trinterud, *American Tradition*, 54. The theological acuity and pious spirit of Frelinghuysen is found in a superb collection of his sermons in *Forerunner of the Great Awakening: Sermons by Theodorus Jacobus Frelinghuysen (1691-1747)*, Joel R. Beeke, ed. (Grand Rapids: Eerdmans, 2000). It is the judgment of W.W. Sweet that the impulse for American Revivalism belongs to Theodorus Frelinghuysen and New Jersey and not to Jonathan Edwards and Massachusetts, to pietism and not to Calvinism. See his *Religion in Colonial America* (New York: Charles Scribner's Sons, 1942), 281-84. See also L. Trinterud, *Biography of Colonial American Presbyterianism* (Philadelphia: Presbyterian Historical Society, 1968) and J. Tanis, *Dutch Calvinistic Pietism in the Middle Colonies. A Study in the Life and Theology of Theodorus Jacobus Frelinghuysen* (The Hague: Martinus Nijhoff, 1967).

[13] Gilbert Tennent, Minister of the Gospel in New Brunswick, New Jersey, "The Danger of an Unconverted Ministry Considered in a Sermon on Mark 6:34, preached at Nottingham in Pennsylvania, March 8, Anno 1739,40" (Philadelphia: Benjamin Franklin, 1740), sermon pamphlet.

[14] In this connection, see the following: R.A. Hasler, "Thomas Shepard: Pastor-Evangelist (1605-1649): A Study in New England Ministry," (Ph.D. diss., Hartford Seminary Foundation, 1964); K.L. Sprunger, "William Ames and the Settlement of Massachusetts Bay," *NEQ* 39 (1966): 66-79; D. Hall, *The Faithful Shepherd: A History of the New England Ministry in the Seventeenth Century* (Chapel Hill: University of North Carolina, 1972); C.E. Hambrick-Stowe, *The Practice of Piety. Puritan Devotional Disciplines in Seventeenth-Century New England* (Williamsburg, VA: University of North Carolina, 1982); H. Stout, *The New England Soul: Preaching and Religious Culture in Colonial New England* (New York: Oxford, 1986); D.B. Rutman, *Winthrop's Boston: Portrait of a Puritan Town* (Chapel Hill: University of North Carolina, 1965); and J.W. Jones, III, "The Beginnings of American Theology: John Cotton, Thomas Hooker, Thomas Shepard and Peter Bulkeley," (Ph.D. diss., Brown University, 1970). A. Whyte tries to cover all bases with the claims he makes for Shepard in *Thomas Shepard, Pilgrim Father and Founder of Harvard. His Spiritual Experience and Experiential Preaching* (London: Oliphant, Anderson & Ferrier, 1909).

Biographical Parallels: Jonathan Edwards and William Ames

The parallels in the lives of these two divines – William Ames and Jonathan Edwards – so separated in time and space, are remarkable. Following spiritual conviction, both experienced profound conversion and became devoted to lives of holiness and vital piety. They received education at those institutions of the time noted for their emphasis on Calvinist orthodoxy, Puritan and non-conforming distinctives, and pietism: Ames at Cambridge (over Oxford) and Edwards at Yale (over Harvard). Establishing for himself a vast reputation at Christ's College, Cambridge, Ames' deepening and maturing convictions became manifest in his staunch resistance and body of literature against the Arminianism, Antinomianism and ecclesiastical trends of the day and this procured Ames his exile to the Netherlands in 1610. Following his advisory position at the Synod of Dort, he wielded a mighty pen from the geographic and intellectual backwater of the recently-formed University of Franeker. It was not long before this school became an international center for learning in theology, philosophy and logic. It was from this base, too, that Ames, the scholar and sometime-pastor did battle for thirteen years with the Dutch Scholasticism and Antinomian tendencies of the day, amidst a continuing Arminian threat. On the other hand, Jonathan Edwards, the pastor and sometime-scholar established a vast reputation for himself from his pulpit and study in Northampton from whence he did battle on the same two fronts: the Antinomianism (if more pronounced than in Ames' time) and rampant Arminianism in the theological and cultural ethos of the Great Awakening. Edwards' convictions earned him dismissal as well and virtual banishment to Stockbridge, the very edge of the frontier. Continuing for eight years to wield tremendous influence from there through pen and pulpit, he was reluctantly pressed to assume the presidency of the College of New Jersey and transitioned from the church to the academy but tragically died from reaction to a smallpox vaccination within a few weeks of his appointment in March 1758. Edwards was fifty-four. A century and a quarter earlier Ames, under pressure from his friend Hugh Peter in Rotterdam and with mixed emotions and some uncertainty decided to leave the academy for the church and accepted an appointment to co-pastor the English-speaking congregation in that city but died in November 1633, only weeks after his appointment, from chills and fever sustained from the late-October flooding of the Maas River. He was fifty seven.[15]

Edwards was preeminently a spokesman for "practical and vital Christianity" said Samuel Finley, writing in 1758.[16] For both these men who shifted so

---

[15] Biographical information on Edwards is drawn from Marsden, *Edwards* and Murray, *Edwards*.

[16] In Jonathan Edwards, "Introduction," *The Great Christian Doctrine of Original Sin*, in *The Works of Jonathan Edwards*, S.E. Dwight and E. Hickman, eds. (London: Westley and Davis, 1834; reprint ed., Edinburgh: Banner of Truth, 1974; reprint ed., 1995),

easily between study and pulpit, the Christian religion was a religion of the head and heart. But, ultimately, for both, Holy Spirit-induced vital piety was the *sine qua non* of the believer's status in Christ. For both Ames and Edwards this status was a covenantal one, which authenticity is demonstrated by true evidences in the believer's covenantal life, experiences examined in the court of one's conscience and anchored in love for God *qua* God. What were the intellectual influences on Edwards, the "foremost theologian in the Reformed tradition"[17] and, in the judgment of some, "the most brilliant of all American theologians?"[18] They were vast, to be sure, and Ames is counted among them.

Direct Amesian Influences in Edwards' Understanding of the Covenant

The Pactum Salutis

In God's justifying work there was a "transaction between the Father and the Son," says Edwards, "that was antecedent to Christ's becoming man, and being made under the law."[19] This lay at the root of the redemptive work of Christ. The application of redemption, said Ames earlier, is effecting the mediating work of Christ in "certain men." This application – the work of the Holy Spirit – depends on three things: the Father's decree and "donation" of Christ, Christ's intention to make satisfaction for those identified by the Father, and the Father's own acceptance of this satisfaction.[20] The pre-temporal covenant of redemption, the agreement between the Father and the Son, for Ames is a surety or guarantee of redemption actualized in time in God's elect. So it was for Edwards. As C. Bogue remarks, "according to Edwards, the covenant of redemption is the foundation, an eternally sure foundation, of the covenant of grace. Had there been no covenant of redemption, there would be no covenant of grace."[21] The covenantal scheme is Edwards' grand design for history and is anchored in the eternal counsel of God. Cosmic redemption is worked out in personal redemption through the covenant of grace. We shall see presently just to what degree Edwards held this as he employed the preeminent spiritual principle of the covenant of redemption (broadly understood as the covenant of

---

1.144; I cite from this edition as *Works* ("Dwight") by volume and page number. Murray assigns this anonymous quote to Finley in *Edwards*, xix.

[17] "Jonathan Edwards, "Notebooks" for *A History of the Work of Redemption*" in *History of the Work of Redemption*, J.F. Wilson, ed., vol. 9, 543, in *The Works of Jonathan Edwards*, P. Miller et al., eds. (New Haven: Yale University, 1957 ff.). This Appendix (pages 543-56) is a reprint, with minor editorial changes, from *Reformation, Conformity, and Dissent: Essays in Honour of Geoffrey Nuttall*, R.B. Knox, ed. (London: Epworth, 1977). Titles and volumes from the Yale edition of Jonathan Edwards' *Works* will be so identified.

[18] Marsden, *Edwards*, 1.

[19] Jonathan Edwards, *Justification by Faith Alone* in *Works* (Dwight), 1.637.

[20] Ames, *Marrow*, 1.24.1-1.24.4.

[21] C.W. Bogue, *Jonathan Edwards and the Covenant of Grace* (Cherry Hill, NJ: Mack Publishing Company, 1975), 111.

grace through history) and applied it to his cosmic teleology in a way Ames never did.

C. Cherry observes that Edwards' only conception of God's indebtedness to man was that of God's self-binding in covenant.[22] In searching for the source of this thought, he jumps back over three generations of Puritan tradition and rightly links Edwards directly to Ames when he asserts that the covenant of grace is "for Edwards, as for William Ames before him, one made between the sinful believer and the sovereign God, not one made between equals."[23] For the old covenant "was a covenant of friendship, so to speak, between the creator and the creature, but this is a covenant of reconciliation between enemies."[24] Edwards, with Ames, considered the covenant as primarily expressive of the believer's relation to God in faith.

The Covenant of Works
Recall that for Ames the conjunction of the law of nature with the moral law in the governance of God over his creatures gives rise to a covenant between a God of promise and threat and an obedient humanity represented by Adam as federal head.[25] Edwards considers the covenant of works and the covenant of grace as unified and as representative of two dimensions of the same covenant-making God. The covenant of works offered justification by works to Adam as the federal head of the race. And the blessings issuing from covenantal obedience prior to the Fall "were evidently given to Adam as the public head of mankind."[26] For Edwards, and Ames before him, the unity of the two covenants lay in their salvific significance. Edwards emphasizes that the first covenant was gratuitous and between two unequals when he says:

> If God had strictly required obedience not only to the moral law and abstaining from the forbidden fruit, but many other positive precepts, without any promise or hopes of reward, it would have been most reasonable that he should obey, and God could no way be accused of injustice if he had bestowed no reward. Much less can fallen man by obedience to God's law deserve of God that he should forgive his sins and should be brought from the state of misery into eternal life.[27]

---

[22] C. Cherry, "The Puritan Notion of the Covenant in Jonathan Edwards' Doctrine of Faith," *CH* 34 (1965): 328-41.
[23] Cherry, "Puritan Notion," 332. If Cherry is suggesting here that all Puritanism between Ames and Edwards held strictly to a dipleuric view of the covenant of grace, he is oversimplifying. Nevertheless, the direct connection drawn from Ames to Edwards is remarkable.
[24] Ames, *Marrow*, 1.24.13.
[25] Ames, *Marrow*, 1.10.9-1.10.32.
[26] Jonathan Edwards, *Notes on the Bible* in *Works* (Dwight), 2.689.
[27] Edwards, "Sermon on Luke 17:9," Yale MSS, cited in Bogue, *Covenant of Grace*, 146.

Ames' teaching on the distinction between the parties of the covenant had led him to the same conclusions. In the covenant between God (as lord) and humanity (as servant), "the moral deeds of the intelligent creature lead either to happiness as a reward or to unhappiness as a punishment. The latter is deserved, the former is not."[28]

Covenant Conditionality
To resolve the inherent tension between the covenant's conditionality and absolutism, Edwards, as Ames before him, demonstrates preference for the "testamental" understanding of the covenant, because of its unconditional and promissory nature. Ames' affirmation of the one-sided nature of the covenant of grace was sufficiently strong that he is judged to be an exception to the otherwise stereotypical alignment of English Puritanism with the Rhineland Reformers who taught covenantal conditionality somewhat more explicitly. God works in grace, humanity responds in obedience. Recall that for Ames, the covenant was a "firm promise" and a "free gift." But it was also about obediently *experiencing* God. So must his entire understanding of theology be taken – covenant faith and covenant obedience, two sides of the same coin.

The dangers Jonathan Edwards considered inherent in covenant terminology resulted in his un-Amesian-style equivocation, a trait which we have seen clearly demonstrated in Perkins.[29] In some of his writing, Edwards explicitly states that faith is the "grand condition" of the covenant. "There is no promise that the covenant of grace belongs to any man, till he has first believed in Christ; for 'tis by faith alone that we become interested in Christ, and the promises of the new covenant made in him."[30] Yet Edwards can also say that "the covenant of grace . . . is indeed without any proper conditions to be performed by us. Faith is not properly the condition of this covenant but the righteousness of Christ."[31] Both Ames and Edwards were unique within the Puritan tradition in explicitly eschewing covenantal conditionality and mutuality as such; yet, equally, both emphasized covenantal obedience.

For Edwards, faith cannot be called the condition of receiving because it is the receiving itself.[32] Bogue demonstrates how Edwards resolves this issue with the help of Turretin and Mastricht. The condition of faith is not meritorious;

---

[28] Ames, *Marrow*, 1.10.10-1.10.11.
[29] On the phrase "justification by faith alone" Edwards states: "Here the great difficulty has been about the import and force of the particle by, or what is that influence that faith has in the affair of justification that is expressed in Scripture by being justified by faith" (Edwards, *Justification by Faith*, 1.623).
[30] Jonathan Edwards, *Religious Affections* in *Works* (vol. 2, Yale), 222.
[31] Jonathan Edwards, "Miscellanies," No. 617, Yale MSS quoted in Bogue, *Covenant of Grace*, 261. Bogue aptly demonstrates the apparent ambiguity with which Edwards wrestled with the whole issue of faith as a condition of the covenant (*Covenant of Grace*, 253-78).
[32] "Miscellanies," No. 2, Yale MSS, cited in Bogue, *Covenant of Grace*, 258.

rather it is instrumental. "Christ and his church are one in respect of the covenant. By Christ's performing the condition of the covenant, the condition is, as it were, performed by them."[33] Faith is a gift of grace and provides covenant entry, or, as S.T. Logan, Jr., puts it (in aligning Edwards' position with that of John Calvin): "union with Christ . . . accomplished by God's sovereign grace" effects an "ontologically grounded" relationship between Christ and the believer.[34]

More strenuously than Edwards, perhaps, and blazing a trail significantly different from that of his teacher and followed by many in the Puritan tradition – a dipleuric notion of the covenant of grace – Ames never defined the covenant in conditional terms, as we have seen. Yet he gave proper notice to both divine action in covenant making and human responsibility in covenant appropriation.[35] Similarly, Edwards held that, having received Christ, other conditions accrue to the covenant member as well: conditions such as love to God, repentance and an obedient spirit.[36] This is unquestionably the "experience" of covenantal living to God that Ames emphasized so much. Finally, like Ames before him, Edwards considers the covenant frame of reference in the eternal and electing counsel of God. Recall both Ames and Edwards were controverting the Arminian threats of their respective ages: Ames amidst the ethos of dead orthodoxy and Antinomianism in the seventeenth-century public church of the Dutch Republic and Edwards in the *zeitgeist* of the Great Awakening and the opposing forces within it in the eighteenth-century American colonies.

The Role of the Will, Once Again
In his teaching on human responsibility in the covenant, Edwards held that "the covenant to be owned or professed, is God's covenant. . . . To own this covenant, is to profess the consent of our hearts to it; . . . Not only . . . the assent of our understandings . . . but . . . the consent of our wills."[37] This is in agreement with the by now familiar but unique Amesian emphasis when he said that the will is the "first and proper subject of theology."[38] Enlightenment of the mind, or "intellectual virtues" direct the will to do right.[39] This divinely-infused inborn principle is the virtuous habit that moves the faculty towards the good. S.H. Lee asserts that Ames' understanding of "habit" – in the doctrinal formu-

---

[33] Bogue, *Covenant of Grace*, 258.
[34] S.T. Logan, Jr., "The Doctrine of Justification in the Theology of Jonathan Edwards," *WTJ* 46 (1984): 26-52.
[35] The interpretation also of J. von Rohr in "Covenant and Assurance in Early English Puritanism," *CH* 34 (1965): 195-203, quoting Ames.
[36] Edwards, *Justification by Faith*, 1.623.
[37] Jonathan Edwards, *An Humble Inquiry into the Rules of the Word of God, Concerning the Qualifications Requisite To a Complete Standing and Full Communion in the Visible Christian Church* in *Works* (Dwight), 1.433.
[38] Ames, *Marrow*, 1.1.9.
[39] Ames, *Marrow*, 2.2.27.

lations and not in the metaphysical sense – includes the "main features" of the Aristotelian-Thomistic conception of the term "habit."[40] But Ames' volitional schema, if emphasized more than in the thought of other Puritans,[41] always sets the divine initiative as prior. Kendall points out that while voluntarism is at the very epicenter of his thought, for Ames, "the will to be godly can only exist in the elect."[42]

Lee avers that Edwards' understanding of habit incorporated this active tendency of the Aristotelian-Scholastic conception, despite the fact that, whereas Ames operated in a philosophical metaphysic of substance and form, Edwards' world was explained in the Newtonian terms of power and motion.[43] The agency of the will was as central to Edwards as it was to Ames. Smith points out, however, that Edwards does not set the will in opposition to the intellect.[44] The intellect is informed by the will which together issue in affections. Cherry draws attention to Edwards' caution that overemphasis on distinct activity of each faculty might destroy the unity of the human subject. For Edwards, "in faith the powers of intellect and will tend to merge into one."[45] The Puritans never set the faculties in opposition to each other either; but they did prioritize them in the faith act. In his caution, Edwards' more advanced scientific mind may have flagged concerns that never occurred to the early Puritans such as Ames. Yet for Edwards as well even as the affections testify to one's covenantal status, so they move the believer towards God in the Christian life.

C.N. Pickell challenges the commonly-held position (argued notably by P. Miller) that there exists a great difference between Jonathan Edwards' conception of the will and that of William Ames.[46] He indicates that the common conception that Ames teaches freedom of the will is grounded in misunderstanding Ames' preparationism. Ames placed strong emphasis on preparation for salvation and on the means of grace. It is argued that because neither Calvin nor Edwards taught such preparationism, Ames has departed from pure Calvinian

---

[40] S.H. Lee, *The Philosophical Theology of Jonathan Edwards* (Princeton: Princeton University, 1988), 24.
[41] Von Rohr, *Covenant of Grace in Puritan Thought*, 69-70.
[42] Kendall, *Calvin and English Calvinism*, 154-56.
[43] Lee, *Philosophical Theology*, 24-46. "Habit or an active power is, for Edwards, a lawlike relation between events or actions and not an accidental quality that inheres in a substance. At this point, Edwards has effectively left the old world of the substance/form metaphysics. Edwards was in all this really only honoring the fundamental methodological concerns of Newtonian science" (*Philosophical Theology of Jonathan Edwards*, 39).
[44] Smith, "Editor's Introduction" in *Religious Affections*, 13.
[45] C. Cherry, *The Theology of Jonathan Edwards: A Reappraisal* (Garden City, NJ: Doubleday, 1966; reprint ed., Bloomington and Indianapolis: Indiana University, 1990), 17.
[46] C.N. Pickell, "The Freedom of the Will in William Ames and Jonathan Edwards," *GR* 5 (1959): 168-74.

roots.[47] From T.H.L. Parker's work on the theology of John Calvin, Pickell demonstrates how Calvin, "at least in passing," teaches *praeparatio fidei*.[48] Pickell also brings to bear the position of E. Emerson who summarizes that "conversion is for Calvin just what Miller says it is for the Covenant Theologians, a reinvigoration of the various capacities of the soul, illuminating the mind and supporting the affections."[49] Furthermore, for Edwards the means of grace are instrumental in exercising volitional liberty. Although Edwards holds that means are vain unless they produce the desired end, "theoretically at least he defends their use."[50] Pickell shows how this, too, is the position of Ames who would never hold that through means alone the creature had a hand in his or her own salvation. It was only the choice of the predestinating God.[51] On a final persuasive note, Ames held that "there is no other cause or reason to be given of our election unto salvation, but only the good pleasure of God. . . . This may serve to refute those, that make God's election to depend upon our faith and perseverance, as a cause or condition requisite."[52]

Pickell astutely observes that preparation was "incipient Arminianism only insofar as men failed to comprehend its design."[53] Consistent Calvinists such as Ames and Edwards would hold that any act of humanity is less than perfect because tainted with original sin. Such spiritual inability does not factor into the Arminian view of freedom of the will.[54] Pickell concludes that "what may ap-

---

[47] Pickell, "Ames and Edwards," 168-74.

[48] T.H.L. Parker, *The Doctrine of the Knowledge of God, A Study of the Theology of John Calvin* (Edinburgh and London: N.p., 1952), 102, cited in Pickell, "Ames and Edwards," 170-71.

[49] E. Emerson, "Calvin and Covenant Theology," *CH* 25 (1956): 139, cited in Pickell, "Ames and Edwards," 170.

[50] Edwards, *Freedom of the Will* in *Works* (vol. 1, Yale), 265-71, cited in Pickell, "Ames and Edwards," 171.

[51] Ames, *Marrow*, 1.26.6.

[52] Ames, *Exposition of Peter* (1642 ed.), 3-4.

[53] Pickell, "Ames and Edwards," 172.

[54] Because this discussion on free will and preparationism will not be re-engaged following this section, I will note here that Petrus van Mastricht addressed this issue as well. Mastricht asks whether regeneration can admit of any preparation. He answers that while the Pelagians and Arminians and their followers believe that "the efficacy of converting grace depends upon the *free will* of man . . . the Reformed admit indeed of preparations in regeneration, taken in a large sense, to signify the same as conversion; thus Perkins in his *Cases of Conscience*, Sect. I, Ch. v, vi, xi. Dr. Ames in his *Cas. Con.* Lib. II. Ch. iv." Mastricht directs the reader to his own doctrinal teaching in which he expands on Ames to add: "regeneration, understood to signify only the *first* implantation of the spiritual life, admits of no preparations, excepting what ariseth from the offers and moral invitations of the external call of the gospel, if you chuse to call that a preparation" (Mastricht, *A Treatise on Regeneration . . . Extracted from his System of Divinity, called Theologia theoretico-practica* [New Haven, CT: Thomas & Samuel Green, 1770], 42. This volume is a translation of Book 6 ("De Redemptionis Applicatione") and the third chapter ("De Redimendorum regeneratione") of Mastricht's *Practica Theolo-*

pear to be theological differences between them are in reality only differences in emphasis. . . . Ames stressed the practical while Edwards stressed the intellectual, but Ames was also intellectual and Edwards practical."[55]

In the lengthy appendix to the only section of the work of Petrus van Mastricht to be translated into English, the translator has inserted a survey "containing Extracts from many celebrated divines of the reformed Church, upon the same subject [of regeneration]."[56] In that survey the thought of Ames (and Mastricht) looms large as the translator rhetorically clarifies some of the more difficult topics in this broad field.[57] In controverting with Bellarmine, Ames asserts: "We hold that together with moral suasion there is joined a real efficiency of God, by which a new principle of spiritual life is effectually wrought in the heart of man, and be at the same time excited to put forth the acts of this life."[58] The editor then provides a lengthy quote from Ames – the section on the will, from *Marrow*, noted earlier – as final and incontrovertible evidence. Mastricht no doubt spoke for all three – himself, Ames, and Edwards – when he asserted the following:

> The will doth naturally follow the *last* dictate of the practical understanding . . . only when the understanding, in its last dictate, judgeth agreeably to the *inclination* of the will. . . . It is therefore in this spiritual propensity of the will, that the seeds of all those graces, which are necessary to salvation are contained.[59]

An enlightened understanding and an unrenewed will profit nothing. For, finally, "the will in this first receiving [of converting grace] plays the role neither of a free agent nor a natural bearer, *but only of an obedient subject*."[60]

Edwards and Ames on the Heart of Informed Piety: Gracious Affections and Conscience

With the will as the locus of faith, his emphasis on activism in covenant compelled Ames to confidently assert that "living well is more excellent that living

---

gia, 657-74. A large part of this volume is devoted to the discussion regarding the relation of will and intellect in the act of regeneration. We have already mentioned Mastricht's preference to see the faith act as more of an act of the soul (combining will and intellect). On preparationism in the thought of early New England, see D.L. Parker, "The Application of Humiliation: Ramist Logic and the Rise of Preparationism in New England," (Ph.D. diss., University of Pennsylvania, 1972) and his "Petrus Ramus and the Puritans: The 'Logic' of Preparationist Conversion Doctrine," *EAL* 8 (1973): 140-62.
[55] Pickell, "Ames and Edwards," 174.
[56] Translator of Mastricht's *Treatise on Regeneration*, "Appendix."
[57] Fiering observes this Ames-Mastricht-Edwards connection as well in *Moral Philosophy*, 140-41.
[58] Ames, *Bellarminus Enervatus*, cited in Fiering, *Moral Philosophy*, 86.
[59] Mastricht, *Treatise on Regeneration*, 26-27.
[60] Ames, *Marrow*, 1.26.25, my emphasis.

happily" although both are within the purview of humanity.[61] With a similar goal in view in *Religious Affections*, Edwards develops his theme of determining the distinguishing marks of a true Christian around a three-point orientation: firstly, love to God on the basis of who and what He is; secondly, living to God as a mark of true piety; and this, thirdly, by supernaturally-enabled holy exercises of the inclination and will of the soul.[62] In each of these foci (insofar as they can be individually distinguished) Edwards has added significant development to three key doctrines first emphasized by Ames in both his *Marrow* and his *Conscience*. What Ames made explicit in Book 2 of *Marrow* and in *Conscience* – distinguishing marks of visible sainthood are examined and uncertainty resolved in the court of one's conscience – was true also of Edwards. In the first line of *Religious Affections* Jonathan Edwards poses the question: "What are the distinguishing qualifications of those that are in favor with God and entitled to his eternal rewards? Or, . . . What is the nature of true religion?"[63] Nearly a century and a quarter earlier, in 1627, Ames had answered in his opening statement of Book 2 of *Marrow*: "Obedience . . . the submissive performance of the will of God for the glory of God."[64]

Love to God
The "first objective ground of gracious affections" for Edwards is the nature of divine things outside of any relation they might bear to self and only for the moral excellency inhering in the transcendent divine.[65] The saint's love for God is ontologically-grounded in God's very nature. God is loved for who God is – the great I AM – outside of any self-interest motivated by, say, God's expression of love towards the sinner in Christ. This conception of love is the foundation for all twelve signs by which true gracious affections can be distinguished.

"Charity, or love," said Ames in 1627, "is the virtue whereby we love God as the chief good. . . . The joy of praising, which is an effect of love, has the same primary object as love, which is this joy's own proper cause. The goodness of God which is manifest specifically in the effects of his kindness is the proper object of love, as it is of praise."[66] God's goodness or moral excellency is for Ames the reason why God is the chief good. Three years later the question is made explicit in *Conscience*:

---

[61] Ames, *Marrow*, 1.1.8.
[62] Edwards, *Religious Affections*, 93-99. W. Breitenbach uses this taxonomy in "Piety and Moralism: Edwards and the New Divinity" in *Jonathan Edwards and the American Experience*, N.O. Hatch and H.S. Stout, eds. (New York: Oxford University, 1988), 177-204.
[63] Edwards, "Author's Preface" in *Religious Affections*, 84.
[64] Ames, *Marrow*, 2.1.1.
[65] Edwards, *Religious Affections*, 240-53.
[66] Ames, *Marrow*, 2.7.1.

Quest. I. *Whether is God to be loved for his goodnesse and perfection in it selfe considered, or for his goodnesse towards us, and benefits conferred upon us?*
1. *A*. 1. The most perfect kind of love stands in this, that we love God for himselfe, that is, that the formall reason of our love, being (as the Schoolemen speake) the lovely nature of God; and that our love be carried towards him, as towards the last end. 1. Because that love is most perfect which is wont to be called the Love of friendship. 2. Because if we love God onely for his goodnesse towards us, then we love him for our selves, and so we love our selves more then God. 3. Because such is the divine love that is betwixt the Father, Sonne, and holy Ghost, *Pro*. 8.30. 4. Because such is the Love of God towards us, forasmuch as there is no good can acrue properly to him from us.
2. *A*. 2. Yet because we are so imperfect that we cannot immediately raise up our minds to the contemplation of Gods perfection, but by those meanes by which the goodnes and perfection of God is made known unto us: and because it is principally made knowne by the communicating of good things, and we are most affected with these good things which are communicated to our selves; therefore the benefits of God to our selves, are also a reason, and as they call them, motives of our love towards God, and in regard of the order are the first, though in regard of dignitie they are not the principall; the last and highest, but such as from which, and by which, we ought to ascend to the divine nature of God itselfe, which is in it selfe, and for it selfe to be loved, and where we must lastly rest, *John* 4.8, 9, 10, 11, 16, 19.[67]

Love must be motivated by the very nature and perfections of the divine. A reciprocity of love for what God has done, a relational love, is nothing short of self-interest and betrays one's love of self over one's love of God. But because of human fallibility, one may express love for God, functionally, for what he has done in grace (what Ames called the "communicating of good things") as long as one, ontologically, loves God for the dignity of Himself. This dignity is demonstrated most clearly in the divine love which binds together the trinity within the Godhead itself. Thus, there is a legitimacy in self-love as motivation for love to God provided it is subordinate to God-love. Both explicitly and in attacking only a particular kind of self-love – the carnal or concupiscent – Edwards demonstrates his agreement with this point.[68]

Edwards, as well, looked to the trinitarian example of love as the unifying force.[69] Love, said Edwards, is so "essential and necessary to the Deity that his nature consists in it."[70] Ames continued his discourse on love for God by asserting that the "signs of love towards God" consisted in loving those things God loved, hating those things God hated and living in community with God's peo-

---

[67] Ames, *Conscience*, 4.10.1-4.10.2.
[68] N. Fiering observes that, for Edwards, self-love is legitimate if it serves love for God (*Jonathan Edwards' Moral Thought and its British Context* [Chapel Hill: University of North Carolina, 1981], 156).
[69] Jonathan Edwards, "Essay on the Trinity," 381, cited in H. Stob, "The Ethics of Jonathan Edwards," in *Faith and Philosophy: Philosophical Studies in Religion and Ethics*, A. Plantinga, ed. (Grand Rapids: Eerdmans, 1964), 111-37.
[70] Edwards, "Essay on the Trinity," 376.

ple, the Church, with whom, together, the will and purposes of God would be pursued.[71] And because God is moral perfection this life is a life of moral holiness. This is the defining feature out of which Ames develops all predications of his casuistry.

Edwards furthered this Amesian principle by emphasizing that community is portrayed in the Godhead "which contains in principle all the materials of the social life and thus portrays in broad outline the whole complicated scheme of virtue."[72] Edwards and Ames agreed on the importance of the church as the community of believers. For both divines, covenantal living is done for love to God *absolutely*; it is, secondly, an expression of obedience for his gratuitous love towards the believer *relationally*. This absolute and relational love are together demonstrated in a life of evangelical, covenantal obedience.

Living to God

Christian practice is the desired and sure result of gracious and holy affections, says Edwards, in discussing the twelfth sign of gracious affections. It is this sign that constitutes the "best evidence of the sincerity of professors to others." But it is much more than that; it is "a distinguishing and sure evidence of grace to persons' own consciences."[73] He continues:

> This is very plain in 1 John 2: 3. "Hereby we do know that we know him, if we keep his commandments." And the testimony of our consciences, with respect to our good deeds, is spoken of as that which may give us assurance of our own godliness. . . . Christian practice . . . is the chief of all evidences that men can have of their own sincere godliness.[74]

Evidence of evangelical obedience to God is absolutely necessary in one born again from above. This sign is the "test of holy practice."[75] Edwards has provided a precise summary of the thrust of Ames in both his *Marrow* and *Conscience*.

Edwards devotes considerably more space to his description of the twelfth sign than he did to any of the others. Experimental religion, he asserts, is taught in Scripture as being demonstrated in Christian practice:

> I think it to be abundantly manifest, that Christian practice is the most proper evidence of the gracious sincerity of professors, to themselves and others; and the

---

[71] Ames, *Marrow*, 4.10.3.

[72] Stob, *Faith and Philosophy*, 128. Stob places Edwards' concern for virtue in the trinitarian nature of the Godhead. For Edwards, "morality is essentially social and as such presupposes relations." And because relations identify the trinitarian nature of God, he is not only absolute but also a moral God (*Faith and Philosophy*, 127-28).

[73] Edwards, *Religious Affections*, 383, 420.

[74] Edwards, *Religious Affections*, 420-21.

[75] J.E. Smith, "A Treatise Concerning Religious Affections, in Three Parts; by Jonathan Edwards, A.M., 1746," *AP* 66 (1988): 222.

> chief of all the marks of grace, the sign of signs, and evidence of evidence, that which seals and crowns all other signs. . . . Practice is the proper proof of the true and saving knowledge of God . . . of repentance . . . of a saving faith . . . of a saving belief in the truth . . . of a true coming to Christ, and accepting of, and closing with him . . . of trusting in Christ for salvation . . . of a gracious love, both to God and men . . . of humility . . . of the true fear of God . . . of true thankfulness . . . of a gracious hope . . . of a truly holy joy . . . of Christian fortitude . . . .[76]

J.E. Smith underscores the peculiar Edwardsean connection between religion and experience. What is basic to Edwards' outlook?

> [The] *fusion of thought and experience*. For Edwards, it is not enough to think and believe that man is dependent on God; one must feel this dependence as a living force which serves to overcome the self-righteousness that stems from belief in one's own self-sufficiency. An idea in religion must not merely be thought of or understood; it must be experienced or felt.[77]

Quoting Edwards' first biographer Samuel Hopkins, Smith asserts that, indeed, Edwards devoted his life to distinguishing between true and false piety by "testing the spirits."[78] Edwards focused on the "major Puritan concern with finding the means of testing or proving the authenticity of souls."[79] This testing, this determination is centered in the human mind – in the understanding – and is that by which the soul "is capable of perception and speculation, or by which it discerns and judges of things."[80] The will, meanwhile, is "that by which the soul is some way inclined with respect to the things it views or considers."[81] Let us again hear Ames introducing *Conscience*:

> The Conscience of man . . . Is a mans judgement of himselfe, according to the judgement of God of him. . . . I call Conscience *Judgement*, First, to shew that it belongs to the Understanding, not to the Will. . . . because all those actions, which in the Scriptures are attributed to mans Conscience, doe properly belong to the reasonable power, or faculty; though the Will by some act or inclination can both command the Understanding to judge, and also follow that judgement. . . . Conscience being referred to *judgement*, it is distinguished from the bare apprehension of truth. For Conscience doth alwaies suppose an assent that is firm and setled. . . . Conscience is not a *contemplative judgement*, whereby truth is simply discerned from falsehood; but a *practicall* judgement, by which, that which a man knoweth is particularly aplyed to that which is either good or evill to him, to the end that it may be a rule within him to direct his will.[82]

---

[76] Edwards, *Religious Affections*, 443-49.
[77] J.E. Smith, "Testing the Spirits: Jonathan Edwards and the Religious Affections," *USQR* 37 (1981-1982): 31.
[78] Smith, "Testing the Spirits," 27.
[79] Fiering, *Moral Philosophy*, 172.
[80] Edwards cited in Stob, *Faith and Philosophy*, 122.
[81] Stob, *Faith and Philosophy*, 122.
[82] Ames, *Conscience*, Preamble to 1.1.1-1.1.3.

When Smith says that for Edwards "an affection is a response of the person accompanied by understanding,"[83] he could have been describing Ames. The most important function of the intellect in the moral life was, for Edwards, the exercise of conscience.[84]

Smith asserts the Edwardsean novelty of judging experience by the use of a sign or some other criterion. But in judging it to be a novelty, he is glossing over a rich Puritan history which had its provenance with Perkins and its refinement in Ames.[85] Vital piety is determined in the court of one's conscience by way of syllogism. Recall from our much earlier discussion that this three-statement construct – the proposition, the assumption and the conclusion – Ames held as the means by which Christian practice is judged to be authentic or not."[86]

Although it is true that Edwards' examination of the distinguishing signs was somewhat less mechanistic and considerably more refined, it cannot be but that his philosophical apparatus, although not explicitly expressed by way of syllogism, followed that of Ames: the use of observable criteria for adjudicating authentic Christian experience, against the propositional truth of Scripture, in the court of conscience. Generalizing greatly but also to the point, N. Fiering is certainly correct when he asserts that the "pietistic impetus" in American Calvinism, although modified, began under the "leading influence" of Ames.[87]

Having examined the role of the (enlightened and illuminated) conscience in distinguishing affections that are gracious from those that are false in the life of evangelical obedience, it now remains, finally, to examine the divine principle at work in this adjudication.

Conscience and Authentic Experience

"Affections that are truly spiritual and gracious, do arise from those influences and operations on the heart, which are *spiritual, supernatural,* and *divine.*" They "arise from the mind's being enlightened, rightly and spiritually to understand or apprehend divine things" and "are attended with a reasonable and spiritual conviction of the judgment, of the reality and certainty of divine things."[88]

Edwards' interest in Ames' *Conscience*, Smith informs us, was primarily for its use in interpreting individual experiences.[89] The point was made above that the adjudication of vital piety was for both Edwards and Ames an overriding concern, each in his own respective theological and ecclesiastical context. Be-

---

[83] Smith, "Testing the Spirits," 33.
[84] Fiering, *British Context*, 62.
[85] J.E. Smith, *Jonathan Edwards: Puritan, Preacher, Philosopher* (London: Geoffrey Chapman, 1992), 31.
[86] Ames, *Conscience*, 1.1.8-1.1.11.
[87] Fiering, *British Context*, 147.
[88] Edwards, *Religious Affections*, 197, 266, 291; describing, respectively, signs one, four and five of truly gracious affections.
[89] Smith, "Editor's Introduction" in *Religious Affections*, 68.

cause deception and hypocrisy lay at the root of inauthentic piety, both divines expended vast amounts of intellectual and literary energy in teaching the ascertainment and uncovering of such affections.

Edwards realized, with Ames before him, that the role of the affections in experimental religion promoted inauthentic Christianity because bereft of supernatural grace. A. Chamberlain develops a key observation first made by Fiering which should be fundamental to our understanding and analysis of *Religious Affections*.[90] This has to do with the usage of the term "hypocrisy." Commenting on Edwards' concern to distinguish Arminian hypocrites – who are "deceived by their outward morality and external religion" – from those who are "deceived with false discoveries and elevations" and make of these a righteousness,[91] Chamberlain remarks:

> Following Thomas Shepard, Edwards called the form of self-deception common among supporters of heart religion, 'evangelical hypocrisy.' It is important to note, however, that Edwards' use of the term 'hypocrisy' and its use by his contemporaries differs from the way in which the term is commonly used today. In modern usage, hypocrites represent themselves to others in a way they know to be false; they deceive others but not themselves. Edwards's hypocrites, however, were not primarily defined by their self-conscious and willful intention to deceive others. . . . Hypocrisy depended on the incongruity between appearance and reality that was created by a claim to grace made in the absence of its corresponding inner gracious condition. Nevertheless, hypocrites were sincere in their professions; they represented themselves to the world in a way they sincerely believed to be accurate and appropriate. In modern usage, 'sincerity' and 'hypocrisy' are opposite conditions, but for Edwards they could easily coexist. A sincere hypocrite was as possible as a sincere convert.[92]

---

[90] Fiering, *Moral Philosophy*, 172.

[91] Edwards, *Religious Affections*, 173.

[92] A. Chamberlain, "Self-Deception as a Theological Problem in Jonathan Edwards's 'Treatise Concerning Religious Affections'," *CH* 63 (1994): 543. The following sampling of New England pastor Thomas Shepard's work say much of his concern, one later shared by Jonathan Edwards: *The Sincere Convert Discovering the Paucity of True Beleevers; and the great difficulty of Saving Conversion* (London: Printed by Thomas Paine for Matthew Symmons, 1640; reprint ed., *The Sincere Convert. Discovering the small Number of True Believers* (n.p., n.d.); *The Sound Beleever or a Treatise of Evangelicall Conversion. Discovering the work of Christs Spirit, in reconciling of a sinner to God* (London: Printed for R. Dawlman, 1645); *Certain Select Cases Resolved Specially tending to the right ordering of the heart, that we may comfortably walk with God in our general and particular Callings* (London: Printed by M. Simmons for John Rothwell, 1648); *The Complete Works of Thomas Shepard*, 3 vols., J.A. Albro, ed. (Boston: Doctrinal Tract & Book Society, 1853; reprint ed., New York: Georg Olms Verlag, 1971); and "The Autobiography of Thomas Shepard," *CSM* 27 (1932): 352-92. See also R.A. Humphrey, "The Concept of Conversion in the Theology of Thomas Shepard (1605-1649)," (Ph.D. diss., Drew University, 1967).

Living on experience (anthropocentric) was infinitely different from living on faith (theocentric). Gracious affections were, by definition, produced by grace. The spirit of discernment requisite to distinguish the true from the false was a supernaturally-infused quality manifest in one's charitable judgment of the affections. Christian practice helped more accurately assess one's spiritual estate, while at the same time functioning as evidential assurance of salvation.

While maintaining with the Puritans that sanctification was the most reliable evidence of justification, Ames' emphasis lay more with the divine nature of the confidence of grace. Sanctification was considered a highly imperfect state: "... all believers have, as it were, a double form – that of sin and that of grace, for perfect sanctification is not found in this life, except in the dreams of some fanatics."[93] Because of the incongruity of the life of sin with the life of grace, assurance is firmly rooted in the justifying grace of God. Ames taught that God's faithfulness is the ground of Christian surety; assurance is founded upon the grace of God.[94] At the same time, expressive of this estate was a holy life which Edwards agreed to be the chief of all the signs of grace. For both Edwards and Ames, divine grace issued in action, an "increase in spiritual appetite" as Edwards put it in his eleventh sign. This is what Ames had in mind when he asserted that "all the faithfull are commanded not onely to beleeve, but also to *make this sure onto themselves* that they doe beleeve."[95]

In the true believer, neglect of this holy life results in a shaken assurance. The hypocrite, however, struggles under no such convicting grace but continues in his or her deluded state. Now Edwards quotes Ames:

> Dr. Ames speaks of it as a thing, by which the peace of a wicked man may be distinguished from the peace of a godly man, "that the peace of a wicked man continues, whether he performs the duties of piety and righteousness or no; provided those crimes are avoided that appear horrid to nature itself." *Cases of Conscience, lib*. III, chap. vii.[96]

Ames' context is this: peace of conscience depends upon obedience which is itself grounded in "that justification which we have by Christ Jesus" as the "principal cause."[97] Inauthentic affections not grounded in that "principal cause" yet providing peace are "a sure evidence of their delusion."[98]

---

[93] Ames, *Marrow*, 1.29.29.
[94] Ames, *Marrow*, 2.6.21.
[95] Ames, *Conscience*, 4.2.18, my emphasis.
[96] Edwards, *Religious Affections*, 175. Smith correctly observes that Edwards' quotation of Ames differs from the posthumous English translation of 1643 which is the edition Edwards possessed and used. Smith concludes that Edwards is either paraphrasing the English or providing his own translation of his 1631 Latin edition. Smith considers the latter more probable because Edwards' own citation here refers to "Lib. III." (*Religious Affections*, 174-75, n. 3).
[97] Ames, *Conscience*, 3.7.1.
[98] Edwards, *Religious Affections*, 174.

Then how do gracious affections differ from these affections that are "false and delusive?" They "are attended with the lamblike, dovelike spirit and temper of Jesus Christ;" they "soften the heart, and are attended and followed with a Christian tenderness of spirit;" and they have "beautiful symmetry and proportion."[99] As he describes this "dovelike spirit" and the holy fear and trembling invoked, he elaborates that the reverence inhering in such a nature is not in opposition to "holy boldness in prayer, and the duties of divine worship."[100] Holy boldness can legitimately issue from a spirit of reverence. With more holy boldness comes less self-confidence.[101] "Dr. Ames," says Edwards, ". . . speaks of a holy modesty in the worship of God, as one sign of true humility."[102] Boldness in divine worship is a legitimate expression of authentic gracious affections.

The "symmetry and proportion of virtues" which results from the infusion of this spirit and nature of Christ involves *uniformity* in the affections. Hypocrites may profess love for Christ but contend with neighbor. They may have affections for some, but bitterness towards others. There may be compassion for one's physical needs but neglect for the spiritual. With some it may be the opposite, for to demonstrate care for souls costs nothing. Some hypocrites are concerned about others' "badness of heart" but consider not the baseness of their own. Some may hate only particular sins, love only particular graces. Religion may come and go in some hypocrites who are religious only in "fits and starts." "And as there is a strange unevenness and disproportion in false affections, at different times; so there often is in different places."[103] Affections may rise in the company of others but evacuate in secret. "Dr. Ames, . . . speaks of it as a thing by which sincerity may be known, 'That persons be obedient in the absence, as well as in the presence of lookers on; in secret, as well, yea more, than in public.'"[104] Consistency, proportionality and "symmetry" of Christian virtues in their modes, locations, and times of expression are the hallmark of gracious and sincere affections. Finally, "because sincerity is a proper quality of obedience"[105] these affections are also reflective of, and issue in, a life of obedience enabled by supernatural influence. Amesian ethics and Edwardsean affections are intertwined, one and the same.

---

[99] Edwards, *Religious Affections*, 344, 357, 365; signs eight, nine and ten of Edwards' distinguishing marks of true gracious affections.
[100] Edwards, *Religious Affections*, 367.
[101] Edwards, *Religious Affections*, 365-66.
[102] Ames, *Conscience*, 3.4.8, cited in Edwards, *Religious Affections*, 362.
[103] Edwards, *Religious Affections*, 374.
[104] Edwards, *Religious Affections*, 365-76, and 374, n. 4, quoting Ames, *Conscience*, 3.5.7.
[105] Ames, *Conscience*, Preamble to 3.5.

Jonathan Edwards and Petrus van Mastricht

Foreword

Joseph Bellamy, a Presbyterian minister from Connecticut and good friend of Jonathan Edwards had communicated some miscellaneous concerns. In his return correspondence of January, 1746/7, Edwards offers some interesting counsel on prudent shepherding before turning to weightier matters:

> As to the books you speak of: Mastricht is sometimes in one volume, a very thick, large quarto; sometimes in two quarto volumes. I believe it could not be had new under eight or ten pounds. Turretin is in three volumes in quarto, and would probably be about the same price. They are both excellent. Turretin is on polemical divinity; on the Five Points, and all other controversial points; and is much larger in these than Mastricht; and is better for one that desires only to be thoroughly versed in controversies. But *take Mastricht for divinity in general, doctrine, practice, and controversy; or as an universal system of divinity; and it is much better than Turretin or any other book in the world, excepting the Bible, in my opinion.*[106]

Happily, six months later Edwards secured a copy of Mastricht and one volume of Turretin for his friend. Still six months later, he wrote Bellamy again, requesting the return of these authors and sharing his intention to use them "in studies on the Arminian controversies."[107]

In his greatest work, *Religious Affections*, Edwards refers to his prime theological source as "the great Mastricht."[108] Even after discounting for the common hyperbole of the day, it is nonetheless true that Petrus van Mastricht was a great influence in the thought of Jonathan Edwards.

---

[106] Edwards, "To the Reverend Joseph Bellamy," *Letters and Personal Writings* in *Works* (vol. 16, Yale), 216-17, my emphasis.

[107] Edwards, *Letters*, 223, 266.

[108] Edwards, *Religious Affections*, 337. The context of this reference to Mastricht is in the course of Edwards' discussion of the sixth sign of gracious affection, evangelical humiliation. Not surprisingly, this discussion generally conforms to that of Ames in *Conscience*, 3.4, but follows in the tradition of the great amplification of Mastricht. My intention is not to identify every place in which Mastricht is mentioned by name. Such citation occurs regularly throughout Edwards' *Works*. For example, in his miscellaneous writings, Edwards consulted Mastricht on difficult theological issues such as: the Christian Sabbath, the reason for Adam's first sin, lapsarianism (here Turretin is consulted as well), and the economic trinity. See *The "Miscellanies"* in *Works* (vol. 13, Yale), 319, 382, 384, 524. In some cases, Edwards considers simply a citation of Mastricht, with no further explanation, as sufficient to address the issue at hand. At other times, Edwards' discussion is entirely indebted to Mastricht's work. See, for example, *"Miscellanies,"* 382, n. 6. In his *Notes on Scripture* in *Works* (vol. 15, Yale), he depends on Mastricht for help in explaining the concept of "sinning against the Holy Ghost" (Heb 10:25-29) and in describing the ascension of Christ (various scriptural passages). See *Notes on Scripture*, 179-80, 298.

Influence of Edwards' History of the Work of Redemption

From his examination of the influence of Ames' thought on American philosophy and theology,[109] Gibbs concludes that although Edwards' early work offers the most "unambiguous witness" to American idealism founded upon the *technologia* taught at Yale (in the form of Ames' *Technometria*), it is notably in Edwards' later works such as *End of Creation, True Virtue,* and *History of the Work of Redemption* that Ames shines through most explicitly.[110] J.E. Smith has summarized that *History of the Work of Redemption* demonstrates a "remarkable interpretation" of biblical and secular sources, in addition to Edwards' literary talents as a preacher.[111] Significantly, he concludes: "If one were to ask, given the total body of what Edwards wrote, what one idea stands out as more important than any other, the answer would have to be the utter sovereignty of God."[112] C.R. Smith asserts that in this work (as well as in many of his other writings) Edwards demonstrates the postmillennial position that he held "consistently" throughout his career.[113] Moreover, it is a progressive, evolutionary, and prophetic historiography.[114] Meanwhile, "Edwards has come nearest of all the world's metaphysicians to reconciling philosophy and religion."[115] J.I. Packer is among many scholars who have written about Edwards' focus on revivals in this work. In Packer's opinion, this work should make Edwards more readable to evangelicals who have dismissed him as unreadable or too philosophical.[116] Note, finally, the judgment of erstwhile Puritan scholar P. Miller:

> The book had a vogue among simple people, who also read Foxe and Bunyan, but by the middle of the 19th century became too primitive for even such an audience. At first sight it is an uncritical retelling of the "Christian epic" – the creation, the Fall, Saul, David, and the prophets, the life of Christ, the Reformation; it ends with a prophecy which is simply old-fashioned chiliasm – the thousand-year reign of Christ, to be followed by the last apostasy, and then the Day of Judgment and the end of the world in flames. Biographers avert their gaze from this tract, as

---

[109] Gibbs, "Introduction" in *Technometry*, 18-63, esp. 61-63.

[110] M.X. Lesser, *Jonathan Edwards: An Annotated Bibliography, 1979-1993*, Bibliographies and Indexes in Religion Studies, no. 30 (Westport, CT: Greenwood, 1994), 3.

[111] Lesser, *Edwards*, 150, summarizing Smith's *Edwards: Puritan, Preacher, Philosopher*.

[112] Lesser, *Edwards*, 150, quoting Smith.

[113] Lesser, *Edwards*, 150, citing C.R. Smith, "Postmillennialism and the Work of Renewal in the Theology of Jonathan Edwards" (Ph.D. diss., Boston College, 1992).

[114] Lesser, *Edwards*, 147, citing M.I. Lowance, Jr. "Sacvan Bercovitch and Jonathan Edwards," *SPAS* 3 (1992): 53-68.

[115] Lesser, *Edwards*, 142, citing W.H. Squires in *The Edwardean: A Quarterly Devoted to the History of Thought in America*, Studies in American Religion, 56 (Lewiston, NY: Edwin Mellen, 1991), 193-256.

[116] Lesser, *Edwards*, 127-28, citing J.I. Packer in "Jonathan Edwards and Revival" in his *A Quest for Godliness: The Puritan Vision of the Christian Life* (Wheaton: Crossway, 1990), 309-27.

though to treat it seriously would be to insult their own intelligence. . . . I agree that if one stops with the surface narrative, *History of the Work of Redemption* sounds like a story book for fundamentalists, and it is hardly to be mentioned with Gibbon, Marx, Spengler, or Toynbee. Measured against modern scholarship, textual criticism, archeology and comparative religions, it is an absurd book, where it is not pathetic.[117]

Miller asserts that the value of the book lies not in its ("absurd") facts but in its revolutionary conceptual framework. Stripping Edwards' work of the facts, and leaving only the method, results in a "pioneer work in historiography," in fact, a "prophetic book."[118]

Introduction to Edwards' History of the Work of Redemption
Jonathan Edwards' "Redemption Discourse" was originally a series of 30 sermons (organized around Isaiah 51:8[119]) summarizing his position on what he considered to be the most fundamental Christian doctrine – God's work of redemption.[120] The book's real uniqueness, it is observed, lies not so much in the material but rather in Edwards' approach.[121] According to Smith, to fully understand the "Discourse" one must first appreciate the sermon form before analyzing it.[122] The familiar Puritan method of sermon preparation is employed by Jonathan Edwards: text, doctrine, and application (or, "improvements,").

---

[117] P. Miller, *Jonathan Edwards* (New York: William Sloan, 1949), 310.

[118] Miller, *Jonathan Edwards*, 311.

[119] "For the moth shall eat them up like a garment, and the worm shall eat them like wool: but my righteousness shall be for ever, and my salvation from generation to generation" (KJV rendering used by Edwards).

[120] J.F. Wilson, "Editor's Introduction" in Edwards' *A History of the Work of Redemption*, 9-10. W.J. Scheick remarks that "Edwards thought of his study as innovative because in it he treats history as an allegory of the conversion experience" ("The Grand Design: Jonathan Edwards' *History of the Work of Redemption*," *Critical Essays on Jonathan Edwards* [Boston: G. K. Hall & Co., 1980], 178).

[121] Wilson, "Editor's Introduction," 13-14, 28-79. Wilson notes that a "typically Puritan" concern had to do with the "application of redemption" – how this might be rendered real in the lives of individual saints (the *ordo salutis*). This often translated into a finely-tuned scheme of personal salvation termed the "morphology of conversion." Essentially, this was a formalization of the Puritan's "scrupulous analysis of the steps to salvation." In this connection, see previous note. This "step-approach" framework Wilson claims to be unique – employing the *ordo salutis* around which to construct covenantal life in these periods. Working out of the ethos of the Great Awakening, Edwards' emphasis is to relate the work of the Holy Spirit through history to successively greater "effusions of grace" displayed in covenant renewal. By building on a distinctly Amesian-Mastrichtian taxonomy for the application of the covenant of grace through time, Edwards explicitly identifies the Old Testament covenant renewal periods as those key components of redemptive history in which the Holy Spirit gratuitously revealed, by increasingly greater degree, the refinements and particulars of the covenant of grace in its anticipatory phase, until the covenant Himself, Christ, appeared.

[122] Wilson, "Editor's Introduction," 33-35.

From Column 3, Table 1 at chapter's end, we note the sermons assigned to the various components of the arrangement of Edwards' discourse. The application of redemption takes place between the fall of humanity and the end of the world or last judgment. This time span is divided into three macro periods.

In Period 1 and Sermon 1, Edwards introduces his scriptural text and develops the doctrine of comfort in the face of persecution.[123] God's faithfulness and everlasting righteousness and resolute intention to achieve salvation for his people are contrasted with the fragility and transitory nature of earthly goods. Sermons 2 through 12 address Christ's work of redemption from the fall to the birth of Christ, followed by application, in Sermon 13. Along similar lines, Period 2 addresses the time of Christ's incarnation to resurrection and, while Sermons 14-16 represent a theological analysis of Christ's life, Sermon 17 is, again, application. Finally, Sermons 18-30 cover Period 3 of this discourse – from the resurrection of Christ to the end of the world, the final two discourses representing associated application.

About twenty to twenty-five per cent of this 30-sermon series is "applied" teaching, or practical use of the doctrine outlined in the narrative account.[124] Wilson stresses that this is not just a history, but a history with a "controlling theological premise," a history that was intended to eventuate in religious practice or conversion.[125] Central to this theological premise is Isaiah 51:8.

The Covenant as Architectonic of History of the Work of Redemption
What inspired Edwards to utilize this particular conceptual framework in sketching out the history of redemption? What peculiarities might surface in his subject matter? These questions will be answered with reference to a comparative analysis of the covenant administration through redemptive history as understood by William Ames, Petrus van Mastricht, and Jonathan Edwards and represented in Table 1.[126]

Table 1, at a glance, demonstrates an earlier assertion that the organizing and conceptual framework used by Petrus van Mastricht is a typical Mastrichtian amplification of the sometimes cryptic William Ames. But now we observe further that Jonathan Edwards' "pioneer work in historiography"[127] is really a facsimile of the "Sketch of Church History" penned by Mastricht. Indeed, Edwards' entire program, from conceptual framework to content, "from the fall of

---

[123] Wilson observes that this scripture assured a "dialectical framework" for the development of the sermon series ("Editor's Introduction," 38).
[124] According to estimates by Wilson ("Editor's Introduction," 36).
[125] Wilson, "Editor's Introduction," 37.
[126] In this table I have included the framework of Francis Turretin as well. In light of Edwards' self-confessed reliance on Turretin for polemics and Mastricht for all else in divinity, it is interesting to observe whose system Edwards follows in the covenantal framework underlying his views on the historical progression of the work of redemption.
[127] Recall P. Miller's earlier comment.

man to the end of the world" reveals, with some modification, a construct almost identical to that of Voet's successor at Utrecht.[128]

With the use of Table 1 we will probe Edwards' use of Mastricht a little more closely. Time is divided into three periods: from the fall to the incarnation, from the incarnation to the resurrection, and from the resurrection to the end of the world. The first period was "preparatory," the second "procuring and purchasing redemption," and the third "accomplishing the great effect or success of that purchase." Like Mastricht before him, Edwards makes further divisions. The New England divine closely follows the *Nadere Reformatie* theologian as both build on Ames' taxonomy by emphasizing the covenant renewal periods in the Old Testament economy. These serve as dividing lines for both Mastricht and Edwards. For from the fall to the incarnation, "for greater clearness and distinctness," Edwards subdivides this period further: "1st, From the fall to the flood. 2d, From thence to the calling of Abraham. 3d, From thence to Moses. 4th, From thence to David. 5th, From David to the captivity in Babylon. 6th, From thence to the incarnation of Christ."[129] But these are more than just dividing lines for organizational precision. As mentioned and more significantly, this particular periodicity reflects a stage in the old covenant economy where Jehovah interposed into the affairs of a sinful covenant people with divine acts of gracious *covenant renewal*. This was Mastricht's justification for

---

[128] Edwards employs the preeminent spiritual principle of the covenant of redemption and broadens it to his cosmic teleology in a way Ames didn't, although it is highly unlikely that Ames would have disagreed with much of this view of redemptive history. We find it difficult to imagine, however, that Ames would have adhered to the typological thinking of Mastricht and Edwards. Wilson observes that Edwards' use of imagery and apocalyptic speculation did not reflect a "conservative typological hermeneutic" (Wilson, "Editor's Introduction," 49). From another angle, P. Wilson-Kastner correctly points to Edwards' spiritual understanding of the covenant when she remarks that Edwards' understanding of history was not Deuteronomic. She argues that this Deuteronomic understanding was common among many Puritans (P. Wilson-Kastner in "Jonathan Edwards: History and the Covenant," *AUSS* 15 [Autumn, 1977]: 205-16). In this view, national disaster was seen as judgment on national disobedience, while national prosperity was the blessing that accompanied obedience. With Edwards, Wilson-Kastner notes, "God's glory was the reason for his sovereignty" in the determination of history, not "human endeavours or responses" ("Jonathan Edwards: History and the Covenant," 211-12). In setting Edwards against what she perceives to be the trend in Puritan covenantal understanding, Wilson-Kastner fails to mention that Ames stood out among the Puritans as having never subscribed to this Puritan notion of covenant as a system of command-response-reward. Further, Ames did not explicitly apply covenant thought to the socio-political realm. The question of the Deuteronomic understanding of covenant as the predominant Puritan view is controvertible. The spiritual dimension was always central to the Puritan conception of the covenant. Covenant thought in the political realm was very popular and undergirded the founding of the Massachusetts Bay Colony.

[129] Edwards, *History of the Work of Redemption*, 127-29.

his periodicity as well. Clearly from Table 1 we can observe the Mastrichtian origins of Edwards' conceptual framework.[130]

The first thing to notice about the content of the work is the already-mentioned significance of the covenant-renewal stages in the history of the old covenant people. In Sermon 3, for example, Edwards remarks that the flood was brought about to destroy God's enemies which was "done in fulfillment of the covenant of grace as it had been revealed to Adam." And "in this God renews with Noah and his sons the covenant of grace."[131] Mastricht remarks that the very first lesson to be learned theologically is that "which we assert as being none other than the teaching or doctrine of living to God, which Noah discovered in his walk with God."[132] The theological significance of this episode in history was the renewal of the covenant of grace, which recommitment was sacramentally assured by the ark and the rainbow.[133] The key theme for both divines is the covenantally-bound promise of God to preserve the church.[134] Edwards interestingly ties this in with the breach of the former Adamic covenant of works which helps explain the necessity of the flood as confirming the faithfulness of God's covenantal promise to Adam:

> The first grant of the earth to Adam was founded on the first covenant, and therefore when the first covenant was broken the right conveyed to him by that first covenant was forfeited and lost.... If the first covenant had not been broken, God never would have drowned the world and so have taken it away from mankind.... [God] gives Noah a new grant of the earth founded on that sacrifice of Christ or that covenant of grace which is by that sacrifice of Christ.....[135]

The recording of biblical history through the various stages, as Edwards delivered these in 30 sermons, is in general conformity with the exposition of Mastricht. While the detail is more copious in Mastricht's long discourse, Edwards' coverage of the history of the church is surely adequate.

We now turn to a brief look at the final period of Edwards' redemption discourse. "From the resurrection to the end of the world." Again, from Table 1 we must first observe the remarkable similarity between the scheme of Edwards and that of Mastricht. The history of redemption is demarcated by seven periods, the events in each of which are very significant in bringing about the

---

[130] Miller remarks that Edwards' interpretation of the first two periods of church history covered by *History of the Work of Redemption* represented the prevailing orthodox view of church history established over the past 1500 years. Edwards' insights into period three, however, were "less securely orthodox and traditional" ("Editor's Introduction" in *History of the Work of Redemption*, 42).
[131] Edwards, *History of the Work of Redemption*, 150, 153.
[132] Mastricht, *Praktikale Godgeleerdheit*, 8.1.743.
[133] Mastricht, *Praktikale Godgeleerdheit*, 8.1.738, 8.1.742-8.1.744.
[134] Mastricht, *Praktikale Godgeleerdheit*, 8.1.745-8.1.747; Edwards, *History of the Work of Redemption*, 148-49.
[135] Edwards, *History of the Work of Redemption*, 152-53.

postmillennial resolution to history in the schemas of both Mastricht and Edwards. The events covered by Edwards are the same as those focused on by Mastricht, but the latter is much more detailed in historical coverage.

The highly typological coverage of Mastricht takes, as point of departure, an exposition of Revelation 6:1-11:19; each of these "ages of the New Testament church" corresponds to the opening of one of the seven seals in this biblical apocalyptic narrative. Mastricht's coverage of the events of church history is exhaustive. For example, each pope, each Roman emperor, each martyr, each church father, each heresy, each heretic, each synod and church council, is named and the significance for the preservation of the church of the respective individual or event is provided. The state and prospects for the learning of theology, the church and her rulers are described. The list is almost endless.[136]

Edwards, however, is much more succinct in his coverage which, as noted, was delivered in the form of thirty sermons preached in the course of one year, 1739. But the periodicity of this last stage, like the larger plan, is almost identical to that of Mastricht. And so is the overall tenor of the work: the preservation of the true church through the events of the world structured around the rise and the fall of Antichrist (the Roman church) and to the end of the world.[137] At one point, Edwards uses imagery from architecture to demonstrate just how architectonic is the covenantal divine master plan for the working out of this grand design.[138] As concerns a deeper meaning of this tome, Scheick remarks that it is to be taken as an allegory for the personal conversion experience.[139]

For his exposition of the last period of the work of redemption, Edwards acknowledges that "we have nothing to guide us but the prophecies of Scripture." While the first period had sacred history as a guide, and, while from the fall of Jerusalem to the present time "we had prophecy together with the accomplishment of it in providence, as related in human histories," now, for this last period, only Scripture prophecy can help. But interpretation of scriptural prophecy requires a certain set of hermeneutical principles. To that end, Edwards notes: "And here I would pass by those things that are only conjectural, or that are supposed by some from those prophecies that are doubtful in their interpretation, and shall insist only on those things that are more clear and evident."[140] As Edwards moves through the final stage of history, from the present to the end of the world, we see the development of a postmillennial view of

---

[136] Edwards, *History of the Work of Redemption*, 152-53. An excellent summary for each period in this "Sketch of Church History" is provided in the section closing the preliminary pages and prior to the beginning of the exposition of Book 1, Chapter 1, "On the Nature of Theology;" cf. the summary of Mastricht in *Practica Theologia*.

[137] See the eminently useful "Outline of the Redemption Discourse" in Appendix A, *History of the Work of Redemption*, 531-42.

[138] Edwards, *History of the Work of Redemption*, 118, 121-22, 148-49, 154-55, 380-81, 510-13, 524-25.

[139] Scheick, "Grand Design," 180.

[140] Edwards, *History of the Work of Redemption*, 456.

history. Every historical event, up to and including the final "happiness of the church" contributes to the one "grand design" of redemption in the covenant of grace.[141]

Behind the schema of Table 1 lies considerable detail which demonstrates that the progressive view of history in Edwards' *History of the Work of Redemption* generally follows that of Mastricht in holding to a renewing and broadening of the covenant of grace, but not without opposition in the form of various trials and persecutions as these have progressed through history. Edwards looked to a future day of wrath when apostasy would heighten in contradistinction to the increased faith of the redeemed. Edwards' unique interest in this was from the perspective of end-time revivals. Indeed, better times were ahead for the church but only after much tribulation. In the closing comments of his thirtieth and last sermon, Edwards states that "the most glorious times for the church are always the most dismal times to the wicked and impenitent . . . ."[142] The advance of this "afflictive model of progress,"[143] for Edwards, was measured by the outpouring of the seven vials in the book of Revelation. The opposing forces (such as the Church of Rome, Islam and all of heathendom) would be finally destroyed by Christ and his church, empowered, as they would be, by the pouring out of the last and seventh vial.[144] Although Mastricht patterned his eschatology after the process of the opening of the seven seals in Revelation 6:1-11:18, the similarities in the millennial outlook of the two divines are great.

C.C. Goen points out that the postmillennial view of the apocalypse was a novelty in eighteenth-century New England.[145] In fact, he observes that the postmillennialism of Edwards was a departure from Calvinism, from the *Westminster Standards* (which are amillennial in import) and from all the creeds of historic Christendom. Goen summarizes the scholarly speculations concerning the source of Edwards' postmillennial views and argues that the biblical commentaries of Daniel Whitby (1638-1725), the work of Charles Daubuz (1673-1717), and that of Moses Lowman (1680-1752) were formative in Edwards' views. It was notably the former who is viewed as the originator of postmillennialism in the form used by Edwards. In this he was followed by his two contemporaries. According to Goen, Edwards was most indebted to Whitby for

---

[141] See Scheick, *Critical Essays on Jonathan Edwards*, for a collection of critical opinion on Edwards' typology, eschatology and apocalyptic views in his *History of the Work of Redemption* and other work. In this volume, some scholars seek to discover the source of Edwards' thought. See particularly 151-96.

[142] Edwards, *History of the Work of Redemption*, 527.

[143] As J.W. Davidson describes it in *The Logic of Millennial Thought: Eighteenth-Century New England* (New Haven: Yale University, 1977), 127-75.

[144] Edwards, *History of the Work of Redemption*, 463-64.

[145] C.C. Goen, "Jonathan Edwards: A New Departure in Eschatology," *Critical Essays on Jonathan Edwards*, 151-66.

his eschatology.[146] "The whole tenor of Edwards' eschatology so comports with the Whitby-Lowman exegesis that one must regard this . . . as the immediate source of his millennial speculations."[147]

While this is not the place for us to dispute the Whitby-Lowman thesis of Goen's, we have shown enough of the close correspondence between Jonathan Edwards and Mastricht before him to give scholars like Goen pause about such emphatic statements.[148] It would appear that Goen, Stein, and others have overlooked the influence of *Nadere Reformatie* divines upon the thought of Edwards. We mentioned in the last chapter the interesting Appendix to Wilhelmus à Brakel's massive work and the postmillennial inclinations of that orthodox and pious soul doctor. G.R. McDermott argues that Lowman probably was familiar with the work of Brakel.[149] In fact, McDermott, we believe correctly, traces the source of seventeenth-century postmillennial thinking, a decidedly non-Calvinian view, to Johannes Cocceius. We have already seen some of the impact and stature that Cocceius, student of Ames, had in the Netherlands of the day. We mentioned as well that his doctrine of covenant abrogations was a thesis involving considerable speculation. Could it be that the Cocceian view of the apocalypse lies at the very root of that of Jonathan Edwards? It is instructive to hear what McDermott has to say on the Whitby-Lowman thesis:

> Edwards' confidence in the progressive nature of history, particularly in this last phase, begs the question of influence on his thinking. Much scholarly attention has been given to the influence of English eschatology, particularly that of Moses Lowman, on Edwards' millennialism. But credit must be given as well to Dutch Reformed scholasticism, which may have influenced Edwards indirectly through Lowman. . . . Lowman studied under disciples of Cocceius (1603-1669) at Leiden and Utrecht from 1698-1710. . . . Typical of consensus thinking was Willem a Brakel's *Redelyk Godsdienst* . . . which proclaimed that history's end was near, though not imminent. . . . Lowman probably knew of Brakel's work. Brakel may have influenced Lowman's view that the destruction of the Church's enemies was gradually being accomplished and would culminate in their total defeat, to be followed by the millennium. Since we know that Edwards "struggled mightily in his notebook with the interpretation of Lowman" . . . we can infer that Dutch eschatology may have influenced Edwards through Lowman.[150]

---

[146] Goen, "Jonathan Edwards: A New Departure," 159-61.
[147] Goen, "Jonathan Edwards: A New Departure," 162.
[148] Goen is supported in his thesis by S.J. Stein who has studied Edwards' notebook on these writings. See Stein, "A Notebook on the Apocalypse," *Critical Essays on Jonathan Edwards*, 166-76.
[149] G.R. McDermott, *One Holy and Happy Society: The Public Theology of Jonathan Edwards* (University Park, PA: Pennsylvania State University, 1992), 79-80.
[150] McDermott, *Public Theology of Jonathan Edwards*, 79-80. The quotation is from S.J. Stein's "Editor's Introduction" in Jonathan Edwards, *Apocalyptic Writings* in *Works*, (vol. 5, Yale), 7. Recall that Petrus van Mastricht taught at Utrecht from 1677 to his death in 1706.

We have shown this to be more than just inference, however. And this position McDermott hypothesizes as well, supported by some of the same facts that underlay our earlier observations.[151] But it is not our purpose to probe into Edwards' eschatology. Rather, we have discovered the covenantal form and general content of *History of the Work of Redemption* to bear close resemblance to the thought of Petrus van Mastricht. As an added bonus we have seen that in eschatology, even where Mastricht wandered off the beaten trail of Calvinism, he was followed by Edwards.

Summary
This section has demonstrated that in key areas the very sentiment of *Religious Affections* borrows from Mastricht. Additionally, the covenantal framework embracing Edwards' "Redemption Discourse" was an updated facsimile, as it were, of Mastricht's work on the history of the church, rather than a new and "revolutionary conceptual framework" as Miller averred. Edwards – indeed, all of New England – had high regard for this chief of *Nadere Reformatie* divines. From its inception, the religion of New England had been saturated with Mastricht's work. Edwards was but following in the earlier footsteps of New England divine John Cotton, who wrote to a ministerial candidate:

> There is nothing that I can with so much plerophorie recommend unto you as a *Mastricht*, his *Theologia theoretico-practica*. That a minister of the gospel may be thoroughly furnished unto every good work, and in one or two quarto volumes enjoy a well furnished library; I know not that the sun has ever shone upon an human composure that is equal to it; and I can heartily subscribe unto the commendation which *Pontanus*, in his *Laudatio Funebris* upon the author has given of it. [*I confidently affirm that it is disposed in that order, abounds in such weighty matter, and is filled with such a copious variety of learning, that I know not whether the world can afford any thing of the kind better studied, and more accurate than this.*] I hope you will, next unto the sacred scriptures, make a *Mastricht* the storehouse to which you may resort continually. But above all things remember the dying words of this true Divine; which he uttered *altissima voce* (with a loud voice and I wish all that study divinity might hear it!) [*that he hath no opinion of any defence of the truth, which sincere piety and holiness of life doth not inseperably accompany*]. The character, I say, of our Author, and his professedly delivering upon this point the general sentiment of the whole reformed church abroad, it is hoped, will weigh so much, in the mind of every one, as to obtain a candid examination of his sentiments, before they reject them.[152]

---

[151] McDermott, *Public Theology of Jonathan Edwards*, 80-81.
[152] "Preface" of translator in *Van Mastricht on Regeneration*, vi-vii; quoting Pontanus, "Oratio in Obitum Petri van Mastricht, Laudatio Funebris," *Practica Theologia*, preliminary pages; "verum de hoc corpore confidenter affirmo, quod eo ordine sit digestum, tantu rerum pondere prægnans & tumidum tanta & tam varia eruditione refertum; ut nesciam, an in illo genere usquam gentium exstet aliquid magis accuratum & elaboratum;" and "porro & hoc altissima voce addidit, se nullo loco & numero habere defensionem, quam sincera pietas & vitæ sanctitas individuo nexu non comitetur;" cf. editor's

Ames and Edwards: Closing Comments

Jonathan Edwards lived at a time when Puritan emphases on covenant and conscience, faith and obedience, were informed by more than a century of development and considered reflection. In the wealth of Ames' system the New England faithful had discovered many veins of gold to be coveted in directing the obedient walk of the redeemed. In pursuit of vital and practical Christianity – Edwards borrowed heavily from Ames both directly and indirectly. He underscored the entirely one-sided gracious covenantal dealings of God with humanity. This commitment to covenant theology Edwards demonstrated, for example, in his Amesian gloss on the *pactum salutis*, on the covenant of works, and on the entirely unconditional nature of the new covenant. With Ames, Edwards placed great emphasis on covenant obedience, not as a condition but rather as evidence of the covenant of grace. Having received Christ, Christians have a responsibility to love God, to repent, and to obedience, and in this the will is supremely active. These Amesian distinctives Edwards applied to the spirit of his age as well – especially in addressing the exigencies of the Great Awakening. As Ames had taught, vital piety was an authentic, experiential Calvinism, measured against the objective standard of scripture. Heart religion was evidenced by Christian practice, "the desired and sure result of gracious and holy affections."

Petrus van Mastricht supplied Jonathan Edwards with a highly-articulated structure of the administration of the covenant of grace through time. It is perhaps here that these successors of the Franeker scholar have most developed the theological heritage left them. When stripped of these (at times speculative) details, however, this was Ames' system, plain and simple: the new covenant looked forward to Christ, centered on Christ, looked back to Christ, and in its contemporary unfolding, looks both forward and backward to Christ again as ultimate fulfilment of the covenant promise awaits.

Amesian principles and teaching are present in other areas of Edwards' thought. For example Edwards depends on Ames' views on the doctrine of the church and on self-examination in preparation for communion, a key matter in the spiritual lives of the pious Reformed. To be sure, Edwards, like Ames before him and like great and innovative thinkers everywhere, borrowed heavily from other divines and philosophers as well. Mr. Shepard is quoted at great length in, for example, *Religious Affections*, much more than Ames. Clearly John Calvin and William Perkins lurk behind Ames, Mastricht, and Edwards, and not at a great distance. Additionally, Edwards received much of the Reformed and Puritan tradition through the mediation of John Cotton. But the central principles of the theoretical and practical theology of the Reformed tradition as furthered and then perpetuated by the defrocked pastor had, as seminal

---

"Introduction," in Peter Van Mastricht, *A Treatise on Regeneration*, Brandon Winslow, ed. (New Haven, CT, 1769; reprint ed., Morgan, PA: Soli Deo Gloria, 2002), xxix.

influence, the thought and priorities of the exiled professor. There is a clear sense in which the entire burden of Edwards' work is pervaded by the incisive, probing and discerning spirit of the *fijnzinnige* Franeker theologian.

Table 1

Respective Schemas of the Administration of the Covenant of Grace Through Redemptive History, 1627-1739

(1)	(2)	(3)	(4)
William Ames (1576-1633) *Medulla Theologica*, 1627	**Petrus van Mastricht** (1630-1706) *Theoretico-Practica Theologia*, 1682-87	**Jonathan Edwards** (1703-1758) *History of the Work of Redemption*, 1739, 1774	**Francis Turretin** (1623-1687) *Institutio Theologiae Elencticae*, 1679-85
BEFORE MOSES	UNDER THE PATRIARCHS	FALL TO INCARNATION (Sermons 1-13)	BEFORE MOSES
Adam to Abraham	Adam to Noah	Fall to Flood	Adam to Abraham
	Noah to Abraham	Flood to Abraham	
Abraham to Moses	Abraham to Moses	Abraham to Moses	Abraham to Moses
MOSES TO CHRIST	UNDER MOSES		MOSES TO CHRIST
	Moses to David	Moses to David	
	David to the Exile	David to Exile	
	Exile to Christ	Exile to Christ	
CHRIST TO END OF THE WORLD	UNDER CHRIST (Ages of the NT Church)	INCARNATION TO RESURRECTION (Sermons 14-17)	CHRIST TO END OF THE WORLD

(1)	(2)	(3)	(4)
William Ames (1576-1633) *Medulla Theologica*, 1627	**Petrus van Mastricht** (1630-1706) *Theoretico-Practica Theologia*, 1682-87	**Jonathan Edwards** (1703-1758) *History of the Work of Redemption*, 1739, 1774	**Francis Turretin** (1623-1687) *Institutio Theologiae Elencticae*, 1679-85
		Incarnation to resurrection	
		RESURRECTION TO END OF WORLD (Sermons 18-30)	
	1st Age: AD 30-100	1) Resurrection to destruction of Jerusalem	
	2nd Age: 100-306	2) To Constantine and fall of Heathendom	
	3rd Age: 306-600	3) To rise of Antichrist	
	4th Age: 600-1050	4) To the Reformation	
	5th Age: 1050-1500	5) To the present	
	6th Age: 1500-present	6) To fall of Antichrist	
		7) In the millennium	
END OF WORLD	UNDER ETERNITY 7th Age: From the second coming to eternity	From the second coming to eternity	

Chapter 11

Summary and Concluding Remarks

It is hard work to truly live *coram Deo*, to fully understand the unity and complementarity of two defining characteristics of the Reformed tradition: the gracious nature of a God who has sought to redeem through unconditional covenant, and the related injunction to live in covenant obedience. More acutely, even though justification is by faith, works have central significance. It is difficult logically, theologically, experientially, and, perhaps most significant of all for the student in the ministry to understand and explain this pastorally. The easy answer is either to live obediently, in the sure knowledge that works count for something, or to live a little more carelessly, for after all, *sola fide*. Christ is owned by virtue of the entirely gracious, unconditional covenant of grace – *sola gratia*. The implications of choosing the one or the other has given rise to some interesting and often unhappy occasions through the history of the church, both in Europe and New England, both in the time of William Ames and in our own day. These implications have often had consequences well beyond the borders of the ecclesiastical world. In other words, the issue is not restricted only to the history of the church.

The strength of the Reformed tradition is that it teaches the unified nature of covenant and life, faith and obedience. It holds to an internally consistent, fully coherent system of covenant theology and informed piety. It teaches that yes, the Christian is called to rejoice in a gracious God, but this is a joyful obedience. This obedience motivates to full enjoyment, but it also devolves upon the believer as a prerequisite in the attainment of humanity's chief end.

William Ames has shown that there is a right way of viewing these issues, a way represented by a unified and coherent system of covenant theology and piety. This is at the center of *sola scriptura*. Only the obedience of Christ has fulfilled the new covenant requirement. Only the obedience of the redeemed meets the new covenant standard. This tension is only successfully resolved in union with Christ – *solus Christus*.

A clearer picture of the thought of William Ames and its significance on the historiographical landscape of the Reformed tradition has emerged. Ames subscribed to the unambiguously unconditional character of the covenant of grace, but this does not absolve one of covenant responsibility. Ames considered obedience as equally paramount and as underlying the experimental life of the covenant child. This obedience manifest itself in an informed piety, the alignment of life with doctrine, the meeting of orthodoxy with orthopraxy, a practical Christian living that demonstrates complete harmony between grace and obedience. Formal structure to such practical obedience was provided by his casuistry. He ascribed to conscience a highly practical and active dimension, active that is, in the directing of the will to Christian activism according to the rule of the ten commandments. This was no reductionist voluntarism: it was, rather, the very center of heart religion, the desire to live a life of humble obedience in recognition of, and thankfulness for, God's gracious covenantal work.

Ames' exposition of the *Heidelberg Catechism* added a new, practical dimension to the work of Zacharias Ursinus and Caspar Olevianus. Comfort is derived not just from the soteriological reality of God's gracious work in Christ (Ursinus' emphasis), but also from the practical application and the rules for living yielded by these soteriological realities. The grace orientation of Ursinus was not undermined by Ames' particular augmentation; rather it was buttressed and rendered more complete by his practical spin.

This awareness of and direct engagement with one of the key formulations of just developing Reformed thought demonstrate Ames' desire to plunge into the theological and ecclesiastical world of his adopted home where presence of a crypto-Protestant spirit and evidence of a theoretical scholasticism jeopardized holy living and pietism. The biblical formulation of Ames' casuistry or moral divinity provided a sound and objective biblical and theological foundation to a living and vital Christianity. The practical emphases stemming from this moral divinity, in conjunction with a humble recognition of the gracious nature of the new covenant, combined to pave the way for the best experiential Calvinism that followed in the Netherlands. This type of Calvinism was the trademark of two chief representatives of the *Nadere Reformatie*, Wilhelmus à Brakel and Petrus van Mastricht. The former has been considered to be the soul doctor of the period and the latter its most prolific and astute theologian. The dependence of the marrow of the *Nadere Reformatie* distinctives of piety and experiential Christianity on the thought of William Ames is vast.

This theological tradition had emigrated to New England, via the Puritans, since the early 1600s. In fact even more: it was an experiential Calvinism that the earliest Puritans taught and practiced and the historical record shows that it was the work of Ames that was both informally and formally at the center of New England thought and life. With the onset of an arid orthodoxy evidenced most clearly by a lack of warm, heart religion, an orthodoxy not entirely unlike that found in the early seventeenth-century Dutch Republic, it was Theodorus Frelinghuysen who re-emphasized the work and thought of the *Heidelberg Catechism*, William Ames, and Wilhelmus à Brakel, and who proved to be the provenance of the Great Awakening which made great progress through men like Gilbert Tennent and Jonathan Edwards. An analysis of Edwards' thought revealed his burden for experimental Calvinism of the sort constructed by William Ames upon whom he depended both directly and through Petrus van Mastricht. The covenant theology of Ames and his concern to maintain the twin biblical principles of faith and obedience in healthy balance as expressed in a vital and living faith, were very much at the center of Edwards' thought.

It is our judgment that as helpful as the Ramist system of logic and method was pedagogically, Ames' dedicated reliance on this system at times curtailed further elaboration. Positively, for Ames Ramism was more than merely a philosophical tool that compels to decision. Rather, in Ramus Ames saw the emphasis on doctrine and life he was seeking as he worked out the faith/obedience nexus. With a Ramist understanding of theology, one could not go wrong because Ramism presented a structure that required an informed decision to act. This is what lies at the heart of an informed piety. For Ames there were two things: what one needs to know and what one needs to do. Despite its shortcomings, the system of the French Huguenot provided the formal structure by which this joint program of knowing and doing, epistemology and ethics, fused together to yield the wonderful harmony of faith and obedience that lies at the center of the Reformed tradition as life is fully lived *coram Deo*.

This study has ironically shown C. Graafland's adjudication to be true; Ames did not leave behind a school. He left much more than that: his thought contributed significantly in formulating the marrow of the Reformed tradition in its understanding of biblical Christianity as holding dear both faith and works, God's divine grace and the believer's obedient response. We concur with Reuter, who averred that theologians and pastors blithely followed Ames' trail without knowing the trailblazer. The seed for the intellectual and spiritual path of the "angelicall doctor" that had been sown in Suffolk, watered at the University of Cambridge, and increased in the Netherlands, received welcome germination in New England where it grew and further flourished in the brilliant and productive mind of Jonathan Edwards, pre-eminent Reformed theologian and pastor. Through him and others he influenced, the thought of the Learned Doctor receives continued harvest and is carried on in the tradition the Reformed venerate today, which has, at center, *soli Deo gloria*.

Bibliography

Primary Sources – William Ames

The Latin works of Guilielmus Amesius are collected in *Guilielmi Amesii Opera Quae Latinè Scripsit, Omnia, in Quinque Volumina Distributa. Cum Praefatione Introductoria Matthiae Netheni*. Amsterdam: Johannes Jansson, 1658-[61].

What follows is a chronological listing of the writing of Ames and the various editions used in the present work. A complete list of Ames' works is found in Sprunger, *Ames*, 1972, 263-66.

1618.   *Coronis ad Collationem Hagiensem*. N.p.
1622.   *A Reply to Dr. Morton's Generall Defence of three nocent ceremonies. The surplice, cross in Baptisme and Kneeling at the receiving of the sacramental elements of Bread & wine*. N.p.
1627.   *Medulla Theologiae, ex sacris literis, earumque interpretibus extracta, & methodice disposita*. Amstelodami: Joannem Janssonium (elaboration of 1623 fragments). [*The Marrow of Sacred Divinity, Drawne out of the holy Scriptures, and the Interpreters thereof, and brought into Method*. London: Printed by Edward Griffin for John Rothwell, 1642. *The Marrow of Theology*. Translated from the 3rd Latin ed., 1629, edited and with an introduction by John D. Eusden. Boston-Philadelphia: Pilgrim, 1968; reprint ed., Grand Rapids: Baker, 1997.]
1625-29. *Scriptum Elenchticum contra Papists vid. Bellarminus Enervatus in 4 Tomos Divisus*. Amstelodami: Joannem Janssonium, 1629.
1629.   *Animadversiones in Synodalia Scripta Remonstrantium*. N.p. [Appearing in 1646 and 1661 as *Anti-Synodalia Scripta*.]
1630.   *De Conscientia, et Eius Iure, vel Casibus, libre quinque*. Amstelodami: Joannem Janssonium. [*Conscience with the Power and Cases Thereof. Devided into V. Bookes*. N.p., 1639; reprint ed., Norwood, NJ: Walter J. Johnson, 1975. *Vyf Boecken van de Conscientie en haar regt of gevallen*. Translated by C.V. Wallendal. Amsterdam: Jan Pieterse Kuypen, 1660.]
1631.   *Technometria, omnium & singularum artium fines adaequatè circumscribens*. N.p. [*Technometria*. London: Milo Flesher, 1633. *Technometry by William Ames*. Haney Foundation Series of the University of Pennsylvania, vol. 24. Translated from the Latin, edited, and with an introduction by Lee. W. Gibbs. Philadelphia: University of Pennsylvania, 1979.]
1633.   *A Fresh Suit Against Human Ceremonies in Gods Worship*. Rotterdam(?): N.p.
1633.   *Sententia de Origene Sabbati & die Dominico*. N.p., 1633.

1635. *Christianæ Cathecheseos Sciagraphia.* Franekeræ: Bernardum A Berentsma. Amsterdam ed., 1660.[*The Substance of Christian Religion: Or, a plaine and easie Draught of the Christian Catechisme, in LII Lectures, on Chosen Texts of Scripture, for each Lords-day of the Year, Learnedly and Perspicuously Illustrated with Doctrines, Reasons and Uses.* London: T. Mabb for Thomas Davies, 1659; Ann Arbor, MI: University Microfilms, 1659. *A Sketch of the Christian's Catechism.* Translated by Todd M. Rester. Introduced by Joel R. Beeke and Todd M. Rester. Grand Rapids: Reformation Heritage, 2008.]

1635. *Explicatio Analytica Utriusque Epistolae Divi Petri Apostoli.* N.p. [*An Analyticall Exposition of both the Epistles of the Apostle Peter, Illustrated by Doctrines Out of Every Text. And Applyed by their Uses, for a further progresse in Holinesse.* Foreword by A.B. London: Edward Griffin for John Rothwell, 1641.]

1643. *Philosophemata.* (Containing "Technometria, omnium & singularum artium fines adaequatè circumscribens" [1631], "Alia technometriae delineatio," "Disputatio theologica adversus metaphysicam" [1629], "Disputatio theologica, de perfectione SS. Scripturae," "Demonstratio logicae verae" [1632], and "Theses logicae.")

1643. *The Workes of the Reverend and Faithfull Minister of Christ William Ames Doctor and Professor of the Famous University of Franeker in Friesland.* (Containing *Divinity, I and II Peter, Conscience.*) London: John Rothwell.

Primary Sources – Other

Alleine, Joseph. *Divers Practical Cases of Conscience Satisfactorily Resolved.* London: Printed for Nevil Simmons, 1672.

Aquinas, Thomas. *Nature and Grace.* Edited and translated by A.M. Fairweather. Library of Christian Classics, vol. 11. Philadelphia: Westminster, 1954.

_____. *Summa Theologiae.* Blackfriars Latin text and English translation with Introduction, Notes, Appendices and Glossaries. 60 vols. New York: McGraw-Hill, 1963-76.

Arminius, Jacobus. *The Works of James Arminius.* Translated from the Latin by James Nichols and W.R. Bagnall. 3 vols. London: Printed for Longman, Hurst, Rees, Orme, Brown and Green, 1825-28; reprint ed., Grand Rapids: Baker, 1956.

The Articles of the Synod of Dort, and its Rejection of Errors: with the History of Events which made way for that Synod, ed. and trans. Thomas Scott. Utica: William Williams, 1831.

Augustine, Aurelius. *A Select Library of the Nicene and Post-Nicene Fathers of the Christian Church.* First Series. Vols. 1-8. Ed. Philip Schaaf. New York:

Christian Literature Co., 1886-90; reprint ed., Grand Rapids: Eerdmans, 1978-79.

Baillie, Robert. *The Letters and Journals of Robert Baillie*. Ed. David Laing. 3 vols. Edinburgh: Robert Ogle, 1841-42.

Baxter, Richard. *A Christian Directory: or, A Summ of Practical Theologie, and Cases of Conscience*. London: By Robert White for Nevil Simmons, 1673.

_____. *The Life of Faith, as it is the Evidence of Things Unseen*. London: Printed by R.W. and A.M. for Francis Tyton and Jane Underhill, 1660.

_____. *The Practical Works of Richard Baxter*. Introduction and life by William Orme. 23 vols. London: James Duncan, 1830; reprint ed. in 4 vols., London: George Virtue, 1857 and Ligonier, PA: Soli Deo Gloria Publications, 1990-91.

Blake, Thomas. *Vindiciae Foederis, or a Treatise of the Covenant of God entered with man-kinde, in the several Kindes and Degrees of it, in which the agreement and respective differences of the Covenant of works and the Covenant of grace, of the old and New Covenant are discust*. London: Printed for A. Roper, 1653.

Bradshaw, William. *English Puritanisme. Containeing: the maine Opinions of the Rigidest Sort of those that are called Puritanes in the realme of England*. N.p. [Amsterdam], 1605.

Brakel, Theodorus à. *De trappen Des Geestelijken Levens*. 8th ed. Amsterdam: Abraham Cornelis, 1670.

_____. *Het geestelijke leven, ende de stand eens geloovigen mensches hier op aarde*. Amsterdam: Abraham Cornelis, 1648.

Brakel, Wilhelmus à. *Redelijke Godsdienst*. 2 vols. (Leiden: D. Donner, 1881).

_____. *Redelyke Godts-Dienst, In welke de Goddelijke Waarheden des Genaden-Verbondts worden verklaart, tegen allerleye partyen beschermt, ende tot de praktijke aangedrongen*. 2 vols. 's-Gravenhage: Cornelis van Dyck, 1700. [*The Christian's Reasonable Service*. Translated by Bartel Elshout. Ed. Joel R. Beeke. 4 vols. Morgan, PA: Soli Deo Gloria Publications, 1992 - 1995.]

Bucer, Martin. *Melanchthon and Bucer*. Ed. Wilhelm Pauck. Library of Christian Classics, no. 19. Philadelphia: Westminster, 1969.

Bulkeley, Peter. *The Gospel-Covenant; or the Covenant of Grace Opened*. 2nd ed., much enlarged, and corrected by the Author. London: Matthew Simmons, 1651.

Bullinger, Henrich. *Compendium Christiane religionis decem librem comprehensum*. Tiguri: apud Frosch, 1556. [*Commonplaces of the Christian Religion compendiously written*. Translated by John Stockwood. London: George Byshop, 1572.]

Burgess, Cornelis. *A Chain of Graces drawn out at length for a Reformation of Manners. Or, A brief Treatise of Virtue, Knowledge, Temperance, Patience,*

Godliness, Brotherly kindness, and Charity, so far as they are urged by the Apostle in 2 Pet. i. 5, 6, 7. London, 1622.

_____. *Vindiciae Foederis, or a Treatise of the Covenant of God entered with man-kinde, in the several Kindes and Degrees of it*. London: A. Roper, 1653.

Burmannus, Franciscus. *Synopsis Theologiae et speciatim oeconomiae foederum Dei ab Initio Saeculorum usque ad Consummationem eorum*. Genevae: sumptibus Joannis Picteti/bibliopol, 1678.

Calvin, John. *Commentaries of Calvin*. 22 vols. Various translators. Edinburgh: for Calvin Translation Society, 1843; reprint ed., Grand Rapids: Baker, 1979.

_____. *Institutes of the Christian Religion*. Translated by Ford Lewis Battles. Ed. John T. MacNeill. 2 vols. Library of Christian Classics, no. 20 and 21. Philadelphia: Westminster, 1960.

_____. *Theological Treatises*. Translated by J.K.S. Reid. Library of Christian Classics, no. 22. London: SCM, 1954.

Cats, Jacob. *Alle de Werken*. Amsterdam, 1658; Amsterdam/Utrecht, 1700.

_____. *Houwelijk Dat is Het Gantschebeleyt des Echten Staets*. Amsterdam, 1655.

Cocceius, Johannes. *Opera Anecdota Theologica et Philologica*. 2 vols. Supplement to 3rd ed. Amstelodami: P. & J. Blaer, 1706.

_____. *Opera Omnia Theologica, Exegetica, Didactica, Polemica, Philologica*. 3rd ed. 10 vols. Amstelodami: P. & J. Blaer, 1701.

_____. *Summa doctrina de foedere & Testamento Dei*. Franeker, 1648. [*De Leere Van het Verbond En Testament Gods*. Translated from the Latin. 2nd printing. Amsterdam: Johannes van Someren, 1689.]

_____. *Summa Theologiae*. N.p., 1662.

Comrie, Alexander. *Een Beknopte Verhandeling van het Verbond der Werken*. Ed. G.H. Kersten. Rotterdam: De Banier, 1932.

_____. *Stellige en Praktikale Verklaaringe van den Heidelbergschen Catechismus volgens de leer en gronden der Hervorming, waarin de waarheden van onzen Godsdienst op en klare en bevindelijke wijze voorgesteld en betoogd worden, de natuurlingen ontdekt, de zoekenden bestuurd, de zwakken vertroost en de sterken tot hun plicht, volgens een Evangelische leiding, opgewekt worden*. Amsterdam: N. Byl, 1753; reprint ed., Barneveld: G.J. van Horssen, 1976.

Confession of Faith, the: the Larger and Shorter Catechisms, with the Scripture Proofs at Large together with The Sum of Saving Knowledge. Inverness: Free Presbyterian Church of Scotland, 1958.

Confession of Faith (1647), the, The Larger Catechism (1648), The Shorter Catechism (1648), The Directory of Public Worship. Toronto: Presbyterian Publications, n.d.

Documenta Reformata: Teksten uit de Geschiedenis van Kerk en Theologie in de Nederlanden sedert de Hervorming. Ed. J.N. Bakhuizen van den Brink et al. 2 vols. Kampen: J.H. Kok, 1960-62.

Edwards, Jonathan. *The Works of Jonathan Edwards.* Ed. Edward Hickman, with a memoir by Sereno E. Dwight. Ed. S.E. Dwight and E. Hickman. 2 vols. London, Westley and Davis, 1834; reprint ed., Edinburgh: Banner of Truth, 1974; reprint ed., 1995.

_____. *The Works of Jonathan Edwards.* Ed. Perry Miller, John E. Smith, and Harry S. Stout. New Haven: Yale University, 1957 – .

Episcopius, Simon. *Antwoord op LXIV Theologische vragen.* Amsterdam: 1648.

Fisher, Edward. *The Marrow of Modern Divinity. Touching both the Covenant of Works and the Covenant of Grace: with their use and end.* 5th ed. London: Printed by R. Ibbitson for G. Calvert, 1647. [Edition with notes by Thomas Boston. London: T. Tegg, 1837.]

Frelinghuysen, Theodorus Jacobus. *Forerunner of the Great Awakening: Sermons by T.J. Frelinghuysen (1691-1747).* The Historical Series of the Reformed Church in America. No. 36. General Editor, Donald J. Bruggink. Ed. Joel R. Beeke. Grand Rapids: Eerdmans, 2000.

Gataker, Thomas. *A Just Defence of Certain Passages in a Former Treatise Concerning the Nature and Use of Lots.* London, 1623.

_____. *Of the Nature and Use of Lots.* London, 1619.

_____. *The Works of Thomas Gataker.* London: Jacob Benjamin, 1659.

Gillespie, George. "Notes of Debates and Proceedings of the Assembly of Divines and Other Commissioners at Westminster, February 1644 to January 1645." *The Presbyterian Armory*, vol. 2. Edinburgh: Robert Ogle, Oliver and Boyd, 1846.

Gomarus, Franciscus. *Opera theologica omnia.* 2nd ed. Amstelodami: Joannis Janssonii, 1664.

Goodwin, T.; Nye, P.; Simpson, S.; Burroughes, J.; Bridge, W. *An Apologeticall Narration of Some Ministers Formerly Exiles in the Netherlands: Now Members of the Assembly of Divines, Humbly Submitted to the Honourable House of Parliament.* London, 1643.

Hales, John. *Letters from the Synod of Dort to Sir Dudley Carlton, the English embasssador at the Hague.* Glasgow: Robert and Andrew Foulis, 1765.

Hellenbroek, Abraham. *Wilhelmus à Brakel.* Leiden: Rouklagte, 1724.

Hommius, Festus. *Het Schat-Boeck Der Verklaringhen over de Catechismus der Christelicke Religie.* Translator and editor. Amsteldam: Joannes van Ravesteyn, 1650.

_____. *Oordeel des Synod: Nationalis Der Gereformeerde Kercken van de Vereenichde Nederlanden.* Dordrecht, 1619.

Hooker, Thomas. *The Covenant of Grace Opened: Wherein These Particulars are Handled: viz. 1. What the Covenant of Grace Is, 2. What the Seales of the Covenant Are, 3. Who are the Parties and Subjects Fit to Receive These*

Seals. From All which Particulars Infants Baptisme Is Fully Proved and Vindicated. London: G. Dawson, 1649.

⎯⎯⎯⎯. The Works of Rev. Thomas Hooker, first minister of Cambridge and of Hartford, Conn. 4 vols. London, 1637-45.

Hoornbeeck, Johannes. *Theologica Practica.* 2 vols. Ultrajecti, Waesberge, 1658.

Keckerman, Bartholomew. *A Manuduction to Theologie.* Translated by T. V[icars]. N.p.: Printed for A. Mathewes, [1620].

Koelman, Jacobus. *De Natuur en Gronden des Geloofs. By wege van een Brief ingeregt ter Vast-stelling van de Staat dergenen die Christus in Geloof Omhelsen.* 2nd ed. 's-Gravenhage: Gerardus Winterswyk: 1724.

Lampe, Friedrich Adolph. *Milch der Wahrheit volgens Anleitung des Heidelberger Katechismus.* s'-Gravenhage: Gerardus Winterwyk, 1750.

Lightfoot, John. "The Journal of the Proceedings of the Assembly of Divines from January 1, 1643 to December 31, 1644; and the Letters to and from Dr. Lightfoot," *The Whole Works of the Rev. John Lightfoot*, vol. 13. Ed. John Rogers Pitman. London: J.F. Dove, 1844.

Linacre, Robert A. A *Comfortable Treatise for the reliefe of such as are Afflicted in Conscience.* London: H. L. for William Leake, 1610.

Lodenstein, Jodocus van. *Beschouwinge van Zion.* Amsterdam: J. Van Hardenburg, 1718.

⎯⎯⎯⎯. *De Heerlykheyd Van en Waar Christelihke Leven. Uytblinkende in God-saligen Wandel, volgens het Geestelijke Licht des Evangeliums, te sien in Jezus heerlyk Voorbeeld, nedrige Geboorte en Armoede, om ons te Wederbaren, en Rijk in God te maken.* Amsterdam: Jacobus Van Hardenburg, 1711.

⎯⎯⎯⎯. *Het Vervolg van den Geestelyken Opwekker, Voor-gestelt in Negen Predicatien.* Amsterdam: Jacobus Van Hardenburg, 1707.

⎯⎯⎯⎯. *J. van Lodensteyn's Negen Predicatien.* Ed. Everardus van der Hooght. Rotterdam: Gebr. Huge, n.d.

Maccovius, Johannes. *Johannes Maccovius Redivivus, seu manuscripta ejus, tertium jam typis exscripta.* Opera Nicolai Arnoldi. Amstelodami: apud Ludovicum & Danielem Elzevirios, 1659.

⎯⎯⎯⎯. *Loci cummunes theologici.* Editio postrema. Opera & Studio Nicolai Arnoldi. Amstelodami: apud Ludovicum & Danielem Elevirios, 1658.

Mastricht, Petrus van. *A Treatise on Regeneration . . . Extracted from his System of Divinity, called Theologia theoretico-practica.* New Haven, CT: Thomas & Samuel Green, 1770; an extract translated from the original Latin edition. [*A Treatise on Regeneration.* Ed. Brandon Withrow. Morgan, PA: Soli Deo Gloria, 2002.]

⎯⎯⎯⎯. *Theoretico-Practica Theologia: Quâ, per singula capita Theologica, pars exegetica, dogmatica, elenchtica & practica, perpetuâ successione conjugantur.* 1682-1687. Expanded edition: Editio nova. Priori multo emendatior, & tertiâ saltem parte auctior. Trajecti ad Rhenum: Prostant apud Gerardum Muntendam, 1698. [*Beschouwende en Praktikale Godgeleerdheit, waarin door alle de Godgeleerde Hoofdstukken henen, het Bybelverklarende, Leerstellige, Wederleggende, en Praktikale deel, door eenen onafgebroken schakel, onderscheidenlyk samengevoegt, voorgestelt word: Hier By Komt een volledig Kort-begrip der Kerklyke Geschiedenisse, een vertoog der Zedelyke, en een schets der Plichtvermanende Godgeleertheit, enz*. Met eene Voorrede [foreword] van den Heer Cornelius van der Kemp, en eene Lyk en Lof-reede [eulogy] van den Heer Henricus Pontanus. Translater unknown. Rotterdam: Hendrik van Pelt, de Wed. P. van Gilst, Jacobus Bosch, en Adrianus Douci, and Utrecht: Jan Jacob van Poolsum, 1749-1753.]

Molinaeus, Petrus. *Anatome Arminianismi, seu enucleatio controversiarum quae in Belgio agitantur: super doctrina de providentia, de praedestinatione, de morte Christi, de natura & gratia*. Editio secunda. Lugduni Batavorum: ex officina Jacobi Marci, 1620. [Pierre du Moulin. *The Anatomy of Arminianisme: or the Opening of the Controversies lately handled in the Low-Countries, concerning the Doctrine of Predestination, of the Death of Christ, of the Nature of Grace*. London: T. S., 1620.]

Nethenus, Matthew. *Praefatio Introductoria*. N.p., 1658.[Translated by Douglas Horton as *Introductory Preface in Which the Story of Master Ames is Briefly Narrated and the Excellence and Usefulness of his Writings Shown* in *William Ames by Matthew Nethenus, Hugo Visscher, and Karl Reuter*. Cambridge: Harvard Divinity School, 1965.]

Olevianus, Caspar. *A Firm Foundation: An Aid to Interpreting the Heidelberg Catechism*. Translated and edited by Lyle D. Bierma. Texts and Studies in Reformation and Post-Reformation Thought. Ed. Richard A. Muller. Grand Rapids: Baker, 1995.

_____. *An Exposition of the Symbole of the Apostles, or rather of the Articles of Faith. In which the chief points of the everlasting and free covenant between God and the faithful is briefly and plainly handled*. Translated by John Field. London: H. Middleton, 1581.

_____. *De substantia foederis gratuiti inter Deum et electos, itemque de mediis, quibus ea ipsa substantia nobis communicavit*. Genevae: apud Eustathius Vignon, 1585.

_____. *Geschriften van Caspar Olevianus. Verklaring van: "De apostolische Geloofsbelijdenis," "Het wezen van het Genadeverbond," "De getuigenissen van het Genadeverbond."* Den Haag: Het Reformatorische Boek, 1963.

Perkins, William. *Prophetica, sive de sacra et unica ratione concionandi*. Cambridge, 1592. [*The Art of Prophesying with The Calling of the Ministry*. With a Foreword by Sinclair B Ferguson. Edinburgh: Banner of Truth Trust, 1996. This combines *The Arte of Prophecying, or, A Treatise concerning the sacred and onely true manner and methode of Preaching* (Cambridge, 1592, 1606), in *Workes*, 2.642-2.673, and *The Calling of the Ministerie* (Cambridge, 1605), in *Workes*, 3.428-3.463).]

———. *The Whole Treatise of the Cases of Conscience Distinguished into Three Bookes*. London: John Legat, Printer to the University of Cambridge, 1606; reprint ed., The English Experience: Its Record in Early Printed Books Published in Facsimile, no. 482. Amsterdam: Theatrvm Orbis Terrarvm Ltd., and New York: Da Capo, Inc., 1972.

———. *The Workes of that Famous and Worthy Minister of Christ in the Universitie of Cambridge, Mr. William Perkins*. 3 vols. London: John Legatt, 1612-1613.

Polansdorf, Amandus Polandus von. *Partitiones theologicae juxta naturalis methodi leges conformatae duobus libris: quorum primis est de fide: altera de bonis operibus*. Editio secunda. Basileae: per Conradum Waldkirchi, 1590. [*The Substance of Christian Religion: Soundly Set Forth in Two Books, by Definition and Partitions, Framed According to the Rules of a Natural Method*. Translated by Thomas Wilcox.. London: John Oxenbridge, 1595].

Preston, John. *The New Covenant, or the Saints Portion: A Treatise Unfolding the all-sufficiencie of God, Man's uprightness, and the Covenant of Grace*. 10th ed. London: Imprinted by I. D. for Nicholas Bourne, 1639.

Ramus, Petrus (Pierre de la Ramée, Peter Ramus). *Dialectique (1555)*. Ed. Michel Dassonville. Geneva: Librairie Droz, 1964.

———. *Oratio de Professione liberalium artium*. Paris, 1563.

———. *Peter Ramus of Vermandois, the King's Professor, his Dialectica in two bookes*. Translated by R. F[age] Gent. London: W. J[ones], 1632; Ann Arbor Michigan: University Microfilms, n.d.

———. *Petri Rami Veromandui pro philosophica Parisiensis academiae disciplina oratio, ad Carolum Lotharinguum Cardinalem*. Parisiis, 1555. [*An Oration by the French Belgian Peter Ramus on Behalf of the Philosophical Training at the University of Paris, Delivered to Charles Cardinal Lorraine.*]

———. *The Art of Logick (Gathered Out of Aristotle and Set in Due Forms) According to his instructions*. Translated by Antony Wooten. London: I. D. for Nicholas Bourne, 1626.

———. *The Logike of the Moste Excellent Philosopher P. Ramus Martyr*. Translated by Roland MacIlmaine (1574). Ed. Catherine M. Dunn. Renaissance Editions, no. 3. Northridge, CA: San Fernando Valley State College, 1969.

Rutherford, Samuel. *Influences of the Life of Grace*. London: T. C. for Andrew Cook, 1659.

———. *The Covenant of Life Opened, or a Treatise of the Covenant of Grace*. Edinburgh: Printed by Andro Anderson for Robert Broun, 1655.

Shepard, Thomas. *Certain Select Cases Resolved Specially tending to the right ordering of the heart, that we may comfortably walk with God in our general and particular Callings*. London: Printed by M. Simmons for John Rothwell, 1648.

_____. "The Autobiography of Thomas Shepard." In *Publications of the Colonial Society of Massachusetts.* Vol. 27. Boston: Colonial Society of Massachusetts, 1932.

_____. *The Complete Works of Thomas Shepard.* Ed. John A. Albro. 3 vols. Boston: Doctrinal Tract & Book Society, 1853; reprint ed., New York: Georg Olms Verlag, 1971.

_____. *The Sincere Convert Discovering the Paucity of True Beleevers; and the great difficulty of Saving Conversion.* London: Printed by Thomas Paine for Matthew Symmons, 1640; reprint ed., *The Sincere Convert. Discovering the small Number of True Believers.* N.p., n.d.

_____. *The Sound Beleever or a Treatise of Evangelicall Conversion. Discovering the work of Christs Spirit, in reconciling of a sinner to God.* London: Printed for R. Dawlman, 1645.

Silesii, Davidis Parei. *Explicationum Catecheticarun D. Zachariae Ursini Silesii.* Neostadii Palatinorim: Excudebat Matthaeus Harnisch, 1593.

Smytegelt, Bernardus. *Des Christens Eenige Troost in Leven en Sterven, of Verklaringe over den Heidelbergschen Catechismus in LII Predicatien; Benevens V Belydenis-Predicatien.* Middelburg: Ottho en Pieter van Thol, Den Haag, en A. L. en M.H. Callenfels, 1747.

Spener, Philip J. *Pia Desideria.* Translated and edited by Theodore G. Tappert. Philadelphia: Fortress, 1964.

Spiljardus, Johannes. *Het Schat-Boeck Der Verklaringhen over de Catechismus der Christelicke Religie.* 2 vols. With an Introduction by Joan van den Honert. Gorinchem: Nicolaas Goetzee, 1736.

Suárez, Francisco, S.J. *Selections from Three Works. De Legibus, AC Deo Legislatore, 1612 Defensio Fidei Catholicae et Apostolicare Adversus Anglicanae Sectae Errores, 1613 de Triplici Virtute Theologica, Fide, Spe, et Charitate, 1621.* Volume Two, The Translation. Prepared by Gwladys L. Williams, Ammi Brown and John Waldron with certain revisions by Henry Davis, S.J. and an Introduction by James Brown Scott. Oxford: Clarendon and London: Humphrey Milford, 1944; reprint ed., Buffalo: William S. Hein & Co., Inc., 1995.

Taffin, Jean. *De boetveerdicheyt des levens, vervaet in vier boeken.* Translated by J. Crucius. Amsterdam, 1620. [*The Amendment of Life, Comprised in Fower Books.* London: G. Bishop, 1595.]

_____. *Des Marques des enfans de Dieu, et des consolations en leurs afflictions.* 1606 ed. [*De merck-teeckenen der kinderen Godts, ende de vertroostinghen in hare verdruckingen.* Translated from the French by J. Viverius. Amsterdam, 1620. *Of the Marks of the Children of God, and of their Comforts in Afflictions.* Translated by Anne Prowse for Thomas Man. London: Thomas Orwin, 1590. *The Marks of God's Children.* Classics of Reformed Spirituality. Translated by Peter Y. De Jong. Edited by James A. De Jong. Grand Rapids: Baker, 2003.]

Teellinck, Willem. *Alle de wercken van Mr. Willem Teellinck*. 3 vols. Utrecht: Johannes van Someren, 1659-64.

———, Theophilus Philopatris, Johannes Teellinck. *Adam rechtschapen, wanschapen, herschapen*. Utrecht, 1659.

————. *De Worstelinge eenes bekeerden Sondaers*. Middelburg, 1631.

————. *Eubulus ofte Tractaet Vervattende Verscheyden Aenmerckingen over de tegenwoordige staet onzer Christelicker Gemeynte*. Ed. D.D. Theodorus and Johannes Teellinck, V.D.M. Utrecht: Hermannus Ribbius, and Johannes van Waesberge, 1657.

————. *Geestelycke couranten voor dit loopende quartier-jaers, over de swarigheden die ons den voorleden somer getroffen hebben, ende hoe wy ons daer tegen te dragen hebben dese winter; beginnende vanden 1 Octob. eyndende inden laetsten Decemb. deses jaers 1625*. 1626. Utrecht: H. Ribbius, H. Specht, en J. van Waesberge, 1655.

————. *Huys-boeck, of te een Voudighe Verklaringhe en toe-eygheninghe, van de Voornaemste Vraeghstucke des Nederlandschen Christelijcken catechismi*. Middelburgh: voor Gillis Horthemels, 1650.

————. *Noord-Sterre, Aenwijsende de rechte streke van de ware Godsalicheyt*. Middelburgh: Hans vander Hellen, 1621. [*The Path of True Godliness*. Classics of Reformed Spirituality. Translated by A. Godbehere. Ed. J. R. Beeke. Grand Rapids: Baker, 2003.]

————. *The Ballance of the Sanctuarie, shewing how we must Behave our selves when wee see and behold the People of God in Miserie and Oppression under the Tyranny of their Enemies*. Translated by C. Harmar. Ed. T. Gataker. London: I. D. for William Sheffard, 1621.

————. *The Christian Conflict and Conquest*. London: John Pawlar for I. Bellamie, 1622.

————. *Zephaniae waerschouwinge* [1623]; *Zions basuyne aengesteken* [1621]; *Weech-schale des heylichdoms* [1621]; *Treur-schrift* [1622]. 1621-1623. Reprint ed. Urk: Willem Teellinck Fonds, 1978.

Tennent, Gilbert. "The Danger of an Unconverted Ministry Considered in a Sermon on Mark 6:34, preached at Nottingham in Pennsylvania, March 8, Anno 1739,40." Philadelphia: Benjamin Franklin, 1740.

Trelcatius, Lucas. *A Briefe Institution of the Common Places of Sacred Divinitie*. Englished by John Gawen. London: Imprinted by T.P. for Francis Burton, 1610.

Turretin, Francis. *Institutes of Elenctic Theology*. Translated by George M. Giger. Ed. James T. Dennison, Jr. 3 vols. Phillipsburg, NJ: P&R, 1992-1997.

Twisse, William. *A briefe Catecheticall Exposition of Christian Doctrine*. London: G. M. for Robert Bird, 1632.

————. *The Doctrine of the Synod of Dort and Arles, reduced to the practise*. Amsterdam, 1631.

Udemans, Godefridus Cornelisz. *Christelycke bedenckingen, die een geloovige ziele dagelycx behoort te betrachten, gestelt op elcke dagh van de week*.

Noch is hier bygevoeght De Leeder van Jacob, dat is: Korte ende Naeckte Afbeeldinghe van den rechten wegh, na den Hemel, in sekere trappen onderscheyden. Dordrecht: Voor F. Boels, 1603.

_____. *Practycke, dat is wercklycke oeffeninge van de Christelijcke hooftdeuchden, gheloove, hope ende liefde*. Dordrecht: Fransoys Boels, 1632.

Ursinus, Zacharias. *A Collection of Certaine Learned and Excellent Discourses: Treating and Discussing Diverse Hard and Difficult Points of Christian Religion*. Collected and published in Latin by D. David Pareus. London: H. L. for John Roysron, 1613.

_____. *The Summe of Christian Religion: Delivered by Zacharias Ursinus in his Lectures Upon the Catechisme*. Translated by Henry Parrie. Oxford: Joseph Barnes, 1587, 1601; reprint ed., London: H. L. for Arthur Johnson, 1645, to which are annexed the *Theologicall Miscellanies* of D. David Pareus. [Most recent translation, lacking Pareus: *The Commentary of Dr. Zachariaz Ursinus on the Heidelberg Catechism*. Translated by George W. Williard. 2nd ed. Columbus: Scott and Bascom, 1852; reprint ed., Phillipsburg, NJ: Presbyterian and Reformed, 1985.]

_____, Festus Hommius, and Jacobus Laurentius. *Het Schat-boeck der verklaringhen over de catechismus der christelicke religie: die in de Gereformeerde Kercken ende scholen van Hoogh- en Neder-Duytslandt gheleert wordt*. Amsteldam: Joannes van Ravesteyn, 1650.

Voetius (or Voet), Gisbertus. *Catechisatie. Dat is Een grondige ende eenvoudige onderwijsinge over de Leere des Christelicken catechismi: Bestaende in Vragen en Antwoorden*. Compiled by Cornelius Poudroyen. N.p., 1653.

_____. *Catechisatie over den Heidelbergschen Catechismus*. Ed. A. Kuyper. 2 vols. Rotterdam: Gebroeders Huge, 1891.

_____. *Disputationes theologicae*. 5 vols. Ultrajecti: apud Joannem à Waesberge, Anonium Smytegelt, 1648-69.

_____. *Geestelijke Verlatingen*. Voortgezet door Johannes Hoornbeeck. Utrecht: Lambert Roeck, 1646; reprint ed., n.p.: Het Traktaat-genootschap "Filippus," 1898. [*Spiritual Desertion*. Classics of Reformed Spirituality. Translated by John Vriend and Harry Boonstra. Ed. M. Eugene Osterhaven. Grand Rapids: Baker, 2003.]

_____. *Proeve van de Kracht der Godzaligheydt*. Utrecht: Simon de Vries, 1656.

_____. *Te asketica sive Exercitia Pietatis*. Gorinchen: Vink, 1654.

Wesley, John A. *A Christian Library: Consisting of Extracts from and Abridgements of the Choicest Pieces of Practical Divinity which have been Published in the English Tongue*. 2nd ed. 30 vols. London: Printed by T. Cordeux, for T. Blanshard, 1819-26.

Westminster Confession of Faith. Inverness: Free Presbyterian Publications, 1958; reprint ed. in large format, Glasgow, 1994.

Whitefield, George. *George Whitefield's Journals*. Compilation of seven previously published works. London: Banner of Truth Trust, 1960.

_____. *The Works of George Whitefield.* 6 vols. London: Printed for Edward and Charles Dilly, 1771.
Williams, George et al., eds. *Thomas Hooker: Writings in England and Holland, 1626-1633.* Harvard Theological Studies, no. 28. Cambridge: University, 1975.
Winthrop, John. *History of New England from 1630-1649.* Ed. James Savage. 2 vols. Boston: Thomas B. Wait & Son, 1825-26.
_____. *Winthrop Papers.* Ed. A.B. Forbes. 5 vols. Boston: Massachusetts Historical Society, 1929-47.
Witsius, Herman. *A Treatise on Christian Faith.* Extracted and translated by Rev. Madan. London: E. Dilly, and T. Fuller, 1761.
_____. *De Oeconomia Foederum Dei cum hominibus libri quattuor.* Editio tertia. Utrecht: Franciscum Halmam, 1694. [*The Oeconomy of the Covenants between God and Man. Comprehending A Complete Body of Divinity.* Translated by William Crookshank, with life of author prefixed. 3 vols. London: Printed for Edward Dilly, 1763.]
_____. *Geestelyke Printen van een onwedergeboorne op syn beste en een wedergeboorne op syn slechtste.* Zeist, 1874.
_____. *Sacred Dissertations on the Apostles' Creed.* Translated with notes by Donald Fraser. 2 vols. Glasgow: Khull, Blackie, & Co., 1823; reprint ed., Reformation Heritage, 2012.
Zanchius, Hieronymus. *De Religione Christianae, Fides: Quam Nunc Demum, Annum Agens LXX, Suo Subeque Familiae Nominae, in Lucem Edendam Curavit.* London: 1605. [*H. Zanchius: His Confession of Christian Religion: Which Now at length being 70 years of Age, He Caused to be Published in the Name of Himself and his Family.* Cambridge: John Legat, 1599.]
_____. *Speculum Christianum or A Christian Survey for the Conscience.* Translated by H.N. London: George Eld, 1614.
_____. *The Doctrine of Absolute Predestination Stated and Asserted.* Translated by A. Toplady. Wilmington: Adam's, 1793; reprint ed., Grand Rapids: Sovereign Grace, 1971.
_____. *The Whole Body of Christian Religion.* Translated by D. Ralph Winterton. London: John Redmayne, 1659.
Zwingli, Huldreich. *The Latin Works and the Correspondence of Huldreich Zwingli.* Ed. Samuel Macaulay Jackson et al. 3 vols. Philadelphia: Heidelberg, 1912-29.
_____. *Zwingli and Bullinger; Selected Translations*, with introductions and notes by G.W. Bromiley. Philadelphia: Westminster, 1953.

Secondary Sources

Aa, Abraham Jacob van der, ed. *Biographisch Woordenboek der Nederlanden.* 21 vols. in 27. Haarlem: J.J. van Brederode, 1852-78.

Ahlstrom, Sidney E. *A Religious History of the American People*. New Haven: Yale University, 1972.

Alexander, Archibald. *Thoughts on Religious Experience*. Philadelphia: Presbyterian Board of Publications, 1844.

Allison, C.F. *The Rise of Moralism: The Proclamation of the Gospel from Hooker to Baxter*. London: Society for Promotion of Christian Knowledge, 1966.

Althaus, Paul. *Die Prinzipien der deutschen-reformierten Dogmatik im Zeitalter der aristotelischen Scholastik*. Leipzig: Deichert, 1914; reprint ed., Darmstadt: Wissenschaftliche Buchgesellschaft, 1967.

Armstrong, Brian G. *Calvinism and the Amyraut Heresy: Protestant Scholasticism and Humanism in Seventeenth-Century France*. Madison: University of Wisconsin, 1969.

_____. *Probing the Reformed Tradition: Historical Studies in Honor of Edward A. Dowey, Jr*. Louisville, KY: Westminster/John Knox, 1989.

_____. "Westphalia, Peace of (1648)." In *The New International Dictionary of the Christian Church*. Ed. James D. Douglas. Revised ed. Grand Rapids: Zondervan, 1978.

Asselt, Willem Jan van. "Amicitia Dei: Een Onderzoek naar de structuur van de theologie van Johannes Coccejus (1603-1669)." Ph.D. diss., State University of Utrecht, 1988.

_____. "*Expromissio or fideiussio*? A Seventeenth-Century Theological Debate Between Voetians and Cocceians About the Nature of Christ's Suretyship in Salvation History." *Mid-America Journal of Theology* 14 (2003): 37-57.

_____. "'Hebraïca Veritas': Zeventiende-Eeuwse Motieven voor de Bestudering van het Hebreeuws door Predicanten." *Kerk en Theologie* 46 (1995): 309-24

_____. et al. *Inleiding in de Gereformeerde Scholastiek*. Zoetermeer: Boekencentrum, 1998.

_____. *Johannes Coccejus. Portret van een zeventiende-eeuws theoloog op oude en nieuwe wegen*. Heerenveen: J.J. Groen en Zoon, 1997.

_____. "Mastricht, Petrus van." In *Biografisch Lexicon voor de Geschiedenis van het Nederlandse Protestantisme*, vol. 5. 5 vols. Ed. D. Nauta et al. Kampen: J.H. Kok, 1978-2001.

_____. and Eef Dekker, eds. *Reformation and Scholasticism: An Ecumenical Enterprise*. Texts and Studies in Reformation and Post-Reformation Thought. Ed. Richard A. Muller. Grand Rapids: Baker, 2001.

_____. "Studie van de gereformeerde scholastiek: Verleden en Toekomst." *Nederlands Theologisch Tijdschrift* 50 (1996): 290-312.

_____. "The Doctrine of the Abrogations in the Federal Theology of Johannes Coccejus (1603-1669)." *Calvin Theological Journal* 29 (1994): 101-16.

_____. *The Federal Theology of Johannes Cocceius (1603-1669)*. Translated by Raymond A. Blacketer. Studies in the History of Christian Thought, no. 100. Leiden: E.J. Brill, 2001.

_____. "The Theologian's Tool Kit: Johannes Maccovius (1588-1644) and the Development of Reformed Theological Distinctions." *Westminster Theological Journal* 68 (2006): 23-40.

Audi, Robert, ed. *The Cambridge Dictionary of Philosophy*. New York: Cambridge University, 1995.

Baarsel, Jan Jacobus van. *William Perkins: Eene Bijdrage tot de Kennis der religeuse ontwikkeling in Engeland, ten tijde van Koningin Elisabeth*. Amsterdam: Ton Bolland, 1975.

Bagchi, David and David C. Steinmetz, eds. *The Cambridge Companion to Reformation Theology*. Cambridge: Cambridge University, 2004.

Baker, Derek. *Reform and Reformation: England and the Continent, c. 1500 - c.1700*. Oxford: Basil Blackwell, 1979.

Baker, J. Wayne. *Heinrich Bullinger and the Covenant: The Other Reformed Tradition*. Athens, Ohio: Ohio University, 1980.

Bakhuizen van den Brink, J.N. et al, eds. *Documenta Reformata: Teksten uit de Geschiedenis van Kerk en Theologie in de Nederlanden sedert de Hervorming*. 2 vols. Kampen: J.H. Kok, 1960-62.

_____. "Engelse Kerkelijke Politiek in de Nederlanden in de Eerste Helft der 17de Eeuw." *Nederlands Archief voor Kerkgeschiedenis* 39 (1952): 132-46.

Balke, Willem. "Het Pietisme in Oostfriesland." *Theologia Reformata* 21 (1978):307-27.

_____. "The Word of God and *Experientia* according to Calvin." In *Calvinus Ecclesiae Doctor*. Ed. W.H. Neuser. Kampen: J.H. Kok, 1978.

Balke, W. and W. van 't Spijker, eds. *Reformed Protestantism: sources of the 16th and 17th centuries on microfiche*. Zug, Switzerland: Inter Documentation Co., 1983.

Bangs, Carl. *Arminius: A Study in the Dutch Reformation*. Nashville: Abingdon, 1971.

Bank, J.H. van de. "Frelinghuysen, Theodorus Jacobus." In *Biografisch Lexicon voor de Geschiedenis van het Nederlandse Protestantisme*. Ed. D. Nauta et al. 5 vols. Kampen: J.H. Kok, 1978-2001.

Barker, William S. *Puritan Profiles: 54 Influential Puritans at the time when the Westminster Confession of Faith was written*. Geanies House, Fearn, Ross-shire: Mentor, 1996.

Barth, Karl. *Church Dogmatics*. 13 vols. Edinburgh: T&T Clark, 1932-67.

_____. *Einführung in dem Heidelberger Katechismus*. Zurich, 1960.

Battis, John Emery. "Troublers in Israel: The Antinomian Controversy in the Massachusetts Bay Colony, 1636-1638." Ph.D. diss., Columbia University, 1958.

Battles, Ford Lewis. *The Piety of John Calvin. An Anthology Illustrative of the Spirituality of the Reformer of Geneva.* Grand Rapids: Baker, 1978.

Beardslee, John Walter, III. "Theological Development at Geneva under Francis and Jean-Alphonse Turretin, 1648-1737." Ph.D. diss., Yale University, 1956.

_____, ed. and trans. *Reformed Dogmatics: J. Wollebius, G. Voetius, and F. Turretin. A Library of Protestant Thought.* New York: Oxford University, 1965; reprint ed., Grand Rapids: Baker, 1977.

Beattie, Francis R., Charles R. Hemphill, and Henry V. Escott, eds. *Memorial Volume of the Westminster Assembly. 1647-1897.* Richmond: The Presbyterian Committee of Publication, 1897.

Beeke, Joel R. *Assurance of Faith: Calvin, English Puritanism and the Dutch Second Reformation.* American University Studies: Series 7, Theology and Religion, vol. 89. New York: Peter Lang, 1994.

_____. "Gisbertus Voetius: Toward a Reformed Marriage of Knowledge and Piety." In *Protestant Scholasticism: Essays in Reassessment.* Ed. Carl R. Trueman and R. Scott Clark. Carlisle, Cumbria: Paternoster, 1999.

_____ and Mark Jones. *A Puritan Theology: Doctrine for Life.* Grand Rapids: Reformation Heritage, 2012.

_____ and Randall J. Pederson. *Meet the Puritans: With a Guide to Modern Reprints.* Grand Rapids: Reformation Heritage, 2006.

_____ and Sinclair Ferguson, eds. *Reformed Confessions Harmonized.* Grand Rapids: Baker, 1999.

Bell, Michael D. "Propter Potestatem, Scientiam, AC Beneplacitum Dei: The Doctrine of the Object of Predestination in the Theology of Johannes Maccovius." Th.D. diss., Westminster Theological Seminary, 1986.

Berkhof, Louis. *Systematic Theology.* 4th ed. Grand Rapids: Eerdmans, 1972.

Bergh, W. van den. *Calvijn Over het Genadeverbond.* 's-Gravenhage: W.A. Beschoor, 1879.

W. Bergsma. "'Slow to hear God's Holy Word'?: Religion in everyday life in early modern Friesland." In *Experiences and explanations: Historical and sociological essays on religion in everyday life.* Ed. L. Laeyendecker, L.G. Jansma, and C.H.A. Verhaar. Leeuwarden: Fryske Akademy, 1990.

Bie, J.P. de, and J. Loosjes, eds. *Biographisch Woordenboek der Protestantsche Godgeleerden in Nederland.* 5 vols. 's-Gravenhage: Martinus Nijhoff, 1907-43.

Bierma, Lyle Dean. trans and ed. *A Firm Foundation: An Aid to Interpreting the Heidelberg Catechism*, Texts and Studies in Reformation and Post-Reformation Thought. Ed. Richard A. Muller. Grand Rapids: Baker, 1995.

_____ et al. *An Introduction to the Heidelberg Catechism: Sources, History, and Theology.* Texts and Studies in Reformation and Post-Reformation Thought. Ed. Richard A. Muller. Grand Rapids: Baker, 2005.

_____. "Covenant or Covenants in the Theology of Olevianus." *Calvin Theological Journal* 22 (1987): 228-50.

_____. "Federal Theology in the Sixteenth Century: Two Traditions?" *Westminster Theological Journal* 45 (1983): 304-21.

_____. *German Calvinism in the Confessional Age: The Covenant Theology of Caspar Olevianus*. Grand Rapids: Baker, 1996; reprint ed., *The Covenant Theology Of Caspar Olevianus*, Grand Rapids: Reformation Heritage, 2005.

_____. "The Covenant Theology of Caspar Olevian." Ph.D. diss., Duke University, 1980.

_____. "The Role of Covenant Theology in Early Reformed Orthodoxy." *Sixteenth Century Journal* 21 (1990): 453-62.

Bizer, Ernst. "Reformed Orthodoxy and Cartesianism." Translated by C. MacCormick. *Journal for Theology and the Church* 2 (1965): 20-82.

Blench, J.W. *Preaching in England in the Late Fifteenth and Sixteenth Century*. Oxford: Basil Blackwell, 1964.

Blok, P.J. *A History of the People of the Netherlands*. Translated by Oscar A. Bierstadt and Ruth Putnam. 4 vols; reprint ed., New York: AMS, 1970.

Bobick, Michael William. "Owen's razor: the role of Ramist logic in the covenant theology of John Owen (1616-1683)." Th.D. diss., Drew University, 1996.

Boeles, W.B.S. *Frieslands Hoogeschool en het Rijks Athenaeum te Franeker*. 2 vols. Leeuwaarden, 1878-1889.

Boer, Johannes de. *De Verzegeling met de Heilige Geest volgens de opvatting van de Nadere Reformatie*. Rotterdam: Bronder, 1968.

Boerkoel, Benjamin J. "Uniqueness Within the Calvinist Tradition: William Ames (1576-1633): Primogenitor of the Theologia Pietatis in English-Dutch Puritanism." Th.M. thesis. Calvin Theological Seminary, 1990.

Bogue, Carl W. *Jonathan Edwards and the Covenant of Grace*. Cherry Hill, NJ: Mack Publishing Company, 1975.

Bohren, R. *In der Tiefe der Zisterne*. Munich, 1990.

Bouwman, Harm. *Willem Teellinck en de Practijk der Godzaligheid*. Kampen: J.H. Kok, 1928; reprint ed., Kampen: De Groot Goudrian, 1985.

Bouwman, Marinus. *Voetius over het gezag der Synoden*. Amsterdam: S.J.P. Bakker, 1937.

Brandt, Geeraerdt. *The History of the Reformation and Other Ecclesiastical Transactions in and about the Low-Countries, from the Beginning of the Eighth Century, down to the Famous Synod of Dort*. 4 vols. London: T. Wood, 1720-23; reprint ed., New York: AMS, 1979.

Bratt, John. *The Rise and Development of Calvinism*. Grand Rapids: Eerdmans, 1959.

Brauer, Jerald C. "Reflections on the Nature of English Puritanism." *Church History* 23 (1954): 98-109.

_____. "Types of Puritan Piety." *Church History* 56 (1987): 39-58.

Bray, John S. "The Value of Works in the Theology of Calvin and Beza." *Sixteenth Century Journal* 4 (1973): 77-86.

Breitenbach, William. "Piety and Moralism: Edwards and the New Divinity." In *Jonathan Edwards and the American Experience*. Ed. Nathan O. Hatch and Harry S. Stout, 177-204. New York: Oxford University, 1988.

_____. "Religious Affections and Religious Affectations: Antinomianism and Hypocrisy in the Writings of Edwards and Franklin (Themes of Morality and True Virtue)." In *Benjamin Franklin, Jonathan Edwards, and the Representation of American Culture*. Ed. Harry S. Stout and Barbara B. Oberg. New York: Oxford, 1993.

Brereton, William. *Travels in Holland, the United Provinces, England, Scotland and Ireland, MDCXXXIV-MDCXXXV*. Ed. Edward Hawkins. Remains, Historical and Literary Connected with the Palatine Counties of Lancaster and Chester, 1844, vol. 1; reprint ed., New York: The Chetham Society, n.d.

Breugelmans, R. *The Auction Catalogue of the Library of William Ames*. Facsimile edition with an Introduction by K.L. Sprunger. Catalogi Redivivi, vol. 6. Utrecht: HES, 1988.

Breward, Ian. "The Life and Theology of William Perkins 1558-1602." Ph.D. diss., University of Manchester, 1963.

_____. "The Significance of William Perkins." *Journal of Religious History* 4 (1966): 113-28.

_____, ed. *The Work of William Perkins*. The Courtenay Library of Reformation Classics, no. 3. Appleford, Abingdon, Berkshire, England: Sutton Courtenay, 1970.

_____. "William Perkins and the Origins of Reformed Casuistry." Puritan and Reformed Studies Conference, 1962. In *Faith and a Good Conscience*. London: A.G. Hasler, 1963.

_____. "William Perkins and the Origins of Reformed Casuistry." *The Evangelist Quarterly* 40 (1968): 3-20.

Brienen, Teunis. et al. *De Nadere Reformatie. Beschrijving van haar voornaamste vertegenwoordigers*. 's-Gravenhage: Boekencentrum, 1986.

_____. *De Prediking van de Nadere Reformatie*. Amsterdam: Ton Bolland, 1974.

_____. "De 22 regels van Willem Teellinck over het maken van preken," *Documentatieblad Nadere Reformatie* 6 (1982): 16-22.

_____ et al. *Nadere Reformatie en het Gereformeerd Piëtisme*. 's-Gravenhage: Boekencentrum, 1989.

_____ et al. *Theologische aspecten van de Nadere Reformatie*. Zoetermeer: Boekencentrum, 1993.

Broes, *De Engelsche Hervormde Kerk, benevens haren invloed op onze Nederlandsche, van den tijd der Hervorming*. 2 vols. Delft: Allart, 1825.

Bromiley, Geoffrey W. *Historical Theology: An Introduction*. Grand Rapids: Eerdmans, 1978.

Bronkema, Ralph. "The Essence of Puritanism." Th.D. diss., Free University of Amsterdam, 1929.

Brook, Benjamin. *The Lives of the Puritans*. 3 vols. London: James Black, 1813; reprint ed., Pittsburgh: Soli Deo Gloria, 1994.

Brown, George, Jr. "Pietism and the Reformed Tradition." *Reformed Review* 23 (1970): 143-53.

Brown, John. *Puritan Preaching in England*. New York: Charles Scribner's Sons, 1900.

_____. *The English Puritans*. London: Cambridge University, 1912.

Brown, Paul Edward. "The Principle of the Covenant in the Theology of Thomas Goodwin." Ph.D. diss., Drew University, 1950.

Bruggink, Donald J. "Calvin and Federal Theology." *Reformed Review* 13 (1959): 15-22.

Buchanan, C. "Catechisms." In *The New International Dictionary of the Christian Church*. Ed. James D. Douglas. Revised ed. Grand Rapids: Zondervan, 1978.

Burgess, Walter H. *John Robinson, Pastor of the Pilgrim Fathers: A Study of His Life and Times*. London: Williams and Norgate, 1920.

Burleigh, J.H.S. *A Church History of Scotland*. Oxford: Oxford University, 1960; reprint ed., Edinburgh: Hope Trust, 1988.

Burrage, Champlin. *The Church Covenant Idea: Its Origin and Its Development*. Philadelphia: American Baptist Publication Society, 1904.

_____. *The Early English Dissenters in the Light of Recent Research (1550-1641)*. 2 vols. Cambridge: Cambridge University, 1912.

Byington, Ezra Hoyt. *The Puritan in England and New England*. Boston: Little, Brown and Co. 1900.

Byrnes, Thomas A. "H. Richard Niebuhr's Reconstruction of Jonathan Edwards' Moral Theology." *Annual of the Society of Christian Ethics*, 1985.

Cadoux, Cecil J. *Philip of Spain and the Netherlands: An Essay on Moral Judgments in History*. London and Redhill: Lutterworth, 1947.

Campbell, Douglas. *The Puritan in Holland, England, and America: An Introduction to American History*. 4th ed. 2 Vols. New York: Harper & Brothers, 1892.

Carden, Allen. *Puritan Christianity in America: Religion and Life in Seventeenth-Century Massachusetts*. Grand Rapids: Baker, 1990.

Carruthers, S.W. *The Everyday Work of the Westminster Assembly*. Philadelphia: Presbyterian Historical Society, 1943.

_____. *The Westminster Confession of Faith*. Manchester: R. Aikman & Son, 1937.

Carson, John L. and David W. Hall. *To Glorify and Enjoy God: A Commemoration of the 350th Anniversary of the Westminster Asssembly*. Edinburgh: Banner of Truth Trust, 1994.

Carter, Alice C. *The English Reformed Church in Amsterdam in the Seventeenth Century*. Amsterdam: Scheltema & Holkema, 1964.

_____. "The Ministry to the English Churches in the Netherlands in the Seventeenth Century." *Bulletin of the Institute of Historical Research* 33 (Nov. 1960): 166-79.

Chalker, William H. "Calvin and Some Seventeenth Century English Calvinists." Ph.D. diss., Duke University, 1961.

Chamberlain, Ava. "Self-Deception as a Theological Problem in Jonathan Edwards's 'Treatise Concerning Religious Affections'." *Church History* 63 (1994): 541-56.

Cherry, Conrad. "The Puritan Notion of the Covenant in Jonathan Edwards' Doctrine of Faith." *Church History* 34 (1965): 328-41.

_____. *The Theology of Jonathan Edwards: A Reappraisal*. Garden City, NJ: Doubleday, 1966; reprint edition with a new introduction by Conrad Cherry and a foreword by Stephen Stein; Bloomington and Indianapolis: Indiana University, 1990.

Clark, R. Scott. "Brief History of Covenant Theology." http://rscottclark.org/2001/09/a-brief-history-of-covenant-theology/. Accessed June 19, 2013.

_____. "Calvin on the *Lex Naturalis*." *Stulos Theological Journal* 6 (1998): 1–22.

_____. "Christ and Covenant: Federal Theology in Orthodoxy." In *Companion to Reformed Orthodoxy*. Ed. Herman Selderhuis. Leiden: Brill, 2013.

Clebsch, William A. Review of *Technometry by William Ames*, by Lee W. Gibbs, ed. and trans. In *Journal of the American Academy of Religion* 48 (1990):124-25.

Clifford, K. "The Reconstruction of Puritan Casuistry." Ph.D. diss., University of London, 1957.

Clouse, R.G. "Thirty Years' War (1618-48)." In *The New International Dictionary of the Christian Church*. Ed. James D. Douglas. Revised ed. Grand Rapids: Zondervan, 1978.

Coffey, John and Paul C.H. Lim, eds. *The Cambridge Companion to Puritanism*. New York: Cambridge University Press, 2008.

Collinson, Patrick. *The Elizabethan Puritan Movement*. Berkeley: University of California, 1967.

Come, Donald R. "John Cotton: Guide of the Chosen People." Ph.D. diss., University of Illinois, 1956.

Commissee voor de Archieven van de Nederlands Hervormde Kerk. *De archieven van de Hervormede Kerk in korte overzichten*. 2 vols. Leiden: E.J. Brill, 1960-74.

Como, David R. *Blown by the Spirit: Puritanism and the Emergence of an Antinomian Underground in Pre-Civil War England*. Stanford: Stanford University, 2004.

Costello, William T. *The Scholastic Curriculum in Early Seventeenth Century Cambridge*. Cambridge: Harvard University, 1958.

Cottrell, Jack. "Covenant and Baptism in the Theology of H. Zwingli." Th.D. diss., Princeton Theological Seminary, 1971.

Cramer, J.A. *De Theologische Faculteit te Utrecht ten tijde van Voetius*. Utrecht: Kemink en Zoon, 1932.

Crocco, Stephen. "Paul Ramsey and the Works of Jonathan Edwards." *Annual of the Society of Christian Ethics*. Ed. H. Beckley. (1992): 157-72.

Cross, F.L. and E.A. Livingstone, eds. *The Oxford Dictionary of the Christian Church*. New York: Oxford University, 1957; reprint ed., 1997.

Cunningham, William. *Historical Theology: A Review of the Principal Doctrinal Discussions in the Christian Church Since the Apostolic Age*. 2 vols. Edinburgh: Clark, 1863; reprint ed., London: Banner of Truth Trust, 1960.

Curtis, Mark H. *Oxford and Cambridge in Transition 1558-1642*. Oxford: Clarendon, 1959.

Dallimore, Arnold. *George Whitefield*. 2 vols. London: Banner of Truth Trust, 1970-80.

Dankbaar, W.F. *Hoogtepunten uit het Nederlandsche Calvinisme in de Zestiende Eeuw*. Haarlem: H.D. Tjeenk Willink & Zoon, 1946.

D'Aubigne, J.H. Merle. *History of the Reformation in Europe in the Time of Calvin*. 8 vols. London: Longmans, Green, and Co., 1863-1878.

Davidson, James West. *The Logic of Millennial Thought: Eighteenth-Century New England*. New Haven: Yale University, 1977.

Davies, Horton. *The Worship of the English Puritans*. London: Dacre, 1948; reprint ed., Morgan, Pennsylvania: Soli Deo Gloria, 1997.

Davis, Brian Richard. "Reformation while tarrying for many: The radical Puritan ecclesiology of William Ames." Ph.D. diss., Southern Baptist Theological Seminary, 2010.

Deal, Max Eugene. "The Meaning and Method of Systematic Theology in Amandus Polanus." Ph.D. diss., University of Edinburgh, 1980.

Deeter, Allen C. *An Historical and Theological Introduction to Philipp Spener's "Pia Desideria.": A Study in Early German*. Ann Arbor: University Microfilms, Inc., 1963.

Dentz, Fred Oudschans. *History of the English Church at the Hague, 1586-1929*. Delft: W.D. Meinema, 1929.

Dickens, A.G. *The English Reformation*. London: B.T. Batsford, 1964.

_____ and John Tonkin. with Kenneth Powell. *The Reformation in Historical Thought*. Cambridge: Harvard University, 1985.

Diemer, N. *Het Scheppingsverbond met Adam (Het Verbond der Werken): bij de Theologen der 16e, 17e, en 18e Eeuw in Zwitserland, Duitsland, Nederland, en Engeland*. Kampen: J.H. Lol, n.d.

Dorsten, J. van, ed. *Ten Studies in Anglo-Dutch Relations*. London: University, for Sir Thomas Brown Institute, 1974.

Douglas, James D., ed. *The New International Dictionary of the Christian Church*. Rev. ed. Grand Rapids: Zondervan, 1978.

Dowey, Edward. *The Knowledge of God in Calvin's Theology*. New York: Columbia University, 1965.

Duker, Arnoldus C. *Gisbertus Voetius*. 3 vols. Leiden: E.J. Brill, 1897-1914.

Edwards, David L. *Christian England*. 2 vols. Grand Rapids: Eerdmans, 1983.
Edwards, Paul, ed. *The Encyclopedia of Philosophy*. 2 vols. New York: MacMillan and Co. and Free, 1967.
Eekhof, A. *De Theologische Faculteit te Leiden in de 17de Eeuw*. Utrecht: G.J.A. Ruys, 1921.
―――――. "Religious Thought and Life in Holland." In *Lectures on Holland for American Students*. Leiden: A.W. Sijthoff's Publishing Company, 1924.
Eeinigberg, Elton M. "The Place of the Covenant in Calvin's Thinking." *Reformation Review* 10 (1957): 1-22.
Eggermont, P. L. "Bibliografie van het Nederlandse Piëtisme in de zeventiende en achttiende eeuw." *Documentatieblad Werkgroep 18e eeuw* 3 (1969): 17-31.
Ehalt, David R. "The Development of Early Congregational Theory of the Church with Special Reference to the Five 'Dissenting Brethren' at the Westminster Assembly." Ph.D. diss., Claremont, 1969.
Emerson, Everett H. "Calvin and Covenant Theology." *Church History* 25 (1956): 136-44.
―――――. *John Cotton*. Boston: Twane, 1990
Encyclopedia Brittanica. "Pensionary." Britannica.com. http://www.britannica.com/EBchecked/topic/450291/pensionary .(Accessed June 18, 2013).
End, G. van der. "Guiljelmus Saldenus." *Theologica Reformata* 12 (1969): 77-90.
Engelberts, Willem J.M. *Willem Teellinck*. Amsterdam: Ton Bolland, 1973.
Erb, Peter C., ed. *Pietists: Selected Writings*. The Classics of Western Spirituality. Ed. Richard J. Payne. New York: Paulist, 1983.
Erickson, Millard J. *Christian Theology*. Grand Rapids: Baker, 1983; reprint ed., 1987.
Etulain, Richard W. Review of *The Marrow of Theology, By William Ames 1576-1633*, trans. John D. Eusden. In *Christian Scholar's Review* 1 (Fall 1970): 60-61.
Eusden, John D. *Puritans, Lawyers, and Politics in Early Seventeenth-Century England*. New Haven: 1958.
―――――. *The Marrow of Theology, William Ames (1576-1633)*. Foreword by Douglas Horton. Translated by John D. Eusden from the 3rd Latin ed., 1629. United Church, 1968; reprint ed., Grand Rapids: Baker, 1997.
Exalto, K. *Beleefd Geloof: Acht schetsen van gereformeerde theologen uit de 17e Eeuw*. Amsterdam: Ton Bolland, 1974.
―――――. *De Kracht der Religie: Tien schetsen van Gereformeerde 'Oude Schrijvers' uit de 17e en 18e Eeuw*. Urk: De Vuurtoren, 1976.
―――――. "Willem Teellinck (1579-1629)." In *De Nadere Reformatie: Beschrijving van haar voornaamste vertegenwoordigers*. Ed. T. Brienen et al. 's-Gravenhage: Boekencentrum, 1986.
Ferguson, Sinclair. "The Westminster Conference, 1976." *The Banner of Truth*, no. 168 (September 1977): 15-22.

_____, David F. Wright and James I. Packer, eds. *New Dictionary of Theology*. Downers Grove, IL: InterVarsity, 1988.

Fieret, W. "Introduction" in *The Christian's Reasonable Service*. Translated by Bartel Elshout. Ed. Joel R. Beeke. 4 vols. Morgan, PA: Soli Deo Gloria Publications, 1992 - 1995.

_____. *Udemans: Facetten uit zijn leven en werk*. Houten, 1985.

Fiering, Norman. *Jonathan Edwards' Moral Thought and its British Context*. Chapel Hill: University of North Carolina, 1981.

_____. *Moral Philosophy at Seventeenth-Century Harvard: A Discipline in Transition*. Chapel Hill: University of North Carolina, 1981.

Florijn, H., ed. *Hollandse Geloofshelden* Utrecht: De Banier, 1981.

Fluent, Mike. "The Marrow of Theology." *Fundamentalist Journal* 5 (July-August 1986): 49-50.

_____. "William Ames, Watchman for Orthodoxy and Purity." *Fundamentalist Journal* 5 (July-August 1986): 47-48.

Foster, Herbert Darling. "Liberal Calvinism: the Remonstrants at the Synod of Dort in 1618." *Harvard Theological Review* 16 (1973): 1-37.

Foxgrover, David. "John Calvin's Understanding of Conscience." Ph.D. diss., Claremont, 1978.

Fulcher, John Rodney. "Puritan Piety in Early New England: A Study in Spiritual Regeneration from the Antinomian Controversy to the Cambridge Synod of 1648 in the Massachusetts Bay Colony." Ph.D. diss., Princeton University, 1963.

Gabbey, A. "Cambridge Platonists." In *Cambridge Dictionary of Philosophy*. Ed. Robert Audi. New York: Cambridge University, 1995.

Galama, Sybrand Haije Michiel. *Het wijsgerig onderwijs aan de Hogeschool te Franeker, 1585-1811*. Franeker: T. Wever, 1954.

Garcia, J.L.A. "Cardinal virtues." In *Cambridge Dictionary of Philosophy*. Ed. Robert Audi. New York: Cambridge University, 1995.

Garrett, Christina H. *The Marian Exiles: A Study in the Origins of Elizabethan Puritanism*. Cambridge: Cambridge University, 1938.

Geesink, W. *Calvinisten in Holland*. Amsterdam, 1887; reprint ed., Genevae: Slatkine Reprints, 1970.

_____. *Gereformeerde Ethiek*. 2 vols. Kampen: J.H. Kok, 1931.

Genderen, J. van. *Herman Witsius: Bijdrage tot de kennis der Gereformeerde Theologie*. 's-Gravenhage: Guido de Brès, 1953.

_____. "Wilhelmus à Brakel (1635-1711)." In *De Nadere Reformatie: Beschrijving van haar voornaamste vertegenwoordigers*. Ed. T. Brienen et al. 's-Gravenhage: Boekencentrum, 1986.

Gent, W. van. *Bibliotheek van oude schrijvers*. Rotterdam: Lindebergs, 1979.

Gerstner, John H. "Theological Boundaries: The Reformed Perspective." In *The Evangelicals: What They Believe, Who They Are, Where They Are Changing*. Rev. ed. Ed. David F. Wells and John D. Woodbridge, 21-37. Grand Rapids: Baker, 1977.

Geyl, Pieter. *The Netherlands in the Seventeenth Century: Part One, 1609-1648*. 2nd ed. New York: Barnes & Noble, 1961.
Gibbs, Lee W. "The Puritan Natural Law Theory of William Ames." *Harvard Theological Review* 64 (1971): 37-57.
Glasius, B. *Geschiedenis der Nationale Synode in 1618 en 1619 gehouden to Dordrecht*. 2 vols. Leiden: E.J. Brill, 1860-61.
_____. *Godgeleerd Nederland: Biographisch Woordenboek van Nederlandsche Godgeleerden*. 3 vols. 's-Hertogenbosch: Gebr. Muller, 1851-56.
Godfrey, W. Robert. "Tensions within International Calvinism: The Debate on the Atonement at the Synod of Dordt, 1618-1619." Ph.D. diss., Stanford University, 1974.
Goen, C.C. "Jonathan Edwards: A New Departure in Eschatology." In *Critical Essays on Jonathan Edwards* by William J. Scheick. Boston: G.K. Hall & Co., 1980.
Goeters, Wilhelm. *Die Vorbereitung des Pietismus in der reformierten Kirche der Niederlande bis zur labadistischen Krisis 1670*. Leipzig: J.C. Hinrichs'sche Buchhandlung, 1911; reprint ed., Amsterdam: Ton Bolland, 1974.
Gordis, Lisa M. *Opening Scripture: Bible Reading and Interpretive Authority in Puritan New England*. Chicago: University of Chicago, 2003.
Gorsel, W. van. *De Ijver voor Zijn Huis: De Nadere Reformatie en haar belangrijkste vertegenwoordigers*. Groede: Pieters, 1981.
Graafland, Cornelis. *De Continuteit en Actualiteit van de Gereformeerde Theologie*. Kampen: Kok, 1972.
_____. "De Gereformeerde Orthodoxie en het Piëtisme in Nederland." *Nederlands Theologisch Tijdschrift* 19 (1965): 466-79.
_____. "De invloed van het Puritanisme op het ontstaan van het Gereformeerde Piëtisme in Nederland." *Documentatieblad Nadere Reformatie* 7 (1983): 1-24.
_____. "De Nadere Reformatie en haar culturele context." In *Met het Woord in de Tijd*. Ed. L. Westland. 's-Gravenhage: Boekencentrum, 1985.
_____. "De Nadere Reformatie en het Labadisme." In *De Nadere Reformatie en het Gereformeerd Piëtisme*. Ed. T. Brienen et al. 's-Gravenhage: Boekencentrum, 1989.
_____. "De toekomstverwachting der Puriteinen en haar invloed op de Nadere Reformatie." *Documentatieblad Nadere Reformatie* 3 (1979): 65-95.
_____. *De Zekerheid van het Geloof: Een onderzoek naar de geloofsbeschouwing van enige vertegenwoordigers van reformatie en nadere reformatie*. Wageningen: H. Veenman en Zonen, 1961.
_____. "De Zekerheid van het Geloof: Een onderzoek naar de geloofbeschouwing van enige vertegenwoordigers van reformatie en nadere reformatie." Th.D. diss., State University of Utrecht, 1961.
_____. "Gereformeerde Scholastiek V: De Invloed van de Scholastiek op de Gereformeerde Orthodoxie." *Theologia Reformata* 30 (1987): 4-25.

_____. "Gereformeerde Scholastiek VI: De Invloed van de Scholastiek op de Nadere Reformatie (1)." *Theologia Reformata* 30 (1987): 109-31.

_____. "Gereformeerde Scholastiek VI: De Invloed van de Scholastiek op de Nadere Reformatie (2)." *Theologia Reformata* 30 (1987): 313-40.

_____. "Het eigene van het Gereformeerd Piëtisme in de 18e eeuw in onderscheid van de 17e eeuw." *Documentatieblad Nadere Reformatie* 11 (1987): 37-53.

_____. "Jodocus van Lodenstein (1620-1676)." In *De Nadere Reformatie: Beschrijving van haar voornaamste vertegenwoordigers*. Ed. T. Brienen et al. 's-Gravenhage: Boekencentrum, 1986.

_____. ""Kernen en contouren van de Nadere Reformatie." In *De Nadere Reformatie: Beschrijving van haar voornaamste vertegenwoordigers*. Ed. T. Brienen et al. 's-Gravenhage: Boekencentrum, 1986.

_____. "Macarius, F.A. Lampe en de Nadere Reformatie (n.a.v.: J.H. van de Bank, Macarius en zijn invloed in de Nederlanden)." *Theologia Reformata* 21 (1978): 56-60.

_____. Nadere Reformatie. G. Voetius, W. à Brakel, J. Verschuir." In *Bij Brood en beker. Leer en gebruik van het heilig avondmaal in het Nieuwe Testament en in de geschiedenis van de westerse kerk*. Ed. W. van 't Spijker et al. Kampen: De Groot Goudrian, 1980.

_____. "Schriftleer en Schriftverstaan in de Nadere Reformatie." In *Theologische aspecten van de Nadere Reformatie*. Ed. T. Brienen et al. Zoetermeer: Boekencentrum, 1993.

_____. *Van Calvijn tot Barth: Oorsprong en ontwikkeling van de leer der verkiezing in het Gereformeerde Protestantisme*. 's-Gravenhage: Boekencentrum, 1987.

_____. *Van Calvijn tot Comrie: Oorsprong en ontwikkeling van de leer van het verbond in het Gereformeerde Protestantisme*. 3 Vols. Zoetermeer: Boekencentrum, 1992-96.

_____. "Van syllogismus practicus naar syllogismus mysticus." In *Wegen en Gestalten in het Gereformeerd Protestantisme*, 105-22. Ed. W. Balke, C. Graafland, and H. Harkema. Amsterdam: Ton Bolland, 1976.

_____. *Ver*antwoord *gereformeerd: Een voortgezet gesprek*. Zoetermeer: Boekencentrum, 1995.

_____, W.J. op 't Hof, F.A. van Lieburg. "Nadere Reformatie: opnieuw een poging tot begrijpsbepaling." *Documentatieblad Nadere Reformatie* 19 (1995): 108.

Graves, Frank P. *Peter Ramus and the Educational Reformation of the Sixteenth Century*. New York: The Macmillan Company, 1912. Text-fiche.

Greaves, Richard L. "John Bunyan and Covenant Thought in the Seventeenth Century." *Church History* 36 (1967): 151-69.

_____. "The Origins and Early Development of English Covenant Thought," *The Historian* 31 (November 1968): 21-35.

Greve, Lionel. "Freedom and Discipline in the Theology of John Calvin, William Perkins, and John Wesley: An Examination of the Origin and Nature of Pietism." Ph.D. diss., The Hartford Seminary Foundation, 1976.
Groenendijk, L.F. "De Oorsprong van de uitdrukking 'Nadere Reformatie.'" *Documentatieblad Nadere Reformatie* 9 (1985): 128-34.
_____. "Jacobus Koelman's actieplan voor de 'Nadere Reformatie.'" *Documentatieblad Nadere Reformatie* 2 (1978): 121-26.
Gustafsson, Berndt. *The Five Dissenting Brethren: A Study of the Dutch Background of Their Independentism.* London: C.W.K. Gloerup, 1955.
Haar, J. van der. *From Abbadie to Young. A bibliographie of English, mostly Puritan Works, Translated i/t Dutch Language.* 2 vols. in 1. Veenendaal: Kool, 1980.
_____. "Nederlandsche theologen onder Engelse puriteinen." *Documentatieblad Nadere Reformatie* 10 (1986): 105-8.
_____. "Puriteinse invloed uit Engeland." *Documentatieblad Nadere Reformatie* 2 (1978): 117-20.
_____. *Schatkamer van de Gereformeerde Theologie in Nederland (c. 1600-1800): Bibliografisch Onderzoek.* Veenendaal: Kool, 1987.
Haley, K.H.P. *The Dutch in the Seventeenth Century.* Norwich, England: Jarrold and Sons Ltd., 1972.
Hall, Basil. "Calvin against the Calvinists." In *John Calvin*, 19-37. Ed. G.E. Duffield. Grand Rapids: Eerdmans, 1966.
_____. "Puritanism: The Problem of Definition." In *Studies in Church History*, vol. 2, 283-96. Ed. G. J. Cumming. London: Nelson, 1965.
Hall, David. *The Faithful Shepherd: A History of the New England Ministry in the Seventeenth Century.* Chapel Hill: University of North Carolina, 1972.
Hall, David W., ed. *The Practice of Confessional Subscription.* Lanham, MD: University Press of America, 1995.
Hamming, R. "Willem Teellinck." *Gereformeerd Theologisch Tijdschrift* 27 (1926-27): 97-115.
Hambrick-Stowe, Charles E. *The Practice of Piety. Puritan Devotional Disciplines in Seventeenth-Century New England.* Williamsburg, VA: University of North Carolina, 1982.
Handy, Robert T. Review of *The Marrow of Theology, By William Ames 1576-1633*, trans. John D. Eusden. In *Union Seminary Quarterly Review* 24 (Fall 1968): 114-15.
Hansen, Maurice G. *The Reformed Church in the Netherlands.* New York: Reformed Church in America, 1884.
Hardy, E.R. Review of *The Marrow of Theology, By William Ames 1576-1633*, trans. John D. Eusden. In *Encounter* 30 (1969): 177.
Harnack, Adolph. *History of Dogma.* Translated from the 3rd German edition by N. Buchanan et al. 7 vols. Boston: Roberts Brothers, 1897.
Haroutunian, Joseph. *Piety versus Moralism.* American Religious Series, No. 4. New York: Henry Holt and Co., 1932.

Harper, George W. "Calvin and English Calvinism to 1649: A Review Article." *Calvin Theological Journal* 20 (1985): 255-62.
Harrison, Graham S. "Jonathan Edwards and the Terms of Admission to Communion." In *The Good Fight of Faith*. Ed. Peter H. Lewis et al. Papers read at the Westminster Conference. Huntingdon, England: London Evangelical, 1971.
Hasler, R.A. "Thomas Shepard: Pastor-Evangelist (1605-1649): A Study in New England Ministry." Ph.D. diss., Hartford Seminary Foundation, 1964.
Hastings, James, ed. *Encyclopedia of Religion and Ethics*. 13 vols. Edinburgh: T.&T. Clark, 1908-26.
Helm, Paul. *Calvin and the Calvinists*. Edinburgh: Banner of Truth Trust, 1982.
_____. "Calvin, English Calvinism and the Logic of Doctrinal Development." *Scottish Journal of Theology* 34 (1981): 179-85.
Heppe, Heinrich. *Die Dogmatik der evangelisch-reformierten Kirche*. Ed. Ernst Bizer. Neukirchen: Kreis Moers, 1958. [*Reformed Dogmatics*. Translated by G.T. Thomson. London: George Allen and Unwin, 1950.]
_____. *Geschichte des Pietismus und der Mystik in der Reformirten Kirche, namentlich der Niederlande*. Leiden: E.J. Brill, 1879.
Heringa, J. "De Twistzaak van den hoogeleeraar Johannes Maccovius, door de Dordrechtsche Synode, ten jare 1619 beslecht." *Archief voor Kerkelijke Geschiedenis, inzonderheid van Nederland* 3 (1831): 503-664.
H.D. Betz et al., eds. *Religion in Geschichte und Gegenwart. Handwörterbuch für Theologie und Religionswissenschaft*. 8 vols. and 1 index vol. 4th ed. Tübingen: Mohr Siebeck Verlag, 1998-2007.
Hesselink, I. John. *On Being Reformed: Distinctive Characteristics and Common Misunderstandings*. Ann Arbor: Servant, 1983.
Hessler, Mark Hunt. "Providence lost: A study of epistemology and religious culture among New England Puritans, 1630-1730." Ph.D. diss., State University of New York, Stony Brook, 1992.
Hetherington, W.M. *History of the Westminster Assembly of Divines*. New York: Robert Carter & Brothers, 1859.
Hindson, Edward, ed. *Introduction to Puritan Theology: A Reader*. Foreword by James I. Packer. Grand Rapids: Baker, 1976.
A History of the Westminster Assembly of Divines, Embracing an Account of its Principal Transactions, and Biographical Sketches of Its Most Conspicuous Members. Philadelphia: Presbyterian Board of Publications, 1841.
Hodge, A.A. *The Confession of Faith*. Philadelphia: Presbyterian Board of Publications, 1869; reprint ed., London: Banner of Truth Trust, 1983.
Hodge, Charles. *Systematic Theology*. 3 vols. Grand Rapids: Eerdmans, nd [1962].
Hoekema, Anthony A. "The Covenant of Grace in Calvin's Teaching." *Calvin Theological Journal* 2 (1967): 133-61.
Hoeksema, Herman. *Reformed Dogmatics*. Grand Rapids: Reformed Free, 1966.

———. *The Triple Knowledge: An Exposition of the Heidelberg Catechism.* 3 vols. Grand Rapids: Reformed Free, 1970.
Hof, Willem Jan op 't. "De Nederlandse vertalers van William Perkins' geschriften voor 1650." *Documentatieblad Nadere Reformatie* 8 (1984): 56-60.
———. *De theologische opvattingen van Willem Teellinck.* Kampen: De Groot Goudriaan, 2011.
———. "De visie op de Reformatie in de Nadere Reformatie tijdens het eerste kwart van de zeventiende eeuw." *Documentatieblad Nadere Reformatie* 6 (1982): 89-108.
——— "Een onbekende zoon van Willem Teellinck." *Documentatieblad Nadere Reformatie* 25 (2001): 84-89.
———. *Engelse piëtistische geschriften in het Nederlands, 1598-1622.* Rotterdam: Lindenberg, 1987.
———. "Gisbertus Voetius' Evaluatie van de Reformatie." *Theologia Reformata* 32 (1989): 211-42.
———. *Het puritanisme. Geschiedenis, theologie en invloed.* Zoetermeer: Boekencentrum, 2001.
———. "Johannes Polyander en Willem Teellinck." *Documentatieblad Nadere Reformatie* 7 (1983) 126-43.
——— "Kennis van hoofd en hart: Dogmatische themas in de Nadere Reformatie." In *Geloofsleer en Geloofs(be)leven in de Nadere Reformatie,* 8-17. 8th Winter Course of the SSNR, 2002-2003.
———. "Taffin, Jean." In *Biografisch Lexicon voor de Geschiedenis van het Nederlandse Protestantisme.* Ed. D. Nauta et al. 5 vols. Kampen: J.H. Kok, 1978-2001.
———. *Voorbereiding en bestrijding.* Kampen: De Groot Goudriaan, 1991.
———. "Willem Teellinck in het licht zijner geschriften." *Documentatieblad Nadere Reformatie* 1 (1977): 3-14, 33-41, 69-76, 105-114; 2 (1978): 1-12, 33-62, 65-88, 97-105; 3 (1979): 33-40, 97-100; 4 (1980): 1-9, 33-38, 97-103; 5 (1981): 1-5, 34, 70-82, 107-108; 6 (1982): 1-4, 37-45; 7 (1983): 25-30, 37-42, 117-25; 8 (1984): 9-17, 37-40, 73-80, 109-113; 9 (1985): 37-42, 73-77, 109-118; 10 (1986): 31-36, 64-66, 73-76.
——— *Willem Teellinck. Leven, geschriften en invloed.* Kampen: De Groot Goudriaan, 2008.
———, C.A. de Niet, and H. Uil. *Eeuwout Teellinck in handschriften.* Kampen: De Groot Goudriaan, 1989.
Hoffecker, W. Andrew. *Piety and the Princeton Theologians. Archibald Alexander, Charles Hodge, and Benjamin Warfield.* Phillipsburg, New Jersey: Presbyterian and Reformed, 1981.
Hoitenga, Jr. Dewey J. *John Calvin and the Will: A Critique and Corrective.* Grand Rapids: Baker, 1997.

Holifield, E. Brooks. *The Covenant Sealed: The Development of Puritan Sacramental Theology in Old and New England, 1570-1720.* New Haven: Yale University, 1974.

Honders, Huibert, Jacob. *Andreas Rivetus als invloedrijk gereformeerd theoloog in Holland's bloeitijd.* 's-Gravenhage: Martinus Nijhoff, 1930.

Howell, Wilbur Samuel. *Logic and Rhetoric in England, 1500-1700.* Princeton: Princeton University, 1956.

Horton, Douglas. "Let Us Not Forget the Mighty William Ames." *Religion in Life* 29 (1960): 434-42.

_____, trans. *William Ames by Matthew Nethenus, Hugo Visscher, and Karl Reuter.* Cambridge: Harvard Divinity School, 1965.

Hsia, R. Po-Chia and Henk van Nierop, eds. *Calvinism and Religious Toleration in the Dutch Golden Age.* Cambridge; Cambridge University, 2002.

Huizinga, Johan H. *Dutch Civilization in the Seventeenth Century.* Translated by Arnold J. Pomerans. London: Collin Sons & Co. Ltd., 1968.

Humphrey, Richard Alan. "The Concept of Conversion in the Theology of Thomas Shepard (1605-1649)." Ph.D. diss., Drew University, 1967.

Isbell, R. Sherman. "The Origin of the Concept of the Covenant of Works." Th.M. thesis, Westminster Theological Seminary, 1976.

Israel, Jonathan I. *Radical Enlightenment: Philosophy and the Making of Modernity, 1650-1750.* Oxford: Oxford University, 2002.

_____. *The Dutch Republic: Its Rise, Greatness, and Fall, 1477-1806.* Oxford: Clarendon, 1995.

Itterzon, G.P. *Franciscus Gomarus.* 's-Gravenhage: Martinus Nijhoff, 1930.

_____. *Het Gereformeerde Leerboek der 17de Eeuw: "Synopsis Purioris Theologiae."* 's-Gravenhage: Martinus Nijhoff, 1931.

_____. *Johannes Bogerman.* Amsterdam: Ton Bolland, 1980.

Janse, L. *Gisbertus Voetius, 1589-1676.* Utrecht: De Banier, 1971.

_____. *Jacobus Koelman, 1632-1695.* Utrecht: De Banier, n.d.

Jensma, G.Th., F.R.H. Smit, and F. Westra, eds. *Universiteit te Franeker: 1585-1811.* Leeuwarden: Fryske Academy, 1985.

Jones, James William, III. "The Beginnings of American Theology: John Cotton, Thomas Hooker, Thomas Shepard and Peter Bulkeley." Ph.D. diss., Brown University, 1970.

Jong, Peter Y. de. ed. *Crisis in the Reformed Churches: Essays in Commemoration of the Great Synod of Dort, 1618-1619.* Grand Rapids: Reformed Fellowship, Inc., 1968.

_____. *The Covenant Idea in New England Theology, 1620-1847.* Grand Rapids: Eerdmans, 1945.

Jonge, Christiaan de. "Franciscus Junius (1545-1602) en de Engelse Separatisten te Amsterdam." *Nederlands Archief voor Kerkgeschiedenis* 59 (1978): 132-59.

Jonker, H. "Reflexen (Gereformeerde scholastiek)." *Theologia Reformata* 30 (1987): 296-307.

Kapic, Kelly M. and Randall C. Gleason, eds. *The Devoted Life: An Invitation to the Puritan Classics*. Downers Grove, IL: InterVarsity, 2004.

Kaajan, H. *De Groote Synode van Dordrecht in 1618-1619*. Amsterdam: N.V. de Standaard, 1918.

Karlberg, Mark W. "Covenant Theology and the Westminster Tradition: A Review Article." *Westminster Theological Journal* 54 (1992): 135-52.

_____. "Reformed Interpretation of the Mosaic Covenant." *Westminster Theological Journal* 43 (1980): 1-57.

Kendall, Robert T. *Calvin and English Calvinism to 1649*. Oxford: Oxford University, 1979.

_____. "Living the Christian Life in the Teaching of William Perkins and His Followers." *Living the Christian Life*, 45-60. London: Westminster Conference, 1974.

_____. "The Puritan Modification of Calvin's Theology." In *John Calvin: His Influence in the Western World*, 199-214. Ed. W. Stanford Reid. Grand Rapids: Zondervan, 1982.

Kirk, Kenneth E. *Conscience and its Problems. An Introduction to Casuistry*. Library of Theological Ethics. Ed. Robin W. Lovin, Douglas F. Ottati, William Schweiker. New ed. Louisville, KY: Westminster, John Knox, 1999.

Kittredge, G.L. "A Note on Dr. William Ames." In *Publications of the Colonial Society of Massachusetts*. Vol. 13. Boston: Colonial Society of Massachusetts, 1910.

Klauber, Martin I. "Continuity and Discontinuity in Post-Reformation Reformed Theology: An Evaluation of the Muller Thesis." *Journal of the Evangelical Theological Society* 33 (1990): 467-75.

_____. "The Use of Philosophy in the Theology of Johannes Maccovius (1588-1644)." *Calvin Theological Journal* 30 (1995): 376-91.

Klunder, Jack D. "The Application of Holy Things: A Study of the Covenant Preaching in the Eighteenth Century Dutch Colonial Church." Ph.D. diss., Westminster Theological Seminary, 1984.

Knappen, Marshall M. *Tudor Puritanism: a Chapter in the History of Idealism*. Gloucester, MA: P. Smith, 1963.

_____, ed. *Two Elizabethan Puritan Diaries*. Chicago: American Society of Church History, 1933.

Knoppers, Laura Lunger, ed. *Puritanism and its Discontents*. Cranberry, NJ: Associated University, 2003.

Knox, R. Bucik, ed. *Reformation, Conformity, and Dissent: Essays in Honour of Geoffrey Nuttall*. London: Epworth, 1977.

Koenigsberger, H.G., George L. Mosse, and G.Q. Bowler. *Europe in the Sixteenth Century*. New York: Longman, 1968; 2nd ed., 1989. 7th printing, 1994.

Krabbendam, Johannes L. *Sharing the Reformed Tradition: the Dutch-North American Exchange, 1846-1996*. Amsterdam: Free University, 1996.

Krahn, C. *Dutch Anabaptism: Origin, Spread, Life and Thought (1450-1600)*. 's-Gravenhage: Boekencentrum, 1968.

Kreeft, P. *A Summa of the Summa*. San Francisco: Ignatius, 1990.
Kromminga, D.H. *The Christian Reformed Tradition: From the Reformation Till the Present*. Grand Rapids: Eerdmans, 1943.
Kromsigt, Johannes Christiaan. *Wilhelmus Schortinghuis. Eene bladzijde uit de geschiedenis van het Pietisme in de Gereformeerde kerk van Nederland*. Groningen: J.B. Wolters, 1904.
Krull, F.A. *Jacobus Koelman: Een kerkhistorische Studie*. Reprint ed., Amsterdam: Ton Bolland, 1972.
Kuiper, B.K. *The Church in History*. Grand Rapids: Eerdmans, 1988.
Kuiper, J. *Geschiedenis van het Godsdienstig en Kerkelijk Leven van het Nederlandsche Volk*. Nijkerek: G.F. Callenbach, 1903.
Kuyper, Abraham, Jr. "Johannes Maccovius." Th.D. diss., Free University of Amsterdam, 1899.
_____. *Johannes Maccovius*. Leiden: D. Donner, 1899.
Laeyendecker, L., L.G. Jansma and C.H.A. Verhaar, eds. *Experiences and Explanations: Historical and Sociological Essays on Religion in Everyday Life*. Leeuwarden: Fryske Akademy: 1990.
Lake, Peter with Michael Questier. *The Anti-Christ's Lewd Hat: Protestants, Papists and Players in Post-Reformation England*. New Haven: Yale University, 2002.
Laman, H.W. *Geloofsbezwaren opgelost door Wilhelmus à Brakel*. Kampen: J.H. Kok, 1929.
Lang, August. *Puritanismus und Pietismus: Studien zu ihrer Entwicklung von M. Butzer bis zum Methodismus*. Beitrage zur Geschichte und Lehre der Reformierten Kirche. Ed. W. Goeters, W. Kolfhaus, A. Lang und O. Weber, vol. 6. Neukirchen: Buchhandlung des Erziehungsvereins Neukirchen Kreis Moers, 1941.
Ledeboer, L.G.C. *Verzamelde Geschriften*. 3 vols. Utrecht: Den Hertog, 1977.
Lee, Brian J. *Johannes Cocceius and the Exegetical Roots of Federal Theology*. Reformed Historical Theology, vol. 7. Gottingen: Vandenhoeck & Ruprecht, 2009.
Lee, Sang Hyun. *The Philosophical Theology of Jonathan Edwards*. Princeton: Princeton University, 1988.
Leith, John H. *Assembly at Westminster: Reformed Theology in the Making*. Richmond: John Knox, 1973.
_____. *Introduction to the Reformed Tradition*. Atlanta: John Knox, 1981.
Lesser, M.X. *Jonathan Edwards: An Annotated Bibliography, 1979-1993*. Bibliographies and Indexes in Religion Studies. No. 30. Westport, CT: Greenwood, 1994.
Letham, Robert W.A. "Reformed Theology." In *New Dictionary of Theology*. Eds. Sinclair Ferguson, David F. Wright and James I. Packer. Downers Grove, IL: InterVarsity, 1988, 569-72.
_____. "The *Foedus Operum*: Some Factors Accounting for its Development." *Sixteenth Century Journal* 14 (1983): 457-67.

Leurdijk, G. "Het begin van de Nadere Reformatie in Holland." *Documentatieblad Nadere Reformatie* 11 (1987): 1-5.

Lewis, Neil. "William of Auvergne." *The Stanford Encyclopedia of Philosophy.* Ed. Edward N. Zalta. Stanford University: Winter 2010 Edition. http://plato.stanford.edu/archives/win2010/entries/william-auvergne/. Accessed June 18, 2013.

Lieberg, F.A. van. *De Nadere Reformatie in Utrecht ten Tijde van Voetius.* Rotterdam: Lindenberg, 1989.

Lillback, Peter A. "Calvin's Covenantal Response to the Anabaptist View of Baptism." In *Christianity and Civilization* 1 (1982): 181-232.

_____. "The Binding of God: Calvin's Role in the Development of Covenant Theology." Ph.D. diss., Westminster Theological Seminary, 1985.

_____. *The Binding of God: Calvin's Role in the Development of Covenant Theology.* Texts and Studies in Reformation and Post-Reformation Thought. Ed. Richard A. Muller. Grand Rapids: Baker, 2001.

_____. "The Continuing Conundrum: Calvin and the Conditionality of the Covenant." *Calvin Theological Journal* 29 (1994): 42-74.

_____. "Ursinus' Development of the Covenant of Creation: A Debt to Melanchthon or Calvin?" *Westminster Theological Journal* 43 (1981): 247-88.

Linde, S. van der. "Calvijn, Calvinisme en Nadere Reformatie." *Documentatieblad Nadere Reformatie* 6 (1982): 73-88.

_____. "De betekenis van de Nadere Reformatie voor Kerk en Theologie." *Kerk en Theologie* 5 (1954): 215-25.

_____. "De Godservaring bij W. Teellinck, D.G. à Brakel en A. Comrie." *Theologia Reformata* 16 (1973): 193-205.

_____. "De Heilige Geest in Reformatie en Nadere Reformatie." In *Leven door de Heilige Geest.* Ed. A. Noordegraaf. Amersfoort: N.p., n.d.

_____. "'De Nadere Reformatie', Een Nieuwe Start." *Theologia Reformata* 29 (1986): 188-97.

_____. "De Prediking van de Nadere Reformatie." *Theologia Reformata* 19 (1976): 6-21.

_____. "Gereformeerde Scholastiek IV: Calvijn." *Theologia Reformata* 29 (1986): 244-66.

_____. "Gisbertus Voetius' Gedachten over de Prediking." *Theologia Reformata* 19 (1976): 256-67.

_____. *Het gereformeerde protestantisme.* Nijkerek: G.F. Callenbach, 1957.

_____. "Het 'Griekse' Denken in Kerk, Theologie en Geloofspraktijk." *Theologia Reformata* 28 (1985): 247-68.

_____. "Het Werk van de Heilige Geest in de gemeente: Een appreciatie van de Nadere Reformatie." *Nederlands Theologisch Tijdschrift* 10 (1956): 1-13.

_____. "Jean Taffin: eerst pleiter voor 'Nadere Reformatie' in Nederland." *Theologia Reformata* 6 (1982): 6-29.

_____. *Jean Taffin: Hofprediker en raadsheer van Willem van Oranje*. Amsterdam: Ton Bolland, 1982.

_____. "Mystiek en bevinding in het Gereformeerde Protestantisme." In *Mystiek en bevinding*. Ed. G. Quispel et al. Kampen: Kok, 1976.

_____. *Opgang en voortgang der reformatie*. Amsterdam: Ton Bolland, 1976.

_____. "Puritanisme en Piëtisme." *Theologia Reformata* 31 (1988): 196-212.

_____. *Vromen en Verlichten: Twee eeuwen Protestantse Geloofsbeleving 1650-1850*. Utrecht: Aartbisschoppelijk Museum Utrecht: 1974.

Lloyd-Jones, D.M. *The Puritans: Their Origins and Successors. Addresses delivered at the Puritan and Westminster Conferences 1959-1978*. Edinburgh: Banner of Truth Trust, 1987.

Lobstein, Paul. *Petrus Ramus als Theologe*. Strassburg: G.F. Schmidts Universitäts-Buchhandlung, 1878.

Logan, Samuel T., Jr. "The Doctrine of Justification in the Theology of Jonathan Edwards." *Westminster Theological Journal* 46 (1984): 26-52.

_____. "Theological Decline in Christian Institutions and the Value of Van Til's Epistemology." *Westminster Theological Journal* (57) 1995: 145-63.

Loon, J.W. van. *Kerkgeschiedenis in Synchronistisch Verband met de Wereldgeschiedenis*. 2nd printing. Amsterdam: Hoveker & Zoon, 1878.

Loonstra, B. *Verkiezing-Verzoening-Verbond. Beschrijving en beoordeling van de leer van het pactum salutis in de gereformeerde theologie*. The Hague: Boekencentrum, 1990.

Los, Frans Johannes. *Wilhelmus à Brakel*. Leiden: G. Los, 1892.

Lovelace, Richard. "Evangelicalism: Recovering a Tradition of Spiritual Depth." *Reformed Journal* 40 (September 1990): 20-25.

_____. *The American Pietism of Cotton Mather*. Grand Rapids: Eerdmans, 1979.

Lowance, Mason I., Jr. "Sacvan Bercovitch and Jonathan Edwards." *Studies in Puritan American Spirituality* 3 (1992): 53-68.

Luthardt, Christopher E. *Geschichte der Christlichen Ethik*. Leipzig, 1893.

MacLear, James F. "The Puritan Party, 1603-1643: A Study in a Lost Reformation." Ph.D. diss., University of Chicago, 1947.

MacMillan, Douglas. "The Connection between 17th Century British and Dutch Calvinism." In *Not by Might nor by Power*, 1988 Westminster Conference Papers, 22-31. Colchester: Christian Design & Print, 1989.

Macauley, George. *Puritan Theology*. 2 volumes. London: James Nisbet & Co., 1872.

Malan, Christian J. *Die Nadere Reformasie*. Potchefstroom: Potchefstroomse Universiteit vir CHO, 1981.

Malone, Dumas, ed. *Dictionary of American Biography*. 20 vols. New York: Charles Scribner's Sons, 1943.

Marest, David D. de. *History and Characteristics of the Reformed Protestant Dutch Church*. 2nd ed. New York: Board of Publications of the Reformed Protestant Dutch Church, 1856.

Markham, Coleman C. "William Perkins' Understanding of the Role of Conscience." Ph.D. diss., Vanderbilt University, 1967.

Marsden, George M. *Jonathan Edwards: A Life*. New Haven & London: Yale University, 2003.

_____. "Perry Miller's Rehabilitation of the Puritans: A Critique." *Church History* 39 (1970): 91-105.

Mather, Cotton. *The Great Works of Christ in America or Magnalia Christi Americana*. 3rd ed., 2 vols. Hartford: Silas Andrus and Son, 1853; reprint ed., Edinburgh: The Banner of Truth Trust, 1979.

McAdoo, H.R. *The Structure of Caroline Moral Theology*. London: Longman's, Green and Co., 1949.

M'Clintock, John and James Strong, eds. *Cyclopaedia of Biblical, Theological and Ecclesiastical Literature*. New York: Harper & Brothers, 1878.

McCoy, Charles S. "Johannes Cocceius: Federal Theologian." *Scottish Journal of Theology* 16 (1963): 352-70.

_____. "The Covenant Theology of Johannes Cocceius." Ph.D. diss., Yale University, 1956.

_____ and J. Wayne Baker. *Fountainhead of Federalism: Heinrich Bullinger and the Covenantal Tradition with a Translation of De testamento seu foedere Dei unico et aeterno (1534) by Heinrich Bullinger*. Louisville, KY: Westminster/John Knox, 1991.

McDermott, Gerald R. *One Holy and Happy Society: The Public Theology of Jonathan Edwards*. University Park, PA: Pennsylvania State University, 1992.

McGiffert, Michael. "From Moses to Adam: the making of the covenant of works (1585-1615)." *Sixteenth Century Journal* 19 (1988): 131-55.

_____. "Grace and works: the rise and division of covenant divinity in Elizabethan Puritanism." *Harvard Theological Review* 75 (1982): 463-502.

_____. *The Paradoxes of Puritan Piety Being the Autobiography and Journal of Thomas Shepard*. Boston: University of Massachusetts, 1972.

_____. "The Perkinsian Moment of Federal Theology." *Calvin Theological Journal* 29 (1994): 117-48

McGrath, Gavin John. "Puritans and the Human Will: Voluntarism within mid-seventeenth century English puritanism as seen in the works of Richard Baxter and John Owen." Ph.D. diss., University of Durham, 1989.

McKee, William Wakefield. "The Idea of Covenant in Early English Puritanism (1580-1643)." Ph.D. diss., Yale University, 1948.

McKim, Donald K. ed. *Major Themes in the Reformed Tradition*. Grand Rapids: Eerdmans, 1992.

_____. "Ramism in William Perkins." Ph.D. diss., University of Pittsburgh, 1980.

_____. *Ramism in William Perkins' Theology*. American University Studies, Series VII, Theology and Religion, no. 15. New York: Peter Lang, 1987.

_____, ed. *Readings in Calvin's Theology*. Grand Rapids: Baker, 1983.

_____, ed. *The Cambridge Companion to John Calvin*. Cambridge: Cambridge University, 2004.

_____. "William Perkins and the Theology of the Covenant." In *Studies of the Church in History*. Ed. Horton M. Davies. Allison Park, PA: Pickwith Publications, 1983, 85-101.

McNeill, John T. "Casuistry in the Puritan Age." *Religion in Life* 12 (1942-43): 76-89.

_____. *Modern Christian Movements*. Philadelphia: Westminster, 1954; reprint ed., New York: Harper & Row, Harper Torchbooks, 1968.

_____, ed. *Readings in Calvin's Theology*. Grand Rapids: Baker, 1983.

_____. *The History and Character of Calvinism*. New York: Oxford University, 1973.

Meertens, P.J. "Godefrides Cornelisz Udemans." *Nederlandsch Archief voor Kerkgeschiedenis* 28 (1936): 65-106.

Merrill, Thomas F., ed. and intro. *William Perkins, 1558-1602. English Puritanist. His Pioneer Works on Casuistry: "A Discourse of Conscience" and "The Whole Treatise of Cases of Conscience."* Nieuwkoop: B. De Graaf, 1966.

Messler, Abraham. *Annals of the American Pulpit*. Ed. William B. Sprague. Vol. 9. New York: Robert Carter & Brothers, 1869; reprint ed., New York: Arno & The New York Times, 1969.

Middlekauff, Robert. *The Mathers: Three Generations of Puritan Intellectuals 1596-1728*. New York: Oxford University, 1971.

Miller, Glenn. "The Rise of Evangelical Calvinism: A Study in Jonathan Edwards and the Puritan Tradition." Th.D. diss., Union Theological Seminary, 1971.

Miller, Perry. *Errand into the Wilderness*. Cambridge: Belknap, 1956.

_____. *Jonathan Edwards*. New York: William Sloane, 1949.

_____. *Orthodoxy in Massachusetts*. Cambridge: Harvard University, 1933; reprint ed., Gloucester, Massachusetts: Peter Smith, 1965.

_____. "'Preparation for Salvation' in Seventeenth-Century New England." *Journal of the History of Ideas* 4 (1943): 253-86.

_____. *Sources for 'The New England Mind: The Seventeenth Century'*. Ed. James Hoopes. Williamsburg, Virginia: The Institute of Early American History and Culture, 1981.

_____. *The Marrow of Puritan Divinity*. Boston: Publications of the Colonial Society of Massachusetts. Vol. 32. 1937.

_____. *The New England Mind: From Colony to Province*. Cambridge: Harvard University, 1953.

_____. *The New England Mind: The Seventeenth Century*. Cambridge: Harvard University, 1939.

Mitchell, Alexander F. *Catechisms of the Second Reformation*. London: James Nisbet & Co., 1886.

———. *The Westminster Assembly, Its History and Standards*. Philadelphia: Presbyterian Board of Publications: 1884.

———, and John Struthers, eds. *Minutes of the Sessions of the Westminster Assembly of Divines*. Edinburgh: William Blackwood and Sons, 1874; reprint ed., Edmonton: Still Waters Revival Books, 1991.

Møller, Jens G. "The Beginnings of Puritan Covenant Theology." *Journal of Ecclesiastical History* 14 (1963): 46-67.

Montgomery, Michael S. *American Puritan Studies: An Annotated Bibliography of Dissertations, 1882-1981*. Bibliographies and Indexes in American History, no. 1. Westport, Connecticut: Greenwood, 1984.

Moore, Susan Hardman. *Pilgrims: New World Settlers and the Call of Home*. London: Yale University, 2007; reprint ed., 2010.

Morgan, Edmund. *The Puritan Dilemma: The Story of John Winthrop*. Boston: Little, Brown and Company, 1958.

———. *Visible Saints*. New York: University, 1963.

Morison, Samuel Eliot. *Harvard College in the Seventeenth Century*. Cambridge: Harvard University, 1936.

———. "Note on the Education of Thomas Parker, of Newbury." In *Publications of the Colonial Society of Massachusetts*. Vol. 28. Boston: Colonial Society of Massachusetts, 1935.

———. *The Founding of Harvard College*. Cambridge: Harvard University, 1935.

———. *The Intellectual Life of New England*. Ithaca: Cornell University, 1956.

Morris, Edward D. *Theology of the Westminster Symbols*. Columbus, Ohio: Champlin, 1900.

Mosse, George L. "Puritan Political Thought and the 'Cases of Conscience'." *Church History* 23 (1954): 109-18.

Motley, John Lothrop. *The Rise of the Dutch Republic*. 3 vols. New York: Harper & Brothers, 1899.

Muller, Richard A. *A Dictionary of Latin and Greek Theological Terms Drawn Principally from Protestant Scholastic Theology*. Grand Rapids: Baker, 1985.

———. *After Calvin: Studies in the Development of a Theological Tradition*. New York: Oxford University, 2003.

———. "Calvin and the "Calvinists": Assessing Continuities and Discontinuities Between the Reformation and Orthodoxy. Part One" *Calvin Theological Journal* 30 (1995): 345-75.

———. "Calvin and the "Calvinists": Assessing Continuities and Discontinuities Between the Reformation and Orthodoxy. Part Two" *Calvin Theological Journal* 31 (1996): 125-60.

_____. *Christ and the Decree: Christology and Predestination in Reformed Theology from Calvin to Perkins*. Durham, NC: Labyrinth, 1986.

_____. "Covenant and Conscience in English Reformed Theology: Three Variations on a 17th Century Theme." *Westminster Theological Journal* 42 (1980): 308-34.

_____. "John Calvin and later Calvinism: the identity of the Reformed tradition." In *The Cambridge Companion to Reformation Theology*. Ed. D.Bagchi and D.C. Steinmetz. New York: Cambridge University, 2004; 3rd printing, 2009, 134-35.

_____. Mullinger, James Bass. *The University of Cambridge*. 3 vols. Cambridge: Cambridge University, 1873-1911.

_____. "Perkins' *A Golden Chaine*: Predestinarian System or Schematized *Ordo Salutis*?" *Sixteenth Century Journal* 9 (1978): 69-81.

_____. *Post-Reformation Reformed Dogmatics: The Rise and Development of Reformed Orthodoxy, ca. 1520 to ca. 1725*. Vol. 1. 2nd ed. Grand Rapids: Baker, 2003.

_____. "Scholasticism and Orthodoxy in the Reformed Tradition: An Attempt at Definition." Inaugural Address. Grand Rapids: Calvin Theological Seminary, 1995.

_____. "The Covenant of Works and the Stability of Divine Law in Seventeenth-Century Reformed Orthodoxy: A Study in the Theology of Herman Witsius and Wilhelmus à Brakel." *Calvin Theological Journal* 29 (1994): 75-100.

_____. "The Federal Motif in Seventeenth Century Arminian Theology." *Nederlands Archief voor Kerkgeschiedenis* 62 (1982): 102-22.

_____. "The Myth of 'Decretal Theology'." *Calvin Theological Journal* 30 (1995): 159-67.

_____. *The Unaccommodated Calvin: Studies in the Foundation of a Theological Tradition*. New York: Oxford University, 2000.

Munson, Charles Robert. "William Perkins Theologian of Transition." Ph.D. diss., Case Western Reserve University, 1971.

Murdock, Kenneth B. *Increase Mather: the Foremost American Puritan*. Cambridge: Harvard University, 1925.

_____. *Literature and Theology in Colonial New England*. Cambridge: Harvard University, 1949.

Murray, Iain H. *Jonathan Edwards: A New Biography*. Edinburgh: Banner of Truth Trust, 1987; reprint ed., 1996.

_____. *Revival and Revivalism: The Making and Marring of American Evangelicalism: 1750-1858*. Edinburgh: Banner of Truth Trust, 1994.

_____. *The Puritan Hope*. London: Banner of Truth Trust, 1971.

Murray, John. "Covenant Theology." *The Encyclopedia of Christianity*. Vol. 3: 199-216. Ed. Philip E. Hughes. Marshallton, Delaware: National Foundation for Christian Education, 1972.

_____. *Principles of Conduct*. Grand Rapids: Eerdmans, 1957; reprint ed., 1994.

Nauta, D. *De Nederlandsche Gereformeerden en het Independentisme in de zeventiende eeuwe*. Amsterdam: H.J. Paris, 1935.

_____. *Het Calvinisme in Nederland*. Franeker: Wever, 1949.

_____ et al., eds. *Biografisch Lexicon voor de Geschiedenis van het Nederlandse Protestantisme*. 5 vols. Kampen: J.H. Kok, 1978-2001.

Neal, Daniel. *The History of the Puritans; or, Protestant Nonconformists; from the Reformation in 1517, to the Revolution in 1688*. 3 vols. London: Thomas Tegg and Son, 1837; reprint ed., Minneapolis: Klock & Klock, 1979.

Neele, Adriaan C. *Petrus van Mastricht (1630-1706): Reformed Orthodoxy: Method and Piety*. Brill's Series in Church History, Wim Janse, ed. Leiden: Brill, 2009.

_____. *The Art of Living to God: A Study of Method and Piety in the* Theoretico-Practica Theologia *of Petrus van Mastricht (1630-1706)*. Perspectives on Christianity Series, no. 8, vol. 1. Pretoria: University of Pretoria, 2005.

Nichols, J. and W.R. Bagnall, trans. *The Works of James Arminius*. 3 vols. London: Printed for Longman, Hurst, Rees, Orme, Brown and Green, 1825-28; reprint ed., Grand Rapids: Baker, 1956.

Niet, C.A. de. *Gijsbertus Voetius. De Praktijk der Godzaligheid*. 2 Vols. Utrecht: De Banier, 1996.

Nobbs, Douglas. *Theocracy and Toleration: A Study in the Disputes in Dutch Calvinism from 1600-1650*. Cambridge: Cambridge University, 1938.

Noll, Mark. *A History of Christianity in the United States and Canada*. Grand Rapids: Eerdmans, 1992.

Noordegraaf, A., ed. *Leven door de Heilige Geest*. Amersfoort: N.p., n.d.

Norton, Arthur Orlo. "Harvard Text-Books and Reference Books of the Seventeenth Century." In *Publications of the Colonial Society of Massachusetts*. Vol. 28. Boston: Colonial Society of Massachusetts, 1935.

Nuttall, Geoffrey F. "English Dissenters in the Netherlands, 1640-1689." *Nederlands Archief voor Kerkgeschiedenis* 59 (1978): 37-54.

_____. *Visible Saints: The Congregational Way, 1640-1660*. Oxford: Basil Blackwell, 1957.

Oberman, Heiko A. *Forerunners of the Reformation: The Shape of Late Medieval Thought Illustrated by Key Documents*. New York: Holt, Rhinehart and Winston, 1966; reprint ed., Philadelphia: Fortress, 1981.

_____. *The Dawn of the Reformation: Essays in Late Medieval and Early Reformation Thought*. Edinburgh: T.&T. Clark, 1986; reprint ed., Grand Rapids: Eerdmans, 1992.

_____. *The Harvest of Medieval Theology: Gabriel Biel and Late Medieval Nominalism*. Grand Rapids: Eerdmans, 1967.

Oki, Hideo. "Ethics in Seventeenth Century English Puritanism." Ph.D. diss., Union Theological Seminary, 1960.

Ong, S.J., Walter J. *Ramus, Method, and the Decay of Dialogue*. Cambridge: Harvard University, 1958.

Orme, William. *The Life and Times of Richard Baxter*. 2 vols. London: James Duncan, 1830.

Oort, J. van. *De Kerkvaders en Reformatie en Nadere Reformatie*. Zoetermeer: Boekencentrum, 1997.

Osterhaven, M. Eugene. "Calvin on the Covenant." *Reformed Review* 33 (1980): 136-49. Reprinted in *Readings in Calvin's Theology*. Ed. Donald K. McKim. Grand Rapids: Baker, 1983.

_____. "The Experiential Theology of Early Dutch Calvinism." *Reformed Review* 27 (1974): 180-89.

_____. *The Spirit of the Reformed Tradition*. Grand Rapids: Eerdmans, 1970.

Ozment, Steven. *Protestants: The Birth of a Revolution*. New York: Doubleday, 1993.

_____, ed. *Reformation Europe: A Guide to Research*. St. Louis: Center for Reformed Research, 1982.

_____. *The Age of Reform 1250-1550: An Intellectual and Religious History of Late Medieval and Reformation Europe*. New Haven: Yale University, 1980.

Packer, James I. "Jonathan Edwards and Revival." In *A Quest for Godliness: The Puritan Vision of the Christian Life*. Wheaton: Crossway Books, 1990.

Parker, David L. "Petrus Ramus and the Puritans: The 'Logic' of Preparationist Conversion Doctrine." *Early American Literature* 8 (1973): 140-62.

_____. "The Application of Humiliation: Ramist Logic and the Rise of Preparationism in New England." Ph.D. diss., University of Pennsylvania, 1972.

Parker, T.H.L. *The Doctrine of the Knowledge of God, A Study of the Theology of John Calvin*. Edinburgh and London, 1952.

Partee, Charles. *The Theology of John Calvin*. Louisville, KY: Westminster John Knox, 2008.

Paul, Robert S. *The Assembly of the Lord: Politics and Religion in the Westminster Assembly and the Grand Debate*. Edinburgh: T.&T. Clark: 1985.

Peile, John. *Biographical Register of Christ's College, 1505-1905 and of the Earlier Foundation, God's House, 1448-1505*. 2 vols. Cambridge: Cambridge University, 1910-1913.

_____. *Christ's College*. London, 1900.

Pelkonen, J.P. "The Teaching of John Calvin on the Nature and Function of Conscience." *Lutheran Quarterly* 21 (1969): 24-88.

Pederson, Randall J. "Puritan Studies in the Twenty-First Century: Preambles and Projections." *Puritan Reformed Journal* 2:2 (2010): 106-20.

Phillips, James M. "Between Conscience and the Law: The Ethics of Richard Baxter (1615-1691)." Ph.D. diss., Princeton University, 1959.

Pickell, Charles N. "The Freedom of the Will in William Ames and Jonathan Edwards." *Gordon Review* 5 (1959): 168-74.

Pincus, Steven C.A. *Protestantism and Patriotism: Ideologies and the making of English foreign policy, 1650-1668.* Cambridge: University of Cambridge, 1996.

Pipa, Joseph A. Jr. "William Perkins and the Development of Puritan Preaching." Ph.D. diss., Westminster Theological Seminary, 1985.

Plantinga, A., ed. *Faith and Philosophy: Philosophical Studies in Religion and Ethics.* Grand Rapids: Eerdmans, 1964.

Platt, John. *Reformed Thought and Scholasticism: The Arguments for the Existence of God in Dutch Theology, 1575-1650.* Studies in the History of Christian Thought. Ed. Heiko A. Oberman, no. 29. Leiden: E.J. Brill, 1982.

Plooij, D. *The Pilgrim Fathers from a Dutch Point of View.* New York: New York University, 1932.

Pointer, Steven R. "The Emmanuel College, Cambridge, Election of 1622: The Constraints of a Puritan Institution." In *Puritanism and its Discontents.* Ed. Laura Lunger Knoppers. Cranberry, NJ: Associated University, 2003.

Porter, H.C. *Puritanism in Tudor England.* New York: MacMillan Co., 1970.

_____. *Reformation and Reaction in Tudor Cambridge.* London: Cambridge University 1958.

Prak, Maarten. *The Dutch Republic in the Seventeenth Century: The Golden Age.* Translated by Diane Webb. Cambridge: Cambridge University, 2005; reprint ed., 2008.

Price, J.L. *Holland and the Dutch Republic in the Seventeenth Century: The Politics of Particularism.* Oxford: Clarendon, 1992.

Prestwich, Menna, ed. *International Calvinism 1541-1715.* Oxford: Clarendon, 1985.

Priebe, Victor Lewis. "The Covenant Theology of William Perkins." Ph.D. diss., Drew University, 1967.

Price, J.L. *Holland and the Dutch Republic in the Seventeenth Century: The Politics of Particularism.* Oxford: Clarendon, 1992.

Prins, P. *Het Geweten: Een Exegetisch-Historisch-Dogmatisch Onderzoek.* Delft: Naamlooze Vennootschap W.D. Meinema, 1937.

Prozesky, Martin H. "The Emergence of Dutch Pietism." *Journal of Ecclesiastical History* 28 (1977): 29-37.

Ramsey, Paul. "Jonathan Edwards and the Splendor of Common Morality." *This World* 25 (1989): 5-25.

Reid, James. *Memoirs of the Lives and Writings of Those Eminent Divines who Convened in the Famous Assembly at Westminster in the Seventeenth Century.* 2 vols. Paisley: Stephen and Andrew Young, 1811; reprint ed., Edinburgh: Banner of Truth Trust, 1982.

Reid, W. Stanford, ed. *John Calvin: His Influence in the Western World.* Grand Rapids: Zondervan, 1982.

Reuter, Karl. *Wilhelm Amesius: der führende Theologe des erwachsenden reformierten Pietismus*. Neukirchen, Kreis Moers: Buchhandlung des Erziehungsvereins, 1940. [Translated by Douglas Horton as *William Ames: The Leading Theologian in the Awakening of Reformed Pietism* in *William Ames by Matthew Nethenus, Hugo Visscher, and Karl Reuter*. Cambridge: Harvard Divinity School Library, 1965.]

Rhoades, Donald Hosea. "Jonathan Edwards: Experimental Theologian." Ph.D. diss., Yale University, 1945.

Ridderbos, Jan. *De Theologie van Jonathan Edwards*. Den Haag: Johann A. Nederbragt, 1907.

Ritschl, Albrecht B. *Geschichte des Pietismus in der reformirten Kirche*. 3 vols. Bonn: Marcus, 1880-86.

Ritter, Joachim et al., eds. *Historisches Wörterbuch der Philosophie*. 13 vols. Basel: Schwabe, 1971-2007.

Robinson, Charles F. and Robin Robinson. "Three Early Massachusetts Libraries." In *Publications of the Colonial Society of Massachusetts*. Vol. 28. Boston: Colonial Society of Massachusetts, 1935.

Robinson, Hastings, ed. *Original Letters Relative to the English Reformation, 1531-1558, Chiefly from the Archives of Zurich*. 2 vols. For the Parker Society. Cambridge: Cambridge University, 1846-47.

Robinson, John. *The Works of John Robinson, Pastor of the Pilgrim Fathers*. Ed. Robert Ashton. 3 vols. London: John Snow, 1851.

Robinson, Lewis Milton. "A History of the Half-Way Covenant." Ph.D. diss., University of Illinois, 1963.

Rohr, John von. "Covenant and Assurance in Early English Puritanism." *Church History* 34 (1965): 195-203.

_____. *The Covenant of Grace in Puritan Thought*. American Academy of Religion, Studies in Religion. Ed. Charley Hardwick and James O. Duke. No. 45. Atlanta: Scholars, 1986.

_____. "The Covenant of Grace in Puritan Thought." *Journal of Religion* 68 (1988): 111-12.

Rose, Elliot. *Cases of Conscience*. Cambridge: Cambridge University, 1975.

Ryken, Leland. *Worldly Saints: The Puritans As They Really Were*. Grand Rapids: Zondervan, 1986; reprint ed., 1990.

Rutman, Darrett B. *Winthrop's Boston: Portrait of a Puritan Town, 1630-1649*. Chapel Hill: University of North Carolina, 1965.

Schafer, Thomas A. "Jonathan Edward's Conception of the Church." *Church History* 24 (1955): 51-66.

Schaff, P. *The Creeds of Christendom, with a History and Critical Notes*. 3 vols. New York: Harper and Brothers, 1877-78.

Schama, Simon. *The Embarassment of Riches: An Interpretation of Dutch Culture in the Golden Age*. London: William Collins & Sons, 1987.

Scheick, William J. "The Grand Design: Jonathan Edwards' *History of the Work of Redemption.*" In *Critical Essays on Jonathan Edwards*. Boston: G.K. Hall & Co., 1980.

Schurman, Anna Maria van. *Whether a Christian Woman Should be Educated and other Writings from her Intellectual Circle*. Edited and translated by Joyce L. Irwin. Chicago: University of Chicago, 1998.

Schweizer, Alexander. "Die Entwickelung des Moralsystems in der Reformirten Kirche," *Theologische Studien und Kritiken*. Zurich, 1850.

Scott, Thomas, trans. and ed. *The Articles of the Synod of Dort, and its Rejection of Errors: with the History of Events which made way for that Synod*. Utica: William Williams, 1831.

Seybolt, Robert Francis. "Student Libraries at Harvard, 1763-1764." In *Publications of the Colonial Society of Massachusetts*. Vol. 28. Boston: Colonial Society of Massachusetts, 1935.

Shaw, Mark R. "The Marrow of Practical Divinity: A Study in the Theology of William Perkins." Th.D. diss., Westminster Theological Seminary, 1981.

Slagboom, D. *Jodocus van Lodensteyn*. Utrecht, 1966.

Smith, Christopher R. "Postmillennialism and the Work of Renewal in the Theology of Jonathan Edwards." Ph.D. diss., Boston College, 1992.

Smith, David H. "Introduction" in *Conscience and Its Problems: An Introduction to Casuistry*. By Kenneth E. Kirk. Library of Theological Ethics. Ed. Robin W. Lovin, Douglas F. Ottati, William Schweiker. New ed. Louisville, KY: Westminster, John Knox, 1999.

Smith, John E. "A Treatise Concerning Religious Affections, in Three Parts; by Jonathan Edwards, A.M., 1746." *American Presbyterians* 66 (1988): 219-22.

_____. "Jonathan Edwards: Piety and its Fruits." In *The Return of Scripture in Judaism and Christianity*. Ed. P. Ochs. New York: Paulist, 1993.

_____. *Jonathan Edwards: Puritan, Preacher, Philosopher*. London: Geoffrey Chapman, 1992.

_____. "Testing the Spirits: Jonathan Edwards and the Religious Affections." *Union Seminary Quarterly Review* 37 (1981-1982): 27-37.

Smithen, Frederick J. *Continental Protestantism and the English Reformation*. London: J. Clarke & Co., 1927.

Sommerville, C.J. "Conversion versus the Early Puritan Covenant of Grace." *Journal of Presbyterian History*, 44 (1966): 178-97.

Song, Young Jae Timothy. "System and Piety in the Federal Theology of William Perkins and John Preston." Ph.D. diss., Westminster Theological Seminary, 1998.

Spijker, W. van 't et al., eds. *De Nadere Reformatie en het Gereformeerde Piëtisme*. 's-Gravenhage: Boekencentrum, 1989.

_____ et al., eds. *De Synode van Dordrecht in 1618 en 1619*. Houten: Den Hertog, 1987, 1994.

_____. "Experientia in reformatorisch licht." *Theologia Reformata* 19 (1976): 236-55.
_____. "Gereformeerde Scholastiek II: Scholastiek, Erasmus, Luther, Melanchthon." *Theologia Reformata* 29 (1986): 7-27.
_____. "Gereformeerde Scholastiek III: Zwingli en Bucer." *Theologia Reformata* 29 (1986): 136-60.
_____. "Gisbertus Voetius (1589-1676)." In *De Nadere Reformatie: Beschrijving van haar voornaamste vertegenwoordigers*. Ed. T. Brienen et al. 's-Gravenhage: Boekencentrum, 1986.
_____. "Guilelmus Amesius (1576-1633)." In *De Nadere Reformatie en het Gereformeerd Piëtisme*. Ed. T Brienen et al. 's-Gravenhage: Boekencentrum, 1989.
_____. "Teellinck's Opvatting van de menselijke wil." *Theologia Reformata* 7 (1964): 125-42.
_____. *Vroomheid en wetenschap bij Voetius*. Apeldoorn: Theologische Universiteit, 1998.
Spitz, Lewis W., ed. *The Reformation: Basic Interpretations*. Lexington/Toronto: D. C. Heath and Company, 1962; reprint ed., 1972.
Sprunger, Keith L. "Ames, Ramus, and the Method of Puritan Theology." *Harvard Theological Review* 59 (1966): 133-51.
_____."Ames, William (1576-1633)." *Oxford Dictionary of National Biography*. Ed. H.C.G. Matthew and Brian Harrison. Vol. 1. Oxford: Oxford University, 2004
_____. *Dutch Puritanism: A History of English and Scottish Churches of the Netherlands in the Sixteenth and Seventeenth Centuries*. Studies in the History of Christian Thought. Ed. Heiko A. Oberman, no. 31. Leiden: E.J. Brill, 1982.
_____. "Other Pilgrims in Leiden: Hugh Goodyear and the English Reformed Church." *Church History* 41 (1972): 46-60.
_____. Review of *Technometry by William Ames*, edited and translated by Lee W. Gibbs. In *Fides et Historia* 12 (1979): 108-9.
_____. "Technometria: A Prologue to Puritan Theology." *Journal of the History of Ideas* 29 (1968): 115-22.
_____. "The Dutch Career of Thomas Hooker." *New England Quarterly* 46 (1973): 17-44.
_____. *The Learned Doctor William Ames: Dutch Backgrounds of English and American Puritanism*. Chicago: University of Illinois, 1972.
_____. *Trumpets from the Tower: English Puritan Printing in the Netherlands, 1600-1640*. Brill's Studies in Intellectual History. Ed. A.J. Vanderjagt, no. 46. Leiden: E.J. Brill, 1994.
_____. "William Ames, A Seventeenth-Century Puritan, Looks at the Anabaptists." *The Mennonite Quarterly Review* 39 (1965): 72-74.

———. "William Ames and the Franeker link to English and American Puritanism." *Universiteit te Franeker: 1585-1811*. Ed. G.Th. Jensma, F.R.H. Smit, F. Westra. Leeuwarden: Fryske Academy, 1985.

———. "William Ames and the Settlement of Massachusetts Bay." *New England Quarterly* 39 (1966): 66-79.

Squires, William Harder. *The Edwardean: A Quarterly Devoted to the History of Thought in America*. Studies in American Religion, no. 56. Lewiston, NY: Edwin Mellen, 1991.

Staehelin, Ernst. *Amandus Polanus von Polandsdorf*. Studien zur Geschichte der Wissenschaften in Basel, no. 1. Basel: Helbing & Lichtenhahn, 1955.

Stearns, Raymond P. *Congregationalism in the Dutch Netherlands: The Rise and Fall of the English Congregational Classis, 1621-1635*. Chicago: The American Society of Church History, 1940.

———. *The Strenuous Puritan: Hugh Peter, 1598-1660*. Urbana, IL: University of Illinois, 1954.

Steenblok, C. *Gisbertus Voetius, zijn leven en werken*. 2nd ed. Gouda: Gereformeerde Pers, 1976.

———. *Voet en de Sabbat*. Gouda: Gereformeerde Pers, 1975.

Stein, Stephen J. "A Notebook on the Apocalypse." In *Critical Essays on Jonathan Edwards* by William J. Scheick. Boston: G.K. Hall & Co., 1980.

———, ed. *The Cambridge Companion to Jonathan Edwards*. New York: Cambridge University, 2007.

Stephen, Sir Leslie and Sir Sidney Lee, eds. *The Dictionary of National Biography*. 22 vols. London: Oxford University, 1949-50.

Steven, William. *The History of the Scottish Church, Rotterdam*. Edinburgh: Wangh & Innes, 1883.

Stichting Studie der Nadere Reformatie (SSNR). *Geloofsleer en Geloofs(be)leven in de Nadere Reformatie*, 8-17. 8th Winter Course of the SSNR, 2002-2003.

Stob, Henry. "The Ethics of Jonathan Edwards." In *Faith and Philosophy: Philosophical Studies in Religion and Ethics*. Ed. A. Plantinga. Grand Rapids: Eerdmans, 1964.

Stoeffler, F. Ernest. ed. *Continental Pietism and Early American Christianity*. Grand Rapids: Eerdmans, 1976.

———. *German Pietism During the Eighteenth Century*. Studies in the History of Religions, no. 24. Leiden: E.J. Brill, 1973.

———. *The Rise of Evangelical Pietism*. Studies in the History of Religions, no. 9. Leiden: E.J. Brill, 1965.

Stoever, William K.B. *'A Faire and Easie Way to Heaven': Covenant Theology and Antinomianism in Early Massachusetts*. Middletown, Connecticut: Wesleyan University, 1978.

Stone, Lawrence. *Broken Lives: Separation and Divorce in England, 1660-1857*. Oxford: Oxford University, 1993.

_____. *Road to Divorce: England, 1530-1987*. Oxford: Oxford University, 1990.

_____. *The Causes of the English Revolution 1529-1642*. London: Routledge & Kegan Paul Ltd., 1972; reprint ed., London: New York: Harper & Row, 1972.

_____. *The Family, Sex and Marriage in England*. New York: Harper & Row, 1979.

_____. *Uncertain Unions: Marriage in England, 1660-1753*. Oxford: Oxford University, 1992.

Stout, Harry. *The New England Soul: Preaching and Religious Culture in Colonial New England*. New York: Oxford, 1986.

_____ and Nathan O. Hatch, eds. *Jonathan Edwards and the American Experience*. New York: Oxford University, 1988.

Stoute, Douglas Andrew. "The Origins and Early Development of the Reformed Idea of the Covenant." Ph.D. diss., Cambridge University, 1979.

Strehle, Stephen. *Calvinism, Federalism, and Scholasticism: A Study of the Reformed Doctrine of Covenant*. Basler und Berner Studien zur historischen und systematischen Theologie, Band 58. New York: Peter Lang, 1988.

Sweet, William Warren. *Religion in Colonial America*. New York: Charles Scribner's Sons, 1942.

Tanis, James. *Dutch Calvinistic Pietism in the Middle Colonies. A Study in the Life and Theology of Theodorus Jacobus Frelinghuysen*. The Hague: Martinus Nijhoff, 1967.

_____. "Reformed Pietism and Protestant Missions." *Harvard Theological Review* 67 (1974): 65-80.

_____. "The Heidelberg Catechism in the Hands of the Calvinistic Pietists." *Reformed Review* 24 (1970-71): 154-61.

Thomas, Keith. "Cases of Conscience in Seventeenth-Century England." In *Public Duty and Private Conscience in Seventeenth-Century England*. Ed. John Morrill, Paul Slack, and Daniel Woolf. Oxford: Oxford University, 1993.

Thompson, Bard et al. *Essays on the Heidelberg Catechism*. Philadelphia: United Church, 1963.

Tichelaar, J.J. "De functie van de praedestinatie in de theologie van Calvijn en Brakel." *Theologia Reformata* 1 (1958): 171-88.

Todd, Margo. "Justifying God: The Calvinisms of the British Delegation to the Synod of Dordt." *Archiv for Reformation History* 96 (2005): 272-90.

_____. "Providence, Chance, and the New Science in Early Stuart Cambridge." *The Historical Journal* 29 (1986): 697-711.

Toon, Peter. *The Emergence of Hyper-Calvinism in English Nonconformity, 1689-1765*. London: The Olive Tree, 1967.

Torrance, James B. "Calvin and Puritanism in England and Scotland - Some Basic Concepts in the Development of 'Federal Theology.'" In *Calvinus Reformator: His Contribution to Theology, Church, and Society*.

Potchefstroom: Potchefstroom University for Higher Education, 1982, 264-77.

———. "Covenant or Contract? A Study of the Theological Background of Worship in Seventeenth-Century Scotland." *Scottish Journal of Theology* 23 (1970): 51-76.

Trevor-Roper, H.R. *Archbishop Laud, 1573-1645*. 2nd ed. London: MacMillan, 1940.

Trimp, J.C. *Jodocus van Lodensteyn, Predicant en dichter*. Kampen: Kok, 1987.

Trinterud, Leonard J. *Biography of Colonial American Presbyterianism*. Philadelphia: Presbyterian Historical Society, 1968.

———, ed. *Elizabethan Puritanism*. New York: Oxford University, 1971.

———. *The Forming of an American Tradition. A Re-examination of Colonial Presbyterianism*. Philadelphia: Westminster, 1949.

———. "The Origins of Puritanism." *Church History* 20 (1951): 37-57.

Trueman, Carl R. "Calvin and Calvinism," in *The Cambridge Companion to John Calvin*. Ed. Donald K. McKim. Cambridge: University of Cambridge, 2004.

——— and R.S. Clark, eds. *Protestant Scholasticism: Essays in Reassessment*. Carlisle, Cumbria: Paternoster, 1999.

Tufft, J.R. "William Perkins, 1558-1602." Ph.D. diss., University of Edinburgh, 1952.

Tukker, C.A. "The Recruitment and Training of Protestant Ministers in the Netherlands in the 16th Century." In *Miscellanea Historiae Ecclesiasticae*, vol. 3. Louvain, 1970.

Tuttle, Julius H. "Library of Dr. William Ames." In *Publications of the Colonial Society of Massachusetts*. Vol. 19 Boston: Colonial Society of Massachusetts, 1911.

Tuuk, H. Edema van der. *Johannes Bogerman*. Groningen: J.B. Walters, 1868.

Veen, Sietse Douwes van. *Voor tweehonderd jaren. Schetsen van het leven onzer Gereformeerde Vaderen*. 2nd ed. Utrecht: Kemink & Zoon, 1905.

Veninga, James Frank. "Covenant Thought and Ethics in the Thought of John Calvin and John Preston." Ph.D., diss., Rice University, 1974.

Verbeek, Theo. *Descartes and the Dutch: Early Reactions to Cartesian Philosophy, 1637-1650*. Carbondale and Edwardsville: Southern Illinois University, 1992.

Verboom, W. *De Catechese van de Reformatie en de Nadere Reformatie*. Amsterdam: Buijten en Schipperheijn, 1986.

———. *De Theologie van de Heidelbergse Catechismus. Twaalf Themas: De Context en de Latere Uitwerking*. Zoetermeer: Boekencentrum, 1996.

Verschoor, J. "Het Geloof bij Brakel en Comrie." *Onder Eigen Vaandel*. 3 (1928): 272-94.

Visscher, Hugo. *Guilielmus Amesius, Zijn leven en werken*. Haarlem: J.M. Stap, 1894. [Translated by Tjaard Georg Hommes and Douglas Horton as *William*

Ames: His Life and Works in *William Ames by Matthew Nethenus, Hugo Visscher, and Karl Reuter*. Cambridge: Harvard Divinity School Library, 1965.]

Visser, H.B. *De Geschiedenis van den Sabbatstrijd onder de Gereformeerden in de Zeventiende Eeuw*. Utrecht: Kemink en Zoon, 1939.

Vliet, Jan van. "Decretal Theology and the Development of Covenant Thought: An Assessment of Cornelis Graafland's Thesis with a Particular View to Federal Architects William Ames and Johannes Cocceius." *Westminster Theological Journal* 63 (2001): 393-420.

_____. "Gambling on Faith: A Holistic Examination of Blaise Pascal's *Wager*." *Westminster Theological Journal* 62 (2000): 33-63.

_____. "Leven voor God in geloof en plichten: De invloed van William Ames op de ontwikkeling van de traditie van de Nadere Reformatie." *Documentatieblad Nadere Reformatie* 29 (2005): 124-54. Translated by I. den Dekker.

Vogelaar, Case. "Bernardus Smytegelt." *The Banner of Truth* 53 (1987): 210-11.

_____. "Father Brakel." *The Banner of Truth* 53 (1987): 66-67.

_____. "Gisbertus Voetius." *The Banner of Truth* 52 (1986): 262-63; 55 (1989): 182-83.

_____. "Johannes Beukelman." *The Banner of Truth* 53 (1987): 264-65.

_____. "Pioneers of the Second Reformation." *The Banner of Truth* 52 (1986): 150-51.

_____. "The Second or 'Further' Reformation." *The Banner of Truth* 52 (1986): 40-41.

Vos, A. "Aristotelianism." In *New Dictionary of Theology*. Eds. Sinclair Ferguson, David F. Wright and James I. Packer. Downers Grove, IL: InterVarsity, 1988, 43-45.

_____. "Scholasticism." In *New Dictionary of Theology*. Eds. Sinclair Ferguson, David F. Wright and James I. Packer. Downers Grove, IL: InterVarsity, 1988, 621-23.

Vos, Geerhardus. *Biblical Theology. Old and New Testaments*. Grand Rapids: Eerdmans, 1948; reprint ed., Edinburgh: Banner of Truth, 1992.

_____. "The Doctrine of the Covenant in Reformed Theology." In *Redemptive History and Biblical Interpretation: The Shorter Writings of Geerhardus Vos*, 234-70. Ed. Richard B. Gaffin, Jr. Phillipsburg, New Jersey, Presbyterian and Reformed, 1980.

Vrijer, Marinus Johannes Antonie de. *Ds. Bernardus Smytegelt en zijn "gerookte riet."* Amsterdam: H. J. Spruyt, 1947.

Waddington, Charles Tzaunt. *Ramus (Pierre de la Ramée) sa vie, ses écrits et ses opinions*. Paris: Librairie de Ch. Meyrueis et Ce, Éditeurs, 1855; reprint ed., Dubuque, Iowa: W.C. Brown, n.d.

Wakefield, Gordon S. *Puritan Devotion: Its Place in the Development of Christian Piety*. London: Epworth, 1957.

Walker, Williston. *Ten New England Leaders*. New York: Silver, Burdette and Co., 1901.

_____, ed. *The Creeds and Platforms of Congregationalism*. New York: Charles Scribner's Sons, 1893.

_____ et al., eds. *A History of the Christian Church*. 4th ed. New York: Charles Scribner's Sons, 1985.

Wallmann, Johannes. *Philipp Jakob Spener und die Anfänge des Pietismus*. Tübingen: Mohr Siebeck, 1970.

Walton, R.C. "The Visible Church: A Mixed Body or a Gathered Church of Visible Saints. John Calvin and William Ames." In *Calvin: Erbe und Auftrug*. Ed. Willem van 't Spijker. Den Haag: Koninklijke Bibliotheek, 1991.

Ward, Samuel and Richard Rogers. Edited and with an introduction by Marshall M. Knappen. *Two Elizabethan Puritan Diaries*. Chicago: American Society of Church History, 1933.

Warfield, Benjamin B. *Biblical and Theological Studies*. Philadelphia: Presbyterian and Reformed, 1968.

_____. *The Westminster Assembly and Its Work*. Cherry Hill: Mack Publishing Co., 1972.

Watkins, Owen C. *The Puritan Experience*. London: Routledge and Kegan Paul, 1972.

Watt, Tessa. *Cheap Print and Popular Piety, 1550-1640*. Cambridge Studies in Early Modern British History. Ed. Anthony Fletcher, John Guy and John Morrill. Cambridge: Cambridge University, 1991.

Weber, Hans C. *Der Einfluss der protestantischen Schulphilosophie auf die orthodox-lutherische Dogmatik*. Leipzig: A. Deichert'sche Verlagsbuchhandlung Nachf, 1908.

Weber, Otto. *Foundations of Dogmatics*. Translated and edited by Darrell L. Guder. 2 vols. Grand Rapids: Eerdmans, 1981-1983. [Translation of *Grundlagen der Dogmatik*. 2 vols. Neukirchen: Verlag der Buchhandlung des Erziehungsvereins, 1955-1962.

Weir, David A. *The Origins of the Federal Theology in Sixteenth-Century Reformation Thought*. Oxford: Clarendon, 1990.

Welles, Judith B. "John Cotton, 1584-1652: Churchman and Theologian." Ph.D. diss., University of Edinburgh, 1948.

Wells, D.F. and J.D. Woodbridge, eds. *The Evangelicals: What They Believe, Who They Are, Where They Are Changing*. Rev. ed. Grand Rapids: Baker, 1977.

Welsby, Paul A. *George Abbot, the Unwanted Archbishop, 1562-1633*. London: SPCK, 1962.

Wendel, François. *Calvin: The Origins and Development of His Religious Thought*. Translated by Philip Mairet. New York: Harper and Row, 1963.

Westland, L., ed. *Met het Woord in de Tijd*. 's-Gravenhage: Boekencentrum, 1985.

Whyte, Alexander. *Thomas Shepard, Pilgrim Father and Founder of Harvard. His Spiritual Experience and Experiential Preaching*. London: Oliphant, Anderson & Ferrier, 1909.

Wilcox, William. "New England Covenant Theology: Its English Precursors and Early American Exponents." Ph.D. diss., Duke University, 1959.

Williams, George H. "The Life of Thomas Hooker in England and Holland, 1586-1633." In *Thomas Hooker*. Harvard Theological Studies, no. 28, 1-35. Cambridge: Harvard University, 1975.

————. "The Pilgrimage of Thomas Hooker (1586-1647) in England, The Netherlands, and New England." *Bulletin of the Congregational Library* 29 (Oct. 1967): 5-15; (Jan. 1968): 9-13.

Wilson-Kastner, Patricia. "Jonathan Edwards: History and the Covenant." *Andrews University Seminary Studies* 15 (1977): 205-16.

Wing, Donald Goddard, ed. *Short-Title Catalog of Books Printed in England, Scotland, Ireland, Wales and British America and of English Books Printed in Other Countries, 1641-1700*. 3 vols. New York: Columbia University, 1945-51.

Wippel, J. F. "Aquinas." In *Cambridge Dictionary of Philosophy*. Ed. Robert Audi. New York: Cambridge University, 1995.

Witt, John Richard de. *Jus Divinum: The Westminster Assembly and the Divine Right of Church Government*. Kampen: J.H. Kok, 1969.

Wood, Thomas. *English Casuistical Divinity during the Seventeenth Century with Special Reference to Jeremy Taylor*. London: Society for the Promotion of Christian Knowledge, 1952.

Woude, Cornelius van der. "Amesius' Afscheid van Franeker." *Nederlands Archief voor Kerkgeschiedenis* 52 (1971-1972): 153-77.

————. *Sibrandus Lubbertus, leven en werken, in het bizonder naar zijn correspondentie*. Kampen: J.H. Kok, 1963.

Wright, Louis B. "William Perkins: Elizabethan Apostle of Practical Divinity." *The Huntington Library Quarterly* 3 (1940): 171-96.

Ziff, Larzer. *The Career of John Cotton, Puritanism and the American Experience*. Princeton: Princeton University, 1962.

Zilverberg, S. B. J. *Geloof en Geweten in de Zeventiende Eeuw*. Bussum, 1971.

INDEXES

Authors

Althaus, P., 24
Armstrong, B.G., 2n.2, 13n.33

Baker, J.W., 27n.1
Bangs, C., 15n.44, 172n.32, 33
Barth, K., 30, 30n.13, 92n.44, 94, 95, 132, 160
Beardslee, J.W., 65n.24
Beeke, J.R., 51n.109, 53n.115, 65n.24, 92n.44, 173n.37, 179, 182, 212n.158
Bell, M.D., 164n.5, 168, 169, 169n.21, 169n.22
Bergsma, W., 14-15
Berkhof, L., 31n.22, 194n.61, 198, 199, 200
Bierma, L.D., 29n.7, 129n.1, 130n.5
Blacketer, R.A., 28n.1
Boeles, W.B.S., 166n.11
Bogue, C., 237, 239
Bouwman, H., 15n.42, 173n.37, 177
Brandt, G., 12n.28
Breitenbach, W., 244n.62
Brereton, W., 112n.34
Breward, I., 29, 30n.12, 51, 76, 81, 88, 126n.91
Brienen, T., 230n.225
Bronkema, R., 181, 181n.78
Brook, B., 184n.90
Brown, J., 181n.78
Buchanan, C., 129n.1

Cadoux, C.J., 109n.20
Campbell, D., 9n.19
Carter, A.C., 16n.48
Chamberlain, A., 249
Cherry, C., 238, 241

Clark, R.S., 28n.4
Clouse, R.G., 13n.33
Costello, W.T., 233n.1
Coy, C.S., 27n.1
Cramer, J.A., 212n.156

Davidson, J.W., 259n.143
Davis, B.R., 17n.53, 56n.133
de Niet, C.A., 223n.202
Duker, A.C., 65n.24
Dankbaar, W.F., 9n.19, 15n.45

Emerson, E., 242
Engelberts, W.J.M., 173n.37, 178
Eusden, J.D., 5n.2, 21n.69, 50, 56n.133, 70, 81, 89n.24, 195n.67, 220n.184, 233n.1
Exalto, K., 173n.36, 230n.225

Ferguson, S.B., 136n.21
Fieret, W., 185n.1
Fiering, N., 233n.1, 243n.57, 245n.68, 248, 249
Foster, H.D., 171n.31

Garcia, J.L.A., 125n.90
Geesink, W., 25n.91, 64n.23, 178n.66, 229n.218
Gerstner, J.H., 2n.2
Geyl, P., 9n.19, 110n.21
Gibbs, L.W., 105n.2, 136n.21, 253
Glasius, B., 171n.31, 213
Godfrey, R.W., 171n.31
Goen, C.C., 259-260
Goeters, W., 24
Goodwin, T., 17n.52
Gordis, L.M., 136n.22

Graafland, C., 25, 85, 85n.1, 86, 87, 92-93, 98, 162n.2, 182, 186n.8, 212n.158, 218n.176, 268
Graves, E.P., 74, 74n.60
Groenendijk, L.F., 162n.2

Hales, J., 19n.59
Haley, K.H.P., 9n.19
Hall, B., 85n.1, 181n.78, 235n.14
Hambrick-Stowe, C.E., 235n.14
Harper, G.W., 61n.10
Hasler, R.A., 235n.14
Helm, P., 61n.10, 85n.1
Heppe, H., 23
Heringa, J., 166n.10
Hesselink, I.J., 2n.2
Hodge, C., 194n.61, 195n.67
Hoekema, A.A., 36n.46, 47, 86, 86n.6
Hoeksema, H., 129n.1, 132, 133, 199, 201n.104
Hoitenga, D.J., Jr., 59n.5, 61n.13
Horton, D., 5n.3, 164n.4
Hsia, R.P.-C., 11n.27, 16n.49
Huizinga, J.H., 9n.19, 10, 15n.45
Humphrey, R.A., 249n.92

Israel, J.I., 9n.19, 15n.45, 162n.1
Itterzon, G.P., 19n.59

Jones, J.W., III, 235n.14

Kaajan, H., 171n.31
Kendall, R.T., 59, 60n.10, 69-70, 83, 241
Kirk, K., 106, 108n.12
Kitteridge, G.L., 21n.68
Klauber, M.I., 86n.1, 166n.10
Knebel, S.K., 59
Kreeft, P., 68n.33

Kuitert, H.M., 86
Kuyper, A., Jr., 164n.4, 166n.11, 167, 169, 199

Laman, H.W., 230n.222
Lee, B.J., 28n.2, 42, 45n.76
Lee, S.H., 240
Leith, J.H., 2n.2, 127
Lesser, M.X., 253n.110
Letham, R.W.A., 2n.2
Lewis, N., 122n.76
Lillback, P.A., 27n.1, 32, 46, 86n.6, 87
Logan, S.T., 80n.85, 240
Loonstra, B., 31n.16
Los, F.J., 185n.1
Lowance, M.I., 253n.114

Markham, C.C., 113n.45
Marsden, G.M., 87, 88, 88n.13, 233n.2
McAdoo, H.R., 107n.8, 118n.62
McCoy, C.S., 92n.44, 95
McDermott, G.R., 260-261
McKim, D.K., 2n.2, 76-77, 79, 114n.47
McNeill, J.T., 182
Merrill, T.F., 107n.8
Messler, A., 234n.8
Miller, P., 29, 29n.11, 57, 87, 88, 88n.13, 233, 234, 241, 242, 253, 254, 257n.130, 261
Møller, J.G., 33
Moore, S. H., 18n.57
Morison, S.E., 233n.1
Mosse, G.L., 118n.62
Motley, J.L., 9n.19
Muller, R.A., 1, 2n.1, 29n.8, 32, 32n.24, 39n.57, 59, 61, 61n.13, 63, 70n.44, 85n.1, 88, 165n.8, 179, 214n.164
Mullinger, J.B., 6n.5
Murray, F.H., 233n.2

Neele, A.C., 211n.154, 219n.180, 225
Nethenus, M., 5n.2
Nobbs, D., 171n.31
Norton, A.O., 233n.1
Nuttall, G.F., 172n.31

Oberman, H.A., 28n.4
Ong, W.J., 7, 7n.14
op 't Hof, W.J., 16n.50, 112n.35, 162n.2, 173n.36, 175n.47, 176n.51, 232n.227
Osterhaven, E.M., 2n.2, 36n.46, 86n.1, 182-183

Packer, J.I., 253
Partee, C., 86n.1
Peile, J., 6n.5
Parker, D.L., 243n.54
Parker, T.H.L., 242
Phillips, J.M., 128n.98
Pickell, C.N., 241, 242
Pipa, J.A., 136n.21
Pointer, S.R., 8n.16
Porter, H.C., 6n.5
Prak, M., 9n.19
Preus, J.S., 28n.6
Price, J.L., 9n.19
Priebe, V.L., 30, 30n.14, 31n.19, 33n.31, 34, 34n.33, 34n.34, 47n.90, 48n.92
Prozesky, M.H., 172, 172n.34

Reuter, K., 5n.2, 23, 24, 56n.133, 90, 62-63, 64, 70n.44, 110, 180, 180n.74, 221
Ritschl, A.B., 23
Robinson, C.F., 233n.1
Robinson, R., 233n.1
Rutman, D.B., 235n.14

Scheick, W.J., 254n.120, 258
Schema, S., 9n.19
Schweitzer, A., 23-14

Seybolt, R.F., 233n.1
Shaw, M.R., 113n.45
Slagboom, D., 231n.225
Smith, C.R., 253, 253n.113
Smith, D.H., 106n.4, 241
Smith, J.E., 246n.75, 247, 248, 253
Song, Y.J.T., 30n.15, 51n.107
Sprunger, K.L., 5n.3, 16n.48, 16n.50, 17n.54, 21n.70, 21n.71, 23, 56n.131, 64, 77, 77n.75, 166n.10, 166n.11, 234n.7, 235n.14
Squires, W.H., 253n.115
Stearns, R.P., 17n.53, 21n.71
Steenblok, C., 65n.24
Stein, S.J., 260n.150
Stob, H., 245n.69, 246n.72
Stoeffler, F.E., 24, 212n.158
Stout, H., 235n.14
Strehle, S., 85n.1
Sweet, W.W., 235n.14

Tanis, J., 235n.12
Thomas, K., 107n.8
Todd, M., 113n.43
Trimp, J.C., 231n.225
Trinterud, L.J., 45n.77, 47, 181n.78, 234n.9, 235n.12
Trueman, C.R., 85n.1
Tufft, J.R., 30n.12
Tuttle, J.H., 126n.91

van Asselt, W.J., 28n.1, 92n.44, 93, 95n.54, 102, 109n.16, 166n.10, 166n.11, 168, 211n.154
van de Bank, J.H., 234n.10
van den Bergh, W., 38n.53, 39n.57
van den Brink, J.N.B., 22
van der Linde, S., 65n.24, 164n.7, 176n.51, 181n.78
van der Tuuk, H.E., 19n.59

van der Woude, C., 21n.70, 164n.6
van Genderen, J., 202n.108
van Gorsel, W., 163n.2
van Lieberg, F.A., 65n.24
van Nierop, H., 11n.27
van Oort, J., 65n.24
van Tellingen, A.E., 212n.155
van 't Spijker, W., 25, 65n.24, 163n.2, 165n.7, 174n.39
van Vliet, J., 107n.6
Verbeek, T., 92n.44
Verboom, W., 129-130, 129n.1, 129n.2, 130n.5, 131, 132, 133, 134n.19, 138, 152, 158
Visscher, H., 5n.2, 24, 90, 112n.38, 113n.43, 170
Von Rohr, J., 42, 240n.35
Vos, A., 71n.45

Walker, W., 16n.47
Walton, R.C., 56n.133
Watt, T., 109n.20
Weber, H.E., 24
Weber, O., 2n.1
Weir, D.A., 28, 28n.2
Whyte, A., 235n.14
Wilson, J.F., 254n.120, 254n.121
Wilson-Kastner, P., 256n.128

Scripture

Genesis, 3
1-3,   32
2:25,   192
3:15,   37, 225
15:6,   219
17,   46
17:1,   219

2 Samuel
7,   143

1 Kings
8:27,   190

Psalms,   132, 140
4,   138, 141, 142
4:6,   139
15,   119n.66
19:8,   217
37:13,   219
119:113,   5
119:66,   36

Proverbs
2:6,   217
4:23,   65
8:30,   245
23:26,   65

Isaiah,   140
50:4,   127n.92
51:4,   217
51:8,   254, 255
53:10,   157
55:3,   46

Jeremiah
22:29-30,   31
31,   38, 68
33:20,   44
33:25,   44

Malachi
3:1,   170

Matthew
7:12,   204, 208
15:9,   206
16:17,   217
21:25,   217
25,   145
25:34,   144
25:41,   144
28:20,   219

John
1:11-12,   220
1:12,   202, 221
1:17,   55
1:18,   217
4:8, 9, 10, 11, 16,
   19,   245
6:45,   217
7:16, 17,   217
9:29,   217
10:17-18,   152
13:17,   219

Acts
5:41,   140
10:42,   209
14:17,   120n.69
24:14-16,   219
24:16,   223

Romans,   131
1:19,   222
1:20,   120n.69
2:15,   115, 222
5:4,   52
6:4,   153
6:13,   192
6:17,   217
7:18,   221
8:29-30,   198

8:35,   137
9:7,   55
12,   66

1 Corinthians
6,   148
6:19,   147
13:1,2,   220
13:12,   120n.69
15,   150n.68

2 Corinthians
3,   38
12:2,   190

Galatians
1:11-12,   217
3,   43
3:28,   54
4:1,   55

Philippians
2:13,   50, 67
3:12,   66
3:20-21,   150

Ephesians
1:4,   89n.25
1:11,   67
1:19-20,   153
4:24,   192
5:22-27,   157
5:25,   226
5:25-27,   226

Colossians
2:2,   217
2:17,   41
2:23,   206
3:10,   192

1 Timothy
1:19,   219

4:6, 217
4:7, 223
4:13, 15, 212n.159
6:2-3, 216
6:3, 217

2 Timothy
1:13, 218, 219
3:16, 17, 217

Titus
1:1, 176, 216
2:12, 127
3:8, 219

Hebrews
5:14, 217
8:8, 44
8:10, 44, 68
9:10, 55
9:15, 43
9:16, 44
10:22, 52
10:23, 52
10:25-29, 252n.108

James, 146
1:2, 140
2:17, 153
1:18, 220
2:22, 154
2:24, 154

1 Peter
2:9, 227n.213
3:15-16, 52

2 Peter
3:3,4, 145

1 John, 119n.66
2:3, 246

3:14, 52
3:19, 52

Revelation, 259
6:1–11:19, 258, 259
6:1-2, 228
6:3-4, 228
6:5-6, 228
6:6-8, 228
6:9-11, 228
6:12, 228
7:1–11:19, 228
20, 211

Subject

Adam, 32-36, 37, 40, 101, 192, 238, 252n.108, 257, 264
adoption, 40, 55, 90, 100, 101, 102, 198, 199, 200, 203, 210
Ambrose, 135
Ames, William, 2, 3, 4, 5, 11. 12n.31, 13, 15, 16-22, 44-50, 64, 77-83, 89, 92n.44, 93, 98, 99, 101, 102, 103, 104, 107, 107n.10, 110-111, 114-119, 119n.66, 121-128, 130, 133, 133-161, 162, 165, 166, 167, 168, 169, 170, 171, 172, 177, 179, 180, 182, 183, 185-232, 228-232, 233-263, 264-267; works, 22-23; *Catechisme*, 22. 135, 136, 141, 149, 154, 156, 157, 158, 159, 215, 222; *Christianae Catecheseos Sciagraphia*, 133; *Conscience*, 22, 108, 110-111, 115, 118, 122-123, 127n.92, 178, 200, 200n.97, 204, 205, 208, 222, 223, 244, 246, 247, 248; *Marrow*, 19, 22, 34, 65, 74, 78, 115, 122, 123, 167, 183, 198, 203, 206, 208, 209, 213, 222, 223, 234, 243, 244, 246; *Medulla Theologica*, 264; *Philosophemata*, 23
Anabaptists, 11, 12n.31
Anastasius of Nicea, 219
Anselm, 64, 120n.69
Anti-Christ, 258, 265
Apostles' Creed, the, 76, 143, 147, 149, 150, 156
Aquinas, Thomas, 71, 72, 78-79, 82, 83, 106, 116, 117, 118, 118n.61, 120, 120n.69, 125, 126n.91, 193, 204

Aristotle, 11, 69, 71, 72, 74, 74n.60, 75, 79, 86, 118, 121, 127, 162, 166, 167, 180
Arminianism, 69, 84, 177, 236, 242n.54
Arminians, 18, 23, 134, 165, 172, 174, 177, 220
Arminius, Jacobus, 15-16, 15n.44, 172, 173
assurance, 50, 53, 58, 62, 90, 101, 107, 119, 119n.66, 131, 137, 140-141, 152, 153, 172, 202, 246, 250
Augustine, 28, 32, 71, 72, 86, 91n.35, 135, 150, 180, 180n.74

Basil, 132
Baxter, Richard, 128, 128n.98
Belgic Confession (1561), 12
Bellarmine, Robert, 13, 23, 126n.91, 166, 243
Bernard, 64
Beza, 60n.10, 61, 62, 64, 76, 89n.24, 98, 172n.32, 220, 234
Biel, Gabriel, 28
Brakel, à, Wilhelmus, 66n.27, 92n.44, 185-210, 185n.2, 186n.5, 228-232, 234, 235, 260, 267
Brethren of the Common Life, the, 12
Bucer, Martin, 45n.77
Bullinger, Heinrich, 28, 28n.2, 45, 45n.77, 86, 88n.21, 172n.32
Bunyan, John, 229, 253

calling (see 'vocation'), 90, 102, 170, 197, 198, 199, 200, 201, 201n.104, 210
Calvin, John, 1, 2, 3, 4, 10, 10n.24, 27, 29, 30-57, 58-61, 62, 68, 69, 70, 75, 80, 81, 82, 83, 86, 91, 91n.35, 93, 98, 102,

103, 117n.56, 130, 132, 159, 160, 164n.7, 168-169, 174, 177-178, 184, 189, 190, 193, 194n.64, 234, 240, 241, 242, 262

Calvinism, 6, 7, 10n.23, 12, 13, 23

Capito, 45n.77

casuistry, 105-128, 178, 179, 206, 208, 214, 222, 234, 266, 267

Cats, Jacob, 109-110

Christ, Jesus, 3, 26, 30, 31, 31n.22, 32, 33, 35, 36, 38, 40, 41, 47, 48, 51, 55, 58, 60, 62, 67, 78, 82, 89, 99, 100, 102, 111, 131n.8, 135, 137, 140, 141, 142, 147, 148, 151, 152, 153, 167n.13, 174, 177, 179, 189, 194-196, 199, 202, 210, 214, 216, 219, 221, 225, 226, 237, 239, 240, 247, 250, 251, 253, 254n.121, 256, 257, 259, 262, 264, 266, 267; as Judge, 143-147; as King, 145, 209; as mediator, 221, 226; as messiah, 221; incarnation, 97, 195, 255, 256, 264, 268; lordship, 3; redeemer, 202, 221;suffering, 157-158

Chrysostom, John, 28, 135

church, 3, 53-57, 58, 76, 91, 100, 123, 147, 152, 157, 158, 174, 175, 182, 195n.67, 196-198, 210, 218, 218n.176, 227, 230, 246, 257, 258, 259, 262

church government, 3, 17n.53

Clement of Alexandria, 135

Cocceius, Johannes, 92-104, 92n.44, 169n.22, 172, 212, 214n.164, 260

community, 3, 16n.49, 53, 56, 86, 123, 230, 246

confession, 119

confessionalism, 13

conscience, 11, 35, 53, 67, 105, 113-119, 121, 123, 125, 137, 190-191, 205, 222-224, 229, 231, 233-263, 246, 247, 248, 248-251

conversion, 6, 7, 182, 199, 200, 235, 236, 242, 258

coram Deo, 3, 106, 123, 181, 266, 268

Cotton, John, 261, 262

covenant, 3, 27, 29, 42-50, 50-53, 53-57, 57-58, 58, 68, 85, 87, 88, 89, 92, 93, 99, 101, 105, 130, 131, 132, 141, 156, 157-158, 182, 192, 196, 197, 206, 214, 225, 233-263, 256n.128, 266, 267; conditionality, 39, 42-50, 58, 192-193, 239-240, 262; of grace, 36-42, 44, 45, 47, 48, 49, 50, 50, 52, 55, 58, 78, 86, 88, 90, 92n.44, 93, 94, 97, 98, 99-100, 102, 103, 179, 183, 186, 188, 189, 193, 194, 196, 197, 198, 204, 209-211, 214, 222, 224, 225, 232, 237, 238, 239, 254n.121, 257, 259, 264, 266; of redemption, 30-31, 31n.22, 57, 99-100, 237, 256n.128; of works, 32-36, 39, 40, 41, 44, 47, 49, 57, 58, 93, 96, 97, 98, 99, 100, 102, 103, 155, 189, 192, 193, 194, 204, 224, 226, 238-240, 257, 262; response, 214; responsibility, 49, 266; theology, 224-228, 225n.210, 262, 266

creation, 99, 111, 157, 182, 189-190, 192, 253

Cyprian, 135

Cyril of Jerusalem, 219

dancing, 112-113
Daubuz, Charles, 259
Decalogue, the (10 commandments; see 'Law'), 123, 124, 128, 132n.8, 147, 149, 154, 157, 193, 204, 206, 223, 267
decretal theology, 85-104, 158
discipline, 3, 20, 100, 157, 197, 198
Dutch Puritanism, 172-180
Dutch Republic, the, 1, 9, 9n.19, 11 13, 25, 69, 84, 108, 124, 133, 135, 162, 180, 184, 234, 267

Edwards, Jonathan, 1, 233-263, 264, 265, 267, 268; *History of the Work of Redemption*, 253-261, 264, 265; *Religious Affections*, 244, 249, 252, 261, 262
Eighty Years' War, 13n.33
election, 37, 43, 51, 51n.109, 58, 67, 86, 87, 88, 91, 101, 156, 157, 182, 188, 240, 242
Erasmus, 10, 10n.24, 107n.10
eschatology, 209, 214, 226, 261
evangelism, 3
experience (experiential), 7, 41, 50, 130, 132, 138, 149, 172-180, 178, 179, 182, 183, 184, 210, 230, 232, 233, 235, 237, 239, 240, 246, 247, 248, 248-251, 258, 262, 266, 267

faith, 27, 39, 40, 43, 47, 48, 49, 51n.107, 52, 53, 54, 55, 58-71, 82-83, 84, 87, 88, 91, 99, 104, 119, 119n.66, 120, 123, 127, 131, 132, 132n.8, 138, 141, 143, 144, 147, 148, 151, 154, 155, 156, 160, 178, 183, 187, 197, 199, 200, 202, 203, 208, 209, 218n.176, 219, 220, 220-222, 225, 230, 231, 238, 239, 240, 242, 247, 250, 259, 266, 268
fall, the, 97, 194, 238, 253, 255, 256, 264
Franeker, 7n.12, 15-16, 19, 20, 56n.131, 74, 77, 84, 99, 107, 162-172, 185, 236
freedom, 11, 39, 41, 55, 103, 203, 241
Frelinghuysen, Theodorus J., 183, 234, 235, 267

gambling, 112-112
Gataker, Thomas, 113, 207, 207n.135
Genevan Psalter, the, 13
glorification, 37, 40, 90, 100, 101, 102, 152n.77, 199, 200, 203, 207, 210
Gomarus, Franciscus, 62, 64
good works, 27, 49, 146, 147n.55, 153-156, 156n.93, 219
Goodwin, Thomas, 229
Gospel, the, 38, 39, 49, 89, 131, 137, 138, 143, 144, 167, 175
grace, 32, 33, 41, 45, 46, 48, 49, 50, 54, 59, 62, 63, 66, 68, 121, 124n.87, 126, 137, 146, 153, 155, 167, 189, 239, 245, 246, 249, 250, 266, 268
gratitude, 138, 153, 156
Great Awakening, the, 236, 240, 254n.121, 262, 267
Great Commission, the, 3
Gregory of Nazianzus, 135

Hampton Court Conference (1604), 8
Heidelberg Catechism, 12, 68, 128, 129-161, 175, 234, 267
Henry of Ghent, 64
Hilary, 135
Holy Spirit, the, 2, 31, 38, 40, 41, 51, 52, 53n.115, 60, 65, 68,

69, 96, 98, 102, 103, 104, 121, 137, 138, 143, 147-149, 150, 152, 156n.93, 167, 199, 201n.104, 203, 214, 237, 245, 252n.108, 254n.121
Hooker, Thomas,   21n.69
hope,   52, 123, 152, 204, 208, 247
humanism,   10, 10n.24
hypocrisy (hypocrites),   249, 250, 251

Irenaeus,   28
imago Dei (image of God),   32, 36, 67, 81

Janszoon, Dirck,   14-15
Jud,   45n.77
judgment,   143-147, 146n.54, 209, 253, 255
justification,   28, 37, 40, 51n.107, 52, 90, 100, 101, 102, 152n.77, 154, 199, 200, 203, 210, 239n.29, 250, 266

Keckermann, Bartholomäus, 127n.93, 167, 221
kingdom of God (of heaven), the, 7n.10, 96, 147

Lasco, à, Johannes,   130
Law (see 'Decalogue, the'),   5, 32, 33, 33n.27, 53, 55, 67, 105, 116, 117, 123, 125, 131n.8, 135, 138, 144, 145, 149, 153, 191, 193, 195, 199, 203-204, 238
Leydekker, Melchior,   25
liturgy,   3
Lodenstein, Jodocus van,   25
Lodewijk, Willem,   14
Lombard, Peter,   76
Lord's Day (see 'Sabbath, the'), 123, 157

Lord's Prayer, the,   153, 205, 208
Lord's Supper, the,   57, 112, 135, 172n.32
love to God,   244-246, 262
Lowman, Moses,   259, 260
Luthardt, C.E.,   24
Luther, Martin,   12, 86, 164n.7
Lutherans,   11, 12n.31, 14

Maccovius, Johannes,   2, 20, 21, 64, 74, 127n.93, 163-166, 167, 168, 169, 171, 220
Major, John,   86
Mather, Cotton,   22, 234
Mather, Increase,   127
Melanchthon,   130, 131, 132
Mennonites,   11, 13, 14
mission,   3

Nadere Reformatie,   25n.93, 162-184, 162n.2, 187, 230n.225, 231, 256, 260, 261, 267

obedience,   27, 32, 33n.27, 34, 45, 47, 48, 49, 50, 53n.115, 58, 63, 66, 68, 69, 82, 84, 87, 89, 104, 122, 123, 125, 126, 127, 160, 166, 177, 179, 183, 192, 193, 199, 201n.104, 220, 222, 225, 230, 232, 238, 244, 246, 250, 256n.128, 262, 266, 267, 268
Oecolampadius, Johannes,   32, 45n.77
Olevianus, Casper,   32, 33, 129n.1, 130, 130n.5, 134n.17, 146n.51, 267
ordo salutis,   37, 40, 51n.107, 52, 53, 58, 90, 94, 95, 98, 100, 101, 102, 103, 121, 198, 199, 200, 201n.104, 210, 211, 214, 225, 227, 227n.213
Origen,   86

orthodoxy, 1, 4, 16, 20, 48, 62, 64, 108-111, 164, 174, 176, 187, 196, 236; early, 1, 4, 59, 158; high, 1, 4; late, 1, 4
Owen, John, 229

papacy, 6, 23
Paris, William, 122, 122n.76, 208n.141
Parker, Thomas, 165, 233n.1
Perkins, William, 6, 7, 7n.10, 27, 29-30, 30-57, 58, 61-63, 64, 67, 69, 75-77, 78, 80, 81, 82, 83, 87, 88, 89, 91, 103, 107, 113, 113-114, 115, 116, 117, 118, 119-121, 122, 125, 126, 136, 151, 167, 174, 175, 177-179, 189, 190, 198n.88, 204, 206, 209, 215, 222, 229, 239, 248, 262
Pietism, 173-174, 180, 180-183, 236
piety, 3, 6, 7, 10n.24, 14, 18, 20, 24, 26, 50, 51n.107, 53, 58, 78, 104, 108, 110, 111, 127, 140, 156, 162, 163, 168, 169, 170, 175, 179, 182, 184, 206, 218n.176, 233-235, 236, 237, 243-251, 244, 247, 248, 250, 262, 266
Polyander, Johannes, 175
post-Reformation, 1, 25, 72, 107, 125, 164
prayer, 10, 131, 138, 140, 147, 153, 204, 222
preaching, 2, 7, 54, 55, 57, 110, 134, 136, 140, 147, 159, 169-170, 174, 198, 201n.104, 215
predestination, 29, 31, 40, 47, 51, 54, 63, 75, 76, 85-90, 91, 91n.35, 93, 94, 100, 101, 102, 104, 157, 188-189, 200, 201, 210
Preston, John, 29, 29n.11

privilege, 11
providence, 99, 120, 189, 192
Puritans, 1, 5, 16, 18, 25, 53n.115, 60, 76, 109, 113, 165n.8, 173, 219n.180, 229, 250, 256n.128
Puritanism, 5, 6, 62, 180-183, 233n.1, 238n.23, 239, 267
Puritan principles, 6

Ramism (Ramist), 6, 15n.44, 20, 21, 23, 40, 63, 71-75, 77, 78, 79, 83, 84, 100, 110n.78, 114n.47, 121, 136n.21, 155, 158, 164n.4, 189, 194, 205, 213, 220, 232, 267, 268
Ramus, Peter, 7, 7n.13, 11, 25, 71, 75, 76, 79-80, 81, 83, 100n.78, 118, 138, 172n.31, 172n.32, 268
reconciliation, 137
redemption, 49, 56, 78, 93-94, 98, 101, 138, 156, 194, 195, 199, 214, 226, 232, 237, 254, 255
Reformation, the, 1, 106, 163, 198, 253, 265
Reformed system, 4, 26, 57, 84, 125, 214, 222, 225n.210, 232
Reformed tradition, 1, 2-4, 33, 48, 56n.131, 127, 206, 230, 232, 233, 234, 235, 262, 266, 268
regeneration, 50, 121, 147, 152n.77, 167, 182, 199, 200, 201n.104, 242n.54, 243
repentance, 47, 48, 89, 119, 147, 199, 200, 240, 247, 262
reprobation, 86, 88, 188
resurrection, 149-153, 152n.77, 256, 265
Robinson, John, 56
Roman Catholics, 11, 13, 14, 15

Sabbath, the (see 'Lord's Day, the'), 36, 111-113, 120, 121,

327

133, 135, 203, 205, 205n.128, 207, 222, 252n.108
sacramentalism,   28
sacraments,   2, 54, 55, 56-57, 99, 100, 123, 135, 197, 203, 203n.114
salvation,   7n.10, 37, 41, 49, 94, 119, 144, 145, 147, 177, 194, 195, 241, 242, 243, 247, 250, 255
sanctification,   37, 40, 51n.107, 52, 90, 97, 98, 100, 101, 102, 182, 198, 200, 203, 205, 210, 229, 250
Satan,   131, 138, 158, 199
Schleiermacher,   24
scholasticism,   24, 62, 63, 71, 72, 164, 164n.7, 165, 165n.8, 167, 169, 260, 267
sin(s),   49, 53, 68, 97, 100, 101, 119, 121, 122, 137, 141, 148, 149, 152, 153, 153, 182, 195n.67, 209, 225, 250
sola fide,   266
sola gratia,   266
sola scriptura,   2, 266
solus Christus,   266
Spener, Jacob,   173-174, 180, 181
Synod of Dordt (1618),   1, 25, 162-172, 171n.31, 236

Taffin, Jean,   175, 175n.51
Teellinck, Willem,   15, 109-110, 111, 162n.2, 163n.3, 172-180, 173n.36, 175n.45, 184, 223
Tennent, Gilbert,   234, 235, 235n.13, 267
Tertullian,   135
testament,   42-50
Theodoret,   135
Thirty Years' War, the,   1
toleration,   11

triple knowledge,   130-133, 134, 153
Turretin, Francis,   185, 194n.61, 252, 255n.126, 264, 265
Tyndale, William,   45

van Mastricht, Petrus,   185, 201n.104, 211-228, 228-232, 242n.54, 243, 252, 252n.108, 255, 257, 258, 259, 260, 260n.150, 261, 262, 264, 265, 267
virtues,   122, 123, 125
vocation (see 'calling'),   3, 156
Voet, Gisbertus,   64, 69, 92n.44, 109, 150n.68, 173, 174, 175, 185, 186, 212, 212n.156, 218n.176, 223, 234, 235, 256
voluntarism,   59-84, 146, 178, 240, 267

Ursinus, Zacharias,   32, 33, 88n.21, 129n.1, 130, 130n.5, 132, 134, 134n.17, 135, 136, 139n.30, 141-152, 150n.68, 153-158, 267

Walaeus, Antonius,   62
Westminster Assembly, the,   60
Westminster catechisms,   128, 143, 159, 160
Whitby, Daniel,   259, 260
Word of God, the (Scripture),   2-3, 14-15, 54, 56, 57, 120, 133, 136, 140, 147, 167, 170, 181, 183, 186, 187, 198, 201n.104, 202, 217
worship,   3, 5, 11, 18, 66, 111, 120, 121, 123, 175, 182, 206, 210, 251

Zanchius,   64, 98
Zwingli, Ulrich,   2, 28, 32, 45, 45n.77, 86